Rick Steves®

PRAGUE

& THE CZECH REPUBLIC

Rick Steves & Jan (Honza) Vihan

CONTENTS

Prague

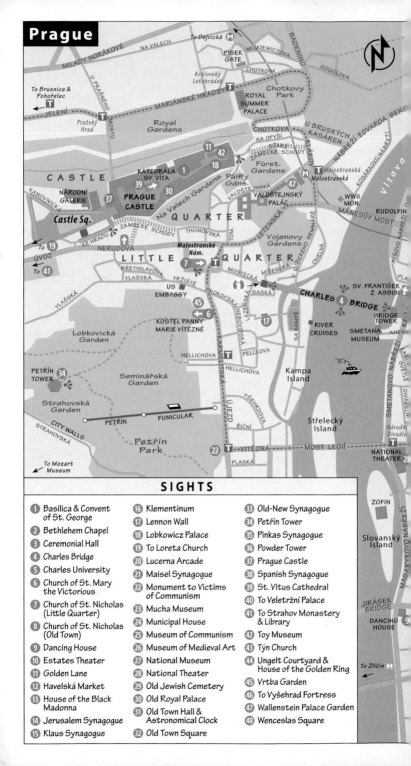

To Dejvická Ⓜ
NA VALECH
MILADY HORÁKOVÉ
PÍSEK GATE
MICKIEWICZOVA
BADENIHO
GOGOLOVA
CHOTKOVA
Královský Letohrádek
ROYAL SUMMER PALACE
Chotkovy Park
U PRAŠNÉHO MOSTU
MARIÁNSKÉ HRADBY
JELENÍ
To Brusnice & Pohořelec
Pražský Hrad
Royal Gardens
CHOTKOVA
U BRUSKÝCH KASÁREN
NA OPYŠI
STARÉ ZÁMECKÉ SCHODY
NÁBŘEŽÍ EDVARDA BENE
Vitava
11 42
Fürst. Gardens
18
KATEDRÁLA SV. VÍTA 1
Pálffy Gdns.
47 Malostranská Ⓣ Malostranská
CASTLE
39
30
NÁRODNÍ GALERIE
37 PRAGUE CASTLE
VALDŠTEJNSKÝ PALÁC
WWII MON.
RUDOLFIN
KANOVNICKÁ
Na Valech Gardens
VALDŠTEJNSKÁ
MÁNESŮV MOST
Castle Sq.
ZÁMECKÉ SCHODY
KE HRADU
THUNOVSKÁ
QUARTER
LETENSKÁ
Vojanovy Gardens
To 19
ÚVOZ
NERUDOVA
Malostranské Nám.
7 Ⓣ
MOSTECKÁ
MÍŠEŇSKÁ
U LUŽICKÉHO SEMINÁŘE
ČIHELNÁ
SV. FRANTIŠEK Z ASSISI
ALŠOVO NÁBŘEŽÍ
To 41
BŘETISLAVOVA
LITTLE
QUARTER
VLAŠSKÁ
TRŽIŠTĚ
US EMBASSY
PROKOPSKÁ
NEBOVIDSKÁ
SASKÁ
CHARLES 4 BRIDGE
BRIDGE TOWER
SMETANA MUSEUM
PLA
45
6
17
RIVER CRUISES
ANENS
VLAŠSKÁ
KOSTEL PANNY MARIE VÍTĚZNÉ
HELLICHOVA
KARMELITSKÁ
NA KAMPĚ
Kampa Island
SVĚTLÉ
Lobkovická Garden
HELLICHOVA
PELCLOVA
KŘÍŽ
DIVADLE
PETŘÍN TOWER 34
Seminářská Garden
VŠEHRDOVA
Střelecký Island
SMETANOVO NÁBŘEŽÍ
Strahovská Garden
PETŘÍN
FUNICULAR
ŘÍČNÍ
ÚJEZD
Národní Divadlo
CITY WALLS
STRAHOVSKÁ
Petřín Park
22 Ⓣ VÍTĚZNÁ
MOST LEGIÍ
NATIONAL THEATER 2
To Mozart Museum
PLASKÁ

ZOFIN
MASARYKOVO NÁBŘEŽÍ
Slovanský Island
JIRÁSEK BRIDGE
DANCING HOUSE 9
To Zličín

SIGHTS

1. Basilica & Convent of St. George
2. Bethlehem Chapel
3. Ceremonial Hall
4. Charles Bridge
5. Charles University
6. Church of St. Mary the Victorious
7. Church of St. Nicholas (Little Quarter)
8. Church of St. Nicholas (Old Town)
9. Dancing House
10. Estates Theater
11. Golden Lane
12. Havelská Market
13. House of the Black Madonna
14. Jerusalem Synagogue
15. Klaus Synagogue
16. Klementinum
17. Lennon Wall
18. Lobkowicz Palace
19. To Loreta Church
20. Lucerna Arcade
21. Maisel Synagogue
22. Monument to Victims of Communism
23. Mucha Museum
24. Municipal House
25. Museum of Communism
26. Museum of Medieval Art
27. National Museum
28. National Theater
29. Old Jewish Cemetery
30. Old Royal Palace
31. Old Town Hall & Astronomical Clock
32. Old Town Square
33. Old-New Synagogue
34. Petřín Tower
35. Pinkas Synagogue
36. Powder Tower
37. Prague Castle
38. Spanish Synagogue
39. St. Vitus Cathedral
40. To Veletržní Palace
41. To Strahov Monastery & Library
42. Toy Museum
43. Týn Church
44. Ungelt Courtyard & House of the Golden Ring
45. Vrtba Garden
46. To Vyšehrad Fortress
47. Wallenstein Palace Garden
48. Wenceslas Square

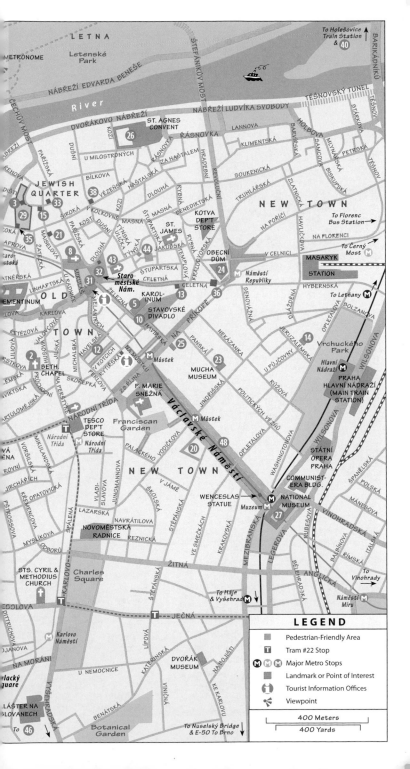

Na zdraví! (Cheers!)

Gothic spires of Týn Church

Domes and towers of Prague's skyline

Mucha stained-glass window, St. Vitus Cathedral, Prague

Charles Bridge with Prague Castle (upper right)

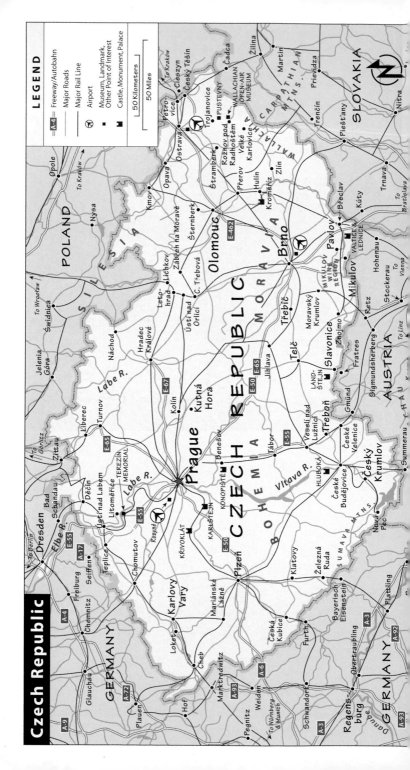

Rick Steves®

PRAGUE

& THE CZECH REPUBLIC

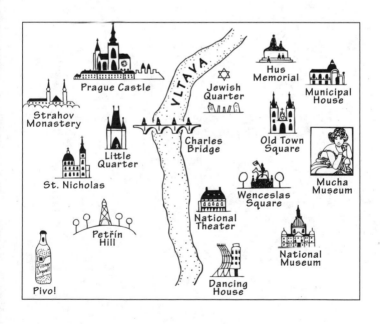

Top Destinations in the Czech Republic

DAY TRIPS:
KUTNÁ HORA,
KARLOVY VARY,
TEREZÍN & CASTLES

PRAGUE

OLOMOUC

SOUTHERN CZECH TOWNS:
TŘEBOŇ, TELČ,
TŘEBÍČ & SLAVONICE

ČESKÝ
KRUMLOV

MIKULOV
WINE REGION

INTRODUCTION

Wedged between Germany and Austria, the Czech Republic is the first stop for many visitors' foray into Eastern Europe. After the fall of communism, the Czech capital, Prague, quickly became one of Europe's most popular destinations. Come see what all the fuss is about...but don't overlook the rest of the country. Even in a quick visit, you can enjoy a fine introduction to the entire Czech Republic.

This book focuses on Prague, but also includes my favorite small-town and back-to-nature destinations in the countryside. If you want to experience the best two weeks that the Czech Republic has to offer, this book has all the information you'll need.

Experiencing Czech culture, people, and natural wonders economically and hassle-free has been my life-long goal as a traveler, tour guide, and writer. This book is selective, including only the top destinations and sights. For example, the Czech Republic has dozens of historic countryside castles, but I take you to only the best (Konopiště, Karlštejn, Křivoklát, and Lednice).

The best is, of course, only my opinion. But after spending much of my life researching Europe, I've developed a sixth sense for what travelers enjoy.

ABOUT THIS BOOK

Rick Steves Prague & the Czech Republic is a personal tour guide in your pocket. Better yet, it's actually two tour guides in your pocket: The co-author and researcher of this guidebook is Honza Vihan, a Prague native with 20 seasons of guiding experience. Together, Honza and I keep this book up-to-date and accurate. For simplicity we've shed our respective egos to become "I" in this book—though at times, you'll know from the intimacy of some of the comments that Honza is sharing his own uniquely Czech perspective.

INTRODUCTION

Map Legend

⅙	Viewpoint	✈	Airport	) (	Tunnel
✦	Entrance	Ⓣ	Taxi Stand		Pedestrian Zone
🛈	Tourist Info	Ⓣ	Tram Stop	------	Railway
WC	Restroom	Ⓜ	Metro Stop	....	Ferry/Boat Route
⌂	Castle	Ⓑ	Bus Stop	⊢—⊢	Tram
⌂	Church	Ⓟ	Parking	⊪⊪⊪⊪⊪	Stairs
▪	Statue/Point of Interest	)(	Mtn. Pass	• • • • •	Walk/Tour Route
◎	Fountain	⬚	Park	--------	Trail

Use this legend to help you navigate the maps in this book.

The first half of this book focuses on Prague, following this format:

Orientation to Prague includes specifics on public transportation, helpful hints, local tour options, easy-to-read maps, and tourist information. The "Planning Your Time" section suggests a schedule for how to best use your limited time.

Sights in Prague describes the top attractions and includes their cost and hours. Major sights have self-guided tours.

The **Self-Guided Walks** cover the Old Town, the New Town's Wenceslas Square, and the peaceful, view-filled Vyšehrad park, pointing out sights and fun stops.

The **Self-Guided Tours** lead you through Prague's most fascinating museums and sights: the Jewish Quarter, Museum of Medieval Art, Mucha Museum, and Prague Castle.

Sleeping in Prague describes my favorite hotels, from good-value deals to cushy splurges.

Eating in Prague serves up a buffet of options, from inexpensive eateries to fancy restaurants.

Shopping in Prague gives you tips for shopping painlessly and enjoyably, without letting it overwhelm your vacation or ruin your budget.

Entertainment in Prague is your guide to fun, including a wide array of concerts and nightclubs—as well as other Czech entertainment options, from the unique Black Light Theater to hockey and soccer games.

Prague Connections outlines your options for traveling to destinations by train, bus, plane, or with a private driver.

The second half of the book, **Beyond Prague,** is devoted to the rest of the Czech Republic. For easy day trips from Prague, consider the towns of Kutná Hora (with bone church) and Karlovy Vary (with famous spa), the Terezín Memorial (concentration camp), and three castles. Farther-flung destinations are each covered as a

Key to This Book

Updates
This book is updated regularly, but things change. For the latest, visit www.ricksteves.com/update.

Abbreviations and Times
I use the following symbols and abbreviations in this book:
Sights are rated:

▲▲▲   Don't miss

▲▲   Try hard to see

▲   Worthwhile if you can make it

No rating   Worth knowing about

Tourist information offices are abbreviated as **TI,** and bathrooms are WCs. Accommodations are categorized with a **Sleep Code** (described on page 202); eateries are classified with a **Restaurant Price Code** (page 210). To indicate discounts for my readers, I include **RS%** in the listings.

Like Europe, this book uses the **24-hour clock.** It's the same through 12:00 noon, then keeps going: 13:00, 14:00, and so on. For anything over 12, subtract 12 and add p.m. (14:00 is 2:00 p.m.).

When giving **opening times,** I include both peak season and off-season hours if they differ. So, if a museum is listed as "May-Oct daily 9:00-16:00," it should be open from 9 a.m. until 4 p.m. from the first day of May until the last day of October (but expect exceptions).

A 📖 symbol in a sight listing means that the sight is described in greater detail elsewhere—either with its own self-guided tour, or as part of a self-guided walk. A 🎧 symbol indicates that a free, downloadable self-guided Rick Steves audio tour is available.

For **transit** or **tour departures,** I first list the frequency, then the duration. So, a train connection listed as "2/hour, 1.5 hours" departs twice each hour, and the journey lasts an hour and a half.

mini-vacation: the pretty town of Český Krumlov; a cluster of distinctly different Southern Czech towns (Třeboň, Telč, Třebíč, and Slavonice); the youthful town of Olomouc; and the scenic Mikulov Wine Region.

Near the end of the book, you'll find these chapters:

Czech History explains the complicated, tumultuous, and ultimately uplifting background of this country.

The **Practicalities** chapter is a traveler's tool kit, with my best travel advice about money, sightseeing, sleeping, eating, staying connected, and transportation.

The **appendix** has the nuts-and-bolts: useful phone numbers and websites, a holiday and festival list, recommended books and

INTRODUCTION

films, a climate chart, a handy packing checklist, and Czech survival phrases.

Throughout this book, you'll find money- and time-saving tips for sightseeing, transportation, and more. Some businesses—especially hotels and walking tour companies—offer special discounts to my readers, indicated in their listings.

Browse through this book, choose your favorite destinations, and link them up. Then have a great trip! Traveling like a temporary local, you'll get the absolute most out of every mile, minute, and dollar. As you visit places I know and love, I'm happy that you'll be meeting some of my favorite Czech people.

Planning

This section will help you get started planning your trip—with advice on trip costs, when to go, and what you should know before you take off.

TRAVEL SMART

Your trip to the Czech Republic is like a complex play—it's easier to follow and to really appreciate on a second viewing. While no one does the same trip twice to gain that advantage, reading this book in its entirety before you go accomplishes much the same thing.

Design an itinerary that enables you to visit sights at the best possible times. Note holidays, festivals, colorful market days, and days when sights are closed or most crowded (all covered in this book).

If you have only a few days for Prague, remember that the impressive sights of the Jewish Quarter are closed on Saturday, and other museums (particularly in the Old Town) are closed on Monday. Monday can also be a problem day outside of Prague, as many Czech museums and castles are closed.

To get between destinations smoothly, read the tips in Practicalities on taking trains and buses, or renting a car and driving. A smart trip is a puzzle—a fun, doable, and worthwhile challenge.

Make your itinerary a mix of intense and relaxed stretches. To maximize rootedness, minimize one-night stands. It's worth taking a long drive after dinner to get settled in a town for two nights. Every trip—and every traveler—needs slack time (laundry, picnics, people-watching, and so on). Pace yourself. Assume you will return.

Reread this book as you travel, and visit local tourist information offices (abbreviated as TI in this book). Upon arrival in a new town, lay the groundwork for a smooth departure; confirm the train, bus, or road you'll take when you leave.

Even with the best-planned itinerary, you'll need to be flexible.

The Czech Republic at a Glance

Best Home Bases

▲▲▲**Prague** Czech capital and one of Europe's most romantic cities, boasting a remarkably well-preserved Old Town, a thriving New Town packed with Art Nouveau, and fascinating 20th-century history.

▲▲**Český Krumlov** Charming Bohemian hill town huddled under a colorful castle and hugging a river bend.

▲**Telč and Southern Czech Towns** Tiny town with spectacular main square that's a good overnight stop for visiting other southern Bohemian towns: Třeboň, surrounded by artificial lakes; Třebíč, with echoes of Jewish history; and—huddled along the Austrian border—Slavonice, with evocative, never-used WWII fortifications.

▲**Olomouc** Moravian cultural capital and thriving university city; nearby are the Rococo château in Kroměříž, and the time-passed, mountainous Wallachia region.

▲**Mikulov Wine Region** Czech Republic's top wine-growing area, with a trio of worthwhile stops: the historical town of Mikulov, the humble village of Pavlov, and the impressive château-and-garden complexes of Lednice and Valtice.

Day Trips from Prague

▲▲**Kutná Hora** Workaday Czech town with an offbeat bone church, stunning cathedral, and silver mining museum.

▲▲**Terezín Memorial** The Nazis' model "Jewish town," now a sobering memorial to the victims.

▲**Konopiště Castle** Neo-Gothic residence of the Archduke Franz Ferdinand, with captivating stories about its former inhabitants.

▲**Karlštejn Castle** Dramatically situated summer residence of Charles IV, with fairy-tale-esque exterior.

Křivoklát Castle Genuinely Gothic hunting palace of Czech kings, later transformed into royal prison.

▲**Karlovy Vary (Carlsbad)** Swanky spa town with grand architecture.

Update your plans as you travel. Get online or call ahead to learn the latest on sights (special events, tour schedules, and so on), book tickets and tours, make reservations, reconfirm hotels, and research transportation connections.

Enjoy the friendliness of the Czech people. Connect with the culture. Set up your own quest for the ultimate characteristically Czech pub. (Anything with an English menu doesn't count.) Once inside, ask the locals to recommend the best beer, and make it your goal to get the most interesting story you possibly can out of them.

Slow down and be open to unexpected experiences. Ask questions—most locals are eager to point you in their idea of the right direction. Keep a notepad in your pocket for confirming prices, noting directions, and organizing your thoughts. Wear your money belt, learn the currency, and figure out how to estimate prices in dollars. Those who expect to travel smart, do.

TRIP COSTS

There are two price tiers in the Czech Republic: Prague, and everywhere else. Outside of Prague, you'll be amazed at the low prices for accommodations, food, transportation, and sightseeing. In Prague, you'll find prices closer to the Western European range. Prague hotels are particularly expensive, often surpassing Western prices. But even in Prague, things that natives pay for—such as transportation and food (in local-style, rather than tourist-oriented, restaurants)—are very affordable. Despite the expense of Prague, if you avoid overpriced restaurants on the main tourist drag, and if you use my listings to stay at only the best-value hotels, a trip to the Czech Republic can still be substantially less expensive than a trip to Western European destinations.

Five components make up your trip costs: airfare to Europe, transportation in Europe, room and board, sightseeing and entertainment, and shopping and miscellany.

Airfare to Europe: A basic round-trip flight from the US to Prague can cost, on average, about $1,000-2,000 total, depending on where you fly from and when (cheaper in winter). If Prague is part of a longer trip, consider saving time and money in Europe by flying into one city and out of another (for example, into Prague and out of Vienna). Overall, Kayak.com is the best place to start searching for flights on a combination of mainstream and budget carriers.

Transportation in Europe: Point-to-point train and bus tickets within the Czech Republic are inexpensive—a second-class train ticket from Prague to the farthest reaches of the country won't run you more than about $20. Renting a car is convenient for exploring the Czech countryside, but doing so is much more expensive than public transportation (allow $230

The Czech Republic's Best Two-Week Trip by Car

Day	Plan	Sleep in
1	Arrive in Prague	Prague
2	Prague	Prague
3	Prague	Prague
4	Day trip to Terezín Memorial	Prague
5	Tour Konopiště Castle en route to Český Krumlov	Český Krumlov
6	Český Krumlov	Český Krumlov
7	To Třeboň, then Telč	Telč
8	Side-trip to Slavonice	Telč
9	Visit Třebíč on the way to Mikulov Wine Region	Mikulov or Pavlov
10	Tour Lednice Château and visit whichever town you're not sleeping in	Mikulov or Pavlov
11	To Olomouc (with time, visit Kroměříž en route)	Olomouc
12	Olomouc (possible side-trip to Wallachia)	Olomouc
13	Visit Kutná Hora on the way back to Prague	Prague
14	Prague	Prague

per week, not including tolls, gas, and supplemental insurance). If you'll be keeping the car for three weeks or more, look into leasing, which can save you money on insurance and taxes for trips of this length. Car rentals and leases are cheapest if arranged from the US. Those with more money than time can consider hiring a car with a private driver (a full-day, round-trip excursion from Prague to Český Krumlov runs about $152; see page 259). Rail passes normally must be purchased outside Europe but aren't necessarily your best option—you may save money by simply buying tickets as you go. For more on public transportation and car rental, see "Transportation" in Practicalities.

Room and Board: You can manage comfortably in Prague on $100 a day per person for room and board. This allows $10 for lunch, $15 for dinner, and $75 for lodging (based on two people splitting the cost of a $150 double room that includes breakfast). Outside Prague, hotel rates plummet to $70 or less for a decent double, and food prices also drop—making $50 a day per person a reasonable budget in the Czech countryside. Even in Prague, students and tightwads can eat and sleep for as little as $40 a day ($25 for a bed, $15 for meals and snacks).

Sightseeing and Entertainment: Sightseeing is inexpensive here. Most sights generally cost about $5-10. A few biggies cost more (such as Prague Castle—$10) or much more (the Jewish Quarter—$20), but that's rare. Most sights offer senior and student discounts; always ask. Figure $20-35 for concerts, Black Light Theater performances, and other splurge experiences. You can hire a private guide for as little as $100 for four hours. An overall average of $30 a day works for most people. Don't skimp here. After all, this category is the driving force behind your trip—you came to sightsee, enjoy, and experience the Czech Republic.

Shopping and Miscellany: Figure $1-2 per stamped postcard, coffee, beer, or ice-cream cone. Shopping can vary in cost from nearly nothing to a small fortune. Good budget travelers find that this category has little to do with assembling a trip full of lifelong memories.

WHEN TO GO

In Prague and the Czech Republic, the "tourist season" runs roughly from Easter through October. July and August have their advantages, with the best weather, longer days (daylight until after 21:00), fewer tourists in Prague than in the peak months of May, June, and September, and busy festivals held in small towns around the country. In spring and fall (May, June, Sept, and early Oct), the weather is milder, and the colors and scents are more powerful. Winter travelers find the concert season in full swing, with re-

The Czech Republic's Best
12-Day Trip by Bus and Train

Day	Plan	Sleep in
1	Arrive in Prague	Prague
2	Prague	Prague
3	Prague	Prague
4	Day trip to Terezín Memorial	Prague
5	To Český Krumlov	Český Krumlov
6	Český Krumlov	Český Krumlov
7	To Telč via Třeboň	Telč
8	To Olomouc via Třebíč	Olomouc
9	Olomouc	Olomouc
10	Return to Prague	Prague
11	Side-trip to Kutná Hora	Prague
12	Prague	Prague

With more time in the Czech Republic, consider a pair of other destinations that are a little more difficult, but still possible, to reach by public transportation: Hikers enjoy Wallachia, which fits easily into the above schedule after Olomouc (make your home base in Trojanovice). Wine lovers head for the Mikulov wine region, easiest to visit between Telč and Olomouc (make your home base in Mikulov or Pavlov).

Beyond the Czech borders, you could visit Budapest, Hungary, and Kraków, Poland—each an easy, direct night-train trip away from Prague (or an even quicker connection from Olomouc). For more on these destinations beyond the Czech Republic, see the current editions of *Rick Steves Budapest* and *Rick Steves Eastern Europe*.

markably fewer tourists—but outside of Prague, many sights are either closed or open on a limited schedule. In December, you'll find Christmas markets on main squares around the country, fragrant with the scent of hot wine with cloves. After a quiet Christmas season, Prague explodes with fun on New Year's Eve, teeming with thousands of Germans and other Europeans. In January and early February, when few tourists come, chances are you will wake up to a Prague silenced by the wistful glimmer of snow, which quickly melts in the Old Town but stays on the ground at Prague Castle and on top of Petřín Hill. Seeing the Charles Bridge blanketed by fresh snow makes the hours spent out in the cold worthwhile. Frequent pub stops, with lots of plum brandy and hot wine, are essential at this time of year—and they bring you closer to local life. Winter can linger, but Prague usually turns green with spring around mid-April. Use the climate chart in the appendix as your Prague weather guide.

INTRODUCTION

∩ Rick Steves Audio Europe ∩

My free **Rick Steves Audio Europe app** is a great tool for enjoying Europe. This app makes it easy to download my audio tours of top attractions, plus hours of travel interviews, all organized into destination-specific playlists.

My self-guided **audio tours** of major sights and neighborhoods across Europe are free, user-friendly, fun, and informative. In Prague, my City Walk audio tour (marked in this book with the ∩ symbol) takes you through the middle of the New Town and Old Town, connecting most of the major landmarks. My audio tours are hard to beat: Nobody will stand you up, the quality is reliable, you can take the tour exactly when you like, and the price is right.

The Rick Steves Audio Europe app also offers a far-reaching library of insightful **travel interviews** from my public radio show with experts from around the globe.

This app and all of its content are entirely free. (And new content is added about twice a year.) You can download Rick Steves Audio Europe via Apple's App Store, Google Play, or the Amazon Appstore. For more information, see www.ricksteves.com/audioeurope.

SIGHTSEEING PRIORITIES

So much to see, so little time. How to choose? Depending on the length of your trip, and taking geographic proximity into account, the following are my recommended priorities:

3 days:	Prague
4-5 days, add:	Your choice of nearby day trips (Kutná Hora, Terezín Memorial, Karlovy Vary, and three castles: Konopiště, Karlštejn, or Křivoklát)
6 days, add:	Český Krumlov (and skip day trips)
8 days, add:	Olomouc
10 days, add:	Třeboň, Telč, and Třebíč, and/or Slavonice
More:	Your choice

This includes nearly everything on the map on page 7. If you don't have time to see it all, prioritize according to your interests. The "Czech Republic at a Glance" sidebar can help you decide where to go (see page 5). This list assumes you're primarily interested in the Czech Republic. But note that Prague also splices neatly into a wider-ranging trip that can include such nearby destinations as Vienna (4.5 hours by train), Budapest (7 hours), Kraków (8 hours), Munich (6.25 hours), and Berlin (4.5 hours).

How Was Your Trip?

Were your travels fun, smooth, and meaningful? You can share tips, concerns, and discoveries at www.ricksteves.com/feedback. To check out readers' hotel and restaurant reviews—or leave one yourself—visit my travel forum at www.ricksteves.com/travel-forum. I value your feedback. Thanks in advance.

KNOW BEFORE YOU GO

Check this list of things to arrange while you're still at home.

You need a **passport**—but no visa or shots—to travel in the Czech Republic. You may be denied entry into certain European countries if your passport is due to expire within six months of your ticketed date of return. Get it renewed if you'll be cutting it close. It can take up to six weeks to get or renew a passport (for more on passports and requirements for the Czech Republic, see www.travel.state.gov). Pack a photocopy of your passport in your luggage in case the original is lost or stolen.

The Czech Republic has joined the open-borders Schengen Agreement, eliminating checks at **border crossings** when traveling to and from neighboring countries. You'll simply zip through the border without stopping. But when you change countries, you still change phone cards, currency, and postage stamps.

Book rooms well in advance if you'll be traveling during peak season (May-June and Sept) or on any major holidays or festivals (see page 482).

Call your **debit- and credit-card companies** to let them know the countries you'll be visiting, to ask about fees, and to request your PIN if you don't already know it. See page 443 for details.

Do your homework if you're considering **travel insurance.** Compare the cost of the insurance to the cost of your potential loss. Also check whether your existing insurance (health, homeowners, or renters) covers you and your possessions overseas. For more tips, see www.ricksteves.com/insurance.

Several **Czech castles** in the countryside (Český Krumlov, Karlštejn´s Chapel of the Holy Cross, and Konopiště) can only be visited with a guided tour, and may offer just a few English tours each day. While you can generally reserve a space the day before (or even the same day), it's worth doing some homework so you can plan your day around joining an English tour. Otherwise, you can join a Czech tour and read the English handout.

If you're planning on **renting a car** in the Czech Republic, bring your driver's license and an International Driving Permit (see page 470).

INTRODUCTION

If you plan to hire a **local guide,** reserve ahead by email. Popular guides can get booked up.

If you're bringing a **mobile device,** download any apps you might want to use on the road, such as translators, maps, transit schedules, and **Rick Steves Audio Europe** (see page 10).

Check for recent updates to this book at www.ricksteves.com/update.

Traveling as a Temporary Local

We travel all the way to the Czech Republic to enjoy differences—to become temporary locals. You'll experience frustrations.

Certain truths we find "God-given" or "self-evident," such as cold beer, ice in drinks, bottomless cups of coffee, "the customer is king," and bigger being better, are suddenly not so true. One of the benefits of travel is the eye-opening realization that there are logical, civil, and even better alternatives. A willingness to go local ensures that you'll enjoy a full dose of Czech hospitality. And with an eagerness to go local, you'll have even more fun.

Europeans generally like Americans. But if there is a negative aspect to the Czech image of Americans, it's that we are loud, wasteful, ethnocentric, too informal (which can seem disrespectful), and a bit naive.

While Czechs look bemusedly at some of our Yankee excesses—and worriedly at others—they nearly always afford us individual travelers all the warmth we deserve.

Judging from all the happy feedback I receive from travelers who have used this book, it's safe to assume you'll enjoy a great, affordable vacation—with the finesse of an independent, experienced traveler.

Thanks, and happy travels!

Rick Steves

Back Door Travel Philosophy

From *Rick Steves Europe Through the Back Door*

Travel is intensified living—maximum thrills per minute and one of the last great sources of legal adventure. Travel is freedom. It's recess, and we need it.

Experiencing the real Europe requires catching it by surprise, going casual..."through the Back Door."

Affording travel is a matter of priorities. (Make do with the old car.) You can eat and sleep—simply, safely, and enjoyably—anywhere in Europe for $100 a day plus transportation costs. In many ways, spending more money only builds a thicker wall between you and what you traveled so far to see. Europe is a cultural carnival, and time after time, you'll find that its best acts are free and the best seats are the cheap ones.

A tight budget forces you to travel close to the ground, meeting and communicating with the people. Never sacrifice sleep, nutrition, safety, or cleanliness to save money. Simply enjoy the local-style alternatives to expensive hotels and restaurants.

Connecting with people carbonates your experience. Extroverts have more fun. If your trip is low on magic moments, kick yourself and make things happen. If you don't enjoy a place, maybe you don't know enough about it. Seek the truth. Recognize tourist traps. Give a culture the benefit of your open mind. See things as different, but not better or worse. Any culture has plenty to share. When an opportunity presents itself, make it a habit to say "yes."

Of course, travel, like the world, is a series of hills and valleys. Be fanatically positive and militantly optimistic. If something's not to your liking, change your liking.

Travel can make you a happier American, as well as a citizen of the world. Our Earth is home to seven billion equally precious people. It's humbling to travel and find that other people don't have the "American Dream"—they have their own dreams. Europeans like us, but with all due respect, they wouldn't trade passports.

Thoughtful travel engages us with the world. It reminds us what is truly important. By broadening perspectives, travel teaches new ways to measure quality of life.

Globetrotting destroys ethnocentricity, helping us understand and appreciate other cultures. Rather than fear the diversity on this planet, celebrate it. Among your most prized souvenirs will be the strands of different cultures you choose to knit into your own character. The world is a cultural yarn shop, and Back Door travelers are weaving the ultimate tapestry. Join in!

CZECH REPUBLIC

Česká Republika

The Czech Republic is geographically small. On a quick visit, you can enjoy a fine introduction while still packing in plenty of surprises. The country has a little of everything for the traveler. Quaint villages? Check. Beautiful landscapes? Check. World-class art? Czech, Czech, and Czech.

While the Czechs have long occupied the lands of the present-day Czech Republic, for most of their history they were treated as second-class citizens, under the thumb of foreign rulers (generally from Germany or Austria). That the Czech nation exists as an independent state today is practically a Cinderella story. So let's get to know the underdog Czechs.

In Czech towns and villages, you'll find a simple joy of life—a holdover from the days of the Renaissance. The deep spirituality of the Baroque era still shapes the national character. The magic of Prague, the beauty of Český Krumlov, and the lyrical quality of the countryside relieve the heaviness caused by the turmoil that passed through here. Get beyond Prague and explore the country's medieval towns. These rugged woods and hilltop castles  will make you feel as if you're walking through the garden of your childhood dreams.

Given their imaginative, sometimes fanciful culture, it's no surprise that the Czechs have produced some famously clever writers—from Franz Kafka (who wrote about a man waking up as a giant cockroach) to Karel Čapek (who wrote about artificially created beings he dubbed "roboti," or robots).

The unique entertainment form of Black Light Theater—a combination of illusion, pantomime, puppetry, and modern dance—exemplifies Czech creativity (see page 243). And beloved Czech characters—such as the smiling Good Soldier Švejk, who befuddles his Austro-Hungarian army officers by cleverly playing dumb, and the ubiquitous little cartoon mole called Krtek—will quickly become familiar, as you'll see them all over the streets of Prague. (For more on Czech lit, see page 152).

Czechs refuse to dumb things down; if you want to visit one of the pretty countryside castles, they'll only let you do it on a thoughtfully guided tour—as if to guarantee that every visitor will come away with a complete appreciation for the place. Education and intellect are important, and academics are honored in Czech society. At the end of communism, the nation elected a poet, playwright, and philosopher, Václav Havel, to serve two terms as president.

Beyond his intellect, voters no doubt also appreciated Havel's independent thinking and bold actions (he had been imprisoned by communist authorities for his activities promoting human rights). Perhaps because they've seen their national affairs bungled by centuries of foreign overlords, many Czechs have a healthy suspicion of authority, and an admiration for those willing to flout it. Other Czechs with a rebellious spirit are national hero Jan Hus (who refused to recant his condemnation of Church corruption, and was burned at the stake), contemporary artist David Černý (whose outrageous stunts are always a lightning rod for controversy), and, of course, the man voted by a wide margin to be the greatest Czech of all time, Jára Cimrman. A fictional character originally created in the 1960s by a pair of radio satirists, Cimrman has taken on a life

CZECH REPUBLIC

Czech Republic Almanac

Official Name: As of 2016, the country's new official short name is Czechia. It's better known as the Česká Republika, born on January 1, 1993, along with Slovakia, when the nation of Czechoslovakia—formed after World War I and dominated by the USSR after World War II—split into two countries.

Population: 10.6 million people. About 64 percent are ethnic Czechs, who speak Czech, and another 5 percent are Moravian. Unlike some of their neighbors (including the very Catholic Poles and Slovaks), Czechs are inclined to be agnostic: One in 10 is Roman Catholic, but the majority (54 percent) list their religion as unaffiliated, and another 35 percent list none.

Latitude and Longitude: 50°N and 15°E (similar latitude to Vancouver, British Columbia).

Area: 31,000 square miles (similar to South Carolina or Maine).

Geography: The Czech Republic comprises three regions (called "lands" here)—Bohemia (Čechy), Moravia (Morava), and a small slice of Silesia (Slezsko). The climate is generally cool and partly cloudy.

Biggest Cities: Prague (the capital, 1.3 million), Brno (378,000), Ostrava (300,000), and Plzeň (167,000).

Economy: The gross domestic product equals about $332 billion (similar to Minnesota). The GDP per capita is approximately $31,600 (compared to $51,490 for the average American). Major moneymakers for the country include machine parts, cars and trucks (VW subsidiary Škoda is a highly respected automaker),

of his own—and today is something of a nationwide practical joke. (For more on Cimrman, see page 74.)

The Czechs' well-studied, sometimes subversive, often world-weary outlook can be perceived by outsiders as cynicism. Czechs have a sharp, dry, often sarcastic sense of humor, and a keen sense of irony. They don't suffer fools lightly...and watching a united nations of clueless tourists trample their capital city for the past generation hasn't done wonders for their patience. Cut the Czechs some slack, and show them respect: Be one of the very few visitors who bothers to learn a few pleasantries—hello, please, thank you—in their language. (See "Czech Survival Phrases" on page 491.) You'll notice the difference in how you're treated.

Of the Czech Republic's three main regions—Bohemia, Moravia, and small Silesia—the best-known is Bohemia. It has nothing to do with beatnik bohemians, but with the Celtic tribe of Bohemia that inhabited the land before the coming of the Slavs. A longtime home of the Czechs, Bohemia, with Prague as its capital, is circled by a naturally fortifying ring of mountains and cut

and beer (the leading brand is Pilsner Urquell). Industrial production declined during the economic slowdown, but not beer consumption, which dropped only minimally (the vast majority of Czech beer is consumed domestically). More than a third of trade is with next-door-neighbor Germany; as a result, Germany's economic health one year generally predicts the Czech Republic's fortunes the next.

Currency: 25 Czech crowns (*koruna*, Kč) = about $1.

Government: From 1948 to 1989, Czechoslovakia was a communist state under Soviet control. Today, the Czech Republic is a member of the European Union (since 2004) and a vibrant democracy, with about a 60 percent turnout for elections. Its parliament is made up of 200 representatives elected every four years and 81 senators elected for six years. The president is selected every five years. No single political party dominates; the current leadership is a coalition of Social Democrats (left), Christian Democrats (center), and an unpredictable one-man populist party. Ailing President Miloš Zeman, elected in 2013 in the first-ever popular presidential vote, is viewed as increasingly out of touch with the public and bent on steering the country's foreign policy toward Russia and China.

Flag: The Czech flag is red (bottom), white (top), and blue (a triangle along the hoist side).

The Average Czech: The average Czech has 1.4 kids (slowly rising after the sharp decline that followed the end of communism), will live 78 years, and has one television in the house.

down the middle by the Vltava River. The winegrowing region of Moravia (to the east) is more Slavic and colorful, and more about the land.

Tourists often conjure up images of Bohemia when they think of the Czech Republic. But the country consists of more than rollicking beer halls and gently rolling landscapes. It's also about dreamy wine cellars and fertile Moravian plains, with the rugged Carpathian Mountains on the horizon. Politically and geologically, Bohemia and Moravia are two distinct regions. The soils and climates in which the hops and wine grapes grow are very different... and so are the two regions' mentalities. The boisterousness of the Czech polka contrasts with the melancholy of the Moravian ballad; the political viewpoint of the Prague power broker is at odds with the spirituality of the Moravian bard.

Only a tiny bit of Silesia—around the town of Opava—is part of the Czech Republic today; the rest of the region is in Poland and Germany. (The Habsburgs lost traditionally Czech Silesia to Prussia in the 1740s, and 200 years later, Germany in turn ceded most of it to Poland.) People in Silesia speak a wide variety of dialects that mix Czech, German, and Polish. Perhaps due to their diverse genes and cultural heritage, women from Silesia are famous for being intelligent and beautiful.

Baby-boomer tourists, who grew up thinking of Prague as a dingy and dangerous outpost of an "Evil Empire," are often surprised at how well the Czech Republic has gotten its act together. But after all, it's been nearly three decades since the Velvet Revolution peacefully overthrew the Soviet puppet regime. Communism seems like ancient history, and the country feels every bit as modern, affluent, safe, and "Western" as any other European country. English is widely spoken, the economy is thriving, roads and railways are in good repair, formerly run-down old buildings are newly gleaming, and locals think about communism only when tourists bring it up.

Ninety percent of the tourists who visit the Czech Republic see only Prague. But if you venture outside the capital, you'll enjoy traditional towns and villages, great prices, a friendly and gentle countryside dotted by nettles and wild poppies, and almost no international tourists. Since the time of the Habsburgs, fruit trees have lined the country roads for everyone to share. Take your pick.

PRAGUE
Praha

ORIENTATION TO PRAGUE

Few cities can match Prague's over-the-top romance, evocative Old World charm...and tourist crowds. Prague is equal parts historic and fun. No other place in Europe has become popular so quickly. And for good reason: Prague—the only Central European capital to escape the large-scale bombing of the last century's wars—is one of Europe's best-preserved cities. It's filled with sumptuous Art Nouveau facades, offers tons of cheap Mozart and Vivaldi concerts, and brews some of the best beer in Europe. Cross the famous Charles Bridge, communing with vendors, artists, tourists, and a stoic lineup of Czech saints in stone. Hike up to the world's biggest castle for a lesson in Czech history and sweeping views across the city's spires and domes.

Appreciate the many layers of Prague's history: It's been the center for the Czech people for a thousand years. In the 1300s, when the Czechs' own ruling dynasty died out, Holy Roman Emperor Charles IV took over...and made the city a world-class capital. Later, Habsburg rulers from Vienna embraced it as a second city of culture. They populated Prague with artists, writers, and composers (most of them German-speaking) and added a Baroque layer (1700-1800), then renovated it (around 1900) in elegant Art Nouveau. When the age of empires ended, and the Czechs and Slovaks finally created their own nation (1918), Prague was the obvious choice as capital. But after World War II, as a Soviet satellite, Prague had no money to modernize. The happy upshot is that, when the city became free of communist rule in 1989, it emerged with its thousand-year ambience intact.

Prague is a photographer's delight. You'll wind through walkable neighborhoods, past statues of bishops and pastel facades adorned with gables, balconies, lanterns, and a zillion little architectural details. Prague itself seems a work of art. Besides its medieval and Baroque look, it's a world of willowy Art Nouveau paintings and architecture. You'll also see rich remnants of its strong Jewish heritage and stark reminders of the communist era. And you'll meet an entrepreneurial mix of locals and expats, each with their own brilliant scheme of how to make money in the tourist trade.

Escape the crowds into the back lanes and pretend you're strolling through the 18th century. Duck into pubs to enjoy the hearty food and good pilsner beer, and tour museums packed with fine art. Delve into one of Europe's top stops.

PLANNING YOUR TIME

A few days in Prague is plenty of time to get a solid feel for the city and enjoy some side-trips. If you're in a rush, you'll need a minimum of two full days (with three nights, or two nights and a night train) for a good introduction to the city. From Munich, Berlin, or Vienna, Prague is a four- to six-hour daytime train ride away; from Budapest, Warsaw, Kraków, or Vienna, you can reach Prague on a handy overnight train.

Keep in mind that Jewish Quarter sights close on Saturday and Jewish holidays. Some museums, mainly in the Old Town, are closed on Monday, as is Veletržní Palace.

Prague in Two or More Days

Here's my suggested plan for fully experiencing Prague in two days. With more time, I've offered more suggestions. Split your nights between beer halls, live music, or Black Light Theater.

Day 1

9:00   Take my Old Town Walk to get oriented to the city's core. Along the way, enter some of the sights (including the Municipal House) and climb at least one of the old towers—at the Old Town Hall, or at either end of the Charles Bridge—to enjoy the view.

13:00   Have lunch either in the Old Town or Little Quarter. Explore the Little Quarter (Kampa Island, Lennon Wall, Little Quarter Square).

15:00   Follow my Jewish Quarter Tour.

Day 2

8:00   Get an early start from your hotel, and zip up to Prague Castle on the tram. Be at St. Vitus Cathedral when it opens at 9:00, then follow my Prague Castle Tour.

11:00   As you leave the castle, tour the Lobkowicz Palace.

12:00   Have lunch in the Little Quarter, below the castle.

13:00   Ride the tram or metro to Vyšehrad park for a pleasant, crowd-free stroll.

14:30   Walk along the river to town and follow my New Town Walk.

15:30   Tour the Mucha Museum or the Municipal House (if you didn't visit it already) to enjoy some Art Nouveau.

16:30   Squeeze in one more museum—perhaps the Museum of Medieval Art or the Museum of Communism.

Note: If you'd rather sleep in today, flip this plan—do Vyšehrad, the New Town Walk, Mucha Museum or Municipal House; then tram up to the castle in the early afternoon (by about 14:00), as the crowds disperse.

Day 3 and Beyond

With more time, fit in additional museums that interest you. If you have at least four days, Prague has a variety of worthwhile day trips at its doorstep. I'd prioritize Kutná Hora (delightful small town with gorgeous cathedral and famous bone church) and/or the Terezín Memorial. Several castles (Karlštejn, Konopiště, and Křivoklát) are worth considering. Český Krumlov is another wonderful destination, but it's a bit far for a day trip—it's much better if you stay overnight.

Prague Overview

PRAGUE BY NEIGHBORHOOD

Residents call their town "Praha" (PRAH-hah). It's big, with about 1.3 million people (swelling to 2 million in the metropolitan area). But during a quick visit, you'll focus on its relatively compact old center.

The Vltava River divides the city in two. East of the river are the Old Town and New Town, the main train station, and most of the recommended hotels. To the west of the river is Prague Castle, and below that, the sleepy Little Quarter. Connecting the two halves are several bridges, including the landmark Charles Bridge.

Think of Prague as a collection of neighborhoods. In fact, until about 1800, Prague actually was four distinct towns with four town squares, all separated by fortified walls. Each town had a unique character, drawn from the personality of its first settlers. Today, much of Prague's charm survives in the distinct spirit of these towns.

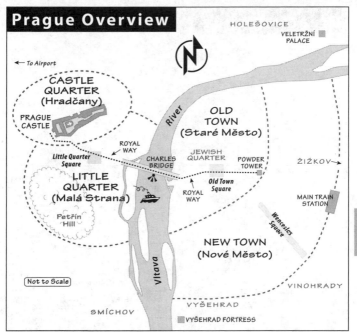

Prague Overview

HOLEŠOVICE

VELETRŽNÍ PALACE

← To Airport

CASTLE QUARTER (Hradčany)

PRAGUE CASTLE

River

OLD TOWN (Staré Město)

ROYAL WAY

CHARLES BRIDGE

JEWISH QUARTER

POWDER TOWER

Little Quarter Square

ŽIŽKOV →

LITTLE QUARTER (Malá Strana)

Old Town Square

ROYAL WAY

MAIN TRAIN STATION

Petřín Hill

Wenceslas Square

NEW TOWN (Nové Město)

Not to Scale

Vltava

VINOHRADY

SMÍCHOV

VYŠEHRAD

VYŠEHRAD FORTRESS

ORIENTATION

Old Town (Staré Město): Nestled in the bend of the river, this is the historic core, where most tourists spend their time. It's pedestrian-friendly, with small winding streets, old buildings, shops, and beer halls and cafés. In the center sits the charming Old Town Square. Slicing east-west through the Old Town is the main pedestrian axis, along Celetná and Karlova streets. Look at a map of the modern road plan to trace the walls that once protected the town; the Powder Tower is a remnant of the wall system that completed a fortified ring, the other half of which was formed by the river.

Within the Old Town, tucked closest to the river, is the **Jewish Quarter** (Josefov), a several-block area with a high concentration of old synagogues and sights from Prague's deep Jewish heritage. It also holds the city's glitziest shopping area (with big-name international designers filling gorgeously restored Art Nouveau buildings).

New Town (Nové Město): Stretching south from the Old Town is the long, broad expanse of Wenceslas Square, marking the center of the New Town. The New Town, shaped like a piece of elbow macaroni, hugs the edge of the Old Town—cutting a swath from riverbank to riverbank. As the name implies, it's relatively new ("only" 600 years old). It's the neighborhood for modern buildings, fancy department stores, and a few communist-era sights.

Wrapping around the New Town, a bit farther from the cen-

ORIENTATION

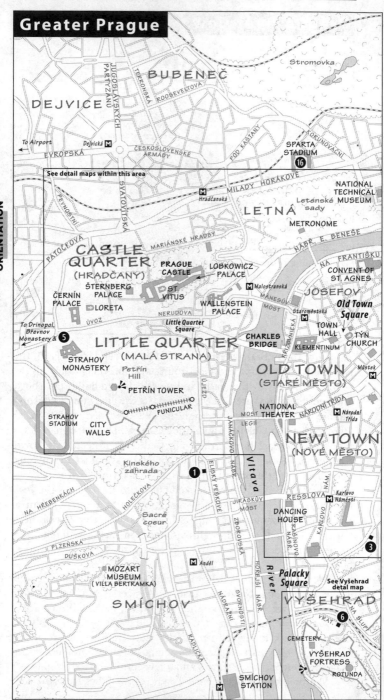

Greater Prague

Stromovka

BUBENEČ

DEJVICE

JUGOSLÁVSKÝCH
PARTYZÁNŮ

TERONSKÁ

ROOSEVELTOVA

KORUNOVAČNÍ

To Airport

Dejvická Ⓜ

EVROPSKÁ

ČESKOSLOVENSKÉ
ARMÁDY

POD KAŠTANY

SPARTA
STADIUM

⑯

MILADY HORÁKOVÉ

NATIONAL
TECHNICAL
MUSEUM

See detail maps within this area

Ⓜ
Hradčanská

PEVNOSTNÍ

SVATOVÍTSKÁ

LETNÁ

Letenské
sady

METRONOME

NÁBŘ. E. BENEŠE

PATOČKOVA

MARIÁNSKÉ HRADBY

CASTLE
QUARTER
(HRADČANY)

PRAGUE
CASTLE

LOBKOWICZ
PALACE

NA
FRANTIŠKU

CONVENT OF
ST. AGNES

ČERNÍN
PALACE

ŠTERNBERG
PALACE

ST.
VITUS

Ⓜ Malostranská

MÁNESŮV
MOST

JOSEFOV

LORETA

WALLENSTEIN
PALACE

Staroměstská Ⓜ

Old Town
Square

To Drinopol,
Břevnov
Monastery &

ÚVOZ

NERUDOVA

Little Quarter
Square

CHARLES
BRIDGE

KŘIŽOVNICKÁ

TOWN
HALL

TÝN
CHURCH

⑤

LITTLE QUARTER
(MALÁ STRANA)

KLEMENTINUM

STRAHOV
MONASTERY

Petřín
Hill

OLD TOWN
(STARÉ MĚSTO)

Můstek
Ⓜ

PETŘÍN TOWER

FUNICULAR

ÚJEZD

MOST
LEGIÍ

NATIONAL
THEATER

NÁRODNÍ TŘÍDA

Národní
Třída Ⓜ

STRAHOV
STADIUM

CITY
WALLS

JANÁČKOVO

NEW TOWN
(NOVÉ MĚSTO)

Kinského
zahrada

ELIŠKY PEŠKOVÉ

Vltava

①

HOLEČKOVA

NÁBŘ.

JIRÁSKŮV
MOST

RESSLOVA

Karlovo
Náměstí Ⓜ

KARLOVO NÁM.

NA HŘEBENKÁCH

Sacré
coeur

ZBOROVSKÁ

DANCING
HOUSE

RAŠÍNOVO NÁBŘ.

③

PLZEŇSKÁ

DUSKOVA

Ⓜ Anděl

MOZART
MUSEUM
(VILLA BERTRAMKA)

HOŘEJŠÍ

River

Palacky
Square

See Vyšehrad
detail map

SMÍCHOV

NÁDRAŽNÍ

SVORNOSTI

NÁBŘ.

VYŠEHRAD

NA SLUPI

V PEVNOSTI

⑥

RADLICKÁ

CEMETERY

SMÍCHOV
STATION

Ⓜ

VYŠEHRAD
FORTRESS

ROTUNDA

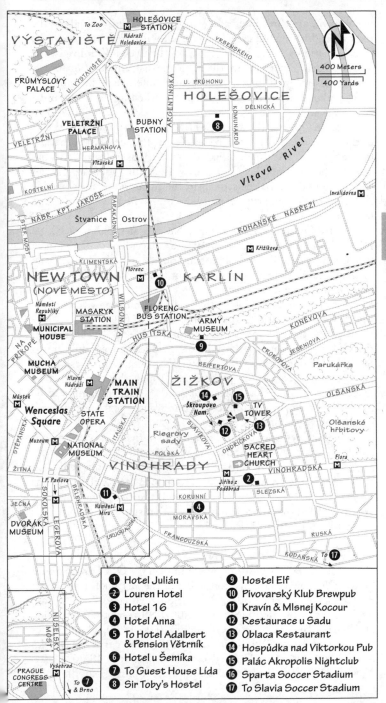

1. Hotel Julián
2. Louren Hotel
3. Hotel 16
4. Hotel Anna
5. To Hotel Adalbert & Pension Větrník
6. Hotel u Šemíka
7. To Guest House Lída
8. Sir Toby's Hostel
9. Hostel Elf
10. Pivovarský Klub Brewpub
11. Kravín & Mlsnej Kocour
12. Restaurace u Sadu
13. Oblaca Restaurant
14. Hospůdka nad Viktorkou Pub
15. Palác Akropolis Nightclub
16. Sparta Soccer Stadium
17. To Slavia Soccer Stadium

ter of town, are three interesting neighborhoods: South along the river is the historic hill called **Vyšehrad,** with great views and the Czechs' national cemetery. Southeast of the river is **Vinohrady,** the former "Royal Vineyards" (as the name means), and now an upscale residential area with some recommended hotels. And just north of that, **Žižkov** is a trendy nightlife zone marked by the city's futuristic TV tower.

Castle Quarter (Hradčany): High atop a hill on the west side of the river stands the massive complex of Prague Castle, marked by the spires of St. Vitus Cathedral. For a thousand years, this has been the neighborhood of Czech rulers (including today's president and foreign minister). Consequently, the surrounding area is noble and leafy, with high art and grand buildings, little commerce, and few pubs.

Little Quarter (Malá Strana): Nestled at the foot of Castle Hill is this pleasant former town of fine palaces and gardens (and a few minor sights). This is Prague's diplomatic neighborhood, made to feel elegant by stately embassies, but lacking some of the funky personality of the Old Town.

Also on the castle side of the river, north of the riverbend, is the **Holešovice** district, home to the Veletržní Palace.

Cutting through the towns—from the Powder Tower through the Old Town, crossing the Charles Bridge, and winding up to St. Vitus Cathedral—is the **Royal Way** (Královská Cesta), the ancient path of coronation processions. Today, this city spine (the modern streets of Celetná, Karlova, and Nerudova) is marred by tacky trinket shops and jammed by tour groups—explore beyond it if you want to see the real Prague.

District System: Prague is administratively carved up into numerical districts (like Budapest, Vienna, and Paris). Almost everything of interest to tourists is in "Praha 1," the old center on both sides of the river, but a few accommodations and attractions are in outlying districts. Addresses include the district number: For example, Veletržní Palace is in the seventh district, so its address is "Dukelských Hrdinů 47, Praha 7."

TOURIST INFORMATION

TIs are at several key locations, including on the **Old Town Square** (in the Old Town Hall, just to the left of the Astronomical Clock; Easter-Oct Mon-Fri 9:00-19:00, Sat-Sun 9:00-18:00; Nov-Easter Mon-Fri 9:00-18:00, Sat-Sun 9:00-17:00); on the castle side of **Charles Bridge** (Easter-Oct daily 10:00-18:00, closed Nov-Easter); and in the Old Town, around the corner from **Havelská Market** (at Rytířská 31, April-Oct Mon-Sat 9:00-19:00, closed Nov-March). For general tourist information in English, dial 221-

714-444 (Mon-Fri 8:00-19:00), or check the useful TI website: www.prague.eu.

The TIs offer maps, a helpful transit guide, and information on guided walks and bus tours. They can book local guides, concerts, and occasionally hotel rooms.

Monthly event guides—all of them packed with ads—include the *Prague Guide* (29 Kč), *Prague This Month* (free), and *Heart of Europe* (free, summer only).

Prague Card: This pricey sightseeing pass covers public transit (including the airport bus); admission or discounts to a number of sights (including a few biggies—such as Prague Castle and Jewish Quarter sights); a free bus tour and river cruise; and discounts to other attractions, including some concerts and guided tours. For most travelers, it's not worth the steep cost (e.g., €48/2 days); check what's included and do the math before you buy (pick up a brochure at the TI, or use the calculator feature at www.praguecard.com).

ARRIVAL IN PRAGUE

Prague has multiple train stations, but most visitors arrive at the main train station (Hlavní Nádraží), on the eastern edge of downtown—a 20-minute walk, short taxi ride, or bus ride to the Old Town Square and many of my recommended hotels. Prague's Václav Havel Airport—12 miles from downtown—is easily connected to the city center by public bus, airport bus, minibus shuttle, and taxis. For details on all of these options, see page 253.

HELPFUL HINTS

Exchange Rate: 25 Kč = about $1

Country Calling Code: 420 (see page 464 for dialing instructions)

Rip-Offs: There's no particular risk of violent crime in Prague, but—as in any heavily touristed city—naive tourists can get taken by con artists. Most scams fall into the category of being charged a two-scoop price for one scoop of ice cream, having extra items appear on your restaurant bill, or not getting the correct change. Jaded salesclerks in the tourist zone know that the 25-to-1 exchange rate mystifies American visitors, and may try to take advantage of your carelessness. Any time you pay for something, make a careful mental note of how much it costs, how much you're handing over, and how much you expect back. Count your change. Beware the "slow count," where clerks give back part of your change, then pause...hoping you'll think they're done and walk away. Wait until you get all the money you're due. Plainclothes policemen "looking for counterfeit money" are con artists—ask to see their badges and they'll shrink away.

Pickpockets: They're abundant in Prague. They can be little children or adults dressed as professionals—sometimes even as tourists with jackets draped over their arms to disguise busy fingers. Thieves work crowded and touristy places in teams—for example, they might create a commotion at the door to a Metro or tram car. Keep your wits about you, assume any big distraction is a smokescreen for theft, and wear a money belt. All of this can sound intimidating, but Prague is safe. Simply stay alert.

Medical Help: A 24-hour **pharmacy** is at Palackého 5 (a block from Wenceslas Square, tel. 224-946-982). For standard assistance, there are two state hospitals in the center: the **General Hospital** (open daily 24 hours, moderate wait time, right above Karlovo Náměstí at U Nemocnice 2, Praha 2, use entry G, tel. 224-962-564) and the **Na Františku Hospital** (on the embankment next to Hotel InterContinental, Na Františku 1, go to the main entrance, for English assistance call Mr. Juřina 7:30-16:30 on weekdays, tel. 222-801-278—serious problems only). The reception staff may not speak English, but the doctors do.

For above-standard assistance in English (including dental care), consider the top-quality **Hospital Na Homolce** (less than 1,000 Kč for an appointment, daily 8:00-16:00 call 252-922-146, for after-hours emergencies call 257-211-111; bus #167 from Anděl Metro station, Roentgenova 2, Praha 5). The **Canadian Medical Care Center** is a small, private clinic with an English-speaking Czech staff at Veleslavínská 1 in Praha 6 (appointment-3,000 Kč, house call-4,500 Kč, halfway between the city and the airport, tel. 235-360-133, after-hours emergency tel. 724-300-301).

Thai massage parlors (which might sound salacious, but are legit) are all the rage in the Old Town. For a more professional fix, contact **Patrick Kočica,** an experienced Hoshino therapist (1,000 Kč/hour, mobile 722-070-703, patrick. kocica@hoshino.cz, www.hoshino.cz).

Bookstores: Shakespeare and Sons is a friendly English-language bookstore with a wide selection of translations from Czech, the latest publications, and a reading space downstairs overlooking a river channel (daily 11:00-19:00, one block from Charles Bridge on Little Quarter side at U Lužického Semináře 10, tel. 257-531-894, www.shakes.cz). In the heart of the Jewish Quarter, the **Franz Kafka Society** has a fine little bookstore

Prague's Best Views

Enjoy the "Golden City of a Hundred Spires" during the early evening, when the light is warm and the colors are rich. Good viewpoints include the following:

- The garden terrace in front of **Strahov Monastery,** above the castle (see page 91);
- The many balconies and spires at **Prague Castle;**
- **Villa Richter** restaurants, overlooking the city from just below the castle past the Golden Lane;
- The top of either tower on **Charles Bridge;**
- The **Old Town Square clock tower** (with a handy elevator);
- **Hotel u Prince's** rooftop dining terrace overlooking the Old Town Square (also with an elevator);
- The steps of the **National Museum** overlooking Wenceslas Square; and
- The top of the **Žižkov TV tower,** offering spaceship views of the city, in the Žižkov/Vinohrady neighborhood east of the city center (150 Kč for elevator to observatory at 300 feet, free access to Oblaca restaurant at 200-foot-level for customers—see page 226).

ORIENTATION

with a thoughtfully curated shelf of Czech lit in English translation—from Kafka to Švejk to tales of the Little Mole (daily 10:00-18:00, Široká 14, tel. 224-227-452).

Maps: A good map of Prague is essential. For ease of navigation, look for one with trams and Metro lines marked, and tiny sketches of the sights (30-70 Kč; sold at kiosks, exchange windows, and tobacco stands). The *Kartografie Praha* city map, which shows all the tram lines and major landmarks, also includes a castle diagram and a street index. It comes in two versions: 1:15,000 covers the city center (good enough for most visitors), and 1:25,000 includes the whole city (worthwhile if you're sleeping in the suburbs).

Also consider getting a mapping app for your smartphone, which uses GPS to pinpoint your location. To avoid data-roaming charges, look for an offline map that can be downloaded in its entirety, such as those offered by **City Maps 2Go** (searchable offline).

Laundry: A **full-service laundry** near most of the recommended hotels is at Karolíny Světlé 11 (200 Kč/8-pound load, wash and dry in 3 hours, Mon-Fri 7:30-19:00, closed Sat-Sun, 200 yards from Charles Bridge on Old Town side, mobile 721-030-446); another laundry is at Rybná 27 (290 Kč/8-pound load, same-day pickup, Mon-Fri 7:00 or 8:00-18:00, closed Sat-Sun, tel. 224-812-641). **Prague Andy's Laundromat** offers both self- and full-service (self-service-160 Kč/load, full service-300 Kč/load—weekdays only, free Internet access, daily 8:00-20:00, near Náměstí Míru Metro stop at Korunní 14, Praha 2, mobile 723-112-693, www.praguelaundromat. cz).

Mini-Markets: These corner convenience stores, generally open daily until midnight, cleverly stock their shelves to fill most of your grocery needs. Many are run by Vietnamese immigrants, who first came here in the 1980s to train in textile factories as part of a communist government program. After the fall of communism, they stayed on. Prices are generally fair. Locals figure if the beer costs less than a Coke, it's a good place to shop.

Bike Rental: Prague has improved its network of bike paths, making bicycles a feasible option for exploring the center of the town and beyond (see http:// mapa.prahounakole.cz for a map). Two bike-rental shops are located near the Old Town Square: **Praha Bike** (daily 9:00-22:00, Dlouhá 24, mobile 732-388-880, www.prahabike. cz) and **City Bike** (daily 9:00-19:00, Královdorská 5, mobile 776-180-284, www.citybike-prague.com). They rent bikes for about 300 Kč for two hours  or 500 Kč a day (1,500-Kč deposit), and also organize guided bike tours. Another shop offers **electric bikes** (590 Kč/half-day, 890 Kč/day, April-Oct daily 9:00-19:00, tours available, just above American Embassy in Little Quarter at Vlašská 15, mobile 604-474-546, www.ilikeebike.com).

Car Rental: You won't want or need to drive within compact Prague, but a car can be handy for exploring the countryside. All the biggies have offices in Prague (check each company's website, or ask at the TI).

Travel Service and Tours: Magic Praha is a tiny travel service run by Lída Jánská. A Jill-of-all-trades, she can help with accommodations and transfers throughout the Czech Republic, as well as private tours and side-trips to historic towns (mobile 604-207-225, www.magicpraha.cz, magicpraha@magicpraha.cz).

GETTING AROUND PRAGUE

You can walk nearly everywhere. Brown street signs (in Czech, but with helpful little icons) direct you to tourist landmarks. For a sense of scale, the walk from the Old Town Square to the Charles Bridge takes less than 10 minutes (depending on crowds).

Still, it's worth figuring out the public transportation system, which helps you reach farther-flung sights (Prague Castle, Vyšehrad, and so on). The Metro is slick, the trams fun, and the taxis quick and easy. Prague's tram system is especially wonderful—trams rumble by frequently and take you just about anywhere. Be bold and you'll swing through Prague like Tarzan. For details, pick up a transit guide at the TI. City maps show the Metro, tram, and bus lines.

By Metro, Tram, and Bus

Excellent, affordable public transit is perhaps the best legacy of the communist era (locals ride all month for 300 Kč).

Tickets: The Metro, trams, and buses all use the same tickets:
- 30-minute **short-trip ticket** *(krátkodobá),* which allows as many transfers as you can make in a half hour—24 Kč
- 90-minute **standard ticket** *(základní)*—32 Kč
- **24-hour pass** *(jízdenka na 24 hodin)*—110 Kč
- **3-day pass** *(jízdenka na 3 dny)*—310 Kč

Buy tickets from your hotel, at Metro stops, newsstand kiosks, or from machines. To avoid wasting time looking for a ticket-seller when your tram is approaching, stock up on tickets before you set out. Since Prague is a great walking town, most find that individual tickets work better than a pass.

Be sure to validate your ticket as you board the tram or bus, or as enter the Metro station, by sticking it in the machine, which stamps a time on it—watch locals and imitate. Inspectors routinely ambush ticketless riders (including tourists) and fine them 700 Kč on the spot.

Schedules and Frequency: Trams run every 5-10 minutes in the daytime (a schedule is posted at each stop). The Metro closes at midnight, and but nighttime tram routes (identified with white numbers on blue backgrounds at tram stops) run all night at 30-minute intervals. You can find more information and a complete route planner in English at www.dpp.cz.

By Tram

Navigate by signs that list the end stations. At the platform, a sign lists all the stops for each tram in order. Remember that trams going one direction leave from one platform, while the other direction might leave from a different platform nearby—maybe across the street or a half-block away. When the tram arrives, open the doors by pressing the green button. Once aboard, validate your ticket in the machine.

As you go, follow along carefully so you'll be ready when your stop comes up. Newer trams have electronic signs that show either the next stop *(příští)*, or a list of upcoming stops. Also, listen to the recorded announcements for the name of the stop you're currently at, followed by the name of the stop that's coming up next. (Confused tourists, thinking they've heard their stop, are notorious for rushing off the tram one stop too soon.) The surest way to know whether it's your stop is to check the platform for a sign that shows the name of the stop.

Handy Trams: These lines are especially useful.

• **Tram #22** is practically made for sightseeing, connecting the New Town with the Castle Quarter (see my "Tram #22 Tour," later, and find the line marked on the Prague Metro map). The tram uses some of the same stops as the Metro (making it easy to get to—or travel on from—the tram route). Of the many stops this tram makes, the most convenient are two in the New Town (Národní Třída, between the bottom of Wenceslas Square and the river; and Národní Divadlo, at the National Theater), two in the Little Quarter (Malostranské Náměstí, on the Little Quarter Square; and Malostranská

Metro stop, near the riverbank), and three above Prague Castle (Královský Letohrádek, Pražský Hrad, and Pohořelec; for details, see page 85 of the Prague Castle Tour chapter).

• **Tram #17** connects Vyšehrad and the New and Old Town embankments (including stops at the National Theater/Národní Divadlo—closest stop to Charles Bridge, and Old Town/Staroměstská) and stretches to the Veletržní stop.

• **Tram #2** connects Malostranská (near the riverbank, on the castle side of the river) with stops along the Old Town embankment (Old Town/ Staroměstská, Charles Bridge/Karlovy Lázně, National Theater/Národní Divadlo), cuts inland along Národní Třída and south to Charles Square/Karlovo Náměstí, and then returns to the river at Výtoň, at the base of Vyšehrad hill.

• **Trams #9** and **#24** are helpful for traveling across town from the main train station and the Wenceslas Square/Václavské Náměstí and Republic Square/Náměstí Republiky stops.

By Metro

The three-line Metro system is handy and simple, but doesn't always get you right to the tourist sights (landmarks such as the Old Town Square and Prague Castle are several blocks from the nearest Metro stops). Although it seems that all Metro doors lead to the neighborhood of Výstup, that's simply the Czech word for "exit."

By Taxi

I find Prague to be a great taxi town and use them routinely. That said, the city has more than its share of dishonest cabbies, so here

are a few tips to avoid being overcharged.

Legitimate local rates are cheap: Drop charge starts at 40 Kč; per-kilometer charge is around 30 Kč; and waiting time per minute is about 6 Kč. These rates are clearly marked on the door, so be sure the cabbie honors them. Also insist that cabbies turn on the meter, and that it's set at the right tariff, or "*sazba*" (usually but not always tariff #1). Unlike in many cities, there's no extra charge for calling a cab—the meter starts only after you get in. Tip by rounding up; locals never tip more than 5 percent.

Have a ballpark idea of what your ride will cost. Figure about 150-200 Kč for a ride between landmarks within the city center (for example, from the main train station to the Old Town Square, or from the Charles Bridge to the castle). Even the longest ride in the center should cost under 300 Kč.

ORIENTATION

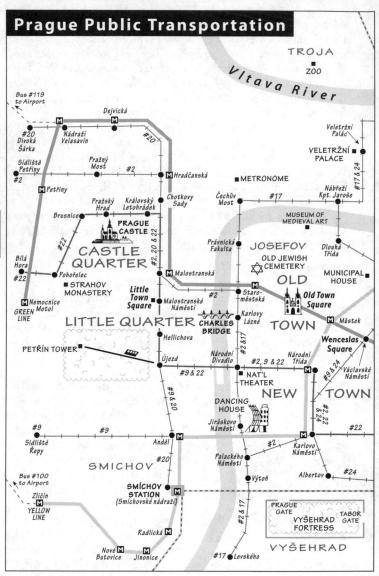

Prague Public Transportation

To improve your odds of getting a fair metered rate, call for a cab (or ask someone at your hotel or restaurant to call for you), rather than hailing one on the street. **AAA Taxi** (tel. 222-333-222) and **City Taxi** (tel. 257-257-257) are the most likely to have English-speaking staff and honest cabbies. I also find that hailing a passing taxi usually gets me a decent price, although at a slightly higher rate than when reserving by phone. Avoid cabs waiting at

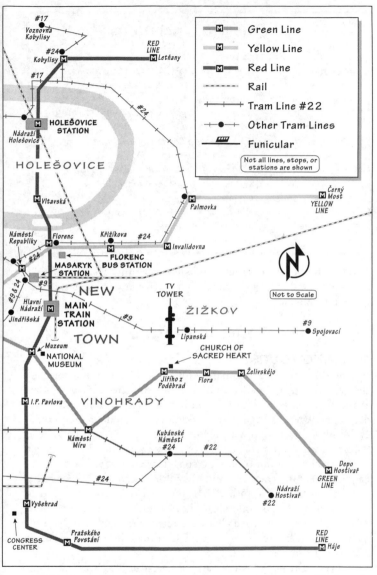

tourist attractions and train stations, who are far more likely to be crooked—waiting to prey on unwary tourists.

And what if the cabbie surprises you at the end with an astronomical fare? If you think you're being overcharged, challenge it. Point to the rates on the door. Get your hotel receptionist to back you up. Pull out your phone and threaten to call the police. (Because of new legislation to curb dishonest cabbies, the police will

Prague Pronunciations

English	Czech
Main train station	Hlavní Nádraží (HLAV-nee NAH-drah-zhee)
Old Town	Staré Město (STAR-eh MYEHS-toh)
Old Town Square	Staroměstské Náměstí (STAR-oh-myehst-skeh NAH-myehs-tee)
New Town	Nové Město (NOH-vay MYEHS-toh)
Little Quarter	Malá Strana (MAH-lah STRAH-nah)
Jewish Quarter	Josefov (YOO-zehf-fohf)
Castle Quarter	Hradčany (HRAD-chah-nee)
Charles Bridge	Karlův Most (KAR-loov most)
Wenceslas Square	Václavské Náměstí (vaht-SLAHF-skeh NAH-myehs-tee)
Vltava River	Vltava (VUL-tah-vah)

ORIENTATION

stand up for you.) Or simply pay what you think the ride should cost—300 Kč should cover you for a long ride anywhere in the center—and walk away.

Tours in Prague

WALKING TOURS

A staggering number of small companies offer walking tours of the Old Town, the castle, and more (for the latest, pick up fliers at the TI). Since guiding is a routine side-job for university students, you'll generally get hardworking young guides at good prices. While I'd rather go with my own local guide (described later), public walking tours are cheaper (4 hours for about 450 Kč), cover themes you might not otherwise consider, connect you with other English-speaking travelers, and allow for spontaneity. The quality depends on the guide rather than the company. Your best bet is to show up at the Astronomical Clock a couple of minutes before 8:00, 10:00, or 11:00, then chat with a few of the umbrella-holding guides there. Choose the one you click with. Guides also have fliers advertising additional walks.

"Free" Tours: As is the case all over Europe, "free" walking tours that are not really free; you're expected to tip your guide (with paper bills rather than coins) when finished. While these tours are fine for the backpacker and hostel crowd (for whom they're designed), the guides are usually expat students (generally from the US or Australia) who memorize a script and give an entertaining performance as you walk through the Old Town, with little respect for serious history. When it comes to guided tours, nothing is free (except for my self-guided audio tour; see page 10).

LOCAL GUIDES

In Prague, hiring a guide is particularly smart (and a ▲▲ experience)—they're twice as helpful for half the price compared with guides in Western Europe. Because prices are usually per hour (not per person), small groups can hire an inexpensive guide for several days. Guides meet you wherever you like and tailor the tour to your interests. Visit their websites for details on various walks, airport transfers, countryside excursions, and other services offered, and then make arrangements by email.

Small Companies

Personal Prague Guide Service's Šárka Kačabová uses her teaching background to help you understand Czech culture, and has a team of personable and knowledgeable guides (600 Kč/hour for 2-3 people, 800 Kč/hour for 4-8 people, fifth hour free, mobile 777-225-205, www.personalpragueguide.com, sarka@me.com).

PragueWalker is run by Katka Svobodová, a hardworking historian-guide who knows her stuff and manages a team of enthusiastic and friendly guides (600 Kč/hour for individuals, families, and small groups; mobile 603-181-300, www.praguewalker.com, katerina@praguewalker.com).

Individual Guides

These generally young guides (which is good, because they learned their trade post-communism) typically charge about 2,000-2,500 Kč for a half-day tour.

Jana Hronková has a natural style—a welcome change from the more strict professionalism of some of the busier guides—and a penchant for the Jewish Quarter (mobile 732-185-180, www.experience-prague.info, janahronkova@hotmail.com). **Zuzana Tlášková** speaks English as well as Hebrew (mobile 774-131-335, tlaskovaz@seznam.cz). **Martin Bělohradský,** formerly an organic chemistry professor, is particularly enthusiastic about fine arts and architecture (mobile 723-414-565, martinb5666@gmail.com). **Jana Krátká** enjoys sharing Prague's tumultuous 20th-century history with visitors (mobile 776-571-538, janapragueguide@gmail.com). Friendly **Petra Vondroušová** designs tours to fit your interests (mobile 602-319-420, www.compactprague.com, petra.vondrous@seznam.cz). To combine a highlights tour with exploration outside the main circuit, contact this book's co-author, **Honza Vihan** (mobile 603-418-148, honzavihan@hotmail.com). **Kamil and Pavlína** run a family business specializing in tours of Prague and beyond. They also provide sightseeing and transport as far as Vienna and Berlin (mobile 605-701-861, www.prague-extra.com, info@prague-extra.com).

My readers have also had good experiences with these guides:

ORIENTATION

Daily Reminder

Sunday: St. Vitus Cathedral at Prague Castle is closed Sunday morning for Mass. Some stores have shorter hours or are closed.

Monday: The Museum of Medieval Art is closed. Most of the other major sights—such as Prague Castle and sights in the Jewish Quarter—are open, but a number of lesser sights, including Týn Church, Church of St. James, Bethlehem Chapel (in winter), House of the Golden Ring, and Sternberg Palace are closed.

   If you're day-tripping today, the three castles—Konopiště, Karlštejn, and Křivoklát—are closed.

   In Prague's Old Town, classical musicians have a jam session at 17:00 at St. Martin in the Wall, and the cover is free at the Roxy music club, where concerts start at 20:00.

Tuesday-Friday: All sights are open.

Saturday: The Jewish Quarter sights are closed. In nearby Terezín, the Crematorium and Columbarium are closed.

Renata Blažková, who has a special interest in the history of Prague's Jewish Quarter (tel. 222-716-870, mobile 602-353-186, blazer@volny.cz); **Václav Štorek,** who specializes in history (mobile 603-743-523, www.storek.guide-prague.cz, vaclavstorek@post.cz); **Petr Zídek** (mobile 721-286-869, www.bohemiantours.cz, petr@bohemiantours.cz); **Andrea Řezníčková** (mobile 777-930-024, www.mypraguetours.com, andrea@mypraguetours.com); and **Darina Krajakova** (krajakova@hotmail.com).

The **TI** also has plenty of local guides (3-hour tour: 1,200 Kč/1 person, 1,400 Kč/2 people, 1,600 Kč/3 people, 2,000 Kč/4 people; desk at Old Town Square TI, arrange and pay in person at least 2 hours in advance, tel. 236-002-562, guides@pis.cz). For a list of yet more guides, see www.guide-prague.cz.

Running Tours Prague are guided by Radim Prahl, a local with an appetite for ultra-marathons; he'll run you past monuments, through parks, and down back alleys at your own pace (1,500 Kč for two people; mobile 777-288-862, www.runningtoursprague.com).

JEWISH QUARTER TOURS

Jewish guides (of varying quality) meet small groups twice daily in season for three-hour tours in English of the Jewish Quarter. **Wittmann Tours** charges an 880-Kč fee that includes entry to the Old-New Synagogue and the six other major Jewish Quarter sights (which cost 480 Kč total), so the tour actually costs only 400 Kč (May-Oct Sun-Fri at 10:30 and 14:00, Nov-Dec and mid-March-

April Sun-Fri at 10:30 only, no tours Sat and Jan-mid-March, minimum 3 people). Tours meet in the little park (just beyond the café), directly in front of Hotel InterContinental at the end of Pařížská street (tel. 603-168-427 or 603-426-564, www.wittmann-tours. com). In addition, several of the **private local guides** recommended earlier do good tours of the Jewish Quarter.

BUS TOURS

Since Prague's sightseeing core (Castle Quarter, Charles Bridge, and the Old Town) is not accessible by bus, I don't recommend any of the city's bus tour companies. (Most are basically walking tours that use buses for pickups and transfers.) For a good once-over of Prague, skip the pricey bus tours and take my "Tram #22 Tour" (see the end of this chapter).

Prague—which is so delightful on foot—really doesn't lend itself to the **hop-on, hop-off bus-tour** formula. These buses give ticket holders 24 hours to hop on and off tour buses that come by every half-hour or so as they circulate through town, stopping at major attractions. An uninspired recorded narration plays along the way. Tickets cost about 450 Kč and may include a one-hour riverboat cruise (described next).

Bus tours can make sense for day trips out of Prague. Several companies have kiosks on Na Příkopě, where you can comparison-shop. **Premiant City Tours** offers 20 different tours, including one to Karlštejn and Konopiště castles (1,950 Kč, 8.5 hours) and a river cruise. The tours have live guides and depart from near the bottom of Wenceslas Square at Na Příkopě 23. Get tickets at an AVE travel agency, your hotel, on the bus, or at Na Příkopě 23 (tel. 224-946-922, mobile 606-600-123, www.premiant.cz). **Wittmann Tours,** listed earlier in "Jewish Quarter Tours," offers an all-day minibus tour to the Terezín Memorial (www.wittmann-tours.com).

Tour salespeople are notorious for telling you anything to sell a ticket. Some tours, especially those heading into the countryside, can be in as many as four different languages. Hiring a local guide, many of whom can drive you around in their car, can be a much better value (described earlier).

BOAT TOURS AND RENTALS

Prague isn't ideal for a **boat tour**—you might spend half the time waiting to go through the locks. Still, the hour-long Vltava River cruises, which leave from near the castle end of

ORIENTATION

ORIENTATION

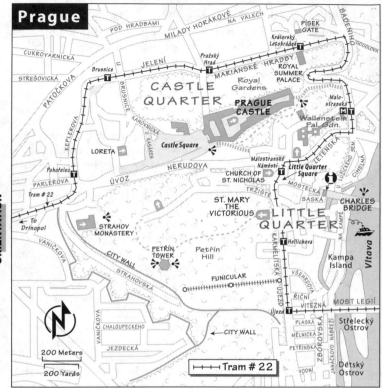

Prague

POD HRADBAMI — MILADY HORÁKOVÉ — NA VALECH — PÍSEK GATE — BADENÍHO — GOGOLOVA
CUKROVARNICKÁ — Brusnice — JELENÍ — Pražský Hrad — MARIÁNSKÉ HRADBY — Královský Letohrádek — ROYAL SUMMER PALACE
STŘEŠOVICKÁ — BRUSNICE — CASTLE QUARTER — Royal Gardens — Malo-stranská
PATOČKOVA — KEPLEROVA — KANOVNICKÁ — U KAŠÁREN — PRAGUE CASTLE — Wallenstein Pal. Gdn.
LORETA — Castle Square — NERUDOVA — Malostranské Náměstí — Little Quarter Square — KLÁROV — LETENSKÁ — U LUŽICKÉHO SEM. — CHELNÍ
Pohořelec — CHURCH OF ST. NICHOLAS — MOSTECKÁ — SASKÁ — CHARLES BRIDGE
PARLÉŘOVA — ÚVOZ — TRŽIŠTĚ — Vltava
Tram # 22 — ST. MARY THE VICTORIOUS — LITTLE QUARTER — NA KAMPĚ
To Dřínopol — STRAHOV MONASTERY — Petřín Hill — Hellichova — KARMELITSKÁ — VŠEHRDOVA — Kampa Island
VANIČKOVA — CITY WALL — PETŘÍN TOWER — FUNICULAR — ŘÍČNÍ — ÚJEZD
STRAHOVSKÁ — VITEZNÁ — MOST LEGIÍ
N — CHALOUPECKÉHO — CITY WALL — Újezd — PLASKÁ — ZBOROVSKÁ — Střelecký Ostrov
200 Meters — VANIČKOVA — JEZDECKÁ — MĚLNICKÁ — PETŘINSKÁ — JANÁČKOVO NÁBŘEŽÍ — Dětský Ostrov
200 Yards — Tram # 22 — VODNÍ

Charles Bridge about hourly, are scenic and relaxing, though not informative (150-200 Kč).

Renting a rowboat or paddleboat on the island by the National Theater is a better way to enjoy the river (worth ▲). You'll float at your own pace among the swans and watch local lovers cruise by in their own boats (40 Kč/hour for rowboats, 60 Kč/hour for paddleboats, bring photo ID for deposit).

TOURS OUTSIDE OF PRAGUE

To get beyond the sights listed in most guidebooks, or for a deeply personal look at the usual destinations, call **Tom and Marie Zahn.** Tom is American, Marie is Czech, and together they organize and lead family-friendly day excursions (in Prague and throughout the country). Their tours are creative and affordable, and they teach travelers how to find off-the-beaten-track destinations on their own. Their specialty is Personal Ancestral Tours & History (P.A.T.H.)—with sufficient notice, they can help Czech descendants find their ancestral homes, perhaps even a long-lost relative. Tom and Marie can also help with other parts of your Eastern European travel by linking you with associates in other countries,

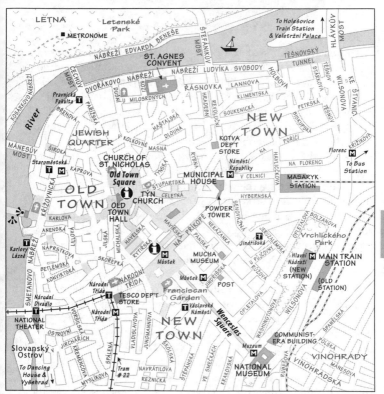

ORIENTATION

especially Germany, Hungary, Poland, Romania, Slovakia, and Ukraine (US tel. 360-450-5959, Czech tel. 257-940-113, www. pathways.cz for tours, www.pathfinders.cz for genealogy research, info@pathfinders.cz).

Reverend Jan Dus, an enthusiastic pastor who lived in the US for several years, now serves a small congregation about 100 miles east of Prague. Jan can design itineraries, and likes to help travelers connect with locals in little towns, particularly in northeastern Bohemia and Moravia. He also has an outstanding track record in providing genealogical services (toll-free US tel. 800-807-1562, www.revjan.com, rev.jan.services@gmail.com).

TOUR PACKAGES FOR STUDENTS

Andy Steves (Rick's son) runs **Weekend Student Adventures** (WSA Europe), offering 3-day and 10-day budget travel packages across Europe including accommodations, skip-the-line sightseeing, and unique local experiences. Locally guided and DIY unguided options are available for student and budget travelers in 12 of Europe's most popular cities, including Prague (guided trips from €199, see www.wsaeurope.com for details).

Tram #22 Tour

A trip on tram #22 makes a good self-guided Prague orientation joyride, worth ▲▲. It runs roughly every 5-10 minutes, and you can hop on and off as you like (32-Kč standard ticket valid for 1.5 hours—see page 31). Be warned: Thieves and plainclothes ticket-checkers like this route as much as the tourists.

Catch the tram in the New Town and ride it over the river and up to the castle (stop: Pohořelec). You'll see how easy it is to use the trams, get the lay of the land, and zip effortlessly up to the castle (saving lots of sweat or a 200-Kč taxi ride).

Start by catching the tram at the **Národní Třída** stop on the same side of Spálená street as the Tesco department store (a Metro stop of the same name is nearby). The tram will turn and rattle along National Street (Národní Třída). Or, since several recommended places to eat and sleep are near the Náměstí Míru stop (four stops before Národní Třída), you could start the tour from there.

At the next stop, **Národní Divadlo,** you'll see the recommended Slavia café (look for the *Kavárna Slavia* sign) facing the National Theater, just before the tram crosses the river. Survey the boat-rental scene (island with rental wharfs) and the romantic beach island, and enjoy a great castle view. The Dancing House (designed by Frank Gehry), while hard to see, is 400 yards upstream.

The next stop, **Újezd,** faces a park. See the Monument to Victims of Communism—the bronze spectral figures descending the steps into the park at the corner (described on page 83). A funicular leads to the Eiffel-like Petřín Tower.

The tram then heads north from the **Hellichova** stop, paralleling Kampa Island on the river side (to the right). On the left side, the tram passes St. Mary the Victorious Church, popular with pilgrims for its Infant Jesus of Prague. As the tram gradually goes uphill, it enters Little Quarter Square. You'll catch a peek-a-boo view of the Charles Bridge off to the right at the end of the street.

The tram stops next at **Malostranské Náměstí** (closest stop to the Charles Bridge), on the Little Quarter's main square, dominated by the Church of St. Nicholas. If you get off here, you can hike up Nerudova street to Prague Castle.

After a short tunnel, the tram passes the Old Town end of the Charles Bridge on the left and the Klementinum (National Library) on the right. From the **Staroměstká** stop, the Old Town Square is 300 yards to the right. Directly ahead across the park is the Rudolfinum, the home of the Czech Philharmonic. The Pinkas Synagogue and the Jewish Quarter are across the tracks from the Rudolfinum.

Next the tram turns left across the bridge and rejoins the old route at Malostranská. Fifteen yards beyond the **Malostranská** stop, on the left, is the entry to the Wallenstein Palace Garden. Behind you, on the right in the park, is a modern memorial to WWII freedom fighters. (Beyond that, a bridge leads across the Vltava River to Josefov, the Jewish Quarter.) The tram now enters the longest stretch between stations—perfect for ticket-checkers to reveal themselves and catch anyone traveling without a valid ticket. Just after the tram completes its climb up the hill and makes a sharp left turn, you'll see the Písecká Brána (Písek Gate, or Sand Gate) on your right, one of the few preserved gates of Prague's Baroque fortification system.

The next stop is **Královský Letohrádek.** Immediately across the street is the Royal Summer Palace, the Royal Gardens leading fragrantly to Prague Castle, and a public WC.

If you're in a hurry to hit the castle sights, jump out at the **Pražský Hrad** stop for the most direct route to the castle entrance. If you've got more time, stay on board for my favorite approach from Pohořelec, coming up soon.

The next stop is **Brusnice,** from which you can explore the Nový Svět (New World) neighborhood, a time capsule of cobblestone streets and tiny houses with no shops or tourists (to reach this area from the stop, walk across the small park that has a statue—just ahead on the left—then go down the steps).

The tram now winds through a greenbelt built along the remains of the city wall. The stop at **Pohořelec** is my preferred approach to the castle and the closest stop to the Strahov Monastery. Hop out here, and it's all downhill (for directions to the monastery, see 85). Or catch a tram going the opposite direction to do this trip in reverse.

Extending the Route: To experience workaday Prague without a hint of tourism, stay on the tram three more stops to **Drinopol.** Browse organic shops and French cheese stores, indicating that this 1930s neighborhood is now populated by cosmopolitan young families. Sit down for a fine, relatively inexpensive meal at the **$$ U Bílého Lva** ("By the White Lion," daily 11:00-24:00, Bělohorská 79, tel. 233-355-909), just on the left as you get off the tram, or choose from a wide array of poppy-seed pastries in the tiny bakery-cum-café across the street.

You can also walk or take the tram two stops farther to **Břevnovský Klášter** (five stops after Pohořelec), a peaceful Benedictine monastery built in a pleasantly simple Baroque style with a garden, low-key restaurant, and the recommended Hotel Adalbert. To get back to the Strahov Monastery and the castle at any point, simply take tram #22 back in the other direction.

ORIENTATION

SIGHTS IN PRAGUE

These sights are arranged by neighborhood for handy sightseeing. Remember that Prague started out as four towns—the Old Town and New Town on the east side of the river, and the Castle Quarter and Little Quarter on the west—and it's still helpful for sightseers to think of the city that way. I've also included a pair of sights outside the city center.

When you see a 📖 in a listing, it means the sight is covered in much more depth in a self-guided walk or tour. This is why Prague's most important attractions get the least coverage in this chapter—we'll explore them later in the book.

Check www.ricksteves.com/update for significant changes that have occurred since this book was published. For tips on sightseeing, see page 448.

The Old Town (Staré Město)

All the sights described here are within a 10-minute walk of the magnificent Old Town Square.

📖 For a self-guided tour of the square and its main landmarks, see the Old Town Walk chapter. 🎧 My Prague City Walk audio tour covers sights in both the Old Town and New Town.

THE OLD TOWN SQUARE AND NEARBY
▲▲▲The Old Town Square (Staroměstské Náměstí)

The focal point for most visits, Prague's Old Town Square is one of the city's top sights. This perfectly preserved living postcard boasts gorgeous showpieces of virtually every architectural era: stout Gothic towers and steeples, boisterous Baroque domes, and frilly Rococo palaces. The square's centerpiece is the **memorial to Jan Hus,** the great Czech philosopher whose criticism

of the Catholic Church sparked religious conflicts long before Martin Luther's time (for more on Hus, see page 103). Hus gazes up at the iconic twin towers of the **Týn Church.** Across the square stands the tower of the **Old Town Hall,** with another Prague symbol, the ludicrously complex **Astronomical Clock,** which uses revolving discs, celestial symbols, and sweeping hands to keep several versions of time.

Old Town Hall Tower and Tour

While this building's most popular feature is its Astronomical Clock, you can pay to see other sights inside. Go through the door to the left of the Astronomical Clock, where the ticket desk shares a space with the TI. From here, continuing deeper into the building, you'll find pay WCs and a bank of elevators.

Ride the elevator to floor 3 to buy your ticket to ascend the **town hall's tower** (via another elevator—if it's busy, you may have to wait a few minutes), with ▲▲ views over Prague's prettiest square (110 Kč, Tue-Sun 9:00-21:00, Mon 11:00-21:00; after 19:00 the entry is through the door immediately to the left of the clock rather than through the TI).

On floor 1, you can take a 45-minute **tour of the Old Town Hall,** which includes a Gothic chapel and a close-up look at the inner guts of the Astronomical Clock, plus its statues of the 12 apostles (100 Kč, or 160-Kč combo-ticket with tower, about 3 tours/day in English—see the schedule at the ticket desk).

▲Týn Church

The twin, multiturreted, fairy-tale-like Gothic towers of the Church of Our Lady Before Týn (its full name) loom over the Old Town Square. While every tourist snaps a photo of this church, consider stepping inside, too. Due to its complex history—first Catholic, then the main Hussite (Protestant) church, then Catholic again—it has an elaborately decorated interior.

Cost and Hours: 30-Kč requested donation, generally open to sightseers Tue-Sat 10:00-13:00 & 15:00-17:00, Sun 10:30-12:00, closed Mon. No photos.

❍ Self-Guided Tour: Look at the facade from the Old Town Square. The Týn Church is the Old Town's main church. It has roots back to the 1100s, though this structure dates from Prague's

SIGHTS

Prague at a Glance

Rather than a checklist of museums, Prague is a fine place to wander around and just take in the fun atmosphere. Plan some worthwhile activities: Take a self-guided tram tour (page 42), hire a local guide (page 37), enjoy a concert (page 244), or go for a scenic paddle on the river (page 39).

In the Old Town

▲▲▲**The Old Town Square** Magical main square of Old World Prague, with dozens of colorful facades, the dramatic Jan Hus Memorial, looming Týn Church, and fanciful Astronomical Clock. **Hours:** Týn Church generally open to sightseers Tue-Sat 10:00-13:00 & 15:00-17:00, Sun 10:30-12:00, closed Mon; clock strikes on the hour daily 9:00-21:00, until 20:00 in winter; clock tower open Tue-Sun 9:00-21:00, Mon 11:00-21:00. See page 44.

▲▲▲**Charles Bridge** Atmospheric, statue-lined bridge that connects the Old Town to the Little Quarter and Prague Castle. **Hours:** Always open and crossable. See page 55.

▲▲▲**Jewish Quarter** Finest collection of Jewish sights in Europe, featuring various synagogues and an evocative cemetery. **Hours:** The quarter can be visited any time; museum sights open April-Oct Sun-Fri 9:00-18:00, Nov-March until 16:30, closed Sat and on Jewish holidays; Old-New Synagogue open Sun-Thu 9:30-18:00, off-season until 17:00, Fri closes one hour before sunset, closed Sat and Jewish holidays. See page 56.

▲▲**Museum of Medieval Art** Best Gothic art in the country, at the former Convent of St. Agnes. **Hours:** Tue-Sun 10:00-18:00, closed Mon, may close sporadically due to budget cuts. See page 58.

▲**Havelská Market** Colorful open-air market that sells crafts and produce. **Hours:** Daily 9:00-18:00. See page 52.

▲**Klementinum** National Library's lavish Baroque Hall and Observatory Tower (with views), visit possible by 45-minute tour only. **Hours:** Tours depart daily every half-hour 10:00-17:30, shorter hours off-season. See page 54.

In the New Town

▲▲**Wenceslas Square** Lively boulevard at the heart of modern Prague. **Hours:** Always open. See page 59.

▲▲**Mucha Museum** Easy-to-appreciate collection of Art Nouveau works by Czech artist Alfons Mucha. **Hours:** Daily 10:00-18:00. See page 60.

▲▲**Municipal House** Pure Art Nouveau architecture, including Prague's largest concert hall and several eateries. **Hours:** Daily 10:00-18:00. See page 66.

▲**Museum of Communism** The rise and fall of the regime, from start to Velvet finish. **Hours:** Daily 9:00-21:00. See page 62.

▲**National Memorial to the Heroes of the Heydrich Terror** Tribute to members of the resistance, who assassinated a notorious Nazi architect of the Holocaust. **Hours:** Tue-Sun 9:00-17:00, closed Mon. See page 70.

In the Little Quarter

▲**Petřín Hill** Little Quarter hill with public art, a funicular, and a replica of the Eiffel Tower. **Hours:** Funicular—daily 8:00-22:00; tower—daily 10:00-22:00, shorter hours off-season. See page 83.

In the Castle Quarter

▲▲▲**St. Vitus Cathedral** The Czech Republic's most important church, featuring a climbable tower and a striking stained-glass window by Art Nouveau artist Alfons Mucha. **Hours:** Daily 9:00-17:00, Nov-March until 16:00, closed Sunday mornings year-round for Mass. See page 88.

▲▲**Prague Castle** Traditional seat of Czech rulers, with St. Vitus Cathedral (see above), Old Royal Palace, Basilica of St. George, shop-lined Golden Lane, and lots of crowds. **Hours:** Castle sights—daily 9:00-17:00, Nov-March until 16:00; castle grounds—daily 5:00-24:00. See page 164.

▲▲**Lobkowicz Palace** Delightful private art collection of a Czech noble family. **Hours:** Daily 10:00-18:00. See page 90.

▲**Strahov Monastery and Library** Baroque center of learning, with ornate reading rooms and old-fashioned science exhibits. **Hours:** Daily 9:00-11:45 & 13:00-17:00. See page 91.

Outside the Center

▲**Vyšehrad** Welcoming, untouristy park at the site of a former hilltop palace, rich with Czech history and great city views. **Hours:** Park always open, though various sights inside (church, cemetery, etc.) close at 18:00 (earlier off-season). See page 95.

SIGHTS

Golden Age, built around 1360 as the university church (by the same architect who did St. Vitus Cathedral at Prague Castle). The fanciful **steeples** (with their forest of sub-steeples) aren't exactly "twins"—they were built a century apart, and one is slightly fatter.

Enter the church by making your way through the cluster of buildings in front of it, entering at #14 (under the arcade that faces the square). The structure is full of light, with soaring Gothic arches. The ornamentation reflects the church's troubled history. Originally Catholic, it was taken over by the Hussites (proto-Protestant followers of Jan Hus, c. 1420-1620), who whitewashed it and stripped it of Catholic icons. When the Catholic Habsburgs retook the church, they encrusted its once elegant and pure Gothic columns with noisy Baroque altars, erected statues of Mary and the saints, and added black-and-gold highlights.

Now do a slow, counterclockwise tour around the church, heading up the right aisle. Midway down the aisle, at the base of a pillar on your left, look for an exquisite carved-wood Baptism-of-Christ **altarpiece.**

At the front-right corner of the church, on the pillar to your right is a brown stone slab showing a man in armor with a beard and ruff collar, his hand resting on a globe. This is **Tycho Brahe** (1546-1601), the first modern astronomer—whom the Habsburgs brought with them while they ruled Prague.

Now circle around to face the stunning **main altar,** topped with a statue of the archangel Michael with a flaming sword. A painting (on the lower level) shows Mary ascending to heaven where (in the next painting up) she's to be crowned. To the right of the altar is a statue of one of Prague's patron saints—John of Nepomuk (always easy to identify thanks to his halo of stars; see page 118).

You're surrounded by the **double-eagle symbol** of the Catholic Habsburgs: on the flag borne by a knight statue on the altar, atop the organ behind you (Prague's oldest), and above you on the ceiling.

Exploring the rest of the church, you'll see lots of reliefs of knights who are buried underfoot, and a number of "marble" altarpieces that are (knock, knock) actually made of wood. Before leaving, read the Catholic spin on the church's history (in the entry vestibule, in English)—told with barely a mention of Hus, whose followers made their home in this building for two centuries.

Heading outside, on the side of the church facing Celetná street, find a **statue of the Virgin Mary** resting on a temporary column in an ignored niche. Catholics are still waiting for a chance to reinstall Mary in the middle of the Old Town Square, where she stood for about 250 years until being torn down in 1918 by a mob of anti-Habsburg (and therefore anti-Catholic) demonstrators.

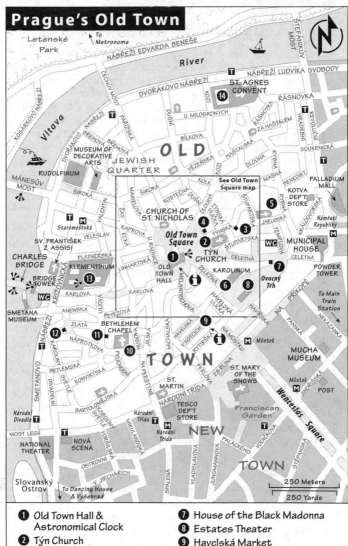

Prague's Old Town

SIGHTS

1. Old Town Hall & Astronomical Clock
2. Týn Church
3. Ungelt Courtyard & House of the Golden Ring
4. Kinský Palace
5. Church of St. James
6. Charles University
7. House of the Black Madonna
8. Estates Theater
9. Havelská Market
10. Bethlehem Chapel
11. Family Museum of Postcards
12. Theater on the Balustrade
13. Klementinum (National Library)
14. Museum of Medieval Art

Sightseeing Strategies

Crowd-Beating Tips Visit Prague Castle either first thing in the morning (be at St. Vitus Cathedral right at 9:00—except Sun morning, when it's closed for Mass) or midafternoon (closes at 17:00 in summer, 16:00 in winter). Hiring your own guide for a historic walk is relatively cheap and allows you to choose a time (evening or early morning) and route to avoid crowds.

Evening Activities Prague Castle's grounds stay open until 24:00 and provide a fanciful people-free zone to wander in the evening. Concerts in the National Theater, Smetana Hall at the Municipal House, and Rudolfinum feature superb artists at bargain prices (see the Entertainment in Prague chapter).

Nearby: Tucked immediately behind Týn Church is a welcome oasis of tranquility in the midst of the Old Town Square hubbub. The courtyard called **Ungelt** was the commercial nucleus of medieval Prague. It once served as a hostel for foreign merchants, much like a Turkish caravanserai. It still bustles with commerce, but now serves mostly tourists (inviting outdoor restaurants, cafés, shops, and hotels).

House of the Golden Ring (Dům u Zlatého Prstenu)

This medieval townhouse is the home of the City of Prague Gallery and its delightful collection of 20th-century Czech art. Since 1900, Czech artists have been refining the subtle differences between dream, myth, and ideal. The English descriptions in each room psychoanalyze this demanding art and recall Prague's role at the forefront of the European avant-garde in the 1930s and again in the 1960s. Notice the absence of Socialist Realism (the  state-sanctioned propaganda art of the communist era): The artists exhibited here chose deeply personal means of expression over regime-sponsored proclamations of universal optimism.

Cost and Hours: 120 Kč, Tue-Sun 10:00-18:00, closed Mon, just left of the entry into Ungelt courtyard as you approach it from the Old Town Square, Ty nská 6, tel. 224-827-0224, www.ghmp. cz. The house's courtyard is home to a lively-with-students café.

Kinský Palace (Palác Kinských)

A meditative space just 10 steps away from the Old Town Square bustle, this modest exhibit of Asian art ranges from Bronze Age China to modern Japan, and from the human-focused art of Buddhism to the flowery and abstract motifs of Islam.

Cost and Hours: 300-Kč combo-ticket also covers Medieval Art Museum, Sternberg Palace, Schwarzenberg Palace, and Veletržní Palace; valid 7 days; open daily 10:00-18:00; Staroměstské Náměstí 12, tel. 224-810-758, www.ngprague.cz.

▲Church of St. James (Kostel Sv. Jakuba)

This fine old medieval church—tucked just behind the Ungelt courtyard—was redecorated head-to-toe in exuberant Baroque following a late-17th-century fire.
Step inside to appreciate the gorgeous space, with its gilded woodwork and bombastic frescoes, and to see the church's main relic, the Madonna Pietatis.

Cost and Hours: Free, Tue-Sun 9:30-12:00 & 14:00-16:00, closed Mon, corner of Malá Štupartská and Jakubská.

☐ For a self-guided tour of the church, see the Old Town Walk chapter.

SOUTH AND EAST OF THE OLD TOWN SQUARE

Between the Old Town Square and the New Town, you'll find several interesting sights.

On Celetná Street

Celetná, a pedestrian-only street, is a convenient and relatively un-crowded way to get from the Old Town Square to the New Town.

Along the way, near the square called Ovocný Trh ("Fruit Market"), you'll find several interesting sights: the Cubist-style **House of the Black Madonna,** with bold and uniquely Czech architecture and a genteel turn-of-the-century café; the historic **Estates Theater;** and the looming, Gothic-flavored **Powder Tower,** marking the course of the former wall that separated the Old Town from the New Town.

☐ All of these are described in greater detail in the Old Town Walk chapter.

On Melantrichova Street

Skinny, tourist-clogged Melantrichova street leads directly from the Old Town Square's Astronomical Clock to the bottom of Wenceslas Square. But even along this most crowded of streets,

Prague's Charles University

Back in the 1300s, Charles University students studied the arts first; the other three faculties (medicine, law, and theology) were secondary subjects. Classes were taught in Latin, and Czechs made up only a fourth of the cosmopolitan student body.

During the chaotic Hussite reforms in the early 1400s, greater Czech control over the university prompted foreign students and professors to leave Prague and found the first German university in Leipzig. Although celebrated as a victory by Czech nationalists, as a result Charles University declined from a European center of learning to a provincial institution.

In the 1600s, the mostly Protestant university was given to the Jesuits. Habsburg Emperor Josef II abolished the Jesuit order in the 1780s, opened the university to non-Catholics, and allowed classes to be taught in to German. Czechs finally won the freedom to study in their own language in 1882, when the university split into two separate schools (the German school dissolved in 1945).

Today, the Charles University campus is intertwined with the Old Town. Though lined with souvenir stalls outside, many buildings hold classrooms that have been animated by lecturers for centuries. Some of the Old Town's most hidden courtyards have provided Czech scholars with their two most essential needs: good beer and space for inspiring conversation.

a genuine bit of Prague remains. Halfway along, don't miss the **Havelská Market,** worth ▲, an open-air marketplace (daily 9:00-18:00). While it's dominated by produce on weekdays, you'll find more souvenirs, puppets, and toys on weekends.

📖 For more on Havelská Market, see the Old Town Walk chapter.

On and near Bethlehem Square (Betlémské Náměstí)

The charming, relatively quiet Bethlehem Square is a pleasantly untouristy chunk of Old Town real estate.

Bethlehem Chapel (Betlémská Kaple)

Holy Roman Emperor Charles IV founded the first university in Prague—and Central Europe—in 1348, and this was its chapel. In about 1400, priest and professor Jan Hus preached from the pulpit here (see the sidebar on page 103). While meant primarily for students and faculty, services were open to the public, and standing-room-only crowds of more than 3,000 were the norm when Hus preached.

Today's chapel is a 1950s reconstruction of the original. Try the unbelievably bad acoustics inside—they demonstrate the sloppy

Charles University has always been a center of Czech political thought. It's where Jan Hus called for reform of the Church. The revolutions of 1618 and 1848 were sparked by university minds; university students rose up against totalitarian regimes in 1939, 1948, and 1968. Student demonstrations incited the Velvet Revolution, which swept communists out of power in November 1989.

The Czech education system itself has yet to fully escape the legacy of authoritarian regimes: Schools focus on memorization, not independent thinking; even at the university level, few students dare to challenge a professor's view. There's also a lack of opportunities within the small country: Most Ph.D. graduates find employment only within their department of study.

Despite these limitations, Charles University still attracts well-qualified Czech and Slovak students. A controversial proposal to begin charging tuition is under debate, but wouldn't solve the problem of more students than available seats. Only a third of those who apply to Czech high schools ("gymnasium") are accepted; of those only half get in to state universities. Those from well-educated (and well-off) families tend to do better in a system that begins selecting students from the age of 11.

SIGHTS

restoration work sponsored by the communists. English info sheets are available for the tiny upstairs exhibit and big chapel.

Cost and Hours: 60 Kč; April-Oct daily 10:00-18:30; Nov-March Tue-Sun 10:00-17:30, closed Mon and for frequent university functions; Betlémské Náměstí, tel. 224-248-595.

More Sights near Bethlehem Square

The tiny **Family Museum of Postcards,** inside Choco Café, is around the corner on Liliová street, which connects Bethlehem Square with Karlova. After learning how the Austro-Hungarian Empire invented the postcard, you can buy your own early-20th-century specimen (40 Kč, Tue-Sun 11:00-19:00, closed Mon, Liliová 4, tel. 222-222-519).

Walk down Liliová street for 30 yards and then turn left into a narrow corridor leading past a church-like structure into the quiet Anenské Náměstí (St. Anne Square), with a black iron grille covering a medieval well in the middle. On the opposite side of the square is the avant-garde **Theater on the Balustrade** (Divadlo Na zábradlí) with a handy café inside (Mon-Fri 10:00-24:00, Sat-Sun from 16:00). It was here that future Czech president Václav Havel found a job as a stagehand in the early 1960s, and wrote and staged the first Czech plays of the absurd (for more on Havel, see

Czechs and Indians

The German writer Karl May used the time he spent in prison for fraud in the 1860s to write stories about the fictional noble Apache chief Winnetou and his German friend Old Shatter-hand (although May didn't visit America until 1908, very late in his life). Ever since, the Czechs have been obsessed with Na-tive Americans. Most kids spend summers at "teepee camps," where they learn about the Native Americans' respect for na-ture, survival skills in the wilderness, courage, and idealized noble spirit. A Czech remake of Johnny Horton's song "Jim Bridger" is an outright celebration of the Sioux victory at Lit-tle Bighorn, and one of the most popular sagas sung around Czech campfires. And Prague's Náprstek Museum of Asian, African, and American Cultures owns attire worn by Lakota Chief Sitting Bull (closed Mon, Betlémské Náměstí 1).

page 155). The embryo-shaped copper drainpipe on the corner of the building symbolizes the traditionally experimental nature of the art performed inside.

If you were to turn and go around the corner with the embryo, you'd pass the second-floor balustrade (the theater's namesake), and head down to the Vltava River. From here you could go to the right along the tram tracks to the Charles Bridge, or go to the left to the National Theater.

Or, instead of heading to the river, you can turn right (as you face the front of the theater), walk to the far end of the square, and enter a passageway. This leads to two connected courtyards and busy Karlova street. The bronze sculpture in the first court-yard, depicting a planet with elliptical orbits modeled around it, is a reminder that Johannes Kepler occupied the adjacent house in the early 1600s. The Czech Astronomical Society runs the small **Kepler Museum** here (60 Kč, Tue-Sun 10:00-18:00, closed Mon, Karlova 4, tel. 608-971-236, www.keplerovomuzeum.cz).

BETWEEN THE OLD TOWN SQUARE AND THE RIVER

Karlova street winds through medieval Prague from the Old Town Square to the Charles Bridge (it zigzags—just follow the crowds and the *Karlův Most* signs). The touristy feeding-frenzy of Prague is at its ugliest along this commercial gauntlet. But try to ignore all of that and appreciate this slice of medieval Prague. If you need an escape, duck into the Klementinum.

▲Klementinum

The Czech Republic's massive National Library borders touristy Karlova street. The contrast could not be starker: Step out of the

most souvenir-packed stretch of Eastern Europe, and enter the meditative silence of Eastern Europe's biggest library.

Cost and Hours: Tour—220 Kč, departs daily every half-hour 10:00-17:30; shorter hours off-season, tel. 733-129-252, www.klementinum. com; strolling down Karlova, turn at the intersection with Liliová through an archway into the Klementinum's courtyard.

Background: Jesuits built the Klementinum in the 1600s to house a new college; they had been invited to Prague by the Catholic Habsburgs to offset the influence of the predominantly Protestant Charles University nearby. The building was transformed into a library in the early 1700s, when the Jesuits took firm control of the university. Their books, together with the collections of several noble families (written in all possible languages...except Czech), form the nucleus of the National and University Library, which is now six million volumes strong. (Note that the Klementinum's Chapel of Mirrors is a popular venue for evening concerts.)

Touring the Klementinum: While much of the Klementinum building is simply a vast library, its magnificent original Baroque Hall and Observatory Tower are open to the public by tour only (45 minutes, in English). You'll belly up to a banister at the end of the ornate library with its many centuries-old books, fancy ceilings with Jesuit leaders and saints overseeing the pursuit of knowledge, and Josef II—the enlightened Habsburg emperor—looking on from the far end. Then you'll climb the Observatory Tower, learning how early astronomers charted the skies over Prague. The tour finishes with a grand Prague view from the top.

▲▲▲Charles Bridge (Karlův Most)

Prague's landmark icon—connecting the two halves of the city across the Vltava River, and lined with statues of Czech saints—

is one of Europe's most famous bridges, and one of its best public spaces. Day and night, the bridge bustles with buskers, tourists, street vendors, school groups, impromptu concerts... and, occasionally, a few Czechs. Make a point to do several laps across the Charles Bridge during your Prague visit, and be sure to slow down and linger as you stroll. Get to know the stony saints who line the bridge. Enjoy the

SIGHTS

360-degree views. Visually trace the hilltop horizon that hems in this gorgeous cityscape. Count spires and domes. Lose yourself in the magic of Prague.

▫ See the Old Town Walk chapter.

Nearby: You can climb the **bridge towers** on both ends of Charles Bridge. The tower on the **Old Town side** of the river (Staroměstská Mostecká Věž, 138 steps) rewards you with some of Prague's best views: a stunning vista of the bridge itself, jammed with people heading for the castle; and 180 degrees away, a perfect panorama that reminds you why Prague is called the "Golden City of a Hundred Spires." On the **Little Quarter side** (Malostranská Mostecká Věž), you can huff up 146 steps for fine views of the bridge, the Little Quarter rooftops, and the castle. If you're trying to decide which to climb, consider that for snapping photos, the light is better if you climb the Old Town tower early in the day, and the Little Quarter tower late in the day (90 Kč to climb each tower, daily 10:00-22:00, March and Oct until 20:00, Nov-Feb until 18:00).

▲▲▲JEWISH QUARTER (JOSEFOV)

The Jewish Quarter is Europe's most accessible sight for learning about an important culture and faith that's interwoven with the fabric of Central and Eastern Europe. Within a three-block radius, several original synagogues, cemeteries, and other landmarks survive, today collected into one big, well-presented museum—the Jewish Museum in Prague. It can get crowded here, so time your visit carefully (early or late is best). All the sights listed below are covered by the same ticket and open the same hours—with one exception: the Old-New Synagogue, which has its own ticket (plus a combo-ticket) and schedule.

▫ See the Jewish Quarter Tour chapter.

Jewish Museum in Prague (Židovské Muzeum v Praze)

The "museum" consists of four synagogues, a ceremonial hall, and a cemetery—each described below. To avoid lines, buy your ticket at a less-crowded sight (such as the Klausen or Spanish synagogues) instead of a more crowded one (such as the Pinkas Synagogue). You can also buy tickets at the Information Center at Maiselova 15 (near the intersection with Siroka street).

Cost and Hours: 300 Kč, or covered by 480-Kč combo-ticket with Old-New Synagogue; 300-Kč audioguide is overkill; April-Oct Sun-Fri 9:00-18:00, Nov-March until 16:30, closed year-round on Sat—the Jewish Sabbath—and on Jewish holidays; their website lists all of their closures (tel. 222-317-191, www.jewishmuseum.cz).

Maisel Synagogue (Maiselova Synagóga): This newly renovated pastel-colored Neo-Gothic synagogue was built as a private place of worship for a wealthy family. It now houses an interactive exhibit on Jewish history in the Czech lands and a few precious objects. During Nazi occupation, this building became a warehouse for a vast collection of Judaica, which Hitler planned to turn into a "Museum of the Extinct Jewish Race"...perhaps explaining why these items, and the Jewish Quarter itself, managed to survive through those dark days.

Pinkas Synagogue (Pinkasova Synagóga): For many visitors, this house of worship—today used as a memorial to the Holocaust victims—is the most powerful of the Jewish Quarter sights. The name of each of the 77,297 Czech Jews who were murdered during the Holocaust is inscribed on the walls, and a somber voice reads those names on an endless loop. Upstairs is an emotionally devastating collection of art created by child inmates at the Terezín concentration camp (outside of Prague). Most of these young artists perished in Nazi death camps.

Old Jewish Cemetery (Starý Židovský Hřbitov): Hiding behind a wall and sitting above the street level, this is where Prague's

Jews buried their dead. Because space in the ghetto was at a premium, and it's against Jewish laws to disturb graves, residents had no choice but to bury bodies on top of bodies—raising the ground level several feet, and squeezing several generations' worth of grave markers onto the top level. A stroll through the crooked tombstones is a poignant experience.

Ceremonial Hall (Obřadní Síň): Sitting at the edge of the cemetery, this small space has an exhibit focusing on Jewish burial rituals.

Klausen Synagogue (Klauzová Synagóga): This 17th-century synagogue is devoted to Jewish religious practices. Exhibits on the ground floor explain the Jewish calendar of festivals. Upstairs is an exhibit on the rituals of Jewish life (circumcisions, bar and bat mitzvahs, weddings, kosher eating, and so on).

Spanish Synagogue (Španělská Synagóga): Called "Spanish" though its design is Moorish (which was all the rage when this was built in the 19th century), this has the most opulently decorated interior of all the synagogues. It marked a time of relative wealth and importance for Prague's Jews, who in this era were increasingly welcome in the greater community and (in many cases) chose to adopt a more reformed approach to worship. Exhibits explain the lives of Czech Jews in the 19th and early 20th centuries, when they believed to be living their best days yet...unaware that the Holocaust was looming.

Nearby: Prague's fine Museum of Medieval Art (see page 58) is just a few blocks from the Spanish Synagogue.

Old-New Synagogue (Staronová Synagóga)

The oldest surviving and most important building in the Jewish Quarter, the Old-New Synagogue goes back at least seven centuries. While the exterior seems simple compared to ornate neighboring townhouses, the interior is atmospherically 13th-century.

Cost and Hours: 200 Kč, or 480-Kč combo-ticket with Jewish Museum of Prague, Sun-Thu 9:00-18:00, off-season until 17:00, Fri closes one hour before sunset, closed Sat and on Jewish holidays, admission includes worthwhile 10-minute tour, tel. 222-317-191, www.synagogue.cz.

NORTH OF THE OLD TOWN SQUARE, NEAR THE RIVER

Stray just a couple of blocks north of the Old Town Square and you'll find a surprisingly tourist-free world of shops and cafés, pastel buildings with decorative balconies and ornamental statues, winding lanes, cobblestone streets, and mosaic sidewalks. It's also home to this fine, underrated museum.

▲▲Museum of Medieval Art (Středověké umění v Čechách a Střední Evropě)

Prague flourished in the 14th century, and the city has amassed an impressive collection of altarpieces and paintings from that age.

Today this art is housed in the former Convent of St. Agnes, which was founded in the 13th century by a Czech princess-turned-nun as the first hospital in Prague. A visit here is a sightseeing twofer: Enjoy the well-presented art in a refreshingly uncrowded setting, and savor the tranquil corridors and cloisters.

Cost and Hours: 300-Kč combo-ticket also covers Sternberg Palace, Schwarzenberg Palace, Kinský Palace, and Veletržní Palace; valid 7 days; convent buildings are free; open Tue-Sun 10:00-18:00, closed Mon; two blocks northeast of Spanish Synagogue, along the river at Anežská 12, tel. 224-810-628, www.ngprague.cz.

📖 See the Museum of Medieval Art Tour chapter.

The New Town (Nové Město)

Enough of pretty, medieval Prague—let's leap into the modern era. The New Town, with Wenceslas Square as its focal point, is today's urban Prague. This part of the city offers bustling boulevards and interesting neighborhoods. Even today, the New Town is separated from the Old Town by a "moat" (the literal meaning of the street called Na Příkopě). As you cross bustling Na Příkopě, you leave the glass and souvenir shops behind, and enter a town of malls and fancy shops that cater to locals and visitors alike. The New Town is one of the best places to view Prague's remarkable Art Nouveau art and architecture, and to learn more about its communist past.

♪ My Prague City Walk audio tour covers sights in both the Old Town and New Town.

WENCESLAS SQUARE AND NEARBY

These sights are on or within a few blocks of the elongated main square of the New Town. The top of the square is the highest point (and farther from the city center); the bottom of the long square is several blocks away, nearer the center.

▲▲Wenceslas Square (Václavské Náměstí)

More a broad boulevard than a square, this city landmark is named for St. Wenceslas (Václav in Czech), whose equestrian statue overlooks the square's top end. Wenceslas Square functions as a stage for modern Czech history: The creation of the Czechoslovak state was celebrated here in 1918; in 1968, the Soviets suppressed huge popular demonstrations (called the Prague Spring) at the square; and, in 1989, more than 300,000 Czechs and Slovaks converged here to demand their freedom (in the Velvet Revolution). Today it's a busy thoroughfare of commerce.

At the top of the square, the **National Museum** (described next) stands behind Wenceslas. Just to the left is an ugly Soviet-era building that housed the **communist parliament,** and later became the post-Cold War headquarters for Radio Free Europe. And in the square just in front of Wenceslas is the poignant **memorial to Jan Palach** (a student who set himself on fire in 1969 to protest the regime) and other victims of communism.

Shopping malls line the square, including (on the left as you look down from the top) the swanky **Lucerna Arcade** (with some interesting public art) and **Světozor Mall** (once a stronghold of rebellion against the communists, and now home to Prague's favorite ice cream stand). And in the streets to the right, you'll find the excellent **Mucha Museum** (described later).

📖 See the Wenceslas Square Walk chapter.

National Museum (Národní Muzeum)

This museum stands grandly at the top of Wenceslas Square. Undergoing a seven-year renovation (which will retain the exterior bullet marks from 1968), the historical building is slated to reopen in 2018. Its interior is richly decorated in the Czech Revival Neo-Renaissance style that heralded the 19th-century rebirth of the Czech nation. However, its collection is dull—a skippable assemblage of Czech fossils and animals. For cost and opening times ask at the TI or check www.nm.cz.

Franciscan Garden (Františkánská Zahrada)

Just a few steps off of Wenceslas Square, this delightful hidden garden is a much-appreciated oasis in the heart of a busy city. While the 17th-century Franciscan monastery that once stood here is long gone, the monks' garden thrives as a favorite escape for local urbanites. Free to enter and always open, it's tucked behind the Světozor Mall near the midpoint of Wenceslas Square.

📖 See the Wenceslas Square Walk chapter.

▲▲Mucha Museum (Muchovo Museum)

This enjoyable little museum features a small selection of the insistently likeable art of Alfons Mucha (MOO-khah, 1860-1939), a founding father of the Art Nouveau movement. It's all crammed into a too-small space, some of the art is faded, and the admission price is steep—but there's no better place to gain an understanding of Mucha's talent, his career, and the influence he's had on the world art scene. And the museum, partly overseen by Mucha's grandson, gives you a peek at some of the posters that made Mucha famous. You'll learn how these popular patriotic banners, filled with Czech symbols and expressing his people's ideals and aspirations, aroused the national spirit. Enjoy decorative posters from his years in Paris, including his celebrated ads for the French actress Sarah Bernhardt. Check out the photographs of his models, which Mucha later re-created in pencil or paint, and be sure to see the 30-minute film on the artist's life.

Cost and Hours: 240 Kč, daily 10:00-18:00, good English

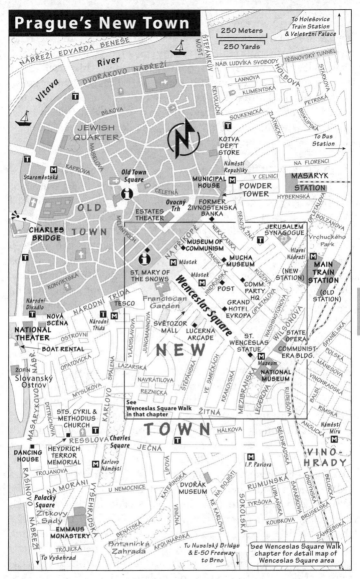

Prague's New Town

250 Meters
250 Yards

To Holešovice
Train Station
& Veletržní Palace

NÁBŘEŽÍ EDVARDA BENEŠE

River

DVOŘÁKOVO NÁBŘEŽÍ

NÁB. LUDVÍKA SVOBODY

TĚŠNOVSKÝ TUNNEL

LANNOVA

HOLBOVA

REVOLUČNÍ

KLIMENTSKÁ

BÍLKOVA

JEWISH
QUARTER

SOUKENICKÁ

ZLATNICKÁ

To Bus
Station

KOTVA
DEP'T
STORE

NA FLORENCI

MASARYK
STATION

Náměstí
Republiky

Y CELNICI

MUNICIPAL
HOUSE

POWDER
TOWER

HYBERNSKÁ

FORMER
ŽIVNOSTENSKÁ
BANKA

JERUSALEM
SYNAGOGUE

Vrchuckého
Park

MUSEUM OF
COMMUNISM

MUCHA
MUSEUM

Hlavní
Nádraží

MAIN
TRAIN
STATION

(NEW
STATION)

ST. MARY OF
THE SNOWS

POST

COMM.
PARTY
HQ

(OLD
STATION)

SIGHTS

Wenceslas Square

TESCO

Franciscan
Garden

GRAND
HOTEL
EVROPA

NÁRODNÍ TŘÍDA

NOVÁ
SCÉNA

Národní
Třída

SVĚTOZOR
MALL

LUCERNA
ARCADE

ST.
WENCESLAS
STATUE

STATE
OPERA

NATIONAL
THEATER

NEW

COMMUNIST-
ERA BLDG.

BOAT RENTAL

Muzeum

ŽOFÍN

Slovanský
Ostrov

NATIONAL
MUSEUM

TOWN

See
Wenceslas Square Walk
in that chapter

STS. CYRIL &
METHODIUS
CHURCH

Charles
Square

JEČNÁ

VINO-
HRADY

DANCING
HOUSE

HEYDRICH
TERROR
MEMORIAL

Karlovo
Náměstí

I.P. Pavlova

Náměstí
Míru

DVOŘÁK
MUSEUM

RUMUNSKÁ

Palacký
Square

Žitkovy
Sady

EMMAUS
MONASTERY

Botanická
Zahrada

Tu Nuselský Dridge
& E-50 Freeway
to Brno

See Wenceslas Square Walk
chapter for detail map of
Wenceslas Square area

To Vyšehrad

descriptions, two blocks off Wenceslas Square at Panská 7, tel. 224-233-355, www.mucha.cz. Peruse the well-stocked gift shop.

⛾ See the Mucha Museum Tour chapter.

Jerusalem Synagogue (Jeruzalémské Synagóga)

Buried deep in a residential district a few blocks off of Wenceslas Square, this colorful synagogue (also known as the Jubilee Synagogue) is a fascinating combination of Moorish Renaissance and

Viennese Art Nouveau styles. It was built from 1905 to 1906 in commemoration of the first 50 years of Franz Josef's liberal, relatively Jewish-friendly rule. Recently restored, still serving the Prague Jewish community, and sparsely visited, this is the most contemplative as well as visually stunning of Prague's synagogues.

Cost and Hours: 80 Kč, April-Oct Sun-Fri 11:00-17:00, closed Sat, closed in winter and on Jewish holidays, between Powder Tower and main train station at Jeruzalémská 7, tel. 222-319-002, www.synagogue.cz/Jerusalem.

ALONG NA PŘÍKOPĚ

At the bottom of Wenceslas Square, the street running to the right is called Na Příkopě. Meaning "On the Moat," this busy boulevard follows the line of the Old Town wall, leading to one of the wall's former gates, the Powder Tower (the black tower spire in the distance). This street is a showcase of Art Nouveau: Be sure to keep your eyes up as you stroll here. City tour buses leave from along this street, which also offers plenty of shopping temptations (including these modern malls: Slovanský Dům at Na Příkopě 22 and Černá Růže at Na Příkopě 12, next door to Mosers, which has a crystal showroom upstairs). I've listed the following sights as you'll reach them as you walk northeast along Na Příkopě from the bottom of Wenceslas Square.

▲Museum of Communism (Muzeum Komunismu)

Tucked away upstairs in a cramped and creaky old mansion, this humble but engaging museum traces the story of communism in Prague: the origin, dream, reality, and nightmare; the cult of personality; and, finally, the Velvet Revolution. Along the way, it gives a thought-provoking review of the Czech Republic's 40-year stint with Soviet economics, "in all its dreariness and puffed-up glory." You'll find propaganda posters and busts of communist All-Stars (Marx, Lenin, and others), and re-created slices of communist life. While dated and faded (like its subject), and lacking high-tech flair, the museum's clever displays and English descriptions evoke the time well—making this Prague's most accessible sight relating to its communist era. (For a contrast to this commercial (but well-done) museum, and an authentic glance at 1950s political persecution, consider a day-trip to the Vojna Memorial near Příbram—see sidebar on page 64.)

Cost and Hours: 190 Kč, daily 9:00-21:00, Na Příkopě 10, tel. 224-212-966, www.muzeumkomunismu.cz.

◑ Self-Guided Tour: The small museum is a one-way, chronological route. This historical overview will help you lace together the exhibits.

Before you enter the display space, stand beneath the giant

red star on the ceiling. It's 1918. World War I ends, and **Czecho-slovakia** is born. But it's weak and divided—with a huge minority of Germans (mostly concentrated in the Sudetenland)—and easily overrun by Adolf Hitler. In the Munich Agreement, the rest of Europe cedes Czechoslovakia to the Nazis.

Now head into the narrow hall that begins the exhibit. At the end of **World War II,** Prague is liberated by the Russian Red Army. On the wave of the postwar pro-Soviet euphoria, a predominantly communist government is elected for a two-year interim term. Hard-pressed from Moscow, the communists do not allow the next scheduled election to take place, and instead exercise their might (via the army, police, and armed workers' guards) to silence dissent and drive democrats out of the government. Soon Prague is speckled with huge statues of communist heroes Lenin and Marx (some are displayed in this room). Find the poster of the first communist president of Czechoslovakia, Klement Gottwald, smiling next to Comrade Stalin.

In the early days of communist rule—even as Stalin ruthlessly coerces compliance—a false optimism percolates. After the big  Lenin and Marx statues, the exhibit illustrates **communist values:** technology (cosmonauts, rocket engines); heavy industry (a cluttered workshop, rousing posters of hardworking laborers from every demographic); education (a re-created classroom, with textbooks using Russia's Cyrillic alphabet—no longer studied today—and a poem on the chalkboard that extols the virtues of the tractor); and hero-worship (the pile of busts of commie bigwigs, and a photo of the 50-foot Stalin statue that overlooked the city until 1962).

Continue into the next section, which considers the insidious effects of communism in **everyday life:** rosy on the outside, but bleak inside. Having rejected the capitalist Marshall Plan to rebuild Europe, postwar Czechoslovakia finds economic recovery slow and difficult. Farms are forcibly collectivized, effectively reducing rather than increasing production. Kulaks (hereditary property owners) are punished and ostracized. After being initially suspicious of sportsmen, the communists embrace sporting events as a Cold War battlefield. All the while, the focus is on heavy industry (steelworks) and weapons (guns, tanks, uranium). The re-created store counter—with a display case that's empty except for packets of the fizzy-drink powder called *šumĕnky*—is juxtaposed with a propaganda poster of a happy mom with a cornucopia of commercial goods in her shopping bag.

The Continuing Legacy of Communism

Czech survivors of communist prisons (honored by the Monument to Victims of Communism) feel a sense of injustice. Following World War II, many Czechs who collaborated with the Nazis were brought to justice. In contrast, after communism fell in 1989, few individuals responsible for the crimes committed by the communist regime faced retribution. In fact, when the country's industrial infrastructure was privatized in the early 1990s, former Communist Party big shots used their connections to take control of some of the country's new capitalist enterprises. Many old party leaders morphed into bosses of the new Czech economy.

The Czech Republic was the first post-communist country to ban secret police informants from public office (a policy called *lustrace*, or "lustration"). They were also the first to outlaw the propagation of communism (and other totalitarian ideologies). Even so, efforts to enforce this legislation have been less than successful. Many former agents have destroyed evidence, while others contend that they were not aware of their own cooperation.

In the early 1990s, stalwart members of the Communist Party fended off attempts at reform and preserved a fossil of an institution that still draws about 10 to 15 percent of the national vote. Today's "vanguards of progress" no longer preach class warfare, but instead blend empty rhetoric ("We have a solution") with vague finger-pointing ("Who took away our hard-won securities?"). To become more palatable to a wider public and to hide their Stalinist roots, they exchanged their unsavory red star

You'll see how the communists attempted to **control** their subjects through propaganda (including some biting anti-USA posters), as well as through careful patrol of the borders.

In the corner, the museum reconstructs a spooky **interrogation office.** The communist government spies on its own people, using informants and secret police (some of them ex-Nazis). Your building janitor, your favorite bartender, even your own family members might be secretly reporting your movements to the authorities. "Enemies of the people" are arrested, interrogated, tortured, and sent to a system of prison camps (see the displayed map). Protests are brutally crushed. Resistance is futile. Or so it seems.

In the adjoining room, watch part of the 20-minute **video** (plays continuously, English subtitles and Czech protest/folk songs)

symbol for a more innocuous pair of cherries (allegedly to recall the Paris Commune of 1871).

Their nostalgic-about-the-good-old-times message registers mainly with Czechs who find it difficult to adapt to a more complex and risk-prone society. Many (including the younger generation) find communism's ordered worldview—familiar since childhood—comfortable and easily comprehensible. Today, they read the newspapers for reassurance that capitalism is responsible for many social ills, that the European Union is German imperialism in disguise, and—in extreme cases—that China is pairing up with Russia to defend humanity.

The idealistic Velvet Revolutionaries of 1989 believed communism would naturally disappear over time—but failed to realize how deeply the years of authoritarian rule had affected Czech society. Today, Communist Party members are routinely re-elected into Parliament by older voters who look nostalgically to the past, and by young voters vote Communist as a form of protest. Visitors surprised by the communist presence in a free Czech Republic can take it as a reminder that difficult experiences take generations to process—especially if kept buried inside.

For a deeper look at the dark legacy and the degree to which today's Czech Republic teaches its young generation about communist crimes (in an age when Prague is again infiltrated by hundreds of empire-minded, history-denying Russian secret agents), consider hiring a local guide to drive you to the **Vojna Memorial** near Příbram (one hour south of Prague). Here a prisoner camp that supplied labor to the local uranium mine from 1949-1951 is thoughtfully re-created (based on former inmates' memories), including a sinister *Prací ke svobodě* ("Work Sets You Free") sign over the entrance (60 Kč, April-Oct Tue-Sun 9:00-17:00, closed Mon; Nov-March Tue-Fri until 16:00, closed Sat-Mon; tel. 326-531-488, www.muzeum-pribram.cz).

SIGHTS

that shows how the Czech people chafed under the big Red yoke from 1969 through 1989. It's mostly footage of demonstrations—and is striking in how little things changed over that 30-year span.

Continuing through the last section, you'll learn more specifics about these **ongoing protests.** In 1968, the Prague Spring reforms attempt to forge a distinctly Czechoslovak socialism with a human face. Soviet tanks crush both the protesters and the spirit of rebellion, and a policy of "normalization" brings back Soviet control. But a few brave freedom fighters refuse to give up: Jan Palach burns himself alive in protest, stoking demonstrations one million strong. Playwright Václav Havel endures repeated prison sentences. And the underground rock band The Plastic People of the Universe challenge the legal framework of Gustav Husák's government.

Finally, you'll walk along a small-scale reproduction of the greatest symbol of communist oppression—the Berlin Wall—and learn about the fall of communism. With Gorbachev's introduction of Glasnost and Perestroika, the Soviet Bloc's days are numbered—and when the Wall comes down in Germany in October 1989, the rest of the Soviet empire is ready to crumble. A few weeks later, 300,000 Czechs and Slovaks gather in Wenceslas Square to demand that the Soviets leave—a peaceful movement known as the Velvet Revolution. Freedom! As a visitor, you feel it when you escape through a hole in the Wall.

Nearby: If you're curious to see communism outside of a museum, take a five-minute walk to the present-day **Headquarters of the Communist Party of Bohemia and Moravia (KSČM).** From the museum, hook around the corner (to the right) and head up Panská street a long block and a half—passing the Mucha Museum—to find Politických Vězňů 9 (on the left). The building—which sits on "Political Prisoners Street" (no joke)—is painted an appropriately peachy shade of red, and protesters have spilled red paint on its threshold. Step inside (go ahead—the door's open) to pick up some propaganda brochures and see party leadership and candidate photos of today's midlevel apparatchiks in bad suits... who seem oblivious to the political (and fashion) changes since 1989. They've swapped the red star with a cheerier symbol—a pair of bright-red cherries, as if voting Communist is like playing a slot machine. Despite heavy public pressure to outlaw this artifact of a hated-by-most era, the Communist Party still commands between 10 and 15 percent of the national Czech vote—mostly from aging, nostalgic voters more concerned about predictability than freedom. More pragmatic Czechs say they're glad the Communists have their own party—it keeps them marginalized, rather than being a vocal fringe that hijacks the agenda of a larger, more influential party.

▲▲Municipal House (Obecní Dům)

The cultural and artistic leaders who financed this Art Nouveau masterpiece (1905-1911) wanted a ceremonial palace to reinforce self-awareness of the Czech nation. Built under Catholic Habsburg rule, it was slathered in patriotic Czech themes to emphasize how the Protestant Czechs were a distinct culture. In 1918, Czechoslovakia's independence was declared from the balcony of this building. While the exterior is impressive, the highlight is the interior—and it's free. The

Municipal House features Prague's largest concert hall, a recommended Art Nouveau café (Kavárna Obecní Dům), and two other restaurants. To extend your Art Nouveau bliss, take a guided tour or attend a concert here.

📖 While the interior is described below, to learn more about the exterior of this fine building, the Old Town Walk chapter.

Cost and Hours: The entrance halls and public spaces are free to enter and explore, open daily 10:00-18:00. For an in-depth look

at all the sumptuous halls and banquet rooms, take advantage of the daily one-hour English **tours** (290 Kč, usually 3/day, departures 11:00-17:00; limited to 35 people—buy your ticket online or as soon as you can from the ground-floor shop where tours depart; Náměstí Republiky 5, tel. 222-002-101, www.obecnidum.cz).

Concerts: Performances are held regularly in the lavish Smetana Hall (schedule on website). Note that many concerts brag they are held in the Municipal House, but are performed in a smaller, less impressive hall in the same building.

➋ Self-Guided Tour: Don't be timid about poking around the interior, which is open to the public. Having lunch or a drink in one of the eateries is a great way to experience the decor, but you can also just glimpse them from the doorway (as you "check out the menu").

Enter under the green, wrought-iron arcade. In the **rotunda,** admire the mosaic floor, stained glass, the woodwork doorway and the lighting fixtures. To the left is the **café** *(kavárna)*—a harmony of woodwork, marble, metal, and glittering chandeliers. Opposite the café is the equally stunning **restaurant** (both described on page 220).

From the rotunda, step into the **lobby,** where you can look up the staircase that leads up to the main concert hall (no tourist access upstairs). Also in the lobby is the box office, selling concert tickets and guided English tours of the building.

Facing the staircase, go right and head **downstairs**—yes, tourists are welcome there. Admire the colorful tiles in the stairwell, and more colorful tiles in the downstairs main room. Look for the plaster model of this building and the adjacent Powder Tower, which shows how the angled facade conceals a surprisingly large performance space. Also check out the **American Bar** (salute the US flags above the bar) and the **Plzeňská Restaurant** (with its dark-wood booths and colorful tile scenes of happy peasants).

Finish your tour by going back upstairs to find the **Moderni-**

SIGHTS

sta shop (tucked to the left as you face the main staircase)—full of fancy teacups and jewelry.

Also upstairs, you may find **temporary exhibits** (usually around 150 Kč), typically about Art Nouveau. This style was heavy on the applied arts (as opposed to fine arts like painting), so you'll see elegant lamps, chairs, prints, and clothes. The period celebrated new technologies, which allowed high-quality objects to be mass-produced for the average Jan and Jana. They're functional and minimal in design, but always beautiful. To reach this space, you're allowed to ascend the main staircase, pass by the guard, and glimpse into the stylish Smetana Hall along the way.

Nearby: Standing sternly next to the Municipal House—and providing a somewhat jarring architectural contrast—is the medieval **Powder Tower,** with one of Prague's trademark trapezoidal rooflines from the Gothic period. This is a good reminder that Na Příkopě was not just a moat, but a heavily fortified wall—and this was its main entrance.

📖 For more on the Powder Tower, see the Old Town Walk chapter.

ALONG NÁRODNÍ TŘÍDA

From the bottom of Wenceslas Square, at the intersection and (nearby Metro stop) called Můstek, you can head west on Národní Třída (in the opposite direction from Na Příkopě) for an interesting stroll through urban Prague to the National Theater and the Vltava River.

Národní Třída and the Velvet Revolution

Národní Třída ("National Street") is where you feel the pulse of the modern city. The street, which connects Wenceslas Square with the National Theater and the river, is a busy thoroughfare running through the heart of urban Prague. In 1989, this unassuming boulevard played host to the first salvo of a Velvet Revolution that would topple the communist regime.

Make your way down Národní Třída until you hit the tram tracks (just beyond the Tesco department store). On the left, look for the photo of President Bill Clinton playing saxophone, with Václav Havel on the side (this is the entrance to **Reduta,** Prague's best jazz club—see page 248); next door are two recommended eateries, **Café Louvre** and **Le Patio.** Just beyond that, you'll come to a short corridor with white arches (now closed). On the street facing outside of the arcade is a simple memorial to the hundreds of students injured inside the corridor by the police in the Velvet Revolution, which took place on November 17, 1989. The monument's open hands and peace signs are a reminder that the terrified students corralled in here by the burly "Red Berets" that night were unarmed and entirely nonviolent.

NEAR THE VLTAVA RIVER

I've listed these sights from north to south, beginning at the grand, Neo-Renaissance National Theater, which is five blocks south of the Charles Bridge and stands along the riverbank at the end of Národní Třída. It's also easy to see these sights in the opposite order, on the long-but-scenic walk back from the hill called Vyšehrad—just hold the book upside-down.

National Theater (Národní Divadlo)

Opened in 1883 with Smetana's opera *Libuše,* this theater was the first truly Czech venue in Prague. From the very start, it was nick-

named the "Cradle of Czech Culture." The building is a key symbol of the Czech National Revival that began in the late 18th century. In 1800, "Prag" was predominantly German. The Industrial Revolution brought Czechs from the countryside into the city, their new urban identity defined by patriotic teachers and priests. By 1883, most of the city spoke Czech, and the opening of this theater represented the birth of the modern Czech nation. It remains an important national icon: The state annually pours more subsidies into this theater than into all of Czech film production. It's the most beautiful venue in town for opera and ballet, often with world-class singers (for more details on performances, see page 245).

Next door (just inland, on Národní Třída) is the boxy, glassy facade of the **Nová Scéna.** This "New National Theater" building, dating from 1983 (the 100th anniversary of the original National Theater building), reflects the bold and stark communist aesthetic.

Across the street from the National Theater is the former haunt of Prague's intelligentsia, the recommended **Kavárna Slavia,** a Viennese-style coffee house that is fine for a meal or drink with a view of the river (described on page 227).

• *Just south of the National Theater, in the Vltava you'll find...*

Prague's Islands

From the National Theater, the Bridge of Legions (Most Legií) leads across the island called **Střelecký Ostrov.** Covered with chestnut trees, this island boasts Prague's best beach (on the sandy tip that points north to Charles Bridge). You might see a fisherman pulling trout out of a river that's now much cleaner than it used to be. Bring a swimsuit and take a dip just a stone's throw from Europe's most beloved bridge.

In the mood for boating instead of swimming? On the next island up, **Slovanský Ostrov,** you can rent a boat (rowboats—40 Kč/hour, paddleboats—60 Kč/hour, bring picture ID as deposit). A lazy hour paddling around Střelecký Ostrov—or just floating sleepily in the middle of the river surrounded by this great city's architectural splendor—is a delightful experience on a sunny day. It's cheap, easy fun (and it's good for you).

• *A 10-minute walk (or one stop on tram #17) south from the National Theater, beyond the islands, is Jirásek Bridge (Jiráskův Most), where you'll find the...*

Dancing House (Tančící Dům)

If ever a building could get your toes tapping, it would be this one, nicknamed "Fred and Ginger" by American architecture buffs. This metallic samba is the work of Frank Gehry (who designed the equally striking Guggenheim Museum in Bilbao, Spain, and Seattle's Museum of Pop Culture). Eight-legged Ginger's wispy dress and Fred's metal mesh head are easy to spot. Some Czechs prefer to think that the two "figures" represent the nation's greatest 20th-century heroes, Jozef Gabčík and Jan Kubiš (see "The Assassination of Reinhard Heydrich" sidebar). A contemporary art gallery occupies unused office space throughout the building (90 Kč, daily 11:00-19:00).

The building's top-floor restaurant, **$$$ Céleste,** is a fine place for a fancy French meal. Whether you go up for lunch (reasonable, 12:00-14:30), a drink (16:00-18:00), or an expensive dinner, you'll be a louse in the Gehry haircut (tel. 221-984-160).

• *Two blocks up Resslova street is the Sts. Cyril and Methodius Church, which contains in its crypt the...*

▲National Memorial to the Heroes of the Heydrich Terror (Národní Památník Hrdinů Heydrichiády)

In 1942, WWII paratroopers Jozef Gabčík and Jan Kubiš assassinated the SS second-in-command Reinhard Heydrich, who controlled the Nazi-occupied Czech lands and was one of the main architects of the Holocaust. In the weeks following his assassination, the two paratroopers hid, along with other freedom fighters, in the crypt of the Greek Orthodox Sts. Cyril and Methodius Church on Resslova street. Today, a modest exhibition in the church's crypt retells their story, along with the history of the Czech resistance movement. Outside, notice the small memorial, including bullet holes, plaque, and flowers on

the street. Around the corner is the entry into the museum and the crypt.

Cost and Hours: 75 Kč, Tue-Sun 9:00-17:00, closed Mon, full history explained in small 25-Kč booklet, 2 blocks up from the Dancing House at Resslova 9A, tel. 224-916-100.

• *Farther up Resslova street is...*

Charles Square (Karlovo Náměstí)

Prague's largest square is covered by lawns, trees, and statues of Czech writers. It's a quiet antidote to the bustling Wenceslas and Old Town squares. The Gothic New Town Hall at the top-left corner of the square has excellent views and labeled panoramic photographs that help you orient yourself. The little parlor across the street has some of the best gelato in town.

• *Back along the riverbank, another long block to the south is...*

Palacký Square (Palackého Náměstí)

Depicted in the dynamic, recently restored, Art Nouveau monument overlooking the square named after him, **František Palacký** (1798-1876) is credited with rescuing the Czech culture from obscurity and, perhaps, oblivion.

By the early 19th century, the Czechs had been living under Austrian Habsburg rule for centuries—and their unique cultural fabric had been all but lost. A historian and politician, Palacký was at the vanguard of the Czech National Revival, a movement that celebrated those old traditions and elevated them as being worthy of respect. Palacký spent 20 years dutifully digging through dusty archives, and singlehandedly revived the memory of Jan Hus (who had been all but completely forgotten by history). Palacký effectively wrote the Czech national narrative still held dear by the people of this country—and, in stoking a flourishing of Czech pride, inspired the construction of the National Theater that still stands proudly just up the embankment. Today he's considered the Father of the Nation—along with Charles IV and Tomáš Garrigue Masaryk (see page 174), one of the three most important figures

The Assassination of Reinhard Heydrich

Visitors to the Sts. Cyril and Methodius Church are reminded of a fascinating slice of Nazi-era intrigue.

In September 1941, Reinhard Heydrich—the SS second-in-command, Hitler's personal favorite, and one of the architects of the Holocaust—volunteered to replace the ineffective Otto Neurath as the governor of the occupied Czech lands. Heydrich acutely understood the role that the Nazi-established Protectorate of Bohemia and Moravia played in the German war effort, as the heavily industrialized territory was home to two of Europe's largest armaments factories (in Plzeň and in Brno).

As a wave of sabotage threatened to disrupt supply lines to the eastern front, a determined Heydrich arrived in Prague, armed with a sinister carrot-and-stick strategy. While increasing worker benefits—bribing the Czech proletariat with meat, shoes, and spa vacations—he also violently lashed out against any hint of resistance or illegal economic activity.

At the same time, the Czechoslovak government-in-exile was suffering a crisis of legitimacy in Britain's eyes. Following the British signing of the Munich Pact (an act of appeasement that would annex Czechoslovakia's Sudetenland area to the Nazis), thousands of Czechs and Slovaks went abroad to fight, and few of those left in the occupied lands were cut out for underground resistance. Moreover, rather than occupying Czechoslovakia, the Nazis were able to rule through a cabinet of willing Czech helpers. Edvard Beneš, the exiled prime minister, appeared to the Allies to be a self-proclaimed spokesperson for a complicit nation.

It was under these circumstances that two paratroopers, Jozef Gabčík and Jan Kubiš, were chosen by British Special Operations and trained in Scotland for a secret and—as they were made to understand from the start—potentially suicidal mission to eliminate Heydrich.

On the morning of May 27, 1942, Heydrich was coming down Kobylisy hill on his daily commute. Just as the unaccompanied open car slowed down at a hairpin turn, Gabčík jumped in front of the car and pointed his Sten machine gun at Heydrich, and pulled the trigger. But the gun jammed. Heydrich, ordering his driver to stop, pulled out his revolver. At that moment, Kubiš, coming in from behind, threw a handmade grenade that missed and exploded outside the car. But the explosion was enough to wound Heydrich, who was transported to a nearby hospital, where he died a few days later. At his funeral—the Nazis' most elaborate funeral ceremony ever—Hitler appeared genuinely distressed, and Heydrich was eulogized as the model for all SS men.

The Nazi response in the Protectorate was brutal. Martial

Jozef Gabčík (left) and Jan Kubis (right)

law was declared, two villages were summarily razed to the ground, and in the ensuing months, 5,000 individuals were executed. A reward was announced for tips leading to the capture of the assassins. Karel Čurda, a member of another paratrooper unit, betrayed his comrades. On June 18, at 4:15 in the morning, the Gestapo surrounded the Sts. Cyril and Methodius Church on Resslova street, where the two paratroopers were hiding. After a two-hour battle, Kubiš, on guard in the nave of the church, was killed along with two other defenders. Gabčík and three other paratroopers committed suicide in the crypt below.

For years, feelings about the Heydrich assassination were mixed. Many regretted the lives lost, and some felt it effectively wiped out Czech underground resistance. The fact that the operation stemmed from British (rather than native or Soviet) roots also became problematic following the communist takeover. The act was officially depicted as shortsighted and symbolic.

Today, historians praise the sacrifice. Days after the assassination, the British government revoked its signature on the Munich Pact, recognizing Czechoslovakia's prewar boundaries; the French followed two months later. Heydrich—whose elimination was one of the most significant acts of resistance in occupied Europe—remains the highest-ranked Nazi official killed while in office. During anniversaries, Czech politicians cover the pavement outside the crypt with wreaths and flowers. And in 2009, the spot of Heydrich's assassination (next to the freeway to Terezín, in the northern part of town) was finally marked with a thoughtful monument.

SIGHTS

Jára Cimrman: The Greatest Czech?

"I am such a complete atheist that I am afraid God will punish me." Such is the pithy wisdom of Jára Cimrman, the man overwhelmingly voted the "Greatest Czech of All Time" in a 2005 national poll. Who is Jára Cimrman? A philosopher? An explorer? An inventor? He is all these things, yes, and much more.

Born in the mid-19th century, Cimrman studied in Vienna before journeying the world. He traversed the Atlantic in a steamboat he designed himself, taught drama to peasants in Peru, and drifted across the Arctic Sea on an iceberg. He invented the lightbulb, but Edison beat him to the patent office by five minutes. It was he who suggested to the Americans the idea for a Panama Canal, though, as usual, he was never credited. Indeed, Cimrman surreptitiously advised many of the world's greats: Eiffel on his tower, Einstein on his theories of relativity, Chekhov on his plays. ("You can't just have *two* sisters," Cimrman told the playwright. "How about three?") Long before the world knew of Sartre or Camus, Cimrman was writing tracts such as *The Essence of the Existence*, which would become the foundation for his philosophy of "Cimrmanism," also known as "nonexistentialism." (Its central premise: "Existence cannot not exist.")

Despite Jára Cimrman's genius, the "Greatest Czech" poll's sponsors had a single objection to his candidacy: He's not real,

of Czech history. The inscription on the monument reads: "To our awakener and leader of the resurrected nation."

The park just upstream from Palacký Square is called **Zítkovy Sady** (named for the architect of the National Theater). While it's often said that Prague was undamaged by the bombs of World War II, this park contains a footnote. Imagine standing here on the night of February 14, 1945. Suddenly, a US warplane screams across the sky, dropping firebombs that leave a flaming trench through the middle of this square, and sowing a path of destruction east through the city center. The pilots were on a bombing run to Dresden, Germany (which was consumed by a firestorm that night), and lost their way—mistaking Prague and its river for their target. In addition to killing more than 700 civilians and destroying more than a hundred homes, the bombers obliterated Prague's biggest synagogue (which was never rebuilt) and severely damaged the 14th-century Benedictine **Emmaus Monastery** (also called the Monastery of the Slavs)—which was rebuilt in the 1960s with a conspicuously modern, crisscross spire that feels out of place in this otherwise architecturally conservative town. The bombing also cleared the way for the Dancing House and other structures in this part of the city that are more modern than the norm.

but the brainchild of Czech humorists Zdeněk Svěrák and Jiří Šebánek, who brought this patriotic Renaissance Man to life in 1967 in a satirical radio play.

How should we interpret the fact that the Czechs chose a fictional character as their greatest countryman over any of their flesh-and-blood national heroes—say, Charles IV (the 14th-century Holy Roman Emperor who established Prague as the cultural and intellectual capital of Europe), or Martina Navrátilová (someone who plays a sport with bright green balls)?

I like to think that the vote for Cimrman says something about the country's enthusiasm for blowing raspberries in the face of authority. From the times of the Czech kings who used crafty diplomacy to keep the German menace at bay, to the days of Jan Hus and his criticism of the Catholic Church, to the flashes of anticommunist revolt that at last sparked the Velvet Revolution in 1989—the Czechs have maintained a healthy disrespect for those who would tell them how to live their lives. Their vote for a fictional personage, says Cimrman's co-creator Svěrák, shows two things about the Czech nation: "That it is skeptical about those who are major figures and those who are supposedly the 'Greatest.' And that the only certainty that has saved the nation many times throughout history is its humor."

SIGHTS

• *At Palacký Square and Zítkovy Sady, cross over and stroll downstream along...*

Prague's Embankment

Much of the city's Vltava-front embankment—especially the stretch between Palacký Square and Vyšehrad—has been gorgeously renovated in recent years, and has become a particularly fine (and untouristy) place to wander. Al fresco cafés and restaurant barges enliven the riverbank on sunny days, and a farmers market bustles on Saturday morning (8:00-14:00). At the southern end of the embankment, you're in the Výtoň neighborhood, at the base of the historic Vyšehrad hill (listed later, under "Outside the Center").

The Little Quarter (Malá Strana)

Huddled under the castle on the west bank of the river, this neighborhood is pleasant, though low on blockbuster sights. The most enjoyable approach from the Old Town is across the Charles Bridge. From the end of the bridge (TI in tower), Mostecká street leads two blocks up to the Little Quarter Square (Malostranské Náměstí) and the huge Church of St. Nicholas. But before you head up there, consider a detour to Kampa Island.

The Little Quarter was one of the original four towns that comprised old Prague. After the original merchant settlement burned down in the 1540s, it rose from the ashes to become a Baroque town of fine palaces and gardens. The Czech and European nobility who settled here took pride in the grand design of their gardens. In the 1990s, after decades of decay, the gardens were carefully restored. While some are open only to the successors of the former nobility—including the Czech Parliament and the American, German, and Polish embassies—many are open to visitors.

BETWEEN CHARLES BRIDGE AND LITTLE QUARTER SQUARE

Kampa Island

One hundred yards from the castle end of the Charles Bridge, stairs on the left lead down to the main square of Kampa Island (mostly

created from the rubble of the Little Quarter, which was destroyed in a 1540 fire). The island features relaxing pubs, a breezy park, hippies, lovers, a fine contemporary art gallery, and river access. From the main square, Hroznová lane (on the right) winds around to a little bridge. The high-water mark at the end of the bridge dates from 1890. The **old water wheel** is the last survivor of many mills that once lined the canal here. Each mill had its own protective water spirit *(vodník)*. The padlocks adorning the bridge are the scourge of romantic spots throughout Europe these days, popular with not-very-creative Romeos who think that clinching a lock onto a bridge proves their enduring love.

• *Fifty yards beyond the bridge (on the right, under the trees) is the...*

Lennon Wall (Lennonova Zeď)

While V. I. Lenin's ideas hung like a water-soaked trench coat upon the Czech people, rock singer John Lennon's ideas gave many locals hope and a vision. When Lennon was killed in 1980, a large wall was spontaneously covered with memorial graffiti. Night after night, the police would paint over the "All You Need Is Love" and "Imagine" graffiti. And day after day, it would reappear. Until independence came in 1989, travelers, freedom lovers, and local hippies gathered here. Silly as it might seem, this wall is remembered as a place that gave hope to locals craving freedom. Even today, while the tension and danger associated with this wall are gone, people come here to imagine. *"John žije"* is Czech for "John lives."

• *From here, continue up to the Little Quarter Square.*

ON OR NEAR LITTLE QUARTER SQUARE

The focal point of this neighborhood, the Little Quarter Square (Malostranské Náměstí), is split into an upper and lower part by the domineering Church of St. Nicholas and its adjacent Jesuit college. A Baroque plague column oversees the upper square. Note that there's a handy Via Musica ticket office across from the plague column (on the uphill side). The lower square was once ruled by an equestrian statue of Marshal Radetzky (of "Radetzky March" fame), a 19th-century Czech military strategist in the service of the Habsburgs.

This hated symbol of support for a foreign monarchy was torn down with Czechoslovak independence in 1918, and was never replaced. But recently, some have suggested erecting a monument to Jára Cimrman, a fictional Czech globetrotter "who had never helped the Habsburgs with anything." In accordance with his wishes, the statue would be carved out of white marble ("In white, I will better resist the pigeons") and would depict Cimrman walking beside (rather than riding) a horse. So far the major obstacle seems to be that, due to the sheer size of the proposed horse, from the upper end of the square you wouldn't be able to see Cimrman, only his rubber boots. For more on Cimrman, see the sidebar.

Church of St. Nicholas (Kostel Sv. Mikuláše)

When the Jesuits came to Prague, they found the perfect piece of real estate for their church and its associated school—right on Little Quarter Square. The church (built 1703-1760) is the best example of High Baroque in town.

Cost and Hours: 70 Kč, daily 9:00-17:00, Nov-Feb until 16:00, opens at 8:30 for prayer.

Visiting the Church: The church's interior is giddy with curves and illusions. Stand directly under the tallest dome and look up. Spin slowly around, greeting four giant statues—the fathers

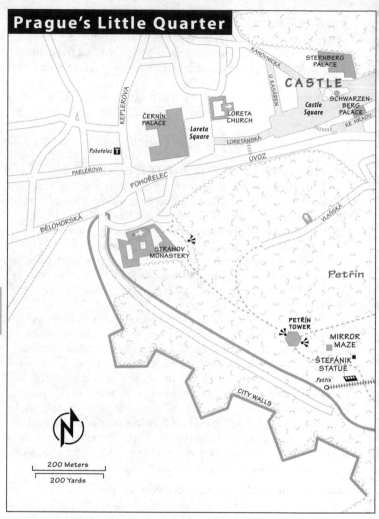

Prague's Little Quarter

SIGHTS

of the Eastern Church. Pan up and see the earthly world merging with heaven above.

The **altar** features a lavish gold-plated Nicholas, flanked by the two top Jesuits: the founder, St. Ignatius Loyola, and his missionary follower, St. Francis Xavier.

Climb up the **gallery** through the staircase in the left transept for a close-up look at a collection of large canvases and illusionary frescoes by Karel Škréta, who is considered the greatest Czech Baroque painter. Notice that at first glance the canvases are utterly dark, but as sunbeams shine through the window, various parts of the painting brighten up. Like a looking glass, the image reflects the light, creating a play of light and dark. This painting technique

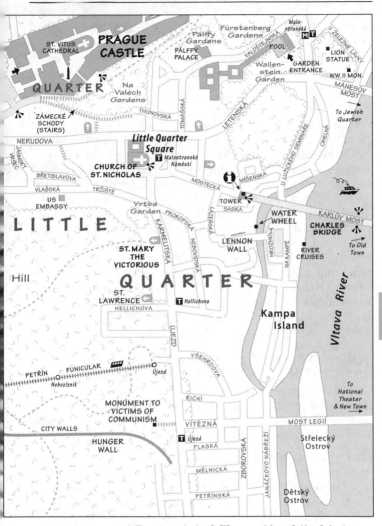

represents a central Baroque belief: The world is full of darkness, and the only hope that makes it come alive emanates from God. The church walls seem to nearly fuse with the sky, suggesting that happenings on earth are closely connected to heaven.

Tower Climb: For a good look at the city and the church's 250-foot dome, climb 215 steps up the bell tower. Closed to the public during the communist times, the deck was used by the secret police to spy on the activities at the nearby embassies of the US, Britain, and West Germany (90 Kč, daily 10:00-22:00, shorter hours in winter, tower entrance is outside the right transept).

Concerts: The church is also an evening concert venue; tickets are usually on sale at the door (490 Kč, generally nightly at 18:00 except Tue, www.stnicholas.cz).

• *From here, you can hike 10 minutes uphill to the castle (and 5 more minutes to the Strahov Monastery).* 📖 *For information on these sights, see the Prague Castle Tour chapter. If you're walking up to the castle, consider going via...*

Nerudova Street

This steep, cobbled street, leading from Little Quarter Square to the castle, is named for Jan Neruda, a gifted 19th-century journalist (and somewhat less-talented fiction writer). It's lined with old buildings still sporting the characteristic doorway signs (such as the lion, three violinists, and house of the golden suns) that once served as street addresses. The surviving signs are carefully restored and protected by law. They represent the family name, the occupation, or the various passions of the people who once inhabited the houses. (If you were to replace your house number with a symbol, what would it be?) In the 1770s, in order to collect taxes more effectively, Habsburg empress Maria Theresa decreed that numbers be used instead of these quaint house names. This neighborhood is filled with old noble palaces, now generally used as foreign embassies and as offices of the Czech Parliament.

NORTH OF LITTLE QUARTER SQUARE, NEAR THE MALOSTRANSKÁ METRO STATION

Twenty yards from the Metro station (go left from the top of the escalator and turn right when you get outside), a few blocks north of Little Quarter Square, is a lovely palace and garden. If you want to reach Little Quarter Square from here, follow Valdštejnská street.

Klárov Park and WWII Monument

In the park between the Malostranska Metro and the river stands the **Memorial of the Second Resistance Movement.** The furled Czech flag honors all those who opposed the Nazis during World War II. Note the dates—1938-1945. Wait—didn't World War II start in 1939? Not for the Czechs. Remember, it was Hitler's 1938 encroachment on the Sudetenland (the border region between Bohemia and Germany) that first alerted the world to Nazi aggression. That threat prompted Britain's Prime Minister, Neville Chamberlain, to sign a peace agreement with Hitler, giving the Nazis this part of Czechoslovakia (and soon the rest) in hopes of achieving "peace in our time." It didn't turn out that way. It took more than 60 years after the end of the war for this monument to all Czechs and Slovaks to be dedicated. During communism, only Czechs and Slovaks who fought alongside the Russians were officially remembered; those who had fought in France, Britain, and

North Africa returned home only to be sent to communist labor camps as "imperialist spies" and erased from the national memory.

At the other end of the park is a **bronze winged lion,** a recent gift from British expats to commemorate the 2,500 Czech and Slovak pilots who fought in the Battle of Britain. While the first memorial was passionately debated until a compromise was found, the lion went up without any public discussion and has been unanimously regarded as a monstrosity.

Wallenstein Palace Garden (Valdštejnská Palac Zahrada)

Of the neighborhood's many impressive palace gardens, this is by far the largest and most beautiful. The complex—consisting of a

palace (generally closed) and the surrounding garden (generally open)—was commissioned during the Thirty Years' War by the Habsburg general and Czech nobleman Albrecht z Valdštejna (or, in German, Albrecht von Wallenstein). It's a testimony to how war can be such a great business for the unscrupulous. For 16 years (1618-1634), the mercenary Albrecht

conspired with all sides involved in the war. He was the banker of the Czech Estates Uprising until he ran off to Vienna with the money to join the Habsburgs. Plundering territories in the name of the Catholic faith, Albrecht followed his own simple rule: half for the emperor, half for me. When Habsburg favors waned, Albrecht secretly negotiated with the Swedes. When desperate Habsburgs put him in charge of their armies once again, he continued to play both sides. Finally, somebody had enough: Albrecht was murdered in his bedroom in 1634.

Cost and Hours: Garden—free; April-Oct Mon-Fri 7:30-18:00, Sat-Sun 10:00-18:00, June-Sept daily until 19:00; closed Nov-March. Palace—usually closed to the public.

Visiting the Palace Garden: The inconspicuous entry to the palace's Wallenstein Garden is by the Malostranská Metro station. The garden, renovated in the late 1990s, features a large pool surrounded by peacocks. The statues that line the central walkway (inspired by Greek mythology) were created by the Danish artist Adriaen de Vries—arguably the best Renaissance sculptor outside of Italy. Notice the elegant classical shapes, a sharp contrast to the chubbiness of the Baroque figures on the Charles Bridge and elsewhere in the city. The original statues were stolen by invading Swedish armies in 1648 and are still in Sweden; the present replicas were cast in the early 1900s.

The Renaissance garden and the palace were built by Italian

architects, just like most of the Little Quarter. The theatrical loggia—the *sala terena*—is a stage for drama and music inspired by Greek amphitheaters. Notice the unusual pairing of columns—at the time, a trendy invention of the Italian architect Andrea Palladio. Inside, the gory depictions of the Trojan War tell you about the taste and character of the owner. (A handy WC is to the left of the amphitheater.) The bizarre grotto wall farther on the left was an expression of an uncertain age. It creates the illusion of caves and holes, stalagmites and stalactites, interspersed with partially hidden stone goblins, frogs, and snakes (count how many you can find). The wall continues into a cage with live owls, completing the transition from dead to living nature. The twisted cries of the owls deepen the surreal sensation of the place.

Exit through the door in the right corner of the garden by the *sala terena*. You'll pass into a small courtyard surrounded by what once was the residential part of the palace. Today, the upper chamber of the Czech Parliament meets inside.

SOUTH OF LITTLE QUARTER SQUARE, TO PETŘÍN HILL

The following sights lie along Karmelitská street, which leads south (along the tram tracks) from Little Quarter Square.

Vrtba Garden (Vrtbovská Zahrada)

This terraced Baroque garden makes for an interesting comparison to the Renaissance garden at Wallenstein Palace, described earlier.

Cost and Hours: 65 Kč, April-Oct 10:00-18:00, closed Nov-March, just south of Little Quarter Square at Karmelitská 25, www.vrtbovska.cz.

• *Continue past the gardens to the...*

Church of St. Mary the Victorious (Kostel Panny Marie Vítězné)

This otherwise ordinary Carmelite church displays Prague's most worshiped treasure, the Infant of Prague (Pražské Jezulátko). Kneel at the banister in front of the tiny lost-in-gilded-Baroque altar, and find the prayer in your language (of the 13 in the folder). Brought to Czech lands during the Habsburg era by a Spanish noblewoman who came to marry a Czech nobleman, the Infant has become a focus of worship and miracle tales in Prague and Spanish-speaking countries. South Americans come on pilgrimage to Prague just to see this one statue. An exhibit upstairs shows tiny embroidered robes given to the Infant, including ones from Habsburg Empress Maria Theresa of Austria (1754) and the country of Vietnam (1958), as well as a video showing a nun lovingly dressing the doll-like sculpture.

Cost and Hours: Free, Mon-Sat 9:30-17:30, Sun 13:00-

18:00, English-language Mass Sun at 12:00, Karmelitská 9, www.
pragjesu.cz.

• *Continue a few more blocks down Karmelitská to the south end of the Little Quarter (roughly where the street, now called Újezd, intersects with Vítězná). Here you find yourself at the base of...*

▲PETŘÍN HILL (PETŘÍNSKÉ SADY)

This hill, topped by a replica of the Eiffel Tower, features several unusual sights.

Monument to Victims of Communism (Pomník Obětem Komunismu)

The sculptural figures of this poignant memorial, representing victims of the totalitarian regime, gradually atrophy as they range up the hillside steps. They do not die but slowly disappear, one limb at a time. The statistics inscribed on the steps say it all: From 1948 until 1989, in Czechoslovakia alone, 205,486 people were imprisoned, 248 were executed, 4,500 died in prison, 327 were shot attempting to cross the border, and 170,938 left the country. For further information, and a suggestion for a half-day trip delving into this dark side of history, see the "The Continuing Legacy of Communism" sidebar earlier in this chapter.

• *To the left of the monument is the...*

Hunger Wall (Hladová Zed')

This medieval defense wall was Charles IV's 14th-century equivalent of FDR's work-for-food projects. The poorest of the poor helped build this structure just to eke out a bit of income.

• *On the right (50 yards away) is the base of a handy* **funicular**—*hop on to reach Petřín Tower (uses tram/Metro ticket, runs daily every 10-15 minutes 8:00-22:00).*

Summit and Tower

The summit of Petřín Hill is considered the best place in Prague to take your date for a romantic city view. Built for an exhibition

in 1891, the 200-foot-tall **Petřín Tower**—an elegant pure Art Nouveau steel and wood structure—is one-fifth the height of its Parisian big brother, which was built two years earlier. But, thanks to this hill, the top of the tower sits at the same elevation as the real Eiffel Tower. Before you climb up, appreciate the tower's sinuous curves. Climbing the 400 steps rewards you with amazing views of the city. Czech couples come to the orchard-filled slope of Petřín Hill each May Day to reaffirm their love with a kiss under a blooming sour-cherry tree. A **mirror maze** next door to the tower is fun for a quick wander if you're already here.

Next to the maze, in front of the cupola-topped observatory, notice the statue of **Milan Rastislav Štefánik** (1880-1919), the charismatic Slovak astronomer and patriot. As a naturalized pilot and general in the French army during World War I, Štefánik assembled the first Czechoslovak units, and worked with Tomáš Garrigue Masaryk and Edvard Beneš to create the nation of Czechoslovakia. After the war Štefánik fought to bring home tens of thousands of Czech and Slovak freedom fighters left stranded in Siberia by the Bolshevik Revolution. Štefánik died in a plane crash in May 1919 in bad weather just outside the newly named Slovak capital of Bratislava. His death eventually proved to be a devastating blow for the unity of the young country. Masaryk, Beneš, and Štefánik are the only 20th-century politicians commemorated with statues in the Czech capital.

Cost and Hours: Tower-105 Kč, mirror maze-75 Kč, both daily 10:00-22:00, shorter hours off-season.

• *To the left of the tower as you face Prague Castle, stairs lead down to a path that swirls left along the hill's contour and takes you directly to the Strahov Monastery, described in the next section.*

The Castle Quarter (Hradčany)

Looming above Prague, dominating its skyline, is the Castle Quarter. Prague Castle and its surrounding sights are packed with Czech history, as well as with tourists. In addition to the castle, I enjoy visiting the nearby Strahov Monastery, which has a fascinating old library and beautiful views over all of Prague.

Castle Square (Hradčanské Náměstí)—right in front of the castle gates—is at the center of this neighborhood. Stretching along the promontory away from the castle is a regal neighborhood that ends at the Strahov Monastery. Above the castle are the Royal Gardens, and below the castle are more gardens and lanes leading down to the Little Quarter (see previous section).

Getting There: You have three options: Ride a **taxi** up (ideally to the top of Nerudova street, just below Castle Square); **walk** up (figure 20 minutes uphill from Charles Bridge, along charming cobbled Nerudova street); or ride the **tram.** Departing from various handy locations around town, tram #22 uses several stops near the castle. The closest stop to Castle Square is Pražský Hrad; two stops farther up is Pohořelec, which works for those who want to tour the Strahov Monastery before the downhill walk to Castle Square. For more on this tram line, see my self-guided tram tour on page 42.

Planning Your Time: Visit the castle early or late to

minimize crowds. For complete outlines of the best castle strategies, see page 168.

OFFICIAL SIGHTS AT PRAGUE CASTLE (PRAŽSKÝ HRAD)

This vast and sprawling complex has been the seat of Czech power for centuries. It collects a wide range of sights, including the country's top church, its former royal palace, a higgledy-piggledy lane, and an assortment of history and art museums. (These are listed here in order, from top to bottom, starting at the main gate.) While it's imposing and a bit intimidating to sightseers, the casual visitor finds that a quick and targeted visit is ideal. The sights listed here are part of the official castle complex, and share opening hours and tickets. Which ticket you choose depends on which sights you want

to enter—so familiarize yourself with the options before buying your ticket.

📖 All of these sights—and a recommended route for connecting them—are covered in far greater detail in the Prague Castle Tour chapter.

Ticket Options: While you can enter the grounds for free, most sights require tickets. For a quick visit, get the 250-Kč "Circuit B" ticket, which hits the highlights (St. Vitus Cathedral, Old Royal Palace, Basilica of St. George, Golden Lane). For a few bucks more, "Circuit A" (350 Kč) adds "The Story of Prague Castle" exhibit and a few other sights worthwhile for those with a healthy interest in history and art. You can buy tickets at three different ticket offices in the castle's second and third courtyards. Climbing St. Vitus Cathedral's Great South Tower requires a separate 150-Kč ticket.

Crowd-Beating Tips: One of the city's most crowded sights, Prague Castle is awash in visitors during peak times (9:30-12:30, especially May-Sept). St. Vitus Cathedral's free to visit vestibule is often packed; sights that require paid entry—including at the cathedral—are less jammed. President Zeman's siege-mentality administration has instituted security checks at the main entrance that add 15 minutes to your wait; consider entering through the Royal Garden (Letohrádek tram stop) or from the Pražský hrad tram stop. For tips on visiting at less-crowded times, and detailed suggestions for structuring your visit, see the Prague Castle Tour chapter.

Tours: Tours in English and an audioguide are available, but I'd skip both in favor of this book's self-guided tour chapter (tours-

Prague Castle Quarter

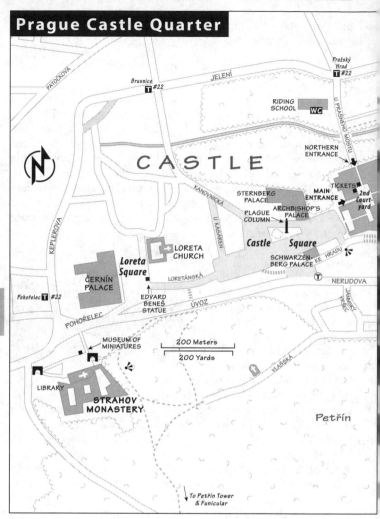

100 Kč plus entry ticket, covers only the cathedral and Old Royal Palace; audioguide-350 Kč plus 500-Kč deposit).

Hours: Castle sights—daily 9:00-17:00, Nov-March until 16:00; castle grounds—daily 5:00-24:00; castle gardens—daily 10:00-18:00 in summer, closed off-season. St. Vitus Cathedral is closed Sunday mornings for Mass, and can be closed unexpectedly at other times. The Great South Tower of St. Vitus Cathedral is open daily 10:00-18:00, until 16:00 in winter, www.hrad.cz.

Castle Square (Hradčanské Náměstí)

Spreading out before the main entrance of the castle, this square is ringed by important buildings (including two that house art gal-

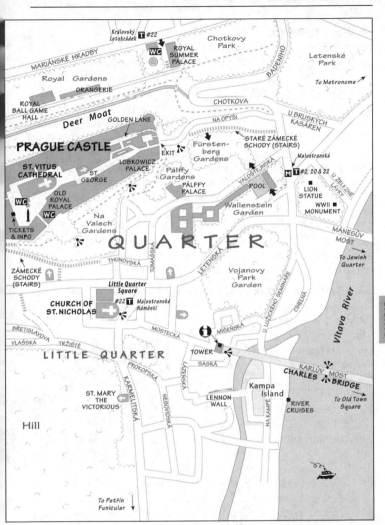

leries—see "Art Museums on Castle Square," later). A statue of the statesman Tomáš Garrigue Masaryk (who led Czechoslovakia after World War I) surveys the scene. Above the gilded gateway to the complex, stone giants battle, while real-life soldiers stand stiffly at attention...until they change the guard with great ceremony at the top of each hour.

To find the castle ticket offices from Castle Square, tiptoe under those giants into the First Courtyard, then under a stone gateway into the Second Courtyard (with a ticket office) and on into the vast expanse of the Third Courtyard (two more ticket offices).

St. Vitus Treasury

Recently opened in the restored Chapel of the Holy Cross (in the castle's Second Courtyard), this pricey-to-view collection shows off the accumulated wealth of the cathedral's ecclesiastical gear. The highlight, dating from Charles IV's reign (1360s), is a golden reliquary in the shape of a cross; used during coronation ceremonies, the cross contains what are supposedly the actual thorns, nails, sponge, rope, and fragments of the cross from Jesus' Crucifixion. You'll also see reliquary busts in the shape of saints (Vitus, Wenceslas, and Adalbert); monstrances slathered in diamonds and other precious stones; chalices; and icons. It's a fine collection, but it's outrageously overpriced. Skip it unless you're a monstrance aficionado.

Cost and Hours: 300 Kč, includes torturously dull audioguide; buy ticket at entrance—not at castle ticket office, which sells only a combo-ticket that adds another museum; daily 10:00-18:00, last entry one hour before closing, tel. 224-372-432.

▲▲▲St. Vitus Cathedral (Katedrála Sv. Víta)

This towering house of worship—with its flying buttresses and spiny spires—is the top church of the Czech people. Many VIPs from this nation's history—from saints to statesmen—are buried here. While it looks old, the front half is the same age as the Empire State Building—Neo-Gothic, built to match the original Gothic back half. You can step into the very congested entry vestibule for a peek at the interior, but it's worth paying for a ticket that lets you go deeper, leave some of the crowds behind, and explore. Inside the soaring nave are stately tombs, reliefs showing the Prague of yore, and the historic Wenceslas Chapel, with the tomb of the most important Czech saint. But for most, the cathedral's highlight is the exquisite stained-glass window by the Art Nouveau great Alfons Mucha, which tells the entire history of Christianity in the Czech lands—from the first missionaries to modern times—with swirling figures, vibrant colors, and powerful symbolism.

📖 For a self-guided tour, see the Prague Castle Tour chapter.

▲Old Royal Palace (Starý Královský Palác)

The traditional seat of Czech power, this feels like a mostly empty historical shell. But its oversized Vladislav Hall—big enough for horseback jousting competitions or bustling markets—is impressive. The smaller, adjoining rooms called the "Czech Office" was the site of a famous defenestration—the Czech way of dealing

The Castle Quarter 89

with unwanted politicians (just throw them out the window). The palace also comes with a balcony offering fine views of the surrounding hillsides, and assorted other royal portraits and bric-a-brac.

The Story of Prague Castle Exhibit (Příběh Pražského Hradu)

For those wanting to dig deeper into the history of Prague and its castle, this exhibit features well-described historical artifacts from the very first Czechs through the imported Habsburg monarchy of the 17th century. As this is the main addition to the pricier "Circuit A" ticket, visit here only if you have a bigger-than-average appetite for history.

▲Basilica and Convent of St. George (Bazilika Sv. Jiří)

The oldest-feeling place at the castle, this atmospheric, dimly lit, stripped-down Romanesque chapel offers a subdued contrast to the big and bombastic spaces elsewhere. Its most significant feature is the tomb of St. Ludmila, the grandmother of St. Wenceslas.

▲Golden Lane (Zlatá Ulička)

Named for the goldsmiths who likely worked here, this medieval merchant street retains its historic aura. When uncrowded, this atmospheric lane—lined with endearing little exhibits on the commerce and customs of a bygone era—is fun

to explore. When busy, as it typically is, it's miserable.

ART MUSEUMS ON CASTLE SQUARE
Sternberg Palace (Šternberský Palác)

This historic mansion is filled with the National Gallery's collection of European paintings. While I'd rather spend my time in the Czech Republic learning about Czech artists (such as Alfons Mucha), those who tour this collection will see minor works by Albrecht Dürer, Peter Paul Rubens, Rembrandt, and El Greco.

Cost and Hours: 300-Kč combo-ticket also covers Schwarzenberg Palace, Museum of Medieval Art, Kinský Palace, and Veletržní Palace; valid 7 days; open Tue-Sun 10:00-18:00, closed Mon; Hradčanské Náměstí 15, www.ngprague.cz.

Schwarzenberg Palace (Schwarzenberský Palác)

Once a home to Czech nobility, this palace is now home to the National Gallery's collection of Czech Baroque paintings and sculpture, displayed in restored rooms that enjoy great views of the city.

Cost and Hours: 300-Kč combo-ticket also covers Sternberg Palace, Museum of Medieval Art, Kinský Palace, and Veletržní Palace; valid 7 days; open Tue-Sun 10:00-18:00, closed Mon; Hradčanské Náměstí 2, www.ngprague.cz.

BELOW THE CASTLE

Extend your visit by dropping by a nobleman's palace and a toy museum with an entire floor devoted to the Barbie doll. These sights require separate admission tickets; they're not included in any castle tickets.

▲▲Lobkowicz Palace (Lobkowiczký Palác)

This palace, at the bottom of the castle complex, displays the private collection of a prominent Czech noble family, including paintings, ceramics, and musical scores. The Lobkowiczes' property was confiscated twice in the 20th century: first by the Nazis at the beginning of World War II, and then by the communists in 1948. In 1990, William Lobkowicz, then a Boston investment banker, returned to Czechoslovakia to fight a legal battle to reclaim his family's property and, eventually, to restore the castles and palaces to their former state. While the National Gallery may seem a more logical choice for the art enthusiast, the obvious care that went into creating this museum, the collection's variety, and the personal insight that it opens into the past and present of Czech nobility make the Lobkowicz worth an hour of your time.

Cost and Hours: 275 Kč, includes audioguide, daily 10:00-18:00, tel. 233-312-925, www.lobkowicz.cz.

Visiting the Palace: A conscientious host, William Lobkowicz himself narrates the delightful, included audioguide. Use the map that comes with your ticket to hone in on the highlights:

The Second-Floor Landing and Room B: As you pass by the portraits of Lobkowicz's ancestors, listen to their stories, including that of Polyxena, whose determination saved the two Catholic governors defenestrated next door (according to family legend, she hid the bruised officials under the folds of her skirt).

Room G: The family loved music. See their instruments, including old lutes. There's the manuscript of Beethoven's *Eroica* symphony (with his last-minute changes). The piece was dedicated to his sponsor—Prince Lobkowicz (see his portrait)—and premiered at the Lobkowicz Palace in Vienna. Nearby is Mozart's handwritten reorchestration of Handel's *Messiah.*

Rooms H-J: The highlights of the museum's paintings include Pieter Bruegel the Elder's magnificently preserved *Haymaking,* from 1565. It's one of the earliest entirely secular landscape paintings in Europe (showing an idyllic and almost heroic connection between peasants and nature). Admire a few paintings of various Lobkowicz castles (by no-name artists), as well as two Canaletto scenes of London's Westminster Abbey and St. Paul's Cathedral.

Eating: The Lobkowicz Palace Café, by the exit, has a creative, cosmopolitan menu and stunning panoramic views of the city (daily 10:00-18:00). The charming young man you may see selling ice cream out front is William's son, Will.

Toy Museum (Muzeum Hraček)

Across the street from Lobkowicz Palace, a courtyard and a long wooden staircase lead to two entertaining floors of old toys and dolls, thoughtfully described in English. You'll see a century of teddy bears, some 19th-century model train sets, old Christmas decor, and an incredible Barbie collection. Find the buxom 1959 first edition, and you'll understand why these capitalistic sirens of material discontent weren't allowed here until 1989.

Cost and Hours: 70 Kč, 120-Kč family ticket, daily 9:30-17:30, WC next to entrance.

ABOVE THE CASTLE: STRAHOV MONASTERY AND LORETA CHURCH

The Strahov Monastery, with its landmark domes, sits above the castle. Remember: If you'd like to combine the monastery with your castle visit, it's easy to ride tram #22 up to the Pohořelec stop (beyond the castle), visit the monastery, enjoy the views, then walk 10 minutes down to Castle Square—passing Loreta Church on the way. (However, if you're rushing to beat the morning crowds at the castle, it's better to head straight for St. Vitus Cathedral in the castle complex, then backtrack to Strahov later.)

▲Strahov Monastery and Library (Strahovský Klášter a Knihovna)

Medieval monasteries were a mix of industry, agriculture, and education, as well as worship and theology. In its heyday, Strahov Monastery had a booming economy of its own, with vineyards, a brewery, and a sizable beer hall—all now open once again. You can explore the monastery complex, check out the beautiful old library, and even enjoy a brew (no longer monk-made, but still refreshing).

Cost and Hours: Grounds—free and always open; library—100 Kč, extra 50 Kč to take photos—strictly enforced, daily

SIGHTS

9:00-12:00 & 13:00-17:00, www.strahovskyklaster.cz. A pay WC is just to the right of the monastery entrance.

Visiting the Monastery and Library: The monastery's **main church,** dedicated to the Assumption of St. Mary, is an originally Romanesque structure decorated by the monks in textbook Baroque (usually closed, but look through the gate inside the front door to see its interior). Notice the grand effect of the Baroque architecture—both rhythmic and theatric. Go ahead, inhale. That's the scent of Baroque.

Buy your ticket in the adjacent building, and head up the stairs to the **library,** offering a peek at how enlightened thinkers in the 18th century influenced learning. The **display cases** in the library gift shop show off illuminated manuscripts, described in English. Some are in old Czech, but because the Enlightenment promoted the universality of knowledge (and Latin was the universal language of Europe's educated elite), there was little place for regional dialects—therefore, few books here are in the Czech language.

Two rooms (seen only from the doors) are filled with 10th- to 17th-century books, shelved under elaborately painted ceilings. The theme of the first and bigger hall is **philosophy,** with the history of Western man's pursuit of knowledge painted on the ceiling. The second hall—down a hallway lined with antique furniture—focuses on **theology.** As the Age of Enlightenment began to take hold in Europe at the end of the 18th century, monasteries still controlled the books. Notice the gilded, locked case containing the *libri prohibiti* (prohibited books) at the end of the room, above the mirror. Only the abbot had the key, and you had to have his blessing to read these books—by writers such as Nicolas Copernicus, Jan Hus, Jean-Jacques Rousseau, and even including the French encyclopedia.

The **hallway** connecting the two library rooms was filled with cases illustrating the new practical approach to natural sciences. In the crowded area near the philosophy hall, find the dried-up elephant trunks (flanking the narwhal or unicorn horn) and one of the earliest models of an electricity generator.

Nearby: That hoppy smell you're enjoying in front of the monastery is the recommended **Klášterní Pivovar,** where they brew beer just as monks have for centuries (in the little courtyard directly across from the library entrance; described on page 224).

Tucked in another courtyard across from the Strahov Monastery, the **Museum of Miniatures** (Muzeum Miniatur) displays 40 teeny exhibits—each under a microscope—crafted by an artist from a remote corner of Siberia. Yes, you could fit the entire museum in a carry-on-size suitcase, but good things sometimes come in very, very small packages—it's fascinating to see minutiae such as a padlock on the leg of an ant (100 Kč, kids-50 Kč, daily 9:00-17:00, Strahovské Nádvoří 11, tel. 233-352-371).

Just below the monastery, don't miss the **garden terrace** (look for the aptly named Bellavista Restaurant), with exquisite views over the domes and spires of Prague. The area just below the restaurant tables is free and open to visitors.

After enjoying the views, take **Loretánská street** to the castle, by way of Loreta Church (described next).

📖 For more details as you walk, see the Prague Castle Tour chapter.

Loreta Church

This church has been a hit with pilgrims for centuries, thanks to its dazzling bell tower, peaceful yet plush cloister, sparkling treasury, and much-venerated Holy House.

Cost and Hours: 150 Kč, daily April-Oct 9:00-17:00, Nov-March 9:30-16:00, audioguide-150 Kč, tel. 220-516-740, www.loreta.cz.

Visiting the Church: Inside, follow the one-way clockwise route. While you stroll along the cloister, notice that the ceiling is painted with the many places Mary has miraculously appeared to the faithful in Europe.

In the garden-like center of the cloister stands the ornate **Santa Casa (Holy House),** considered by some pilgrims to be part of Mary's home in Nazareth. Because many pilgrims returning from the Holy Land docked at the Italian port of Loreto, it's called the Loreta Shrine. The Santa Casa is the "little Bethlehem" of Prague. It is the traditional departure point for Czech pilgrims setting out on the long, arduous journey to Europe's most important pilgrimage site, Santiago de Compostela, in northwest Spain. Inside, on the left wall, hangs what some consider to be an original beam from the house of Mary. It's overseen by a much-venerated statue of the Black Virgin. The Santa Casa itself

SIGHTS

might seem like a bit of a letdown, but generations of believers have considered this to be the holiest spot in the country.

The small **Baroque church** behind the Santa Casa is one of the most beautiful in Prague. The decor looks rich—but the marble and gold are all fake. From the window in the back, you can see a stucco relief on the Santa Casa that shows angels rescuing the house from a pagan attack in Nazareth and making a special delivery to Loreto in Italy.

Continue around the cloister. In the last corner, on the left wall of the chapel, is **"St. Bearded Woman"** (Svatá Starosta). This patron saint of unhappy marriages is a woman whose family arranged for her to marry a pagan man. She prayed for an escape, sprouted a beard...and the guy said, "No way." While she managed to avoid the marriage, it angered her father, who crucified her. The many candles here are from people suffering through uncivil unions.

Take a left just before the exit and head upstairs, following signs to the **treasury**—a room full of jeweled worship aids (well-described in English). The highlight here—in the heavily fortified room that feels like a bank vault—is a monstrance (Communion wafer holder) from 1699, with more than 6,000 diamonds.

Enjoy the short **carillon concert** at the top of the hour; from the lawn in front of the main entrance, you can see the racks of bells being clanged. (At the exit, you'll see a schedule of upcoming *pout*—pilgrimages—departing from here.)

ROYAL SUMMER PALACE AND ROYAL GARDENS

These minor sights, above Prague Castle, are only worth visiting if you get off tram #22 at Královský Letohrádek (the Royal Summer Palace is across the street from this stop, WC at gate).

Royal Summer Palace (Královský Letohrádek)

This gift of love is like a Czech Taj Mahal, presented by Emperor Ferdinand I to his beloved Queen Anne. It's the purest Renaissance building in town. You can't go inside, but the building's detailed reliefs are worth a close look. In good Renaissance style, they're based on classical, rather than Christian, stories. The one depicted here is Virgil's *Aeneid*. The fountain in front of the palace features the most elaborate bronze work in the country. (For a trip to Tibet, stick your head under the bottom of the fountain. The audio rainbow you hear is the reason it's called the Singing Fountain.)

• *From here, set your sights on the cathedral's lacy, black spires marking the castle's entrance. Stroll through the...*

Royal Gardens (Královská Zahrada)

Once the private grounds and residence (you'll see the building) of the communist presidents, these were opened to the public with the coming of freedom under Václav Havel (free, April-Oct daily 10:00-18:00, closed Nov-March). Walk through these gardens (with lovely views of St. Vitus Cathedral) to the gate, which leads you over the moat and into Castle Square, the entrance to the vast castle complex.

Outside the Center

While the tourist's Prague is mostly contained in the Old Town, New Town, Little Quarter, and Castle Quarter, just outside this core is a modern art collection at Veletržní Palace (north of the New Town, across the river).

In the opposite direction, south of the New Town, is the peaceful park at Vyšehrad. With a 17th-century fortress and views overlooking the city, Vyšehrad provides a welcome break from the Prague bustle and a wonderful setting for a contemplative stroll any time of day.

Veletržní Palace

Just north of the river from the New Town, Veletržní Palace holds an extensive, fun-to-wander modern art collection, with pieces by artists both Czech and international (lesser-known works by Van Gogh, Picasso, Toulouse-Lautrec, Gauguin, and more).

Cost and Hours: 300-Kč combo-ticket also covers Museum of Medieval Art, Sternberg Palace, Schwarzenberg Palace, and Kinský Palace; valid 7 days; open Tue-Sun 10:00-18:00, closed Mon; Dukelských Hrdinů 47 (Praha 7), tel. 224-301-122, www.ngprague.cz.

Getting There: You can reach Veletržní Palace by tram #17 from Národni Divadlo or Staroměstská; get off at the Veletržní Pálac stop. You can also hire a taxi, or take the Metro to Vltavská, then walk a few minutes.

▲Vyšehrad

If you're looking to escape the tourists—while digging more deeply into Czech culture and history (and also enjoy fine city views)—head for the hilltop fortress-turned-park called Vyšehrad (VEE-sheh-rahd),

just south of the center. While there, ogle the dynamic statues of Bohemian folkloric figures and dip into the National Cemetery to pay your respects to Czech greats such as Mucha and Dvořák.

Cost and Hours: The park is free to enter and open all the time (though the church closes at 18:00 and the cemetery closes as early as 17:00 off-season). To get there, ride the Metro to the Vyšehrad stop and hike five minutes downhill.

📖 See the Vyšehrad Walk chapter.

OLD TOWN WALK

Staré Město

Nestled in the bend of the river is Prague's compact, pedestrian-friendly Old Town. A boomtown since the 10th century, the Old Town has long been the busy commercial quarter, filled with merchants, guilds, and supporters of the Church reformer Jan Hus (who wanted a Czech-style Catholicism). Today it's Prague's tourism ground zero, jammed with tasteful landmarks and tacky amusements alike.

This walk starts in the heart of the neighborhood, the Old Town Square. From here we'll snake through the surrounding neighborhood, get a glimpse of the New Town (at Wenceslas Square), and end at the river, on Charles Bridge—one of the most atmospheric spots in all of Europe. Along the way, we'll see Baroque statues, Art Nouveau facades, and a curious old clock. And we'll learn the story of how the Czech people have courageously fought against foreign oppression, from Habsburgs to Nazis to Soviet communists.

Orientation

Length of This Walk: Allow two to three hours for this walk. It's a great overview of sights you may want to visit in depth later.

When to Go: The Old Town Square and surrounding streets are packed midday, and never really quiet. A huge bottleneck occurs in front of the Astronomical Clock near the top of each hour, but as soon as the show's over, the tourists disperse quickly.

Getting There: This walk begins right on the Old Town Square, Prague's centerpiece.

Týn Church: 30-Kč requested donation, generally open to sightseers Tue-Sat 10:00-13:00 & 15:00-17:00, Sun 10:30-12:00, closed Mon.

Old Town Hall Tower: 110 Kč, Tue-Sun 9:00-21:00, Mon 11:00-21:00.

Church of St. James: Free, Tue-Sun 9:30-12:00 & 14:00-16:00, closed Mon.

Municipal House: Free to view entrance halls and public spaces; daily 10:00-18:00; tours—290 Kč, usually 3/day, departures 11:00-17:00.

Museum of Communism: 190 Kč, daily 9:00-21:00.

Havelská Market: Open-air market open daily 9:00-18:00, produce best on weekdays; more souvenirs, puppets, and toys on weekends.

Klementinum: Baroque Hall and Observatory Tour by tour only, 220 Kč, departs daily every half-hour 10:00-17:30, shorter hours off-season.

Charles Bridge Tower Climb: 90 Kč, daily 10:00-22:00, March and Oct until 20:00, Nov-Feb until 18:00.

Services: Pay WCs are common throughout Prague's Old Town; for example, in the Old Town Hall or at the square's Kotleta Restaurant.

Starring: Prague's showpiece main square, fine old churches, architectural landmarks, and the spunky Czech spirit.

The Tour Begins

• *Plant yourself anywhere in the Old Town Square, and survey the scene.*

OLD TOWN SQUARE

Take in the essence of modern Prague, a city of 1.3 million people and the capital of the Czech Republic. The vast square is ringed with colorful buildings; dotted with towers, steeples, and statues; lined with cafés; and alive with people. Street performers provide a constant soundtrack. Horse carriages and Segways zip through constantly—a reminder that Prague is as much a city of yesterday as a city of today.

This has been a market square since the 11th century. It became the nucleus of the Old Town (or Staré Město) in the 13th century, when its Town Hall was built. In past times, it would have been the site of commerce, parades, demonstrations, and executions. Today, the old-time market stalls have been replaced by outdoor cafés and the tackiest breed of souvenir stands. But under this shallow surface, the square hides a magic power to evoke the history that has passed through here.

• *Begin with the square's centerpiece, the...*

❶ Memorial to Jan Hus

This monument is an enduring icon of the long struggle for Czech freedom. In the center, Jan Hus—the religious reformer who has

become a symbol of Czech nationalism—stands tall. Hus, born in 1369, was a Prague priest who stood up to both the Catholic Church and the Austrian Habsburg oppressors. His defiant stance—as depicted so powerfully in this monument— galvanized the Czech people, who rallied to fight not just for their religious beliefs but for independence from foreign control.

But Hus was about a century ahead of his time. He was arrested, charged with heresy, excommunicated, and, in 1415, burned at the stake. His followers picked up the torch and fought on for two decades in the Hussite Wars, which killed tens of thousands and left Bohemia a virtual wasteland.

Surrounding Hus's statue are the Hussite followers who battled the Habsburgs. One patriot holds a cup, or chalice. This symbolizes one of the changes the Hussites were fighting for: the right of everyone (not just priests) to drink the wine at Communion. Look into the survivors' faces—it was a bitter fight. In 1620, their rebellious cause was brutally crushed by the Catholic Habsburgs at the pivotal Battle of White Mountain fought outside Prague— effectively ending Czech independence for three centuries.

As we'll see on this walk, Jan Hus was the linchpin in Czech history. Before him was the Golden Age of great kings (c. 1200-1400). After him came centuries of foreign domination. But the story ends well. Huddled just behind Jan Hus are a mother and her children—representing the ultimate rebirth of the Czech nation.

Each subsequent age has interpreted Hus to its liking: For Protestants, Hus was the founder of the first Protestant church (though he was actually an ardent Catholic); for revolutionaries, this critic of the Church's power was a proponent of social equality; for nationalists, this Czech preacher was the defender of the language; and for communists, Hus was the first ideologue to preach the gospel of socialism. But regardless of who was in power, Hus' importance to the Czech people has never wavered.

OLD TOWN

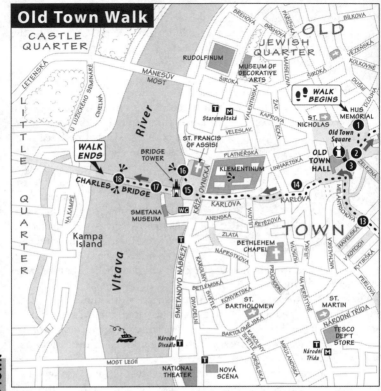

Old Town Walk

• *Stepping away from the Hus Memorial, stand in the center of the Old Town Square, and take a 360-degree...*

❷ Old Town Square Orientation Spin-Tour

Whirl clockwise to get a look at Prague's diverse architectural styles: Gothic, Renaissance, Baroque, Rococo, and Art Nouveau. Remember, Prague was largely spared the devastating aerial bombardments of World War II that leveled so many European cities (like Berlin, Warsaw, and Budapest). Few places can match the Old Town Square for Old World charm.

Start with the green domes of the Baroque **Church of St. Nicholas.** Originally Catholic, now Hussite, this church is a popular venue for concerts. The Jewish Quarter is a few blocks behind the church, down the uniquely tree-lined "Paris Street" (Pařížská)—which also has the best lineup of Art Nouveau houses in Prague, and arguably in all of Europe.

Spin to the right. Behind the Hus Memorial is a fine yellow building that introduces us to Prague's wonderful world of Art Nouveau: pastel colors, fanciful stonework, wrought-iron balco-

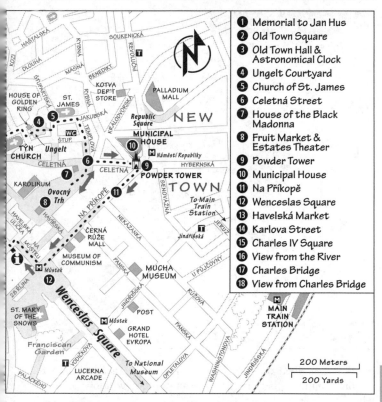

nies, colorful murals—and what are those statues on top doing? Prague's architecture is a wonderland of ornamental details.

Continue spinning a few doors to the right to the large, red-and-tan Rococo **Kinský Palace,** which displays the National Gallery's Asian arts collection (and has a handy WC in the courtyard).

Farther to the right is the towering, Gothic **Týn Church** (pronounced "teen"), with its fanciful twin spires. It's been the Old Town's leading church in every era. In medieval times, it was Catholic. When the Hussites took power (c. 1420-1620), they made it the headquarters of their faith. After the Hussite defeat, the Habsburgs returned it to Catholicism. The symbolism tells the story: Between the church's two towers, find a golden medallion of the Virgin Mary. Beneath that is a niche—now empty. But in Hussite times, a golden chalice stood there, symbolizing their cause. When the Catholics triumphed, they melted down the chalice and made it into this golden image of Mary. The church

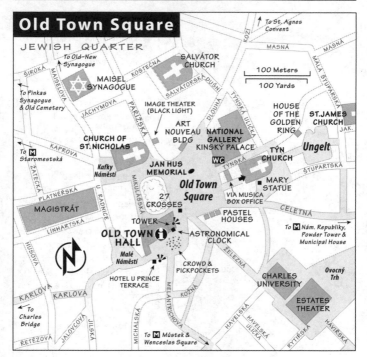

Old Town Square

JEWISH QUARTER

To Old-New Synagogue

MAISEL SYNAGOGUE

SALVÁTOR CHURCH

100 Meters

100 Yards

To Pinkas Synagogue & Old Cemetery

IMAGE THEATER (BLACK LIGHT)

HOUSE OF THE GOLDEN RING

ST. JAMES CHURCH

ART NOUVEAU BLDG

NATIONAL GALLERY KINSKÝ PALACE

CHURCH OF ST. NICHOLAS

To Staroměstská

Kafky Náměstí

JAN HUS MEMORIAL

TÝN CHURCH

Ungelt

WC

MAGISTRÁT

27 CROSSES

Old Town Square

MARY STATUE

VIA MUSICA BOX OFFICE

PASTEL HOUSES

TOWER

OLD TOWN HALL

ASTRONOMICAL CLOCK

To Nám. Republiky, Powder Tower & Municipal House

Malé Náměstí

CROWD & PICKPOCKETS

HOTEL U PRINCE TERRACE

CHARLES UNIVERSITY

Ovocný Trh

To Charles Bridge

ESTATES THEATER

To Můstek & Wenceslas Square

interior (described on page 45) is uncharacteristically bright for a Gothic building because of its clear Baroque windowpanes and whitewash.

The row of pastel houses in front of Týn Church has a mixture of Gothic, Renaissance, and Baroque facades. If you like live music, check out the convenient **Via Musica box office** near the church's front door to find out all your options (see page 241); we'll pass it later on this walk.

Spinning right, to the south side of the square, take in more **glorious facades,** each a different color with a different gable on top—step gables, triangular, bell-shaped. The tan house at #16 has a steepled bay window and a mural of St. Wenceslas on horseback; Albert Einstein once lectured at the light-orange house at #18.

Finally, you reach the pointed 250-foot-tall spire marking the 14th-century **Old Town Hall.** The tower is Neo-Gothic. In the 19th century, a building was constructed on the square's west side that once stretched from the Old Town to the Church of St. Nicholas. Then, in the last days of World War II, Ger-

Jan Hus and the Early Reformers

Jan Hus (c. 1369-1415) lived and preached more than a century before Martin Luther (1483-1546), but they had many things in

common. Both were college professors as well as priests. Both drew huge public crowds as they preached in their university chapels. Both condemned Church corruption, promoted local religious autonomy, and advocated for letting the common people participate more in worship rituals. Both established their national languages. (It's Hus who gave the Czech alphabet its unique accent marks so that the letters could fit the sounds.) And, by challenging established authority, both got in big trouble.

Hus was born in the small southern Bohemian town of Husinec, and moved to Prague to study at the university. He served as a rector at Charles University starting in 1402. Preaching from the pulpit in Bethlehem Chapel (still open to the public and described on page 52), Hus drew inspiration from the English philosopher John Wycliffe (c. 1320-1384), who was an early advocate of reforming the Catholic Church to strip the clergy of its power.

Hus' revolutionary sermons drew huge crowds of reverent but progressive-minded Czechs. He proposed that the congregation should be more involved in worship (for example, be allowed to drink the wine at Communion) and have services and scriptures written in the people's language, not in Latin. Even after he was excommunicated in 1410, Hus continued preaching his message.

In 1414, the Roman Catholic Church convened the Council of Constance to grapple with the controversies of the day. First they posthumously excommunicated Wycliffe, proclaiming him a heretic and exhuming his corpse to symbolically burn at the stake. Then they called Hus to Constance, where on July 6, 1415, they declared him a heretic. After refusing to recant his beliefs and praying that God would forgive his enemies, Hus was tied to a stake and burned alive. But by this time, Hus' challenging ideas had been embraced by many Czechs, and sparked the bloodiest civil war in the country's history.

This early Catholic precursor to the Counter-Reformation kept things under control for generations. But in the 16th century, a German monk named Martin Luther found a more progressive climate for these same revolutionary ideas. Thanks to the new printing press, Luther was able to spread his message cheaply and effectively. While Hus loosened Rome's grip on Christianity, Luther orchestrated the Reformation that finally broke it. Today, both are honored as national heroes as well as religious reformers.

man tanks knocked it down...to the joy of many Prague citizens who considered it an ugly 19th-century stain on the medieval square.

Approach the Old Town Hall. At the base of the tower, near the corner of the tree-filled park, find **27 white crosses** inlaid in the pavement. These mark the spot where 27 Protestant nobles, merchants, and intellectuals were beheaded in 1621 after the Battle of White Mountain—still one of the grimmest chapters in the country's history.

• *Around the left side of the tower are two big, fancy, old clock faces, being admired by many, many tourists.*

❸ Old Town Hall and Astronomical Clock

The Old Town Hall, with its distinctive trapezoidal tower, was built in the 1350s, during Prague's Golden Age. Check out the ornately carved Gothic entrance door to the left of the clock; a bit farther to the left is another door, leading to the TI, a pay WC, and the ticket desk for the clock tower elevator and Old Town Hall tours (both described on page 45).

For now, turn your attention to that famous **Astronomical Clock.** See if you can figure out how it works. Of the two giant dials on the tower, the top one tells the time. It has a complex series of revolving wheels within wheels, but the basics are simple. Read this while you're waiting for the clock to spring to life:

The two big, outer dials tell the time in a 24-hour circle. Of these, the inner dial is stationary and is marked with the Roman numerals I-XII twice, starting at the top and bottom of the dial—noon and midnight. The colorful background of this dial indicates the amount of daylight at different times of day: The black circle surrounded by orange at the bottom half (from XII "p.m." to IV "a.m.") is nighttime, while the blue top half is daytime, and the shades of gray and orange between them represent dawn and dusk.

Meanwhile, the outer dial (with the golden numbers on a black band) lists the numbers 1 through 24, in a strange but readable Bohemian script. But because this uses the medieval Italian method of telling time—where the day resets at sunset—the 1 is not at the top, but somewhere in the lower-right quadrant of the Roman dial. The Roman numeral that the Bohemian 1 lines up with tells you the time of last night's sunset (typically between IV and VIII "p.m.").

The "big hand" (with the golden sun on it) does one slow sweep each 24-hour period, marking the time on both dials.

Now pay attention to the offset inner ring, marked with the zodiac signs. This ring both rotates on its own, and moves around the outer dial, so the sunny "big hand" also lands on today's zodiac sign. And the "little hand" (with a blue moon) appears in this month's zodiac—is the moon in Taurus?

If all this seems complex to us, it must have been a marvel in the early 1400s, when the clock was installed. Remember that back then, everything revolved around the Earth (the fixed middle background—with Prague marking the center, of course). The clock was heavily damaged during World War II, and much of what you see today is a reconstruction.

The second dial, below the clock, was added in the 19th century. It shows the signs of the zodiac, scenes from the seasons of a rural peasant's life, and a ring of saints' names. There's one for each day of the year, and a marker on top indicates today's special saint. In the center is a castle, symbolizing Prague.

Four statues flank the upper clock. These politically incorrect symbols evoke a 15th-century outlook: The figure staring into a mirror stands for vanity, a Jewish moneylender holding a bag of coins is greed, and (on the right side) a Turk with a mandolin symbolizes hedonism. All these worldly goals are vain in the face of Death, whose hourglass reminds us that our time is unavoidably running out.

The clock strikes the top of the hour and puts on a little glockenspiel show daily from 9:00 to 21:00 (until 20:00 in winter). As

the hour approaches, keep your eye on Death. First, Death tips his hourglass and pulls the cord, ringing the bell, while the moneylender jingles his purse. Then the windows open and the 12 apostles shuffle past, acknowledging the gang of onlookers. Finally the rooster at the very top crows and the hour is rung. The hour is often wrong because of Daylight Saving Time (completely senseless to 15th-century clockmakers). I find an alternative view just as interesting: As the cock crows, face the crowd and snap a photo of the mass of gaping tourists.

Before moving on, stand at the Astronomical Clock and get oriented. You're at the axis of several main streets. To the right and left are Celetná and Karlova streets, which form the main east-west spine through the Old Town. Behind you is Melantrichova street, which leads south to Wenceslas Square. We'll be traversing all of these on our walk.

• *Let's leave the Old Town Square. Our next stop is directly behind the Týn Church: Cross through the square and head down the street along*

A Little Walking History

As you're walking through living Czech history, you'll note a theme that runs throughout: how the tiny Czech nation has had to constantly fight to survive amid more powerful neighbors.

The nation was born under the duke Wenceslas, who unified the Czech people 1,100 years ago. Prague's medieval Golden Age peaked under Charles IV (c. 1350), who built many of the city's best-known monuments. Over the next centuries, the Czechs were forever struggling to maintain their proud heritage. First, they defied the pope, led by religious reformer Jan Hus. Then they chafed under the yoke of the Austrian Habsburgs. Finally, in the historic year 1918, the modern nation of Czechoslovakia was created. Unfortunately, that nation was trampled yet again—first by Nazis, then, due to the gullibility of its leading politicians and a shortsighted 1946 popular vote, by the communist Soviet Union. In 1989, huge protests peacefully tossed out the communists in the Velvet Revolution.

Rising nationalist feelings in Slovakia in the early 1990s helped lead to the peaceful dissolution of Czechoslovakia into the Czech Republic and Slovakia on January 1, 1993. In 1999, both countries joined NATO, followed in 2004 by the EU, and in 2007 the Schengen Agreement abolished border passport controls.

the left side of the church (*Týnska*) for about 100 yards, passing the convenient **Via Musica box office**. A bit farther along, on the left, you'll pass the **House of the Golden Ring**, worth considering if you're curious about 20th-century Czech art (see page 50).

Continue straight through a sturdy gate, into a courtyard called...

❹ Ungelt

This pleasant, cobbled, quiet courtyard of upscale restaurants and shops is one of the Old Town's oldest places. During the Bohemian Golden Age (c. 1200-1400), it was a multicultural hub of international trade. Prague—located at the geographical center of Europe—attracted Germans selling furs, Italians selling fine art, Frenchmen selling cloth, and Arabs selling spices. They converged on this courtyard, where they could store their goods and pay their customs (which is what *Ungelt* means, in German). In return, the king granted them protection, housing, and a stable for their horses. By day, they'd sell their wares on the Old Town Square. At night, they'd return here to drink and exchange news from their native lands. Notice that, to protect the goods, there are only two entrances to the complex. After centuries of disuse, the Ungelt has been marvelously restored—a great place for dinner, and a reminder that Prague has been a cosmopolitan center for most of its history.

• *Exit the Ungelt at the far end. Just to your left, across the street, is the...*

❺ Church of St. James (Kostel Sv. Jakuba)

Perhaps the most beautiful church interior in the Old Town, the Church of St. James has been the home of the Minorite Order

almost as long as merchants have occupied Ungelt. A medieval city was a complex phenomenon: Commerce, prostitution, and a life of contemplation existed side by side. (I guess it's not that much different from today.)

Step inside (or, if it's locked, peek through the glass door). Artistically, St. James is a stunning example of how simple medieval spaces could be rebuilt into sumptuous feasts of Baroque decoration. The original interior was destroyed by fire in 1689; what's here now is an early 18th-century remodel. The blue light in the altar highlights one of Prague's most venerated treasures—the bejeweled Madonna Pietatis. Above the *pietà*, as if held aloft by hummingbird-like angels, is a painting of the martyrdom of St. James.

Proceed grandly up the central aisle, enjoying a parade of gilded statues and paintings under a colorfully frescoed ceiling telling stories of Virgin Mary's life. When you reach the altar at the front, turn around and notice how the church suddenly becomes simpler without all that ornamentation. Prague's grandest pipe organ fills the back wall.

As you leave, look for the black, shriveled-up arm with clenched fingers (hanging by a chain from a metal post 15 feet above and to the left of the door). According to legend, a thief attempted to rob the Madonna Pietatis from the altar, but his hand was frozen the moment he touched the statue. The monks had to cut off his arm to get the hand to let go. The desiccated arm now hangs here as a warning.

• *Exiting the church, do a U-turn to the left (heading up Jakubska street, along the side of the church, past some rough-looking bars). After one block, turn right on Templova street. Head two blocks down the street (passing a nice view of the Týn Church's rear end, and some deluxe toilets) and go through the arcaded passageway, where you emerge onto...*

❻ Celetná Street

Since the 10th century, this street has been a corridor in the busy commercial quarter—filled with merchants and guilds. These days, it's still pretty commercial, and very touristy.

OLD TOWN

Here on Celetná street, you're surrounded by a number of buildings with striking facades. To the left is the medieval Powder Tower—we'll head there soon. Straight ahead of you is a Baroque balcony supported by four statues. Many facades are Neoclassical—pastel colors, with arches over doorways, pediments over windows, and hints of scrollwork and garlands. It's little wonder that, when movie-makers want to film a movie set in frilly Baroque times (such as the movie about Mozart, *Amadeus*), they often choose Prague. In fact, we'll see a historic Mozart-era theater in just a moment.

• *To your right is a striking, angular building called the...*

❼ House of the Black Madonna (Dům u Černé Matky Boží)

Back around the turn of the 20th century, Prague was a center of avant-garde art second only to Paris. Art Nouveau blossomed here (as we'll soon see), as did Cubism.
The Cubist exterior is a marvel of rectangular windows and cornices—stand back and see how masterfully it makes its statement while mixing with its neighbors...then get up close and study the details. The interior houses a Cubist café (the recommended Grand Café Orient, one flight up the parabolic spiral staircase)—complete with cube-shaped chairs and square-shaped rolls. The Kubista gallery on the ground

floor shows more examples of this unique style. This building is an example of what has long been considered the greatest virtue of Prague's architects: the ability to adapt grandiose plans to the existing cityscape.

• *The long, skinny square that begins just to the left of the House of the Black Madonna is the...*

❽ Fruit Market (Ovocný Trh) and the Estates Theater

This long, narrow square with a bulge in the middle is typical of medieval Central European market towns. Market stalls would pop up along the busy main drag right in the center of town—making it easy to see how a town can swell as it grows. While no fruit vendors still sell their wares here, this square has retained its traditional name.

The green-and-white building squatting in the middle of the square—right at the bulge—is the **Estates Theater** (Stavovské Divadlo). Built by a nobleman in the 1780s, this

Classicist building was the prime opera venue in Prague at a time when an Austrian prodigy was changing the course of music. Wolfgang Amadeus Mozart premiered *Don Giovanni* in this building (with a bronze statue of Il Commendatore duly flanking the main entrance on the left), and he directed many of his works here. Prague's theatergoers would whistle arias from Mozart's works on the streets the morning after they premiered. Today, the Estates Theater (part of the National Theater group) continues to produce *The Marriage of Figaro, Don Giovanni,* and occasionally *The Magic Flute.* This building is generally seen as a German theater. In fact, for a time the Habsburgs forbade plays here in the Czech language. In the late 1800s, the Czechs built the National Theater in the New Town to celebrate Czech culture—with no regard for their German-speaking rulers. (For more on composers who worked in Prague, see page 69.)

• *Backtrack a few steps to Celetná street, turn right, and head about 50 yards to the...*

❾ Powder Tower

The big, black, 500-year-old Powder Tower was the main gate of the old town wall. It also housed the city's gunpowder—hence the

name. This is the only surviving bit of the wall that was built to defend the city in the 1400s. (Though you can go inside, it's not worth paying to tour the interior.)

The Powder Tower was the city's formal front door—the road from Vienna entered here. Picture the scene two centuries ago, when Habsburg Empress Maria Theresa had just been crowned Queen of Bohemia. As she returned home in triumph, she passed through the Powder Tower gate.

Go back 500 years and look up at the impressive Gothic-carved welcoming committee, reminding all of the hierarchy of our mortal existence: Reading from the bottom up, you'll see artisans flanking Prague's coat of arms, a pair of Czech kings with seals of alliance with neighboring regions, angels with golden wings, and saints flanking Christ in majesty. The tower is topped with one of Prague's signature styles—a trapezoidal roof.

• *Pass regally through the Powder Tower. In so doing, you're leaving the Old Town. You emerge into a big, busy intersection. To your left is the Municipal House, a cream-colored building topped with a green dome. Find a good spot where you can view the facade.*

Prague: The Queen of Art Nouveau

Prague is Europe's best city for Art Nouveau. That's the style of art and architecture that flourished throughout Europe around 1900. It was called "nouveau"—or new—because it was associated with all things modern: technology, social progress, and enlightened thinking. Art Nouveau was neo-nothing, but instead a fresh answer to all the revival styles of the late-19th century, and an organic response to the Eiffel Tower art of the Industrial Age.

By taking advantage of recent advances in engineering, Art Nouveau liberated the artist in each architect. Notice the curves and motifs expressing originality—every facade is unique. Artists such as Alfons Mucha believed that the style should apply to all facets of daily life. They designed everything from buildings and furniture to typefaces and cigarette packs.

Prague's three top Art Nouveau architects are Jan Koula, Josef Fanta, and Osvald Polivka (whose last name sounds like the Czech word for "soup"). Think "Cola, Fanta, and Soup"—easy to remember and a good way to impress your local friends.

Though Art Nouveau was born in Paris, it's in Prague where you'll find some of its greatest hits: the Municipal House and nearby buildings, Grand Hotel Evropa (on Wenceslas Square), the exuberant facades of the Jewish Quarter, the Jerusalem Synagogue, and—especially—the work of Prague's own Alfons Mucha. You can see his stained-glass window in St. Vitus Cathedral (at Prague Castle—page 88), and the excellent Mucha Museum (near Wenceslas Square—page 60). Mucha's masterpiece, *The Slav Epic,* is out of the country on a world tour through 2019.

⑩ Municipal House (Obecní Dům)

The Municipal House, which celebrated its centennial in 2011, is the "pearl of Czech Art Nouveau." Art Nouveau flourished during the same period as the Eiffel Tower and Europe's great Industrial Age train stations.

The same engineering prowess and technological advances that went into making those huge erector-set rigid buildings were used by artistic architects to create quite the opposite effect: curvy, organically flowing lines, inspired by vines and curvaceous women. Art Nouveau was a reaction against the sterility of modern-age construction. Look at the elaborate wrought-iron balcony—flanked by bronze Atlases hefting their lanterns—and the lovely stained glass (like in the entrance arcade).

Mosaics and sculptural knickknacks (see the faces above the windows) made the building's facade colorful and joyous. Study the bright mosaic above the balcony, called *Homage to Prague.* A symbol of the city, the goddess Praha presides over a land of peace and high culture—an image that stoked cultural pride and nationalist sentiment. On the balcony is a medallion showing the three-tower castle that is the symbol of Prague.

The Municipal House was built in the early 1900s, when Czech nationalism was at a fever pitch. Having been ruled by the Austrian Habsburgs for the previous 300 years, the Czechs were demanding independence. This building was drenched in patriotic Czech themes. Within a few short years, in 1918, the nation of Czechoslovakia was formed—and the independence proclamation was announced to the people right here, from the balcony of the Municipal House.

The interior of the Municipal House has perhaps Europe's finest Art Nouveau decor. It's free to enter and wander the public areas. Check out the Art Nouveau café and restaurant near the entrance. Go downstairs to another restaurant for a peek. Enjoy the colorful mosaic designs, razzle-dazzle chandeliers, and curvaceous wooden chairs. While to really appreciate the building you must attend a concert here or take one of the excellent tours offered throughout the day, any visit here gets a sweet dose of Art Nouveau. (For a self-guided tour of the Municipal House interior, see page 66.)

• *Before moving on, note the building across the street, the **Divaldo Hibernia**, where concerts are held.*

Now head west down Na Příkopě (to the left as you face the Powder Tower) toward the Metro station about 200 yards away. Enjoy the sights of...

⓫ Na Příkopě, the Old City Wall

The street called Na Příkopě was where the old city wall once stood. More specifically, the name Na Příkopě means "On the Moat," and you're walking along what was once the moat outside the wall. To your right is the Old Town. To the left, the New. Look at your city map and conceptualize medieval Prague's smart design: The city was protected on two sides by its river, and on the other two sides by its walls (marked by the modern streets called Na Příkopě, Revoluční, and Národní Třída). The only river crossing back then was the fortified Charles Bridge.

Though the moat and city wall are now long gone, there's still a strong divide between the Old Town and the New Town. Na Příkopě—with its modern buildings, banks, and workaday franchise stores—is more New than Old. It's bustling and lively, without a hint of the trouble Prague endured in the mid-20th century.

Many of Prague's top shopping malls are along this strip, as well as the **Museum of Communism** (at #10, tucked down a courtyard on your left; for a self-guided tour, see page 62). This homage to the proletariat is nestled, ironically, between a McDonalds and a casino (somewhere, Lenin is rolling over in his grave). For four decades (1945-1989), the Czech people suffered under a communist government, under the thumb of the Soviet Union.

Remember, at the end of World War II, it was the Soviet Union that liberated Eastern Europe—including Czechoslovakia—from the Nazis. The Soviets used propaganda and intimidation to infiltrate the governments of their satellite states...and didn't leave.

Pause for a moment—immersed in all of this modern commerce—and ponder the hard times under communism: Prague became a gray and bleak world of decrepit buildings. Consumer goods were scarce—customers waited in line for hours for a tin of pineapple or a bottle of ersatz Coke. Statues were black with soot, and on Charles Bridge—so busy today—there was nothing but a few shady characters trying to change money. At the train station, frightened but desperate locals would meet arriving foreigners and offer to rent them a room, hoping to earn enough Western cash to buy batteries or Levis at one of the hard-currency stores. Life seemed hopeless. In the spring of 1968, the Czechs tried to rise up, enacting government reforms that came to be called "Prague Spring." But Soviet tanks rumbled into Prague and crushed the rebellion. It wasn't until a generation later, in 1989, that the sad tale finally had its happy ending...and it happened just steps away from here, at our next stop.

• *Continue up Na Příkopě street to an intersection (and nearby Metro stop) called Můstek. To your left stretches the vast expanse of the wide boulevard called...*

⓬ Wenceslas Square—the New Town
Wenceslas Square—with the National Museum and landmark statue of St. Wenceslas at the very top—is the centerpiece of Prague's New Town. This square was originally founded as a thriving horse market. Today it's a modern world of high-fashion stores, glitzy shopping malls, fine old facades (and some jarringly modern ones), fast-food restaurants, and sausage stands.

Picture the scene on this square on a cold November night in 1989: The Berlin Wall has fallen, and a student protest in Prague has been put down violently—the last straw for a city that was fed up with the oppressive communist system. Each night for a week and a half, hundreds of thousands of freedom-loving Czechs fill Wenceslas Square, jangling their key chains and demanding their freedom. Finally, the

formerly jailed poet/philosopher/dissident Václav Havel appears on a balcony to announce the end of communism. The crowd celebrates wildly, having overthrown the rule of an "Evil Empire" without firing a shot...a feat that has come to be known as the Velvet Revolution. (For more on the Velvet Revolution, landmarks of Wenceslas Square, and New Town—see the ☐ Wenceslas Square Walk chapter; if you'd like to take that walk now, you can walk 10 minutes up to the starting point at the top of the square, or you can just hop on the Metro and go one stop, to Muzeum.)

• *Let's plunge back into the Old Town and return to the Old Town Square. Turn about face, and head downhill (north) on the street called Na Můstku—"along the bridge" that crossed the moat* (příkopě) *we've been following until now.*

Walk down Na Můstku. After one touristy block, it jogs slightly to the left and becomes Melantrichova. As the many shops of lively Melantrichova street clearly demonstrate, the bleak communist era is already ancient history. Today, Prague thrives, amid an Old World ambience. A block farther along, on the left, is...

⓫ Havelská Market

This open-air market, offering crafts and produce, was first set up in the 13th century for the German trading community. Though

heavy on souvenirs these days (especially on weekends), the market still feeds hungry locals and vagabonds cheaply. Lined with inviting benches, it's an ideal place to enjoy a healthy snack—and merchants are happy to sell a single vegetable or piece of fruit. The market is also a fun place to browse for crafts. It's a homegrown, homemade kind of place; you'll often be dealing with the actual artist or farmer. The many cafés and little eateries circling the market offer a relaxing vantage point from which to view the action.

• *Continue along Melantrichova street. Eventually—after passing increasingly tacky souvenir shops and a "museum of sex machines"—Melantrichova curves right and spills out at the Old Town Square, right by the Astronomical Clock. At the clock, turn left down Karlova street. The rest of our walk follows Karlova (though the road twists and turns a bit) to the Charles Bridge, where our tour ends. Begin by heading along the top of the Small Market Square (Malé Náměstí, with lots of outdoor tables), then follow Karlova's twisting course—Karlova street signs keep you on track, and Karlův Most signs point to the bridge. Or just follow the crowds.*

⑭ Karlova Street

Although traffic-free, Karlova street is utterly jammed with tourists as it winds toward the Charles Bridge. But the route has plenty of historic charm if you're able to ignore the contemporary tourism. As you walk, look up. Notice historic symbols and signs of shops, which advertised who lived there or what they sold. Cornerstones, designed to protect buildings from careening carriages, also date from centuries past.

The touristy feeding-frenzy of today's Prague is at its ugliest along this commercial gauntlet. Obviously, you'll find few good values on this drag. Locals have a disdain for the many Russian-owned shops selling *matryoshka* nesting dolls, furry hats, and other things that have nothing to do with Czech culture.

Keep walking toward Charles Bridge. After the street jogs right to cross Husova, many of the buildings you'll see on your right are associated with Prague's **Charles University.** Behind the souvenir stalls lie venerable classrooms and lecture halls. The hidden courtyards have provided Czech scholars with their two most essential needs: a space for inspiring conversation and good beer. Imagine Prague in the late 1500s, when it was the center of the Holy Roman Empire, and one of the most enlightened places in Europe. The astronomers Tycho Brahe (who tracked the planets) and his assistant Johannes Kepler (who formulated the laws of motion) both worked here. Charles University has always been at the center of Czech political thinking and revolutions, from Jan Hus in the 15th century to the passionately patriotic Czech students who swept communists out of power in the Velvet Revolution. Today, Charles University still attracts the best and brightest. For Czech students, tuition is free. (For more on Charles University, see page 52.)

The **Klementinum** (which once housed the university's library) is the large building that borders Karlova street on the right. Just past the intersection with Liliová, where the street opens into a little square, turn right through the archway (at #1) and into a tranquil courtyard that feels an eternity away from the touristy hubbub of Karlova. Locals enjoy using this courtyard as the key link of a less-crowded shortcut between Charles Bridge and the Old Town Square. You can also visit the Klementinum's impressive Baroque interior on a guided tour (see page 54).

• *Karlova street leads directly to a tall medieval tower that marks the start of Charles Bridge. But before entering the bridge, stop on this side of the river. To the right of the tower is a little park with a great view of both the bridge and the rest of Prague across the river. While it's officially called Křižovnické Náměstí, I think of it as...*

⓰ Charles IV Square—The Bohemian Golden Age

Start with the statue of the bridge's namesake, **Charles IV** (1316-1378). Look familiar? He's the guy on the 100-koruna bill. Charles

was the Holy Roman Emperor who ruled his vast empire from Prague in the 14th century—a high-water mark in the city's history. The statue shows one of Charles' many accomplishments: He holds a contract establishing Charles University, the first in central Europe. The women around the pedestal symbolize the school's four traditional subjects: theology, the arts, law, and medicine.

Charles was the preeminent figure in Europe in the Late Middle Ages, and the father of the Prague we enjoy today. His domain encompassed the modern Czech Republic, and parts of Germany, Austria, and the Low Countries.

Charles was cosmopolitan. Born in Prague, raised in Paris, crowned in Rome, and inspired by the luxury-loving pope in Avignon, Charles returned home bringing Europe's culture with him. Besides founding Charles University, he built Charles Bridge, Charles Square (where you're standing), much of Prague Castle and St. Vitus Cathedral, and the New Town (modeled on Paris). His Golden Bull of 1356 served as Europe's constitution for centuries (and gave anti-Semite Charles first right to the property of Jews). Power-hungry, he expanded his empire through networking and shrewd marriages, not war. Charles traded ideas with the Italian poet Petrarch and imported artists from France, Italy, and Flanders (inspiring the art of the Museum of Medieval Art—see page 58). Under Charles, Prague became the most cultured city in Europe. Seemingly the only thing Charles did not succeed in was renaming Prague: He wanted it to be called "New Jerusalem."

Now look up at the **bridge tower** (which you can climb for won-

OLD TOWN

derful views—see page 55). Built by Charles, it's one of the finest Gothic gates anywhere. The statuary shows the 14th-century hierarchy of society: people at street level, above them kings, and bishops above the kings. Speaking of hierarchy, check out Charles' statue from near the street. From this angle, some think the emperor looks like he's peeing on the tourists. Which reminds me, public toilets are nearby.

• *Stroll to the riverside, belly up to the bannister, and take in the...*

⑯ View from the River

Before you are the Vltava River and Charles Bridge. Across the river, atop the hill, is Prague Castle topped by the prickly spires of St. Vitus Cathedral. **Prague Castle** has been the seat of power in this region for over a thousand years, since the time of Wenceslas. By some measures, it's the biggest castle on earth. Given the castle's long history, it's no wonder that, when the nation of Czechoslovakia was formed in 1918, Prague Castle served as the "White House" of its new president. If you tour the castle, you also get access to historic St. Vitus Cathedral, which was begun by Charles IV. The cathedral has the tomb of Wenceslas as well as a stunning Art Nouveau stained-glass window by Alfons Mucha. (For details, 📖 see the Prague Castle Tour chapter.)

The **Vltava River** is better known by its German name, Moldau. It bubbles up from the Šumava Hills in southern Bohemia and runs 270 miles through a diverse landscape, like a thread connecting the Czech people. As we've learned, the Czechs have struggled heroically to carve out their identity while surrounded by mightier neighbors—Austrians, Germans, and Russians. The Vltava is their shared artery. The name "Prague" comes from the word "threshold," because the city was born at a convenient place to cross the wide river and enter a new place.

The **view of Charles Bridge** from here is photogenic to the max. The historic stone bridge, commissioned in 1342, connects the Old Town with the district called the Little Quarter at the base of the castle across the river. The bridge is almost seven football fields long, lined with lanterns and 30 statues, and bookmarked at each end with medieval towers (both climbable).

• *Now wander onto the bridge. Make your way slowly across the bridge, checking out several of the statues, all on the right-hand side.*

⓱ Charles Bridge

Among Prague's defining landmarks, this much-loved bridge offers one of the most pleasant and entertaining strolls in Europe. Musi-

cians, artisans, and a constant parade of people make it a festival every day. You can come back and back to this bridge enjoying its charms differently at various times of day. Early and late, it can be enchantingly lonely. It's a photographer's delight during that "magic hour," when the sun is low in the sky.

The impressively expressive statues on either side of the bridge depict saints. Today, half of these statues are replicas—the originals are in city museums, safe from the polluted air (and some are in the casemates below the hill called Vyšehrad; 📖 see the Vyšehrad Walk chapter).

Pause at the **third statue** on the right. Originally, there were no statues on the bridge, only a cross. You can still see that cross incorporated into this crucifixion scene. The rest of the bridge's statues were added when the Habsburg Catholics ruled in the 17th and 18th centuries. After the Hussite years, the Habsburgs wanted to make sure the saints overlooked and inspired the townsfolk each day as they crossed what was still the only bridge in town. This statue has a gilded Hebrew inscription from the Book of Isaiah celebrating Christ: "Holy, holy, holy is the Lord of hosts." The inscription was paid for by a fine imposed on a member of Prague's Jewish community who was accused of mocking this cross.

Continue two more statues to see **Cyril and Methodius,** the two brothers who brought Christianity to this area around 865. Born in Thessaloniki (part of northern Greece today), Cyril and Methodius are credited with introducing Christianity not only to the Czechs, but to all Slavs; you'll see them revered from here to Dubrovnik, Warsaw, and Vladivostok. In this statue, they're bringing a pagan and primitive (bare-breasted) Czech woman into the Christian fold.

Now continue on, past the next statue, and find a small **brass relief** showing a cross with five stars embedded in the wall of the bridge (it's just below the little grate that sits on top of the stone bannister). The relief depicts a figure floating in the river, with a semicircle of stars above him. This marks the traditional spot where St. John of Nepomuk, the national saint of the Czech people, is believed to have been tossed off the bridge and into the river.

Charles Bridge: Past and Present

Bridges had previously been built at this location, as the tower from the earlier Judith Bridge attests (it's the smaller of the two bridge towers at the far end), but all were washed away by floods. After a major flood in 1342, Emperor Charles IV commissioned an entirely new structure, which was designed and built by architect Peter Parler. Initially called the Stone Bridge, it was Prague's only bridge across the Vltava River for more than 400 years.

The bridge has long fueled a local love of legends—including one tied to numbers. According to medieval records, the bridge's foundation was laid in 1357. In the late 1800s, an amateur astronomer noticed a curious combination of numbers, leading to a popular theory about Charles IV. Charles is known to have been interested in numerology and astrology, and was likely aware of the significance of this date: the ninth of July at 5:31 in the morning. Written out in digits—as the year, month, day, hour, and minute—it's a numerical palindrome: 135797531. It's said that Charles must have chosen that precise moment (which also coincides with a favorable positioning of the Earth and Saturn) to lay the foundation stone

of the bridge. Further "corroboration" of this remarkable hypothesis was provided by the discovery that the end of the bridge on the Old Town side aligns perfectly with the tomb of St. Vitus (in the cathedral across the river) and the setting sun at summer solstice. In the absence of accurate 14th-century records, this intriguing proposition has delighted the modern Czech imagination. The number "135797531" is bound to remain celebrated as the adopted birthday of Prague's most beloved structure.

But even the most auspicious numbers could not protect the bridge from periodic damage caused by floods, ice, and shoddy repairs. In 2010, an ambitious reconstruction project was completed, leaving the bridge cleaner—and stronger—than ever before.

For the rest of that story, continue two more statue groups to the bronze Baroque statue of **St. John of Nepomuk,** with the five golden stars encircling his head. This statue always draws a crowd. John was a 14th-century priest to whom the queen confessed all her sins. According to a 17th-century legend, the king wanted to know his wife's secrets, but Father John dutifully refused to tell. The shiny plaque at the base of the statue shows what happened next: John

was tortured and eventually killed by being thrown off the bridge. The plaque shows the heave-ho. When he hit the water, five stars appeared, signifying his purity. Notice the date on the inscription—1683. This oldest statue on the bridge was unveiled on the supposed 300th anniversary of the martyr's death. Traditionally, people believe that touching the St. John plaque will make a wish come true. But you get only one chance in life to make this wish, so think carefully before you commit.

You'll find statues to John on squares and bridges throughout the Czech Republic. Why? It's not clear. Some historians claim it's because Czechs were being forcibly converted to Catholicism. Nepomuk became the rallying national symbol—"OK, we'll convert, but our patron saint must be Czech." Others argue that Nepomuk was a propaganda figure used by Catholic leaders to give locals an attractive alternative to Jan Hus.

Whatever the reason, the Czech people are especially devoted to several patron saints who—even if you're an atheist—serve as a rallying point for Czech national identity. For example, directly across from John is **St. Ludmila,** who raised her grandson to become St. Wenceslas—the 10th-century duke-turned-saint who first united the Czech people (and whose statue is found at the far end of the bridge).

• *A good way to end this walk is to enjoy the city and river view from near the center of the bridge. Stand here and survey your surroundings.*

⓲ View from Charles Bridge

First, look **upstream.** Notice the icebreakers immediately below. They protect the abutments upon which the bridge sits, as river ice has historically threatened its very survival. Look farther upstream for the tiny locks on the right side. While today's river traffic is limited to tourist boats, in earlier times timber, lashed like rafts, was floated down the river. On the left, farther upstream, by the next bridge, is a building with a gilded crown atop its black dome. That's the National Theater. The rentable paddleboats plying the water are a romantic way to get a little exercise (see page 39).

Now, cross over and look **downstream.** Scan from right to left. You'll see the modern Four Seasons Hotel—that's the black roof, doing a pretty good job of fitting in. Farther down (with the green roof), is the large Neo-Renaissance concert hall of the Czech Philharmonic. Across the river and up the hill is a red needle of a giant metronome (currently stopped). It stands at the spot where a 50-foot-tall granite Joseph Stalin—flanked by eight equally tall deputies—stood from 1955 to 1962. To the right of Stalin's former perch (hiding under the trees and worth the climb on a hot summer day) is Prague's most popular beer garden. Finally, capping the hill, follow the line of noble palaces that leads to the spire of the cathedral. It stands at the center of the castle, which—for a thousand years—has been the political heart of this nation.

And beneath your feet flows the majestic Vltava River, the watery thread that has—and always will—connect the proud Czech people.

• *From here, you can continue across the bridge to the Little Quarter (Kampa Island, on your left as you cross the bridge, is a tranquil spot to explore; for more on sights in this area, see page 76). Across the bridge and a 10-minute walk to the right is the Malostranská stop for the Metro or for the handy tram #22. You can also hike (or ride tram #22) up to the castle from here. Or retrace your steps across the bridge to enjoy more time in the Old Town.*

Ahoj!

JEWISH QUARTER TOUR

Josefov

The fluctuating fortunes of Eastern Europe's Jews are etched in the streets of Prague's historic Jewish Quarter. This three-block area in the Old Town has been home to a Jewish community for a thousand years. The neighborhood features several impressive synagogues (including the oldest medieval one in Europe), an evocative cemetery, a powerful memorial honoring Czech Jews murdered in the Holocaust, and engaging exhibits on Jewish customs and tradition.

All but one of the sights are part of the **Jewish Museum in Prague** (Židovské Muzeum v Praze) and are treated as a single attraction. The remaining sight is the **Old-New Synagogue.** For me, this is the most interesting collection of Jewish sights in Europe, and—despite the high admission cost—well worth seeing.

Orientation

Cost: You have three options: **Ticket #1** ("Jewish Town of Prague")-480 Kč, covers all six Jewish Museum sights plus the Old-New Synagogue; **Ticket #2**-300 Kč, covers Jewish Museum sights only; **Ticket #3**-200 Kč, covers the Old-New Synagogue only. Tickets are good for a week.

Buy your ticket at the Information Center at Maiselova 15 (near the intersection with Široka street). You can also buy tickets at the Klausen, Spanish, or Pinkas synagogues.

Hours: The six **museum** sights are open April-Oct Sun-Fri 9:00-18:00, Nov-March until 16:30, closed year-round on Sat and Jewish holidays; check the website for a complete list of holiday closures, especially if you are visiting in the fall. The Old-New Synagogue is open Sun-Thu 9:00-18:00, off-season until 17:00, Fri closes one hour before sunset, closed Sat and Jewish holidays (admission includes worthwhile 10-minute tour).

Avoiding Lines: The Pinkas Synagogue can be packed, especially 9:30-12:00, so be there right as it opens or later in the day. To save time in line, buy your ticket in advance at the other less-crowded locations. Also see "Planning Your Time," later.

Dress Code: Men are expected to cover their heads when entering a synagogue or cemetery. While you'll see many visitors ignoring this custom, it's respectful to borrow a museum-issued yarmulke.

Getting There: The Jewish Quarter is an easy walk from Old Town Square, up delightful Pařížská street (next to the green-domed Church of St. Nicholas). The Staroměstská Metro stop is just a couple of blocks away.

Information: Jewish Museum in Prague—tel. 222-317-191, www.jewishmuseum.cz; Old-New Synagogue—tel. 222-317-191, www.synagogue.cz.

Tours: The neighborhood is easy to see on your own using this chapter, and you'll find thoughtful information in English posted throughout the quarter. **Guided tours** are probably unnecessary (though I've listed one option—Wittmann Tours—on page 38; see also the local guides listed on page 37, some of whom specialize in Jewish Quarter tours). The **audio-guide** (300 Kč, must leave ID) is probably more information than you'll need.

Length of This Tour: Allow three hours (which can be split over several days—your ticket is good for a week). With limited time, focus on the Old-New Synagogue (for the ambience); the Pinkas Synagogue and Old Jewish Cemetery (for the history); and the Klausen Synagogue (for its exhibits).

Photos: While *No Photo* signs are posted everywhere, photos without flash seem to be allowed (except during prayer times at the Old-New Synagogue). Photography is permitted in the cemetery if you pay a 40-Kč fee.

Services: A café and WCs are at the ticket office at Maiselova 15.

Nearby: The fine Museum of Medieval Art (page 58) is only a few blocks from the Spanish Synagogue.

Starring: The synagogues and cemetery of a faith and culture that has left its mark on Prague.

PLANNING YOUR TIME

Your ticket comes with a map that locates the sights and lists admission appointments—the times you'll be let in if it's very busy. (Ignore the times unless it's extremely crowded.) You'll notice plenty of security, which can slow down entry.

You can see the sights in any order. This plan works well: Buy your ticket at the Information Center, then start with the Maisel Synagogue—its museum-like exhibits give a good introduction to Jewish history. Next is the Jewish Quarter's most popular (and crowded) sight, the Pinkas Synagogue, a sobering reminder of Holocaust victims. This leads into the Old Jewish Cemetery, crowded with tombstones. The small Ceremonial Hall covers burial rites, and the Klausen Synagogue has more informative exhibits. Break for coffee, then visit the Old-New Synagogue to soak up its majestic, medieval ambience. Finish with the ornately decorated Spanish Synagogue and its fine exhibits that bring Jewish history up to the moment.

Alternatively, you could plan your time around the crowded Pinkas Synagogue. Ideally, be there right as it opens, to avoid the crowds. A more leisurely option (involving some backtracking) is to see the sights in roughly chronological order: Start with the Old-New Synagogue (medieval ambience), then the Klausen and Maisel (with their helpful museum displays), and the Spanish Synagogue (modern Jewish history). Then, late in the day when the crowds have died down, finish with the powerful Pinkas.

BACKGROUND

The Jewish people from the Holy Land (today's Israel and Palestine) were dispersed by the Romans nearly 2,000 years ago. Over

the centuries, their culture survived in enclaves throughout the world; it was said that "the Torah was their sanctuary, which no army could destroy."

Jews first came to Prague in the 10th century. The least habitable, marshy area closest to the bend was allotted to the Jewish community. The Jewish Quarter's main intersection (Maiselova and Široká streets) was the meeting point of two medieval trade routes. For centuries, Jews coexisted—at times tensely—with their non-Jewish Czech neighbors.

During the Crusades in the 12th century, the pope declared that Jews and Christians should not live together. Jews had to wear yellow badges, and their quarter was walled in and became a ghetto (minority neighborhood) of wooden houses and narrow lanes. In the 16th and 17th centuries, Prague had one of the biggest ghettos in Europe, with 11,000 inhabitants. Within its six gates, Prague's Jewish Quarter was a gaggle of 200 wooden buildings.

Faced with institutionalized bigotry and harassment, Jews relied mainly on profits from moneylending (forbidden to Christians) and community solidarity to survive. While their money bought them protection (the kings taxed Jewish communities heavily), it was often also a curse. Throughout Europe, when times got tough and Christian debts to the Jewish community mounted, entire Jewish communities were evicted or killed. The worse pogroms were in 1096 and in 1389, when around 3,000 Jews were killed.

In 1781, Emperor Josef II, motivated more by economic concerns than by religious freedom, eased much of the discrimination against Jews. In 1848, the Jewish Quarter's walls were torn down, and the neighborhood—named Josefov in honor of the emperor who provided this small measure of tolerance—was incorporated as a district of the Old Town.

In 1897, ramshackle Josefov was razed and replaced by a new modern town—the original 31 streets and 220 buildings became 10 streets and 83 buildings. They leveled the medieval-era buildings (except the synagogues) and turned this into perhaps Europe's finest Art Nouveau neighborhood. Here (and all along this walk) you'll enjoy stately facades with gables, turrets, elegant balconies, mosaics, statues, and all manner of architectural marvels. By the 1930s, Prague's Jewish community was prospering.

But then World War II hit. Of the 55,000 Jews living in Prague in 1939, just 10,000 survived the Holocaust to see liberation in 1945. And in the communist era—when the atheistic regime was also anti-Semitic—recovery was slow.

Today there are only 3,000 "registered" Jews in the Czech Republic, and of these, only 1,700 are in Prague. (There are probably more Jewish people here, but after their experiences with the Nazis and communists, it's understandable that many choose not to register.) Today, in spite of their tiny numbers, the legacy of Prague's Jewish community lives on. While today's modern grid plan has replaced the higgledy-piggledy medieval streets of old, Široká ("Wide Street") remains the main street. A few Jewish-themed shops and restaurants in the area add extra ambience to this (otherwise modern) neighborhood.

The Tour Begins

• *Start at the center of the neighborhood, the intersection of Maiselova and Široká streets. If you haven't yet read the historical "Background" section, above, this is a good place to do so.*

A half-block south on Maiselova street is the...

❶ Maisel Synagogue (Maiselova Synagóga)

Recently renovated in gentle pastel colors, this synagogue was built as a private place of worship for the Maisel family during the late 16th century.

Prague's Jewish Quarter

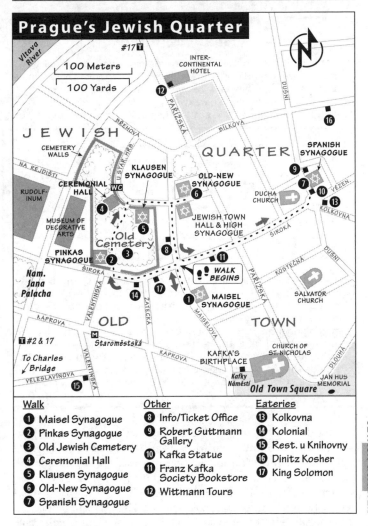

Walk
1. Maisel Synagogue
2. Pinkas Synagogue
3. Old Jewish Cemetery
4. Ceremonial Hall
5. Klausen Synagogue
6. Old-New Synagogue
7. Spanish Synagogue

Other
8. Info/Ticket Office
9. Robert Guttmann Gallery
10. Kafka Statue
11. Franz Kafka Society Bookstore
12. Wittmann Tours

Eateries
13. Kolkovna
14. Kolonial
15. Rest. u Knihovny
16. Dinitz Kosher
17. King Solomon

JEWISH QUARTER

This was a "Golden Age" for Prague's Jews, when Habsburg rulers lifted the many bans and persecutions against them. Maisel, the wealthy financier of the Habsburg king, lavished his riches on the synagogue's Neo-Gothic interior.

Before entering, notice the facade featuring the Ten Commandments top and center (standard in synagogues). Below that is the symbol for Prague's Jewish community: the Star of David, with the pointed hat local Jews wore here through medieval times. Notice how the facades on the adjacent two apartment blocks include hints of ramparts, crenulations, and Neo-Gothic windows to match the style of the synagogue.

The Synagogue

A synagogue is a place of public worship, where Jews gather to pray, sing, and read from the Torah. Most synagogues have similar features, though they vary depending on the congregation.

The synagogue generally faces toward Jerusalem (so in Prague, worshippers face east). At the east end is an alcove called

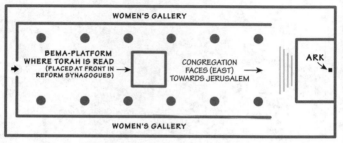

the **ark,** which holds the Torah. These scriptures (the first five books of the Old Testament) are written in Hebrew on scrolls wrapped in luxuriant cloth. The other main element of the synagogue is the **bema,** a platform from which the Torah is read aloud. In traditional Orthodox synagogues (like some in the Jewish Quarter), the bema is near the center of the hall, and the reader stands facing the same direction as the congregation. (In other branches of Judaism, the bema is at the front, and the reader faces the worshippers.) Orthodox synagogues have separate worship areas for

Inside, the interactive exhibit retraces a thousand years of Jewish history in Bohemia and Moravia. Well-explained in English, topics include the origin of the Star of David, Jewish mysticism, the Golem legend, the history of discrimination, and the creation of Prague's ghetto. Pre-WWII photographs of small-town synagogues from the region are projected on a large screen. Notice the eastern wall, with the holy ark containing a precious Torah mantel. Look for the banner of the Prague Jewish Butchers' Guild, the emblem of the Cobblers' Guild, a medieval seal ring, and the bema grillwork from Prague's demolished Zigeuner Synagogue.

As beautiful as these items are, the exhibit's emphasis is more on teaching history than displaying artifacts, perhaps because the Nazis and the communist regime had a habit of using synagogues as storehouses and showplaces for decontextualized art objects. In World War II, this synagogue became a warehouse for Jewish artifacts after the Nazis ordered Jewish synagogues to send their riches—Torah scrolls, books, menorahs—to Prague to be part of a Jewish museum. Some think Hitler had a more sinister plan: to

men and women, usually with women in the balcony.

The synagogue walls might be decorated with elaborate pat-

terns of vines or geometric designs, but never statues of people, as that might be seen as idol worship. A lamp above the ark is always kept lit, as it was in the ancient temple of Jerusalem, and candelabras called menorahs also recall the temple. Other common symbols are the two tablets of the Ten Commandments given to Moses or a Star of David, representing the Jewish king's shield.

At a typical service, the congregation arrives at the start of Sabbath (Friday evening). As a sign of respect toward God, men don yarmulkes (small round caps). As the cantor leads songs and prayers, worshippers follow along in a book of weekly readings. At the heart of the service, everyone stands as the Torah is ceremoniously paraded, unwrapped, and placed on the bema. Someone—the rabbi, the cantor, or a congregant—reads the words aloud. The rabbi ("teacher") might give a commentary on the Torah passage.

Services similar to this have gone on in Prague's Jewish Quarter for a thousand years.

eliminate the Jews altogether, then preserve their precious things in a "Museum of the Extinct Jewish Race." The communists, for their part, displayed these objects with little attention to their historical or ritual context.

• *Return to Široká street and turn left—following the cemetery wall—to find the...*

❷ Pinkas Synagogue (Pinkasova Synagóga)

A site of Jewish worship since the 16th century, this synagogue is certainly historic. But these days it's best known as a poignant memorial to the victims of the Nazis.

Enter and go down the steps leading to the **main hall** of this small Gothic synagogue. Aaron Meshulam Horowitz, a prosperous merchant and man of influence in his day, built the synagogue in 1535. Notice the old stone-and-wrought-iron bema in the middle, the niche for the ark at the far end, the crisscross vaulting overhead, and the Art Nouveau stained glass filling the place with light.

But the main focus of this synagogue is its walls, inscribed with the handwritten **names** of 77,297 Czech Jews sent to the gas chambers at Auschwitz and other camps. Czech Jews were especially hard hit by the Holocaust. More than 155,000 of them passed through the nearby Terezín camp alone. Most died with no grave marker, but they are remembered here.

The names are carefully organized: Family names are in red, followed in black by the individual's first name, birthday, and date of death (if known) or date of deportation. You can tell by the dates that families often perished together.

The names are gathered in groups by hometowns (listed in gold, as well as on placards at the base of the wall). Prague's dead fill the main hall. On the ark wall is a list of the ghettos and extermination camps that received Czech Jews—Terezín, as well as Dachau, Bergen-Belsen, and the notorious Oświęcim (Auschwitz). As you ponder this sad sight, you'll hear the somber reading of the names alternating with a cantor singing the Psalms.

Among the names are the grandparents of (Prague-born) former US Secretary of State Madeleine Albright—Arnost and Olga Korbel, listed at the far end of the long wall.

Climb eight steps into the **women's gallery,** where (as is typical in traditional synagogues) the women worshipped separately from the men. On the left wall, upper part, find some names in poor condition. These are some of the oldest. You see, the name project began in the 1950s. But the communist regime closed the synagogue and erased virtually everything. With freedom, in 1989, the Pinkas Synagogue was reopened and the names had to be rewritten. These are originals.

On your way out, watch on the right for the easy-to-miss stairs up to the small **Terezín Children's Art Exhibit.** Well-described in English, these drawings were made by Jewish children imprisoned at Terezín, 40 miles northwest of Prague. This is where the Nazis shipped Prague's Jews for processing before transporting them east to death camps. Thirty-five thousand Jews died at Terezín, and many tens of thousands more died in other camps.

Of the 8,000 children transported from Terezín, only 240 survived until liberation. Their art looks like something from your typical elementary school—until you recall the tragic circumstances in which it was created. The collection is organized into poignant themes: dreams of returning to Prague; yearning for a fantasized Holy Land; sentimental memories of the simple times before imprisonment; biblical and folkloric tales focusing on the themes of good and evil; and scenes of everyday life at Terezín. Perhaps saddest of all are the photographs of a few of these young artists. (Terezín makes an emotionally moving day trip from Prague; see page 277.)

• *Exiting the Pinkas Synagogue, the visit leads up several stairs into the adjoining cemetery.*

❸ Old Jewish Cemetery (Starý Židovský Hřbitov)

Enter one of the most wistful scenes in Europe—Prague's Old Jewish Cemetery, and meander along a path through 12,000 evocative

tombstones. They're old, eroded, inscribed in Hebrew, and leaning this way and that. A few of the dead have larger ark-shaped tombs. Most have a simple epitaph with the name, date, and a few of the deceased's virtues. Among the dead buried here are Aaron Meshulam Horowitz (builder of the Pinkas Synagogue), Mordecai Maisel (of the Maisel Synagogue), and Rabbi Loew (of golem fame; see "From Golems to Robots" sidebar).

From 1439 until 1787, this was the only burial ground allowed for the Jews of Prague. Over time, the graves had to be piled on top of each other—seven or eight deep—so there are actually closer to 85,000 dead here. Graves were never relocated because of the Jewish belief that, once buried, a body should not be moved. Layer by layer, the cemetery grew into a small plateau. And as things settled over time, the tombstones became crooked. Tune into the noise of passing cars outside, and you realize that you're several feet above the modern street level—which is already high above the medieval level.

People place pebbles on honored tombstones. This custom, a sign of respect, shows that the dead have not been forgotten and recalls the old days, when rocks were placed upon a sandy gravesite to keep the body covered. Others leave scraps of paper that contain prayers and wishes. The most popular tombstone on which to place pebbles, coins, and paper is the reddish tomb found alongside the wall (the path leads right by it). This is the burial site of Prague's beloved Rabbi Loew. The cemetery is called Beth Chaim in Hebrew, meaning "House of Life."

• *The cemetery visit spills out at the far end, right at the entrances to the Ceremonial Hall (on your left) and Klausen Synagogue (right).*

❹ Ceremonial Hall (Obřadní Síň)

This rustic stone tower (1911) was a mortuary house used to prepare the body and perform purification rituals before burial. The inside is painted in fanciful, flowery Neo-Romanesque style. It's filled with a worthwhile exhibition on Jewish medicine, death, and burial traditions. A series of crude but instructive paintings (c. 1780, hanging on walls throughout the house) show how the "burial brotherhood" took care of the ill and buried the dead. As all are equal before God, the rich and poor alike were buried in embroidered linen shrouds similar to the one you'll see on display.

• *Next door is the...*

❺ Klausen Synagogue (Klauzová Synagóga)

The 17th-century Baroque-style synagogue is impressive and historic—again, locate the bema, the ark, and the women's gallery above—but the focus here is the displays on Jewish religious practices.

Ground-floor displays touch on Jewish holidays. The bema displays a Torah (the first five books of the Old Testament) and the solid silver pointers used when reading it—necessary since the Torah is not to be touched. Now start at the entrance and work clockwise. In the first big, horizontal display case, the biggest book is a Torah (1444) associated with the great medieval philosopher Maimonides. The second display case has shofar horns, blown ritually during Jewish high holy days. Up in the elevated area, the ark contains elaborately wrapped

Torah scrolls ornamented with silver. In the next cases you'll see a seder plate, used to serve the six traditional foods of Passover; a tiny "Omer Calendar," an ingenious device used to keep track of the holidays; and a palm frond *(lulav),* waved when reciting a blessing during the holiday of Sukkot. At the back of the synagogue are objects from the Prague community, including menorahs used in both synagogues and the Hanukkah celebration.

Upstairs, exhibits illustrate the rituals of everyday Jewish life. It starts at birth. There are good-luck amulets to ensure a healthy baby, and a wooden cradle that announces, "This little one will become big." The baby is circumcised (see the knife) and grows to celebrate a coming-of-age Bar or Bat Mitzvah around age 12 or 13.

Marriage takes place under a canopy, and the couple sets up their home—the exhibit ends with some typical furnishings.

• *Exiting the synagogue, turn right and go one block down to the...*

❻ Old-New Synagogue (Staronová Synagóga, a.k.a. Altneuschul)

For more than 700 years, this has been the most important synagogue and the central building in Josefov. Built in 1270, it's the

oldest synagogue in Eastern Europe (and some say the oldest still-working synagogue in all of Europe). The name likely comes because it was "New" when built, but became "Old" when other, newer synagogues came on the scene. The exterior is simple, with a unique saw-tooth gable. Standing like a bomb-hardened bunker, it feels as though it has survived plenty of hard times.

As you enter, you descend a few steps below street level to 13th-century street level and the medieval world.

The **interior** is pure Gothic—thick pillars, soaring arches, and narrow lancet windows. If it looks like a church, well, the architects were Christians. The stonework is original, and the woodwork (the paneling and benches) is also old. This was one of the first Gothic buildings in Prague.

Seven centuries later, it's still a working synagogue. There's the stone bema in the middle where the Torah is read aloud, and the ark at the far end, where the sacred scrolls are kept. To the right of the ark, one chair is bigger, with a Star of David above it. This chair always remains empty out of respect for great rabbis of the past. Where's the women's gallery? Here, women worshipped in rooms that flanked the hall, watching the service through those horizontal windows in the walls.

The big red banner rising above the bema is (a copy of) a gift from Charles IV, given in honor of the Jewish community's service to the crown. For centuries it has been proudly carried by the Jewish community during parades. On the banner is a Star of David and the Hebrew prayer at the heart of the service: "Hear, O Israel..." Within the Star of David is pictured the yellow-pointed hat that Jewish men were obliged to wear.

Twelve is a popular number in the decor, because it symbolizes the 12 tribes of Israel: There are 12 windows, 12 vines in the frieze at the base of the bema, 12 bunches of grapes carved over the entrance, and so on. While Nazis routinely destroyed synagogues, this most historic synagogue in the country survived because the

From Golems to Robots

One of Judaism's most popular legends is associated with the Old-New Synagogue. Around 1600, Rabbi Loew (who was indeed a real person) wanted to protect Prague's Jews from persecution. So he created a creature out of Vltava River clay, known as the golem. He placed a stone called the *šém* ("word" in Hebrew) in the golem's forehead (or, some say, under his tongue), bringing the beast to life.

The golem guarded the ghetto, but—in keeping with the Jewish custom of reserving the Sabbath as the day of rest—Rabbi Loew always removed the *šém* on Friday night. But one day he forgot, the golem went on a rampage, and Rabbi Loew had to remove the *šém* for good. He hid the golem in the attic of the Old-New Synagogue, where it's said to be to this day. The attic is closed to tourists, but you can circle around behind the building to see an iron-rung ladder that leads to the still-dangerous lair of the golem. Meanwhile, believers in such legends remain convinced that the *šém* can still be found somewhere in the streets of Prague—keep an eye out.

The story of the golem inspired the early 20th-century Czech writer Karel Čapek to write his play *R.U.R.*, about artificially created beings who eventually turn on their creators. To describe the creatures, he coined the Czech word *roboti*, "workers"—which was quickly absorbed into English as "robot."

Nazis intended it to be part of their "Museum of the Extinct Jewish Race."

Jews were not permitted in the stonemasons' guild, but it's nonetheless taken as a sign of how well Prague's Jews were doing that guild members built this Jewish place of worship (the same stonemasons also built the nearby Convent of St. Agnes). Notice that they outfitted the ceiling with clumsy five-ribbed vaulting. The builders were good at four-ribbed vaulting, but it wasn't right for a synagogue, because it resulted in a cross.

Before leaving, check out the **lobby** (the long hall where you show your ticket). It has two fortified old lockers—in which the most heavily taxed community in medieval Prague stored its money in anticipation of the taxman's arrival.

• *The Spanish Synagogue is four blocks from here. Before moving on, check out the building next door (where they sell the tickets for the Old-New Synagogue). This is where Prague's Jews were rounded up before being shipped off to Terezín.*

To reach the Spanish Synagogue, head up Maiselova street (toward Old Town Square), and turn left on Široká, which leads to the...

❼ Spanish Synagogue (Španělská Synagóga)

In its size and ornateness, this building is typical of many synagogues built around Central Europe in the late 1800s. With the formation of the Austro-Hungarian Empire in 1867, Jews were finally granted full rights. Many Jews prospered, as evidenced by this beautiful synagogue.

Before entering, circle around the left side of the building for a better view of the facade. It's called "Spanish" but the style is re-

ally Moorish: horseshoe arches atop slender columns, different colored stone, elaborate tracery, and topped with pseudo-minarets. Though the building is relatively new, it stands on the site of Prague's oldest synagogue (from c. 1150), which burned down during the horrific pogrom of 1389.

Inside, the decor is exotic and awe-inspiring. Intricate interweaving designs (of stars and vines) cover every inch of the red-gold and green walls and ceiling. A rose window with a stylized Star of David graces the ark.

The new synagogue housed a new movement within Judaism—a Reform congregation—which worshipped in a more modern way. The bema has been moved to the front of the synagogue, so the officiant faces the congregation. There's also a prominent organ (upper right) to accompany the singing.

Displays of Jewish history bring us through the 18th, 19th, and tumultuous 20th centuries to today. In the 1800s, Jews were increasingly accepted and successful in the greater society. But tolerance brought a dilemma—was it better to assimilate within the dominant culture or to join the growing Zionist homeland movement? To reform the religion or to remain orthodox?

Upstairs, the **balcony exhibits** focus on Czech Jews in the 1900s. Start in the area near the organ, which explains the modern era of Jewish Prague, including the late 19th-century development of Josefov. Then work your way around the balcony, with exhibits on Jewish writers (Franz Kafka), philosophers (Edmund Husserl), and other notables (Freud). This intellectual renaissance came to an abrupt halt with World War II and the mass deportations to Terezín (see more sad displays on life there, including more children's art and a box full of tefillin prayer cases). The final displays bring it home: After 2,000 years of living away from their Holy Land roots, the Jewish people had a homeland—the modern nation of Israel. Finish your visit across the landing in the **Winter Synagogue,** showing a trove of silver—Kiddush cups, Hanukkah lamps, Sabbath candlesticks, and Torah ornaments. This collection

JEWISH QUARTER

got its start in the early 20th century, when the Jewish Museum was formed—and began its important work of preserving places and artifacts that otherwise might have been forever lost.

• *Our walk is over. Next door to the Spanish Synagogue is the* **Robert Guttmann Gallery** *of temporary exhibits, which is included in your combo-ticket.*

Also next to the Spanish Synagogue is a fun, bizarre, photo-op-friendly statue meant to (somehow) depict the writer **Franz Kafka.** *Kafka was a Jew who lived most of his life near here. Fans can find a plaque on the wall where he was born (at the corner of Maiselova and the aptly named Náměstí Franze Kafky, a block south of the Maisel Synagogue, near the Church of St. Nicholas).*

MUSEUM OF MEDIEVAL ART TOUR

Středověké umění v Čechách a Střední Evropě

The former Convent of St. Agnes houses the Museum of Medieval Art in Bohemia and Central Europe. Its collections focus on the 14th century—Prague's Golden Age. The religious art displayed in this Gothic space, gathered from churches across Central Europe, is a testament to the rich cultural life of the period. Each exquisite piece is well-lit and thoughtfully described in English. Your visit includes both the Museum of Medieval Art and the historic convent.

There's a lot to like about this sight: It's never crowded; the fine building is interesting to explore; and it sits in one of the less touristed parts of the Old Town, a pleasant stroll from the Old Town Square. Still, many visitors might find the art itself to be, well, pretty boring—room after room of similar-looking paintings and statues of Madonnas-and-Children. Use my quick tour to see the collection's highlights, then browse to your interests and explore the convent buildings.

Orientation

Cost and Hours: 300-Kč combo-ticket also covers Sternberg Palace, Schwarzenberg Palace, and Veletržní Palace, valid for 7 days; convent buildings—free.

Hours: Tue-Sun 10:00-18:00, closed Mon.

Getting There: The museum is two blocks northeast of the Spanish Synagogue, along the river at Anežská 12. The easy 15-minute walk from the Old Town Square shows off some of the best of the Old Town. Exit the square from the northeast (uphill) corner, walking down Dlouhá street. Continue straight, passing the busty statue by David Černý (who also did the upside-down Wenceslas, see page 153), as the street changes names to Kozí. At the five-way intersection, turn 90 degrees left and find the very narrow alleyway, also called Kozí. Head down this cozy, leafy, bird-chirping lane. Can it get more atmospheric? Turn right on U Milosrdných, then veer left down narrow Anežská, to the museum entrance at #12.

Information: Tel. 224-810-628, www.ngprague.cz.

Length of This Tour: One hour.

Starring: Medieval altar sculptures and paintings, exhibited in a historic cloister.

BACKGROUND

It's 1350. Central Europe is emerging from a time of political turmoil, and outbreaks of the Black Death are giving people plenty to pray about. A thousand miles to the southwest, humble Italian craftspeople in Tuscany are knocking on the door of the Renaissance, which will begin in just a few generations.

Medieval art is reaching its pinnacle—perhaps nowhere as much as here in the Bohemian heartland. Like a candle struggling to stay lit in the darkness, the enlightened-before-his-time King Charles IV is putting his hometown of Prague on the map. Importing culture and know-how from his far-and-wide travels, Charles cultivates a respect for the arts. The finely executed altarpieces and other ecclesiastical art that decorate the humble small-town and countryside churches throughout Charles' realm demonstrate a level of artistic skill and cultural sophistication surprising for this time and place.

A fine sampling of these great medieval artworks are collected in this museum, the former Convent of St. Agnes. Like medieval art everywhere in Europe, it focuses on Mary, Christ, and the saints, but keep an eye out for some distinctive Bohemian features. Look for Madonnas with S-curvy bodies and warm smiles, the unique elements of Bohemia's "Beautiful Style." Recognize Bohemian art's folk roots—crude figures with spindly bodies who nevertheless express deep emotion. Learn a few new Czech painters—these "Masters" may be anonymous to us today, but they were the Michelangelos of their era. And finally, realize how essentially un-Bohemian this art is—joyously incorporating shining Byzantine icons, eye-opening Italian 3-D, and lush French landscapes. This is cosmopolitan art of what was one of Europe's most sophisticated cultures.

The Tour Begins

Entering from the courtyard, take a moment to get oriented at the **model of the complex** in the entrance hall: You're standing in the building with the swooping roof. The heart of the convent was an open-air courtyard surrounded by a covered, arcaded cloister. The complex also includes (as you can see) the Church of Christ the Salvator, which we'll visit at the end of this tour.

• *Head into the cloister and turn left to find the ticket office. Then go back the way you came, cross through the entrance lobby, and climb upstairs (following* exhibition *signs) to the top (second) floor, and start with...*

THE MUSEUM

• *Follow the arrows for a chronological sweep through Gothic art history, starting in the first room.*

Aspects of Mary (Room A)

The room features many variations on the mother of Jesus, who was adored in medieval Europe. You'll see statues and paintings of her smiling, sitting, or standing; being thoughtful, playful, or majestic; with or without a crown; cradling her baby or on her own. The first works date from the early 1200s, when this place was a world of women—the Convent of St. Agnes and the austere Order of Poor Clares.

Vyšší Brod Paintings (Room B)

These gold-backed paintings tell the story of Christ, medieval-style. In the *Annunciation,* the angel kneels before Mary and an-

nounces (you can actually read his words) *Ave gratia plena...*"Hail, full of grace." In the *Nativity,* Mary gives birth in a flimsy, and crudely drawn, shack. But the anonymous, Bohemian artist, known only as the Master of Vyšší Brod (the monastery where these panels originated), is experimenting with Italian-style perspective—there's a definite foreground (the couple with water basin) and background (grazing animals). The Master tells Jesus' story through his Crucifixion and up to the *Resurrection*—a remarkable painting of Christ in a brilliant red robe rising above astonished soldiers.

Bohemian art in the mid-1300s is surprisingly cosmopolitan (especially considering it was done in the depths of the Black Death, which killed a third of Europe). Bohemian artists combined local folk art with Italian poses, French love of nature, and Byzantine gold-leaf backgrounds.

Also in Room B, several statues (by the similarly anonymous Master of the Michle Madonna) give Mary a new twist—the slight S-curve of the body called *contrapposto.*

Master Theodoric (Room C)

A half-dozen paintings here give a snapshot of Prague's Golden Age. Around 1350, Emperor Charles IV (see page 426) was remaking Prague into an imperial city. He hired Theodoric of Prague—the country's first "name" artist—to paint 129 saints for a chapel at Karlštejn Castle (see page 295), of which a few have been moved here. These are real people. Compared with the scrawny figures of his contemporaries, these saints are massive. They fill the frames of the wooden panels they're painted on, some even spilling over the frame. They're life-size (or bigger) and zoomed-in to show them from the waist-up, as if they're peering out of windows at us.

In the second painting, Charlemagne—the first Holy Roman Emperor—holds the same coronation objects used by his namesake, Charles IV: golden scepter, orb, and shield with the double-headed eagle. The shield even stands "outside" the frame, giving a sense of 3-D. The hand of Theodoric is everywhere: his signature beard style, thick outlines, brilliant colors, and "soft-focus" features. Notice these characteristics in the other paintings as well. Theodoric proves that Bohemian art holds its own against the work of pre-Renaissance Italian greats like Giotto.

• *Pass through Room D (where a few Madonna statues are really starting to rock that S-curve), Room E (with the glorious, much-copied* Madonna of Roudnice *painting, by the Master of the Třeboň Altarpiece), and Room F—then turn right into Room G.*

The Beautiful Style (Rooms G, H)

As Prague became increasingly more cosmopolitan (c. 1400), foreign artists arrived, bringing the International Style—or, as it's known in its Bohemian version, the Beautiful Style. These works are deliberately graceful, with delicate, curved lines.

The *Madonna from the St. Vitus Cathedral* (midway down Room G, on the left) is a classic example. Rather than being stiff and straight, this Mary is S-curved to the max—

her head tilts one way, her body the other. She presents Jesus to the congregation, and both look directly out with coy expressions. Mary's heavy, dark robe has elaborate, deep creases, showing off the artist's mastery of light and shadow. The complex composition—note how Mary's head and Jesus' body parallel each other—demonstrates a deliberate artfulness that marks the Beautiful Style. The painting, which once stood in St. Vitus Cathedral, was famous in its day. Churches everywhere had a copy. The ornate wooden frame may be original.

The next gallery (Room H) is lined with Madonna statues in the Beautiful Style (or as scholars often call this type of statue, a *Schöne Madonna*). She smiles sweetly, her body sways seductively, her deeply creased robe is luxuriant, and Jesus squirms playfully in her arms. In churches all across Central Europe, worshippers were treated to these happy, "beautiful" (and once colorfully painted) images of an inviting saint—a vision of how the worlds of the spirit and flesh could unite harmoniously.

• *But here on earth, the harmony of the Czech Golden Age was about to be shattered by religious warfare. For the next episode, backtrack and exit Room G, turning right into a large, long hall filled with—you guessed it—more altarpieces.*

Foreign Influence (Rooms J, K, L)

Jan Hus' attempts to reform the church plunged the Czech people into decades of war and division. It sent many Hussites into a frenzy of violent protest and iconoclasm—storming churches to destroy paintings and statues. The Czech nation was invaded and eventually dominated by foreign powers. Homegrown Bohemian art would never be the same.

The large hall is filled with altarpieces from the post-Hus world. There's some glorious stuff, as the art comes more in line with international trends. Discerning art historians see the influence of German artists (such as Cranach) and of Italian art, with its blossoming realism and 3-D perspective. The rest of us can just browse through these large, impressive, colorful works. Some highlights are the *St. George Altar*, the *Puchner Ark*, the *Lamentation of Christ from Žebrák*, and two works that show the influence of Cranach: the *Litoměřice Altar* and a *Madonna and Child* by the artist known only as Monogrammist IW, for the initials found on his paintings.

• *Before leaving the hall, take note of the staircase in the middle of the room. This exit leads to the "churches"—that is, the convent buildings you can visit after the museum. But first, two final artworks. Exit the large hall at the far end, entering rooms that display...*

MUSEUM OF MEDIEVAL ART

Some Foreign Masterpieces (Rooms M, N)

Room M displays lots of wooden altar statues and a glass case with woodcut prints. The four biggest prints are from Albrecht Dürer's fascinating and famous *Apocalypse* series (1511). Finish your visit at the very end of Room N with an impressive wood-carved altarpiece by Monogrammist IP. In both works, it's easy to admire how these great German artists could render the medieval mindset with such meticulous Renaissance realism. With the world moving on, the Golden Age of Bohemian art, with its stylized visions of heaven, was relegated to the past.

• *And we'll move on, too—museum tour over. To reach the convent, backtrack into the large hall and take that staircase down. You'll spill out on ground level, into one of the courtyards of the convent. Turn right and go into the* **refectory** *to read about the...*

CONVENT OF ST. AGNES

In the year 1211, an Italian teenager named Clare met the charismatic St. Francis of Assisi. She immediately decided to dedicate herself to a life of Christian poverty and contemplation. She cut off her hair and went barefoot. Soon, she attracted a group of like-minded women, and they called themselves the Poor Clares. Their holy reputation spread.

In 1233, Princess Agnes, the daughter of a Bohemian king, established a branch of the Poor Clares in Prague. To house the new order of nuns, she built this complex—a convent, churches, the city's first hospital—all of it state-of-the-art.

Here in the refectory, the women ate meals, and also wove and copied manuscripts. They prayed many times a day. The nuns were known for their secret healing elixir (called "swallow water"), which they sold to the rich and gave to the poor. Though the Clares lived in strict poverty and humble contemplation, their order was warmed by the humanist spirit preached by St. Francis.

The convent flourished for around 150 years. But it all ended suddenly in the early 1400s with Jan Hus. During the anti-Catholic strife and Hussite wars, the Clares fled, and the convent was ravaged. Over the next 500 years, the building underwent several incarnations—as an arsenal, a Dominican monastery, and public housing for the poor. The structures declined until a mid-20th-century renovation restored its original look. The Convent of St. Agnes was one of the first Gothic buildings in Bohemia, and now it's the oldest Gothic building in Bohemia.

You can wander through the (mostly empty) rooms surrounding the courtyard. As you explore, imagine how the Poor Clares once lived here, secluded from the outside world.

• *In the corner to the right as you leave the refectory, you'll find the hallway into the other half of the complex and its big, empty church. Posted information may confusingly talk about various chapels ("Chapel of the Virgin Mary," "Chapel of Mary Magdalene," "Church of St. Francis"), but it's basically just the one church with a few adjoining rooms.*

Church of Christ the Salvator and the Přemysl Crypt

During Agnes' time, the convent's church became the official burial place for the ruling Přemysl family. (Other Přemysls lie buried in

St. Vitus and the nearby St. George's Basilica; see page 186.) The Přemyslid dynasty ruled Prague for nearly five centuries (c. 850-1306). Their royal burial chapel here was once glorious, but over time, the building was damaged and the tombs lost. Today the place is a bare shell. But on the floor, you'll find plaques marking two rediscovered Přemyslid graves (about 15 paces apart, one in the back of the nave and the other in the adjoining hall). **Kunigund** (labeled *Cunegundis, 1202-1248)* was the granddaughter of the great Frederick I Barbarossa, Holy Roman Emperor. She married **Wenceslas I** (labeled *Venceslaus I, 1205-1253)*, who, despite the name similarity, was not the 10th-century St. Wenceslas, but rather the king who annexed Austria and saved Bohemia from the Mongol hordes of Genghis Khan. The couple fathered Ottokar II, who ushered in the Bohemian Golden Age. Though the Přemyslid dynasty would end in 1306, Ottokar II's great-grandson (on the maternal side) would take up the ruling mantle as the famed Charles IV.

• *On the left side of the church nave is a side room. This was...*

Agnes' Oratory

This humble room is where Agnes Přemysl—the daughter of the king, and one of the most sought-after women in Europe—spent her days.

Agnes (1211-1282) was born the year Clare met Francis. Well-educated in convent schools, the Přemysl princess was dangled as a potential bride in several politically expedient marriages—to the powerful son of the Holy Roman Emperor, to the king of England, and finally to the emperor himself. But they all fell through, and she became a bride of Christ.

Agnes was well connected. Her father was King Přemysl Ottokar I, who united the warring Bohemians. Her brother was Wenceslas I (see above), and her nephew became Ottokar II. Agnes exchanged letters with Clare of Assisi, inviting five Italian nuns to come north to help found the first Clarist convent north of the Alps, with Agnes as mother superior.

When Agnes died, some speculate that she was buried here. Her remains were lost, but a legend says that whenever they are found, the Czech nation will enter a new Golden Age.

In 1989, Agnes was canonized by Pope John Paul II (who loved to promote the Slavic faithful). Since local celebrations of her sainthood on November 26 coincided with the Velvet Revolution, Agnes has since been regarded as the patron of the renascent Czech democracy.

• *When you're done exploring, leave this restful place and head back out into the bustle of Prague.*

MUSEUM OF MEDIEVAL ART

WENCESLAS SQUARE WALK

Václavské Náměstí

Though the Old Town gets all the attention (and all the tourists), the New Town—and particularly its main square—is more the people's Prague. In the 14th century, the king created this new town, tripling the size of what would become Prague. This short walk focuses on the New Town's centerpiece, Wenceslas Square— once the horse market of this busy working-class district. Along the way, we'll see sights associated with the square's great moments in history, including the watershed protests of 1989 that helped create the modern nation.

Orientation

Length of This Walk: Allow an hour.

When to Go: As this walk doesn't focus on sights with limited hours, it can be done at any time—and may work particularly well in the evening, after other sights have closed.

Getting There: The walk starts at the very top of Wenceslas Square, in front of the National Museum; the nearest Metro stop is called Muzeum. If you're coming from the Old Town, it's probably easiest just to hike the length of the square up to the top to start the walk.

Eating: This walk passes a popular ice-cream parlor. Dozens of other eateries are nearby (see my recommendations on page 218).

Starring: Urban bustle, a secluded garden, and a thousand years of Czech history—from St. Václav to Václav Havel.

The Walk Begins

• *At the top of Wenceslas Square, stand under the huge statue of "Good King Wenceslas" on a horse.*

WENCESLAS SQUARE

Join Wenceslas as he gazes proudly down this long, broad square. It's actually more like a boulevard busy with cars, with a park-like median right down the middle. It's a huge expanse, covering more than 10 acres. Stand here, and take in the essence of modern Prague.

Think of how this place has served as a kind of national stage for important events in the history of the Czech people. In 1918, it was here that jubilant crowds gathered to celebrate the end of World War I and the subsequent creation of modern Czechoslovakia. During World War II, this was the scene of Nazi occupation, and then of rioting Czechs who drove the Nazis out. In the spring of 1968, the Czechs gathered here to protest against their next set of oppressors, the communist Soviets. These "Prague Spring" reforms gained international attention, but eventually Soviet tanks rumbled into town and crushed the rebellion. Then in 1989, more than 300,000 Czechs and Slovaks converged right here to reclaim their freedom once again.

Which brings us to today. Survey the square for a snapshot of "the now." You'll see businesspeople, families, Dumpster divers, security guards, hipsters, and students. It sums up the changes and rapid transformation of society here over the past 100 years.

• *But let's go back to the very beginning. Turn your attention now to the big equestrian statue of...*

❶ Duke Wenceslas I

The "Good King" of Christmas-carol fame was actually a wise and benevolent 10th-century duke. Václav I (as he's called by locals) united the Czech people, back when this land was known as Bohemia. A rare example of a well-educated and literate ruler, Wenceslas Christianized and lifted the culture. He astutely allied the powerless Czechs with the Holy Roman Empire. And he began to fortify Prague's castle as a center of Czech government. After his murder in 929, Wenceslas was canonized as a saint. He became a symbol of Czech nationalism (and appears on

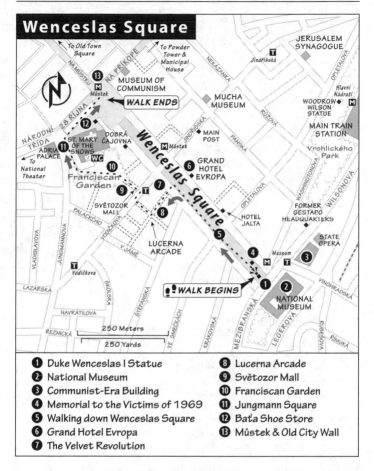

Wenceslas Square

- To Old Town Square
- To Powder Tower & Municipal House
- JERUSALEM SYNAGOGUE
- *Jindřišská*
- NA PŘÍKOPĚ
- NEKÁZANKA
- MUSEUM OF COMMUNISM
- **WALK ENDS**
- *Můstek*
- MUCHA MUSEUM
- RŮZOVÁ
- *Hlavní Nádraží*
- WOODROW WILSON STATUE
- MAIN TRAIN STATION
- NÁRODNÍ TŘÍDA
- 28 ŘÍJNA
- ST. MARY OF THE SNOWS
- DOBRÁ ČAJOVNA
- JINDŘIŠSKÁ
- MAIN POST
- *Můstek*
- PANSKÁ
- Vrchlického Park
- WASHINGTONOVA
- ADRIA PALACE
- To National Theater
- WC
- Franciscan Garden
- GRAND HOTEL EVROPA
- OPLETALOVA
- FORMER GESTAPO HEADQUARTERS
- WILSONOVA
- VLADISLAVOVA
- JUNGMANNOVA
- PALACKÉHO
- VODIČKOVA
- SVĚTOZOR MALL
- Wenceslas Square
- HOTEL JALTA
- STATE OPERA
- LAZARSKÁ
- *Vodičkova*
- V JÁMĚ
- LUCERNA ARCADE
- *Muzeum*
- VINOHRADSKÁ
- ŠKOLSKÁ
- ŠTĚPÁNSKÁ
- **WALK BEGINS**
- NATIONAL MUSEUM
- LEGEROVA
- RUBEŠOVA
- RÍMSKÁ
- NAVRÁTILOVA
- MEZIBRANSKÁ
- VE SMEČKÁCH
- KRAKOVSKÁ
- ŘEZNICKÁ
- **250 Meters**
- **250 Yards**

1. Duke Wenceslas I Statue
2. National Museum
3. Communist-Era Building
4. Memorial to the Victims of 1969
5. Walking down Wenceslas Square
6. Grand Hotel Evropa
7. The Velvet Revolution
8. Lucerna Arcade
9. Světozor Mall
10. Franciscan Garden
11. Jungmann Square
12. Baťa Shoe Store
13. Můstek & Old City Wall

the 20-Kč coin). Later kings knelt before his tomb to be crowned. And he remains an icon of Czech unity whenever the nation has to rally. Like King Arthur in England, Wenceslas is more legend than history, but he symbolizes the country's birth.

Legend has it that when the Czechs face their darkest hour, Wenceslas will come riding out of Blaník Mountain (east of Prague) with an army of knights to rescue the nation. In 1620, when Austria stripped the Czechs of their independence, many people went to Blaník Mountain to see whether it had opened up. They've done the same at other critical points in their history (in 1938, 1948, and 1968), but Wenceslas never emerged. Although the Czech Republic seems to be living its most prosperous days since the Middle Ages, many Czechs remain characteristically cynical: If Wenceslas hasn't come out yet, the worst times must still lie ahead...

The statue is surrounded by the four other Czech patron saints.

The Prague Spring and Its Fall

In January 1968, the Slovak politician Alexander Dubček replaced the aging apparatchiks at the helm of the Communist Party of Czechoslovakia. Handsome and relatively youthful, Dubček's brand was that of a smiling playboy; he appeared on magazine covers in his speedo, about to dive into a swimming pool. Young Czechs and Slovaks embraced Dubček as a potential hero of liberalization.

In April, Dubček introduced his "Action Program," designed to tiptoe away from strict and stifling Soviet communism and forge a more moderate Czechoslovak variation. Censorship eased, travel restrictions were relaxed, state companies began forming joint ventures with Western firms, money poured into the sciences, and a newspaper called "Tomorrow" (rather than "Today")

became the most popular in the country. Plays put on at the Semafor Theater (in today's Světozor mall) lampooned Brezhnev and his ilk. During this so-called "Prague Spring," optimism soared.

But then, around midnight on August 20, 1968, the thundering sound of enormous airplanes ripped across the floodlit rooftops of Prague. The Soviets had dispatched over 200,000 Warsaw Pact troops to invade Czechoslovakia, airlifting tanks right into the capital city. Dubček and his team were arrested and taken to Moscow. Czechs and Slovaks—now living in a police state—were terrified as they took to the streets, boycotting and striking. Tanks rolled through Wenceslas Square, spraying protesters with bullets...some of which are still embedded in the National Museum's pillars. Over the course of the occupation, 72 Czechs and Slovaks were killed.

Dubček stepped down and went into internal exile, and his successor—the hardliner Gustáv Husák—immediately pursued a policy of "normalization." People who refused to sign a petition commending the "Russian Liberation" were fired from their jobs, and forced to find worse ones. Some protesters—including Jan Palach—set themselves on fire to protest against the regime. Tens of thousands of Czechs and Slovaks reluctantly emigrated to the West, fearing what might come next.

While the ill-fated tale of the Prague Spring is pessimistic, it provides an insightful bookend to what happened 21 years later: The children of the generation that suffered Czechoslovakia's bitterest disappointment brought about its greatest success.

WENCESLAS SQUARE

Notice the focus on books. A small nation without great military power, the Czechs have thinkers as national heroes, not warriors.

And this statue is a popular meeting point. Locals like to say, "I'll meet you under the horse's tail" (though they use a cruder term).

• *Circle behind the statue and stand below that tail, and turn your attention to the impressive building at the top of Wenceslas Square.*

❷ National Museum

The building is grand and the interior is rich, though the collection itself is pretty dull (for details, see page 60). The building dates

from the 19th century, back when there was no unified Czech nation—just Czech-speaking peasants and two-bit, wannabe-German aristocrats living under the auspices of Austria's Habsburg Empire. But throughout Europe, the mid-19th century was a time of national resurgence. Bold structures like this Neo-Renaissance building were a way to show the world that the Czech people had a distinct culture, a heritage of precious artifacts, and that they deserved their own nation.

Look closely at the columns on the building's facade. Those light-colored patches are covering holes where Soviet bullets hit during the 1968 crackdown. The repair masons did an intentionally sloppy job, so that dark moment could never be plastered over and forgotten.

• *To the left of the National Museum (as you face it) is a...*

❸ Communist-Era Building

This ugly, modern structure once housed the rubber-stamp Czechoslovak Parliament back when it voted in lock-step with Moscow. At

its base, under the canopy, is a statue from those days, in the style known as Socialist Realism. As was typical, it shows not just a worker...but a triumphant worker.

Between 1994 and 2008, this building was home to Radio Free Europe. After communism fell, RFE lost some of its funding and could no longer afford its Munich headquarters. In gratitude for its broadcasts—which had kept the people of Eastern Europe in touch with real news—the Czech government offered this building to RFE for 1 Kč a year. But as RFE energetically beamed its American message deep into the Muslim world from here, it drew attention—and threats—from Al-Qaeda. In 2009, RFE moved to a new fortress-like headquarters at an easier-to-defend locale farther from the center. Now this is an annex of the National Museum.

In addition to this building, the communist authorities built the nearby Muzeum Metro stop (the crossing point of two Metro lines) and the busy highway that runs between the top of the square and the National Museum. Fortunately, Soviet buildings like this one are quite rare in Prague. Because there was almost no WWII bombing in the city center, the communists had little opportunity to rebuild. Although Prague fell into disrepair, it was spared the ugly Soviet-style wholesale replacement of heavily bombed cities like Warsaw or Moscow.

Since the communists checked out, city leaders have struggled with the legacy of this heavy-handed Soviet infrastructure. During the Cold War, the ambitious master plan was to use this busy highway to link the city's inner and outer freeway rings. After 1989, the project moved forward again, with EU funding; one particularly welcome idea was to reroute this highway underground. But the recent economic crisis stalled Prague's "Big Dig," canceling unfinished tunnels—meaning that cars, trucks, and motorbikes will continue to spew their fumes on the museum's facade (the most polluted spot in the city).

Along the busy street just past the communist-era building (hard to see from here) is the **State Opera,** which was built in the 1880s as the New German Theater—at a time when Prague's once-dominant German population was feeling neglected after the opening of the Czechs' National Theater across town. Facing this from across the road is a Neoclassical, almost fascistic building that was the local Gestapo headquarters during Nazi times. This chilling juxtaposition—high culture and control—pretty much sums up the Czechs' love/hate relationship with their powerful German and Austrian neighbors.

• *Start walking down Wenceslas Square. Pause about 30 yards along, at the little patch of bushes. In the ground on the downhill side of those bushes is a...*

❹ Memorial to the Victims of 1969

After the Russian crackdown of 1968, a group of patriots wanted to stand up to the powerful Soviet occupation. One was a young philosophy student named Jan Palach. He decided that the best way to stoke the flame of independence was to set himself on fire. On January 16, 1969, Palach stood on the steps of the National Museum and ignited his body for the cause of Czech freedom. He died a few days later in a hospital ward. A month later, another student did the same thing, followed by another. Czechs are keen on anniversaries, and—20 years after Palach's brave and patriotic act, in 1989—Czechs gathered here for a huge demonstration. A sense of new possibility swept through the city, and 10 months later, the communists were history.

• *Continue down Wenceslas Square. Our next stop is the median in front of Grand Hotel Evropa. It's the ornate, yellow building about 300 yards down Wenceslas Square, on the right.*

➎ Walking down Wenceslas Square— the New Town

Wenceslas Square is part of Prague's New Town, one of the four traditional quarters. Prague got its start in the ninth century at the castle. It spilled across the river to the Old Town, which was fortified with a city wall. By the 1300s, the Old Town was bursting at the seams. King Charles IV expanded the town outward, tripling the size of Prague. Wenceslas Square, a central feature of the New Town, was originally founded as a horse market.

As you walk, notice the architecture. Unlike the historic Old Town, nearly everything here is from the past two centuries. Wenceslas Square is a showcase of Prague's many architectural styles: You'll see Neo-Gothic, Neo-Renaissance, and Neo-Baroque from the 19th century. There's curvaceous Art Nouveau from around 1900. And there's the modernist response to Art Nouveau—Functionalism from the mid-20th century, where the watchword was "form follows function" and beauty took a back seat to practicality. You'll see what's nicknamed "Stalin Gothic" from the 1950s communist era; a good example of that is the Hotel Jalta building, halfway downhill on the right (the sandy facade with lots of balconies). And there are forgettable glass-and-steel buildings of the 1970s.

On the right-hand side of Wenceslas Square is ➏ **Grand Hotel Evropa.** It's the one with the dazzling yellow Art Nouveau exterior and plush café interior full of tourists. Take a peek inside. If you're a fan of Art Nouveau, you'll want to also check out Prague's Municipal House (near the bottom of Wenceslas Square; see page 66) and the Mucha Museum (just up the street behind this hotel, and described in the 🕮 Mucha Museum Tour chapter).

Opposite Grand Hotel Evropa (that is, on the left side of the square), find the Marks & Spencer building, which has a **balcony** on it (partly obscured by tree branches).

• *Standing here in the center of Wenceslas Square, look up at that balcony and take a moment to consider the events of November 1989.*

❼ The Velvet Revolution

Picture the scene on this square on a cold November night in 1989. Czechoslovakia had been oppressed for the previous 40 years by communist Russia. But now the Soviet empire was beginning to crumble, jubilant Germans were dancing on top of the shattered Berlin Wall, and the Czechs were getting a whiff of freedom.

Czechoslovakia's revolution began with a bunch of teenagers, who—following a sanctioned gathering—decided to march on Wenceslas Square (see sidebar). After they were surrounded and beaten by the communist riot police, their enraged parents, friends, and other members of the community began to pour into this square to protest. Night after night, this huge square was filled with more than 300,000 ecstatic Czechs and Slovaks who believed freedom was at hand. Each night they would jangle their key chains in the air as if saying to their communist leaders, "It's time for you to go home now." Finally they gathered and found that their communist overlords had left—and freedom was theirs.

On that night, as thousands filled this square, a host of famous people appeared on that balcony to greet the crowd. There was a well-known priest and a rock star famous for his rebellion against authority. There was Alexander Dubček, the hero of the Prague Spring reforms of 1968. And there was Václav Havel, the charismatic playwright who had spent years in prison, becoming a symbol of resistance—a kind of Czech Nelson Mandela. Now he was free. Havel's voice boomed over the gathered masses. He proclaimed the resignation of the Politburo and the imminent freedom of the Republic of Czechoslovakia. He pulled out a ring of keys and jingled it. Thousands of keys jingled back in response. It was their symbolic way of saying: The communists have packed up and left, and now we're free to unlock our chains.

In previous years, the communist authorities would have sent in tanks to crush the impudent masses. But by 1989, the Soviet empire was collapsing, and the Czech government was shaky. Locals think that Soviet head of state Mikhail Gorbachev (mindful of the Tiananmen Square massacre a few months before) might have made a phone call recommending a nonviolent response. Whatever happened, the communist regime was overthrown with hardly any blood being spilled. It was done through sheer people power—thanks to the masses of defiant Czechs who gathered here

The Velvet Revolution of 1989

On the afternoon of November 17, 1989, 30,000 students gathered in Prague's New Town to commemorate the 50th anniversary of the suppression of student protests by the Nazis, which had led to the closing of Czech universities through the end of World War II. Remember, this was just a few weeks after the fall of the Berlin Wall, and the Czechs were feeling the winds of change blowing across Central Europe. The 1989 demonstration—initially planned by the Communist Youth as a celebration of the communist victory over fascism—spontaneously turned into a protest *against* the communist regime. "You are just like the Nazis!" shouted the students. The demonstration was supposed to end in the National Cemetery at Vyšehrad (the hill just south of the New Town). But when the planned events concluded in Vyšehrad, the students decided to march on toward Wenceslas Square...and make some history.

As they worked their way north along the Vltava River toward the New Town's main square, the students were careful to keep their demonstration peaceful. Any hint of violence, the demonstrators knew, would incite brutal police retaliation. Instead, as the evening went on, the absence of police became conspicuous. (In the 1980s, the police never missed a chance to participate in any demonstration...preferably outnumbering the demonstrators.) At about 20:00, as the students marched down Národní Třída toward Wenceslas Square, three rows of policemen suddenly blocked the demonstration at the corner of Národní and Spálená streets. A few minutes later, military vehicles with fences on their bumpers (having crossed the bridge by the National Theater) appeared behind the marching students. This new set of cops compressed the demonstrators into the stretch of Národní Třída between Voršilská and Spálená. The end of Mikulandská street was also blocked, and policemen were hiding inside every house entry. The students were trapped.

At 21:30, the "Red Berets" (a special anti-riot commando force known for its brutality) arrived. The Red Berets lined up on both sides of this corridor. To get out, the trapped students had to run through the passageway as they were beaten from the left and right. Police trucks ferried captured students around the corner to the police headquarters (on Bartolomějská) for interrogation.

The next day, university students throughout Czechoslovakia decided to strike. Actors from theaters in Prague and Bratislava joined the student protest. Two days later, the students' parents—shocked by the attacks on their children—marched into Wenceslas Square. Sparked by the events of November 17, 1989, the wave of peaceful demonstrations ended later that year on December 29, with the election of Václav Havel as the president of a free Czechoslovakia.

Václav Havel: An Authentic Life

Václav Havel (1936-2011) was a playwright first and a politician second. Author of more than 20 absurdist plays, Havel served as the first president of post-communist Czechoslovakia and was later elected to two terms as president of the Czech Republic.

At heart, Havel was an unassuming writer-critic—but circumstances propelled him into the roles of political dissident and humanitarian. Banned from Czech theater in the aftermath of the 1968 Prague Spring, Havel became an enemy of the communist state and was repeatedly jailed. Though public channels of expression were closed to him, his controversial essays and plays were circulated secretly, both to Warsaw Pact countries and to the West.

While staring down Czechoslovakia's communist regime during the 1989 Velvet Revolution, Havel and his fellow revolutionaries took to the streets with the chant, "Truth and love must prevail over lies and hatred." Havel acted as leader of the informal human-rights group Charter 77, which challenged the regime's suppression of Czech citizens. Their opposition began in defense of the right to freedom of expression—specifically, of a Czech counter-culture rock group, Plastic People of the Universe—that in 1976 was put on trial and convicted of disturbing the peace, essentially for performing

peacefully in Wenceslas Square, and Slovaks doing the same in Bratislava. They called it "The Velvet Revolution."

• *Look downhill to the bottom of Wenceslas Square. We'll be heading there eventually. But we'll take a less-touristed detour to the left, with some interesting things to see.*

Opposite Grand Hotel Evropa is a shopping mall called the Lucerna Arcade. Use the entry marked Pasáž Rokoko *and walk straight in. Continue about 100 yards straight through the mall until you find a horse hanging from the ceiling.*

❽ Lucerna Arcade

This grand mall retains some of its Art Deco glamor from the 1930s. But that's not its most notable feature. In the middle of it all, you'll see a sculpture—called

without a permit. In Charter 77's manifesto, Havel persuasively argued that if one person's freedom is violated, everyone's freedom is violated. Through his writings, he articulated a message of hope and strength, stressing the importance of becoming a community "living in truth" and strong enough to stop conforming to Soviet ideologies.

The idea that so inspired the martyr Jan Hus and his 14th-century followers was the heretical realization that each human being has an intrinsic capacity to know what a just, free, and beautiful life is. Six centuries later, Václav Havel used his plays to explore what happens to a human being who rejects the guidance of this inner compass. His characters fixate on the abstractions of various mundane "truths" while forgetting their moral obligations to themselves and others. Havel saw love and truth not just as political slogans, but as everyday principles, and was himself catapulted by life into parts he had not scripted.

After serving two terms, Havel returned to his art, continuing to explore the ideas of freedom and morality. His death in 2011 at age 75 was marked by three days of national mourning and the renaming of Prague Airport as Václav Havel Airport Prague.

Havel will long be remembered for his clever use of art as a medium for political expression. In 2012, the Human Rights Foundation established the Václav Havel Prize for Creative Dissent. Prominent activists who have received this honor include Ai Weiwei (China), the Ladies in White (a Cuban opposition group), and Pussy Riot (a Russian punk rock protest group).

Wenceslas Riding an Upside-Down Horse—hanging like a swing from a glass dome. David Černý, who created the statue in 1999, is one of the Czech Republic's most original contemporary artists. Always aspiring to provoke controversy, Černý has painted a menacing Russian tank pink, attached crawling babies to the rocket-like Žižkov TV tower, defecated inside the National Gallery to protest the policies of its director, and sank a shark-like Saddam Hussein inside an aquarium. His art hoax *Entropa*—created for the European Union on behalf of the Czech Republic—insulted many EU nations with its satirical symbolism (Bulgaria was represented by squat toilets, Germany consisted of twisted autobahns hinting at a swastika, and so on).

The grand staircase leading up from beneath the suspended sculpture takes you to a lavish 1930s Prague **cinema,** which shows mostly art-house films in their original language with Czech subtitles. The same staircase leads up to the swanky, Art Deco **Café Lucerna,** with windows overlooking this atrium. And in the basement, there's the popular **Lucerna Music Bar,** which hosts '80s and '90s video parties on weekends, and concerts on other nights (see page 248).

• *From the horse, turn right and head for the side exit (passing the entrance to the Lucerna Music Bar on your left). After you exit into the open air, jog a bit to the right across busy Vodičkova street (with a handy tram stop), where you'll find the entrance to the Světozor mall—it's a few steps to the right, by the* Kino Světozor *sign. Go on in.*

❾ Světozor Mall

As you enter the mall, look up, at a glass window from the 1930s advertising Tesla, a now-defunct Czech radio manufacturer. The

window lends a retro brightness to the place. On the left, pause at the always-busy Ovocný Světozor ("World of Fruit"), every local's favorite ice-cream joint (their specialty is banana-strawberry). They also sell cakes, milkshakes, and "little breads"—delightful Czech-style open-face sandwiches—really cheap. English menus are available on request. While licking your cone, ponder this: This nondescript space once housed the Theatre of the Seven Small Forms (known as the Semafor Theater), the center of the unprecedented creative outburst of the Czech culture that culminated in what became known as the Prague Spring (see sidebar).

• *Walk under the* Tesla *sign to leave the mall. As you exit, turn left immediately to enter the gates of the peaceful...*

❿ Franciscan Garden

Ahhh! This garden's white benches and spreading rosebushes are a universe away from the fast beat of the city, which throbs behind

the buildings corralling this little oasis.

The peacefulness reflects the purpose of its Franciscan origin. St. Francis, the founder of the order, thought God's presence could be found in nature. In the 1600s, Prague became an important center for a group of Franciscans from Ireland. Enjoy the herb garden and children's playground. (And a WC is just out the far side of the garden.) The park is a popular place for a discreet rendezvous; it's famous among locals for kicking off romances.

Looming up at the far end of the garden is a tall, truncated building that looks like it's been chopped in half. When the New Town was founded, its leaders commissioned **St. Mary of the Snows Church**—with its elegant white Gothic walls and lofty apse—to rival St. Vitus Cathedral, across the river. Like St. Vitus, construction halted with the religious wars of the 1400s; unlike St. Vitus, it never resumed. (If you want to peek inside, we'll pass the entrance soon.)

• *Exit the garden at the opposite corner from where you entered (past the little yellow gardening pavilion—which now houses a design boutique—and the herb garden). You'll pass a handy pay WC, then pop out through a big gate into...*

⓫ Jungmann Square (Jungmannovo Náměstí)

The statue depicts **Josef Jungmann** (1773-1847), who revived the Czech language at a time when it was considered a simple peasants' tongue. (If you'd like to step into St. Mary of the Snows' tranquil interior—an airy silence permeated by the damp smell of centuries-old stucco—look for the entrance directly behind Jungmann's rear end.) To the left as you face Jungmann is the decadent, almost overly ornamented Adria Palace—which served as Václav Havel's "base camp" during those electrifying two weeks in November of 1989.

Turn right past the statue, and follow the black paving stones as they cut through the skinny square. Ahead and on the right, look for the ⓬ **Baťa shoe store,** one of the big entrepreneurial success stories of prewar Czechoslovakia. By making affordable but good-quality shoes, Tomáš Baťa's company thrived through the Depression years, only to be seized by the communists after World War II. The family moved their operation abroad, but have now reopened their factory in their hometown of Zlín. Today, Baťa shoes remain popular with Czechs—and international fashionistas.

Just to the right of the shoe store, near the corner of the square, notice the zigzag **Cubist lamppost**—one of many such flourishes scattered around this city, from the brief period when this experimental, uniquely Czech style was in vogue. Just beyond the lamppost is a hidden beer garden that huddles around the base of the church.

• *Keep following those black paving stones through the glassed-in gallery next to the Baťa shoe store. You'll emerge near the bottom of Wenceslas Square.*

⓭ Můstek and the Old City Wall

The bottom of the Square marks the border between the Old Town and New Town. You'll notice the Metro stop Můstek, meaning "Bridge." You used to have to cross a bridge here, then pass through a fortified gate, to enter the Old Town, which was surrounded by a protective wall and moat. (You can detour down into the Můstek Metro station to actually see the original Old Town gate in the wall.) The Old Town and New Town were officially merged in 1784.

Let's finish the walk by bringing Czech history up to the moment. The Soviets were tossed out in the 1989 Velvet Revolution. Then the Czech Republic and Slovakia peacefully separated in the "Velvet Divorce" of 1993. Through the 1990s, the fledgling Czech Republic was guided by President Václav Havel, that former key-jingling playwright. In 2004, the Czech Republic became a member of the European Union. Today, Prague is home to more than one in ten Czechs. The Czech people, while not without problems, are enjoying a growing economy and a strong democracy. And Prague is understandably one of the most popular tourist destinations in Europe.

• *Our walk is done. Here at Můstek, you have many options: Continue straight ahead into the Old Town; turn right along Na Příkopě street (the former moat) to visit the Museum of Communism, Mucha Museum, or Municipal House; or go left along Národní street to the National Theater and the river. For places farther afield, you can hop on the Metro at Můstek. The rest of Prague is yours to enjoy.*

MUCHA
MUSEUM TOUR

Muchovo Museum

Famous in his time but woefully underappreciated outside his homeland today, Alfons Mucha (1860-1939) was an enormously talented Czech artist who wowed the art world as he harnessed and developed the emerging style of Art Nouveau.

Mucha's slinky theater posters—which graced the streets of Paris at the turn of the century—earned him international fame. He could have done anything, but he chose to return to his home country and use his talent to celebrate Czech culture. He created his masterpiece, the *Slav Epic*—a series of huge paintings depicting epic events in the lives of the Slavs (on tour through 2019). While the *Slav Epic* represents the zenith of Mucha's career, this small but endearingly earnest museum is the best place to appreciate his artistic evolution, and the early works that put him on the map.

Orientation

Cost and Hours: 240 Kč, daily 10:00-18:00, tel. 224-233-355, www.mucha.cz.

Getting There: It's at Panská 7, two blocks east of Wenceslas Square.

Length of This Tour: One hour, including time to watch the

MUCHA MUSEUM

Alfons Mucha and the *Slav Epic*

Alfons Mucha (1860-1939) was born in the small Moravian town of Ivančice. He studied in Vienna and Munich, worked for a while in Moravia, then went to Paris to seek his fortune. After suffering as a starving artist, he was hired to design a poster for a play starring the well-known French actress Sarah Bernhardt. Overnight, Mucha was famous. He forged an instantly recognizable style: willowy maidens with flowing hair amid flowery designs and backed with a halo-like circle. His pastel pretties appeared on magazine covers, wallpaper, carpets, and ad campaigns hawking everything from biscuits to beer. Mucha's florid style helped define what became known as Art Nouveau.

But even as he pursued a lucrative (if superficial) career, Mucha was thinking about his native land. While preparing the Bosnian Pavilion for the Paris Exposition of 1900, he traveled widely through Slavic lands, soaking up the culture, history, and traditions. Inspired to immortalize great moments in Slavic history on a grand scale, Mucha convinced the Chicago industrialist Charles Crane to bankroll his project.

At age 50—after years of living abroad—Mucha returned to his homeland. For his studio, he rented a chateau big enough to accommodate huge canvases. In 1928, on the 10th anniversary of modern Czechoslovakia, Mucha's lifework—the *Slav Epic*—was unveiled. A series of 20 thrilling, movie-screen-sized canvases, the *Slav Epic* tells the entire story of the Slavic people, from their humble beginnings in Ukrainian forests to the optimism of the post-WWI era, when Slavic nations (like the Czechs and Slovaks) created their own modern states (Czechoslovakia) for the first time.

But the response was lukewarm. In the experimental age of Picasso, Mucha's representational style was out of fashion. And with the rise of fascism in the 1930s, Mucha's overt Slavic nationalism came under attack. In 1939, German tanks rumbled into Czechoslovakia. The Nazis considered Slavs an inferior race. They arrested the patriot Mucha—now 79 years old—and he was interrogated by the Gestapo. He died a few weeks later.

During World War II, Mucha's canvases were rolled up and hidden away and, in the process, damaged. In 1963, after years of restoration, the paintings were displayed in the obscure Czech town of Moravský Krumlov, near Mucha's birthplace; in 2011, they were brought to Prague's Veletržní Palace where Czechs and tourists alike could appreciate his grand vision. The masterpiece paintings are now on a world tour through 2019.

30-minute film at the end (usually starts at the top and bottom of the hour).
Starring: The early posters and artistic process of Alfons Mucha.

The Tour Begins

• *Follow the chronological exhibit, section by section.*

❶ Timeline and Decorative Panels

Entering the museum, look left (in front of the window) to see a **timeline** of Mucha's life, along with **photos** showing the artist, his

wife Maruška, and some of the luminaries they hung out with—from painter Paul Gauguin (seated, pantsless, at Mucha's beloved organ) to Czechoslovak President Tomáš Garrigue Masaryk to composer Leoš Janáček.

Mucha's fame was hard-earned. It was the result of innate talent, hard work, and—at a few crucial moments—pure dumb luck. Mucha was born in the Moravian village of Ivančice, and almost from his infancy, he displayed prodigious artistic talent. After studying in Vienna, Mucha rode the train back to his homeland and hopped off where he happened to run out of money: in the Moravian village of Mikulov, where a local aristocrat hired him to decorate a newly built estate. That count's cousin later employed Mucha, and was impressed enough to bankroll the young artist's studies in Paris.

Mucha arrived in Paris just in time for the banquet years at the turn of the 20th century. It was a flourishing of world-class artistic and literary talent rarely seen in history—when geniuses like Toulouse-Lautrec, Gauguin, Picasso, Hemingway, Gertrude Stein, and many others were rattling around the grand old city, creating a "bohemian" culture of a very different sort from the one Mucha knew. These artists—whose paths often crossed—found inspiration as they experimented with the arts, drugs, and whatever else they could get their hands on.

Across from the photos are several **decorative posters,** which were some of the earliest works that gained Mucha some acclaim. These employ many of the signature flourishes that would define Mucha's style throughout his career: willowy maidens with flowing hair and gowns, curvaceous poses, and flowers in their hair. The ladies intertwine in the foliage around them, framed by Tiffany-glass backdrops, and radiating pastel tones. You'll see *The Four Flowers* (framed in Gothic windows), *The Four Times of Day,* and *The Four Arts.* Notice how, rather than the conventional method of depicting each figure with a concrete symbol (such as a paintbrush for painting, or an instrument for music), Mucha simply evokes a mood in each scene. For example, the flowers of the "painting" maiden radiate rainbows.

Philosophically, Mucha believed that art wasn't to be elevated and kept at arm's length in a museum; rather, he wanted it to be shared and experienced in everyday life. These panels were designed to be mass-produced, to decorate urbanites' cramped flats. Mucha enjoyed the idea that, through his works, people could enjoy flowers inside, even in the wintertime. Throughout the collection, you'll see how Mucha's works toe the line between advertising and what we'd more conventionally call "art." As the gap separating "pop culture" and just plain "culture" has blurred even more in our own age, Mucha's works provide an interesting point of reflection.

• *The next section is dedicated to...*

❷ Parisian Posters

Turn your attention to the tall, skinny *Gismonda* **poster** at the far end of the room—the result of another extremely lucky stroke for Mucha. It's Paris, on the day after Christmas, 1894.

Mucha—the low man on the totem pole at his design firm—is the lone artist on duty, while the more senior designers are enjoying some holiday time off. Unexpectedly, Sarah Bernhardt—perhaps the most famous theater actress who has ever lived—asks for a poster to be designed to promote her new play. In just a week, working under intense pressure, Mucha cranks out this poster, which is plastered all over town on New Year's Day. Mucha becomes, literally, an overnight sensation. When Parisians start stealing the posters for themselves, it's clear Mucha is on to something. Bernhardt signs him to a six-year contract, and he's the most in-demand artist in town.

The poster was as revolutionary as it was typical of Mucha's emerging style: tall, vertical, hazy pastels, slinky curlicues. Survey the **other posters**—advertising theater presentations (starring Bernhardt and others), art installations, even tobacco (Job). The posters are lithographs, a printing process popularized in late-19th-century Paris (think Toulouse-Lautrec's ads for cancan shows). The artist draws on a stone slab with a grease crayon (or traces onto a greasy film), then coats the slab with water. The ink sticks to the greasy areas and is repelled by the watery parts. It was easy to crank out cheap (but exquisite) four-color posters—intended as throwaway advertising, but soon accepted as high art. Think about how in our age, movie posters (like Drew Struzan's iconic posters for the *Star Wars* and *Indiana Jones* series), album covers, and comic-book characters decorate dorm rooms and rec rooms far more than any other artwork of the past 50 years. Increasingly, mass-produced art—accessible, eye-catching, and linked with fond memories of entertainment—is the art that really matters to the masses.

Before moving on, notice (in the windows) **photos of models** that Mucha posed, lit, photographed, and painstakingly copied for his works. You'll see several figures wearing detailed costumes. As photography was a relatively new medium in Mucha's day, this was a revolutionary tool that would have been unknown to previous generations of artists.

During this same period, Mucha grows more ambitious. He doesn't just do posters—he also designs pavilions for the 1900 Paris World Exposition. A Renaissance man in Art Nouveau times, Mucha dabbles in everything. And he's ready to share his expertise with the world.

• *Continuing past the Parisian posters, the room narrows. On the left wall are excerpts from...*

❸ Documents Decoratifs

Mucha is a sensation, and can't meet the demand all by himself. In keeping with his mission to spread art to the masses, in 1902 Mucha publishes a collection of 72 prints called *Documents Deco-ratifs*—essentially a how-to manual for Art Nouveau. Notice how, no matter the subject—from furniture to stained glass to jewelry to semi-erotic nudes—Mucha approaches the subject with his consis-tent (and consistently eye-pleasing) style. This guy literally wrote the book on his chosen art form.

• *On the right wall are more posters, but now with Czech themes.*

❹ Czech Posters

Mucha and his wife Maruška meet in Paris, and move for a while to the US—mostly to earn money to finance his planned magnum opus, the *Slav Epic*. But in 1910, they return to Bohemia—and get even more caught up in Czech patriotism. These are the wan-ing days of the Austro-Hungarian Empire (which kept the Czech culture and language firmly under its thumb), and the burgeoning Czech National Revival has already inspired generations of Czechs to celebrate what makes their culture unique.

While working on the *Slav Epic* at his Bohemian country-side chateau, Mucha designs posters that commemorate Czech culture while promoting specific events: The Moravian Teachers' Choir took the Czech music of Janáček and others on the road. The Sokol ("Falcon") athletic movement had emerged during Austro-Hungarian times as an important exhibition of Czech strength and pride. And the Lottery of National Unity (in 1912) was used to raise funds for Czech language education (in an age where German was the official language and given strongly preferential treatment in schools). Notice the consistent use of Slavia, a mythical goddess who blesses these proceedings. Mucha's fragile Parisian maidens have become stout Czech peasants and strong workers; when it comes to Slavic women, power equals beauty—strong is sexy. In comparison, examine the contrasting figures Mucha uses in the lottery poster: The stubborn young girl, eagerly gripping her pencil and pad, dares you to help her learn Czech—and will surely grow into one of the strong women we see elsewhere. But in the hazy background behind her, the goddess Czechia is as withered as the tree she sits upon—wasting away from years of neglect.

At the end of the room—between posters promoting cultural events (including an installation of Mucha's own *Slav Epic*)—is the much-reproduced **Princess Hyacinth**, reclining in a chair with a frank, unflinching gaze. This Czech ballet—composed by a Czech, in the Czech language, starring a Czech actress—premiered in the Czech National Theater (a symbol of the Czech National Revival) in 1911...all of which would have been nearly unthinkable in the Austrian town of "Prag" just a few decades earlier.

• *Continue into the next room, which you'll circle counterclockwise, starting on your right.*

❺ Paintings

While we've mostly seen Mucha the draftsman so far, he was also a talented painter (the medium he used for his masterpiece, the *Slav Epic*). The giant canvas *Star* (also called *Woman in the Wilderness)*—in which a starving Russian peasant woman kneels and gazes up at a bright star—might as well be a study for the *Slav Epic*. As in that masterwork, here Mucha demonstrates his emotional connection to all Slavic peoples. This was painted in 1923, as the Czechs were living one of their historical high-water marks, the post-WWI creation of the state of Czechoslovakia. But at that same time, post-Bolshevik Revolution Russia was suffering from famine—and here, Mucha hasn't forgotten his eastern comrades.

• *The area at the end of the hall is a collection of Mucha's...*

❻ Drawings and Pastels

Even his rudimentary sketches demonstrate an innate sense of design—from jewelry to a very early sketch of his stained-glass

window of Cyril and Methodius, in St. Vitus Cathedral (looking more rigidly geometrical than the final, more fluid version). Look carefully in the showcases in the middle of the room, which display (among other items) pages of books that Mucha illustrated. In the first case, find the Crucifixion that Mucha drew as a precocious eight-year-old. (His mother claimed that he could draw even before he could walk—she gave him a pencil to scrawl artfully on the floor.) In the second case, at the far end, find the banknotes and medals that Mucha designed for the budding nation of Czechoslovakia. Having already earned his fame and fortune, much of Mucha's output in his later years was essentially donating his time and talent to celebrate his homeland and build national pride. In the smaller display cases along the window are Mucha's sketchbooks, offering a glimpse at how he turned small-scale motifs into larger masterworks.

At the end of the room (you've been hearing it this whole time) is an excellent 30-minute **movie** that narrates Mucha's life, culminating in the decades he spent executing his *Slav Epic*. It's in English, and plays generally at the top and bottom of each hour.

• *Finally, circling back the way you came, you'll find items from Mucha's...*

❼ Studio

The desk, easel, and chair (in which Mucha is seated in the most famous portrait photograph of him) came from his studio. On the wall are more photographs of his models, many of them nude.

• *After this revealing look at Mucha and his works, consider a visit to the Art Nouveau interiors of the Municipal House, where Mucha designed and painted the Mayor's Salon.*

PRAGUE CASTLE TOUR

Pražský Hrad

For more than a thousand years, Czech leaders—from kings and emperors to Nazis, communists, and presidents—have ruled from Prague Castle. When Christianity arrived in the Czech lands, this promontory—stretching on an east-west axis overlooking the Vltava River—proved a perfect spot for a church and, later, the cathedral (which, according to custom, had to be built with the altar pointing east). Later, the nobles built their representative palaces in proximity to the castle to compete with the Church for influence on the king. Even today, you feel like clip-clopping through this neighborhood in a fancy carriage.

This large complex contains a number of worthwhile sights: the castle itself (the grounds, gardens, and Old Royal Palace interior), St. Vitus Cathedral (stained glass and royal tombs), and a museum on the castle's history. With more time, you can step inside the historic Basilica of St. George, peruse the Golden Lane shops, wander through the Royal Gardens, climb the cathedral tower for the view, or tour a variety of other museums.

A visit to the castle combines nicely with a couple of sights that lie just above it—the Strahov Monastery and Loreta Church. To see them, follow the (optional) "Part 1" circuit outlined below. To start with the castle complex, begin at "Part 2."

Orientation

Cost: Admission to the castle grounds is free, but you need a ticket to enter the sights. Most visitors choose "Circuit B" (250 Kč), which covers the highlights: St. Vitus Cathedral, the Old Royal Palace, the Basilica of St. George, and the Golden Lane. The more comprehensive "Circuit A" (350 Kč) adds a few sights, most notably The Story of Prague Castle exhibit, which interests those with a healthy appetite for history (but may bore others—read the description below before buying a ticket). Tickets are good for two days.

By the way, it's free to enter the vestibule of St. Vitus Cathedral to get a look at its impressive interior. But to get a close-up of its stained-glass windows and historic tombs, you'll need a ticket.

Hours: Castle sights—daily April-Oct 9:00-17:00, Nov-March 9:00-16:00; castle grounds—daily 5:00-24:00; castle gardens—daily 10:00-18:00 in summer, closed off-season. On Sunday, St. Vitus Cathedral is closed until noon for Mass. Be warned that the cathedral can close unexpectedly for special services (check the event calendar at www.katedralasvatehovita.cz or call 724-933-441 to confirm).

Buying Castle Tickets: There are three ticket offices (each marked by a green *"i"*): two in the Second Courtyard, and one in the Third Courtyard (in front of the cathedral). Lines can be long at one and nonexistent at the next, so if it's crowded, check all three. Hang on to your ticket; you must present it at each sight.

Crowd-Beating Tips: Prague Castle is one of the city's most crowded sights. Huge throngs of tourists turn the grounds into a sea of people during peak times (9:30-12:30, especially May-Sept). The most cramped area is the free-to-enter vestibule inside St. Vitus Cathedral; any sight that you pay to enter—including other parts of the cathedral—will be less jammed. For detailed suggestions for structuring your visit, see "Planning Your Time," later.

Security checks at various gates around the castle complex add to your wait during peak times; lines may be shorter at the northern entrance (near the Pražský Hrad and Královský Letohrádek tram stops; see "Getting There," next page) than at the crowded Castle Square entrance. Even the police acknowledge that there are more-likely targets than Prague Castle; the checkpoints are mostly a political show on the part of Czech President Zeman's siege-mentality administration.

Other Sights on This Tour: The most significant are the **Strahov Monastery** (100 Kč, 50 Kč to take photos, daily 9:00-12:00

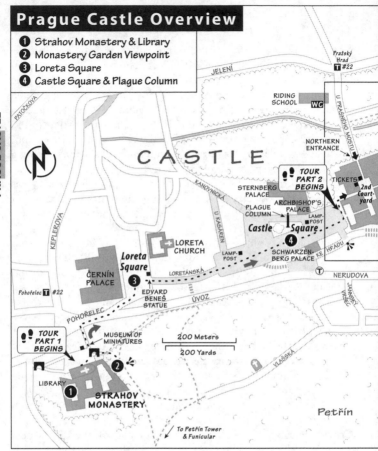

Prague Castle Overview

① Strahov Monastery & Library
② Monastery Garden Viewpoint
③ Loreta Square
④ Castle Square & Plague Column

& 13:00-17:00) and **Loreta Church** (150 Kč, daily April-Oct 9:00-17:00, Nov-March 9:30-16:00).

More Sights on and near the Castle Grounds: Additional sights at the castle are covered by their own, separate tickets, and have their own hours: the **St. Vitus Treasury in the Chapel of the Holy Cross** (300 Kč, daily 10:00-18:00, last entry one hour before closing) and climbing the **Great South Tower of St. Vitus Cathedral** (150 Kč, daily 10:00-18:00, until 16:00 in winter). Nearby sights include **Lobkowicz Palace** (275 Kč, daily 10:00-18:00) and the **Toy Museum** (70 Kč, daily 9:30-17:30).

Getting There: The tram is easy—choose your stop according to which part of the castle you want to reach. Alternatively, you could hike up, or ride a taxi.

  By Tram: Tram #22 takes you up to the castle (see page 42 for my self-guided tram tour, which ends at the castle).

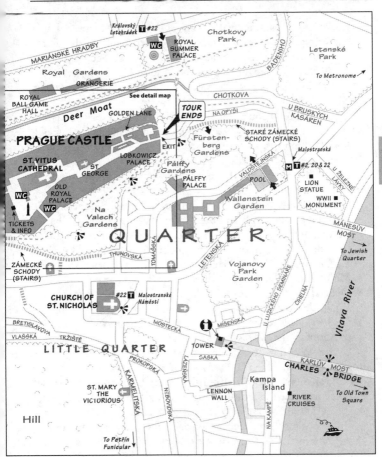

Catch it at one of these three convenient stops: the Národní Třída stop (between Wenceslas Square and the National
Theater in the New Town); in front of the National Theater
(Národní Divadlo, on the riverbank in the New Town); and
at Malostranská (the Metro stop in the Little Quarter). If you
plan to take the tram back to town after your castle visit, bring
an extra ticket with you, as there's no handy place to buy one
at the castle—and inspectors can be ruthless about checking
tourists.

After rattling up the hill, the tram makes three **stops**
near the castle (see map on page 86):

Královský Letohrádek allows a scenic but slow approach
through the Royal Gardens to the bridge near the castle's
northern entrance. A security check is at the garden entry,
by the Summer Palace and Královský Letohrádek tram stop.
Pražský Hrad offers the quickest commute to the castle—from

the tram stop, simply walk along U Prašného Mostu and over the bridge, past the stonefaced-but-photo-op-friendly guards at the northern entrance, and into the castle's Second Courtyard (Part 2 of our tour begins nearby, on Castle Square).

Pohořelec is best if you'd like to start with the Strahov Monastery, then hike down to the castle.

By Taxi: If you tell your driver to take you to "the castle," the taxi ride is a long way around—and expensive. Instead, have the cab drop you off just under the castle at the top of Nerudova street (at the little square under the staircase) and climb 200 yards up the pedestrian-only cobblestone street from there.

By Foot: The fairly steep, uphill, three-quarter-mile walk takes about 20 minutes from the river. From Charles Bridge, follow the main cobbled road (Mostecká) to Little Quarter Square, marked by the huge, green-domed Church of St. Nicholas. (Alternatively, you could take the Metro to Malostranská, then walk down Valdštejnská street to Little Quarter Square.) From Little Quarter Square, hike uphill along Nerudova street. After about 10 minutes, a steep lane on the right leads to Castle Square (and the starting point for this tour's Part 2). If you continue straight, Nerudova becomes Úvoz and climbs to the Strahov Monastery.

Information: Tel. 224-371-111, www.hrad.cz.

Tours: Hour-long **tours** in English depart from the main ticket office near the cathedral entrance about three times a day, but the basic tour covers only the cathedral and Old Royal Palace (100 Kč plus entry ticket, tourist.info@hrad.cz). An **audioguide** is available from the ticket offices (350 Kč plus 500-Kč deposit). I'd skip it in favor of the tour in this chapter.

Length of This Tour: Seeing the castle complex takes two to three hours (depending how long you linger); adding the Strahov Monastery and Loreta Church takes about an hour; and touring the Lobkowicz Palace adds yet another hour.

Eateries: The castle complex has several forgettable cafés scattered within it, but good eateries are nearby: between the castle and Strahov Monastery, and also near the castle-complex exit (see map on page 222, with listings on page 224). I like the scenic, creative café at Lobkowicz Palace (see page 90).

Starring: Europe's biggest castle, a fine cathedral with a stained-glass Mucha masterpiece, and grand views over the city.

PLANNING YOUR TIME

Minimize the effect of crowds and maximize your enjoyment by following one of these plans.

Early-Bird Visit: Leave your hotel no later than 8:00 (earlier is even better). Ride tram #22 up to the Pražský Hrad stop (or leave yourself time to walk through the Royal Gardens, and get off at Královský Letohrádek), then use the northern entrance to the complex's Second Courtyard and buy your tickets. For this option, start with Part 2 of this chapter's tour. See **Castle Square,** and most important, be sure that you're standing at the front door of **St. Vitus Cathedral** when it opens at the stroke of 9:00. For 10 minutes, you'll have the sacred space to yourself...then, on your way out, you'll pass a noisy human traffic jam of multinational tour groups clogging the entrance. Visit the rest of the castle sights at your leisure: the Old Royal Palace, the Basilica of St. George, and the Golden Lane.

To see the **Strahov Monastery** and/or **Loreta Church** after your castle visit, backtrack uphill (either by foot, or by hopping back on tram #22 at a lower stop—near the castle, or even from the Malostranská stop near the river).

Afternoon Visit: Ride tram #22 to the Pohořelec stop. Tour the Strahov Monastery, then drop by Loreta Church on your way to Castle Square. By the time you hit the sights, the crowds should be thinning out (if St. Vitus is jammed, circle back later). The only risk here is running out of time to enter all the sights (which close at 17:00 in summer, or 16:00 in winter); in summer, I'd start at Strahov no later than 14:00.

Nighttime Visit: Least crowded of all is nighttime. True, the sights are closed, but the castle grounds are free, safe, peaceful, floodlit, and open late. The tiny, normally jammed Golden Lane is empty and romantic at night—and no ticket is required.

The Tour Begins

If you're opting for the afternoon visit, begin here with Part 1 and the Strahov Monastery. If you're doing the early-bird visit and starting at Castle Square, skip down to Part 2 of this tour; you can head back up to the Strahov Monastery and Loreta Church later.

PART 1: STRAHOV MONASTERY AND NEARBY

Twin Baroque domes high above the castle mark the Strahov Monastery. After getting off at the Pohořelec tram stop, follow the tracks for 50 yards, take the pedestrian lane that rises up beside the tram tracks, and enter the fancy gate on the left near the tall red-brick wall. You'll see the twin spires of the monastery; the library entrance is on the little square with the monastery church.

❶ Strahov Monastery and Library (Strahovský Klášter a Knihovna)

This fine old monastery has perched on the hill just above Prague

Castle since the 12th century. In the Middle Ages, monasteries like this one weren't simply places for prayerful reflection. Industrious monks served their community as keepers of knowledge (in the form of this monastery's atmospheric, antique library) and producers of both beer and wine. Inhaling deeply, you'll detect a sweet, hoppy fragrance from the recommended Klášterní Pivovar ("Monastery Brewery"), which still operates just across the way. (For details on visiting the monastery's library, see page 91.)

From the library, turn downhill—appreciating the generous shade of the venerable **linden trees** lining the walkways. In pagan times, various Slavic peoples believed that the linden *(lipa)*—which can live for centuries and grow to massive size—had sacred powers. A linden often stood in the main square, and a linden sapling would be planted to celebrate special occasions. Many of the great Eastern Orthodox icons were painted on linden wood. Even in modern times, after more than a millennium of Christianity, the Czechs (and many of their Slavic cousins) still embrace the linden as a national symbol. Here in the Czech Republic, the linden is often used as a symbol of independence; you'll spot linden trees and heart-shaped leaves around the city.

• *Continue downhill through the gate. On the right, just after the Bellavista Restaurant, look for a terrace with arguably the finest views in Prague.*

❷ Monastery Garden Viewpoint

From the public perch beneath the restaurant tables, you can see St. Vitus Cathedral (the heart of the castle complex), the green dome

of the Church of St. Nicholas (marking the center of the Little Quarter), the two dark towers fortifying both ends of the Charles Bridge, and the fanciful black spires of the Týn Church (in Old Town Square). On the horizon is the modern Žižkov TV and radio tower (conveniently marking the liveliest nightlife zone in town—see page 226). Begun in the 1980s, the tower was partly meant to jam Radio Free Europe's broadcast from Munich. By the time it was finished, communism was dead, and Radio Free Europe's headquarters had moved to Prague. Panning right...is that Paris in the distance? No, it's **Petřín Tower,** a mini-Eiffel Tower offering expansive views over Prague (see page 83).

• *From here, it's about a 10-minute walk to Castle Square. Backtrack uphill through the gate, then take a hard right. You'll pass the intriguing Museum of Miniatures—with literally microscopic art (see description on page 92)—on your left, before continuing straight through the small hole in the wall and down the stairs. Emerging at the broad street, turn right, then bear left at the fork. (Avoid the right/downhill fork, which takes you steeply down Úvoz street back to the river.) You'll arrive at the parking lot that fills Loreta Square. Pause at the circular plaza with the statue, overlooking the church.*

❸ Loreta Square (Loretánské Náměstí)

The square is dominated by the beautiful Baroque **Loreta Church.** Popular with pilgrims, the church hides a surprise inside its court-

yard: what's purported to be part of Mary's house from Nazareth. If you have time and an interest in pilgrim churches, buy a ticket and visit the grounds (described on page 93).

On the uphill (left) side of the square is the **Černín Palace** (Černínsky Palác). Once home to a cosmopolitan Czech family, it was turned into the Ministry of Foreign Affairs in 1918. This building was the unfortunate site of a modern-day defenestration. (As we'll learn at the castle, a "defenestration" is a uniquely Czech solution to political discord by literally throwing the offending politician out a window.) On March 10, 1948, soon after the communists took over, popular Czechoslovak politician **Jan Masaryk** was found dead in this building's courtyard, below a palace bathroom window. A charismatic piano player-turned-Secretary of State—and the son of Tomáš Garrigue Masaryk, Czechoslovakia's first president (see sidebar on page 174)—Jan Masaryk was an important symbol of Czech democracy. His death snuffed out the tiny remaining hope that his people still had for regaining some control of their country. While authorities at the time ruled it a suicide, an independent forensic examination in the 1990s confirmed foul play. The most likely theory is that Masaryk was killed by the Soviet secret police, who had learned of Masaryk's plans to leave the country and represent it while in exile. Masaryk, who up to that time had been indispensable even to the communists, had become a liability.

In May 2005, a controversial memorial to Czechoslovakia's second president, **Edvard Beneš,** was unveiled in front of the ministry. While the brilliant young Beneš was instrumental in securing international backing for the new country as Czechslovakia's

first Secretary of State, his subsequent actions as president between 1935 and 1948 (much of that time in exile in London) tarnished his legacy. Arrogant, aloof, and gullible, during the war years Beneš cozied up with Stalin, and after the war he masterminded the eviction of more than 2 million Germans from Czechoslovakia (see sidebar on page 324). Take a moment to psychoanalyze the smaller-than-life-size statue, a recasting of a 1947 work by Karel Dvořák. His drooping shoulders suggest weakness and make his suit look a size too big. His crossed arms are a psychological "tell," indicating that he's closed off and withdrawn. And the look of worry and deep regret etched into his deeply furrowed brow hardly suggests a strong leader.

• *Continue downhill along Lore-tánská. After one long block, the street opens into a square dominated by an elaborate green lamppost. Continue through the square to find the lamppost's twin, which stands at the entrance to Castle Square. This marks the west end of the huge castle complex. You can't miss the* **main entrance:** *a gateway with a golden arch, guarded by two*

fighting-giant statues and two real-life soldiers in their blue-and-white guardhouses.

❹ Castle Square (Hradčanské Náměstí)

You're standing at the tip of the medieval iceberg called Prague Castle. It's a 1,900-foot-long series of courtyards, churches, and palaces, covering 750,000 square feet—by some measures, the largest castle on earth. In the center of the complex sits St. Vitus

Cathedral (the two prickly steeples you see rising above the buildings).

The stoic **guards** at the main entrance make a great photo-op, as does the changing of the guard (on the hour from 5:00-23:00). In fact, there's a guard-changing ceremony at every gate: top, bottom, and side. The best ceremony and music occurs at noon, at the top gate.

Now turn around and survey the broad expanses of Castle Square.

Enjoy the awesome city view and the entertaining bands that play regularly at the gate. (If the Prague Castle Orchestra is playing, say hello to friendly, mustachioed Josef, and consider buying the group's CD—it's terrific.) From the square, stairs lead down to the Little Quarter.

Castle Square was the focal point of medieval power. The arch-bishop lived (and still lives) in the **Archbishop's Palace**—the ornate, white-and-yellow Rococo palace on the right. Above the doorway is the coat of arms of Prague's archbishops: three white goose necks in a red field. (The portal on the left leads to the Stern-berg Palace art museum, described on page 89.)

On the left side of the square, the building with a step-gable roofline is **Schwarzenberg Palace,** where the aristocratic Rožmberk family, of Český Krumlov, "humbly" stayed when they were visiting from their country estates. When the Schwarzenberg family inherited the Krumlov estates, it was their turn to stay in the palace. Notice the envelope-shaped patterns stamped on the exterior. These Renaissance-era adornments etched into wet stuc-co—called sgraffito—decorate buildings throughout the castle, all over Prague, and across the Czech Republic. Today the castle is an art museum with a collection of Baroque-era Czech paintings and sculpture (see page 90).

The black Baroque sculpture in the middle of the square is a **plague column.** Erected as a token of gratitude to Mary and the saints for saving the population from epidemic disease, these columns are an integral part of the main squares of many Habsburg towns.

Closer to you, near the overlook, the statue of a man in a business suit (marked *TGM*) honors the father of modern Czechoslovakia: **Tomáš Garrigue Ma-saryk** (1850-1937). At the end of World War I, Masaryk—a former university prof and pal of Woodrow Wilson—united the Czechs and the Slovaks into one nation and became its first presi-

Tomáš Garrigue Masaryk (1850-1937)

Tomáš Masaryk was the George Washington of Czechoslovakia. He founded the first democracy in Eastern Europe at the end of World War I, uniting the Czechs and the Slovaks to create Czechoslovakia. Like Václav Havel 70 years later, Masaryk was a politician whose vision extended far beyond the mountains enclosing the Bohemian basin.

Masaryk, from a poor servant family in southern Moravia, earned his Ph.D. in sociology in Vienna, studied in Leipzig, then became a professor of philosophy at Charles University of Prague. By then, he was married to American Charlotta Garrigue, a social revolutionary from a prominent New York family. (The progressive Tomáš took her family name as part of his own.) Through Charlotta, Masaryk was introduced to America's high society, including a young Princeton professor named Woodrow Wilson.

Masaryk was greatly impressed with America, and his admiration for its democratic system became the core of his evolving political creed. He traveled the world and served in the Vienna parliament. At the outbreak of World War I, while most other

dent (see sidebar). He was the only 20th-century leader to actually live inside Prague Castle.

PART 2: PRAGUE CASTLE (PRAŽSKÝ HRAD)
• *Let's enter the castle. Veer left through the security checkpoint and emerge into the...*

❺ Second Courtyard
To your right is the **Chapel of the Holy Cross.** This holds the St. Vitus Treasury exhibit, which displays precious reliquaries and liturgical objects dating as far back as the reign of Charles IV (covered by a separate ticket and skippable for most visitors; see the description on page 88).

Just to the left of the chapel, the modern green awning (with the golden-winged cat) marks the entrance to the **offices of the Czech president.**

Two **ticket offices** (with information desks) are in this courtyard, diagonally across from the chapel. You'll need a ticket for our next few sights, so if the line isn't too long, buy one now. (Or duck

PRAGUE CASTLE

Czech politicians stayed in Prague and supported the Habsburg Empire, 64-year-old Masaryk went abroad in protest and formed a highly original plan: to create an independent, democratic republic of Czechs and Slovaks. Masaryk and his supporters recruited an army of 100,000 Czech and Slovak soldiers who were willing to fight with the Allies against the Habsburgs, establishing a strong case to put on his friend Woodrow Wilson's Oval Office desk.

On the morning of October 28, 1918, news of the unofficial capitulation of the Habsburgs reached Prague. Supporters of Masaryk's idea quickly took control of the city and proclaimed the free republic. As the people of Prague tore down double-headed eagles (a symbol of the Habsburgs), the country of Czechoslovakia was born.

On November 11, 1918, four years after he had left the country as a political unknown, Masaryk arrived in Prague as the greatest Czech hero since the revolutionary priest Jan Hus. The dignified old man rode through the masses of cheering Czechs on a white horse. He told the jubilant crowd, "Now go home—the work has only started." Throughout the 1920s and 1930s, Masaryk was Europe's most vocal defender of democratic ideals against the rising tide of totalitarian ideologies.

Masaryk is one of only three foreign leaders (along with Gandhi and Churchill) to have a statue in Washington, DC.

into the Third Courtyard—our next stop—to see if the ticket office there is less busy.)

• *Now head for St. Vitus Cathedral. You'll walk through another passageway, and emerge into the Third Courtyard, facing the impressive façade of St. Vitus Cathedral. Even without a ticket, tourists can step into the church entryway for a nice (if very crowded) view of the nave—but it's worth paying to see the whole church.*

❻ St. Vitus Cathedral (Katedrála Sv. Víta)

This Roman Catholic cathedral is the Czech national church—it's where kings were crowned, royalty have their tombs, the relics of saints are venerated, and the crown jewels are kept. Since A.D. 930, a church has stood on this spot, marking the very origins of the Czech nation. (The letters below correspond to the cathedral map on page 179.)

❹ **Entrance Façade:** The two soar-

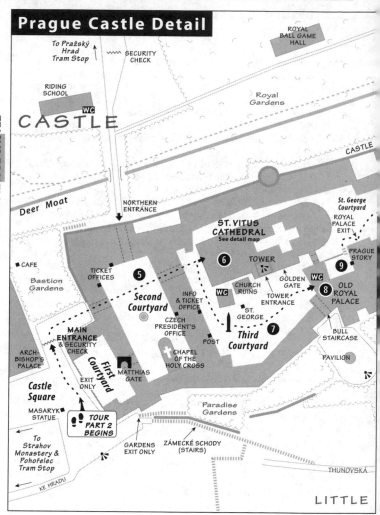

Prague Castle Detail

ing towers of this Gothic wonder rise 270 feet up. The ornate facade features pointed arches, elaborate tracery, Flamboyant pinnacles, a rose window, a dozen statues of saints, and gargoyles sticking their tongues out.

So what's up with the four guys in modern suits carved into the stone, as if supporting the big round window on their shoulders? They're the architects and builders who finished the church six centuries after it was started. Even though church construction got underway in

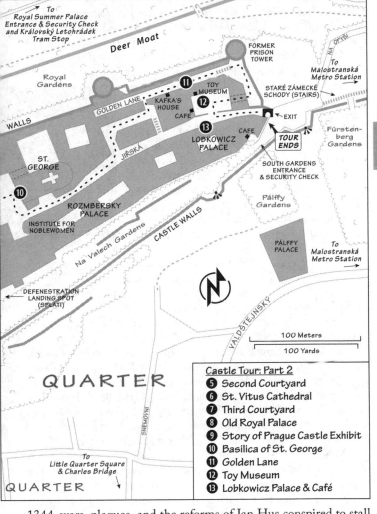

To
Royal Summer Palace
Entrance & Security Check
and Královský Letohrádek
Tram Stop

Deer Moat

FORMER
PRISON
TOWER

Royal
Gardens

To
Malostranská
Metro Station

11

TOY
MUSEUM

STARÉ ZÁMECKÉ
SCHODY (STAIRS)

GOLDEN LANE

KAFKA'S
HOUSE

12

WALLS

CAFE

EXIT

Fürsten-
berg
Gardens

13

CAFE

JIRSKA

LOBKOWICZ
PALACE

TOUR
ENDS

ST.
GEORGE

SOUTH GARDENS
ENTRANCE
& SECURITY CHECK

10

ROZMBERSKY
PALACE

Pálffy
Gardens

INSTITUTE FOR
NOBLEWOMEN

Na Valech Gardens

CASTLE WALLS

PÁLFFY
PALACE

To
Malostranská
Metro Station

DEFENESTRATION
LANDING SPOT
(SPLAT!)

VALDSTEJNSKY

N

100 Meters

100 Yards

QUARTER

SNEMOVNI

To
Little Quarter Square
& Charles Bridge

QUARTER

Castle Tour: Part 2
5 Second Courtyard
6 St. Vitus Cathedral
7 Third Courtyard
8 Old Royal Palace
9 Story of Prague Castle Exhibit
10 Basilica of St. George
11 Golden Lane
12 Toy Museum
13 Lobkowicz Palace & Café

PRAGUE CASTLE

1344, wars, plagues, and the reforms of Jan Hus conspired to stall its completion. Finally, fueled by a burst of Czech nationalism, Prague's top church was finished in 1929 for the 1,000th Jubilee anniversary of St. Wenceslas. The entrance facade and towers were the last parts to be finished.

• *Enter the cathedral. If it's not too crowded in the free entrance area, work your way to the middle of the church for a good...*

6 View down the Nave: The church is huge—more than 400 feet long and 100 feet high—and flooded with light. Notice the intricate "net" vaulting on the ceiling, especially at the far end. It's the signature feature of the church's chief architect, Peter Parler (who also built the Charles Bridge).

• *Now make your way through the crowds and pass through the ticket turnstile (left of the roped-off area). The third window on the left wall is worth a close look.*

🔵 **Mucha Stained-Glass Window:** This masterful 1931 Art Nouveau window was designed by Czech artist Alfons Mucha and executed by a stained-glass craftsman (if you like this, you'll love the Mucha Museum in the New Town—see page 60).

Mucha's window was created to celebrate the birth of the Czech nation and the life of Wenceslas. The main scene (in the four central panels) shows Wenceslas as an impressionable child kneeling at the feet of his Christian grandmother, St. Ludmila. She spreads her arms and teaches him to pray. Wenceslas would grow up to champion Christianity, uniting the Czech people.

Above Wenceslas are the two saints who first brought Christianity to the region: Cyril (the monk in black hood holding the Bible) and his older brother, Methodius (with beard and bishop's garb). They baptize a kneeling convert.

Follow their story in the side panels, starting in the upper left. Around A.D. 860 (back when Ludmila was just a girl), these two Greek missionary brothers arrive in Moravia to preach. The pagan Czechs have no written language to read the Bible, so (in the next scene below), Cyril bends at his desk to design the necessary alphabet (Glagolitic, which later developed into Cyrillic), while Methodius meditates. In the next three scenes, they travel to Rome and present their newly translated Bible to the pope. But Cyril falls ill, and Methodius watches his kid brother die.

Methodius carries on (in the upper right), becoming bishop of the Czech lands. Next, he's arrested for heresy for violating the pure Latin Bible. He's sent to a lonely prison. When he's finally set free, he retires to a monastery, where he dies mourned by the faithful.

But that's just the beginning of the story. At the bottom center are two beautiful (classic Mucha) maidens, representing the bright future of the Czech and Slovak peoples.

Mucha employs other symbolism. Ludmila stands for the past, while the young Wenceslas represents the hope and future of a nation. Notice how master designer Mucha draws your attention to these two figures through the use of colors—the dark blue on the outside gradually turns into green, then yellow, and finally the gold of the woman and the crimson of the boy in the center. In Mucha's color language, blue stands for the past, gold for the mythic, and red for the future. Besides all the meaning, Mucha's art is simply a

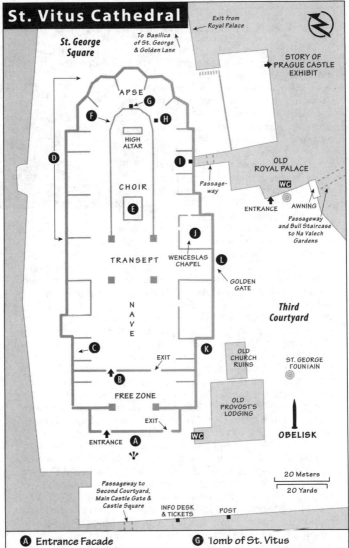

St. Vitus Cathedral

Exit from Royal Palace

To Basilica of St. George & Golden Lane

St. George Square

STORY OF PRAGUE CASTLE EXHIBIT

PRAGUE CASTLE

APSE

G

F

H

HIGH ALTAR

D

I

OLD ROYAL PALACE

WC

Passage-way

ENTRANCE

AWNING

CHOIR

E

Passageway and Bull Staircase to Na Valech Gardens

J

WENCESLAS CHAPEL

L

TRANSEPT

GOLDEN GATE

N A V E

Third Courtyard

C

EXIT

K

OLD CHURCH RUINS

ST. GEORGE FOUNTAIN

B

FREE ZONE

EXIT

OLD PROVOST'S LODGING

OBELISK

ENTRANCE

A

WC

Passageway to Second Courtyard, Main Castle Gate & Castle Square

INFO DESK & TICKETS

POST

20 Meters

20 Yards

- **A** Entrance Facade
- **B** View down the Nave
- **C** Mucha Stained-Glass Window
- **D** Old Church
- **E** Royal Mausoleum
- **F** Relief of Prague
- **G** Tomb of St. Vitus
- **H** Tomb of St. John of Nepomuk
- **I** Royal Oratory
- **J** Wenceslas Chapel
- **K** Tower Entrance
- **L** Last Judgment Mosaic

The Catholic Church in Prague

In stark contrast to the Poles, the freedom-loving Czechs never fully accepted the powerful Catholic Church. They traditionally associated Catholicism with the Habsburgs and Austria—a foreign import. The communists took advantage of this sentiment, and did everything short of banning the Church to uproot the faith of the relatively few practicing Czech Catholics. In the early 1950s, most monks and priests, including the archbishop, were arrested and sent to prisons, from which they were not released until the thawing

that came with the Khrushchev era. A wise old priest remembers his 13 years in a labor camp as "a fascinating, well-spent time in the company of some truly great minds."

During the communist era, Church property was confiscated, churches quickly deteriorated, churchgoers were persecuted, and many priests had to become confidants of the secret police in order to continue their service. Ironically, by persecuting Catholics, the communists gave the Church an opportunity to improve its reputation with the Czechs. From 1946 through 1989, two successive charismatic archbishops of Prague—Cardinals Beran (a survivor of several Nazi labor camps) and Tomášek—became local heroes by frequently standing up to the regime. The communists forced Beran into exile; he is now buried in the crypt of St. Peter's Basilica in Rome. By the 1980s, Tomášek, Beran's handpicked successor, was one of the prominent Czechs who spoke out against communism (along with Václav Havel).

After 1989, many Czechs returned to the Catholic faith. The trend peaked in 1992 when Tomášek died (he's now buried under the Mucha window in St. Vitus Cathedral). Since then, the Church's hold has steadily declined. For now, many parishes are served by Polish missionaries with heavy accents.

The Church is also facing challenges from "new" and fashionable spiritual movements, such as Buddhism, which are drawing Czechs in moderate numbers. But even within these movements, the Czechs remain on the secular side.

joy to behold. (And on the bottom, the tasteful little ad for *Banka Slavie*, which paid for the work, is hardly noticeable.)

• *Continue circulating around the church, following the one-way, clockwise route.*

❿ **The Old Church:** Just after the transept, notice there's a slight incline in the floor. That's because the church was constructed in two distinct stages. You're entering the older, 14th-century

Gothic section. The front half (where you came in) is a Neo-Gothic extension that was finally completed in the 1920s (which is why much of the stained glass has a modern design). For 400 years—as the nave was being extended—a temporary wall kept the functional altar area protected from the construction zone.

• *In the choir area (on your right), soon after the transept, look for the big, white marble tomb surrounded by a black iron fence.*

❺ Royal Mausoleum: This contains the remains of the first Habsburgs to rule Bohemia, including Ferdinand I, his wife Anne, and Maximilian II. The tomb dates from 1590, when Prague was a major Habsburg city.

• *Just after the choir, as you begin to circle around the back of the altar, watch on your right for the fascinating, carved-wood...*

❻ Relief of Prague: This depicts the aftermath of the Battle of White Mountain, when the Protestant King Frederic escaped

over the Charles Bridge (before it had any statues). Carved in 1630, the relief gives you a peek at old Prague. Find the Týn Church (far left) and St. Vitus Cathedral (far right), which was half-built at that time. Back then the Týn Church was Hussite, so the centerpiece of its facade is not the Virgin Mary (more of a Catholic figure), but a chalice, a symbol of Jan Hus' ideals. The old city walls—now replaced by the main streets of the city—stand strong. The Jewish Quarter is the flood-prone zone along the riverside below the bridge on the left—land no one else wanted. The weir system on the river—the wooden barriers that help control its flow—survives to this day.

• *Circling around the high altar, you'll see various...*

Tombs in the Apse: Among the graves of medieval kings and bishops is that of **❼ St. Vitus,** shown as a young man clutching a book and gazing up to heaven. Why is this huge cathedral dedicated to this rather obscure saint, who was martyred in Italy in A.D. 303 and never set foot in Bohemia? A piece of Vitus' arm bone (a holy relic) was supposedly acquired by Wenceslas I in 925. Wenceslas built a church to house the relic on this spot, attracting crowds of pilgrims. Vitus became quite popular throughout the Germanic and Slavic lands, and revelers danced on his feast day. (He's now the patron saint of dancers.) At the statue's feet is a rooster, because the saint was thrown into a boiling cauldron along with the bird (the Romans' secret sauce)...but he miraculously survived.

A few steps farther, the big silvery tomb with the angel-borne canopy honors ❽ **St. John of Nepomuk.** Locals claim it has more than a ton of silver (for more on St. John of Nepomuk and his halo of stars, see page 55).

Just past the tomb, on the wall of the choir (on the right), is another finely carved, circa-1630 **wood relief** depicting an event that took place right here in St. Vitus: Protestant nobles trash the cathedral's Catholic icons after their (short-lived) victory.

Ahead on the left, look up at the ❾ **royal oratory,** a box supported by busy late-Gothic, vine-like ribs. This private box, connected to the king's apartment by a corridor, let the king attend Mass in his jammies. The underside of the balcony is morbidly decorated with dead vines and tree branches, suggesting the pessimism common in the late Gothic period, when religious wars and Ottoman invasions threatened the Czech lands.

• *From here, walk 25 paces and look left through the crowds and door to see the richly decorated chapel containing the tomb of St. Wenceslas. Two roped-off doorways give visitors a look inside. The best view is from the second one, around the corner and to the left, in the transept.*

❿ **Wenceslas Chapel:** This fancy chapel is the historic heart of the church. It contains the tomb of St. Wenceslas, patron saint of the Czech nation; it's where Bohemia's kings were crowned; and it houses (but rarely displays) the Bohemian crown jewels. The chapel walls are paneled with big slabs of precious and semiprecious stones. The jewel-toned stained-glass windows (from the 1950s) admit a soft light. The chandelier is exceptional. The place feels medieval.

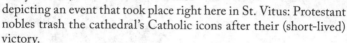

The tomb of St. Wenceslas is a colored-stone coffin topped with an ark. Above the chapel's altar is a statue of Wenceslas, bearing a lance and a double-eagle shield. He's flanked by (painted) angels and the four patron saints of the Czech people. Above Wenceslas are portraits of Charles IV (who built the current church) and his beautiful wife. On the wall to the left of the altar, frescoes depict the saint's life, including the episode

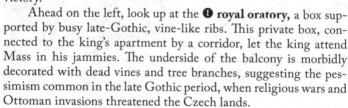

where angels arrive with crosses to arm the holy warrior. (For more on Wenceslas, see page 59.)

For centuries, Czech kings were crowned right here in front of Wenceslas' red-draped coffin. The new king was handed a royal scepter, orb, and sword, and fitted with the jeweled St. Wenceslas crown made for Charles IV. While Wenceslas is considered the eternal ruler of the Czech lands, later kings were loaned his crown and authority. These precious objects are kept locked away behind a door in the corner of the chapel. The door (and the iron safe behind it) has seven locks whose seven keys are held by seven bigwigs (including the Czech president), who must all meet here when someone needs to get inside.

• *Leave the cathedral, turn left (past the public WC), and survey the...*

❼ Third Courtyard

The **obelisk** was erected in 1928—a single piece of granite celebrating the 10th anniversary of the establishment of Czechoslovakia and commemorating the soldiers who fought for its independence. It was originally much taller, but broke in transit—an inauspicious start for a nation destined to last only 70 years.

From here, you get a great look at the sheer size of St. Vitus Cathedral and its fat green **tower** (325 feet tall). Up there is the Czech Republic's biggest **bell** (16.5 tons, from 1549), nicknamed "Zikmund." In June 2002 it cracked, and two months later the worst flood in recorded history hit the city—the locals saw this as a sign. As a nation sandwiched between great powers, Czechs are deeply superstitious when it comes to the tides of history. Often feeling unable to influence their own destiny, they helplessly look at events as we might look at the weather and other natural phenomena—trying to figure out what fate has in store for them next. You can view the bell as you climb up the 287 steps of the tower to the observation deck at the top (❽ buy ticket and enter near sculpture of St. George—a 1960s replica of the 13th-century original). A few steps to the left you can survey the ruins of the first basilica of St. Vitus from the 11th century, protected under a green roof.

It's easy to find the church's **Golden Gate** (for centuries the cathedral's main entry)—look for the glittering ❾ 14th-century mosaic of the Last Judgment. The modern, cosmopolitan, and ahead-of-his-time Charles IV commissioned this monumental decoration in 1370 in the Italian style. Jesus oversees the action, as some go to heaven and some go to hell. The Czech king and queen kneel directly beneath Jesus and six patron saints. On coronation day, royalty would walk under this arch, a reminder to them (and their subjects) that even those holding great power are not above God's judgment. See the grilled windows above this entryway? That's where the royal crown and national jewels are stashed.

Across from the Golden Gate, in the corner, notice the copper, scroll-like **awning** supported by bulls. This leads to a fine garden just below the castle. The stairway, garden, and other features around the castle were designed by the Slovene architect Jože Plečnik. Around the turn of the 20th century, Prague was considered the cultural standard-bearer of the entire Slavic world—making this a particularly prestigious assignment.

• *In the corner of the Third Courtyard, near the copper awning, is the entrance to the Old Royal Palace. In the lobby, there's a WC with a window shared by the men's and women's sections—meet your partner to enjoy the view.*

❽ Old Royal Palace (Starý Královský Palác)

Since the ninth century, this has been the seat of the Bohemian princes. The highlight of the palace building (dating from the 12th century) is the large **Vladislav Hall**—200 feet long, with an impressive vaulted ceiling of vine-shaped (late-Gothic) tracery. This hall, used by the old nobility, served many purposes. It could be filled with market stalls, letting aristocrats shop without actually going into town. It was big enough for jousts—even the staircase (which you'll use as you exit)  was designed to let a mounted soldier gallop in. Beginning in the 1500s, nobles met here to elect the king. The tradition survived into modern times. As recently as the 1990s, the Czech parliament crowded into this room to elect their president.

On your immediate right, enter the two small Renaissance rooms known as the **"Czech Office."** From these rooms (empty today except for their 17th-century porcelain heaters), two governors used to oversee the Czech lands for the Habsburgs in Vienna. Head for the far room, wrapped in windows. In 1618, angry Czech Protestant nobles poured into these rooms and threw the two Catholic governors out the window. An old law actually permits this act—called defenestration—which usually targets bad politicians. An old print on the glass panel shows the second of Prague's many defenestrations. The two governors landed—fittingly—in a pile of horse manure. Even though they suffered only broken arms and bruised egos, this event kicked off the huge and lengthy Thirty Years' War.

As you re-enter the main hall, go to the far end and out on the **balcony** for a sweeping view of Prague. Then head for the door immediately opposite. It opens into the **Diet Hall,** with a fine Gothic ceiling, a crimson throne, and benches for the nobility who once served as the high court. Notice the balcony on the left where scribes recorded the proceedings (without needing to mix with the aristocrats). The portraits on the walls depict Habsburg rulers, including Maria Theresa and Joseph II dressed up as George Washington (both wore the 18th-century fashions of the times), and the display case on the right contains replicas of the Czech crown jewels.

Return to the main hall; the next door to your right is the exit. Head down those horseback stairs. As you exit outside, pause at the door you just came through to consider the subtle yet racy little Renaissance knocker. Go ahead—play with it for a little sex in the palace (be gentle).

• *The next sight requires the "Circuit A" ticket; if you don't have one, skip down to the next stop.*

Otherwise, as you exit the Royal Palace, hook left around the side of the building and backtrack a few steps uphill to find stairs leading down to...

❾ The Story of Prague Castle Exhibit (Příběh Pražského Hradu)

This museum of old artifacts (with good English descriptions) is your best look at castle history and its kings, all housed in the cool Gothic cellars of the Old Royal Palace. Throughout the exhibit, models of the castle show how it grew over the centuries.

Origins (Room 1): In this low-ceilinged medieval room, you'll learn about prehistoric finds (mammoth bones) and the first settlers (c. 800), churches, and fortifications, and see ivory hunting horns of the first kings.

Patron Saints (Room 2): Czechs trace their origins as a people to several early saints. The first was St. Wenceslas, and you can admire (what may be) his actual chain-mail tunic and helmet. He was raised Christian by his grandmother, Ludmila (view her supposed clothes), and went on to found the original St. Vitus church. St. John of Nepomuk (no artifacts here) lies buried in the church's most ornate tomb.

Archaeological Finds (Room 3): Look through the metal floor to see the foundations of the 12th-century palace. An adjoining room displays ecclesiastical gear, documents relating to the history of the church, and (upstairs) bones from early funerals.

Golden Age of Bohemia (Room 4): In this large hall are numerous artifacts from 1200 through 1400. First comes the kings of the Přemysl family (including Ottokar II), then the dynasty of Charles IV and his IV wives.

Habsburg Rulers (Room 5): With Bohemia under Austrian rule, Prague briefly became the Habsburg capital in the 1520s (Turks were pounding on the gates of Vienna). When the Habsburgs returned to Vienna, Prague declined. But then Emperor Rudolf II moved the Habsburg court for one last time from Vienna to Prague (1583-1612), bringing with him current art styles (Mannerism—the transition from Renaissance to Baroque) and leading-edge scientists (astronomers Tycho Brahe and Johannes Kepler).

In this area, a display on the Czech coronation ceremony (always held in St. Vitus) includes fine replicas of the Bohemian crown jewels—scepter, orb, and crown (the originals are exhibited only on special occasions). They're a reminder that Prague Castle has been the center of the Czech state for more than a millennium.

There's also an exhibit that shows how construction of St. Vitus Cathedral—for many years stymied—was finally jump-started in the 19th century and completed.

• *Directly across the courtyard from the rear buttresses of St. Vitus is a very old church with a pretty red facade. This is the...*

❿ Basilica of St. George (Bazilika Sv. Jiří)

Step into one of the oldest structures at Prague Castle to see Prague's best-preserved Romanesque church and the burial place of Czech royalty. The church was found-

ed by Wenceslas' dad around 920, and the present structure dates from the 12th century. (Its Baroque facade came later.) Inside, the place is beautiful in its simplicity. Notice the characteristic thick walls and rounded arches. In those early years, building techniques were not yet advanced enough to use those arches for the ceiling—it's made of wood instead.

This was the royal burial place before St. Vitus was built, so the tombs here contain the remains of the earliest Czech kings. Climb the stairs that frame either side of the altar to study the area around the apse. St. Wenceslas' grandmother, Ludmila, was reburied here in 925. Her stone tomb is in the space just to the right of the altar. Inside the archway leading to her tomb, look for her portrait. Holding a branch and a book, she looks quite cultured for a 10th-century woman.

As you exit the church, you'll pass some small exhibits about the layers of history at this site.

• *Notice the building across the lane from the basilica (with the columned and curved portico)—this was Maria Theresa's* **Institute for Noble-women***, created in the 1750s to empower and educate aristocratic but impoverished ladies.*

Now continue walking downhill on that lane. You'll see the basilica's Romanesque nave and towers—a strong contrast to the pretty Baroque facade. Farther down, to the left, were the residences of soldiers and craftsmen, and to the right, tucked together, were the palaces of Catholic nobility who wanted both to be close to power and able to band together should the Protestants grab the upper hand. The next street on the left leads up to the popular Golden Lane. As you pass through the entry turnstiles, the crowds turn right, but don't overlook the sights to your left (including a tiny café).

⓫ Golden Lane (Zlatá Ulička)

The tiny, old, colorfully painted buildings of this picturesque street originally housed castle servants, and perhaps goldsmiths. Now

they house displays on the olden days—medieval torture, alchemy, armor, medieval clothing—and re-creations of a classic pub and a goldsmith's workshop. Well-written English texts explain the history of the lane and its cannon towers, which served as prisons. Other small buildings are now gift shops selling old-timey products. At various points along the lane, you can climb up to a very cramped corridor that runs atop the houses; in this area, you'll find an armory and access to a tower with mediocre views (at the left end) and a measly torture collection (one cluttered room with unexplained torture tools, near the WC, in the middle).

The houses themselves were occupied until World War II—Franz Kafka lived briefly (1916-1917) at #22, just to the right as you enter. Kafka moved in the year after publication of his most famous book, *The Metamorphosis* (elevator pitch: man wakes up as cockroach). He moved out just as he became engaged and showed the first signs of the tuberculosis that would eventually kill him. A few years after his time here, he wrote an (unfinished) book called *The Castle*, which may have been inspired by his own castle days.

At the bottom of the lane (past the last house, #12), tourists get flushed down a tight, stepped corridor. Before leaving, notice the tiny **cinema** room nearby that shows clips from classic Czech black-and-white films.

The Rest of the Castle

Our tour is over. But remember there are a number of other sights to see in the complex—some free; some requiring a ticket.

The stepped corridor at the end of Golden Lane will deposit you at a rampart walkway next to a round tower, once a famous prison. A small gate to the right leads to a courtyard with the ⑫ **Toy Museum** (see page 91). Across the street is the ⑬ **Lobkowicz Palace,** with a few top-notch paintings, a Beethoven manuscript, and an aristocratic ambience (see page 90). For more Castle Quarter sights, see page 84.

And, if you haven't yet visited the **Strahov Monastery**—up above the castle complex, and described at the start of this walk—you could either walk up, or head down to Malostranská and ride a tram back up to Pohořelec from there (both options explained next).

LEAVING THE CASTLE COMPLEX

Tourists squirt slowly through a fortified door at the bottom end of the castle. A scenic rampart just below the lower gate offers a commanding view of the city. From there, you can head to the nearest Metro/tram station, Strahov Monastery, Little Quarter, or Castle Square.

To the Malostranská Metro/Tram Station: You can follow the 700-some steps down the steep lane called Staré Zámecké Schody ("Old Castle Stairs") directly back to the riverbank. Or you can turn right about halfway down the steps to visit the Fürstenberg Gardens, with 3,500 flowering plants and 2,200 rose bushes (80 Kč, April-Oct daily from 10:00 until one hour before sunset). Alternatively, for a gentler descent, start heading down the steep lane. About 40 yards below the castle exit, a gate on the left leads you through a scenic vineyard and past the recommended Villa Richter restaurants (see page 224) to the station.

To the top of the Little Quarter or Castle Square (and Strahov Monastery): As you leave the castle gate, take a hard right and stroll through the long, delightful park (free, daily 10:00-18:00 or later, closed Nov-March). Along the way, notice the Modernist layout of the Na Valech Gardens, designed by the 1920s court architect, Jože Plečnik of Slovenia. Halfway through the long park is a viewpoint overlooking the terraced Pálffy Gardens (80 Kč, same hours as park). You can zigzag down through these gardens into the Little Quarter. Or, if you want to walk to Castle Square, continue uphill along the castle  wall and through the garden to the square. You can hike up to the Strahov Monastery from here.

VYŠEHRAD WALK

For a park-like break from the big city, fine views, and a special insight into Czech culture and history, consider this easy walk through Vyšehrad (VEE-sheh-rahd), a park just south of the New Town with a 17th-century fortress overlooking Prague. You'll ride the Metro to the top of the park and stroll through ramparts and trees with locals, past monuments and commanding views, then gradually head downhill, eventually ending up in the area known as Výtoň. From here, an easy walk along the river or a tram ride takes you back into the tourist action.

A visit to Vyšehrad is more meaningful if you remember that Prague has never been a purely "Czech" city, but a crossroads where various powerful influences have mixed their linguistic, religious, and cultural agendas. From the Roman Catholic Church to the Germanic culture of the Holy Roman and Habsburg empires, the Czechs were often second-class citizens in their own capital. Vyšehrad is the place (even more than Prague Castle) that they've always considered their own—a stronghold of Czech culture.

Orientation

Length of This Walk: Allow two hours.

When to Go: This walk works during the day, but is also appealing in the evening. Note that although the area is romantically lit at night, most of the interiors (including the cemetery) are closed after 18:00.

Getting There: Take the Metro to the Vyšehrad stop.

Information: Tel. 241-410-348, www.praha-vysehrad.cz.

Vyšehrad Gallery: 30 Kč, daily 10:00-18:00 except closed Jan-Feb.

Basilica of Sts. Peter and Paul: 30 Kč, daily 10:00-18:00.

National Cemetery: Free, daily 8:00-19:00, March-April and Oct until 18:00, Nov-Feb until 17:00.
Casemates: Viewable with 20-minute tour, 60 Kč, tours depart daily 10:00-17:00 at the top of the hour.
Starring: Grand views and stories of a grand history.

The Walk Begins

• *The Vyšehrad Metro exit leads directly to a terrace with a balcony (on your right) overlooking the city. Take a few minutes to appreciate the...*

❶ View of Prague

Survey the scene. The tall, modern bridge was built in the 1970s to accommodate both the Metro and cars. To test whether it could carry its designed load, the first vehicles to cross the bridge were a battalion of tanks. Along the opposing slopes you can discern the brick fortifications of the New Town (one of the last places in Prague that these fortifications have been preserved). Now turn around. The gigantic glass-and-concrete building is the **Congress Center.** Finished in the early 1980s, it was originally designed to house Communist Party conventions but quickly came to be considered the ugliest building in town. In 1999, several former Warsaw Pact countries (including the Czech Republic) joined NATO, and the Congress Center became the first place in Eastern Europe to host a NATO summit.

• *It's about a five-minute walk to the park entrance: Follow the granite bannister the length of the Congress Center building, angling down the ramp. Track the brown* Vyšehrad *signs along a residential street down to the fortress walls. Pause a moment to notice the walls, made with a*  *combination of red brick and white* opuka, *Prague's native limestone. Now enter through a gate on the right. You'll pop out in a charming park, where you can orient yourself at the map on an info post to your right.*

❷ Old Vyšehrad Map

The map shows the layout of this 17th-century fortress, built in the shape of a pentagon with a bastion at every corner. The only access was from the east, along a fortified corridor with double gates. You are standing just inside the outer one, called the Tábor Gate.

Archaeological records show that Vyšehrad once housed a royal palace and an astounding number of churches. By the 10th century, this place had become a Slavic alternative to Prague Castle—which felt closer to the Vatican than to the local culture. Unfortunately, much of what was once here was destroyed by looters in 1420 during the Hussite Wars.

Two and a half centuries later, the Habsburgs chose this more-or-less empty site to serve as the city garrison. Despite the high construction costs, the fortress never saw real fighting. The Austrians remained at Vyšehrad until the 1840s.

Once the soldiers departed, another gate was blasted through the walls on the north side to create an easier connection to the New Town (this walk will take you around the ramparts and out through that gate). The fortress was eventually turned into a park that became popular with Romantic Czech artists, who walked the ramparts daydreaming about their nation's mythic history. The less that remained of the Romanesque and Gothic past, the better, leaving that much more to the imagination and stirring the Czech soul inside artists like the composer Bedřich Smetana. Just as it had centuries before, Vyšehrad became the Slavic alternative to the city's dominant culture (this time, Germanic).

• *Continue along the cobbled street. On the right, notice a tiny piece of a Gothic gate, a reminder of the pre-Hussite period. As you walk above the tennis courts and approach a second gate (the Leopold Gate), look up at the* **double-headed eagle**—*the coat of arms of the Habsburgs, who ruled in Prague for 300 years. Once through the gate, stop on the corner under a horse-chestnut tree to survey the little round...*

➌ Rotunda of St. Martin

This 11th-century Romanesque rotunda, constructed out of Prague's native limestone, is named for St. Martin, patron saint of soldiers, horses, riders, geese, and vintners. St. Martin's feast day falls on November 11 and is celebrated with roast goose and the year's first wine. On this day, St. Martin arrives on a white horse, signifying snow and the coming of winter.

• *Take the lane across the way from the chapel, under the chestnut tree. When the path forks, turn right, left, and right again to reach the ramparts. Walk the length of the wall and find a place to pause to enjoy...*

➍ Vltava River Views

You are looking south, or upstream. Bohemia, one of three regions that make up the Czech Republic (the others are Moravia and Silesia), is defined by its watershed. The region is essentially a big basin with mountains at its edges and Prague right in the middle. The

Vltava originates in the south—at the border with Germany—and collects the waters from the south, east, and west before it flows into the Elbe River about 30 miles north of Prague. The Elbe breaks its way through the sandstone formations at the northern Czech/German border, marking the only place where water leaves Bohemia. It then flows through Dresden, on to Hamburg, and empties into the North Sea.

The TV tower on the horizon marks the spot where the Vltava meets up with two big rivers, one from the east and one from the west. The hill above the confluence was once the largest Celtic settlement in the country (Bohemia derives its name from the Celtic tribe that used to inhabit the area). Celts were the first to recognize Prague's strategic location at a time when waterways were the main or only means of transportation. The two main products that traveled downstream were Austrian salt (Bohemia lacks its own salt) and wood from the border mountains.

The name of the river, Vltava, comes from the old Germanic for "wild awa," meaning wild waters. Moldau—what Germans call the river today—is a variant of the same word. The rapids that gave the river its name disappeared in the 1950s and '60s under a series of dams that were, among other things, built to protect Prague from flooding. But in 2002, the dams were unable to rein in massive flood waters during what was the country's biggest recorded flood.

• *Turn right and follow the ramparts to the end, where you'll find yourself on a bluff overlooking the river.*

❺ Bluff with More Prague Views

Down below, find the wooden house flanked by yachts. This is Prague's oldest rowing club. Next, locate the island across the way. In 1896, the first soccer match between Sparta and Slavia was played on the island's meadow, marking the start of the biggest sports rivalry in the country. Just to the right, the large **mansion** topping a little hill of its own belongs to Karel Gott (literally "God" in German)—the never-fading Czech pop star whose fame has persisted from the 1950s to today (imagine if Elvis was still alive). The mansion is just a little uphill from Villa Bertramka, where Mozart stayed with friends during his visits to Prague.

Down below, perched on a cliff on this side of the river, are the ruins of a **guard house** for customs collectors. Popular legend has reinvented it as the bathhouse of Princess Libuše, Prague's

mythic founder. As the tale goes, Libuše led her Slavic people down from the plains north of Prague and decided to build a castle at Vyšehrad. Upon reaching the rocky hill, Libuše sent her men into the valley to ask about the name of the place where they had just arrived. The men encountered some charcoal makers. While standing in the doorway, they were told that they were "on the threshold" *(práh)*. This popular interpretation of the etymology of the city's name is indicative of the way locals perceive Prague: as

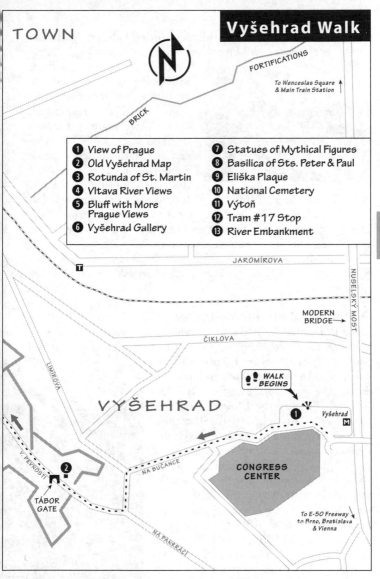

a place of encounter between East and West, and between Latin culture and Slavic heritage.

• *Walk downhill through the tiny vineyard. To the right is a delightful park café—good for a beer and a sandwich (indoor and outside seating). Carry on to the left to...*

⑥ Vyšehrad Gallery

Vyšehrad Gallery has small exhibits featuring local artists. It also boasts more city views. From here study the sprawling Prague

Castle in the distance, with its five noble palaces crowned by a cathedral. Just across the river from you is the smokestack of the Staropramen brewery (marked with a big *A*). Depending on the direction of the wind, you may be able to smell the malt. High up on the hill (look for the elevated lights) is a 200,000-seat stadium that has hosted mass calisthenics gatherings (called Sokol) since the 1930s. During the communist years, these were adapted into even more grandiose gatherings that took place every five years.

• *Walk toward the church through a park dotted with deciduous trees typical of the Czech Republic: linden, oak, alder, and ash. This is where you'll find a few...*

⑦ Statues of Mythical Figures

Stand in the middle of the four 19th-century statues, which give shape to some old Slavic legends. The first group, nearest the church, depicts **Princess Libuše** with an outstretched hand and closed eyes, prophesizing the great future of the city. Her husband, **Přemysl the Plower,** holds (of course) a plow in his hands. Together they founded a historic dynasty that ruled from Prague for more than four centuries.

Diagonally across from that couple is a statue of a stout man with a mustache kneeling in front of a beautiful girl. These are **Ctirad** ("the honor-loving one") and **Šárka** ("the twilight girl"), the main protagonists of a 1,500-year-old battle of the sexes. According to the myth of "The Maidens' War," the women knew that they would be unable to beat Ctirad—the most powerful fighter—and his men on the battlefield. So instead, they used trickery: One summer day, they tied the beautiful Šárka to a tree, naked, and hid in the woods to await Ctirad and his men. When they arrived, Ctirad stopped to help the girl, who told him that she had been left there to die as a traitor. Ctirad untied her, gave her some clothes, and sent his men to a nearby meadow to drink honey mead. Ctirad asked Šárka about the golden horn around her neck, and she encouraged him to try it. The sound of the horn signaled the women, who jumped out of the woods, killed the drunk men, and took Ctirad as their prisoner, eventually tearing his limbs apart on a large wheel and tossing him into a gully to die a slow death. The men lost the war, and ever since women have ruled most Czech households. As for Šárka, she eventually went mad and jumped off a cliff on the western edge of town.

In another version of the legend, Ctirad crawled away and his broken limbs eventually healed. He then secretly reunited with Šárka just in time to head off her suicidal leap. The two then went on to found the "Prague race" (people fond of factual argument but averse to war) while the rest of mankind remains mired in the merciless war of the sexes.

• *Continue to the nearby...*

❽ Basilica of Sts. Peter and Paul

The Neo-Gothic Basilica of Sts. Peter and Paul was built on the site of earlier Romanesque and Baroque churches. Until the 18th century, Vyšehrad was so important that this church and its priest answered directly to the pope (not to the bishops and archbishops of Prague). On the front facade are statues of Peter and Paul, along with mosaics depicting Cyril and Methodius, the Macedonian saints who first brought Christianity to the Slavs in their own language (rather than in Latin). The interior features circa-1900 Art Nouveau frescoes and richly decorated Neo-Gothic windows. Most of the chapels hold Baroque altars; the most precious of these is the first one on the right by Karel Škréta, dedicated to the patrons of Czech lands.

• *Head back outside, and face the facade of the church. Over your right shoulder, about 10 feet up on the corner of the building, look for the...*

❾ Eliška Plaque

This honors a 14th-century queen who was in many ways responsible for Prague's Golden Age. Eliška's brother was the final heir

VYŠEHRAD

of the Czechs' homegrown Přemysl dynasty—and when he was assassinated, that dynasty officially died out with him. But Eliška had entered into a strategic marriage with the powerful Count of Luxembourg, and had nurtured their son, Charles, to have a deep appreciation for his Czech roots. In fact, others in the court grew concerned that Charles was too attached to Czech ways, and sent him to travel and study in Paris and Italy. But when Charles took the Bohemian throne—and later become the Holy Roman Emperor—he chose to make Prague his capital, and built a famous bridge, a university, and much more. Much of the greatness of Prague that you're enjoying today is thanks to that man, Charles IV...and to his mom.

• *As you face the church, turn left to enter the...*

⑩ National Cemetery

Since the 1870s, major Czech cultural figures have been buried here, including Mucha, Smetana, and Dvořák (a map at the cemetery gate shows the locations of their graves). The most important tomb, at the far-right end as you enter, is **Slavín** (meaning "ground of glory")—a large monument capped by angels and dedicated to many cultural VIPs, including Mucha. Smetana's tomb faces Slavín. The word *Rodina,* which you'll see inscribed on gravestones, means family.

• *Leave the graveyard through a gate just after the Slavín monument, turn left, and follow the cemetery wall. At the corner, continue straight down the steps, which lead out of the fortress through a big brick gate. Built into the gate are impressive 18th-century* **military casemates.** *These passageways lead to a chapel-like space (designed for ammunition storage), with six original statues from the Charles Bridge (viewable by tour only).*

Follow the wide, cobbled lane as if you were arriving from Austria 150 years ago. You'll exit the park onto Vratislavova street, which leads downhill, through the neighborhood called...

⓫ Výtoň

On your way to your tram stop, slow down to appreciate this very local-feeling residential neighborhood, which was once a quarter of sailors and fishermen.

About three short blocks down, on the right at #19, notice the faded Art Nouveau house with the red-and-white life preserver in the window. Peek into **Hostinec U Zlaté Kotvy** ("Golden Anchor Guest House")—a spit-and-sawdust fishermen's pub, with simple wood paneling, vintage maps, and photos of lighthouses on the walls. Many who lived in this neighborhood were raftsmen who'd lash together logs from wooded hills in the hinterlands, then float them safely for sale here in Prague.

Keep following Vratislavova as it heads downhill, then curves left. Pause at the park in front of the railway trestle, and look left down the street (Libušina) that forks off toward the river—about halfway down the block on the right, the white house at #3 is one of a smattering of homes in this neighborhood built in the uniquely Czech **Cubist style** of the early 20th century.

Cut through the park and follow the rail trestle to the river. Crossing under the trestle and the busy street that parallels it, you'll see the ⓬ **stop for tram #17** in the middle of the riverside road.

On the corner next to that, sunken into the grassy lawn, is a red-roofed yellow house. This **former customs house** is the only original building that survives from when this was a seamen's quarter. (Today it houses a museum of river commerce.) Like Josefov, the rest of this neighborhood was torn down in the late 19th century and replaced with townhouses more in keeping with the styles of the time—like the Art Nouveau and Cubist houses we've seen in the last few blocks.

Before hopping on the tram, consider crossing the street from the customs house and climbing down the stairs to enjoy Prague's utterly delightful ⓭ **river embankment.** This recently spiffed-up area has become a thriving people zone, with cafés and snack stands filling the walkways and the barges that are lashed nearby—in good weather, there are few more enjoyable places to simply enjoy the city without tourists. And on Saturday mornings, it's even more fun, thanks to a farmers' market (8:00-14:00).

• *From here, it's a straight shot up the riverbank to the town center. Several worthwhile sights are along or near the embankment road; if you're not in a hurry, consider stopping off at some of them. You can enjoy walking the mile and a half up the embankment from here to the Charles Bridge, or you can hop on* **tram #17** *to zip between the stops that interest you. These sights are described in detail starting on page 44 of the "Sights in Prague" chapter:*

• **Palacký Square** *and the adjacent Zítkovy Sady Park, with a* dynamic monument to František Palacký and some fascinating WWII history (Palackého Náměstí tram stop);

• Frank Gehry's **Dancing House** and, just inland, the powerful **National Memorial to the Heroes of the Heydrich Terror** in the crypt of Sts. Cyril and Methodius Church (Jiráskovo Náměstí tram stop);

• the **National Theater,** and—just to the south—the **islands** in the middle of the Vltava, including paddleboat rentals (Národní Divadlo tram stop);

• the **Charles Bridge** (Karlovy Lázně stop); and

• the **Jewish Quarter** (Staroměstská stop).

VYŠEHRAD

SLEEPING IN PRAGUE

Peak months for hotels in Prague are May, June, and September. Easter and New Year's are the most crowded times, when prices are jacked up a bit. Here I've assigned rankings based on peak season pricing. But, if you're traveling in July or August, you'll find rates generally 15 percent lower, and from November through March, about 30 percent lower. It's often possible to negotiate a discount off the official rack rate (a hotel's highest, published rate). Most rack rates are given in euros, so the actual price in crowns may differ somewhat due to currency fluctuations. For tips on hotel rates and deals, making reservations, and other accommodation options—including apartments and other short-term rentals—see page 450.

OLD TOWN HOTELS AND PENSIONS

You'll pay higher prices to stay in the Old Town, but for many travelers, the convenience is worth the expense. These places are all within a 10-minute walk of the Old Town Square.

$$$$ Hotel Metamorphis is a splurge, with solidly renovated rooms in Prague's former caravanserai (hostel for foreign merchants in the 12th century). Its breakfast room is in a spacious medieval cellar with modern artwork. Some of the street-facing rooms, located above two popular bars, are noisy at night (Malá Štupartská 5, tel. 221-771-011, www.hotelmetamorphis.cz, hotel@metamorphis.cz).

$$$$ Hotel Maximilian is a sleek, mod, 71-room place with Art Deco black design; big, plush living rooms; and all the business services and comforts you'd expect in a four-star hotel. It faces a church on a perfect little square just a short walk from the action (Haštalská 14, tel. 225-303-111, www.maximilianhotel.com, reservation@maximilianhotel.com).

$$$$ Design Hotel Jewel Prague (U Klenotníka), with 11

Sleep Code

Hotels are classified based on the average price of a standard double room with breakfast in high season. I've given *very* rough conversions to dollars using 25 Kč = $1.

$$$$ **Splurge:** Most rooms over 3,400 Kč (roughly $135)
$$$ **Pricier:** 2,600-3,400 Kč ($105-135)
$$ **Moderate:** 1,800-2,600 Kč ($70-105)
$ **Budget:** 1,000-1,800 Kč ($40-70)
¢ **Backpacker:** Under 1,000 Kč ($40)
RS% **Rick Steves discount**

Unless otherwise noted, credit cards are accepted, hotel staff speak basic English, and free Wi-Fi is available. Comparison-shop by checking prices at several hotels (on each hotel's own website, on a booking site, or by email). For the best deal, *book directly with the hotel*. Ask for a discount if paying in cash; if the listing includes **RS%,** request a Rick Steves discount.

modern, comfortable rooms in a plain building, is three blocks off the Old Town Square (RS%, no elevator, Rytířská 3, tel. 224-211-699, www.hoteljewelprague.com, info@jewelhotel.cz).

$$$ Brewery Hotel u Medvídků ("By the Bear Cubs") has 43 comfortable rooms in a big, rustic, medieval shell with dark wood furniture. Upstairs, you'll find lots of beams—or, if you're not careful, they'll find you (RS%, "historical" rooms cost slightly more, apartment available, Na Perštýně 7, tel. 224-211-916, www.umedvidku.cz, info@umedvidku.cz, manager Vladimír). The pension runs a popular beer-hall restaurant with live music most Fridays and Saturdays until 23:00—request an inside room for maximum peace.

$$ Green Garland Pension (U Zeleného Věnce), on a central cobbled lane, has a warm and personal feel rare for the Old Town. Located in a thick 14th-century building with open beams, it has a blond-hardwood charm decorated with a woman's touch. The nine clean and simply furnished rooms are two and three floors up, with no elevator (RS%, family room, Řetězová 10, tel. 222-220-178, www.uzv.cz, pension@uzv.cz).

$$ Hotel Haštal is next to Hotel Maximilian (listed earlier) on the same quiet, hidden square in the Old Town. A popular hotel even back in the 1920s, this family-run place has been renovated to complement the neighborhood's vibrant circa-1900 architecture. Its 31 rooms are comfortable and insulated against noise (RS%, free tea, coffee, and wine, air-con, Haštalská 16, tel. 222-314-335, www.hastal.com, info@hastal.com).

Hotels in Prague's Old Town

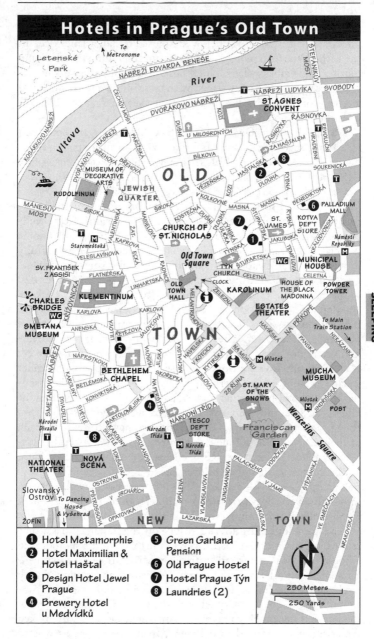

1 Hotel Metamorphis
2 Hotel Maximilian & Hotel Haštal
3 Design Hotel Jewel Prague
4 Brewery Hotel u Medvídků
5 Green Garland Pension
6 Old Prague Hostel
7 Hostel Prague Týn
8 Laundries (2)

250 Meters
250 Yards

SLEEPING

UNDER THE CASTLE, IN THE LITTLE QUARTER

The first and third listings below are buried on quiet lanes deep in the Little Quarter, among cobbles, quaint restaurants, rummaging tourists, and embassy flags. Hotel Julián is a 10-minute walk up the river on a quiet and stately street, with none of the intense medieval cityscape of the others. For locations, see the map on page 222, unless otherwise noted.

$$$$ Vintage Design Hotel Sax's 22 rooms are decorated in a retro, meet-the-Jetsons fashion. With a fruity atrium and a distinctly modern, stark feel, this is a stylish, no-nonsense place (RS%, air-con, elevator, free tea and pastries daily at 17:00, Jánský Vršek 3, tel. 257-531-268, www.sax.cz, hotel@sax.cz).

$$$ Hotel Julián is an oasis of professional, predictable decency in an untouristy neighborhood. Its 33 spacious, fresh, well-furnished rooms and big, homey public spaces hide behind a noble Neoclassical facade. The staff is friendly and helpful (RS%, family rooms, air-con, elevator, plush and inviting lobby, summer roof terrace, parking lot; Metro: Anděl, then take tram #6, #9, #12, or #20 to the left as you leave Metro station for two stops; Elišky Peškové 11, Praha 5, reservation tel. 257-311-150, www.hoteljulian.com, info@julian.cz). Free lockers and a shower are available for those needing a place to stay after checkout (while waiting for an overnight train, for example). For the location, see the map on page 24.

$$$ Dům u Velké Boty ("House at the Big Boot"), on a quiet square in front of the German Embassy, is the rare quintessential family hotel in Prague: homey, comfy, and extremely friendly. Charlotta, Jan, and their two sons treat every guest as a (thirsty) friend, and the wellspring of their stories never runs dry. Each of their 12 rooms is uniquely decorated, most in a tasteful, 19th-century Biedermeier style (RS%, cheaper rooms with shared bath, family rooms, cash only, children up to age 10 sleep free—toys provided, Vlašská 30, tel. 257-532-088, www.dumuvelkeboty.cz, info@dumuvelkeboty.cz). There's no hotel sign on the house—look for the splendid geraniums that Jan nurtures in the windows.

$$ Residence Thunovská, just below the Italian embassy on a relatively quiet staircase leading up to the castle, rents six rooms in a house that once belonged to the Mannerist artist Bartholomeus Sprangler. The all-renovated rooms are historic and equipped with kitchenettes and Italian furniture. The original chimney that runs through the house is inscribed with the date 1577, and the rest of the house is not much younger. The manager, Dean, a soft-spoken American who married into Prague, treats his guests as trusted friends (RS%, breakfast extra—served in the next-door café, Thunovská 19, look for the Consulate of San Marino sign, reception open 9:00-19:00, otherwise on-call, tel. 257-531-189, mobile 721-855-880, www.prague-apartments.org, thunovska@volny.cz).

AWAY FROM THE CENTER

Sleeping just outside central Prague can save you money—and gets you away from other tourists and into more workaday residential neighborhoods. The following listings are great values compared with the downtown hotels listed above, and are all within a short tram or Metro ride from the center. For locations, see the map on page 24, unless otherwise noted.

Beyond Wenceslas Square

These hotels are in urban neighborhoods on the outer fringe of the New Town, beyond Wenceslas Square. But they're still within several minutes' walk of the sightseeing zone and are well-served by trams.

$$$ **Louren Hotel,** with 27 rooms, is a quality four-star, business-class hotel in an upscale, circa-1900 residential neighborhood (Vinohrady) that has become popular with Prague's expat community (RS%, air-con, elevator, 3-minute walk to Metro: Jiřího z Poděbrad, or tram #11, Slezská 55, Praha 3, tel. 224-250-025, www.louren.cz, reservations@louren.cz).

$$$ **Hotel 16** is a sleek and modern business-class place with an intriguing Art Nouveau facade, polished cherry-wood elegance, high ceilings, and 14 fine rooms (RS%, triple-paned windows, free tea, back rooms facing the garden are quieter, air-con, elevator, limited free parking, 10-minute walk south of Wenceslas Square, Metro: I.P. Pavlova, Kateřinská 16, Praha 2, tel. 224-920-636, www.hotel16.cz, hotel16@hotel16.cz).

$$ **Hotel Anna** offers 26 bright, simple, pastel rooms and basic service. It's a bit closer to the action—just 10 minutes by foot east of Wenceslas Square (elevator, Budečská 17, Praha 2, Metro: Náměstí Míru, tel. 222-513-111, www.hotelanna.cz, sales@hotelpro.cz).

The Best Values, Farther from the Center

These accommodations are a 10- to 20-minute tram ride from the center, but once you make the trip, you'll see it's no problem—and you'll feel pretty smug saving $50-100 a night per double by not sleeping in the Old Town. Hotel Adalbert is on the grounds of an ancient monastery, and Pension Větrník is adjacent, with two of Prague's best-preserved natural areas (Star Park and Šárka) just a short walk away. Hotel u Šemíka and Guest House Lída are within a stone's throw of peaceful Vyšehrad Park, with its legendary castle on a cliff overlooking the Vltava River.

$$ **Hotel Adalbert** occupies an 18th-century building in the Břevnov Monastery (one of the Czech Republic's oldest monastic institutions, founded in 993). The monastery complex is the ultimate retreat for those who come to Prague for soul-searching or just a quiet place away from the bustle. Join the Benedictine monks

for morning (7:00) and evening (18:00) Mass in the St. Margaret Basilica, a large and elegant Baroque church decorated with unusual simplicity. You can help yourself in the monastery fruit orchard and eat in the atmospheric monastery pub (Klášterní Šenk). The hotel itself caters primarily to business clientele and takes ecology seriously: recycling, water conservation, and free tram tickets for guests. I prefer the first-floor rooms, as some of the attic rooms—room numbers in the 200s—feel a bit cramped (free parking, halfway between city and airport at Markétská 1, Praha 6, tram #22 to Břevnovský Klášter; 5 minutes by tram beyond the castle, 20 minutes from Old and New Towns; tel. 220-406-170, www. hoteladalbert.cz, recepce@hoteladalbert.cz).

$ **Hotel u Šemíka,** named for a heroic mythical horse, offers 18 rooms in a quiet residential neighborhood just below Vyšehrad Castle and the Slavín cemetery where Dvořák, Mucha, and Čapek are buried. It's a 10-minute tram ride south of the Old Town (RS%, apartment available; from the center, take tram #3, #17, or #21 to Výtoň, go under rail bridge, and walk 3 blocks uphill to Vratislavova 36; Praha 2, tel. 221-965-610, www.usemika.cz, usemika@ usemika.cz).

$ **Pension Větrník** fills an attractive white-and-orange former 18th-century windmill in one of Prague's most popular residential areas, right next to the Břevnov Monastery and midway between the airport and the city. Talkative owner Miloš Opatrný is a retired prizewinning Czech chef. Although the elder Miloš no longer cooks, his namesake grandson has followed in his footsteps—on request, the younger Miloš will gladly prepare an unforgettable meal for you. The six rooms here are the pride of the Opatrný family, who live on the upper floors. The garden has a red-clay tennis court—rackets and balls are provided (U Větrníku 1, Praha 6; airport bus #179 stops near the house, tram #18 goes straight to Charles Bridge, both take 20 minutes; tel. 220-513-390, www.pensionvetrnik.cz, pension@vetrnik1722.cz).

$ **Guest House Lída,** with 12 homey and spacious rooms, fills a big house in a quiet residential area farther inland, a 15-minute tram ride from the center. Jan, Jitka, Jiří, and Jana Prouzas—who run the place—are a wealth of information and know how to make people feel at home (family rooms, top-floor family suite with kitchenette, cash only, pay parking, Metro: Pražského Povstání; exit Metro and turn left on Lomnického between the Metro station and big blue-glass ČSOB building, follow Lomnického for 500 yards, then turn left on Lopatecká, go uphill and ring bell at Lopatecká 26; Praha 4, tel. 261-214-766, www.lidabb.eu, info@ lidabb.eu). The Prouzas brothers also rent two **apartments** across the river, an equal distance from the center).

HOSTELS IN THE CENTER

It's tough to find a double for less than 2,500 Kč in the old center. But Prague has an abundance of fine hostels—each with a distinct personality, and each excellent in its own way for anyone wanting a cheap dorm bed or an extremely simple twin-bedded room for a reasonable price. For travelers seeking low-priced options, keep in mind that hostels are no longer the exclusive domain of backpackers. The first two hostels below are centrally located, but lack care and character; the last two are found in workaday neighborhoods and have atmospheric interiors.

¢ **Old Prague Hostel** is a small, well-worn place on the second and third floors of an apartment building on a back alley near the Powder Tower. The spacious rooms were once apartment bedrooms, so it feels less institutional than most hostels, but the staff can be indifferent and older travelers might feel a bit out of place. The TV lounge/breakfast room is a good hangout (private rooms available, in summer reserve 2 weeks ahead for doubles, a few days ahead for bunks; Benediktská 2, see map on page 203 for location, tel. 224-829-058, www.oldpraguehostel.com, info@oldpraguehostel.com).

¢ **Hostel Prague Týn**—quiet, mature, and sterile—is hidden in a silent courtyard two blocks from the Old Town Square. The management is very aware of its valuable location, so they don't have to bother being friendly (private rooms available, reserve one week ahead, Týnská 19, see map on page 203 for location, tel. 224-808-301, www.hostelpraguetyn.com, info@hostelpraguetyn.com).

¢ **Sir Toby's** is in a 1930s working-class neighborhood—a popular residential and dining-out area that's a 12-minute tram ride from the center. The owners have taken great pains to stamp the place with character: hardwood floors, a back garden with tables made out of sewing machines, rooms filled with vintage 1930s furniture and photographs, an on-site pub, and a friendly staff (private rooms available; from the Main Train Station, take Metro line C red to the Vltavska stop, then tram #1, #14, or #25 to Dělnická; at Dělnická 24, Praha 7, see map on page 24 for location, tel. 246-032-610, www.sirtobys.com, info@sirtobys.com). The owners also run two contemporary-design hostels in Vinohrady.

¢ **Hostel Elf,** a 10-minute walk from the main train station or one bus stop from the Florenc Metro station, is fun-loving, ramshackle, covered with noisy, self-inflicted graffiti, and the wildest of these hostels. They offer cheap, basic beds, a helpful staff, and creative services—free luggage room, no lockout, free tea and coffee, cheap beer, and a terrace (private rooms available, reserve four days ahead, Husitská 11, Praha 3, take bus #133 or #207 from Florenc Metro station for one stop to U Památníku, see map on page 24 for location, tel. 222-540-963, www.hostelelf.com, info@hostelelf.com).

ROOM-BOOKING SERVICES

Prague is awash with fancy rooms on the push list; private, small-time operators with rooms to rent in their apartments; and roving agents eager to book you a bed and earn a commission. You can save about 30 percent by showing up without a reservation and finding accommodations upon arrival. However, it can be a hassle, and you won't likely get your ideal choice. If you're coming in by train or car, you'll encounter booking agencies. They can almost always find you a reasonable room, and, if it's in a private guesthouse, your host can even come and lead you to the place. Be clear on the location before you make your choice.

Athos Travel has a line on 200 properties ranging from hostels to five-star hotels, most of which are in the Old Town (best to arrange in advance during peak season, can also help with last-minute booking off-season, tel. 241-440-571, www.a-prague.com, info@a-prague.com). Readers report that Athos is aggressive with its business policies—although there's no fee if you cancel well in advance, they strictly enforce penalties on cancellations within 48 hours.

Touristpoint, at the main train station (Hlavní Nádraží), is another booking service (daily 8:00-22:00). They represent a slew of hotels and small pensions (moderately priced pension doubles in the Old Town, budget doubles a Metro ride away). You can reserve online, using your credit card as a deposit (tel. 224-946-010, www.touristpoint.cz, info@touristpoint.cz), or just show up at the office and request a room.

Lída Jánská's **Magic Praha** can help with accommodations (mobile 604-207-225, www.magicpraha.cz, magicpraha@magicpraha.cz; see "Helpful Hints" on page 27). Lída also rents a well-situated apartment with a river view near the Jewish Quarter.

EATING IN PRAGUE

A big part of Prague's charm is found in wandering aimlessly through the city's winding old quarters, marveling at the architecture, watching the people, and sniffing out fun restaurants. You can eat well here for relatively little money. What you'd pay for a basic meal in Vienna or Munich will get you a memorable dining experience in Prague. In addition to meat-and-potatoes Czech cuisine, you'll find trendy, student-oriented bars and lots of fine ethnic eateries. For ambience, the options include traditional, dark Czech beer halls; elegant Art Nouveau dining rooms; and hip, modern cafés.

Remember, there are two parallel worlds in Prague: the tourist town and the real city. Generally, if you walk just a few minutes away from the tourist flow, you'll find better value, atmosphere, and service. The more touristy a place is, the more likely you'll pay too much—either in inflated prices or because waiters pad the bill. It's smart to closely examine your itemized bill and understand each line. At touristy places, they may automatically tack on a 10 percent service charge; if you see this, there's no need to tip extra. If service is not included, locals tip by rounding up (usually 5 to 10 percent for good service—but never more). But stubborn tourists have trained local servers to expect American-size tips (15 percent or more) from their American customers. Not wanting to contribute to this overtipping epidemic, I still tip on the lower, local end of the scale. While many places accept credit cards, I usually pay for meals in cash—it seems to make waiters happier.

I've listed eating and drinking establishments by neighborhood. Most of the options—and highest prices—are in the Old Town. For a light meal, consider one of Prague's many cafés (see page 227). Many of the places listed here are handy for an efficient lunch, but may not offer fine evening dining. Others make

Restaurant Price Code

I've assigned each eatery a price category, based on the average cost of a typical main course. Drinks, desserts, and splurge items (steak and seafood) can raise the price considerably. I've given *very* rough conversions to dollars using 25 Kč = $1.

$$$$ Splurge: Most main courses over 500 Kč (roughly $20)

$$$ Pricier: 250-500 Kč ($10-20)

$$ Moderate: 120-250 Kč ($5-10)

$ Budget: Under 120 Kč ($5)

In the Czech Republic, a pub, basic sit-down eatery, and less-touristy café or teahouse is **$**; a typical restaurant—or a fancy café with coffee over 50 Kč and tea over 100 Kč—is **$$**; an upscale restaurant is **$$$**; and a swanky splurge is **$$$$**.

less sense for lunch, but are great for a slow, drawn-out dinner. Read the descriptions to judge which is which.

Unlike most European countries, the Czech Republic permits smoking in restaurants and cafés. I've noted those that are either more or less smoky than the norm. For general advice on eating in the Czech Republic, including details on tipping, budget meals, and Czech cuisine and beverages, see page 456.

Fun, Touristy Neighborhoods: Several areas are pretty and well-situated for sightseeing, but lined only with touristy restaurants. While these places are not necessarily bad values, I've listed only a few of your many options—just survey the scene in these spots and choose whatever looks best. **Kampa Square,** just off the Charles Bridge, feels like a small-town square. **Havelská Market** is surrounded by colorful little eateries, any of which offer a nice perch for viewing the market scene while you munch. The massive **Old Town Square** is the place to nurse a drink or enjoy a meal while watching the tide of people, both tourists and locals, sweep back and forth. There's often some event on this main square, and its many restaurants provide tasty and relaxing vantage points.

Traditional Czech Places: It's getting difficult to find a truly Czech pub in the historic city center, as many cheap student pubs have been replaced by shops and hotels that make more money. Most Czechs no longer go to "traditional" eateries, preferring the cosmopolitan taste of the world to the mundane taste of sauerkraut. As a result, ancient institutions with "authentic" Czech ambience have become touristy—but they're still great fun, a good value, and respected by locals. Expect wonderfully rustic spaces, smoke, surly service, and reasonably good, inexpensive food. Understand every line on your bill. I've listed several of these characteristically Czech eateries throughout this chapter.

Dining with a View: For great views, consider these options, all described in detail in the following pages: **Hotel u Prince's terrace** (rooftop dining above a fancy hotel, completely touristy but with awesome views); **Villa Richter** (next to Prague Castle, above Malostranská Metro stop); **Bellavista Restaurant** at the Strahov Monastery; **Petřínské Terasy** and **Nebozízek** (next to the funicular stop halfway up Petřín Hill); and **Čertovka** in the Little Quarter (superb views of the Charles Bridge). Another lofty dining perch is the **Oblaca** restaurant and café 200 feet up in the Žižkov TV tower east of downtown (see page 226). For the best cheap riverside dinner, have a picnic on a paddleboat (see page 39). There's nothing like drifting down the middle of the Vltava River as the sun sets, while munching on a picnic meal and sipping a beer with your favorite travel partner.

Cheap-and-Cheery Sandwich Shops: All around town you'll find modern little sandwich shops (like the Panería chain) offering inexpensive fresh-made sandwiches (grilled if you like), pastries, salads, and drinks. You can get the food to go, or eat inside at simple tables.

Groceries and Farmers Markets: Ask your hotelier for the location of the nearest grocery store; it'll probably be small, stocked with what you need, and close by. Or check out the farmer-supplied grocery called **Grunt,** which offers lots of fresh products (in the Old Town at Národni 21).

Farmers markets crop up around the city and tantalize picnickers. Apart from vegetables, you'll find quality cheeses, juices, cakes, coffee, and more (www.farmarsketrziste.cz). The most central and touristy is the **Havelská Market** in the Old Town (also has handicrafts, daily 9:00-18:00, see page 113) The most scenic is the **Náplavka** ("River Landing") market on the Vltava embankment, just south of the Palacký Bridge; the original and biggest market is on **Vítězné Náměstí** at the Dejvická Metro stop (both Sat 8:00-14:00). A smaller farmers market enlivens the heart of the trendy **Žižkov** neighborhood on Wednesday, Friday, and Saturday mornings (at Metro stop Náměstí Jiřího z Poděbrad—you could combine a visit with a trip up the nearby Žižkov TV tower). And another is on **Republic Square** (Náměstí Republiky) from Tuesdays through Fridays, at the entrance to the Old Town (www.farmarsketrhyprahy1.cz).

IN THE OLD TOWN
Traditional Czech
$$ Restaurace u Provaznice ("By the Ropemaker's Wife") has all the Czech classics, peppered with the story of a once-upon-a-time-faithful wife. (Check the menu for details of the gory story.) Natives congregate under bawdy frescoes for the famously good

Prague Restaurants in Old & New Towns

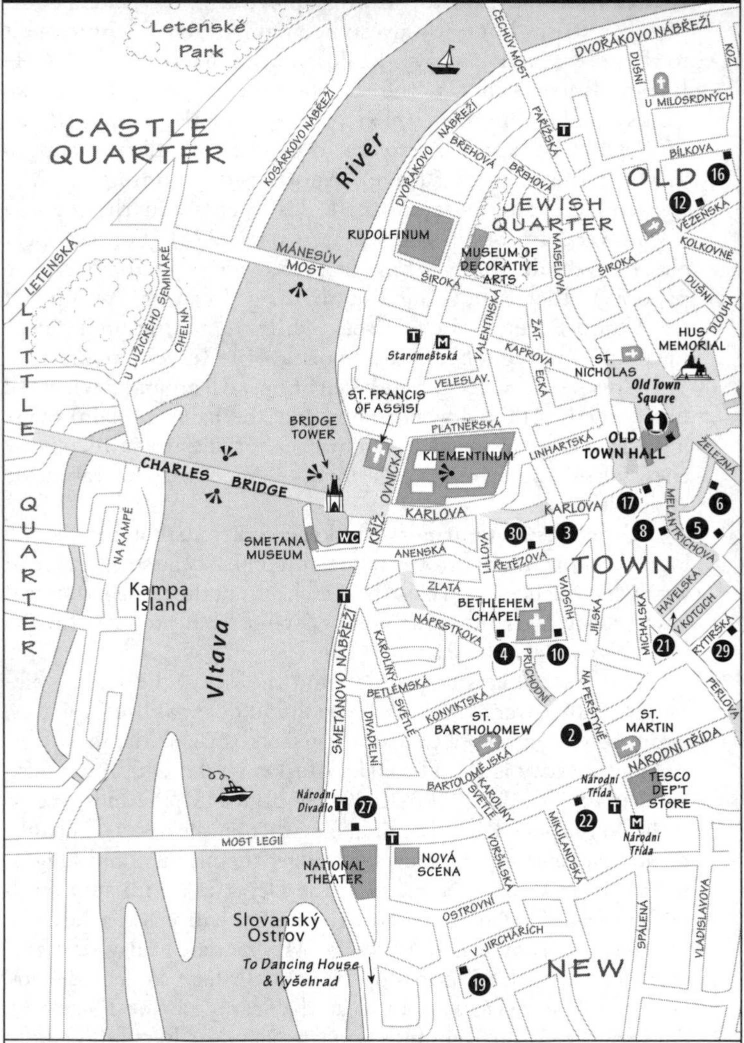

EATING

1. Restaurace u Provaznice
2. U Medvídků Beer Hall
3. U Zlatého Tygra Pub
4. Restaurace u Betlémské Kaple
5. Česká Kuchyně
6. Restaurace Mlejnice
7. Lokál Restaurant
8. Country Life Vegetarian Restaurant
9. Beas Cafeteria
10. Klub Architektů
11. Chez Marcel
12. Amici Miei Restaurant
13. Ariana Afghan Restaurant
14. Indian Jewel
15. James Joyce Irish Pub
16. La Casa Blú
17. Hotel/Restaurant u Prince Terasa
18. Restaurace u Pinkasů

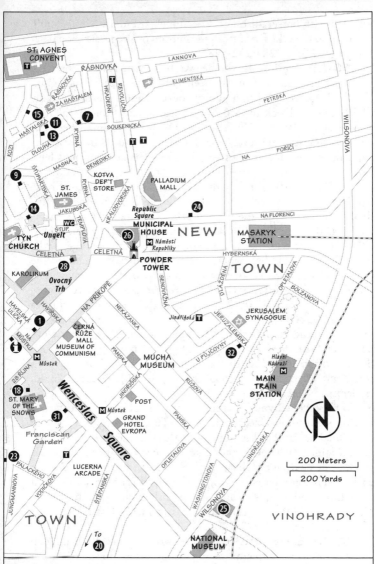

EATING

⑲ Hospoda u Nováka	㉗ Kavárna Slavia
⑳ To Pivovarský Dům	㉘ Grand Café Orient
㉑ Havelská Market	㉙ Café Café
㉒ Le Patio & Café Louvre	㉚ Café Montmartre & Ebel Coffee House
㉓ Pasha Kebab Turkish Restaurant	㉛ Dobrá Čajovna Teahouse
㉔ Brasserie La Gare	㉜ Čajový Klub
㉕ Kavárna Muzeum Café	
㉖ Municipal House Eateries	

"pig leg" with horseradish and Czech mustard (daily 11:00-24:00, a block into the Old Town from the bottom of Wenceslas Square at Provaznická 3, tel. 224-232-528).

$$ U Medvídků ("By the Bear Cubs") started out as a brewery in 1466 and is now a flagship beer hall of the Czech Budweiser. The one large room is bright, noisy, touristy, and a bit smoky (daily 11:30-23:00, a block toward Wenceslas Square from Bethlehem Square at Na Perštýně 7, tel. 224-211-916). The small beer bar next to the restaurant (daily 16:00 until late) is used by university students during emergencies—such as after most other pubs have closed.

$ U Zlatého Tygra ("By the Golden Tiger") has long embodied the proverbial Czech pub, where beer turns strangers into kindred spirits, who cross the fuzzy line between memory and imagination as they tell their hilarious life stories to each other. Today, "The Tiger" is a buzzing shrine to one of its longtime regulars, the writer Bohumil Hrabal, whose fictions immortalize many of the colorful characters that once warmed the wooden benches here. Only regulars have reserved tables. To get a spot, arrive around opening time (daily 15:00-23:00, just south of Karlova at Husova 17, tel. 222-221-111).

$ Restaurace u Betlémské Kaple, behind Bethlehem Chapel, is not "ye olde" Czech. It has light wooden decor, cheap lunch deals, and fish specialties that attract natives and visitors in search of a good Czech bite for good Czech prices (daily 11:00-23:00, Betlémské Náměstí 2, tel. 222-221-639).

$ Česká Kuchyně ("Czech Kitchen") is a blue-collar cafeteria serving steamy old Czech cuisine. It's fast, practical, cheap, and traditional as can be. Pick up your tally sheet as you enter, grab a tray, point to whatever you'd like, and keep the paper to pay as you exit. It's extremely cheap...unless you lose your paper. As you enter, you'll come across serving stations in this order: salads, fruit dumplings and sweets, soups, main dishes, and finally, drinks (daily 9:00-20:00, very central, across from Havelská Market at Havelská 23, tel. 224-235-574).

$$ Restaurace Mlejnice ("The Mill") is a fun little pub strewn with farm implements and happy eaters, located just out of the tourist crush two blocks from the Old Town Square. They serve hearty traditional and modern Czech plates. Reservations are smart in the evening (daily 11:00-24:00, between Melantrichova and Železná at Kožná 14, tel. 224-228-635, www.restaurace-mlejnice.cz/en).

$$ Lokál ("The Neighborhood Dump") is a hit with residents for its good-quality Czech classics. Filling a long, arched space, the restaurant plays on customers' nostalgia: The stark interior is a deliberate 1980s retro design, and the waiters have been instructed to be curt (but not impolite)—just as if they were serving in one of Prague's notorious train station "dumps." Reservations are smart (daily 11:00 until late, ask for English menu at the front by the tap, Dlouhá 33, tel. 222-316-265, www.lokal-dlouha.ambi.cz/en). The same group has a smaller branch, **Lokál u Bílé Kuželky,** in the Little Quarter (see listing later).

Vegetarian and Modern
These hip and trendy places have a fun, youthful vibe.

$$ Country Life Vegetarian Restaurant is a bright, easy, nonsmoking cafeteria with a well-displayed buffet of salads and hot veggie dishes. It's midway between the Old Town Square and the bottom of Wenceslas Square. They're serious about their vegetarianism, serving only plant-based, unprocessed, and unrefined food. Its quiet dining area is elegant for a cafeteria, with a few tables outside in the courtyard (pay by weight, Sun-Thu 9:00-20:30, Fri 9:00-17:00, closed Sat, through courtyard at Melantrichova 15/Michalská 18, tel. 224-213-366).

$$ Beas Cafeteria, a little vegetarian restaurant, is ruled by a Punjabi chef. Diners grab a steel tray and scoop up whatever looks good, typically various choices of *dal* (lentils) and *sabji* (vegetables) with rice or *chapati* (pancakes). The food is sold by weight—you'll likely spend 130 Kč for lunch. Tucked away in a courtyard behind the Týn Church, this place is popular with university students and young professionals (Mon-Fri 11:00-20:00, Sat-Sun from 12:00, Sun until 18:00, Týnská 19, mobile 608-035-727).

$$$ Klub Architektů, next to Bethlehem Chapel, is a modern hangout in a cave-like medieval cellar that also has straw-chair seating outside. The fun menu includes excellent original dishes, hearty salads, Moravian wines, and Slovak beer (daily 11:30-24:00, Betlémské Náměstí 169, tel. 224-248-878).

Beware that two popular Prague vegetarian restaurants, **Lehká Hlava** ("Clear Head") and **Maitrea** (a.k.a. "Buddha of the Future"), are owned by Antonín Koláček, a former manager of a state-controlled brown coal company (and more recently a Buddhist philanthropist) who was convicted in 2013 in a Swiss court as the mastermind behind a 1990s fraudulent privatization scheme that robbed the country of at least three billion crowns.

Ethnic Eateries and Bars
Dlouhá, the wide street leading away from the Old Town Square behind the Jan Hus Memorial, is lined with ethnic restaurants catering mostly to cosmopolitan locals. Within a couple of blocks, you can eat your way around the world. From Dlouhá, wander the Rámová/Haštalská/Vězeňská area to survey a United Nations of eateries: You'll find French (**Chez Marcel** at Haštalská 12); Italian

Czech Beer

Czechs are among the world's most enthusiastic beer *(pivo)* drinkers—adults drink an average of 80 gallons a year. The pub is a place to have fun, complain, discuss art and politics, talk hockey, and chat with locals and visitors alike. Whether you're in a *restaurace* (restaurant), *hostinec* (pub), or *hospoda* (bar), a beer will land on your table upon the slightest hint to the waiter, and a new pint will automatically appear when the old glass is almost empty (until you tell the waiter to stop). Order beer from the tap *(točené* means "draft," *sudové pivo* means "keg beer"). A *pivo* is large (0.5 liter—17 oz); a *malé pivo* is small (0.3 liter—10 oz).

The Czechs perfected a Bavarian's invention—Pilsner-style lager—in nearby Plzeň and the result, Pilsner Urquell, is on tap in many local pubs. But the Czechs produce plenty of other good beers; most of the famous brands, including Krušovice, Gambrinus, Staropramen, and Kozel, are owned internationally. Budvar, from the town of Budějovice ("Budweis" in German), is the last state-owned (and as locals like to point out, mismanaged) brewery. For years, the Czech and the American breweries disputed the "Budweiser" brand name. The solution: Czech Budweiser is sold under its own name in Europe, China, and Africa, while in America it is marketed as Czechvar.

(the expensive **Amici Miei** at Vězeňská 5, which prides itself on fresh *pesci* and *frutti di mare*); and Afghan (**Ariana** at Rámová 6).

These places deserve special consideration:

Indian: $$$ Indian Jewel, in the Ungelt courtyard behind the Týn Church, is the best place in Prague to find a full Indian menu that actually tastes Indian. Located in a pleasant, artfully restored courtyard, this is my choice for outdoor dining, with seriously executed sub-Continental classics and good-value lunch specials (daily specials, daily 11:00-23:00, Týn 6, tel. 222-310-156).

Irish: $ James Joyce Irish Pub may seem like a strange recommendation in Prague—home of some of the world's best beer—but it has the kind of ambience that locals (and few tourists) seek out. Expats have favored this pub (formerly known as Molly Malone's) for Guinness ever since the Velvet Revolution enabled the Celts to return to one of their homelands. Worn wooden floors, dingy walls, and the Irish manager transport you right into the heart of blue-collar Dublin—a popular place for young Czechs to seek jobs

The big degree symbol on beer bottles doesn't indicate alcohol content. Instead, it is a measurement used by brewers to track the density of certain ingredients. As a rough guide, 10 degrees is about 3.5 percent alcohol, 12 degrees is about 4.2 percent alcohol, and 11 and 15 degrees are dark beers. The most popular Czech beers are about as potent as German beers and only slightly stronger than typical American brews.

Each establishment has only one brand of beer on tap; to try a particular kind, look for its sign outside. A typical pub serves only one brand each of 10-degree, 12-degree, and dark beer. Czechs don't mix beer with anything, and they don't hop from pub to pub (in one night, it is said, you must stay loyal to one woman and to one beer). *Na zdraví* means "to your health" in Czech.

While the trend for much of the last 20 years has been for the biggest beer corporations to buy up or edge out the smaller companies, Czechs have been moving beyond "eurotaste" beers to creative microbrews. Now, more and more restaurants are making their own beer or serving beer only from independent breweries.

On the other hand, alcoholism is cited as the chief cause of homelessness in the country, leading many to question the ethics of a culture in which beer costs less than bottled water.

in the high-tech industry before the recession (daily 11:00 until late, U Obecního Dvora 4, tel. 224-818-851).

Latin American: $$ La Casa Blů, with cheap lunch specials, Mexican plates, Staropramen beer, and greenish mojitos, is your own little pueblo in Prague. It's one of the last student bastions in the Old Town. Painted in warm oranges and reds, energized by upbeat music, and guarded by creatures from Mayan mythology, La Casa Blů attracts a fiesta of happy eaters and drinkers (Mon-Sat 11:00-23:00, Sun 14:00-23:00, nonsmoking, on the corner of Kozí and Bílkova, tel. 224-818-270).

In the Jewish Quarter

These eateries are well-placed to break up a demanding tour of the Jewish Quarter—all within two blocks of each other on or near Široká (see map on page 125). Also consider the nearby ethnic eateries listed above.

$$$ Kolkovna, the flagship restaurant of a chain allied with Pilsner Urquell, is big and woody yet modern, serving a fun mix of

EATING

Czech and international cuisine—ribs, salads, cheese plates, and beer. It feels a tad formulaic...but not in a bad way (a bit overpriced, daily 11:00-24:00, across from Spanish Synagogue at V Kolkovně 8, tel. 224-819-701).

$$ Kolonial ("Bicycle Place"), across the street from the Pinkas Synagogue, has a modern interior playing on the bicycle theme, six beers on tap, and an imaginative menu drawing from Czech, French, Italian, and Spanish cuisine (daily specials, daily 9:00-24:00, Široká 6, tel. 224-818-322).

$ Restaurace u Knihovny ("By the Library"), situated steps away from the City and National libraries as well as the Pinkas Synagogue, is a favorite lunch spot for locals who work nearby. The cheap daily lunch specials consist of seven variations on traditional Czech themes. The service is friendly, and the stylish red-brick interior is warm (daily 11:00-23:00, nonsmoking at lunch, on the corner of Veleslavínova and Valentinská, mobile 732-835-876).

$$$ Dinitz Kosher Restaurant, around the corner from the Spanish Synagogue, is the most low-key and reasonably priced of the kosher restaurants in the Jewish Quarter (Shabbat meals by prepaid reservation only, Sun-Thu 11:30-22:30, Fri 11:30-14:30, Bílkova 12, tel. 222-244-000, www.dinitz.cz). For Shabbat meals, the fancier **$$$ King Solomon Restaurant** is a better value (Široká 8, tel. 224-818-752, www.kosher.cz).

Dining with an Old Town Square View

The **$$$$ Hotel u Prince Terasa,** atop the five-star hotel facing the Astronomical Clock, is designed for foreign tourists. A sleek elevator takes you to the rooftop terrace, where every possible inch is used to serve good food (international with plenty of fish) from their open-air grill. The view is arguably the best in town—especially at sunset. The menu is a fun but overpriced mix, with photos that make ordering easy. Being in such a touristy spot, rude waiters are experts at nicking you with confusing menu charges; don't be afraid to confirm exact prices before ordering. This place is also great for a drink at sunset or late at night (fine salads, daily until 24:00, brusque staff, outdoor heaters, Staroměstské Náměstí 29, tel. 224-213-807, no reservations possible).

IN THE NEW TOWN
Traditional Czech

$$ Restaurace u Pinkasů, founded in 1843, is known among locals as the first place to serve Pilsner beer. You can sit in its traditional interior, in front to watch the street action, or out back in a garden shaded by the Gothic buttresses of the St. Mary of the Snows Church. While the prices are straightforward, some of the waiters could win the rudest-service award (daily 9:00-24:00, near the bottom of Wenceslas Square, between the Old Town and New Town, Jungmannovo Náměstí 16, tel. 221-111-150).

$ Hospoda u Nováka, behind the National Theater, is emphatically Czech, with few tourists. It takes good care of its regulars (you'll see the old monthly beer tabs in a rack just inside the door). Nostalgic communist-era signs are everywhere. During that time, pubs like this were close-knit communities where regulars escaped from the depression of daily life. Today, the U Nováka is a bright and smoky hangout where you can still happily curse whatever regime you happen to live under. While the English menu lists the well-executed Czech classics, it doesn't list the cheap daily specials—ask (daily 10:00-23:00, V Jirchářích 2, tel. 224-930-639).

$$ Pivovarský Dům ("The Brewhouse"), on the corner of Ječná and Lípová, is popular with locals for its rare variety of fresh beers (yeast, wheat, and fruit-flavored), fine classic Czech dishes, and an inviting interior that mixes traditional and modern (daily 11:00-23:00, reservations recommended in the evenings, variety of beer mugs sold; walk up Štěpánská street from Wenceslas Square for 10 minutes, or take tram #22 for two stops from Národní to Štěpánská; Lípová 15, tel. 296-216-666, www.pivovarskydum. com).

Modern and Ethnic

$ Pivovarský Klub ("The Brew Club," related to Pivovarský Dům, above) serves the widest selection of Czech microbrews in town in a modern, blond-wood restaurant. Every week different beers are featured on tap on the ground floor, while small breweries hold regular presentations in the basement (daily 11:30-23:30, evening reservations recommended; about 50 yards on the left along Křižíkova from Florenc Metro station, Křižíkova 17, see map on page 24 for location, tel. 222-315-7770, www.pivovarskyklub.com).

$$$ Le Patio, on the big and busy Národní Třída, has a hip, continental feel. But for a place that also sells furniture (head straight back and down the stairs), it definitely needs comfier dining chairs. Hanging lanterns and live music (Fri-Sat) contribute to the pleasant atmosphere. Dishes are from India, France, and points in between, and a serious vegetarian option is always available (daily 8:00-23:00, Národní 22, tel. 224-934-375).

$ Pasha Kebab Turkish Restaurant, near the bottom of Wenceslas Square, has American fast-food-chain ambience, good ingredients, and wonderful, authentic ready-to-eat Turkish dishes (daily 10:00-22:00, a block from Můstek Metro stop, just beyond Franciscan garden at Jungmannova 27, tel. 224-948-481).

$$ Brasserie La Gare, just off Republic Square (Náměstí Republiky), opened with the mission to prove to Czechs that French food can be simple and inexpensive. The menu includes such classics as *escargots de Bourgogne* and coq au vin. The red-hued, modern interior also contains a French bakery and a deli (lunch specials, daily 11:00-24:00, V Celnici 3, tel. 222-313-712).

$ Kavárna Muzeum, in the former communist parliament building (now part of the National Museum) at Wenceslas Square, offers daily menus, freshly roasted coffee, soups, and sandwiches in a pleasant, kid-friendly setting (daily 10:00-19:00, Vinohradská 1, tel. 224-284-511).

Art Nouveau Splendor in the Municipal House

The Municipal House (Obecní Dům), the sumptuous Art Nouveau concert hall, has three restaurants: a café, a French restaurant, and a

beer cellar (all at Náměstí Republiky 5). The dressy café, **$$$ Kavárna Obecní Dům,** is drenched in chandeliered, Art Nouveau elegance and offers the best value and experience here. Light, pricey meals and drinks come with great atmosphere and bad service (daily 7:30-23:00, live piano or jazz trio 16:00-20:00, tel. 222-002-763). The fine and formal **$$$$ French restaurant** in the next wing oozes Mucha elegance (daily 12:00-16:00 & 18:00-23:00, tel. 222-002-777). The **beer cellar** is overpriced and touristy (daily 11:30-23:00).

IN THE LITTLE QUARTER

These characteristic eateries are handy for a bite before or after your Prague Castle visit.

$$ Malostranská Beseda, in the impeccably restored former Town Hall, weaves together an imaginative menu of traditional Czech dishes (both classic and little known), vegetarian fare, and fresh fish. It feels a bit sterile and formulaic, but that follows a local trend. You can choose among three settings: the nonsmoking ground-floor restaurant on the left; the café on the right (serves meals, but it's OK to have only coffee or cake); or the packed beer hall downstairs, where Pilsner Urquell is served well (daily 11:00-23:00, Malostranské Náměstí 21, tel. 257-409-112). The restaurant has a recommended music club upstairs.

$$ Lokál u Bílé Kuželky ("By the White Bowling Pin"), a branch of the Old Town's recommended Lokál restaurant, is the best bet for quick, cheap, well-executed Czech classics on this side of the river (Mon-Fri 11:30-24:00, Sat-Sun 12:00-22:00, nonsmoking section, Míšeňská 12; from the Charles Bridge, turn right around the U Tří Pštrosů Hotel just before the Little Quarter gate; tel. 257-212-014).

$$ Lo Veg Restaurant, on the top two floors and a tiny terrace of a narrow medieval house, serves vegan variations on Czech classics as well as Asian fare. The setting is a tasteful mix of Renaissance roof beams, Balinese art, and gorgeous vistas (daily 11:30-22:00, Nerudova 36, mobile 702-901-060).

$$ Green Spirit Vegetarian Bistro and Café, on a quiet walnut tree-shaded patio next to the Gothic walls of St. Lawrence Church, is a snug, family-run place with an eclectic menu including burritos, pizzas, cakes, and salads (Mon-Fri 10:00-20:00, Sat-Sun from 11:00, Hellichova 14, tel. 257-317-459).

$$ Pastař ("The Pasta Maker"), across the bridge from the National Theater, is serious about freshly made pasta, pickled vegetables, and fresh-squeezed juices. It's part of a larger Czech trend of relying on small producers "with a story." Their deli bistro, with its cheeses and olives, can stock you up for a boating or riverside picnic (daily 11:30-23:00, Malostranské Nábřeží 558, mobile 777-009-108).

$ U Zavěšenýho Kafe a Divadlo Pokračuje ("By the Hanging Coffee" and "The Show Goes On"), just below Loreta Square

on the way to the castle, is a creative little pub/restaurant that has attracted a cult following among Prague's cognoscenti. You can "hang" a coffee here for a local vagabond by paying for an extra coffee on your way out (daily 11:00-24:00, Loretánská 13, mobile 605-294-595).

$ U Hrocha ("By the Hippo"), a small authentic pub with tar dripping from its walls, is packed with beer drinkers. Expect simple, traditional meals—basically meat starters with bread. Just below the castle near Little Quarter Square (Malostranské Náměstí), it's actually the haunt of many members of parliament, which is around the corner (daily 12:00-23:00, chalkboard lists daily meals in English, Thunovská 10, tel. 257-533-389).

$$ Vinograf Wine Bar is a small, intimate place with just eight tables. It's run by Czech wine-lover Karel, who enjoys helping visitors appreciate his wines. He prepares a daily list of Czech wines available by the glass and serves meat-and-cheese plates for wine tasters who'd like a light meal (daily 16:00-24:00, a few steps off the end of Charles Bridge at Míšeňská 8, next to Lokál, tel. 603-116-085).

$$$$ Čertovka, down an alley so narrow that it requires a signal to regulate foot traffic, offers outdoor seating on two small

Restaurants & Hotels in the Little Quarter & Castle Quarter

EATING

Eateries & Entertainment

1. Malostranská Beseda Restaurant & Club
2. Lokál U Bílé Kuželky & Vinograf Wine Bar
3. Lo Veg Restaurant
4. Green Spirit Vegetarian Bistro & Café
5. Pastař Restaurant
6. U Zavěšenýho Kafe a Divadlo Pokračuje
7. U Hrocha Pub
8. Čertovka
9. Cukrkávalimonáda Bistro
10. Restaurant Savoy
11. Petřínské Terasy Restauran
12. Nebozízek Restaurant
13. Bellavista Restaurant
14. Villa Richter Eateries
15. Klášterní Pivovar
16. Host Restaurant
17. Hostinec u Černého Vola Pub
18. Malý Buddha Veggie Rest.
19. U Labutí Restaurant
20. Café Salmovský Palác
21. Kavárna ve Šternberském Paláci
22. Kavárna Nový Svět
23. Lobkowicz Palace Café

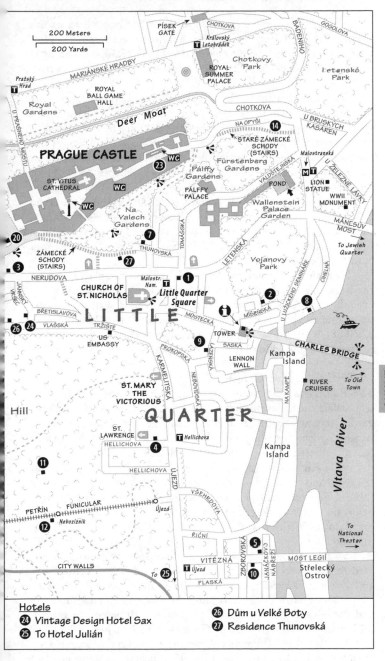

200 Meters
200 Yards

PÍSEK GATE
CHOTKOVA
Královský Letohrádek
Chotkovy Park
Letenský Park
BADENIHO
GOGOLOVA
ROYAL SUMMER PALACE
MARIÁNSKÉ HRADBY
Pražský Hrad
Royal Gardens
ROYAL BALL GAME HALL
CHOTKOVA
Deer Moat
NA OPYŠI
STARÉ ZÁMECKÉ SCHODY (STAIRS)
14
U BRUSKÝCH KASÁREN
PRAGUE CASTLE
WC
23
Fürstenberg Gardens
Pálffy Gardens
Malostranská
M T
LION STATUE
WWII MONUMENT
U ŽELEZNÉ LÁVKY
ST. VITUS CATHEDRAL
WC
WC
PÁLFFY PALACE
Na Valech Gardens
TOMÁŠSKÁ
Wallenstein Palace Garden
POND
VALDŠTEJNSKÁ
MÁNESŮV MOST
20
ZÁMECKÉ SCHODY (STAIRS)
27
THUNOVSKÁ
7
LETENSKÁ
Vojanovy Park
To Jewish Quarter
3
NERUDOVA
CHURCH OF ST. NICHOLAS
Malostr. Nam.
Little Quarter Square
1
U LUŽICKÉHO SEMINÁŘE
CHELNÁ
JÁNSKÝ VRŠEK
BŘETISLAVOVA
LITTLE
MOSTECKÁ
MÍŠEŇSKÁ
2
8
26
24
VLAŠSKÁ
TRŽIŠTĚ
TOWER
1
US EMBASSY
PROKOPSKÁ
9
SASKÁ
CHARLES BRIDGE
Kampa Island
LAZENSKÁ
LENNON WALL
NA KAMPĚ
RIVER CRUISES
To Old Town
ST. MARY THE VICTORIOUS
KARMELITSKÁ
NEBOVIDSKÁ
QUARTER
Hill
ST. LAWRENCE
Hellichova
4
Kampa Island
HELLICHOVA
HELLICHOVA
ÚJEZD
Vltava River
11
VŠEHRDOVA
PETŘÍN
FUNICULAR
Újezd
ŘÍČNÍ
To National Theater
12
Neboziznk
5
ZBOROVSKÁ
VÍTĚZNÁ
MOST LEGII
JANÁČKOVO NÁBŘ.
IZMADNÍ
Střelecký Ostrov
CITY WALLS
To
25
Újezd
PLASKÁ
10

EATING

<u>Hotels</u>
24 Vintage Design Hotel Sax
25 To Hotel Julián
26 Dům u Velké Boty
27 Residence Thunovská

terraces right on the water, with some of the best views of the Charles Bridge. Given the location, the prices are reasonable, but waiters don't bother being nice (daily 11:30-23:30, off the little square at U Lužického Semináře 24, no reservations taken, arrive early to claim a spot, tel. 257-534-524).

$$ Cukrkávalimonáda ("Sugar, Coffee, Lemonade") is part restaurant and part patisserie, serving big salads, ciabatta sandwiches, artful pastries, and freshly squeezed juice in a setting mixing old and new decor. The bistro—an oasis just a block away from the tourist crush—is 50 yards down the first street to the left after you exit the Charles Bridge (Mon-Sat 9:00-23:00, Sun 9:00-19:00, Lázeňská 7, tel. 257-225-396).

$$$ Restaurant Savoy, at the foot of the Legií Bridge, is the closest you'll get to Parisian food culture in Prague—with exquisite dishes, thoughtful service, and elegant Art Deco surroundings (lunch specials, Mon-Fri 8:00-22:30, Sat-Sun 9:00-22:30, Vítězná 5, tel. 257-311-562).

Near the Funicular, on Petřín Hill: These two places are near the funicular stop halfway up Petřín Hill, and offer great views over the city. **$$$ Petřínské Terasy** has woody seating indoors, or outside on the terrace (daily 12:00-23:00; Petřín 393, tel. 257-320-688), while **$$$$ Nebozízek** is more modern, with glassed-in seating (cash only, daily 11:00-23:00, Petřín 411, tel. 257-315-329).

IN THE CASTLE QUARTER

$$$ Bellavista Restaurant is in the garden of the Strahov Monastery, where the abbot himself would come to meditate in a peaceful garden setting. You'll pay for the amazing city views, but if the weather's nice, this is a good value, with traditional grilled meats, pasta, and salads (daily 11:00-24:00, tel. 220-517-274).

Villa Richter, at the end of the castle promontory (closest to the river) and surrounded by newly replanted vineyards, consists of three classy restaurants, each with killer Prague views. Forty yards below the lower castle gate, you'll see a gate leading to a vineyard. Stroll downhill through the vineyard and you'll come upon three distinct restaurants (all open daily 10:00-23:00, tel. 257-219-079). At **$$$ Panorama Pergola,** a string of outdoor tables lines a vineyard terrace overlooking the city (wine, sandwiches, cold plates, and hot views). **$$$$ Piano Nobile** is more pretentious, with Italian and French dishes and romantic white-linen tables indoors and out—it's the perfect place to propose (three-course meals). **$$$ Piano Terra** serves more affordable Czech dishes.

$$ Klášterní Pivovar ("Monastery Brewery"), founded by an abbot in 1628 and reopened in 2004, has two large rooms and a pleasant courtyard. This is the place, though touristy, to taste a range of unpasteurized beers brewed on the premises, including amber, wheat, and IPA. The wooden decor and circa-1900 news-paper clippings (including Habsburg Emperor Franz Josef's "Proc-lamation to My Nations," announcing the beginning of the First World War) evoke the era when Vienna was Europe's artistic capi-tal, Prague was building its faux Eiffel Tower, and life moved much slower. To accompany the beer, try the strong beer-flavored cheese served on toasted black-yeast bread (daily 10:00-22:00, Strahovské Nádvoří 301, tel. 233-353-155). It's directly across from the en-trance to the Strahov Library (don't confuse it with the enormous, tour group-oriented Klášterní Restaurace next door, to the right).

$$$ Host Restaurant is hidden in the middle of a staircase that connects Loretánská and Úvoz streets. This spot, which boasts super views of the Little Quarter and Petřín Hill, has a modern black-and-white design and an imaginative menu. For a good deal, try asking for the "business lunch" *menu* that's advertised only in Czech (daily 11:30-22:00, as you go up Loretánská, watch for stairs leading down to the left at #15—just before the arcaded passage-way, mobile 728-695-793).

$ Hostinec u Černého Vola ("By the Black Ox") is a smoky, dingy old-time pub—its survival in the midst of all the castle splendor and tourism is a marvel. It feels like a kegger on the banks of the river Styx, with classic bartenders serving up Kozel beer (tra-ditional "Goat" brand with excellent darks) and beer-friendly gut-bomb snacks (fried cheese, local hot dogs). The pub is located on Loretánská (50 yards from Loreta Church, no sign outside, sniff for cigarette smoke and look for the only house on the block without an arcade, daily 10:00-22:00, English menu on request, tel. 220-513-481).

$$ Malý Buddha ("Little Buddha") serves delightful food—especially vegetarian—and takes its theme seriously. You'll step into a mellow, low-lit escape of bamboo and peace, where you'll be served by people with perfect complexions and almost no pulse to the no-rhythm of meditative music. Eating in their little back room is like dining in a temple (Tue-Sun 12:00-22:30, closed Mon, nonsmoking, between the castle and Strahov Monastery at Úvoz 46, tel. 220-513-894).

$$ U Labutí ("By the Swans") offers Czech food for a good price in a tranquil courtyard, just across from the Plague Column on Castle Square (daily 10:00-22:00, Hradčanské Náměstí 11, tel. 220-511-191).

$ Café Salmovský Palác, just behind the Tomáš Masaryk statue on Castle Square, has a terrace with great city views and rea-sonably priced (given the location) soups, pasta, and coffee (daily 10:00-18:00, Hradčanské Náměstí 1, mobile 725-816-267).

$ Kavárna ve Šternberském Paláci is the locals' getaway from the tourist scene on Castle Square. It's tucked behind the Archbishop's Palace (go through the gateway to the left of the palace, then pass through the ticket office). They serve soup or goulash with bread and drinks in a quiet courtyard at unbeatable prices. Check out the garden with stunning sculptures that's through the door on the left corner of the courtyard (Tue-Sun 10:00-18:00, closed Mon, Hradčanské Náměstí 15, mobile 721-138-290).

$ **Kavárna Nový Svět** ("New World Café"), on a quiet lane down from the Loreta Church, offers a tasty break from the tourist crowds for cake and coffee (Thu-Tue 11:00-20:00, closed Wed, Nový Svět 2).

AWAY FROM THE CENTER

To rub elbows with hip locals, try these spots in Vinohrady and Žižkov. For locations, see the map on page 24.

$$ **Kravín** ("Cowshed") and **Mlsnej Kocour** ("Cat"), two slick, modern places on Vinohrady's park-like central square, cater to expats and a young professional crowd looking to escape the traditional (read: tired) Czech restaurant scene—but who can't entirely let go of their mothers' cherished classics. Czech staples using fresh, small-farm-raised ingredients are interspersed with steaks, burgers, tortillas, lamb, and boar (both open daily 11:00-24:00, weekday lunch *menu* until 15:00, Náměstí Míru 18, tel. 222-540-524, Belgická 42, tel. 222-541-584).

$ **Restaurace u Sadu,** dark and dingy, is decorated with old typewriters, radios, meat grinders, skis, and sleds. It serves cheap beer and decent food indoors on aged green tablecloths or outside on wooden tables. The way that Czechs of all generations drink beer in this classic blue-collar pub hasn't changed a beat since the 1920s (daily 10:00 until late, on Škroupa Square below Žižkov TV tower at Škroupovo Náměstí 5, Metro: Náměstí Jiřího z Poděbrad, tel. 222-727-072).

$$$ **Oblaca** ("The Clouds"), the restaurant 200 feet up in the Žižkov TV tower, is expensive, but it comes with a Sputnik's-eye view (daily 8:00-24:00, less-expensive café open 8:00-17:00, Mahlerovy Sady 1, Metro: Náměstí Jiřího z Poděbrad, tel. 210-320-086).

$ **Hospůdka nad Viktorkou,** named for this neighborhood's soccer team, is around the corner on Bořivojova street. This quintessential Žižkov pub features occasional live performances by local bands, a warm glassed-in terrace in the winter, and a little courtyard with a shady canopy of chestnut trees in the summer (daily 15:00-24:00, English menu available, Bořivojova 79, tel. 222-722-557).

CAFÉS

Dripping with history, these places in the Old Town and New Town are as much about the ambience as they are about the coffee. Most cafés also serve sweets and light meals. For locations, see the map on page 213.

$$ Kavárna Slavia, across from the National Theater (facing the Legií Bridge on Národní street), is a fixture in Prague,

famous as a hangout for its literary elite. Today, it's tired and clearly past its prime, with an Art Deco interior, lousy piano entertainment, and celebrity photos on the wall. But its iconic status makes it a fun stop for a coffee—skip the food (daily 8:00-23:00, sit as near the river as possible, Smetanovo Nábřeží 2, tel. 224-218-493). Notice the *Drinker of Absinthe* painting on the wall (and on the menu)—with the iconic Czech writer struggling with reality.

$$ Grand Café Orient is only one flight up off busy Celetná street, yet a world away from the crush of tourism below. Located in the Cubist House of the Black Madonna, the café is upstairs and fittingly decorated with a Cubist flair. With its stylish, circa-1910 decor toned to dark green, this space is full of air and light—and a good value as well. The café takes its Cubism seriously: Traditionally round desserts are served square (sandwiches, salads, vanilla squares and other desserts, great balcony seating, Mon-Fri 9:00-22:00, Sat-Sun from 10:00, Ovocný Trh 19, at the corner of Celetná near the Powder Tower, tel. 224-224-240).

$$ Café Café, just off to the right from the main drag connecting the Old Town and Wenceslas Square, serves salads, sandwiches, and cakes in a fancy setting (daily 9:00-23:00, Rytířská 10, tel. 224-210-597).

$$ Café Montmartre, on a small street parallel to Karlova, combines Parisian ambience with unbeatable Czech prices for coffee (no food served). Dreamy Czech minds found their quiet asylum here after Kavárna Slavia (listed earlier) and other longtime favorites either closed down or became stuck in their past. The main room is perfect for discussing art and politics; the intimate room behind the courtyard is where you recite poetry to your partner (Mon-Fri 9:00-23:00, Sat-Sun from 12:00, Řetězová 7, tel. 222-221-244).

$ Ebel Coffee House, next door to Café Montmartre, prides itself on its wide assortment of fresh brews from every coffee-bean-growing country in the world, inviting cakes, sandwiches, and a colorful setting that delights the mind as much as the caffeine (daily 9:00-22:00, Řetězová 3, tel. 224-895-788).

$$ Café Louvre is a longtime elegant favorite (opened in 1902 and maintaining its classic atmosphere) that still draws an energetic young crowd that's crazy about their cheesecake and hot chocolate. From the big and busy Národní street, you walk upstairs into a venerable world of newspapers (including in English) on sticks and waiters in vests and aprons. The back room has long been the place for billiard tables (100 Kč/hour). An English flier tells its history (two-course lunch offered 11:00-15:00, good gluten-free options, open daily 8:00-23:30, Národní 22, tel. 224-930-949).

TEAHOUSES

Many Czechs are bohemian philosophers at heart and prefer the mellow, smoke-free environs of a teahouse to the smoky, traditional beer hall. Young Czechs are much more interested in traveling to exotic destinations like Southeast Asia, Africa, or Peru than to Western Europe, so the Oriental teahouses set their minds in vacation mode. For locations, see the map on page 213.

While there are teahouses all over Prague, a fine example in a handy New Town locale is Prague's original one, established in 1991—just after freedom arrived. **$ Dobrá Čajovna** ("Good Teahouse"), only a few steps off the bustle of Wenceslas Square, takes you into a very peaceful world that elevates tea to an almost religious ritual. You'll be given an English menu—which lovingly describes each tea—and a bell. The menu lists a world of tea (very fresh, prices by the small pot), "accompaniments" (such as Exotic Miscellany), and light meals "for hungry tea drinkers." When you're ready to order, ring your bell to beckon a tea monk—likely a member of the Lovers of Tea Society (Mon-Fri 10:00-21:30, Sat-Sun 14:00-21:30, near the base of Wenceslas Square, opposite McDonald's at Václavské Náměstí 14, tel. 224-231-480).

For a taste of tea from Prague's newly emerging Chinese middle class (rather than from some Czech's vision of Asia), head to **$ Čajový Klub** ("Tea Club"), just down the street from the Jerusalem Synagogue. Creatively run by a man from Beijing, here you'll find red cherry-wood decor, expertly served tea, and the freshest green leaves in town (Mon-Sat 10:00-21:00, closed Sun, Jeruzalémská 10, tel. 222-721-072).

SHOPPING IN PRAGUE

Prague's entire Old Town seems designed to bring out the shopper in visitors. Puppets, glass, crystal, and garnets (deep-red gemstones) are traditional; these days, fashion and design (especially incorporating the city's rich Art Nouveau heritage) are also big business.

I haven't listed specific hours for each shop. Most are open on weekdays from 9:00 until 17:00 or 18:00—and often longer, especially for tourist-oriented shops. Some close on Saturday afternoons and/or all day Sunday. I've noted a few unusual cases, and I've also listed websites for many shops—so you can window-shop your options in advance from home.

Naturally, a shop that sells several different types of souvenirs (glass, garnets, puppets, T-shirts, magnets, and more, all under one roof) is probably more interested in making a sale than in quality. If you're buying a big-ticket item, such as fine crystal or a garnet necklace, go to a place that specializes in doing one thing well. Quality glass or garnets should be packaged in the original box, marked with the date and item number (usually on a label on the bottom of the box).

For information on VAT refunds (for purchases of more than 2,001 Kč—about $80) and customs regulations, see page 447.

SHOPPING STREETS IN THE CENTER
Later in this chapter, I've listed several specific shops that could be worth a detour. But if you'd like to simply window-shop in the tourist zone, consider the following streets. (Keep in mind that any shop in the city center caters primarily to tourists—most locals do their serious shopping in the suburbs.)

Ungelt, the courtyard tucked behind the Týn Church just off of the Old Town Square, is packed with touristy but decent-quality

shops. Material has a fine selection of contemporary-style bead jewelry, and Botanicus is an excellent herbal cosmetics shop (both described later). Fajans Majolica has traditional blue-and-white Czech pottery (www.fajans.cz); and V Ungeltu is a cluttered shop with wooden toys and marionettes. The other marionette shop here—Hračky, Loutky—is a step up in quality (but for even finer craftsmanship, see the shops mentioned in the "Czech Puppets" section, later).

Michalská, a semihidden lane right in the thick of the tourist zone, has a variety of shops (from the Small Market Square/ Malé Náměstí near the Astronomical Clock, go through the big stone gateway marked *459*). After a gauntlet of tacky crystal shops, you'll find a lane with Sanu Babu (a wildly popular chain selling Nepalese, Tibetan, and Indian fashion—all the rage among young Czechs); Art Deco Galerie (with carefully selected secondhand vintage clothes and decor from the 1920s through 1960s); the Prague Gallery (with piles of starving-artist-type paintings of Prague); Leander (the factory shop for a prestigious Czech porcelain manufacturer); Coco Vintage; and De.Fakto (a minimalist home decor shop worth exploring for a glimpse at sleek Czech urban living).

On **Havelská** street, you can browse the open-air Havelská Market, a touristy but enjoyable place to shop for inexpensive handicrafts and fresh produce (daily 9:00-18:00, two long blocks south of the Old Town Square; for details see page 52).

Celetná, exiting the Old Town Square to the right of Týn Church, is lined with big stores selling all the traditional Czech goodies. Tourists wander endlessly here, mesmerized by the window displays. Several of my recommended shops have branches along Celetná, including Blue (contemporary glass, at #2); a store specializing in Turnov garnets (at #8); and Manufaktura (natural cosmetics and handmade souvenirs, at #12).

Na Příkopě, the mostly pedestrianized street following the former moat between the Old Town and the New Town, has the city center's handiest lineup of modern shopping malls. The best is Slovanský Dům ("Slavic House," at #22), where you'll wander past a 10-screen multiplex deep into a world of classy restaurants and designer shops surrounding a peaceful, park-like inner courtyard. Černá Růže ("Black Rose," at #12) has a great Japanese restaurant around a small garden; Moser's flagship crystal showroom is also here (described later). The Galerie Myslbek, directly across the street, has fancy stores in a space built to Prague's scale. Na Příkopě street opens up into Republic Square (Náměstí Republiky)—boasting Prague's biggest mall, Palladium, hidden behind a pink Neo-Romanesque facade. Across the square is the communist-era brown steel-and-glass 1980s department store Kotva ("Anchor"), an obsolete beast on the verge of extinction.

Národní Třída (National Street), which continues past Na Příkopě in the opposite direction (toward the river), is less touristy and lined with some inviting stores. The big **Tesco** department store in the middle (at #26) sells anything you might need, from a pin for a broken watchband to a swimsuit (Mon-Sat 7:00-21:00, Sun 8:00-20:00).

Karlova, the tourist-clogged drag connecting the Old Town Square to the Charles Bridge, should be avoided entirely. Shops along here sell made-in-China trinkets at too-high prices to lazy and gullible tourists.

CZECH PUPPETS

The first puppets were born on the Indian subcontinent and soon found their way to Europe and Southeast Asia. Czechs have treasured the art of puppets for centuries; at times of heavy German influence in the 18th century, traveling troupes of puppeteers kept the Czech language and humor alive in the countryside. While the language of "legitimate theater" had to be German, Czech was tolerated if it came out of a puppet's mouth. Others say that in the distant past, superstitious actors were afraid to take on another person's personality—for fear they'd become possessed—so it was safer to act through a puppet.

For generations, Czech grandfathers felt obliged to bequeath to their grandsons an assembly of their own linden-wood-carved designs. (The power of puppetry peaked between 1938 and 1989, when the Czechs were ruled by a series of puppet governments.) Today, the puppet comedy duo Špejbl and Hurvínek, who have their own permanent stage in Prague, are the greatest Czechs for kids from Japan

SHOPPING

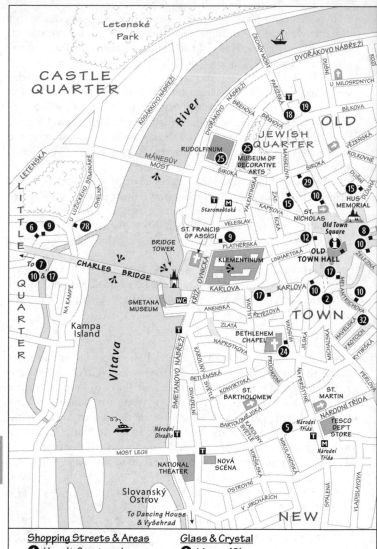

<u>Shopping Streets & Areas</u>
1. Ungelt Courtyard
2. Michalská
3. Celetná
4. Na Příkopě
5. Národní Třída

<u>Puppets</u>
6. Marionety Truhlář & Galerie Michael
7. To Loutky

<u>Glass & Crystal</u>
8. Moser (2)
9. Artěl Glass (3)
10. Blue (5)
11. More Crystal Shops
12. Galerie GOF+FA

<u>Jewelry</u>
13. Turnov Granát Co-op (3)
14. Studio Šperk
15. More Garnet Shops (3)
16. To Koralky

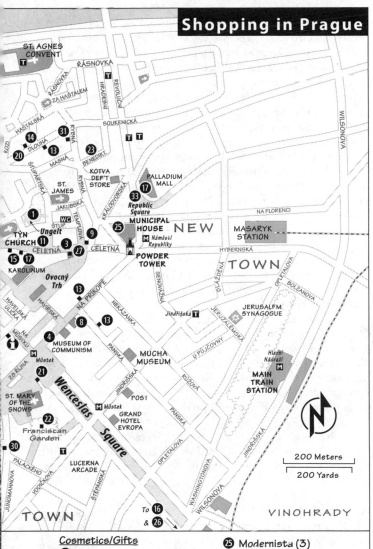

Shopping in Prague

Cosmetics/Gifts
17 Manufaktura (5)

Fashion/Design
18 Pařížská Street
19 Elišky Krásnohorské St.
20 Dlouhá Street
21 Baťa Shoes
22 Tribu
23 Benediktská Street
24 Futurista Universum

25 Modernista (3)
26 To Modernista Pavilon
27 Kubista

Books/Maps/Posters
28 Shakespeare & Sons
29 Franz Kafka Society
30 Kiwi Map Store
31 ProVás Posters

Outdoor Markets
32 Havelská Market
33 Republic Square Market

SHOPPING

to Patagonia. Filmmaker Jan Švankmajer (see page 485) has turned wooden characters into Oscar-winning film stars.

It takes a rare artist to turn pieces of wood into nimble puppets, and prices for the real deal can reach into the thousands of dollars. But given that puppets have a glorious past and vibrant present in the Czech Republic, even a simple jester, witch, or Pinocchio can make a thoughtful memento of your Czech adventure. You'll see cheap trinket puppets at souvenir stands across town. Buying a higher-quality keepsake is more expensive (starting in the $100 range). Here are a few better options to consider:

At **Marionety Truhlář**, Pavel has been selling handmade puppets (his own production, as well as ones from other Czech craftspeople) since 1993. He also sells do-it-yourself kits for 1,000 Kč. You can peruse his selection at his shop near the Little Quarter end of Charles Bridge (look right as you near the tower, U Lužického Semináře 5), or take part in a workshop at his office in Vinohrady (Boleslavská 11, www.marionety.com). **Galerie Michael,** just a few doors down from Pavel's Little Quarter shop at U Lužického Semináře 7, is worth comparison-shopping while you're in the area (www.marionettesmichael.cz).

Another excellent store is the no-name **loutky** ("Puppets") shop at the top of Nerudova, at #51. Here, the puppets are displayed by artist, with options ranging from cheap-but-working plastic and plaster creations (from 300 Kč) to professional mechanical wooden marionettes (starting at 4,000 Kč). The smaller puppets are packed into compact boxes and are easily transportable. They also have two more showrooms a few doors down at #45 and #47 (www.loutky. cz).

Closer to the Old Town Square, **Hračky, Loutky** ("Toys, Puppets") is conveniently located in the Ungelt courtyard, just to the right as you are about to exit in the direction of the Church of St. James.

GLASS AND CRYSTAL

The Bohemian landscape is blessed with an abundance of just the right natural resources for making glass: heavily forested hills rich with deposits of certain minerals and timber for powering fires, and plenty of running water. Ever since the Renaissance, Prague has been known for its exquisite glass and crystal.

Glass plus lead equals crystal. Legally, to be called "crystal" (or "lead crystal"), it must contain at least 24 percent lead oxide, which lends the glass that special, prismatic sparkle. The lead also adds weight, makes the glass easier to cut, and produces a harmonious ringing when flicked. ("Crystal glass" has a smaller percentage of lead.)

Historically, people used lead crystal vessels to store and serve food and drink. But now we know that lead is a poison, and these days, it's recommended that you use it carefully: It's fine for short-term use, provided you wash it carefully beforehand, and don't leave it in contact with food or drink for extended periods of time (that is, more than a few hours).

Some shops advertise "lead-free" glass (or "lead-free crystal")—a different process that replaces the lead oxide with safer minerals, while retaining the glittering qualities of true crystal.

Crystal or glass may be decorated in various ways. It may be cut with facets (like on a diamond), which are engineered to emphasize the glass' reflective qualities. The most traditional Czech cut-glass pattern has starbursts in circles, set very close together in a lace-like pattern. (Naturally, a hand-cut item is much more expensive than machine-cut.) Or it can be engraved with an image or pattern—designed to showcase the image itself rather than the sparkle of the glass. Glass can be stained with a color—originally done to disguise impurities, but now considered desirable in itself. And sometimes a design is painted onto the glass with enamel.

Survey your choices if you're serious about buying. Moser (described below) is the top-of-the-top; Sklo Bohemia and Kavalier—sold around town—are good, midrange brands for everyday glassware. Items sold at tacky tourist shops without a clear label can be of lesser quality, and may be glass masquerading as crystal.

Moser, in business since 1857, is the most famous Czech brand—and one of the most expensive. You'll see their shops all over Prague and throughout the country. Their flagship store, with a museum-quality showroom, is at the Černá Růže shopping mall at Na Příkopě 12. The Moser branch on the Old Town Square (in the row of shops in front of the Týn Church, near the start of Celetná street) has a small museum in the cellar (www.moser-glass.com).

Artěl, recommended later, has a small but eye-pleasing selection of Art Nouveau- and Art Deco-inspired glassware, which they call "crystal couture" (for locations, see listing later).

Blue is a chain specializing in sleek, modern designs—many of them in the namesake hue. Locations include several within a few steps of the Old Town Square (at Malé Náměstí 13, Pařížská 3, Melantrichova 6, and Celetná 2), one near the Little Quarter end of Charles Bridge (Mostecká 24), and at the airport (www.bluepraha.cz).

Celetná street is lined with touristy glass shops, some with a wide selection suitable for a surgical strike for a crystal souvenir.

But for something a bit more refined and specialized, consider one of the shops listed earlier.

For a unique, experiential take on Czech glass, visit Antonin Manto-Mrnka's **Galerie GOF+FA.** In addition to visiting a showroom of the artist's works, you can arrange for a workshop experience to actually learn the basics of glassmaking and make your own glass art to take home (on the Small Market Square at Malé Náměstí 6, www.mantogallery.com).

Or consider venturing an hour beyond Prague to the **Rückl Glassworks** in Nižbor (see page 300).

JEWELRY: GARNETS AND BEADS

Bohemian Garnets *(Granát):* These blood-colored gemstones have unique refractive—some claim even curative—properties. Garnets

have long been mined in the mountainous north and northeast of Bohemia (particularly near the town of Turnov). This region was the major source of garnet gems from the Renaissance through the Victorian Age, but is now largely mined out. Much of the authentic Bohemian garnet jewelry you'll see today is Victorian-era—these traditional hand-crafted designs pack many small garnets together on one piece.

If you buy garnet jewelry, shop around, use a reputable dealer, and ask for a certificate of authenticity to avoid buying a glass imitation (these are common). A *"granát Turnov"* label is a good indicator of quality.

Of the many garnet shops in Prague's shopping districts, **Turnov Granát Co-op** has the largest selection. It's refreshingly unpretentious, with a vaguely retro-communist vibe (shops at Dlouhá 28, Panská 1, and inside the Pánská Pasáž at Na Příkopě 23; www.granat.eu). **J. Drahoňovský's Studio Šperk** is a more upscale-feeling shop with more creative designs (Dlouhá 19, www.drahonovsky.cz). Additional shops specializing in Turnov garnets are at Dlouhá 1, Celetná 8, and Maiselova 3.

Costume Jewelry and Beads: You'll see *bižutérie* (costume jewelry) advertised all over town. Round, glass beads—sometimes called Druk beads—are popular, and can range from large marble-sized beads to minuscule "seed beads." The biggest producer of glass beads is Jablonex, from the town of Jablonec nad Nisou. A handy spot to check out some stylish, modern pieces is **Material,** in the Ungelt courtyard behind Týn Church. They have a fun selection of seed beads, as well as some finer pieces (www.i-material.com). **Koralky,** one of the best-supplied bead shops in Prague, is a bit farther out; take the Metro's green line to the Jiřího z Poděbrad stop (Vinohradská 76, www.koralky.cz).

ORGANIC COSMETICS AND HANDMADE GIFTS
Manufaktura is your classy, one-stop shop for good-quality Czech gifts, and sells a variety of organic cosmetics and bathroom products (lotions, perfumes, shampoos, soaps, potpourri), all made from ingredients produced locally. They also have a thoughtfully assembled selection of traditional items such as rustic ceramic cups and bowls, straw ornaments, painted eggs, wooden toys, and "blueprint" Moravian fabrics—all handmade in the Czech Republic. You'll find many branch locations in Prague, including several near the Old Town Square (at Melantrichova 17, Celetná 12, and Karlova 26); at Republic Square (in the Palladium mall); near the Little Quarter end of the Charles Bridge (Mostecká 17); in the main train station; and even along Prague Castle's Golden Lane (www.manufaktura.cz).

Botanicus is similar but a little smaller, with a range of all-natural, fragrant natural soaps, lotions, perfumes, and essential oils. Their Prague branch is in the Ungelt courtyard behind Týn Church. They also have locations in Český Krumlov and Karlovy Vary (www.botanicus.cz).

FASHION AND DESIGN
Czechs have a unique sense of fashion. One popular trend is garments that are adorned with embroidery, leather, beads, hand-painted designs, or other flourishes—all handmade and therefore unique. Shops selling these come and go, and in many cases several small designers work together and share a boutique—look for an "atelier." Vintage clothes are also as popular among young Czech hipsters as they are with their American counterparts.

You'll find the highest concentration of shops from high-class, international designers (Gucci, Prada, Bulgari, Louis Vuitton, Dolce & Gabbana, and the whole gang) along or near the elegant, Art Nouveau **Pařížská street** that runs through the Jewish Quarter. Several designer shops cluster at the intersection of Pařížská and Široká, with another clump farther down, at the big plaza in front of Hotel InterContinental.

For a look at high fashion with a Czech accent, focus on some of the side-streets in the Jewish Quarter that run parallel to Pařížská. One block over, **Elišky Krásnohorské street** has the most engaging lineup of unpretentious local fashion, including the young, hip La Gallery Novesta—a group of Czech and Slovak clothing and shoe designers (at #9); and Navarila, an atelier of Martina Nevařilová, who designs both casual and dressy clothes, jewelry, and handbags (at #4, www.navarila.cz). A block farther east, more boutiques line **Dušní street.**

A short walk away, **Dlouhá street**—which exits the Old Town Square near the Jan Hus statue—offers more Czech designers. In the block after the intersection with Dušní, you'll see three upscale boutiques in a row: Natali Ruden, Klára Nademlýnská, and Beata Rajská. Farther along on Dlouhá, you'll find a wider variety of shops: home decor (Nobis Life, Apropos), an old-fashioned cigar and pipe shop, and—at the far end of the street—the recently restored Palác Dlouhá (at #3a). This grand space features a trendy little warren of upscale food shops (butcher, open-face sandwiches, deli, wine, raw bar, and more).

On and Near Wenceslas Square: Fashionistas are sometimes surprised to learn that the famous and well-respected **Baťa** shoe brand is not Italian, but Czech (for the story, see page 155 of my Wenceslas Square Walk); their seven-story flagship store, on Wenceslas Square (at #6), is nirvana for shoe lovers. Nearby, one of the pavilions inside the Franciscan Garden (hiding just off of Wenceslas Square) houses **Tribu,** a fun and youthful fashion boutique with clothes, jewelry, and other unique pieces (www.tribu.cz).

Funky Hipster Design: Benediktská, a tiny street tucked in a quiet corner of the Old Town, has a little cluster of creative boutiques. **Kuráž** is a small but fun-to-explore collection of Czech and Slovak designers, with jewelry, accessories, clothes, and home decor (at #7, www.kuraz.cz). Across the street, **Eterno Moderno** showcases fun, handmade design—very Czech chic (at #4, www.2008. cz). The **ProVás** vintage poster store, described later, is nearby.

ART NOUVEAU DESIGN SHOPS

Prague is Europe's best Art Nouveau city—and several shops give you a chance to take home some of that eye-pleasing style, in the form of glasswear, home decor, linens, posters, and other items.

Artěl—a chain owned by an American (Karen Feldman) who fell in love with Prague and its unique sense of style—is thoughtfully curated. Specializing in glass with Art Nouveau, Art Deco, and floral motifs, her shops offer a range of other good-quality gifts, including jewelry by local designers. There are three locations (www.artelglass.com): The flagship store is a block from the Municipal House, at Celetná 29; their "Concept Store"—smaller, but with more upscale items—is on the Old Town side of Charles Bridge, at Platnéřská 7; and another branch is at the Little Quarter end of Charles Bridge (at U Lužického Semináře 7; look down on the right as you cross the bridge). Karen also wrote a fun, insightful, design-oriented guidebook called *Prague: Artěl Style.*

Futurista Universum, tucked around the right side of the Bethlehem Chapel in the Old Town, has a fun, modern selec-

Shopping in Prague 239

tion of glass, jewelry, and other design pieces—all original, by local designers (shares an entrance with the recommended Klub Architektů restaurant at Betlémské Náměstí 5a, www.futurista.cz).

Modernista, with a handy location downstairs inside the Municipal House, has a fine selection of Art Nouveau and Art Deco jewelry, glassware, wooden toys, books, and so on. They also have branches in the Rudolfinum and Museum of Decorative Arts, both near the river (north of the Charles Bridge). Their flagship store is in the **Modernista Pavilon,** a sleek, gorgeously restored former train station that's also home to a variety of trendy fashion and home-decor shops. It's farther out, in the Vinohrady neighborhood, but it's worth a visit if you appreciate their aesthetic (closed Sun, between the National Museum and Žižkov at Vinohradská 50, near the Vinohradská Tržnice stop on tram #11, www.modernista.cz).

Kubista, in the House of the Black Madonna, has a fun-to-peruse selection of Czech Cubist dishes, jewelry, furniture, books, and more (closed Mon, Ovocný Trh 19, www.kubista.cz).

BOOKS, MAPS, POSTERS, AND MUSIC
Try **Shakespeare and Sons** (with a big selection in the Little Quarter) or **Franz Kafka Society** (with a smaller selection in the Jewish Quarter), both open daily and described on page 28. **Kiwi Map Store,** near Wenceslas Square, is Prague's best source for maps and travel guides (Jungmannova 23).

ProVás is a poster shop stocking a wide array of unique posters—originals, reprints, and lots of vintage ads from the 1920s (closed Sat-Sun, Rybná 21, www.agenturaprovas.cz).

For tips on buying Czech **music,** see the sidebar on page 248.

OTHER FUN SOUVENIR IDEAS
Far cheaper than fine Czech crystal is old-fashioned **porcelain.** The most traditional pattern has a blue design on a white base—often in the shape of an onion *(cibulak).*

Czechs love cartoons: You'll see stuffed animals and other depictions of their favorite character, **Krtek** (a.k.a. Krteček, "Little Mole"), all over town.

If you enjoy a good brain-teasing puzzle, look for the **"hedgehog in the cage"** *(ježek v kleci).* The Czech answer to a Rubik's cube, this is a spiny ball set inside a cylinder made of bars. Your challenge: Free the hedgehog. You can even find this as a garnet necklace.

Keep an eye out for a **"fishlet"**—a simple pocketknife that folds up into a sardine-shaped housing. This is nostalgic for Czechs who grew up using them during communist times, when the Pioneers (similar to Boy and Girl Scouts) were a big part of their for-

SHOPPING

mative years. (If you buy one, pack it in your checked luggage when you fly home.)

Several shops and stands (e.g., at the Havelská Market) sell **"kitchen witches"**—a doll that you hang in your kitchen for good luck. While not uniquely Czech (it's a very old custom spanning much of Northern Europe), these can be a fun memento of your trip.

Pražská Čokoláda (Prague Chocolate) is a family business with a century-old tradition of producing all kinds of spiced-up munchies (served with a smile at branches including Nerudova 46, Thunovská 19 in the Little Quarter, Železná 2 in the Old Town, and at the airport).

What Not to Buy: Many Prague souvenir shops sell very non-Czech (especially Russian) items to tourists who don't know better. Amber may be pretty, but—considering it's found along the Baltic Sea coast—obviously doesn't originate from this landlocked country. (The amber you'll see sold is mostly Russian and Polish.) Stacking dolls, fur hats, and vodka flasks also fall into this category.

ENTERTAINMENT IN PRAGUE

Prague booms with live and inexpensive theater, classical music, jazz, and pop entertainment. Everything is listed in several monthly cultural events programs (free at TIs).

You'll be tempted to gather fliers as you wander through town. Don't bother. To really understand all your options (the street Mo-

zarts are pushing only their own concerts), drop by a **Via Musica** box office. There are two: One is next to Týn Church on the Old Town Square (daily 10:30-19:30, tel. 224-826-969), and the other is in the Little Quarter across from the Church of St. Nicholas (daily 10:30-18:00, tel. 257-535-568). A posted event schedule clearly shows everything that's playing today and tomorrow, including tourist concerts, Black Light Theater, and marionette shows, with photos of each venue and a map (www.viamusica.cz). If you don't see a posted list of today's events, just ask for it.

Ticketpro sells tickets for the serious concert venues and most music clubs (English-language reservations tel. 296-329-999, www.ticketpro.cz). Ticketpro has several outlets: at Rytířská 31 (daily 8:00-12:00 & 12:30-16:30, between Havelská Market and Estates Theater); in the Lucerna Arcade (daily 9:30-18:00, on Wenceslas Square, opposite Grand Hotel Evropa); and in the privately run Tourist Center at Rytířská 12 (Mon-Fri 11:00-19:00, closed Sat-Sun). As with most ticket box offices, you'll pay about 30 Kč extra per ticket.

Locals dress up for the more "serious" concerts, opera, and

Entertainment in Prague

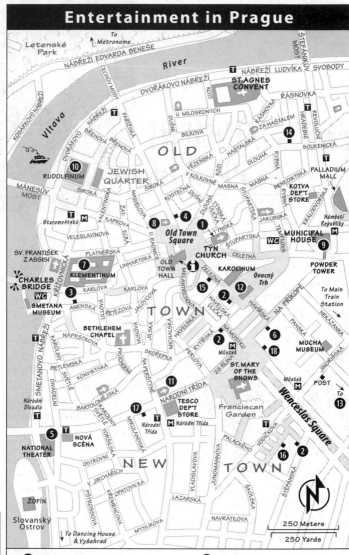

1　Via Musica Box Office
2　Ticketpro (3)
3　Ta Fantastika Theater
4　Image Theater
5　National Theater & Laterna Magika
6　Srnec Theater
7　Klementinum (Chapel of Mirrors)
8　Church of St. Nicholas
9　Municipal House (Smetana Hall)
10　Rudolfinum
11　St. Martin in the Wall
12　Estates Theater
13　To State Opera
14　Roxy Club
15　Agharta Jazz Club
16　Lucerna Music Bar
17　Reduta Jazz Club
18　Bontonland Music Shop

ballet, but many tourists wear casual clothes—as long as you don't
show up in shorts, sneakers, or flip-flops, you'll be fine.

BLACK LIGHT THEATER

A kind of mime/modern dance variety show, Black Light Theater
has no language barrier and is, for some, more entertaining than a
classical concert. Unique to Prague, Black Light Theater originated in the 1960s as a playful and mystifying theater of the absurd.
These days, aficionados and critical visitors lament that it's becoming a cheesy variety show, while others are uncomfortable with the
sexual flavor of some acts. Still, it's an unusual theater experience
that many enjoy. Shows last about an hour and a half. Avoid the
first four rows, which get you so close that it ruins the illusion.
Each of these four theaters has its own spin on what Black Light is
supposed to be. (The other Black Light theaters advertised around
town aren't as good.)

Ta Fantastika tries to be poetic, with haunting puppetry and
a little artistic nudity, but it's less "fun" than some of the others.
Of these choices, it takes itself perhaps the most seriously (680 Kč,
Aspects of Alice nightly at 18:00 and 21:30, reserved seating, near
east end of Charles Bridge at Karlova 8, tel. 222-221-366, www.
tafantastika.cz).

Image Theater has more mime and elements of the absurd,
and tries to incorporate more dance along with the illusions. They
offer the most diverse lineup of programs, including a "best of"
and several short-term, themed shows—recent topics have been
African safari and outer space. Some find Image's shows to be a bit
too slapsticky for their tastes (480 Kč, nightly at 20:00, open seating—arrive early to grab a good spot, just off Old Town Square at
Pařížská 4, tel. 222-314-448, www.imagetheatre.cz).

Laterna Magika, in the big, glassy building next to the National Theater, mixes Black Light techniques with film projec-

tion, dance, and other elements
into a multimedia performance that
draws Czech audiences. Because the
theater is used for other types of performances as well, this Black Light
show is staged less frequently than
some of the others—but if they have
a performance while you're in town,
they're well worth considering (680
Kč; *Wonderful Circus, Legends of Magic, Graffiti;* typically 3-4 nights
a week at 20:00, tel. 224-931-482, www.laterna.cz).

Srnec Theater is an ensemble run by founder Jiří Srnec (credited with inventing the Black Light Theater concept in 1961) and
his son. Fittingly, this is the most "back-to-basics" options—while

ENTERTAINMENT

narratively simplistic, it revels in the childlike, goofy wonder of the effects. Their primary show, *Anthology*, traces the development of the art over the past 50 years; they also plan additional shows in the future (380-680 Kč, generally weekly at 20:00, in the same courtyard as the Museum of Communism and the McDonald's at Na Příkopě 10, mobile 774-574-475, www.srnectheatre.com).

CLASSICAL CONCERTS

Each day, six to eight classical concerts designed for tourists fill delightful Old World halls and churches with music of the crowd-pleasing sort: Vivaldi, Best of Mozart, Most Famous Arias, and works by the famous Czech composer Antonín Dvořák. Concerts typically cost 400-1,000 Kč, start anywhere from 13:00 to 21:00, and last about an hour. Typical venues include two buildings on the Little Quarter Square (the Church of St. Nicholas and the Prague Academy of Music in Liechtenstein Palace), the Klementinum's Chapel of Mirrors, the Old Town Square (in a different Church of St. Nicholas), and the stunning Smetana Hall in the Municipal House. Musicians vary from excellent to amateurish.

To ensure a memorable venue and top-notch musicians, choose a concert in one of three places—the Municipal House's Smetana Hall, the Rudolfinum, or the National Theater—featuring Prague's finest ensembles (such as the Prague Symphony Orchestra or Czech Philharmonic).

The **Prague Symphony Orchestra** plays in the gorgeous Art Nouveau Municipal House. Their ticket office is on the right side of the building, on U Obecního Domu street opposite Hotel Paris (Mon-Fri 10:00-18:00, tel. 222-002-336, www.fok.cz). A smaller selection of tickets is sold in the information office inside the Municipal House.

The **Czech Philharmonic** performs in the classical Neo-Renaissance Rudolfinum in the Jewish Quarter. Their ticket office is on the right side of the Rudolfinum, under the stairs (250-1,000 Kč, open Mon-Fri 10:00-18:00, and until just before the show starts on concert days, on Palachovo Náměstí on the Old Town side of Mánes Bridge, tel. 227-059-352, www.ceskafilharmonie. cz).

Both orchestras perform in their home venues about five nights a month from September through June. Most other nights these spaces are rented to agencies that organize tourist concerts of varying quality for double the price. Check first whether your visit coincides with either ensemble's performance.

You'll find tickets for tourist concerts advertised and sold on the street in front of these buildings. Although the music may not be the finest, these concerts do allow you to experience music in one of Prague's best venues on the night of your choice. This is especially worth considering if you want to enjoy classical music in the Municipal House when the Symphony Orchestra isn't in town (but make sure your concert takes place in the building's Smetana Hall rather than in the much smaller Grégr Hall).

Both the Municipal House and Rudolfinum also act as chief venues for the Prague Spring, Prague Proms, and Dvořák's Prague music festivals (see "Festivals," later).

Jam Session: A good bet is the session held every Monday at 17:00 at **St. Martin in the Wall,** where some of Prague's best musicians gather to tune in and chat with one another (400 Kč, Martinská 8, just north of the Tesco department store in the Old Town).

Buskers: The **Prague Castle Orchestra,** one of the city's most entertaining acts, performs regularly on Castle Square. This trio—Josef on flute, Radek on accordion, and Zdeněk on bass—plays a lively Czech mélange of Smetana, swing, old folk tunes, and 1920s cabaret songs. Look for them if you're visiting the castle (see page 85), and consider picking up their fun CD. They're also available for private functions (mobile 603-552-448, josekocurek@volny.cz).

OPERA AND BALLET

A handy ticket office for the three following theaters is in the little square (Ovocný Trh) behind the Estates Theater, next to a pizzeria.

The **National Theater** (Národní Divadlo), on the New Town side of Legií Bridge, is best for opera and ballet. Enjoy its Neo-

Renaissance interior (300-1,000 Kč, shows from 19:00, tel. 224-912-673, www.narodni-divadlo.cz).

The **Estates Theater** (Stavovské Divadlo) is where Mozart premiered and personally directed many of his most beloved works (see page 51). *Don Giovanni, The Marriage of Figaro,* and *The Magic Flute* are on the program a couple of times each month (800-1,400 Kč, shows from 20:00, between the Old Town Square and the New Town on a square called Ovocný Trh, tel. 224-214-339, www.narodni-divadlo.cz).

The **State Opera** (Státní Opera), formerly the German Theater, is less architecturally rewarding than the National Theater. Operas by non-Czech composers are typically performed here (400-1,200 Kč, at 19:00 or 20:00, 101 Wilsonova, on the busy street between the main train station and Wenceslas Square, see map on page 61, tel. 224-227-693, www.narodni-divadlo.cz).

Mozart, Smetana, Dvořák, and More

The three major composers connected with Prague—Mozart, Smetana, and Dvořák—have museums that are dedicated to their lives and work.

Wolfgang Amadeus Mozart (1756-1791)

During his frequent visits to Prague, Mozart lodged with his friends in the beautiful, small Neoclassical Villa Bertramka, now the **Mozart Museum.** The Salzburg prodigy felt more appreciated in Prague than in his homeland, and this villa, set in a peaceful garden, gives one the sense of the surroundings in which Mozart stayed. But there's not much to see inside, as almost all the original interior furnishings are now housed at the Czech Museum of Music (where some are on display). Unless you're an absolute Mozart fan, there's little reason to make the trek (50 Kč, daily 10:00-17:00, closed Nov-Feb; Metro: Anděl, then a 10-minute walk along a busy street to Mozartova 169; tel. 241-493-547, check www.mozartovaobec.cz for occasional concerts).

Bedřich Smetana (1824-1884)

A statue of Smetana, the father of Czech classical music, is seated in front of the **Smetana Museum,** listening intently to the rapids of the Vltava River near the Charles Bridge (museum entry-50 Kč, Wed-Mon 10:00-17:00, closed Tue, Novotného Lávka, Praha 1, tel. 224-229-075). Like Richard Wagner in Germany, Smetana aimed to stir the Romantic nationalist spirit of the Czechs. His finest work, the cycle of symphonic poems called *My Country (Má Vlast)*, was inspired by places and myths important to the Czech people. *Vltava*, the most beautiful of the poems, is played to get your attention as trains arrive in stations.

FESTIVALS

World-class musicians are in town during these musical festivals: **Prague Spring** (mid-May-early June, www.festival.cz), **Prague Proms** (mid-June-late July, www.pragueproms.cz), the newer **Dvořák Prague** (Sept, www.dvorakovapraha.cz), and the **International Jazz Festival** (autumn, www.agharta.cz).

MUSIC CLUBS

Young locals keep Prague's many music clubs in business. Most clubs are neighborhood institutions with decades of tradition, generally holding only 100-200 people. Live rock and Bob Dylan-style

Antonín Dvořák (1841-1904)

Dvořák is the Czech Republic's best-known composer. For three years, Dvořák directed the National Conservatory in New York, during which time he composed his most famous work, the *New World Symphony (Z Nového Světa)*. Dvořák's advice to his students was to look for inspiration in America's authentic melodies (African American spirituals and Native American music) rather than in European models. Dvořák's gentle opera of a water nymph, *Rusalka*, is considered by many to be the best Czech opera and is often performed in Prague's National Theater.

The **Dvořák Museum** is located in Villa America, a building designed by Prague's most prolific Baroque architect, K. I. Dientzenhofer. It was the first of his structures to be built in the city and was purchased by the Dvořák Society in 1932 (museum entry-50 Kč, Tue-Sun 10:00-17:00, closed Mon, Ke Karlovu 20, Praha 2, see map on page 61, tel. 224-923-363).

Other Composers

Two other important composers from Czech lands are the moderns, Mahler and Janáček. **Gustav Mahler** (1860-1911), a Jew from Jihlava (see page 360), was a pioneer of atonal music. His best works are *Symphony No. 1: Titan* and *The Song of the Earth*, both inspired by the sounds of the Moravian woods and fields. **Leoš Janáček** (1854-1928), arguably the most original and least accessible Czech composer, was stimulated by language—its flow and abrupt pauses. He's known for his *Symphonietta* and *Lachian Dances (Lašské Tance)*, as well as the operas *Cunning Little Vixen (Příhody Lišky Bystroušky)* and my favorite, *Jenůfa*—both perennials in the National Theater's repertoire.

folk are what younger generations go for. A number of good jazz clubs attract a diverse audience, from ages 18 to 80. In the last decade, world music has also become hugely popular: Roma (Gypsy) bands, Moravian poets, African drummers, Cuban boleros, and Moroccan divas often sell out even the largest venues. You can buy tickets at the club, or, for most places, at a Ticketpro office (described earlier). If you like jazz, I've listed some fine options; avoid the Jazzboat (advertised by commission-hungry hotels), which has mediocre musicians and high prices.

Buying Czech Music

While the most convenient places to get CDs of classical music are the shops in the **Via Musica** and **Rudolfinum** ticket offices, you'll find a larger selection and other genres at the huge **Bontonland** music and video store, at the bottom of Wenceslas Square (enter from the mall with the big *Kenvelo* sign on the outside). In the classical music section, you'll find many interpretations of Czech works. For the best renditions, look for music performed by the Czech Philharmonic.

For contemporary, lighter music, get a CD by Čechomor (*Metamorphosis* is their best). This band, which began by playing traditional Czech music at weddings and funerals, synthesized the sound of folk ballads and has since become one of the most popular groups in the country. Jiří Pavlica and Hradišťan keep the music of Moravia alive; Věra Bíla and Ida Kellarová capture the lively spirit of the Roma (Gypsies). Some cool Czech contemporary groups are Psí Vojáci, Neočekávaný Dýchánek, and Už Jsme Doma. Of course, you can also purchase many of these musical recommendations digitally.

In the Old Town

Roxy, a few blocks from the Old Town Square, features live bands from outside the country twice a week—anything from Irish punk to Balkan brass. On other nights, the floor is taken over by experimental DJs spinning a healthy dose of Japanese pop (cover from 100 Kč, no cover on Mon, concerts start at 20:00, disco at 22:00, easy to book online and pick up tickets at the door, Dlouhá 33, tel. 224-826-296, www.roxy.cz).

Agharta Jazz Club, which showcases some of the best Czech and Eastern European jazz, is just steps off the Old Town Square in a cool Gothic cellar. Inside they also sell a wide selection of Czech jazz CDs (250-Kč cover, shows start nightly at 21:00, Železná 16, tel. 222-211-275, www.agharta.cz).

In the New Town

Lucerna Music Bar, at the bottom of Wenceslas Square, is popular for its '80s and '90s video parties on Friday and Saturday nights. The scene is a big, noisy dance hall with a giant video screen. Young and trendy, the Lucerna is cheap, and even older visitors mix in easily with the crowd of half locals, half tourists (about 100-Kč cover, music starts around 21:00, in the basement of Lucerna Arcade, Vodičkova 36, tel. 224-217-108, www.musicbar.cz). On other nights the Lucerna often hosts concerts (tickets 300-500 Kč, starts at 21:00).

The small **Reduta Jazz Club,** with cushioned brown sofas stretching along mirrored walls, launches you straight into the

ENTERTAINMENT

1960s-era classic jazz scene (when jazz provided an escape for trapped freedom lovers in communist times). The top Czech jazzmen—Stivín and Koubková—regularly perform. President Bill Clinton once played the sax here (about 300 Kč; live jazz, blues, swing, or big band every night from 21:30; on Národní street next to Café Louvre, tel. 224-933-486, www.redutajazzclub.cz).

In the Little Quarter

Malostranská Beseda, at the bottom of the Little Quarter, was known in the communist era for playing host to underground rock bands, semilegal bards, and daring jazzmen—a stark contrast to the regime-pampered pop stars. Beseda—with its tight, steamy, standing-room-only space—is the only club in the center with daily live performances. The crowd tends to be a bit older than at other clubs (150-300-Kč cover depending on band, shows from 21:00, Malostranské Náměstí 21, see map on page 222, www.malostranska-beseda.cz, tel. 257-409-123). The building also houses a recommended restaurant and beer hall.

In Žižkov

This hip neighborhood has Prague's highest concentration of cool pubs.

Palác Akropolis is *the* home of Czech independent music. Originally a 1920s movie theater, in the 1990s it was turned into a chill-out lounge, a literary café, and two halls that offer a mix of concerts, disco, and theater (advance ticket sales at café, Mon-Fri 10:00-24:00, Sat-Sun from 16:00, corner of Kubelíkova and Fibichova, under Žižkov TV tower, Metro: Jiřího z Poděbrad, see map on page 24, tel. 296-330-913, www.palacakropolis.cz).

SPORTS

Prague's top sports are soccer (that's "football" here) and hockey. Surprisingly, the Czechs have often been a world power in both. The soccer season usually runs from February to May and August to November with games held Friday, Saturday, or Sunday afternoons. The hockey season runs from September to April on Tuesday, Friday, and Sunday nights. With the exception of matches between the top two Czech soccer teams (Sparta and Slavia), both soccer and hockey games are rarely sold out—just show up at the stadium 15 minutes before the game starts.

Soccer

Czech fans are proud of their national soccer team, which recently reached the knockout stages of the 2016 Euro Cup. Within the Czech Republic, the two oldest and most successful soccer clubs are the bitter Prague rivals AC Sparta and SK Slavia. Sparta's 1970s-era stadium is at Letná (behind the giant Metronome ticking above the river in Letenské Park). Slavia's much newer Eden stadium (c. 2008) is in Vršovice (12 stops from the National Theater on tram #22). Other Czech teams occasionally challenge the supremacy of the two S's. The strongest has been FC Viktoria Plzeň (Pilsen), which won the league title in 2015 and 2016 and also was the last Czech club to qualify for the highly lucrative, 32-club European Champions League.

Two other Prague teams in the top Czech league are FK Dukla—formerly an army team from the communist era (making Czech soccer famous across the globe in the 1960s even though it had no fan base) and its opposite—the fan-owned, traditional Bohemians.

Hockey

AC Sparta also fields a top contending hockey team which plays in the state-of-the-art Sazka Arena (right at the Českomoravská Metro stop). Between 1996 and 2010, the Czech national hockey team won six world championships, and in 1998, took the gold medal at the Olympic Games in Nagano, Japan. However, Czech hockey's golden generation has retired—and younger players have been slow to fill the gap. Following a disappointing performance at the 2010 Vancouver Olympics, the Czech team managed to pull off a major upset by beating the fired-up Russians to win the 2010 World Championship. That was the last time Czechs had a shot at the gold medal.

Many players make a name for themselves in America's National Hockey League, where more than two dozen native Czechs currently take the ice; think of Jaromír Jágr (see sidebar), third on NHL's all-time scoring list, and Dominik "The Dominator" Hašek, a top goaltender (who played 16 seasons in the NHL before retiring from US hockey).

Back in the communist days, ice hockey was the only place where Czechoslovaks could mete out payback on their Soviet oppressors (ice hockey is also the most popular sport in Slovakia). The hockey rink is still where Czechs are proudest about their nationality. If you're here in May during the hockey championships, join locals cheering their team in front of a giant screen on the Old Town Square, or on a main square wherever you are in the country.

Sports on the Old Town and Wenceslas Squares

When there are sporting events of great interest (such as hockey and soccer championships), the Old Town Square plays host to huge TV screens, beer and bratwurst stands, and thousands of Czechs. The warm and friendly scene is like a big family gathering. Some fans lie on the cobblestones up front and focus on the game,

The Magic of "68"

In the National Hockey League he is a hockey legend (currently third on the all-time scoring list); in the generally agnostic Czech Republic he is a near deity. His name is Jaromír Jágr.

In addition to his talent, what makes Jaromír Jágr's appeal so potent is the timing of his meteorite rise to stardom. The Iron Curtain fell three months before Jágr turned 18, making him among the first Czech players eligible for the NHL draft without having to defect. He was drafted in 1990 by the Pittsburgh Penguins—the youngest player in the NHL.

At the start of his NHL career, Jágr bet on the magic of a date, choosing "68" for his jersey number (to memorialize the 1968 Prague Spring crushed by the Soviets). After that invasion, the hockey rink became a substitute battlefield for the two nations. Not only was hockey the national game in both the land of Big Brother and its tiny satellite, it was also a hard-hitting sport that demanded strength, skill, and discipline from an early age.

Born to a family of hard-working peasants—whose lands had been co-opted by the communists—little Jágr dreamed of becoming a pop star or a great hockey player. Discovering that he couldn't sing, he stayed on the ice all day, playing against (and often beating) kids several years his senior. At 16 Jágr was already playing for the national team.

On entering the NHL, Jágr's timing proved perfect again. In his first season he linked up with American and Canadian hockey greats Ron Francis and Mario Lemieux, who became his mentors. In 1991, as the Pittsburgh Penguins battled the Minnesota North Stars for the Stanley Cup, the entire Czech nation stayed up all night to watch Jágr's big win. A year later Jágr led his team to a repeat (his last Stanley Cup ring). In 1998 Jágr helped the Czech Republic win gold in the Nagano Olympics.

The good times didn't last. Jágr was sold by the bankrupt Penguins and gained a reputation as a spoiled superstar as he bounced from team to team. But with age came maturity. The oldest player in the NHL, Jágr now plays for the Florida Panthers, mentoring younger teammates. At age 44 he scored the most points of any player on a regular-season, conference-winning team and was awarded the Bill Masterton Memorial Trophy—given to the NHL's most dedicated player.

Back home, Jágr is considered one of the greatest hockey players of all time. He owns his hometown team, and six-year-old kids—who could well be his grandchildren—ask their coaches to lace their skates "the same way Jágr does."

while others mill around in the back and just enjoy the party.

Major running and biking events (such as the Prague International Marathon at the beginning of May) finish in the Old Town Square. The two biggest sporting events on Wenceslas Square are the Prague Pole Vault and a cycling competition that uses the square as a lap. The bottom of Wenceslas Square is sometimes set up for soccer, basketball, and beach volleyball tournaments. Both squares are also used for pop and folk concerts and for political rallies. These events are fine opportunities to feel the pulse of the Czech capital.

PRAGUE CONNECTIONS

Centrally located Prague is a logical gateway between Western and Eastern Europe. It's also the hub for trains and buses in the Czech Republic—from here, rail lines and expressways fan out like spokes on a wheel. This chapter covers arrivals and departures by train, bus, plane, and car. You'll find handy Czech train and bus schedules at www.idos.cz. For train schedules across Europe, use the German-rail website at www.bahn.com.

By Train

Prague's **main train station** (Hlavní Nádraží; "Praha hl. n." on schedules) serves all international trains; most trains within the Czech Republic, including high-speed SC Pendolino trains; and buses to and from Nürnberg and Munich. Trains serving Berlin also stop at the secondary **Holešovice station** (Nádraží Holešovice, located north of the river). Upon arrival, get money. Both stations have ATMs (best rates) and exchange bureaus (rotten rates).

To get a better geographical picture, remember that the Czech Republic is a country of landlocked, would-be sailors (recall the greeting *"ahoj"*). Accordingly, the four main international rail lines connect Prague to the closest ports on the four seas: the **North Sea Line** to Hamburg (7 hours) via Dresden and Berlin; the **Baltic Line** to Gdańsk (11 hours, one change) via Warsaw; the **Black Sea Line** to Varna (40 hours, one change) via Budapest and Belgrade; and the **Adriatic Line** to Split (20 hours, two changes) via Vienna and Zagreb.

MAIN TRAIN STATION (HLAVNÍ NÁDRAŽÍ)
The station is a busy hive of shops and services; posted maps help you find your way. Three parallel tunnels connect the tracks to the

arrival hall. Taking any of these, you'll first reach a low-ceilinged corridor with several services: To the right are an exchange office with Internet booths, a variety of handy picnic-supply shops, and the "official" taxi stands (avoid these rip-off cabbies—explained later).

Continuing straight past this corridor, you'll reach the waste-of-space main hall, where you'll find four Metro entrances in the center (two for each direction; see "Getting from the Main Station to Your Hotel," later). One **ATM** is along the right wall; two more are in front of the ticketing area under the central stairs. **Lockers** are in the corner under the stairs on the right and a **Billa supermarket** is in the corner under the stairs to the left.

The **Touristpoint** office—at the left end of the main hall (as you face the tracks)—offers a last-minute room-finding service, books car rentals, and sells maps, international phone cards, sightseeing tours, and adrenaline experiences (daily 8:00-22:00, tel. 224-946-010, www.touristpoint.cz, info@touristpoint.cz). Perhaps most importantly, they're willing to call you a taxi to avoid the "official" crooks out front: The driver will meet you at the desk.

Buying Tickets: For most trains, head for the **Czech Railways (České Dráhy) ticket office**—marked *ČD Centrum*—in the middle of the main hall under the stairs. The regular ticket desks are faster if you already know your schedule and destination, but not all attendants speak good English. For more in-depth questions, look for the tiny **ČD Travel** office, on the left as you enter the main office, which sells both domestic and international tickets, and is more likely to provide help in English (Mon-Fri 9:00-18:00, Sat until 14:00, closed Sun, shorter hours in winter, tel. 972-241-861, www.cd.cz/en).

The **RegioJet travel office,** with desks at both sides of the main ticket office, sells international train tickets from the DB (Deutsche Bahn—German railways) system and offers various DB deals and discounts. RegioJet also runs its own trains to Olomouc and Košice, Slovakia, and sells a variety of domestic (e.g., to Český Krumlov) and international (Vienna) bus tickets without a commission (Mon-Fri 5:00-19:45, Sat-Sun from 6:45, tel. 539-000-511, www.regiojet.cz). Despite its name, RegioJet does not sell plane tickets.

The **Leo Express ticket office,** across the hall from the ČD Centrum, sells tickets for its new Swiss-made trains to Olomouc and Košice (www.le.cz).

Bus Stops: To reach the bus stops for the AE bus to the airport and the DB buses to Nürnberg and Munich, simply find your way up to the Art Nouveau hall (explained later) and head outside.

Deciphering Schedules: Platforms are listed by number and—confusingly—sometimes also by letter. *S (sever)* means "south"—the corridor to the left as you face the tracks; *J (jih)* means "north"—the corridor to the right. But in practice, you can take any corridor and walk along the platform to your train. Also on schedules, *B1* means the bus platform (upstairs and out front), while *1B*—used by Leo Express trains—is the shorter track at the far-right end of platform 1.

A Bit of History: If you have time to kill waiting for a train, go exploring. First named for Emperor Franz Josef, the station was later renamed for President Woodrow Wilson (see the commemorative **plaque** in the main exit hall leading away from the tracks, and the large bronze **statue** in the park in front of the station). The Czechs appreciate Wilson's promotion of self-determination after World War I, which led to the creation of the free state of Czechoslovakia in 1918. Under the communists (who weren't big fans of Wilson), it was bluntly renamed Hlavní Nádraží—"Main Station." They enlarged the once-classy Art Nouveau station and painted it the compulsory dreary gray with reddish trim.

For a glimpse at the station's genteel pre-communist times, find your way up into its original **Art Nouveau Hall** (from the

main concourse, look for up escalators with *Historical Building of the Station* signs). You'll emerge to stand under a grandly restored dome with elaborate decorations, providing an almost shocking contrast to the businesslike aura of the rest of the station.

One more interesting historical site is at platform 1 (sector B), where you'll find a touching statue of a British gentleman with a young child. This **monument** honors the people of Great Britain who took in Czech and Slovak kids during World War II, offering them a safe home while their home country was in danger of attack.

Getting from the Main Station to Your Hotel

Even though the main train station is basically downtown, getting to your hotel can be a little tricky.

On Foot: Most hotels I list in the Old Town are within a 20-minute walk of the train station. Exit the station into a small park, walk through the park, and then cross the street on the other side. Head down Jeruzalémská street to the Jindřišská Tower and tram stop, walk under a small arch, then continue slightly to the right down Senovážná street. At the end of the street, you'll see the Powder Tower—the grand entry into the Old Town—to the left. Alternatively, Wenceslas Square in the New Town is a 10-minute walk—exit the station, cross the park, and walk to the left along Opletalova street.

CONNECTIONS

By Metro: The Metro is easy. The entrance is right inside the station's main hall—look for the red *M* with two directions: *Háje* or *Letňany*. To purchase tickets from the machine by the Metro entrance, you'll need Czech coins (get change at the change machine in the corner near the luggage lockers, or break a bill at a newsstand or grocery). Validate your ticket in the yellow machines *before* you go down the stairs to the tracks. To get to hotels in the Old Town, catch a Háje-bound train to the Muzeum stop, then transfer to the green line (direction: Dejvická) and get off at either Můstek or Staroměstská; these stops straddle the Old Town. The next stop, Malostranská, is handy for hotels in the Little Quarter. For details on Prague's public transit, see page 31.

Taxi: The fair metered rate into the Old Town is about 200 Kč; if your hotel is farther out or across the river, it should be no more

than 300 Kč. Avoid the "official" taxi stand that's marked inside the station: These thugs routinely overcharge arriving tourists (and refuse to take locals, who know the going rate and can't be fooled). Instead, to get an **honest cabbie,** exit the station's main hall through the big glass doors, then cross 50 yards through a park to Opletalova street. A few taxis are usually waiting there in front of Hotel Chopin, on the corner of Jeruzalémská street. Alternatively, the Touristpoint office, described earlier, can call a taxi for you (AAA Taxi—tel. 222-333-222; City Taxi—tel. 257-257-257). Before getting into a taxi, always confirm the maximum price to your destination, and make sure the driver turns on the meter. For more pointers on taking taxis, see page 33.

By Tram: The nearest tram stop is to the right as you exit the station (about 200 yards away). Tram #9 (headed away from railway tracks) takes you to the neighborhood near the National Theater and the Little Quarter, but isn't useful for most Old Town hotels.

HOLEŠOVICE TRAIN STATION (NÁDRAŽÍ HOLEŠOVICE)

This station, slightly farther from the center, is suburban mellow. The main hall has the same services as the main train station, in a more compact area. On the left are international and local ticket windows (open 24 hours) and an information office. On the right is an uncrowded café with Internet access (daily 8:00-19:30). Two ATMs are just outside the first glass doors, and the Metro is 50 yards to the right (follow signs toward *Vstup*, which means "entrance"; it's three stops to Hlavní Nádraží—the main station—or four stops to the city-center Muzeum stop). Taxis and trams are outside to the right (allow 300 Kč for a cab to the center).

TRAIN CONNECTIONS

All international trains pass through the main station (Hlavní Nádraží); some also stop at Holešovice (Nádraží Holešovice). Di-

rect overnight trains connect Prague to Vienna, Budapest, Kraków, and Warsaw. For tips on rail travel, see Practicalities.

From Prague's Main Station to Domestic Destinations: Konopiště Castle (train to **Benešov**, 2/hour, 1 hour, then 1.5-mile walk to castle), **Karlštejn** (2/hour, 40 minutes, then a

20-minute steep uphill hike to castle), **Křivoklát** (hourly, 1.5 hours total, transfer in Beroun to infrequent local train), **Kutná Hora** (11/day, 1 hour, more with change in Kolín; to reach Kutná Hora's town center or bone church, you'll need to transfer to a local train), **Terezín** (train to Bohušovice, nearly hourly, 1-1.5 hours, then 5-minute taxi or bus ride—the direct bus from near Holešovice station is better), **Karlovy Vary** (every 2 hours, 3.25 hours), **Český Krumlov** (8/day, 1/day direct, 3.5 hours—bus is faster and cheaper, but may be booked up), **České Budějovice** (almost hourly, 2.5 hours), **Třeboň** (7/day, 2.5 hours, transfer at Veselí nad Lužnicí—get off at Třeboň-Lázně, not Třeboň-Město), **Telč** (3/day, 4-5 hours, requires 2 changes, bus is better), **Třebíč** (nearly hourly, 4-5 hours, transfer in Brno, bus is better), **Slavonice** (first take bus to Telč, 5/day Mon-Fri, 3/day Sat-Sun, 2-3 hours; then 1-hour train to Slavonice, 5/day), **Olomouc** (at least hourly, 2-3 hours; use Olomouc for connections to **Wallachia**), **Valtice** (hourly, 4 hours, 1 transfer), **Břeclav** (with connections to **Mikulov Wine Region;** 9/day direct, 3 hours, most from Holešovice station), **Brno** (every 2 hours direct, 2.5 hours, more with changes).

From Prague's Main Station to International Destinations: Berlin (6/day direct, 4.5-5 hours), **Dresden** (every 2 hours, 2 hours), **Nürnberg** (1/day with change in Cheb, 5 hours, bus is better—see below), **Munich** (3/day direct, 6 hours; bus is better—see next page), **Frankfurt** (3/day, 7-8 hours, 2 changes, more options with bus to Nürnberg), **Cologne** (bus to Nürnberg or Mannheim, then change to train, 7.5-9 hours total), **Vienna**—Vídeň in Czech (6/day direct, 4 hours, more with 1 change; 1 night train, 7 hours), **Paris** (5/day, 10.5-12 hours; 1 direct bus, 16 hours), **Budapest** (5/day direct, 7 hours; more with 1 change; 1 night train, 8.5 hours), **Kraków** (1/day with change to bus in Ostrava, 5.5 hours; 2/day with 2 changes, 7-8 hours; 1 night train via Auschwitz, 8 hours),

Warsaw (1/day direct, 8 hours; 3/day with change in Ostrava, 7.5 hours; 1 night train, 9 hours).

By Bus

Prague's main bus station is at Florenc, east of the Old Town (Metro: Florenc). But some connections use other stations, including Roztyly (Metro: Roztyly), Na Knížecí (Metro: Anděl), Holešovice (Metro: Nádraží Holešovice), Hradčanská (Metro: Hradčanská), or the main train station (Metro: Hlavní Nádraží). Be sure to confirm which station your bus uses.

From Prague by Bus to: Terezín (hourly, 1 hour, departs from Holešovice), **Český Krumlov** (10/day, 3.5 hours, some from Florenc, others leave from Na Knížecí or Roztyly), **Břeclav** (with connections to **Mikulov Wine Region;** 1-2/hour from Florenc, fewer on weekends, 5-6 hours, train is better—see previous page), **Brno** (2/hour from Florenc, 2.5 hours), **Nürnberg,** Germany (6/day via IC Bus, 3.75 hours, covered by rail passes, departs in front of main train station), **Munich,** Germany (4/day via ExpressBus, 5 hours, covered by rail passes, departs from main train station), **Budapest** (1-4/day via Orange Ways, not covered by rail passes, 6.5-7.5 hours, www.orangeways.com).

By Plane

VÁCLAV HAVEL AIRPORT

Prague's modern, tidy, user-friendly Václav Havel Airport (formerly Ruzyně Airport) is located 12 miles (about 30 minutes) west of the city center. Terminal 2 serves destinations within the EU except for Great Britain (no passport controls); Terminal 1 serves Great Britain and everywhere else. The airport has ATMs (avoid the change desks), desks promoting transportation services (such as city transit and shuttle buses), kiosks selling city maps and phone cards, and a TI (airport code: PRG, airport tel. 220-113-314, operator tel. 220-111-111, www.prg.aero/en).

If you're flying out of Václav Havel Airport and need to process a VAT refund (see page 446), get your papers stamped at customs *before* you go through security. In Terminal 1, customs is located in the far left-hand corner of the departure hall, next to the oversize baggage desk. At Terminal 2, customs is immediately to the right of the security check. You can cash in your refund at a Travelex office (minus a 4 percent fee): In Terminal 1, these are located both before and after security. In Terminal 2, Travelex has a booth *before* security only (just to the left).

Getting from the Airport to Your Hotel

Getting between the airport and downtown is easy. Leaving either airport terminal, you have four options, listed below from cheapest to priciest:

Dirt Cheap: Take bus #119 to the Nádraží Veleslavín stop (10 minutes), then take the Metro into the center (another 10 minutes, 32 Kč, buy tickets at info desk in airport arrival hall). This is also fastest as it avoids traffic jams.

Budget: Take the airport express (AE) bus to the main train station, or to the Masarykovo Nádraží Station near Republic Square—Náměstí Republiky (50 Kč, runs every half-hour daily 5:46-21:16, 40 minutes, look for the *AE* sign in front of the terminal and pay the driver, www.cd.cz/en). From either station, you can take the Metro, hire a taxi, or walk to your hotel. The Masarykovo Nádraží stop is slightly closer to downtown.

Moderate: Take the Čedaz minibus shuttle (from exit F at Terminal 1 or exit E at Terminal 2) to the Náměstí Republiky (Republic Square) station, at the entrance to the Old Town. The shuttle stop is on V Celnici street, across the street from Hotel Marriott and near the recommended Brasserie La Gare (pay 130 Kč directly to driver, daily 7:30-19:00, 2/hour, 30 minutes, info desk in arrival hall).

Expensive: Catch a taxi. Cabbies wait at the curb directly in front of the arrival hall. Or book a yellow AAA taxi through their office in the airport hall—you'll get a 50 percent discount coupon for the trip back (book your return trip by calling 222-333-222). AAA taxis wait in front of exit D at Terminal 1 and exit E at Terminal 2 (metered rate, generally 500-600 Kč to downtown).

By Private Car Service

Mike's Chauffeur Service is a reliable, family-run company with fair and fixed rates around town and beyond. Friendly Mike's motto is, "We go the extra mile for you." If Mike is busy, he'll send one of his colleagues—all of whom speak English (round-trip fares, with waiting time included, prices valid through 2018 with this book: Český Krumlov-3,800 Kč, Terezín-1,900 Kč, Karlštejn-1,700 Kč, Karlovy Vary and Pilsner Urquell brewery in Plzeň-3,800 Kč, 4 percent surcharge for credit-card payment; these prices for up to 4 people, minibus for up to 8 also available; tel. 241-768-231, mobile 602-224-893, www.mike-chauffeur.cz, mike.chauffeur@cmail.cz). On the way to Český Krumlov, Mike will stop at no extra charge at Hluboká Castle and/or České Budějovice, where the original Bud beer is made. Mike can also arrange a local guide for your time in many of these places. And for day trips from Prague, Mike can bring bicycles along and will pedal with you.

Mike also offers "Panoramic Transfers" to **Vienna** (7,000 Kč, depart Prague at 8:00, arrive Český Krumlov at 10:00, stay up to 5 hours, 1-hour scenic Czech riverside-and-village drive, then a 2-hour autobahn ride to your Vienna hotel, maximum 4 people); **Budapest** (9,500 Kč via Bratislava or Český Krumlov, 6 hours); and **Kraków** (9,300 Kč direct, or 9,800 Kč with a stop at Auschwitz; these prices include all road taxes). Mike can also pick you up in any of these cities and bring you to Prague. Check Mike's website for special deals on last-minute transfers, including super-cheap "deadhead" rides when you travel in the opposite direction of a full-fare client.

BEYOND PRAGUE

DAY TRIPS FROM PRAGUE

*Kutná Hora • Terezín Memorial •
Konopiště • Karlštejn • Křivoklát •
Karlovy Vary (Carlsbad)*

Prague has plenty to keep a traveler busy, but don't overlook the interesting day trips in the nearby Bohemian countryside. Within a short bus or train ride of Prague (in different directions), you'll find a rich medieval town, a sobering concentration camp memorial, three grand castles, a swanky spa resort, and a variety of other stopovers.

Kutná Hora

Kutná Hora (KOOT-nah HO-rah) is a re-freshingly authentic, yet unmistakably gor-geous town that sits on top of what was once Europe's largest silver mine. In its heyday, the mine was so productive that Kutná Hora was Bohemia's "second city" after Prague. Much of Europe's standard coinage was minted here, and the king got a 12 percent cut of every penny. In addition to financing much of Prague's grand architecture, these precious de-posits also paid for Kutná Hora's particularly fine cathedral. But by about 1700, the mining and minting petered out, and the city slum-bered.

Once rich, then ignored, Kutná Hora is now appreciated by tourists looking for a handy side-trip from Prague. While most visitors come here primarily for the famous, offbeat Sedlec Bone Church, the delightful town itself trumps it—with one of the fin-est Czech churches outside of Prague (St. Barbara's Cathedral), a

Day Trips

breathtaking promenade overlooking the valley, a fascinating silver mine, and a cute, cobbled town center with pretty pastel houses.

All in all, underrated Kutná Hora makes a strong case for the title of "best Czech stop outside of Prague." Unlike dolled-up Český Krumlov, Kutná Hora is a typical Czech town. The shops on the main square cater to locals, and the factory between the Sedlec Bone Church and the train station—since the 1930s, the biggest tobacco processor in the country—is now Philip Morris' headquarters for Central Europe. Kutná Hora is about as close to quintessential Czech life as you can get.

GETTING TO KUTNÁ HORA

The town is 45 miles east of Prague. Direct trains from Prague stop at Kutná Hora's main train station, two miles from the town cen-

Day Trips from Prague at a Glance

▲▲**Kutná Hora** Finely preserved yet down-to-earth city, once home to the world's largest silver mine, now best known for an opulent cathedral—built with riches from the mining bonanza—and an evocative chapel decorated with human bones. See page 262.

▲▲**Terezín Memorial** Walled town and fortress that served as a WWII internment camp and Gestapo prison; today, both house poignant memorials. See page 277.

▲**Konopiště Castle** Former residence of the Habsburg Archduke Franz Ferdinand and his Czech bride, with the most lived-in-feeling interior (and most interesting historical tour) of any Czech castle. See page 291.

▲**Karlštejn Castle** Popular castle—built by Charles IV just outside Prague—with perhaps the country's most dramatic exterior. See page 295.

▲**Karlovy Vary** (Carlsbad) Genteel, architecture-packed spa town where well-heeled Russian and German tourists stroll manicured riverfront promenades sipping icky (but healthy) spring water. See page 304.

Křivoklát Castle Set in a pretty, forested, relatively untouristed countryside, this Back Door alternative to Karlštejn has a nearly-as-fine interior and a lively workshop courtyard in summer (but is farther out, and has fewer options for English-speaking visitors). En route, the Rückl Glassworks in Nižbor offers traditional Czech crystal manufacturing; nearby Lány—with Tomáš Garrigue Masaryk's grave—is a modern-day pilgrimage site for Czech patriots. See page 298.

ter (11/day, 1 hour; other trains are slower and require transfer in Kolín). From the main station, a local train shuttles visitors in just a few minutes to Sedlec Station (near the Sedlec Bone Church), then to the central Město Station (near the rest of the sights). After getting off at the main station, follow the passage beneath the tracks to the cute little yellow local train. For train schedules, see www.jizdniradyidnes.cz.

In Prague, make sure to buy a ticket to "Kutná Hora Město" rather than "Kutná Hora hl. n." (the main station)—the price is nearly the same, and this gives you the flexibility to get off and on at any of the three Kutná Hora stations.

PLANNING YOUR TIME

For the most efficient visit, head to the Sedlec Bone Church first, then explore the town center of Kutná Hora. Kutná Hora is quiet on Sundays, when most shops are closed.

Here's my suggested plan: At Kutná Hora's main train station, transfer to the local train. Get off at its first stop (Kutná Hora Sedlec), and walk five minutes to the Bone Church. After your visit, head to St. Barbara's Cathedral in the town center via tourist minivan, taxi, or public bus. After touring the cathedral, follow my self-guided walk to the Czech Museum of Silver and take an English-language mine tour (consider booking ahead online or by phone, or simply drop by in advance to sign up). At the end of the day, walk to Město Station (about 15 minutes) to catch the train back to Kutná Hora's main train station, where you'll transfer to a train back to Prague.

Orientation to Kutná Hora

For a relatively small town (about 20,000 people), Kutná Hora is tricky to navigate: It's long and skinny, with a spaghetti of lanes spilling across the summit of a promontory that stretches from the main train station, past the Bone Church, to the historical center.

TOURIST INFORMATION

The main TI is on **Palacký Square** (Palackého Náměstí), housed in the same building as the Alchemy Museum (April-Sept daily 9:00-18:00; Oct-March Mon-Fri until 17:00, Sat-Sun until 16:00; tel. 327-512-378, www.kutnahora.cz). It offers Internet access and also rents bicycles (220 Kč/day, mobile 605-802-874).

A small TI kiosk, with handy WCs, is in front of the **cathedral;** you can also hire a local guide here. Reserve ahead if you can (500 Kč/hour Tue-Sun, no tours Mon, tel. 327-516-710, mobile 736-485-408, infocentrum@kh.cz).

ARRIVAL IN KUTNÁ HORA

The **Kutná Hora Sedlec Station** is a short walk from the Bone Church. From the station, head one block down the street perpendicular to the tracks, passing a large church on your right (a cathedral that predates the mine and the town). Cross the main street and find the small Bone Church in the middle of the cemetery directly ahead.

If you're skipping the Bone Church (or not visiting it first), stay on the train to the **Kutná Hora Město Station** in the valley. From there, hike up to St. Barbara's Cathedral (about 20 minutes) to find the start of my self-guided Kutná Hora walk.

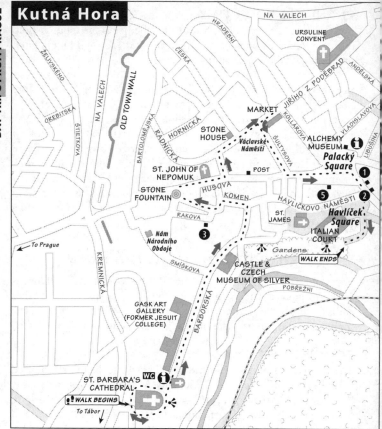

Kutná Hora Walk

This self-guided walk connects virtually all the sights in the historical center in a near-loop (Kutná Hora's most famous attraction—the Bone Church—is on the outskirts of town, and listed on page 271). Before you get too far into the walk, call or drop by the Czech Museum of Silver to book a spot on the 1.5-hour, claustrophobic mine tour. No stop on this walk is more than 10 minutes from the museum, so you can bail out and head for your tour at any point and easily resume the walk later.

• *Begin in the inviting park surrounding the cathedral.*

St. Barbara's Cathedral and Park: Rising like three pointy tents from a forest of buttresses, St. Barbara's strikes an exquisite Gothic profile. This culmination of Czech Gothic architecture was funded with a "spare no expense" attitude by a town riding the crest of a wave of mining wealth. Be sure to tour the **cathedral's interior**

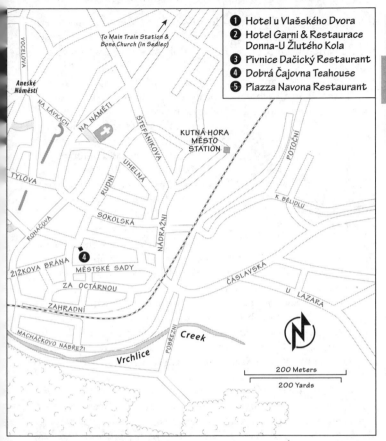

① Hotel u Vlašského Dvora
② Hotel Garni & Restaurace Donna-U Žlutého Kola
③ Pivnice Dačický Restaurant
④ Dobrá Čajovna Teahouse
⑤ Piazza Navona Restaurant

(see listing, later)—but also take the time to do a slow lap around the pristine park that surrounds it.

Behind the church's apse, belly up to the **viewpoint** for an orientation to the city. From left to right, visually trace the historical center that perches along the promontory's crest: The long former Jesuit College now houses a modern art museum. The big, gray building that plunges down the cliff is the town's "little castle" *(Hrádek)*, with the Czech Museum of Silver. And the spire to the right of that bookends this walk. Surveying this scene, think about the history of a town made very, very rich by the glittering deposits it sits upon. Wealthy as it was, this was still an industrial town: The river below was so polluted they called it "Stink" in Czech. Notice the vineyards draping the hill. Kutná Hora is closer to Moravia (the eastern Czech Republic) than it is to Prague—here, you're beginning to see the transition from beer country in Bohemia to the wine country of Moravia.

• *After circling the church, walk along the grand...*

Terrace: Just before you head along the panoramic promenade, notice the handy TI in the little house on the left. Then stroll

regally along the stately white building, which now houses the modern and contemporary **GASK** art collection (see listing, later). The statues of saints that line the terrace are a reminder of the building's Jesuit past. The Jesuits arrived here in 1626 with a mission: to make the Protestant population Catholic again. These chubby sandstone figures, just like those on the Charles Bridge in Prague, were initially commissioned as Counter-Reformation propaganda pieces.

Near the end of the terrace, continue following the broad cobbled footpath downhill...and keep an eye out for an army of white-jacketed, white-helmeted miners trudging up the hill for their daily shift. Or maybe they're tourists, about to explore the former silver mine at the **Czech Museum of Silver,** which occupies the big building on your right (see listing, later).

• *At the little park in front of the museum, take the left (level) fork, following* Stone Fountain *signs. When you hit the bigger street (with lots of parked cars), turn left (uphill, on Rejskova), and bear left around the big drab building. You'll emerge into a little square (Rejskovo Náměstí), with a big and impressive...*

Stone Fountain (Kamenná Kašna): The intensive mining under Kutná Hora released arsenic and other toxins, poisoning the water supply. This means that the city struggled with obtaining clean drinking water, which had to be brought to town by a sophisticated system of pipes, then stored in large tanks. At the end of the 15th century, the architect Rejsek built a 12-sided, richly decorated Gothic structure over one of these tanks. Although

no longer functioning, the fountain survives unchanged—the only structure like it in Bohemia.

• *Facing the fountain, hook right around the corner and head down Husova street. On the left, you'll pass the stately town library (Městská Knihovna), then the gorgeous late–Baroque/Rococo Church of St. John of*

Nepomuk (named for the ever-popular Czech patron saint). Turn left up the street after this church (Lierova). At the top of the street, turn right on Václavské Náměstí (Kutná Hora's own Wenceslas Square). On your left, you'll spot the frilly decorations on the...

Stone House (Kamenný Dům): Notice the meticulous detail in the grape leaves, branches, and animals on this house's facade and up in its gable. Talented Polish craftsmen delicately carved the brittle stone into what was considered a marvel of its time. Skip the boring museum of local arts and crafts inside.

• *Continue past the house as the street opens up into a leafy and inviting square. For a slice of authentic Czech life, continue straight when the street narrows again; a half-block down on your right, under the* tržnice *sign, is the town's humble...*

Market: This double row of stalls selling fake Nike shoes and cheap jeans is as much a part of Czech urban life today as farmers markets were in the past. Many of the stalls are run by Vietnamese immigrants, the Czech Republic's third-largest minority (after Slovaks and Poles). Many came here in the 1970s as part of a communist solidarity program that sent Vietnamese workers to Czech textile factories. They learned the language, adapted to the environment, and, after 1989, set off on a road to entrepreneurial suc-

cess that allowed them to bring over friends and relatives (Mon-Fri 7:30-16:45, shorter hours Sat, closed Sun).

• *Backtrack a few steps uphill, then turn left to walk down through the postcard-perfect Šultysova street, with a towering plague column at its center. Turn left at the street past the column, enjoying the pretty, colorful arcades. You'll emerge into the lively main square.*

Palacký Square (Palackého Náměstí): Beautiful but still somehow local, this square enjoys colorful facades, tempting al fresco restaurant tables, and generous public benches. Across the square on the left, notice the **TI;** inside the same building is the **Alchemy Museum** (described later).

• *Exit the square at the far-right corner, following the traffic-free street (in the gap between buildings, toward the green house). You'll enter...*

Havlíček Square (Havlíčkovo Náměstí): The monuments on this leafy, parklike square are a Who's Who of important Czech patriots.

Straight ahead, the stone statue with his arm outstretched is **Karel Havlíček** (1821-1856), the founder of Czech political journalism (and the square's namesake). From Kutná Hora, Havlíček ran an influential magazine highly critical of the Habsburg government. In 1851, he was forced into exile and detained for five years in the Tirolean Alps under police surveillance. His integrity is reflected by the quote inscribed on the statue: "You can try to bribe me with favors, you can threaten me, you can torture me, yet I will never turn a traitor." His motto became an inspiration for generations of Czech intellectuals, most of whom faced a similar combination of threats and temptations. Havlíček (whose name means "little Havel") was much revered in the 1970s and 1980s, when the *other* Havel (Václav) was similarly imprisoned for his dissent.

Below and to the right, the bronze, walrus-mustachioed statue in front of the big building honors the founder of Czechoslovakia, **Tomáš Garrigue Masaryk** (1850-1937; see sidebar on page 174). Circle around behind the pedestal to see the brief inscription tracing the statue's up-and-down history, which parallels the country's troubled 20th-century history: erected by Kutná Hora townspeople on October 27, 1938 (the eve of Czechoslovakia's 20th birthday); torn down in 1942 (by occupying Nazis, who disliked Masaryk as a symbol of Czech independence); erected again on October 27, 1948 (by freedom-loving locals, a few months after the communist coup); torn down again in 1957 (by the communists, who considered Masaryk an enemy of the working class); and erected once again on October 27, 1991. Notice that the Czechs, ever practical, have left a blank space below the last entry.

Masaryk stands in front of the **Italian Court** (Vlašský Dvůr). Step inside its fine courtyard. This palace, located on the site where Czech currency was once made, became Europe's most important mint and the main residence of Czech kings in the 1400s. It's named for the Italian minters who came to Kutná Hora to teach the locals their trade. Most of the present-day building is a 19th-century reconstruction. Today, it hosts a moderately interest-ing museum on minting and local history. While the main Gothic hall (now a wedding chamber) and the Art Nouveau-decorated St. Wenceslas Chapel are interesting, you can visit them only with a 40-minute guided tour (rarely in English; Czech tour comes with English handout; April-Sept daily 9:00-18:00, shorter hours Oct-March).

Exiting the courtyard of the Italian Court, turn right and watch on the wall to your right for a small bronze tablet showing a hand flashing a peace sign, covered with barbed wire. This is an unassuming little **memorial** to the victims of the communist regime's misrule and torture.

Continue straight down the steps into a little park, and then turn right to reach a great **viewpoint**. It overlooks the distinctive roof of the cathedral and the scenic valley below.

• *Your walk is finished. If you're headed for your tour at the Czech Museum of Silver, take this scenic route: Walk back up to Havlíček Square, circle around the Italian Court, curl along the downhill side of St. James' Church, and enjoy the views. Eventually the view terrace dead-ends at a little lane that bends right and uphill, depositing you at the museum.*

If you're headed back to Prague, it takes about 15 minutes to walk to the Kutná Hora Město train station from Havlíček Square. Head downhill past the park, which funnels you between two buildings. Take the first left on Roháčova, then the first right on Sokolská. When you reach the wide cross-street (Nádražní), turn left and follow the train tracks to the little pink station.

Sights in Kutná Hora

For sightseeing efficiency, start with the Bone Church on the outskirts, then return to the center of town (with the cathedral, silver mine/museum, and my self-guided walk).

ON THE OUTSKIRTS

▲▲Sedlec Bone Church (Kostnice v Sedlci)

Located about a mile and a half outside of the town's historical center, the Sedlec Bone Church sits in a serene graveyard and looks

unassuming from the outside. But inside, it's filled with the bones of 40,000 people—stacked into neat, 20-foot-tall pyramids decorating the walls and ceilings. The 14th-century plagues and 15th-century wars provided all the raw material necessary for the monks who made these designs.

Cost and Hours: 90 Kč, daily April-Sept 8:00-18:00, March and Oct 9:00-17:00, Nov-Feb 9:00-16:00, good 40-Kč audioguide adds 15 minutes of commentary to make it more meaningful, tel. 327-561-143, www. kostnice.cz.

Visiting the Church: Stand outside the church. This is a place of reflection. The cemetery here was "seeded" with holy earth brought from Jerusalem, which made this sacred ground. Demand was high, and corpses that could no longer pay the rent (i.e., those who lacked surviving relatives with enough disposable income for postmortem real estate) were "evicted." What to do with the bones? Recycle them as church decorations with a message.

The monks, who first placed these bones 400 years ago, were guided by the belief that in order to live well, one must constantly remember death (*memento mori*—"what we are now, someday you shall be"). They also wanted to remind viewers that the earthly church was a community of both the living and the dead, a countless multitude that would one day stand before God. Later bone stackers were more interested in design than theology...as evidenced by the many show-off flourishes you'll see around the church.

Approach the church. Ignore the dull upper chapel, and head down below (look for the *kostinec* sign). Flanking the stairwell are two giant chalices made of bones (a symbol of Jan Hus' egalitarian approach to worship).

Downstairs, on either side are giant stacks of bones, reaching up to the top of the Gothic vaults (there are six such bone-pyramids in this small chapel). The skulls are neatly arranged on top, in the belief that this closeness to God would serve them well when Jesus returns to judge the living and the dead. Straight ahead dangles a chandelier, which supposedly includes at least one of every bone in the human body. In the glass case on the right (by the pillar), see the skulls with gnarly holes and other wounds. These belonged to soldiers who died fighting in the Hussite Wars—a boom time for this cemetery.

Finally, head into the left wing of the church, where you'll find a giant coat of arms of the aristocratic Schwarzenberg family—decorated with the skull of an Ottoman invader (a fearsome foe of the time), whose "eye" is being pecked out by a raven made of human bones.

Your visit is over. Go outside and head into town, thankful all of your limbs are intact.

Getting from the Church to Town: The Bone Church runs a **tourist minivan** that can shuttle you from the church to sights in town (35 Kč/person, 3-person minimum or pay the entire 105-Kč fee, April-Sept 9:00-18:00, Oct-March until 17:00, inquire at the desk, mobile 731-402-307). Ask the shuttle bus to drop you off at the park surrounding St. Barbara's Cathedral.

If the shuttle is on a break, church staff can call a **taxi,** which costs no more than 150 Kč to the cathedral. Another option is public **bus** #F01 (on weekdays) or #F07 (on weekends), which runs from near the Bone Church to a stop near the cathedral (12 Kč, pay driver, 2/hour Mon-Fri, 1/hour Sat-Sun, 20 minutes).

IN THE CENTER
▲▲St. Barbara's Cathedral (Chrám Sv. Barbory)

The cathedral was founded in 1388 by miners, who dedicated it to their patron saint. The dazzling interior celebrates the town's sources of wealth, with frescoes featuring mining and minting. This church was a stunning feat of architecture by two Gothic geniuses of Prague, Matyáš Rejsek and Benedict Ried. And, like Prague's cathedral, it sat unfinished and sealed off for centuries, until it was finally completed in the early 20th century.

Cost and Hours: 60 Kč, daily 9:00-18:00, shorter hours Nov-March, audioguide-40 Kč, tel. 327-515-796, www.khfarnost.cz.

Visiting the Cathedral: While this tour covers the highlights, you can ask to borrow slightly more detailed info sheets at the ticket desk or rent the more in-depth audioguide.

Head inside, walk to the middle of the main nave, and just take it all in. Intricate, lacy vaulting decorates an impossibly high ceiling that's also decorated with the coats of arms of local miners. This is the epitome of Gothic: a mind-bogglingly tall nave supported by flying buttresses that create space for not one, but two levels of big windows; pointed arches where the columns converge; and an overall sense of verticality and light.

Take in the gorgeous **high altar**—a Last Supper scene of carved and painted wood. Then circle clockwise around the apse, past Baroque altars. Tune into the fine **stained-glass windows** (throughout the church) by František Urban, a somewhat less talented contemporary of Alfons Mucha, who nevertheless employs a similarly eye-pleasing Art Nouveau flair to illustrate scenes from church history. (A tiny version of this church's distinctive triple-pointed roofline appears in the background of several windows.)

Continue around the apse. The second-to-last chapel, called the **Smíšek Chapel,** is an artistic highlight. The late-Gothic frescoes—*The Arrival of the Queen of Sheba, The Trial of Trajan,* and especially the fresco under the chapel's window depicting two men with candles—are the only remaining works of a Dutch-trained master in Gothic Bohemia. The final chapel, called the **St. Wenceslas Chapel,** has frescoes under the windows showing miners going about their daily labor.

Continue up the side nave. Midway along, look for the **miner statue** on a pillar on your right. He's wearing a typical white miner's

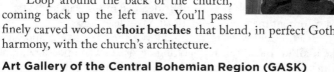

coat. White fabric was the cheapest option (as it required no dyes), and was easier to see in the dark. The leather mat wrapped around his waist made it easier for him to slide down chutes inside the mine. Most miners were healthy, unattached men in their 20s. An average of five miners died each day—from cave-ins, collapsing scaffolding, built-up poisonous gases, fires, and so on. At the back wall of the long chapel on your left, notice the precious frescoes from 1463 showing two people minting coins.

Loop around the back of the church, coming back up the left nave. You'll pass finely carved wooden **choir benches** that blend, in perfect Gothic harmony, with the church's architecture.

Art Gallery of the Central Bohemian Region (GASK)

The huge, former Baroque Jesuit college—which stretches from the cathedral all the way to the castle—was recently restored and converted into an art museum. It boasts the second-biggest exhibition space in the country (after the National Gallery in Prague), filled with ever-changing temporary exhibits of 20th- and 21st-century art.

Cost and Hours: Combo-ticket for all exhibits-200 Kč, single exhibit-80 Kč, April-Dec Tue-Sun 10:00-18:00, March Tue-Sun until 17:00, closed Mon year-round and Jan-Feb, Barborská 51, www.gask.cz.

▲Hrádek Castle and the Czech Museum of Silver (České Muzeum Stříbra)

Located in Kutná Hora's 15th-century Hrádek ("little castle"), the Czech Museum of Silver offers a fascinating look at the primary source of local wealth and pride. Over the centuries, this mine produced some 2,500 tons of silver, copper, and zinc. Today you can visit the facility only with a 1.5-hour tour, which lets you do some spelunking in the former miners' passages that run beneath the entire town center. Note that the tour involves some tight squeezes and may be overwhelming if you're claustrophobic. Also bring some warm clothing—mines are cold.

Cost and Tours: The English tour of the mine (Route II) costs 120 Kč; Route I, which includes only the aboveground museum, is pointless. You can book tours online only two or more days in advance. Better yet, call ahead (the day before or the morning of your visit) to ask when English tours are scheduled—wait through the Czech recording and ask to speak to someone in English. Without advance reservations, drop by the museum soon after you arrive in

Kutná Hora to find out the schedule and reserve. Tel. 327-512-159, www.cms-kh.cz.

Hours: May-Sept Tue-Sun 10:00-18:00, April and Oct Tue-Sun until 17:00, Nov Tue-Sun until 16:00, closed Mon year-round and Dec-March.

Visiting the Museum and Mine: First, your guide takes you to see an intriguing horse-powered winch that once hoisted 2,000 pounds of rock at a time out of the mine. You'll learn the two methods miners used to extract the precious ore: either by hammering with a chisel or pick, or by setting a fire next to a rock—heating it until it naturally cracked.

Then you'll don a miner's coat and helmet, grab a bulky communist-era flashlight, and walk like the Seven Dwarves through the town center to a secret doorway. It's time to climb deep into the mine for a wet, dark, and claustrophobic tour of the medieval shafts that honeycomb the rock beneath the town—walking down 167 steps, traversing 900 feet of underground passages (but it feels even longer), then walking back up 35 steps.

Along the way, you'll see white limestone deposits in the form of mini-stalagmites and stalactites, and peer down into a 26-foot-deep pool of crystal-clear water. Squeezing through very tight passages, you'll feel like (fill in your own childbirth joke here). The mine holds a steady, year-round temperature of 54 degrees Fahrenheit while fat drops of condensation fall continually from the ceiling thanks to the nearly 100 percent humidity. Prepare for the moment when all the lights go out, plunging you into a darkness as total as you'll ever experience. You'll understand why miners relied on their other senses. For instance, when silver was struck, it made a telltale sound and smelled faintly like garlic.

Finally, ascending to ground level, your guide will explain safety mechanisms at the surface, and walk you through the smelting and minting processes that turned those raw deposits into coins for an entire continent.

Alchemy Museum (Muzeum Alchymie)

The only one of its kind in the Czech Republic, situated in the surprisingly deep medieval cellars of this otherwise unassuming house, this museum features a laboratory dedicated to the pursuit of *prima materia* (primal matter). The English descriptions do a good job explaining the goals and methods of alchemy and the fate of its failed practitioners. The rare Gothic tower in the rear of the house is set up as an alchemist's study (complete with ancient books), looking much as it did when a prince used this vaulted space in his quest to purify matter and spirit.

Cost and Hours: 60 Kč, daily 9:00-18:00, Oct-March until

17:00, on the main square in the same building as the TI, tel. 327-512-378.

Sleeping and Eating in Kutná Hora

($$$$ = Splurge, $$$ = Pricier, $$ = Moderate, $ = Budget)

Sleeping: Although one day is enough for Kutná Hora, staying overnight saves you money (hotels are much cheaper here than in Prague) and allows you to better savor the atmosphere of a small Czech town.

$ Hotel u Vlašského Dvora and **Hotel Garni** are two renovated townhouses run by the same management. Furnished in a mix of 1930s and modern style, the hotels come with access to a fitness center and sauna. Hotel Garni is slightly nicer (a few steps off main square at Havlíčkovo Náměstí 513, tel. 327-515-773, www.vlasskydvur.cz).

Eating: $$ Pivnice Dačický has made a theme of its namesake, a popular 17th-century author who once lived here. Solid wooden tables rest under perky illustrations of medieval town life, and a once-local brew, also named after Dačický, flows from the tap. They serve standard Czech fare, as well as excellent game and fish. While its regulars still come here for the cheap lunch specials, during tourist season the crowd is mostly international. Service can be slow when a group arrives (daily 11:00-23:00, Rakova 8, tel. 327-512-248, mobile 603-434-367, www.dacicky.com).

$$ Dobrá Čajovna Teahouse also offers the chance to escape—not to medieval times, but to a Thai paradise. Filled with tea cases, water pipes, and character, this place is an ideal spot to dawdle away the time that this ageless town has reclaimed for you. On weekdays, they serve vegetarian lunch specials (Mon-Fri 11:00-22:00, Sat-Sun from 14:00, Havlíčkovo Náměstí 84, mobile 777-028-481).

$ Restaurace Donna-U Žlutého Kola ("Yellow Wheels") serves the fastest, tastiest Czech dishes in town, attracting a local crowd. There's a long menu in English, but the lunch specials are only listed on a separate sheet in Czech. When the weather's nice, sit in the shady courtyard behind the restaurant (daily, lunch specials until 15:00, on Havlíčkovo Náměstí, right above Hotel Garni, tel. 327-512-749).

$$ Piazza Navona features irritating English-language advertising ("the only true Italian restaurant in town"), but it still draws loyal customers thanks to its decent food and superb location on the main square (daily, Palackého Náměstí 90, tel. 327-512-588).

Kutná Hora Connections

To return to Prague, hop on a local train from Kutná Hora Město Station, near the historical center (or Kutná Hora Sedlec Station if you end your day at the Bone Church), and take it to the Kutná Hora main station for your train transfer to Prague. Note that the best Prague connection runs only about every two hours, so check schedules carefully; other options require an additional change and take much longer.

Terezín Memorial

Terezín (TEH-reh-zeen), an hour by bus from Prague, was originally a fortified town named after Habsburg Empress Maria Theresa (it's called "Theresienstadt" in German). It was built in the 1780s with state-of-the-art, star-shaped walls designed to keep out the Prussians. In 1941, the Nazis removed the town's 7,000 inhabitants and brought in 58,000 Jews, creating a horribly over-crowded ghetto. Ironically, the town's medieval walls, originally meant to keep Germans out, were later used by Germans to keep the Jews in. As the Nazis' model "Jewish town" for deceiving Red Cross inspectors, Terezín fostered the illusion that its Jewish in-mates lived relatively normal lives—making the sinister truth all the more cruel.

Compared to other such sights in Eastern and Central Europe (such as Auschwitz or Mauthausen), Terezín (worth ▲▲) feels dif-ferent: First, it focuses less on the Nazis' ruthless and calculated methods, and instead celebrates the arts and culture that thrived here despite the conditions—imbuing the place with a tragic hu-manity. Second, the various museums, memorials, and points of interest are spread over a large area in two distinct parts: a drab grid of a town and the original fortress (across the river, a short walk away). This means you're largely on your own to connect the dots and flesh out the story (use my self-guided tour to help).

To lift your spirits after a sobering visit, consider side-tripping to the vibrant historic town of Litoměřice, just three miles away (see page 289).

GETTING THERE

The camp is about 40 miles northwest of Prague. It's most convenient to visit Terezín by **bus** (described next) or **tour bus** (see page 39).

Buses to Terezín leave about hourly from Prague's Holešovice train station (Nádraží Holešovice, on Metro line C). When you get off the Metro (coming from the city center), head toward the front of the train, go upstairs, turn right, and walk to the end of the corridor. You'll see bus stands directly ahead, outside the station. The Terezín bus departs from platform 7 (direction: Litoměřice, pay driver). You'll arrive in Terezín an hour later at the public bus stop on the main square, across from the TI and around the corner from the Museum of the Ghetto. Some buses also stop earlier, by the Small Fortress. The driver and fellow passengers may tell you to get off there, but my self-guided tour works best if you begin at the stop in town (after the bus passes a field of crosses on your right and travels across the river).

Two different companies (Busline and Kavka) run this route; for schedules that include both companies, see www.jizdnirady.idnes.cz—you want "Terezín LT" (be sure to check the return schedule, too; for details on getting back to Prague, see "Terezín Connections," later).

PLANNING YOUR TIME

Because the sights are scattered, plan on lots of walking, and give yourself plenty of time: Three hours is barely enough for a minimal visit (and requires skipping some sights); allow at least four hours to quickly see everything, and more like six to really delve in. Your understanding of Terezín becomes immeasurably deeper with the help of a local guide (for a list of Prague-based guides, see page 37).

With more time, stop in the nearby attractive town of Litoměřice (described later) for lunch before returning to Prague.

ORIENTATION TO TEREZÍN

Cost: The 210-Kč combo-ticket includes all parts of the camp.

Hours: Most sights, including the Museum of the Ghetto, Magdeburg Barracks, and Hidden Synagogue, are open daily 9:00-18:00, Nov-March until 17:30. The Columbarium and Crematorium are closed Sat. The Crematorium is open daily 10:00-18:00, Nov-March until 16:00; the Small Fortress is open daily 8:00-18:00, Nov-March. until 16:30.

Tours: Guided tours in English are offered if enough people request them; call ahead to get the schedule and reserve a spot (included in entry).

Information: Terezín's town **TI,** in the corner of the Town Hall that faces the Prague bus stop, has staff that are helpful and speak English (Sun 9:00-15:00, Mon-Thu 8:00-17:00, Fri 8:00-13:30, closed Sat, Náměstí ČSA 179, tel. 416-782-616, www.terezin.cz). In their window, you'll find handy information (such as the Prague bus schedule and directions to town landmarks). Museum information—tel. 416-782-225, mobile 606-632-914, www.pamatnik-terezin.cz.

Eating: Avoid the stale sandwiches in the **Museum of the Ghetto's** dingy basement cafeteria, where most tour guides inexplicably bring their clients. The **Small Fortress** has a **$** cafeteria.

In Terezín town, **$$ Pizzeria Na Obzoru** ("On the Horizon") serves pasta, steaks, and creamy risottos on its pastel-colored, sailor-themed ground floor or in a brick-and-stone vaulted cellar (daily 11:00-22:00, one block up the street from the hidden synagogue at Dlouhá 24, mobile 731-771-841). **$ Atypic Restaurant** offers Czech canteen classics popular with students and employees of the museum, served on an airy terrace or in the cramped interior with a peek into the kitchen (daily 9:30-21:00, Máchova 91, tel. 416-782-780).

For more recommendations, see the "Eating in Litoměřice" section on page 290.

BACKGROUND

Terezín was the Nazis' model "Jewish town," a concentration camp dolled up for propaganda purposes. Here, in a supposedly "self-governed Jewish resettlement area," Jewish culture seemed to thrive, as "citizens" put on plays and concerts, published a magazine, and raised their families. But it was all a carefully planned deception, intended to convince Red Cross inspectors that Jews were being treated well. The Nazis even coached prisoners on how to answer the inspectors' anticipated questions.

The Nazi authorities also used Terezín as a place to relocate elderly and disabled Jews from throughout the Third Reich—so the ghetto was filled with prisoners not only from the Czech lands, but from all over Europe.

In the fall of 1944, the Nazis began transporting Jews from Terezín to even more severe death camps (especially Auschwitz) in large numbers. Virtually all Terezín's Jews (155,000 over the course of the war) ultimately ended up dying—either here (35,000) or in extermination camps farther east.

One of the notable individuals held at Terezín was Viennese artist Friedl Dicker-Brandeis. This daring woman, a leader in the Bauhaus art movement, found her life's calling in teaching children freedom of expression. She taught the kids in the camp to distinguish between the central things—trees, flowers, lines—and

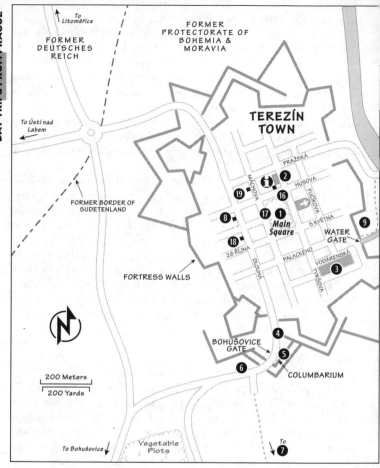

peripheral things, such as the conditions of the camp. In 1944, Dicker-Brandeis volunteered to be sent to Auschwitz after her husband was transported there; she was killed a month later.

Of the 15,000 children who passed through Terezín from 1942 to 1944, fewer than 100 survived. The artwork they created at Terezín is a striking testimony to the cruel horror of the Holocaust. In 1994, Hana Volavková, a Terezín survivor and the director of the Jewish Museum in Prague, collected the children's artwork and poems in the book *I Never Saw Another Butterfly*. Selections of the Terezín drawings are also displayed and well-described in English in Prague's Pinkas Synagogue (described on page 57).

Of the cultural activities that took place at Terezín, the best known was the children's opera *Brundibár*. Written just before the war, the antifascist opera premiered secretly in Prague at a time when Jewish activities were no longer permitted. From 1943 to

Terezín

FORTRESS WALLS

SMALL FORTRESS

To Prague

New Ohře River

<u>Sights</u>
① Main Square
② Museum of the Ghetto
③ Magdeburg Barracks
④ Railway Tracks
⑤ Columbarium
⑥ Memorial Halls
⑦ To Crematorium, Cemeteries & Memorial to Soviet Soldiers
⑧ Hidden Synagogue
⑨ Dry Moat
⑩ National Cemetery
⑪ Gatehouse

⑫ Model Prison Cells, Washroom & Gavrilo Princip's Cell
⑬ History & Art Museum
⑭ Fourth Courtyard
⑮ Execution Ground & Mass Grave

<u>Other</u>
⑯ Bus to/from Prague
⑰ Bus to/from Litoměřice
⑱ Pizzeria Na Obzoru
⑲ Atypic Restaurant
⑳ Cafeteria

1944, the play, performed in Czech, ran 55 times in the camp. After the war it was staged internationally, and was rewritten and published in the US in 2003 as a children's book by Tony Kushner and Maurice Sendak (whose version later appeared on Broadway).

◑ SELF-GUIDED TOUR

The Terezín experience consists of two parts: the walled town of Terezín, which became a Jewish ghetto under Hitler; and (a half-mile walk east, across the river) the Small Fortress, which was a Gestapo prison camp for mostly political prisoners of all stripes (including non-Jewish Czechs). The complete tour involves about four miles of walking (including the walk from the town to the Small Fortress, then back again to catch your return bus to Prague). Pace yourself. If you want to cut it short, I've suggested sections that you could skip.

Terezín Town

• *The bus from Prague drops you off at Terezín town's spacious...*

Main Square (Náměstí Československé Armády): Today Ter-ezín feels like a workaday, if unusually tidy, Czech town, with a tight grid plan hemmed in by its stout walls. And for much of its history, that's exactly what it was. But when Hitler annexed Czechoslovakia, he evicted the residents to create a ghetto for Jews forcibly transplanted here from Prague and elsewhere. Because it started out as a pretty town, rather than a gloomy prison or custom-built

concentration camp, the Nazi authorities cultivated Terezín as a "model" to illustrate to the outside world how good the Jews had it here. (For more details, see "Background," earlier.)

Begin your tour by mentally filling the (now mostly empty) square with thousands of Jewish inmates, all wearing their yellow *Juden* Star of David patches. Picture the giant circus tent and barbed-wire fence that stood on this square for two years during the war. Inside, Jewish workers boxed special motors for German vehicles being used on the frigid Soviet front. As part of year-long preparations for the famous Red Cross visit (which lasted all of six hours on June 23, 1944), the tent and fence were replaced by flower beds (which you still see on the square today) and a pavilion for outdoor music performances.

• *The helpful little TI is across the street from the bus stop. Just around the corner—in the yellow former schoolhouse that faces the adjacent square—is the...*

Museum of the Ghetto: This modern, concise, well-presented museum, with artifacts and insightful English descriptions, sets the stage for your Terezín visit. You can buy the Terezín combo-ticket here (and ask about the day's film schedule—explained below). You'll find two floors of **exhibits** about the development of the Nazis' "Final Solution." The ground floor includes some evocative memorials (such as a stack of seized suitcases and a list of Terezín's victims). The exhibit upstairs illuminates life in the ghetto with historical documents (including underground publications and letters—inmates were allowed to mail one per month), items belonging to inmates, and video footage of survivors' testimonies. In the stairwell are large illustrations of ghetto life, drawn by people who lived here.

In the basement is a theater showing four excellent **films.** One film documents the history of the ghetto (31 minutes), offering a helpful, if dry, overview of the sights you'll see. Two others (14 and 20 minutes) focus on children's art in the camp, and the last

Petr Ginz, Young Artist and Writer

Born in 1928 to a Jewish father and non-Jewish mother, Prague teenager Petr Ginz excelled at art and was a talented writer who penned numerous articles, short stories, and even a science-fiction novel. Petr was sent to the concentration camp at Terezín in 1942, where he edited the secret boys' publication *Vedem (We Are Ahead)*, writing poetry and drawing illustrations, and paying contributors with food rations he received from home.

Some of Petr's artwork and writings were preserved by Terezín survivors and archived by the Jewish Museum in Prague. In 2003, Ilan Ramon, the first Israeli astronaut and the son of a Holocaust survivor, took one of Petr's drawings—titled *Moon Country*—into space aboard the final, doomed mission of the space shuttle Columbia.

The publicity over the Columbia's explosion and Petr's drawing spurred a Prague resident to come forward with a diary he'd found in his attic. It was Petr's diary from 1941 to 1942, hidden decades earlier by Petr's parents and chronicling the year before the teen's deportation to Terezín. *The Diary of Petr Ginz* has since been published in more than 10 languages.

In the diary, Petr matter-of-factly documented the increasing restrictions on Jewish life in occupied Prague, interspersing the terse account with dry humor. In the entry for September 19, 1941, Petr wrote, "They just introduced a special sign for Jews" alongside a drawing of the Star of David. He continued, "On the way to school I counted 69 'sheriffs,'" referring to people wearing the star.

Petr spent two years at Terezín before being sent to Auschwitz, where he died in a gas chamber. He was 16.

is a 10-minute montage of clips from *Der Führer schenkt den Juden eine Stadt (The Führer Gives a City to the Jews)*, by Kurt Gerron. Gerron, a Berlin Jew, was a 1920s movie star who appeared with Marlene Dietrich in *Blue Angel*. Deported to Terezín, Gerron in 1944 was asked by the Nazis to produce a propaganda film. The resulting film depicts healthy (i.e., recently arrived) "Jewish settlers" in Terezín happily viewing concerts, playing soccer, and sewing in their rooms—yet an unmistakable, deadly desperation radiates from their pallid faces. The only moment of genuine emotion comes toward the end, when a packed room of children applauds the final lines of the popular anti-Nazi opera *Brundibár*: "We did not let ourselves down, we chased the nasty Brundibár away. With a happy song, we won it all." Even the Nazis were not fooled: Gerron and his wife were shipped to Auschwitz, and the film was never shown in public.

• *To learn more about living conditions in the camp, return to the main square and continue straight past it, along Tyršova street. A few blocks down, just before the wall, on the left you'll find the...*

Magdeburg Barracks: Peek inside the large courtyard (you'll recognize it as the "soccer stadium" in Gerron's film), then contin-

ue upstairs and follow the one-way, counterclockwise loop. First you'll see a meticulously restored dormitory, complete with three-tiered beds, suitcases, eyeglasses, dolls, chessboards, sewing kits...and utterly no privacy. After Terezín's residents were evicted and Jews were imported in huge numbers, every available space was converted from single-family apartments to outrageously cramped slumber mills like this. Jaunty music lures you around the corner to the first of several rooms celebrating the arts here at Terezín. You'll see exhibits on composers, artists, and writers, who expressed their creativity even in these horrifying conditions. These include profiles of individuals (such as young Petr Ginz—see sidebar) and a wide variety of stirring art illustrating life in the ghetto. Near the end is a room reproducing the camp cabaret stage, where inmates entertained each other.

• *With limited time or energy, consider skipping the next several stops, which take a long, if poignant, detour outside the walls. Jump ahead to the moat (see "Dry Moat," later) by leaving the barracks, turning right, and walking 100 yards to a brick gate. (If you do decide to skip the following stops, you can easily fit in the Hidden Synagogue at the end, before hopping on your bus back to Prague, as it's one block from the main square.)*

To continue the full tour, exit the barracks, turn left, and walk until you dead-end at the city wall. Turn right and walk along the inside of the stout wall to the far corner. Slicing through the hole in the wall are the remnants of...

Railway Tracks: In the early years of the camp, Jews arrived at the train station in the nearby town of Bohušovice and then had

to walk the remaining 1.5 miles to Terezín. This was too public a display for the Nazis, who didn't want townspeople to observe the transports and become suspicious (or to try to interact with the inmates in any way). So the prisoners were forced to construct a railway line that led right to Terezín...and then back out again to Auschwitz.

• *Follow the tracks outside the wall.*

Columbarium and Memorial Halls: Exiting the wall, on the left is a Columbarium, where the Nazis deposited cardboard boxes containing the ashes of dead prisoners. The Germans originally promised that the remains would be properly buried after the war, but in 1945, to erase evidence, the ashes of Terezín victims were dumped into the Ohře River. Farther along, past the little pension/café and across the bridge, on the right you will find Jewish and Christian ceremonial halls and the main morgue.

• *When the main road swings right, take the left turn (marked* Krematorium*) and walk past bucolic vegetable plots and fruit gardens, and along a driveway lined with pointy poplar trees, to reach the...*

Crematorium and Cemeteries: The low-lying yellow building (to the left of the monumental menorah) is the **crematorium,**

 where Nazis would burn the bodies of those who died here. Step inside to see a small exhibit on death and burial in the ghetto (explaining that, over time, single graves in coffins gave way to mass graves, then to simply burning bodies en masse and dumping the ashes in the river). Then head into the chilling main chamber, where four ovens were kept busy cremating bodies.

Outside, surrounding the crematorium is a **Jewish cemetery** with the bodies of those who died before cremation became the norm. Farther to the right (as you face the crematorium) is a **Russian cemetery** and a **Memorial to Soviet Soldiers.** The Soviets liberated Terezín without a fight as the Nazis retreated, on May 8, 1945. But just days before, an epidemic of typhus had spread through the camp. In the weeks after the war ended, scores of Soviet soldiers and medical workers who tried to contain the epidemic died, along with hundreds of former prisoners.

• *Retrace your steps back through the wall, and continue straight ahead past the train tracks, up Dlouhá street. After three blocks, watch on the left for the low-profile green house at #17. Ring the bell to be admitted to the fascinating...*

Hidden Synagogue: Inside you'll find a courtyard; the bakery that used to be here hid the synagogue behind it. This is the only one of the camp's eight hidden synagogues that survived. The atmospheric space is still inscribed with two Hebrew captions, which are translated as "May my eyes behold, how You in compassion return to Sinai," and "If I forget Jerusalem, may my tongue rot and my right arm fall off." These words indicate that the prayer room belonged to a congregation of Zionists (advocates of a Jewish state), who, one would expect, were specifically targeted by the Nazis.

Upstairs, a few prisoners lived in a tight attic space. Even though the cramped rooms (reconstructed with period items) seem impossibly small, they were a far better accommodation than the mass housing in which most prisoners were interned. It's thought that a group of craftsmen who labored in a nearby workshop were "lucky" enough to live here.

• *Leaving the synagogue house, turn right, and at the corner, turn left to pop out at the main square. To proceed to the Small Fortress, head down Tyršova as if you're going to the Magdeburg Barracks. Before you get there, turn left along the park, then continue one block up Palackého to the brick gate. You'll cross a bridge over a...*

Dry Moat: Imagine this moat filled with plots of vegetables, grown by starving Jews for well-fed SS officers. Turn left and walk along the moat. The top of the fortification walls on the other side were once equipped with benches and pathways.

• *When you reach the main road, turn right across the New Ohře River (the original course of the river was diverted here when Terezín was built). After about five minutes, you'll come to a blocked-off, tree-lined driveway and the prison camp.*

Terezín Prison Camp

• *On the right side of the driveway is the wedge-shaped...*

National Cemetery: The remains of about 10,000 victims of Terezín (including 2,386 individual graves; the rest were moved here from mass graves elsewhere) fill this cemetery, which was created after the war's end. The sea of headstones powerfully illustrates the scope of the crime that took place here. No-tice that, in addition to the giant Star of David (closer to the fortress), a  cross towers over the cemetery. This is a reminder that we've left the Jewish ghetto and are about to enter a very different part of the Terezín complex. From 1940 to 1945, this fortress functioned as a Gestapo prison, through which 32,000 inmates passed (of whom nearly 10 percent died here)—chiefly members of the Czech resis-tance and communists. While the majority of the camp's victims

weren't Jewish, the 1,500 Jews interned here were treated with particular severity.

• *Now head under black-and-white-striped gate.*

Gatehouse: Inside the gate, on the left, is a modest museum about the pre-WWII history of this fortress. If you need a break before continuing, you could pause at the handy cafeteria. The wood-and-metal chandeliers inside were produced by Jewish workers for the SS officers who once dined in these two rooms.

• *Continuing into the central part of the fortress, watch on the left for a turnstile into a long, skinny side courtyard. Go in and head to the end of the courtyard, under the notorious* Arbeit Macht Frei *sign painted above an arched gate (a postwar replica of the viciously sarcastic "Work will set you free" sign that was displayed at all camps). Go under this gate to reach a courtyard ringed with...*

Model Prison Cells: Step into some of the barracks on the right side of the courtyard to see tight, triple-decker bunks where

prisoners were essentially stacked at bedtime. Halfway down the courtyard, under the *Block-A* sign, peek into the medical cell.

At the far end, the washroom in the right-hand corner (by #15) was built solely for the purpose of fooling Red Cross inspectors. Go ahead, turn the faucets: No pipes were ever installed to bring in water.

The shower room two doors to the left, on the other hand, was used to fool the Jews. Here they got used to the idea of communal bathing, so they wouldn't be suspicious when they were later taken to similar-looking installations at Auschwitz. (There were no gas chambers at Terezín—most of the deaths here were caused by malnutrition, disease, and, to a lesser extent, execution.)

Before the Nazis, the Austrian monarchy used the Small Fortress as a prison. In the little side courtyard next to the shower room, look for a ghostly doorway with a plaque that recalls the most famous prisoner from that time, Bosnian Serb **Gavrilo Princip,** whose assassination of Archduke Franz Ferdinand and his wife Žofie in 1914 sparked World War I (see sidebar on page 293). Princip died here in 1918 of tuberculosis; of the six Sarajevo conspirators imprisoned here, only two survived.

• *Return through the* Arbeit Macht Frei *gate, then back out into the for-*

tress' central yard. Turn left and continue deeper into the complex. The large building on your right is marked by Muzeum *signs.*

Museum: The ground floor of this building features an exhibit about the Nazi-era history of the Small Fortress. Photographs and brief descriptions identify many of the individuals who were imprisoned—and in many cases, executed. Upstairs is a gallery of paintings by prominent Czech artists, mostly focusing on themes of camp life (and a few about the Spanish Civil War).

• *Back out in the main yard, continue straight ahead, through two gateways in a row. You'll emerge into the wide, eerie...*

Fourth Courtyard: Here you'll have more opportunities to step into former prison cells that flank the yard; some of these house temporary exhibits. At the far end, you'll find a plaque in the ground listing the 17 countries whose citizens perished at Terezín.

• *Returning to the fortress' main yard once more, turn right and follow the long buildings. Turn right to find the...*

Execution Ground and Mass Grave: This is where firing squads executed somewhere between 200 and 300 of Hitler's enemies. Many of Terezín's victims were buried in mass graves along the fortress ramparts. After the war, these remains were moved to the National Cemetery we saw on the way into the fortress.

• *Our tour ends here. As you ponder Terezín, remember the message of all such memorials: Never again.*

TEREZÍN CONNECTIONS

The bus for **Prague** leaves from Terezín's main square (hourly, 1 hour, pay driver). To continue from Terezín to **Dresden,** Germany, take a taxi or bus (3/hour, 5 minutes, pay driver) from Terezín's main square to the Bohušovice station, then take the local train from Bohušovice to Ústí (2/hour, 30 minutes), where you can catch the international express train (every 1-2 hours, 1 hour). For bus and train schedules, see www.idos.cz.

Near Terezín: Litoměřice

With a bustling, beautifully restored Renaissance square, Litoměřice (lee-TOH-myer-zheet-seh, pop. 26,000, known in German as Leitmeritz), located three miles north of Terezín, is a perfect lunch spot to lift your spirits after the bleakness of the camp. During the communist era, Litoměřice had the only seminary in the country. Today, there are still two huge Baroque churches here. Linger on the main square, Mírové Náměstí, and experience the pulse of this friendly, untouristy Czech town.

Buses from Prague to Terezín continue on to Litoměřice (buses returning to Prague stop first in Litoměřice, then Terezín). If arriving by bus from Terezín, get off at the first stop after the bridge; from here it's a two-minute, slightly uphill walk to the main square. Easier yet, it's a five-minute taxi trip between the Terezín Memorial and Litoměřice (about 200 Kč). The staff at Terezín's Museum of the Ghetto ticket office will be happy to call a taxi for you (taxi based in Terezín—mobile 606-833-480, taxi based in Litoměřice—mobile 777-286-406).

Visiting Litoměřice: From the main square, several small streets filled with bakeries and convenience shops radiate outward. The onion-shaped tower is south, and the higher part of the square is due west. Stroll around and get lunch on the square. After lunch, climb up the onion-shaped tower of the **Town Hall** (the guide in the tower loves to talk).

On the square at #24, the **Litoměřice Church Museum,** part of the North Bohemian Art Gallery, is a tiny, beautiful temple of arts in two parts. In the four rooms that face the square, you'll find the highlights of the bishop's collection—800-year-old statues of the evangelists, a Lucas Cranach original, and Karel Skreta's Baroque masterpiece *St. Matthew with an Angel.* The narrow Renaissance house in the back houses the only Art Brut/Naïve Art collection in the Czech Republic. The artists displayed here deliberately defy all trends, taking the perspective that art is first and foremost an expression of an authentic internal need that should not be governed by current tastes or commercial interests. Highlights include Jan Kutalek's *Tree of Life* on the patio and Alois Kučera's lindenwood relief *Pub With Drinkers* in the topmost attic room. Through a narrow window here, you can also enjoy the best views of the river and the cathedral (30 Kč, Tue-Sun 9:00-12:00 & 13:00-18:00, until 17:00 Oct-March, closed Mon year-round, a few doors to the right of Town Hall, tel. 416-732-382).

The short street next to the Town Hall leads onto the city walls, with good views. The statue at the viewpoint depicts the Romantic poet **Karel Hynek Mácha** (1810-1836), who wrote the most famous Czech poem, "Máj." He died in Litoměřice. In the fall of 1938, as Litoměřice was ceded to Hitler as part of the Sudetenland, local Czech patriots exhumed and carried away Mácha's body to prevent German nationalists from desecrating his grave. A year later, reburial of the remains at the Slavín cemetery atop Prague's Vyšehrad hill inspired student-led anti-occupation protests that resulted in a German crackdown, including the closing of Czech universities. In

November of 1989, demonstrating students were headed for the grave of Mácha to mark the 50th anniversary of these events when they suddenly decided that they were tired of the communists...and started the Velvet Revolution.

Eating in Litoměřice: **$$ Gurmánie Pasta & Grill & Café,** at the top of the square, is a hip bistro with a wide selection of soups, salads, sandwiches, and cakes. They sautée pasta and vegetables with fresh red beet juice while you watch (daily 7:00-22:00, weekday specials, no English menu—ask the counter staff to translate, tel. 416-536-131).

The vault-ceilinged, plastic-tabled **$ U Draka** eatery on the corner across from Gurmánie cooks up old Czech canteen classics for a 60+ crowd determined to live like the 1980s never ended (Mon-Fri 6:30-17:30, closed Sat-Sun, no English menu and no English spoken—just point at what you want).

$$ U Zlatého Bažanta is the best—if somewhat tired-looking—choice for a proper sit-down meal, particularly if the weather is good enough to sit at the square-side tables. Try venison stew, wild boar steak, or braised beef cheek, and wash it down with a Slovak beer (daily 8:30-22:00, English menu doesn't include daily specials—ask, next to Town Hall, tel. 416-732-454).

Litoměřice Connections: To reach Litoměřice's bus station for the trip back to Prague (hourly, 1 hour), walk east on the main street (Dlouhá) down from the square to an intersection, cross it, and continue in the same direction along Na Kocandě street (an easy 10-minute walk). The train station is nearby (though buses to Prague are preferable, as the train requires a transfer). For bus and train schedules, see www.idos.cz.

Konopiště Castle

Konopiště (KOH-noh-peesh-tyeh) was the Neo-Gothic residence of the Archduke Franz Ferdinand d'Este—the heir to the Austro-Hungarian Empire, whose assassination sparked World War I. Located 30 miles south of Prague, it's workable either as a day trip or on the way to Český Krumlov.

While it's the least visually arresting of the castles near Prague, its interior has some captivating stories to tell about its former inhabitants. Enjoyable for anyone, Konopiště is worth ▲ for most. But it's a must for Habsburg aficionados—historians find it worth ▲▲▲.

Construction of the castle began in the 14th century, but today's exterior and furnishings date from about 1900, when Franz Ferdinand renovated his new home. As one of the first castles in Europe to have an elevator, a WC, and running water, Konopiště shows "modern" living at the turn of the 20th century.

Those who lived at Konopiště played a role in one of the most important moments in European history: Franz Ferdinand's assassination in Sarajevo (chillingly illustrated by items displayed inside the castle). The shooting eventually meant the end of the age of hereditary, divine-right, multiethnic empires—and the dawn of a Europe of small, nationalistic, democratic nation-states. Historians get goose bumps at Konopiště, where if you listen closely, you can almost hear the last gasp of Europe's absolute monarchs.

The castle interior is only viewable via a guided tour. There are several tour options, but the best is Route 3 (limited space, so call ahead to reserve; explained later, under "Orientation to Konopiště").

GETTING TO KONOPIŠTĚ

By Train: Trains from Prague's main station drop you in Benešov (2/hour, 1 hour, www.idos.cz); a well-marked trail goes from the station to the castle (1.5 miles). To walk to the castle, as you exit the Benešov train station, turn left and walk along the street parallel to the railroad tracks. Turn left at the first bridge you see crossing over the tracks. Along the way you'll see trail markers on trees, walls, and lampposts—one yellow stripe between two white stripes. Follow these markers. As you leave town, watch for a marker with an arrow pointing to a path in the woods. Take this path to bypass the castle's enormous parking lot, which is clogged with souvenir shops and bus fumes.

By Car: Konopiště is about a 45-minute drive from Prague and a two-minute detour off of the main route to Český Krumlov (head east toward Brno on the D-1 expressway; take exit #21 toward *Benešov/České Budějovice/Linz;* after about 15 kilometers, watch for the Konopiště turnoff on the right). Bypass the first, giant parking lot (ringed by restaurants); a bit farther along, on the left near the lake, is a smaller lot that's closer to the castle. From either lot, hike uphill about 10-15 minutes to Konopiště.

ORIENTATION TO KONOPIŠTĚ

Cost and Tours: The recommended Route 3 is 320 Kč (described later, under "Visiting the Castle"); Routes 1 and 2 are 220 Kč apiece; all three cost 690 Kč. Space on Route 3 is limited to eight people per hour: It's best to reserve a spot in advance by calling one day ahead or on the morning of your visit (worth the 20-Kč extra charge). All tickets are 30 percent cheaper if you join a Czech-speaking tour (but renting the English audioguide costs 50 Kč—effectively negating most of your savings). Tel. 317-721-366, www.zamek-konopiste.cz.

Hours: May-Aug Tue-Sun 9:00-12:30 & 13:00-17:00; Sept Tue-Fri 9:00-16:00, Sat-Sun until 17:00; April and Oct Tue-Fri until 15:00, Sat-Sun until 16:00; closed Mon year-round and Nov-March.

VISITING THE CASTLE

While there are three different tour options, **Route 3** is the most intimate and interesting. It takes you through the rooms where Franz Ferdinand, his Czech bride Žofie, and their three kids lived while waiting for Uncle Franz Josef to expire. When the communists took over, they simply threw drop cloths over the furniture and let the place sit, untouched, for decades. Now everything has been meticulously restored (with the help of 1907 photographs)—launching you right into a turn-of-the-20th-century time capsule.

The tour takes you through halls upon halls of hunting trophies (each one marked with the place and date of the kill), paintings of royal relatives (including an entire wall of Italian kings—relations of Franz Ferdinand's Neapolitan mother), and photographs of the many places they traveled and the three kids as they grew up. The tour includes Franz Ferdinand's dressing room (with his actual uniform and his travel case all packed up and ready to go); his private study (which feels like he just stepped away from his desk for a cup of coffee); the living room (with 1,180 pairs of antlers on the

Archduke Franz Ferdinand (1863-1914)

Archduke Franz Ferdinand was born to the brother of the Habsburg emperor (Franz Josef) and a Neapolitan princess. After his cousin died under "mysterious circumstances," Franz Ferdinand was thrust into the role of heir apparent to the throne of the Austro-Hungarian Empire—one of the biggest realms Europe has ever seen. But he had to be patient: His Uncle Franz Josef took the throne in 1848 and would hold onto it for nearly 70 years. In fact, he outlived his nephew.

While he waited, Franz Ferdinand kept himself busy by spending time at his bachelor pad in Konopiště. At a ball in Vienna, he met a gorgeous but low-ranking Czech countess, Žofie Chotková (also known by her German name, Sophie). The couple danced all night. After long years of a secret courtship, Franz Ferdinand announced his intentions to make Žofie his wife. His uncle was displeased—Žofie was "only" aris-tocratic, and the expected path for the heir apparent would be to marry a Western European princess. He insisted on a morganatic marriage so that Žofie could never be an empress and none of the children could inherit the throne. These family squabbles cemented Franz Ferdinand and Žofie's preference for living at Konopiště.

While waiting for a succession that would never arrive, Franz Ferdinand threw himself into his hobbies with an ob-sessive-compulsive zeal. He traveled around the world twice—partly for diplomatic reasons, but largely to pursue his passion for exotic hunting. Shooting at anything in sight—deer, bears, tigers, elephants, and crocodiles—he killed about 300,000 animals in all, a few thousand of whom stare morbidly at you from the walls at Konopiště. Franz Ferdinand and Žofie were also devoted parents, raising three children: young Žofie, Max, and Ernesto.

In the Kaiser's Pavilion on the grounds of Konopiště, Franz Ferdinand met with German Kaiser Wilhelm and tried to talk him out of plotting a war against Russia. Wilhelm argued that a war would work to the mutual benefit of Germany and Austria: Germans wanted colonies, and the Austro-Hungarian Empire—crippled by the aspirations of its many nationalities—could use a war to divert attention from its domestic prob-lems. But Franz Ferdinand foresaw that war would be suicidal for Austria's overstretched monarchy.

Soon after, Franz Ferdinand and Žofie went to Sarajevo, in the Habsburg-annexed territories of Bosnia and Herzegov-ina. On that trip, young Gavrilo Princip, a Bosnian Serb sepa-ratist, shot the Habsburg archduke who so loved shooting, as well as Žofie. Franz Ferdinand's assassination ironically gave the Germans (and their pro-war allies in the Austro-Hungarian administration) the pretext for starting the war against Serbia and its ally, Russia. World War I soon broke out. The event Franz Ferdinand had tried to prevent was, in fact, sparked by his death.

walls); the private dining room (with the table set for an intimate family dinner for five); the master bedroom (with its huge bed); the children's bedrooms, playrooms, and classroom (with their toys and books still on the shelves); three bathrooms with running water and flushing toilets; and—in the final room—a glass display case containing the dress Žofie was wearing that fateful day in Sarajevo (including her still-blood-stained corset). Down the hall are the royal couple's death masks, Franz Ferdinand's bloody suspenders, and the actual bullet that ended Žofie's life.

Route 2—which covers the oldest wing of the castle—is also worth considering, and provides the most comprehensive look into the castle, its history, and celebrated collections. You'll see the oversized elevator (with a couch to make the family comfortable on the 45-second ride upstairs), the library, and the staggeringly large armory collection. Route 1, covering some other rooms, the hunting hall, and the balcony, is the least interesting.

Other Sights at the Castle: Your tour ticket includes two quirky additional sights that are worth poking into. Franz Ferdinand's Shooting Range, just off of the castle courtyard, offers a quick glimpse at the emperor-in-waiting's elaborate system of moving targets; a video demonstrates how the various targets would move around to keep his skills sharp. The Museum of St. George, tucked beneath the long terrace (around the side of the palace), displays Franz Ferdinand's collection of hundreds of sculptures and paintings of St. George slaying the dragon...taking a theme to an extreme.

While the stretch between the parking lot and the castle entrance is overrun by tour groups, the gardens and the park are surprisingly empty. In the summer, the flowers and goldfish in the rose garden are a big hit with visitors. The peaceful 30-minute walk through the woods around the lake (wooden bridge at the far end) offers fine castle views.

Tucked away in the bushes behind the pond is a pavilion coated with tree bark, a perfect picnic spot. This simple structure, nicknamed the Kaiser's Pavilion, was the site of a fateful meeting between the German Kaiser Wilhelm and the Archduke Franz Ferdinand (see the sidebar on page 293).

Eating at Konopiště Castle: Three touristy restaurants sit under the castle, and a café and restaurant are in the castle courtyard, but I'd rather bring picnic supplies from Prague (or buy them at the grocery store by the Benešov train station). While the crowds wait to pay too much for lousy food in the restaurants, you'll enjoy the peace and thought-provoking ambience of a picnic in the shaded Kaiser's Pavilion. Or eat cheaply on Benešov's main square (try $ U Zlaté Hvězdy—"The Golden Star").

Karlštejn Castle

One of the Czech Republic's most popular attractions, Karlštejn Castle (KARL-shtayn) perches high on a stony bluff overlooking its one-street town. From a distance, it's a striking, fairy-tale castle—but there's little to see inside.

Frankly, a visit here can be more trouble than it's worth: Whether you arrive by train or by car, you'll face a half-mile, rather steep hike up to the castle, past an obnoxiously touristy gauntlet of crystal and souvenir shops as intense as Karlova street in Prague. Like other Czech castles, you can see the interior only with a tour—but although the guides strain to make the place interesting, there's not much to say.

For many visitors, the best option may be a quick photo-op, without going inside. It's free to hike up to the courtyard, and you can even continue to the adjacent Well Tower for great views back on the main castle and over the town that fills the gully below. You can also hike in the forested hills surrounding the castle (described later).

GETTING TO KARLŠTEJN

By Train: The castle, 20 miles southwest of Prague, is accessible by train (2/hour, 40 minutes, then a 20- to 30-minute walk; depart from Prague's Main Station in the direction of Beroun, www.idos.cz). When you leave the Karlštejn station, turn right, walk to the next road, turn left, and cross the bridge over the river. From here, follow the pedestrian-only street as it twists up, up, up to the castle.

By Car: Head west from Prague toward Plzeň, and watch for the brown *Karlštejn* signs marking the turnoff. You'll drive through the countryside to the castle, park in the pay lot across the street from the town's main road, and then walk the rest of the way up.

ORIENTATION

Cost and Tours: If you want to tour the castle, opt for **Route II** (300 Kč, departs hourly, 15 people maximum). The 1.5-hour tour is lengthy, but it's the only way to reach the one thing inside worth seeing: the much-venerated Chapel of the Holy Cross (though you only get a few minutes in there; see route description later, under "Visiting the Castle"). The tour requires an advance reservation—check the schedule and book on their website, or send an email with the date you'd like to visit (tel. 274-008-154 or 274-008-155, www.hradkarlstejn.cz, rezervace@stc.npu.cz). They'll reply with an available time slot and instructions for how to pay the 30-Kč/person reservation fee by credit card. **Route I** is nowhere near as interesting (270 Kč, no reservation required, bigger groups, shorter tour).

Hours: May-Sept Tue-Sun 9:00-12:00 & 12:30-18:00, closed Mon except in July-Aug, when it's open daily; March-April and Oct Tue-Sun 9:00-12:00 & 13:00-17:00, closed Mon; Nov-Feb Sat-Sun 10:00-12:00 & 13:00-15:00, closed Mon-Fri.

Eating at Karlštejn: On the way up to the castle are several restaurants and a good bakery (about halfway on the right coming from the train station; stock up on their *koláče* and cabbage rolls before scaling the castle).

To get a post-castle meal while avoiding tourists altogether, immediately after exiting the castle gate, turn left on a forest path marked by a red stripe between two white stripes. In 10 minutes, you gradually descend into a valley with a small road and a creek. Continue along the road for about 100 yards to **$$$ Pension and Restaurant Pod Dračí Skalou ("Under the Dragon's Rock"),** with an imaginative menu that includes game from the nearby woods. From mid-September until November 11 they serve the special "St. Martin" roasted goose, and from November 11 (St. Martin's Day) until February, the year-round game selection is expanded into a "feast of game" (daily 11:00-23:00, Karlštejn 130, mobile 723-845-844). To get back to the train station, just follow the road and the creek down to town.

BACKGROUND

Karlštejn ("Charles' Castle") was built in just 17 years by Charles IV around 1350 as a summer residence, and to house the crown jewels of the Holy Roman Empire. The architecture is designed to reflect the journey of the human soul: from life (the lower castle), through purgatory (the shorter Marian Tower), and finally to paradise (the Chapel of the Holy Cross—which housed the crown jewels—at the top of the Great Tower). Later, during the Hussite Wars, Jan Hus' followers encamped on the hills surrounding the fortress, planning to attack Karlštejn, steal the crown jewels, and name a Protestant king—but they failed. If Karlštejn looks "Transylvanian," that's because it was remodeled in a fanciful, Romantic style in the 19th century. The version you see today, while dramatic, is far from authentic. (They call it "pseudo-Gothic," but I think of it as "pseudo-Epcot.")

VISITING THE CASTLE

On the **Route II** tour, you'll receive an introduction with some historical illustrations before hiking up and through the two towers. First is the squatter **Marian Tower**, featuring a queen's bedroom-turned-chapel, with some valuable frescoes and a tiny chapel whose walls are lined with precious stones.

Next you'll cross a high wooden bridge to the **Great Tower**, where you'll see a dull lapidarium (collection of historic stone fragments) before huffing up several flights of stairs to the **Chapel of the Holy Cross,** a genuinely evocative space in which you'll have just a few minutes. Built to house the crown jewels, this smallish but exquisite chapel is decorated with 129 portraits of medieval European monarchs. (Habsburg Empress Maria Theresa borrowed some, and apparently lost one—since she never returned it.) The ceiling, made of gilded stucco, glitters to represent the stars in the sky. And the lower walls are encased in precious sheets of deepred jasper (representing the blood of Christ) and purple amethyst (symbolizing royalty).

Hiking around Karlštejn: The castle sits in the middle of a national forest preserve with limestone formations. I've outlined two hiking options, both of which start at the well-marked trail that turns off to the left immediately after the castle gate (look for markers with one red stripe between two white stripes).

One option is to follow the trail five miles through woods and past a waterfall to the magically set **Svatý Jan pod Skalou** ("St. John under the Rock"). This is a former monastery with a healing spring; the water bubbles from a spectacular rock with a cross on its top. Climb up the path by the monastery for great views, or try the excellent restaurant in the former school here (Hotel Obecná Škola, May-Sept Sun-Thu 11:00-18:00, Fri-Sat until 22:00; Oct-April Thu-Sun 11:00-18:00, closed Mon-Wed; mobile 603-916-114). From here, a direct bus takes you to Zličín Station, the end of Prague's Metro line B, in 30 minutes (check the schedule at www.idos.cz).

For a shorter, three-mile hike, walk along the same red-marked trail for about two miles, then turn left immediately after you cross a creek onto the yellow-marked trail (yellow stripe between two white stripes). After one mile you'll reach the town of **Srbsko** ("Serbia"), where you'll find two restaurants, a grocery store, and a train station (the same line as Beroun-Karlštejn-Prague).

Křivoklát Castle

Křivoklát (KREE-vohk-laht), an original 14th-century castle, is beautiful for its simplicity and setting, amid the hills and deep woods near the lovely Berounka River valley. Křivoklát is a connoisseur's castle—I think of it as a rustic, less trampled (if less striking) alternative to the overrun Karlštejn. It also has a particularly cozy setting, nestled deep in a primeval forest, overlooking a meandering river valley. While it's less accessible to international tourists (most visitors are Czechs, and English speakers get little respect)...that's the point. Come to this Back Door castle if you enjoy the journey—on a train line along a pastoral river valley—as much as the destination. Note that outside of the peak summer months (June-Aug), the castle can be pretty dead, especially on weekdays.

GETTING TO KŘIVOKLÁT

Trains leave Prague's Main Station for Beroun (hourly, 40 minutes), running through the delightful valley of the dreamy Berounka River. In Beroun, transfer to the cute little motor train to Křivoklát (dubbed by Czech hikers the "Berounka Pacific"; only 2 morning departures, allow 1.5 hours total for trip from Prague). From Křivoklát's train station, it's a 10-minute walk uphill to the castle. At the train station, confirm the return schedule—in the afternoon, a local train leaves almost hourly. For train schedules, see www.idos.cz.

ORIENTATION

Cost and Tours: The recommended short tour costs 170 Kč in English or 120 Kč if you go with a Czech group. While English tours may be available in summer, they are rare at other times; you can try calling ahead to ask if any English tours are scheduled, but you should count on taking the Czech tour and buying the printed English descriptions (30 Kč). It's 80 Kč to enter the main castle courtyard and to walk the castle walls on your own without a tour (this option offered daily in June-Aug, Sat-Sun only off-season). Tel. 313-558-440, www.krivoklat.cz.

Hours: May-Sept Tue-Sun 9:00-12:00 & 13:00-17:00, closed Mon; April and Oct Tue-Sun 10:00-16:00, closed Mon; Nov-

Dec Sat-Sun 10:00-15:00, closed Mon-Fri; Jan-March Mon-Sat 10:00-15:00, closed Sun.

Sleeping and Eating at Křivoklát: ¢ Hotel and $ Restaurant Sýkora, below the castle near the train station, has been a favorite among Czech hikers since the 1930s. If you want to stay for an evening concert in the castle courtyard or for a hike in the nearby woods, sleep in one of the hotel's 11 renovated rooms (tel. 313-558-114, www.hotel-sykora.krivoklatsko. com, hotel.sykora@krivoklatsko.com, only Czech and German spoken).

You can also stay at **¢ Křivoklát Castle,** either in a spartan castle room with an arched ceiling and adjacent kitchen or in the more comfortable former police station immediately outside the castle gate (no breakfast, reserve well in advance through the castle office, tel. 313-558-440, krivoklat@ krivoklat.cz). **$$ Restaurace U Jelena,** also below the castle, primarily serves game in an upscale dining room.

BACKGROUND

Originally a hunting residence of Czech kings, Křivoklát was later transformed into a royal prison that "entertained" a number of distinguished guests, among them the most notorious alchemist of the 1500s, Englishman Edward Kelly. Later the Habsburgs sold the castle to the Wallenstein family, and the property eventually passed down to the Fürstenbergs. It was lightly renovated by the 19th-century Romantics, but retains more of its original Gothic soul than Karlštejn. In 1929, just before the stock market crash, the Czechoslovak state bought this former royal residence for a grand sum—it's one of a few castles that the government purchased, rather than seized.

VISITING THE CASTLE

To get inside, you have two tour options. The recommended short tour, about 45 minutes, includes the Gothic chapel and the king's audience hall, with delicately arched ceilings. In the chapel, check out the 12 monster-animals representing cardinal vices, which are minutely carved at the end of the prayer benches. The long tour, about 80 minutes, includes the 19th-century wing added by the Fürstenberg family.

In summer, Křivoklát comes alive with craftspeople—woodcarvers, blacksmiths, glassblowers, and basket weavers—who work as if it were the 15th century. The absence of tacky souvenir shops, the plain Gothic appearance, and the background noise of hammers and wood chisels give Křivoklát an engaging character (and makes this a good place to shop for a thoughtful gift).

Hiking Around Křivoklát: Several nature trails loop through

Křivoklát National Park: Saving the Czech Republic's Diverse Forests

The Czech Republic's fifth national park may someday be created in the Křivoklát hills. While the country's four other parks lie in relatively remote locations, the proposed 250-acre Křivoklát National Park is within a one-hour bike ride of the Zličín endpoint of the Prague subway system. The ongoing survival of such a diverse and extensive forest ecosystem so close to the big city would be a miracle in heavily industrialized Central Europe.

A thousand years ago, the canyons and rocky hills of the Křivoklát region made it the favorite hunting grounds of the Czech kings, who discouraged local settlement for the next five centuries. The royals eventually gave up Křivoklát, more people moved in, and logging increased with the demand for wood and charcoal. But the Fürstenberg family, who took ownership of Křivoklát in the 18th century, carefully replanted with deciduous trees that matched the forests' original composition.

The communists stripped the visionary Fürstenbergs of their possessions and attempted to introduce large stands of fast-growing, imported spruce trees at Křivoklát, as they had in other parts of the Czech Republic (spruce can be harvested quickly for timber and paper-making). But local foresters and biologists defied the communists by continuing to protect Křivoklát's mix of native broadleaf trees.

In 1989, political changes opened the future of all the Czech Republic's forestlands to public debate. The so-called "spruce

the forests and hills near the castle. You'll see examples of the castle's namesake: rock-perched, spectacularly crooked pines (*křivoklát* means "warped log"—think Chinese landscape painting). Pick up a map or ask for directions in the forest rangers' information office down on the main road near Hotel Sýkora (daily 9:00-16:00).

Towns near Křivoklát

NIŽBOR

This village, which straddles the valley of the Berounka River, lies between Beroun and Křivoklát (it's the third stop on the little motor train after Beroun).

Visiting Nižbor: The main reason to stop in Nižbor is **Rückl Glassworks,** where you can witness the step-by-step production of traditional Czech crystal. As you get off the train, return to the first rail crossing—the entrance to the glassworks is just across the tracks (100 Kč; May-Sept Mon-Fri 9:30-14:30, closed Sat-Sun; Oct-April Mon-Sat 9:30-12:00, closed Sun; if an English-speak-

monocultures" created by the communists came under increasing criticism, as they proved prone to windstorms and bark beetle infestations (which have increased with rising temperatures over the last two decades).

The state-run company that manages half of the country's forests says it aspires to long-term sustainability, but has been slow to discard the failed practices of the past. Cutting down groves of beech woods and planting battalions of spruce trees is a lot easier—and more profitable—than selectively protecting native plants.

There is a movement to designate Křivoklát as a national park, which could preserve its distinctive nature for future generations. It has been a "protected natural area" managed by the state-run company since 1978, but national parks are administered by the ministry of environment and are subject to strict pan-European regulations. The logging lobby and conservationists are both pressing their cases on the matter to the Czech Parliament.

For now, those who visit Křivoklát can experience Czech forests as they used to be—with a magnificent diversity of oak, beech, ash, alder, elm, maple, fir, pine, and even the infamous spruce—by hiking from Lány to Křivoklát (15 miles; see page 303 for details) or by strolling up the hill and into the woods from Nižbor's Rückl Glassworks (2-4 miles; see page 300 for details).

ing guide isn't available, you'll be asked to tag along with a tour-bus group; factory shop and café open same hours, tel. 311-696-248, mobile 605-229-205, www.ruckl.cz). Tours last about 45 minutes and end in the gift shop, of course.

The small **castle** perched on the hill across the river houses a modest exhibit on Celtic archaeology. Nižbor was an important Celtic settlement just before the Christian era (50 Kč, May-Oct daily 10:00-17:00, closed Nov-April, tel. 311-693-100). The trailhead for a three-mile loop **trail** covering these Celtic sights (mainly in an open field) is immediately across the bridge in front of the Co-op supermarket.

Or, if you are in the mood for exploring the diversity of the forests, consider the following **woodland trail** (marked by signs—with a blue stripe between two white stripes—on trees, fences, and lampposts; 4 miles round-trip). Coming out of the glassworks gate, walk straight past the Keltovna restaurant and along the railroad tracks. After 100 yards, follow the blue-and-white marks and turn left up the hill, through a row of family houses. In another 100 yards you'll reach the edge of the forest. The trail then takes you over a small hill and down about a half-mile into a canyon with a creek, through a landscape that could soon be part of the Czech Republic's newest national park (see sidebar on page 300). As you gaze at the surrounding slopes, notice the variety of trees: verdant ashes and alders growing along the moist creek-bed, leafy beeches on the lower slopes, and hardy oaks and pines clinging to the dry, rocky hilltops. It's about two miles to the end of the canyon; walk as far as you'd like or retrace your steps along the same route back to Nižbor.

Eating in Nižbor: $$ Zastávka ("Old Railroad Pub") is a meticulously designed, 19th-century, railroad-themed eatery where you can sit on an old loading ramp or inside what seems like a wooden compartment. On weekends the place is packed with Czech bikers; if it's crowded, for quicker service order just soup and a drink (daily 10:00-22:00, mobile 727-860-680).

Continuing to Křivoklát: If you purchased a train ticket through to Křivoklát, you can get back on the Beroun motor train without purchasing a new ticket (check schedule carefully, trains go every 1-2 hours).

LÁNY

The village of Lány, about 15 miles north from Křivoklát Castle, is close to patriotic Czech hearts. The castle in Lány (closed to the public) served as the Czech "Camp David" for Tomáš Garrigue Masaryk (the first president of Czechoslovakia, between the World Wars) and Václav Havel (the contemporary "father of the Czech Republic" and first post-communist president of the nation). Subsequent presidents have continued the tradition.

Masaryk and his family are buried in Lány's simple village cemetery. Masaryk's humble grave on a hill in the middle of the fields is a pilgrimage place for freedom-loving Czechs. The communists, wanting to erase Masaryk from the nation's memory, destroyed all statues of him (such as the one in Kutná Hora—described on page 270) and barely mentioned his name in history textbooks. During the communist era, Czechs risked their careers by coming here on the Czech Independence Day to put candles on Masaryk's grave. Imagine: Every year, on October 28, the police sealed off all roads to the village of Lány, and anyone who wanted access had to show an ID card. When you arrived at work the next morning, the boss would be waiting at the door, asking, "Where were you yesterday—and why?"

After 1989, Václav Havel—the symbol of the new Czech freedom—strove to restore dignity to the presidency. He went back to the tradition of the first Czech president, making Lány his home away from home. Havel's weekend sojourns here symbolized a return to Czech self-governance. (For more on Havel, see the sidebar on page 152.)

Getting to Lány: The bus leaves Prague's Hradčanská Metro station for the Lány/Kladno district (6/day, fewer on weekends, 1 hour, direction: Rakovník). The bus first stops at the village green, then at the cemetery. A good plan is to catch the bus that leaves Prague at 8:50 on weekdays, and return to Prague on the one that departs from Lány's cemetery at 16:25. Check the schedule at www.idos.cz. There is no public transportation from Lány to Křivoklát Castle—it's a long but doable hike.

Sights in Lány: The **T.G. Masaryk Museum** (Muzeum T.G.M.), situated in an old wooden barn, follows Masaryk's life (1850-1937) in a re-created early 20th-century atmosphere. Before becoming the first President of Czechoslovakia (see sidebar on page 174), Masaryk was a sociology professor, a member of the Austrian Parliament, and an advocate of Czechoslovak independence during World War I. Special focus is devoted to two events that defined his public persona: his defiant defense of Leopold Hilsner—a Jewish shoemaker accused of "ritual murder" of a Catholic girl in 1889, and his challenge to the validity of the nationalistic Czech epic poems *Rukopisy Královedvorský a Zelenohorský (Manuscripts of Dvůr Králové and Zelená Hora)*, which supposedly dated from medieval times but have since been proved to be forgeries (50 Kč, April-Oct Tue-Sun 9:00-17:00, Nov-March Tue-Sun 10:00-16:00, closed Mon year-round; captions in Czech only—pick up an English handout at the counter; located across from the castle entrance, www.muzeumtgm.cz).

The **Castle Park,** adjacent to the castle, offers the opportunity to walk in the footprints of Czech presidents, who have used this as a working retreat for a century. Stroll the pleasant English-style park and a part of a hunting preserve that brings to mind medieval kings (15 Kč, Easter- Oct Sat-Sun 10:00-18:00, Wed-Thu from 14:00, closed Mon-Tue and Fri).

Eating in Lány: At the **$$ Narpa Restaurant** on the village green, servers in rustic attire offer three soups and five main courses on a rotating basis (daily 10:00-22:00, kitchen open 11:00-16:00, mobile 731 732 899).

Hike to Křivoklát Castle: Consider making the 15-mile hike from Lány to Křivoklát Castle. From the cemetery, it's a five-minute walk to the trailhead on the main square, around which you will also find two grocery stores for stocking up on supplies—there are no restaurants or stores until Křivoklát. With the help of a good map, follow the well-marked trail through woods and meadows (look for markers with one red stripe between two white stripes on trees, walls, and fences). This hike takes you through all the varieties of forests in Eastern Europe (beech, birch, poplar, oak, pine, spruce, fir), past a hidden 1950s dam, and to some stunning vistas. The *Praha–Západ* and *Křivoklátsko* hiking maps are excellent (sold in most Prague bookstores).

Karlovy Vary (Carlsbad)

Enough cutesy villages and fairy-tale castles: For a look at an upper-crust side of the Czech Republic, pay a visit to the famous spa town of Karlovy Vary (KAR-loh-vee VAH-ree)—better known by its English name, Carlsbad. Nestled in a wooded valley, where opulent Art Nouveau facades face a gurgling river and several springs bubble up hot and healing mineral water from deep underground, Karlovy Vary is a pristine and memorable spot. In the mostly traffic-free center, aging and aching spa pilgrims seek a cure for their pains by strolling from one thermal spring to another, filling little teapot-shaped cups with piping-hot mineral water, then sitting, sipping, and munching wafer cookies while watching the world go by, immersed in fanciful, over-the-top-elegant architecture. It's a slightly surreal scene that seduces you to join in.

Some visitors are turned off that Karlovy Vary doesn't feel as "authentically Czech" as other destinations in this book. "Karlsbad" made its (German) name as a (German) spa town, and today it's largely Russian-owned and crawling with tourists from anywhere but the Czech Republic. It's a gorgeous but soulless husk of a town where the cops are so ritzy, they ride Segways. But others enjoy its dazzling setting, stellar architecture, relaxed tempo, and unique spa rituals.

PLANNING YOUR TIME

Karlovy Vary sits between Prague and the German border. Unless you're serious about relaxing, it's not worth an overnight—and may not be worth the long side-trip from the capital (3.5 hours each way by train, 2 hours by car). But it can be a fun and fascinating stopover if connecting Prague and Germany. You can get a good look at Karlovy Vary in just a few hours. Stroll through town, from one end to the other, and join in the water-sipping ritual.

Orientation to Karlovy Vary

Karlovy Vary (pop. 50,000) fills the picturesque valley of the Teplá ("Warm") River, which trickles from the hills down into the Ohře River. Confusingly, the "upper" end of town—at the landmark Grandhotel Pupp—is to the south, while the train station and lower-lying modern town center lies to the north.

TOURIST INFORMATION

The town has two TIs (tel. 355-321-176, www.karlovyvary.cz): One is very central, in the pedestrian zone near the Market Colonnade (Lázeňská 14), while the other is between the train station and the center, on the traffic-free Masaryka street (at #53).

ARRIVAL IN KARLOVY VARY

By Train: From the train station, it's an easy and scenic one-mile walk into the town center: Exit the station to the left, cross the busy street, then find the pedestrianized Masaryka street behind the red Becherovka headquarters. This passes the TI on the way into town.

Better yet, start at the top of Karlovy Vary and work your way back down. From the city bus terminal (5-minute walk from train station), take bus #2, which loops on the slopes above town, then stops at Lázně I (the Imperial Spa, just above Grandhotel Pupp) and at Divadelní Náměstí (near the Hot Spring Colonnade, in the center of town). The bus runs every 20 minutes. To reach the city bus terminal, follow the walking directions above to Masaryka, then take the first left down Zeyerova. It's in front of the pretty, yellow former market hall.

By Car: Several pay parking lots and garages are well-marked around town—though driving through the town center isn't worth the hassle (lots of pedestrian-only lanes, so you'll be routed to roads higher up in the hills). It's simpler to park in the Tržnice pay-and-display lot near the bus terminal/old market hall described above, at the lower entrance to town, then ride the bus to the top of town and saunter back down (if that lot's full, another one is across the street, up the hill, and behind the trees, near a row of market stalls).

Sights in Karlovy Vary

I've divided the town into three zones: upper (near Grandhotel Pupp), middle (near the colonnades), and lower (between the town center and the train station). While I prefer starting at the top and working down, you can also do it vice versa—or, if time is short, just focus on the central area (bus #2 takes you to either place). Be sure to slow down and simply enjoy the grand architecture—lots of Neo-Baroque, Art Nouveau, and other eye-pleasing styles from the late 19th and early 20th centuries, when this resort town boomed after a major train line connected it to Prague. Keep an eye out for two main architectural features: the **colonnades,** where you'll find the hot-water springs; and the grand old **spa** buildings *(lázně),* numbered 1 through 5.

▲Upper Area

Anchoring the top of town is the can't-miss-it **Grandhotel Pupp,** an over-the-top confection. Appropriately, it was built by a German candy magnate and has been immortalized in several international films. Along with other locations around Karlovy Vary, the hotel stood in for "Montenegro" in the 2006 James Bond film *Casino Royale,* and it was where Queen Latifah blew through her life savings in 2006's *Last Holiday.* Fittingly, the town

hosts the prestigious Karlovy Vary International Film Festival each July. The building was designed by the Viennese architect duo Ferdinand Fellner and Hermann Helmer, who also did many of the town's other landmarks. While slightly faded today, the Pupp still feels stately. If you keep a low profile, it's generally fine to stroll through the lobby—enjoying the chandeliered elegance and giant black-and-white photos of illustrious guests. Their genteel café sells famously decadent cakes and not-*too*-outrageously-priced coffee (Mírové Náměstí 2, tel. 353-109-111, www.pupp.cz).

Just to the right of the hotel, at the end of the little uphill Marianská lane, a **funicular** departs every 15 minutes to ascend to the crest of the wooded hill. Here, an elevator takes you to the top of the Diana Tower, with views over the surrounding forested hills and some of the hotels that scamper up the steep slopes.

Before descending to the town center, consider a five-minute detour upriver to the **Imperial Spa** (Císařské Lázně, also known as "Spa 1"—labeled *Lázně I).* Sitting in a park facing a statue of Charles IV, this building was once the favored place for Habsburg Emperor Franz Josef to take the waters. These days it's awaiting a studs-out renovation, but if it's still open, you can pay a modest fee to climb up to its exquisite former exercise room: a high-ceilinged riot of handsomely carved wood, which feels more like a ballroom.

The streets between this area and the town center—especially the parallel embankment promenades, **Stará ("Old") Louka** and **Nová ("New") Louka**—are lined with big-ticket shops and more fine facades from a bygone era of opulence. From here, the central area described next is about a 10-minute downhill stroll. Along the way, you'll pass the gorgeous town theater (Mestní Divadlo, with its Neo-Renaissance arches and swaying mansard roof).

▲▲Central Area

The most interesting spa action takes place in the central area just below the pretty, Baroque, pale-green **Church of St. Mary Mag-**

dalene (Kostel Svaté Máří Magdalény; peek through the gate to see its interior).

Built in the 1970s with a stern communist-concrete aesthetic, the **Hot Spring Colonnade** (Vřídelní Kolonáda) is nevertheless a good place to begin your visit to the springs of Karlovy Vary. Inside, vendor stands sell the two main items you need to fully experience the scene: a spa cup and some wafer cookies (see sidebar on page 308). Once equipped, head through the colonnade to find several taps continuously gurgling hot water from the first of Karlovy Vary's springs. Don't miss the glass atrium where a natural, steaming geyser spurts dramatically 20 feet into the air.

Across from the Hot Spring Colonnade is a pleasant pedestrian street called Tržiště, dominated by the delicate, frilly architecture of the **Market Colonnade** (Tržní Kolonáda), with four more springs to sample. Just above the Mill Colonnade, marked by a bold Gothic tower, is the entrance to the **Castle Spa** (Zámecké Lázně), the priciest and most upscale of Karlovy Vary's public spas (see sidebar on page 308).

Farther along, Tržiště passes the **TI**; nearby, look for the entrance to a free **elevator** that zips you up to the Karl IV restaurant, where the adjacent public terrace provides a fine view over town.

Just downstream is one of Karlovy Vary's most impressive architectural features, the **Mill Colonnade** (Mlýnská Kolonáda). The only one that feels like a true colonnade, this awe-inspiring forest of stout columns and rounded arches over a sleek marble floor is scattered with

six more springs to sample. This colonnade—and the riverfront

Taking the Waters in Karlovy Vary

Karlovy Vary is famous for the 16 different natural springs scattered around its town center. Thirteen of these dispense drinkable natural thermal water that's between 107 and 164 degrees Fahrenheit. Sipping this salty, sulfurous stuff supposedly soothes arthritic and digestive pain. While some visitors come equipped with a systematic treatment plan, I enjoy just strolling aimlessly and taste-testing from a few different springs. But sip in moderation: Locals warn that first-timers who chug too much find that it can work all too well in moving along the digestive tract. (Field trips here are typically punctuated by multiple emergency bathroom stops on the way home.)

Traditionally, people taking the waters use a special cup called a *becher,* shaped like a miniature, flattened teapot. Fill your *becher,* then sip gingerly through the combined handle/spout (giving the steaming fluid a chance to cool off). While you could use an empty bottle, it's fun to invest in a souvenir drinking cup to do it in style; the cheapest ones start at around 100 Kč and are guaranteed to break in your luggage.

To kill the powerful mineral aftertaste, munch on the delicious **spa wafers** *(oplatky)*. Resembling salad-plate-sized com-

terrace park in front of it—are made for lingering. Just downriver is the splendid Neo-Moorish facade of **Spa #3** (look for *Lázně III*).

Lower Area

Between the town center and the train station, at the grand hotel adjoining the Dvořák Gardens (Dvořákovy Sady), don't miss the dazzling wooden **Orchard Colonnade** (Sadová Kolonáda).

Farther downriver is the unfortunate **Hotel Thermal**—a heavy-handed, concrete-communist behemoth that's totally (and intentionally) at odds with the spare-no-expense aesthetic of its surroundings. It does, however, run a public swimming pool with fine views over Karlovy Vary's valley (on the hill just behind the hulking building).

Nestled in the middle of the flower-filled Smetana Gardens (Smetanovy Sady) is the **Elisabeth Spa** (Alžbětiny Lázně)—also called Spa #5 *(Lázně V)*.

munion wafers, these sweet cookies come in a variety of flavors and have a thin layer of filling inside. They're cheap, tasty, and even better when heated up on a big press that looks like a waffle iron.

While most visitors are here to drink the waters, you can bathe in them too (be sure to bring a swimsuit). Most of the town's spas are inside hotels, and open only to guests, but there are three public options: The fanciest is the Castle Spa, marked by the Gothic tower in the pedestrianized town center (across from the Hot Spring Colonnade and behind the Market Colonnade, www.zamecke-lazne.com). The Elisabeth Spa, in a grandly crumbling old building at the lower end of town, is more affordable (www.spa5.cz). And the ugly Hotel Thermal, dominating the lower part of town, has an outdoor swimming pool high on the adjacent bluff that's partly fed by spring water. As this one doesn't offer other spa treatments, it's the most lowbrow but most scenic option (www.thermal.cz).

In addition to the thermal springs, Karlovy Vary is near and dear to all Czech hearts for producing two of the country's favorite drinks. Becherovka, the herbal digestif that's second only to beer as the Czech national drink, is distilled here. And Mattoni mineral water—the country's top-selling brand (and, according to aficionados, the best)—bubbles up from a spring in a nearby village. Some people call Becherovka and Mattoni "the 14th and 15th drinkable springs of Karlovy Vary."

While the grand building that houses it has seen better days, the spa facilities have been modernized.

Connecting the Smetana Gardens to the train station is the delightfully pedestrianized **Masaryka street,** lined with both top-end and workaday shops. At the train-station end of the street, you'll find the **Jan Becher Museum,** where a 40-minute guided tour explains the process for distilling the pungent, herbal Czech firewater called Becherovka (open daily, 1-3 tours/day in English—call ahead or check online for schedule, more frequent tours in Czech, www.becherovka.cz). The adjoining Becherplatz restaurant is a warren of highly decorated, borderline-kitschy beer halls and cellars, and a handy place to grab a bite to eat (tel. 353-599-999, www.becherplatz.cz).

NEAR KARLOVY VARY

If you have a car and time to spare, consider these two stops.

Moser Glassworks

For those captivated by Czech crystal, a visit to this sleek, state-of-the-art facility on the outskirts of Karlovy Vary is a pilgrimage. In addition to perusing the stunning showroom, you can visit a museum celebrating the glassmaker's finest works and take a 30-minute tour of the glassworks (open daily, call or check website for tour times and reservation information; at Kapitana Jaroše 46/19 in the Dvory neighborhood just west of the town center, exit from highway toward Cheb; tel. 353-416-132, www.moser-glass.com). For more on Czech crystal, see page 234 of the Shopping in Prague chapter.

Loket

This charming and scenic village is a beautiful six-mile hike or an easy nine-mile drive west of Karlovy Vary (figure about 15 minutes, drive toward Cheb). While smaller and not as endearing as Český
Krumlov, it has a similar and even
more stunning setting—perched on
a steep and bulbous spit of land, almost entirely surrounded by a nearly
180-degree bend in the Ohře River.
(*Loket* means "elbow.") The writer
Johann Wolfgang von Goethe was

a frequent visitor here, making it popular among German tourists. As you drive into town, circle around for the fine views, then head over the bridge and park on the main square. Lose yourself in the tidy pedestrianized lanes, or hike up to the rustic, lived-in-feeling castle for a modest town history exhibit and nice views (walk around at your leisure with English descriptions, or pay more to join a guided tour, www.hradloket.cz). Hardy hikers can make their way from Karlovy Vary to Loket through the wooded hills, following a six-mile nature trail (get details and check return bus times at the Karlovy Vary TI).

ČESKÝ KRUMLOV

Krummau

Surrounded by mountains, lassoed by its river, and dominated by its castle, this enchanted town mesmerizes visitors. When you see its awe-inspiring castle, delightful Old Town of cobbled lanes and shops, and easy canoeing options, you'll understand why having fun is a slam-dunk here. Romantics are floored by its spectacular setting; you could spend all your time doing aimless laps from one end of town to the other.

The sharp bends in the Vltava provide natural moats, so it's no wonder Český Krumlov has been a choice spot for eons. Celtic tribes settled here a century before Christ. Then came Germanic tribes. The Slavic tribes arrived in the ninth century. The Rožmberks (Rosenbergs)—Bohemia's top noble family—ran the city from 1302 to 1602. You'll spot their rose symbol all over town.

The 16th century was the town's Golden Age, when Český Krumlov hosted artists, scientists, and alchemists from across Europe. In 1588, the town became home to an important Jesuit college. In 1602, the Rožmberks ran out of money to fund their lavish lifestyles, so they sold their territory to the Habsburgs—who ushered in a more Germanic period. After that, as many as 75 percent of the town's people were German—until 1945, when most Germans were expelled (for more on this era and its repercussions, see the sidebar on page 324).

Český Krumlov's rich mix of Gothic, Renaissance, and Baroque buildings is easy to miss. As you wander, be sure to look up...notice the surviving details in the fine stonework and pretty gables. Step into shops. Snoop into back lanes and tiny squares. Gothic buildings curve with the winding streets. Many precious Gothic and Renaissance frescoes were whitewashed in Baroque times (when the colorful trimmings of earlier periods were way out of style). Today, these frescoes are being rediscovered and restored.

Český Krumlov is a huge tourist magnet, which makes things colorful and easy for travelers. At times it can feel like a medieval theme park—but fortunately there are still hidden nooks and sleepy back alleys to make the place feel genuine.

PLANNING YOUR TIME

It's easy to enjoy Český Krumlov without ever paying to enter a sight (morning and evening are best for strolling without crowds). But a tour of the Baroque Theater at the castle is worth considering. If you want to join an English tour, reserve first thing in the morning (call ahead or visit in person), then build your day around your visit time. While you're at it, consider booking an English tour of the castle interior. Those who hate planning ahead on vacation can join a Czech tour of the theater or castle anytime (English information sheets provided). And visits to the newly restored synagogue and Seidel Photo Studio Museum bring more recent history alive.

A paddle down the river to Zlatá Koruna Abbey is a highlight (three hours), and a 20-minute walk up to the Křížový Vrch (Hill of the Cross) rewards you with a fine view of the town and its unforgettable riverside setting. Other sights are worthwhile only if you have a particular interest (Viennese artist Egon Schiele, brewery tour, puppets, and so on).

Many sights are closed on Monday, though the major attraction—the town itself—is always open. Evenings are for atmospheric dining and drinking.

Orientation to Český Krumlov

Český Krumlov (CHESS-key KROOM-loff) means, roughly, "Czech Bend in the River." Calling it "Český" for short sounds silly to Czech speakers (since dozens of Czech town names begin with "Český")—rather, they call it "Krumlov."

The city is extremely easy to navigate. The twisty Vltava River, which makes a perfect S through the town, ropes the Old Town into a tight peninsula. Above the Old Town is the Castle Town. Český Krumlov's one main street starts at the isthmus and winds through the peninsula, crossing a bridge before snaking through the Castle Town, the castle complex (a long series of courtyards), and the castle gardens high above. I've narrated this route on my self-guided walk. The main square, Náměstí Svornosti—with the TI, ATMs, and taxis—dominates the Old Town and marks the center of the peninsula. All recommended restaurants, hotels, and sights are within a few minutes' walk of this square.

TOURIST INFORMATION

The helpful TI is on the **main square** (daily 9:00-18:00, June-Aug until 19:00, shorter hours in winter, tel. 380-704-622, www.ckrumlov.info). The 129-Kč *City Guide* book includes a fine town and castle map. The TI has a baggage-storage desk and can check train and bus schedules. Ask about concerts, city walking tours in English, and canoe trips on the river. They rent an audioguide featuring a self-guided town walk (100 Kč, one hour). A second, less-crowded TI—actually a private business—is in the lowest courtyard of the **castle** (daily 9:00-18:00, tel. 380-725-110).

Český Krumlov Card: This 200-Kč card, sold at the TI and participating sights, covers entry to the Round Tower, Castle Museum (but not castle tours), Egon Schiele Art Center, Museum of Regional History, and Seidel Photo Studio Museum. Do the math to decide if it makes sense for you.

ARRIVAL IN ČESKÝ KRUMLOV

By Train: The train station is a 20-minute walk from town (turn right out of the station, then walk downhill onto a steep cobbled path leading to an overpass into the town center). Taxis are standing by to zip you to your hotel (about 100 Kč), or call 602-113-113 to summon one.

By Bus: The bus station is just three blocks away from the Old Town. To walk from the bus-station lot to the town center, follow the "walking man" signs out of the lot to *Centrum*, veer right and downhill on the small road, and cross the main road past the Co-op grocery. Figure on 60 Kč for a taxi from the station to your hotel.

By Car: Parking lots ring the town center, each one marked by a blue *P* sign. If your hotel is in the mostly traffic-free center, you'll be allowed to drive in (gingerly passing hordes of tourists) and park on the main square just long enough to drop off your bags and get directions to one of the outer lots. The flow of traffic is one-way: Enter at the east end of town, on Horní street, then exit across two bridges at the south end of town, on Linecká street (get details from your hotel before you arrive).

HELPFUL HINTS

Exchange Rate: 25 Kč = about $1

Country Calling Code: 420 (see page 464 for dialing instructions)

Festivals: Locals drink oceans of beer and celebrate their medieval roots at big events such as the Celebration of the Rose (Slavnosti Růže), where blacksmiths mint ancient coins, jugglers swallow fire, mead flows generously, and pigs are roasted on open fires (late June, www.ckrumlov.info). The summer also brings a top-notch international music festival, with performances in pubs, cafés, and the castle gardens (mid-July-mid-Aug, www.festivalkrumlov.cz). During St. Wenceslas celebrations, the square becomes a medieval market and the streets come alive with theater and music (late Sept). Reserve a hotel well in advance if you'll be in town for these events.

Bike Rental: You can rent bikes at the **train station** (150 Kč/day with train ticket, prices slightly higher otherwise, tel. 380-715-000), **Vltava Sport Service** (see listing under "Canoeing and Rafting the Vltava" on page 329), and the recommended **Hostel 99.**

Tours in Český Krumlov

Walking Tours

Since the town itself, rather than its sights, is what it's all about here, taking a guided walk is the key to a meaningful visit. The TI sells tickets for several different guided walks. No reservations are necessary—just meet in front of the TI on the main square and pay the guide. Confirm times when you visit, as schedules can change. The **Old Town Tour** offers the best general town introduction (300 Kč, daily at 12:30, 1.5 hours); in peak season, this tour extends to include the castle exteriors (490 Kč, April-Oct daily at 14:30). There's also a nighttime version (departing between 19:30 and 20:30, depending on the season). For a self-guided town walk, consider the TI's audioguide (see "Tourist Information," earlier).

Local Guides

Oldřiška Baloušková studied in California before starting a family back in her hometown, which she knows through and through (500 Kč/hour, mobile 737-920-901, oldriskab@gmail.com). **Jiří (George) Václavíček,** a gentle and caring man who perfectly fits mellow Český Krumlov, is a joy to share this town with (500 Kč/hour, mobile 603-927-995, www.krumlovguide.com, jiri.vaclavicek@gmail.com). **Karolína Kortušová** is an enthusiastic, experienced guide with great organizational skills. Her company, Krumlov Tours, can set you up with a good local tour guide, palace and theater admissions, river trips, and more (guides-500 Kč/hour, mobile 723-069-561, http://krumlovtours.com, info@krumlovtours.com).

Český Krumlov Walk

The town's best sight is its cobbled cityscape, surrounded by a babbling river and capped by a dramatic castle. Most of Český

Krumlov's modest sights are laced together in this charming self-guided walk from the top of the Old Town, down its spine, across the river, and up to the castle. The walk begins at a fine viewpoint...and ends at an even better one. I've divided it into two parts: downhill, through the Old Town to the river; then uphill, ascending through the castle complex on the other side. You can also do the two parts on different days. The second half of the walk makes a useful spine for organizing a visit to the castle quarter.

THE OLD TOWN

• *Start at the bridge over the isthmus, which was once the fortified grand entry gate to the town (see map on page 316). For the best view, step down to the little terrace in front of the restaurant gate.*

Horní Bridge: From this "Upper Bridge," note the natural fortification provided by the tight bend in the river. Trace the river to your right, where it curves around the last building in town, with a smokestack. This is the Eggenberg Brewery, makers of Český Krumlov's very own hometown brew (with daily tours—see page 328). Behind that, on the horizon, is a pile of white apartment high-rises—built in the last decade of the communist era to solve a housing shortage (many homes were demolished after their German owners were forced out at the end of World War II—see page 324). To the left of the brewery stands a huge monastery (with the pointy red steeple; not generally open to the public). Behind that, on Kleť Mountain—the highest hilltop—stands a TV tower and a world-class astronomical observatory and research center.

Head back up to the middle of the bridge. Look down and left, then down and right. Notice how the Vltava wraps entirely around the town center. Rafters take about a half-hour to circle around the Old Town peninsula, beginning and ending under this bridge.

• *Head into town on...*

Horní Street: As you step off the bridge, Český Krumlov's aptly named "Upper Street" passes the **Museum of Regional History** on the right (see page 327). Just past the museum, a little garden overlook affords a fine castle view.

Immediately across the street (on the left), notice the Renais-

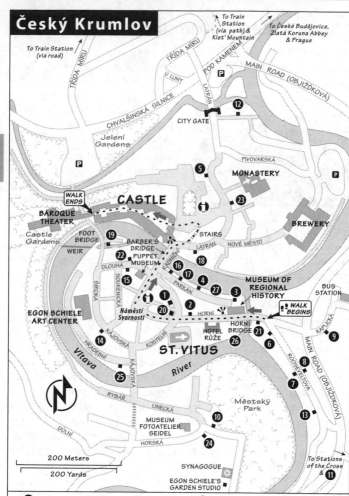

Český Krumlov

1. Castle View Apartments
2. Hotel Konvice
3. Hotel Mlýn
4. Pension Olšakovský
5. Pension Danny
6. Hotel Garni Myší Díra & Maleček Boat Rental
7. Pension Teddy
8. Pension Anna
9. Pension Gardena
10. Pension U Kapličky
11. To Pension Kříž
12. Hostel 99 & Hospoda 99 Rest.
13. Krumlov House Hostel
14. Na Louži Restaurant
15. Cikánská Jizba
16. Krčma u Dwau Maryí
17. Laibon Restaurant
18. Kolektiv
19. Rybářská Restaurace
20. Krčma v Šatlavské
21. Restaurace Barbakán
22. Krumlovská Picka & CK Shuttle Office
23. Dobrá Čajovna Teahouse
24. Coffee Roasting Company
25. Vltava Sport Service
26. Start Quickie River Float
27. End Quickie River Float & Start Abbey/Borsov Floats

sance facade of **Hotel Růže:** This former Jesuit college hides a beautiful courtyard, now filled with artistic vendor stands. Pop inside to shop or just admire its decoration of faux sgraffito "bricks," made by scratching into an outer layer of one color of plaster to reveal a different color beneath. This style was all the rage during the town's boom time, and we'll be seeing several more examples on this walk.

• *Walk another block down the main drag, until you reach steps on the left leading to the...*

Church of St. Vitus: Český Krumlov's main church was built as a bastion of Catholicism in the 15th century, when the Roman Catholic Church was fighting the Hussites. The 17th-century Baroque high altar shows a totem of religious figures: the Virgin Mary (crowned in heaven); St. Vitus (above Mary); and, way up on top, St. Wenceslas, the patron saint of the Czech people—long considered their ambassador in heaven. The canopy in the back, though empty today, once supported a grand statue of a Rožmberk atop a horse. The statue originally stood at the high altar. (Too egotistical for Jesuits, it was later moved to the rear of the nave, and then lost for good.) Notice the empty organ case. While the main organ is out for restoration, the cute little circa-1716 Baroque beauty is getting plenty of use (photos of the restoration work on the far wall; generally open daily 8:30-16:30, Sunday Mass at 9:30, daily Mass at 17:00 in the winter chapel; tel. 724-937-121).

• *Continuing on Horní street, you'll come to the...*

Main Square (Náměstí Svornosti): Lined with a mix of Renaissance and Baroque homes of burghers (all built on 12th-century Gothic foundations), the main square has a grand charm. The Town Hall (the crenellated white building, on the right) flies both the Czech flag and the town flag, which shows the rose symbol of the Rožmberk family, who ruled the town for 300 years.

Imagine the history that this square has seen: In the 1620s, the town was held by the (very Catholic) Habsburgs, just as Lutheran Protestantism was rising to threaten Catholic Europe. Krumlov was a seat of Jesuit power and learning, and the intellectuals of the Roman church allegedly burned books on this square. Later, when there was a bad harvest, locals blamed witches—and burned them, too. Every so often, terrible plagues rolled through the countryside. In a nearby village, all but two residents were killed by a plague.

But the plague stopped before devastating the people of Český

Krumlov, and in 1715—as thanks to God—they built the plague monument that stands on the square today (on the left). Much later, in 1938, Hitler stood right here before a backdrop of long Nazi banners to celebrate the annexation of the Sudetenland. And in 1968, Russian tanks spun their angry treads on the roads to this square to intimidate locals who were demanding freedom. Today, thankfully, this square is part of an unprecedented time of peace and prosperity for the Czech people.

• *From the main square, walk down Radniční street (on the right, just past the Town Hall) and cross the...*

Barber's Bridge (Lazebnický Most): This wooden bridge, decorated with two 19th-century statues, connects the Old Town and the Castle Town. On the right side stands a statue of St. John of Nepomuk, who's also depicted by a prominent statue on Prague's Charles Bridge. Among other responsibilities, he's the protector against floods. In the great floods in August 2002, the angry river submerged the bridge (but removable banisters minimized the damage). Stains just above the windows of the adjacent building show how high the water rose.

• *The second part of the walk involves lots of uphill hiking—but it's worth it to see the castle courtyards and dramatic views.*

KRUMLOV CASTLE

Big and imposing, the town castle boasts several fine courtyards, spectacular viewpoints, and gorgeous gardens—all of which are open to the public, free to enter, and fun to roam (though some areas may be closed on Mon). This part of the walk focuses on those public spaces, leading you from Barber's Bridge, through the heart of the castle, and up to a picturesque viewpoint just before the gardens. The castle also has several individual sights (Round Tower, Castle Museum, Upper Castle, Baroque Theater) that can be laced into this walk but require paid admission and/or a reserved tour (for details, see listings under "Sights in Český Krumlov," later).

• *Cross the bridge and head up shop-lined Latrán street, which bends to the right. Just after that bend, look for the stairs on your left (in front of the gray-and-white building). Head up, passing under a stone arch with the wood-carved rose symbol of the Rožmberk family (see sidebar). You'll emerge into the castle's...*

First (Lower) Courtyard: This is just the first of many courtyards that bunny-hop up through the castle complex. This was the site for workers and industry (stables, smithy, brewery, pharmacy,

Parting of the Roses

A five-petal rose is not just the distinctive mark of Český Krumlov and the Rožmberk rulers (literally, "Lords from the Rose Mountain"). You'll find it, in five-color combinations, all over South Bohemia.

A medieval legend, depicted inside Český Krumlov's castle, explains the division of the roses in the following way: A respected nobleman named Vítek split the property he had accumulated during his lifetime among five sons. Each son was also assigned his own coat of arms, all of which shared the motif of a five-petal rose. The oldest son, Jindřich, received a golden rose in a blue field, along with the lands of Hradec and Telč. Vilém received a silver rose in a red field, with the lands of Landštejn and Třeboň. Smil was given a blue rose in a golden field and the lands of Stráž and Bystřice. Vok kept his father's coat of arms, a red rose in a white field, and became the lord in Rožmberk and Český Krumlov. Finally, the out-of-wedlock Sezima had to make do with a black rose and the tiny land of Ústí.

Over generations, the legend—which is corroborated by historical sources—served as a constant warning to the ambitious Rožmberks not to further split up their land. The Lords from the Rose Mountain were the rare Czech noble family that, for 300 years, strictly adhered to the principle of primogeniture (the oldest son gets all, and younger sons are subservient to him). Unlike Vítek, the patriarch, each successive ruler of the Rožmberk estates made sure to consolidate his possessions, handing more to his eldest son than he had received. As a result, the enterprising Rožmberks grew into the most powerful family in Bohemia. In 1501, their position as "first in the country after the king" became law.

and so on)—convenient for aristocratic needs, but far enough away to keep noises and smells at bay.

Looking up, you can't miss the strikingly colorful **Round Tower** that marks the location of the first castle, built here to guard the medieval river crossing. With its 16th-century Renaissance paint job colorfully restored, it looks exotic, featuring fancy astrological decor, terra-cotta symbols of the zodiac, and a fine arcade.

• *Head up to the former drawbridge. Look over the sides of the bridge. Spot any bears?*

Bear Pits (Medvědí Příkop): These hold a family of European brown bears, as they have since the Rožmberks added bears to their coat of arms in the 16th century to demonstrate their (fake) blood relation to the distinguished Italian Orsini family (whose name means "bear-like"). Featured on countless coats of arms, bears have long been totemic animals for Europeans. Pronouncing the animal's real name was taboo in many cultures, and Czechs still refer to bears only indirectly. For example, in most Germanic languages the word "bear" is derived from "brown," while the Slavic *medvěd* literally means "honey eater."

Near the top of the bridge, notice the gently worded sign suggesting that—rather than toss down your junk-food leftovers—you add a few coins in the collection slot to finance "more varied meals and delicacies" for the bears.

• *Continue through the gateway into the...*

Second Courtyard: Here you'll spot more of the sgraffito (Renaissance faux features scraped into wet plaster) that decorates

much of the castle. To your left, at the bottom of the courtyard, is the entrance to the **tower climb** and the **Castle Museum.** Farther up on the left is the **ticket office** for castle tours, including the Baroque Theater—stop in now (if you haven't already) to see about a tour.

• *From here, things get steep as we enter the...*

Heart of the Castle Complex: Head up the bridge, noticing the little view terrace on the left—the first of several along here. You'll emerge into the **Third Courtyard**, then (after a corridor) the **Fourth Courtyard.** Nicely preserved paintings enliven their blocky facades. Wrapped around these courtyards is the castle proper, a mighty Renaissance building sometimes called the Upper Castle (interiors open to visitors—notice the meeting points for various tour options). Continuing straight out through the end of the Fourth Courtyard, you'll cross the breathtaking **Cloak Bridge**—a triple-decker, statue-lined, covered bridge spanning a vast gorge and connecting the castle firmly with the gardens that sprawl behind it. Enjoy the views—but believe it or not, even better ones are coming up.

Notice the **Baroque Theater,** at the far end of the bridge, which still uses traditional methods for moving scenery and producing sound effects. Aspects of this back-in-the-day stagecraft still survive on Broadway today. This is one of only two such original theaters in Europe.

• *After the bridge, continue uphill through the...*

Fifth Courtyard: Really more of a pathway, this connects the castle to its gardens. Walk along the white wall—with peekaboo windows—until you are almost at the gate up top. High on the wall to the right, notice the **sundial.** Check the time: It's dead-on...except for Daylight Savings Time, which was unknown to medieval timekeepers. Notice that the sundial cuts into one of the faux windows, painted on the lower level of the building to create Renaissance symmetry.

Now step through the low-profile door directly across from the sundial. You'll emerge at a spectacular **viewpoint** that takes in the entire town, its curving river, and even the colorful tower and most of the castle complex you just came through. Jockey your way through the selfie-snapping crowd and drink it in. (Or literally drink, at the little adjacent bar.)

• *Our walk is finished. But if you still have stamina, you can consider exploring the **castle gardens**—they're just uphill, through the gate from the Fifth Courtyard. (While the castle exterior is open all the time, the garden is open daily 8:00-19:00, with shorter hours off-season.)*

Sights in Český Krumlov

KRUMLOV CASTLE COMPLEX (KRUMLOVSKÝ ZÁMEK)

No Czech town is complete without a castle—and now that the nobles are gone, their mansions are open to us common folk. Český

Krumlov is no different. Its immense Krumlov Castle complex, one of the largest in Central Europe, perches on a rock promontory overlooking the Vltava River and the town. The original Gothic castle took shape here in the 13th century, and eventually the Rožmberk, Eggenberg, and Schwarzenberg families each inherited it in turn. In successive waves of additions and renovations, they built it into the splendid Renaissance/Baroque property you see today.

The following sights are listed in the order you'll reach them as you climb up through the complex (ideally following my self-guided walk, earlier). The Round Tower and Castle Museum can be visited at your leisure, while other castle interiors—including the excellent Baroque Theater—can only be seen with a guided tour (see next). On a quick visit, the only sight I'd bother paying admission for is the theater.

Reservations for Baroque Theater and Upper Castle: It's worth the 10 Kč reservation fee to hold a slot on an English tour of the Upper Castle interior or the Baroque Theater (the theater is the castle attraction most likely to sell out). To book ahead, stop by the ticket office in person, or call 380-704-721 to check English tour times and reserve a space. No other castle sights require (or accept) reservations.

Information: Tel. 380-704-711, www.castle.ckrumlov.cz.

▲Round Tower (Zâmecká Věž) and Castle Museum (Hradní Muzeum)

These two sights share a ticket office at the bottom of the castle's middle courtyard. While neither is a must, both are worth considering if you want a peek inside the castle without committing to a guided tour. These are also the only castle sights open on Mondays (in peak season).

Colorfully impressive from the outside, the **tower** is also fun to climb. Twist up the 163 well-worn wood and stone steps to the top, where you'll be rewarded with grand, 360-degree views over the town, the rest of the castle complex, and happy boaters floating on the river.

The exhibits at the **Castle Museum** focus on key moments in the lives of the town's various ruling families: Rožmberks, Eggenbergs, and Schwarzenbergs. Be sure to pick up the good, included audioguide as you enter. You'll see a hall of aristocratic portraits; the offices, bedrooms, and dining rooms of the various inhabitants; and a modest religious treasury, armory, and musical instruments collection. At the end you can sit in old-timey cinema seats and watch archival footage of the castle's residents from the 1920s and 1930s.

Cost and Hours: Tower 50 Kč, museum 100 Kč, combo-ticket for both 130 Kč; both open daily 9:00-17:00, June-Aug until 18:00, closed Mon in Nov-March; last entry one hour before closing.

▲Upper Castle (Horní Hrad)

While the Upper Castle grounds are free to explore, you'll need to take a tour to access the interiors. Two different tour routes give you a glimpse of the places where the Rožmberks, Eggenbergs, and Schwarzenbergs dined, studied, worked, prayed, entertained, and slept. (By European standards, the castle's not much, and the tours move slowly.) Imagine being an aristocratic guest here, riding the dukes' assembly line of fine living: You'd promenade through a long series of elegant spaces and dine in the sumptuous dining hall before enjoying a concert in the Hall of Mirrors, which leads directly to the Baroque Theater (described next). After the play, you'd go out into the château garden for a fireworks finale.

Cost and Hours: Choose from Tour I (Gothic and Renaissance rooms, of the most general interest) or Tour II (19th-century castle life). Tours run June-Aug Tue-Sun 9:00-12:00 & 13:00-18:00, spring and fall until 17:00, closed Mon and Nov-March. Tours in Czech cost 150 Kč, leave regularly, and include an adequate flier in English that contains about half the information imparted by the guide. English tours are preferable, but cost more (250 Kč), run less frequently, and are often booked solid. Pay to reserve a slot in advance; see "Reservations for Baroque Theater and Upper Castle," earlier, for details. You'll be issued a ticket with your tour time printed on it. Be in the correct courtyard at that time, or you'll be locked out.

▲▲Baroque Theater (Zámecké Divadlo)

Europe once had several hundred Baroque theaters. Using candles for light and fireworks for special effects, most burned down. Today, only two survive in good shape and are open to tourists: one at Stockholm's Drottningholm Palace; and one here, at Krumlov Castle. During the 45-minute tour, you'll sit on benches in the theater and then go under the stage to see the wood-and-rope contraptions that enabled scenes to be scooted in and out within seconds (while fireworks and smoke blinded the audience). It's a lovely little theater with an impressive 3-D effect that makes the stage look deeper than it really is, but don't bother with the tour unless you can snare a spot on an English one. The theater is used only once a year for an actual performance, attended by Baroque theater enthusiasts.

Cost and Hours: 300 Kč for English tour, 250 Kč for Czech tour, tours Tue-Sun May-Oct, no tours Mon and Nov-April; English departures at 10:00, 11:00, 13:00, 14:00, and 15:00. Due to the theater's fragility, groups are limited to 20 people, and English tours generally sell out. Reserve ahead—see "Reservations for Baroque Theater and Upper Castle," earlier.

Castle Gardens (Zámecká Zahrada)

This lovely, 2,300-foot-long garden crowns the castle complex. It was laid out in the 17th century, when the noble family would have it lit with 22,000 oil lamps, torches, and candles for special occasions. The lower part is geometrical and symmetrical—French

The Expulsion
of Ethnic Germans from Czechoslovakia

For seven centuries, Czech- and German-speaking people jointly inhabited and cultivated the lands of Bohemia, Moravia, and Silesia. Then, during the 19th century, the growing importance of ethnic identity resulted in tensions between these communities and fierce competition between their institutions. Running up to World War I, animosity rose so high that Czech and German soccer clubs from Prague refused to compete against each other. This charged situation was made worse by the German- and Hungarian-dominated Habsburg monarchy, which treated local Slavs (Poles, Slovaks, Croats, Slovenes, and Serbs) as second-class citizens.

The end of World War I handed the Slavs an unprecedented opportunity to claim the land for themselves. The principle that gave countries such as Poland, Czechoslovakia, and Yugoslavia independence was called "self-determination": Each nation had the right to its own state within the area in which its people formed the majority. But the peoples of Eastern Europe had mixed over the centuries, making it impossible to create functioning states based purely on ethnicity. In the case of Bohemia—which became Czechoslovakia—the borders were drawn along historical boundaries. While the country was predominantly Slavic, areas with overwhelming German majorities remained.

Ethnic Germans in Czechoslovakia were never wholehearted supporters of the newly centralized, Slavic-majority democracy. While politically engaged in the new country, Nazi propaganda appealed to them amidst Hitler's rise to power and an economic downturn that was particularly harsh for their communities. In 1935, 63 percent of Germans in Czechoslovakia voted for the Sudeten Nazi Party, enabling Hitler to appeal to international powers on their behalf, using the principle of self-determination. The 1938 Munich Agreement ceded the German-speaking areas of Czechoslovakia to the Third Reich, and ethnic Czechs were forced to leave those areas.

Over the course of World War II, many Czechs came to believe that peaceful coexistence with Germans in a single state would be impossible. As the war wound down, Czechoslovakia's exiled president Edvard Beneš traveled to Washington and Moscow, securing backing for a state-organized expulsion of more than 2.2 million ethnic Germans still living in Czechoslovakia. Throughout 1945 and 1946, Czechoslovak soldiers carried out the "transfer" orders: They would typically enter a German-speaking town or village, take a few prisoners, and then threaten to execute the hostages unless everyone of German descent left. The expulsions sometimes turned violent: In June 1945, an army captain and a head of a revolutionary unit ordered their men to execute 2,000 ethnic German civilians, including children, near the town of Saatz.

While Beneš and most Czechs at the time considered the expulsion of ethnic Germans as just revenge for the war and historical injustices, the communists saw an opportunity for the future: The emptied region was to become a revolutionary laboratory. Ironically, the Czechs regained "their" land, but in the process eroded their freedom; meanwhile the Germans lost the land in which their ancestors lay buried, but gained a chance to build a prosperous democracy in their new home.

For the next 40 years, the "transfer" of ethnic Germans was a taboo subject, as the communist anti-Nazi propaganda machine continued as if the war had never ended. After 1989, the issue was reluctantly broached by politicians on both sides of the border, as it threatened to derail the otherwise excellent relations between the Czech and German governments. Toward 2004, tensions again rose, as Czech politicians resisted demands for reparations from Sudeten Germans in Berlin and Brussels, who held that such repayment should be a precondition to Czech entry into the European Union.

Over the last decade, the subject finally became depoliticized. Former German residents have continued to visit their old homes, sharing the stories of their trauma with young Czechs, who—having grown confident in their freedom—are able to take a more nuanced view of their country's history. In 2015, the Sudeten German Association stepped back from its support for repatriates' legal claims. A year later, the Czech Minister of Culture Daniel Herman delivered a speech at the annual Sudeten German convention in Nurnberg, addressing the audience as "dear compatriots" and expressing regret over the events of 1945 and 1946. An act that would have amounted to a political suicide just ten years earlier was positively received by the Czech public. Seventy years after a traumatic divorce, a door to reconciliation finally opened.

garden-style. The upper part is wilder—English garden-style. Both are delightful.

Cost and Hours: Free, open May-Sept Tue-Sun 8:00-19:00, April and Oct until 17:00, closed Mon and Nov-March.

OTHER SIGHTS IN TOWN

Egon Schiele Art Center (Egon Schiele Art Centrum)

This classy contemporary **art gallery** has temporary exhibits, generally featuring 20th-century Czech artists. The top-floor permanent collection celebrates Viennese artist Egon Schiele (pronounced "Sheila"), whose mother was born in Český Krumlov and who repeatedly worked here. A friend of Gustav Klimt and an important figure in the Secession movement in Vienna, Schiele lived a short life, from 1890 to 1918. His cutting-edge lifestyle and harsh art of graphic nudes didn't always fit the conservative, small-town style of Český Krumlov, but townsfolk are happy today to charge you to see this relatively paltry collection of his work.

A 15-minute walk south along the river takes you to Egon Shiele's intimate **garden studio,** which serves coffee and displays works by contemporary artists painted on the premises.

Cost and Hours: Art gallery—160 Kč, includes garden studio, galley open daily 10:00-18:00, café, Široká 71; garden studio—30 Kč or covered by gallery ticket, June-Aug Tue-Sun 11:00-17:00, closed Mon and Sept-May, follow the river south from the Art Center, Linecká 343; tel. 380-704-011, www. schieleartcentrum.cz.

▲Seidel Photo Studio Museum (Museum Fotoatelier Seidel)

This fully preserved, meticulously renovated 1905 Art Nouveau villa featuring original furnishings, a garden, and 100-year-old photo equipment offers a welcome respite from the crowds and the ubiquitous Middle Ages. The museum, set in the home and studio of Josef Seidel (1859-1935) and his son František (1908-1997), features more than 100,000 of their original photographs of life in this mountainous region—the Bőhmerwald (Bohemian Forest)—between 1880 and 1950. Josef Seidel was unique among his contemporaries in focusing on just one region, and was the first in the country to use autochrome. Allowed to remain in Český Krumlov during and after World War II when many Germans in the country were evicted (see sidebar), František continued his father's photography business, remaining here until his death in 1997. After his wife died in 2003, the town bought the house and converted it into a delightful museum and a cultural center for cross-border understanding. Restored, functional equipment offers hands-on experience with the process of photography during the late 19th and early 20th centuries. You can literally smell the history.

Cost and Hours: 130 Kč, includes English audioguide; daily May-Sept 9:00-18:00, shorter hours off-season; Linecká 272, across the river south of Old Town, mobile 736-503-871, www. seidel.cz.

Synagogue

Completed in 1910 in a mixture of architectural styles, this synagogue served the small Jewish community of Český Krumlov and neighboring villages. In 1938, there were 200 congregants here, but only two members of the area's Jewish community came back after World War II. Terribly run-down for decades after the war, the synagogue was restored to its former glory in 2015 by the Prague Jewish community, with funding from the European Union and German and Austrian sponsors. It contains an exhibit on its history, and hosts concerts and contemporary art exhibits.

Cost and Hours: 50 Kč, daily 10:00-18:00, Za Soudem 282, across the river south of Old Town, mobile 601-590-213, www. synagoga-krumlov.cz.

Eating: The **$ Café Synagoga,** with an assortment of cakes, occupies the former basement residence of the rabbi's family and an adjacent peaceful garden.

Nearby: Egon Schiele's garden studio (see the Egon Schiele Art Center listing, earlier) is nearby. From the synagogue entrance, turn left on a path up the hill, then left again on a narrow path leading to a gate, and then go down the stairs through terraced gardens.

Museum of Regional History
(Regionální Muzeum v Českém Krumlově)

This small museum gives you a quick look at regional costumes, tools, and traditions. When you pay, pick up the English translation of the displays (it also includes a lengthy history of Krumlov). Start on the top floor, where you'll see a Bronze Age exhibit, old paintings, a glimpse of noble life, and a look at how the locals rafted lumber from the Böhmerwald mountains all the way to Vienna (partly by canal). Don't miss the fun-to-study ceramic model of Český Krumlov in 1800 (note the extravagant gardens high above the town). The lower floor comes with fine folk costumes and domestic art.

Cost and Hours: 50 Kč, Tue-Sun 9:00-12:00 & 12:30-17:00, July-Aug until 18:00, closed Mon, Horní 152, tel. 380-711-674, www.muzeumck.cz.

ČESKÝ KRUMLOV

Puppet Museum and Fairy Tale House
(Muzeum Loutek a Pohádkový Dům)

In three small rooms, you'll view fascinating displays of more than 200 movable creations (overwhelmingly of Czech origin, but also some from Burma and Rajasthan). At the model stage, children of any age can try their hand at pulling the strings on their favorite fairy tale. For more on Czech puppets, see page 231.

Cost and Hours: 80 Kč, daily June-Aug 10:00-18:00, shorter hours off-season, tel. 723-325-262, Radniční 29, www.krumlovskainspirace.cz.

▲Eggenberg Brewery Tour

This may be one of the most intimate and accessible brewery tours in this land that so loves its beer. Tucked into a river bend on the

edge of town, Eggenberg's spunky little brewery has an authenticity that can't be matched by the big, soulless corporate breweries (such as Pilsner Urquell, in Plzeň, or the Czech Budweiser, in nearby České Budějovice). This is your chance to learn about the beer-making process at a facility where they're still using the same giant copper vats from 1915. While some of the facility has recently been modernized (and ongoing works may reroute the tour a bit), you'll still see lots of vintage equipment, including the original brew house (still in service), the fermentation vats, the cellars used for aging, and the bottling plant. Your tour ends with a visit to the pub, where you can sample some brews, including a "smoky" dark beer (Nakouřený Švihák), made with malt that tastes like salami, then aged for 100 days.

Cost and Hours: 100 Kč for the tour only, 130 Kč for tour and two tastes in the pub, 170 Kč for tour and four-pack of your choice of bottled beers to take away, 200 Kč includes everything; one-hour English tours daily at 11:00 year-round, also at 14:00 in May-Oct, tel. 380-711-426, www.eggenberg.cz.

Getting There: It's just a short stroll up Nové Město street from the main drag below the castle. During ongoing reconstruction, you may instead have to loop around town to the back entrance on Pivovarska—about a 10-minute walk.

ACTIVITIES

Český Krumlov lies in the middle of a valley popular for canoeing, rafting, hiking, and horseback riding. Boat-rental places are convenient to the Old Town, and several hiking paths start right in town. Serious hikers should consider a hike up the mushroom- and blueberry-filled Kleť mountain.

▲▲▲Canoeing and Rafting the Vltava

Splash a little river fun into your visit by renting a rubber raft or fiberglass canoe for a quick 30-minute spin around Český Krum-

lov. Or go for a three-hour float and paddle through the Bohemian forests and villages of the nearby countryside. You'll end up at Zlatá Koruna Abbey (described later), from where rafting companies will shuttle you back to town—or provide you with a bicycle to pedal back on your own along a bike path. This is a great hot-weather activity. Though the river is far from treacherous, be prepared to get wet.

You'll encounter plenty of inviting pubs and cafés for breaks along the way. There's a little whitewater, but the river is so shallow that if you tip, you can simply stand up and climb back in. (When that happens, pull the canoe up onto the bank to empty it, since you'll never manage to pour the water out while still in the river.)

Choose from a kayak, a canoe (faster, less work, more likely to tip), an inflatable raft (harder rowing, slower, but very stable), or a retro-style raft made of logs. Prices are per boat (2-6 people) and include a map, a waterproof container, and transportation to or from the start and end points. Here are your options:

Quickie Circle-the-Town Float: The easiest half-hour experience is to float around the city's peninsula, starting and ending on opposite sides of the tiny isthmus. Heck, you can do it twice (500 Kč for 2 people in a canoe or raft).

Three-Hour Float to Zlatá Koruna Abbey: This is your best basic trip, with pastoral scenery, a riverside pub about two hours down on the left, and a beautiful abbey as your destination (about 9 miles, 800 Kč for 2 people including pick-up). From there you can bike back or catch a shuttle bus home—simply arrange a return plan with the rental company.

Full-Day Float to Boršov: This takes you anoth-
er four hours past the Zlatá Koruna Abbey, floating lazily through

a pristine valley below the ruined Dívčí Kámen Castle (about 16 miles, 1,200 Kč for 2 people including pick-up).

Rental Companies: Several companies offer this lively activity. The handiest and also busiest are **Půjčovna Lodí Maleček Boat Rental** (long hours daily April-Oct, closed Nov-March, at recommended Pension Myší Díra, Rooseveltova 28, tel. 380-712-508, www.malecek.cz, lode@malecek.cz) and **Vltava Sport Service** (daily April-Sept 9:00-17:00, closed Oct-March, Hradební 60, tel. 380-711-988, www.ckvltava.cz). **Expedicion** offers similar services, plus airport transfers and car rental, with fewer crowds (Soukenická 33, mobile 720-107-171, http://expedicion.cz). Vltava and Expedicion also rent mountain bikes (300 Kč/day) and can bring a bike to the abbey for you to ride back.

Hiking

For an **easy 20-minute hike** to the Křížový Vrch (Hill of the Cross), walk to the end of Rooseveltova street, cross at the traffic light, then head straight for the first (empty) chapel-like Station of the Cross. Turning right, it's easy to navigate along successive Stations of the Cross until you reach the white church on the hill (closed), set in the middle of wild meadows. Looking down into the valley at the medieval city nestled within the S-shaped river, framed by the rising hills, it's hard to imagine any town with a more powerful *genius loci* (spirit of the place). The view is best at sunset.

For a **longer hike,** start at the trailhead by the bear pits below the castle. Red-and-white trail markers guide you on an easy six-mile hike around the neighboring slopes and villages. The green-and-yellow stripes mark a five-mile hiking trail up Kleť Mountain—with an altitude gain of 1,800 feet. At the top, you'll find the Kleť Observatory, the oldest observatory in the country (and still a leading astronomical center). On clear days, you can see the Alps (observatory tours-50 Kč, hourly July-Aug Tue-Sun 10:30-15:30, April-June Sat-Sun only, closed Sept-March and Mon year-round, www.hvezdarna.klet.cz).

Horseback Riding

Head about a mile out of town, beyond the Křížový Vrch (Hill of the Cross), for horseback rides and lessons at Slupenec Horseback Riding Club.

Cost and Hours: 300 Kč for one hour outdoors or in the ring, 2,200 Kč for all-day ride, Tue-Sun 10:00-15:00, closed Mon, helmets provided, Slupenec 1, worth a taxi trip, tel. 723-832-459, www.jk-slupenec.cz.

Roma in Eastern Europe

Numbering 12 million, the Roma people constitute a bigger European nation than the Czechs, Hungarians, or the Dutch. (The term "Gypsies," previously the common name for this group, is now considered derogatory and inaccurate.)

Descended from several low north-Indian castes, the Roma began to migrate through Persia and Armenia into the Ottoman Empire a thousand years ago. Known for their itinerant lifestyle, expertise in horse trading, skilled artisanship, and flexibility regarding private property, the Roma were both sought out and suspected in medieval Europe.

The Industrial Revolution threatened the Roma's traditional livelihoods, making their wandering lifestyle difficult to sustain. In the 1940s, Hitler sent hundreds of thousands of Roma to the gas chambers. In the occupied Protectorate of Bohemia and Moravia (Czechoslovakia minus the Sudetenland that had been annexed to Germany), Hitler had the help of Czech policemen who ran the two Roma "transfer" camps in Lety and Hodonín, where hundreds died even before being transported to Auschwitz. Only 10 percent of the protectorate's 5,000-strong pre-war Roma population survived.

After the war, tens of thousands of Roma from eastern Slovakia were relocated into the Sudetenland. At this time, the communist governments in Eastern Europe required Roma to speak the country's major language, settle in towns, and work in new industrial jobs. Rather than producing well-adjusted citizens, the result was an erosion of time-honored Roma values, as the policy shattered traditionally cohesive communities. It left the new Roma generation prone to sexual, alcohol, and drug abuse, and filled state-run orphanages with deprived Roma toddlers.

When the obligation and right to work disappeared with the communist regimes in 1989, rampant unemployment and dependence on welfare joined the list of Roma afflictions. As people all over Eastern Europe found it difficult to adjust to the new economic realities, they again turned on the Roma as scapegoats. Many Roma now live in segregated ghettos. Those who make it against the odds and succeed in mainstream society typically do so by turning their backs on their Roma heritage.

In this context, the Roma in Český Krumlov are a surprising success story. The well-integrated, proud Roma community here (numbering 1,000, or 5 percent of the town's population) is considered a curious anomaly even by experts. Their success could be due to a number of factors: the legacy of the multicultural Rožmberks, the fact that almost everyone in Český Krumlov is a relative newcomer, or maybe it's how local youngsters, regardless of skin color, tend to resolve their differences over a beer in the local "Gypsy Pub" (Cikánská Jizba), with a trendy Roma band setting the tune.

ČESKÝ KRUMLOV

CESKÝ KRUMLOV

Shopping

In recent years, Krumlov has become a shopping heaven, with a continuous line of gifts, toys, and handicrafts shops along its main street and spilling into the back alleys. The arts market in the renaissance courtyard of the Hotel Růže near the main square is the most scenic and fun to delve into.

NEAR ČESKÝ KRUMLOV

Zlatá Koruna Abbey (Klášter Zlatá Koruna)

This Cistercian abbey was founded in the 13th century by a Bohemian king to counter the growing influence of the Vítek family, the ancestors of the mighty Rožmberks. As you enter the grounds, notice the magnificent central linden tree, with its strange, cape-like leaves; it's said to have been used by the anti-Catholic Hussites when they hanged the monks. The one-hour tour takes you through the rare two-storied Gothic Chapel of the Guardian Angel, the main church, and the cloister, while a 10-minute tour takes you to the abbot's chapel with the original Gothic Zlatá Koruna Madonna, the most treasured painting in the region. After the order was dissolved in 1785, the abbey functioned briefly as a village school, before being turned into a factory during the Industrial Revolution. Damage from this period is visible on the cloister's crumbling arches. The Gothic interiors adjacent to the ticket office serve as exhibition space for Český Krumlov's school of the arts, displaying the imaginative creations of the school's 6- to 18-year-old students (free).

Cost and Hours: 100 Kč for one-hour tour in Czech, generally runs every half-hour, pick up English leaflet; 20 Kč for the 10-minute Madonna tour; April-Oct Tue-Sun 9:00-16:00, June-Aug until 17:00, closed Mon and Nov-March, call 380-743-126 to arrange English tour, www.klaster-zlatakoruna.eu.

Getting There: Drivers can reach the abbey in about 10 minutes from Český Krumlov (head north out of town and follow route #39). But it's more fun to get there by raft or canoe—the abbey is directly above the river at the end of a three-hour float (see "Canoeing and Rafting the Vltava," earlier).

Sleeping in Český Krumlov

Krumlov is filled with small pensions and hostels. Summer is busy all around. While you can generally find a room in a modern pension in the outskirts upon arrival, book months ahead to stay in the heart of town.

Sleep Code

Hotels are classified based on the average price of a standard double room with breakfast in high season. I've given *very* rough conversions to dollars using 25 Kč = $1.

$$$$ **Splurge:** Most rooms over 3,400 Kč (roughly $135)

$$$ **Pricier:** 2,600-3,400 Kč ($105-135)

$$ **Moderate:** 1,800-2,600 Kč ($70-105)

$ **Budget:** 1,000-1,800 Kč ($40-70)

¢ **Backpacker:** Under 1,000 Kč ($40)

RS% **Rick Steves discount**

Unless otherwise noted, credit cards are accepted, hotel staff speak basic English, and free Wi-Fi is available. Comparison-shop by checking prices at several hotels (on each hotel's own website, on a booking site, or by email). For the best deal, *book directly with the hotel*. Ask for a discount if paying in cash; if the listing includes **RS%**, request a Rick Steves discount.

IN THE OLD TOWN

$$$ Castle View Apartments rents seven diverse apartments. These are the best-equipped rooms I found in town—the bathroom floors are heated, all come with kitchenettes, and everything's done just right. Their website describes each stylish apartment; the "view" ones really do come with eye-popping vistas (RS%, apartment sleeps up to 6, breakfast at a nearby hotel, Šatlavská 140, mobile 731-108-677, www.castleview.cz, info@castleview.cz).

$$ Hotel Konvice is run by a German couple—and their three children—with a personal touch. Each room is uniquely decorated (a block above the main square at Horní 144, tel. 380-711-611, www.boehmerwaldhotels.de, info@stadthotel-krummau.de).

BELOW THE MAIN SQUARE

Secluded Parkán street, which runs along the river below the square, has a hotel and a row of small pensions. These places have a family feel and views of the looming castle above.

$$$ Hotel Mlýn, at the end of Parkán, is a tastefully furnished hotel with more than 30 rooms and all the amenities (elevator, pay parking, Parkán 120, tel. 380-731-133, www.hotelmlyn.eu, info@hotelmlyn.eu).

$ Pension Olšakovský, which has a delightful breakfast area on a terrace next to the river, treats visitors as family guests (free parking, Parkán 114, mobile 604-430-181, www.olsakovsky.cz, info@olsakovsky.cz).

CESKÝ KRUMLOV

AT THE BASE OF THE CASTLE

A quiet, cobbled pedestrian street (Latrán) runs below the castle just over the bridge from the Old Town. Lined with cute shops, it's a 10-minute walk downhill from the train station.

$ Pension Danny is a little funky place, with homey rooms and a tangled floor plan above a restaurant (in-room breakfast, Latrán 72, tel. 603-210-572, www.pensiondanny.cz, recepce@pensiondanny.cz).

BETWEEN THE BUS STATION AND THE OLD TOWN

Rooseveltova street, midway between the bus station and the Old Town (a four-minute walk from either), is lined with several fine little places, each with easy free parking. The key here is tranquility—the noisy bars of the town center are out of earshot.

$$ Hotel Garni Myší Díra ("Mouse Hole") hides 11 bright and woody Bohemian contemporary rooms overlooking the Vltava River just outside the Old Town (prices include transfer to/from bus or train station, Rooseveltova 28, tel. 380-712-853, www.hotelmysidira.com). The no-nonsense reception, which closes at 20:00, runs the recommended boat rental company (Půjčovna Lodí Maleček, at the same address), along with a similar pension with comparable prices, **Villa Margarita,** farther along Rooseveltova.

$ Little **Pension Teddy** offers three deluxe rooms that share a balcony overlooking the river and have original 18th-century furniture. Or stay in one of four modern-style rooms, some of which also face the river (cash only, staff may be unhelpful, pay parking, Rooseveltova 38, tel. 777-713-277, mobile 724-003-981, www.pensionteddy.cz, info@pensionteddy.cz).

$ Pension Anna is well-run, with two doubles, six apartments, and a restful little garden. Its apartments are spacious suites, with a living room and stairs leading to the double-bedded loft. The upstairs rooms can get stuffy during the summer (pay parking, Rooseveltova 41, tel. 380-711-692, www.pensionanna-ck.cz, pension.anna@quick.cz). If you book a standard double and they bump you up to an apartment, don't pay more than the double rate.

OUTSIDE THE CITY CENTER

$ Pension Gardena has 16 spacious, airy rooms in two adjacent, tactfully renovated historical buildings. A family business with a garden, it's on the way into town from the bus station just a hundred yards above Horní Bridge (Kaplická 21, tel. 380-711-028, mobile 607-873-974, www.pensiongardena.com, gardena@seznam.cz).

$ Pension U Kapličky, on a quiet street adjacent to a chapel and a city park, consists of two artistically designed apartments in an unusually shaped medieval house. Jitka, a teacher of stone carving at the local arts academy and one of the last old-timers to still call central Český Krumlov home, lives downstairs and bakes pastries for breakfast (reserve months ahead, Linecká 60, mobile 606-434-090, www.ckrumlov.cz/ck/ukaplicky, ukaplicky@ckrumlov.cz).

$ Pension Kříž, with five rooms in a new, tastefully decorated house, is tucked away in a quiet, modern villa district under the Křížový Vrch (Hill of the Cross), just a five-minute walk from Horní Bridge (Křížová 71, mobile 775-421-012, www.penzion-kriz.cz, ubytovani@penzion-kriz.cz)

HOSTELS

Of the hostels in town, Hostel 99 (closest to the train station) is clearly the high-energy, youthful party place. Krumlov House (closer to the bus station) is more mellow. Both are well-managed, and each is a five-minute walk from the main square.

¢ Hostel 99's picnic-table terrace looks out on the Old Town. While the gentle sound of the river gurgles outside your window late at night, you're more likely to hear a youthful international crowd having a great time. The hostel caters to its fun-loving young guests, offering a day-long river rafting and pub crawl, with a free keg of beer each Wednesday (private rooms available, laundry, use the lockers, no curfew or lockout, recommended Hospoda 99 restaurant, 10-minute downhill walk from train station or two bus stops to Spicak, Vezni 99, tel. 380-712-812, www.hostel99.cz, hostel99@hotmail.com).

¢ Krumlov House Hostel is take-your-shoes-off-at-the-door, shiny, hardwood-with-throw-rugs mellow. Efficiently run by a Canadian/American couple, it has a hip and trusting vibe and feels welcoming to travelers of any age (private rooms and apartments available, breakfast available July-Aug only, well-stocked guest kitchen, laundry, Rooseveltova 68, tel. 380-711-935, www.krumlovhostel.com, info@krumlovhostel.com). The hostel sponsors "WriteAway," a literary retreat for traveling writers (http://writeaway.literarybohemian.com).

Eating in Český Krumlov

Krumlov, with a huge variety of creative little restaurants, is a fun place to eat. In peak season the good places fill up fast, so make reservations or eat early.

$$ Na Louži seems to be everyone's favorite Czech bistro, with 40 seats (many at shared tables) in one 1930s-style room decorated with funky old advertisements. They serve good, inexpensive, unpretentious local cuisine and hometown Eggenberg beer on tap (daily 10:00-23:00, Kájovská 66, tel. 380-711-280).

Restaurant Price Code

I've assigned each eatery a price category, based on the average cost of a typical main course. Drinks, desserts, and splurge items (steak and seafood) can raise the price considerably. I've given *very* rough conversions to dollars using 25 Kč = $1.

$$$$ **Splurge:** Most main courses over 500 Kč (roughly $20)

$$$ **Pricier:** 300-500 Kč ($10-20)

$$ **Moderate:** 100-300 Kč ($5-10)

$ **Budget:** Under 100 Kč ($5)

In the Czech Republic, a pub, basic sit-down eatery, and less-touristy café or teahouse is **$**; a typical restaurant—or a fancy café with coffee over 50 Kč and tea over 100 Kč—is **$$**; an upscale restaurant is **$$$**; and a swanky splurge is **$$$$**.

$$ Cikánská Jizba ("Gypsy Pub") is a Roma tavern filling one den-like, barrel-vaulted room. The Roma staff serves Slovak-style food (most of the Czech Republic's Roma population came from Slovakia). Český Krumlov has a long Roma history. While this rustic little restaurant—which packs its 10 tables under a mystic-feeling Gothic vault—won't win any culinary awards, you never know what festive and musical activities will erupt, particularly on Friday nights, when Milan's son's band, Cindži Renta ("Wet Rag"), performs here (daily 13:00-24:00; off-season Mon-Sat 17:00-24:00, closed Sun; 2 blocks toward castle from main square at Dlouhá 31, tel. 380-717-585).

$$ Krčma u Dwau Maryí ("Tavern of the Two Marys") is a characteristic old place with idyllic riverside picnic tables, serving ye olde Czech cuisine and drinks. The fascinating menu explains the history of the house and makes a good case that the food of the poor medieval Bohemians was tasty and varied. Buck up for buckwheat, millet, greasy meat, or the poor-man's porridge (daily 11:00-23:00, Parkán 104, tel. 380-717-228).

$$ Laibon, while still a top choice for a filling vegetarian meal, has a chef who is evidently not inclined to calibrate her spices or rely exclusively on fresh ingredients (beware of canned pea soup). Settle down in the meditative inside or head out onto the castle-view river terrace and observe the raft-and-canoe action while you eat (daily 11:00-23:00, Parkán 105).

$$ Kolektiv tries to inject some modern sophistication into this olde town. It has a stark minimalist interior, a chalkboard menu, well-executed light café fare with some international flavors, a good cocktail selection, and stylish—if stuffy—service (daily 8:00-20:00, Fri-Sat until 21:00, Latrán 13, across from the castle stairs, tel. 776-626-644).

$$ Rybářská Restaurace ("Fisherman's Restaurant") doesn't look particularly inviting from the outside, but this is *the* place in town to taste fresh carp and trout. Choose between indoor tables under fishnets or riverside picnic benches outside, and ask about their cheap daily specials that feed the floating Czech crowds (daily 11:00-22:00, on the island by the millwheel, mobile 723-829-089).

$$$ Krčma v Šatlavské is an old prison gone cozy, with an open fire, big wooden tables under a rustic old medieval vault, and tables outdoors on the pedestrian lane. It's great for a late drink

or roasted game (cooked on an open spit). *Medovina* is hot honey wine (daily 12:00-24:00, on Šatlavská, follow lane leading to the side from TI on main square, mobile 608-973-797).

$$$ Restaurace Barbakán is built into the town fortifications, with a terrace hanging high over the river. It's a good spot for old-fashioned Czech cooking and beer, at the top of town and near the recommended Rooseveltova street accommodations (open long hours daily, reasonable prices, Horní 26, tel. 380-712-679).

$$ Hospoda 99 Restaurace serves good, cheap soups, salads, and meals. It's the choice of hostelers and locals alike for its hamburgers, vegetarian food, Czech dishes, and cheap booze (meals served 10:00-22:00, bar open until 24:00, at Hostel 99, Vezni 99, tel. 380-712-812). This place is booming until late, when everything else is hibernating.

$ Krumlovská Picka, a tiny, atmospheric place on the island by the millwheel, offers takeout pizza and freshly baked-and-filled baguettes. Cuddle near the oven inside or picnic on the outside terrace (daily 12:00-23:00, Dlouhá 97).

$ Dobrá Čajovna is a typical example of the quiet, exotic-feeling teahouses that flooded Czech towns in the 1990s as alternatives to smoky, raucous pubs. Though directly across from the castle entrance, it's a world away from the tourist hubbub. As is so often the case, if you want to surround yourself with locals, don't go to a traditional place...go ethnic. With its meditative karma inside and a peaceful terrace facing the monastery out back, it provides a relaxing break (daily 13:00-22:00, Latrán 54, mobile 777-654-744).

$ Coffee Roasting Company, on the corner of Linecká just past the Seidel Photo Studio Museum, is a tiny local place far away from the crowds and dead serious about the quality of its cakes and fair-trade brews (daily 10:00-19:00).

Český Krumlov Connections

BY PUBLIC TRANSPORTATION

Almost all trains to and from Český Krumlov require a transfer in the city of **České Budějovice**, a transit hub just to the north. Buses, on the other hand, are direct. Bus and train timetables are available at www.idos.cz.

If you have time in České Budějovice between connections, consider a visit to the town's gigantic medieval main square, Náměstí Přemysla Otakara II (about a six-block walk from the station). Store your bags in lockers at the train station, then exit the station to the right, cross the street at the crosswalk, and head straight down Lannova třída (which becomes Kanovnická street) to the square.

By Train

From Český Krumlov by Train to: České Budějovice (6/day, 45 minutes), **Prague** (8/day, 1/day direct, 3.5 hours; bus is faster and cheaper, but may be booked and doesn't allow a stopover in Budějovice), **Vienna** (6/day with changes in Budějovice and Linz, 5 hours), **Budapest** (6/day with changes in Budějovice and Linz, 7 hours).

By Bus

The Český Krumlov bus station, a five-minute walk out of town, is just a big parking lot with numbered stalls for various buses (bus info tel. 380-711-190). Student Agency (www.studentagency. cz) and Leo Express (www.le.cz) have online reservation and ticket systems, the newest buses, and a free drink for passengers.

From Český Krumlov by Bus to: Prague (10/day, 3.5 hours; tickets can be bought at the Český Krumlov TI), **České Budějovice** (transit hub for other destinations; hourly, 40 minutes).

From České Budějovice by Bus to Třeboň, Telč, and Třebíč: A bus goes from České Budějovice to the Moravian city of **Brno** (3/day Mon-Fri, 2/day Sat-Sun, 4-4.5 hours). Along the way, it stops at **Třeboň** (in 30 minutes), **Telč** (in 2.5 hours), and **Třebíč** (in 3.5 hours).

BY SHUTTLE SERVICE

From Český Krumlov to Austria and Beyond: Several companies offer handy shuttle service. The best of the bunch is CK Shuttle, with free Wi-Fi on board and affordable fares: 800 Kč per person one-way to **Vienna** (4/day, 3.5 hours), **Salzburg** (4/day, 3 hours), **Hallstatt** (3/day, 3 hours), or **Prague** (3/day, 2.5 hours). They can also take you to Linz (where you can hop on the speedy east-west main rail line through Austria), Budapest, Munich, and other places. They offer door-to-door service to and from your hotel, and once you book on their website and receive a confirmation, your departure is guaranteed (office at Dlouhá 95, www.ckshuttle. cz). Another reliable option is Sebastian Tours (higher prices, mobile 607-100-234 or 608-357-581, www.sebastianck-tours.com, sebastiantours@hotmail.com).

ROUTE TIPS FOR DRIVERS
From Prague to Český Krumlov

Figure about 2.5 hours for the drive from the capital to Český Krumlov. Getting an early start lets you make several interesting stopovers en route (the best is Konopiště Castle).

Leave Prague toward Brno on the D-1 expressway. About 20 kilometers east of the city, exit for *Benešov/České Budějovice/Linz*. After about 15 kilometers, you'll find the turnoff for **Konopiště Castle** on the right (for parking tips and a castle description, see page 291; it's worth calling ahead to reserve a tour at this castle).

Beyond Konopiště, the road becomes an expressway, and—about 40 kilometers after the castle—you'll see signs for **Tábor.** This historic small city, a stronghold of the Hussites, is worth considering if you'd like to stretch your legs or have lunch on the pleasant main square.

To visit, follow blue *P* and *Centrum* signs, park in the handy garage, walk up the big yellow staircase, and stroll five minutes through the cobbled town to Žižkovo Náměstí, the main square. Standing in the middle is a statue of the square's namesake, Jan Žižka (the Hussite main military man), with his trademark eye patch and mysterious hood. Ringing the square are some modest museums (including a top Hussite Museum in the country with limited English), a towering church, and some al fresco restaurants. Returning to your car, continue south through Tábor and follow signs to rejoin the expressway, in the direction of České Budějovice.

About 50 kilometers south of Tábor, as you're approaching  České Budějovice, keep an eye out for the turnoff to **Hluboká Castle** (Zámek Hluboká)—a striking, English-style, romanticized-Gothic palace perched on the hill above the town of Hluboká nad Vltavou. If you're up for a steep 10-minute hike that leads to a fine photo op, turn off and carefully track *Hluboká nad Vltavou* signs through the bucolic Czech countryside. After passing through the modern part of Hluboká nad Vltavou, you'll cross the river, then wind around behind the hill, where you can pay to park along the old town's main street (near the church steeple), just below the castle.

From here, you can huff up to what looks like a little Bohemian Windsor: a fanciful faux fortress with crenellations and fantasy ramparts. Snap a photo from the rose garden out front, and consider a drink in the glassed-in winter garden café next to the palace. The show-off interior is far more opulent than Konopiště's but less historically significant (www.zamek-hluboka.eu). The helpful town TI is a good place to pick up a map of the area or get directions (directly across the street from the path up to the castle).

Continuing, you'll go through the city of **České Budějovice**, famous as the home of the original, Czech-brewed Budweiser beer (see page 216 for the story). You can tour the brewery (at the northeastern corner of town, www.budejovickybudvar.cz), but it's a large-scale, corporate-feeling experience—the fine Eggenberg Brewery in Český Krumlov offers a much more intimate tour.

Speaking of which: From České Budějovice, follow signs for *Linz;* some ten minutes out of town you'll reach the turnoff for Český Krumlov.

From Český Krumlov to Třeboň, Telč, Třebíč, or Slavonice

To reach any of these towns, first head north from Český Krumlov (following signs in the direction of *České Budějovice*). After crossing the Vltava river in Rájov, exit to the right toward *Římov*. Head straight through Římov, then follow signs to *Komařice* and *Strážkovice*. After Strážkovice, turn right to Borovany. From here, track signs to **Třeboň**. Approaching town, you'll start to see the lakes that define the Třeboň landscape. Turn off the main road, following the blue *P/Centrum* signs. You'll twist through the outskirts, go through a dramatic gate and past the pointy steepled Dean Church, then skirt across the bottom of the main square and go back out another gate; the pay parking lot is just outside the gate on your right, by the canal.

To continue on to any of the other towns, leave (or continue past) Třeboň toward *Jindřichův Hradec,* passing more lakes and wetlands, and a big solar farm. If your next stop is **Telč,** continue to Jindřichův Hradec, and follow Telč signs from there (about an hour away). **Třebíč** is another 40 minutes' drive past Telč.

If you want to cut through the countryside to **Slavonice** (about 50 minutes from Třeboň), turn off before Jindřichův Hradec, on the right, toward *Nová Bystřice*. Take twisty backcountry roads to that town, in which you'll find signs to

Landštejn and *Slavonice*. On this road, you'll pass a turnoff for the dramatically set ruins of the Landštejn Castle—guarding the three-corner meeting point of Bohemia, Moravia, and Austria (see page 374). Just before entering Slavonice, watch on the left for the low-profile turnoff to the WWII bunkers (see page 372). Then head into Slavonice. (Note: From Slavonice, it's an easy 30-minute drive north to Telč, via Dačice.)

SOUTHERN CZECH TOWNS

Třeboň • Telč • Třebíč • Slavonice

Many travelers to the southern part of the country visit only Český Krumlov. While that's a delightful destination, several nearby towns—straddling the regions of Bohemia and Moravia—are less packaged, more authentic, and, for many, equally worthwhile. Escape the crowds of Prague and Český Krumlov and immerse yourself in a bucolic countryside of rolling hills, workaday townscapes, vibrantly colorful main squares and village greens, convivial beer gardens, and an endearing (and well-deserved) local pride. While the economy boomed here in the 1500s, the Industrial Revolution largely bypassed this sleepy region sandwiched between the large centers of Pilsen, Prague, and Brno to the north and the Danube Valley to the south. This part of the Czech Republic boasts the lowest population density in Central Europe. A popular local slogan runs: "South Bohemia: God-forgotten country, thank God."

The following four towns are the most worthy of consideration. Třeboň is an inviting medieval burg famous for its peat spas, network of man-made lakes, and fish specialties. Tiny Telč has the Czech Republic's most impressive main square. Busy Třebíč is home to the country's most intact historic Jewish quarter. And Slavonice is a sleepy Renaissance gem with a genuine artistic community. Near the Austrian border, it feels like it's perched at the end of the world.

GETTING AROUND

By Public Transportation: If you were to draw a line between České Budějovice (the capital of South Bohemia) and Brno (the capital of Moravia), you'd go right through the "Three Ts": Třeboň, Telč, and Třebíč. A bus follows this route, stopping in all three (3/day Mon-Fri, 2/day Sat-Sun; České Budějovice to Třeboň—30 minutes, to Telč—2.5 hours, to Třebíč—3.5 hours, to Brno—4-4.5

hours). You can reach České Budějovice easily by direct train from Prague (almost hourly, 2.5 hours) or from Český Krumlov (6/day, 1 hour). In České Budějovice, the bus and train stations are next to each other. Direct buses also connect Třeboň, Telč, and Třebíč to Prague and other destinations; see "Connections" for each destination. To reach **Slavonice,** change in Telč to catch the train (6/day, 1 hour). For bus and train schedules, see www.idos.cz.

By Car: While doable by public transit, this region is a delight by car—each of these towns is within an hour's drive from the next through scenic countryside. For pointers, see "Route Tips for Drivers" in the Český Krumlov chapter (page 339).

PLANNING YOUR TIME

This area makes a good stopover on the way from Český Krumlov to points farther east (Olomouc, the Mikulov Wine Region, or even Vienna, Bratislava, or Poland). If taking public transit, bus departures will dictate the amount of time you spend in each town—on weekdays you could reasonably leave Český Krumlov early in the morning, visit Třeboň and Telč, and arrive in Třebíč by evening.

Driving gives you more flexibility. Because towns are fairly close, it's possible to string together a few of them in a long day. Depart Český Krumlov early and stop at your choice of towns before returning to Český Krumlov for the night. With more time, consider sleeping in one of the towns. For village relaxation and hiking, spend the evening in Telč. For a bigger, more city-like feel, consider Třebíč. Slavonice, a bit out of the way and not as eye-catching as Telč, is worthwhile as a slow-paced art-, nature-, and history-packed base for those seeking to escape not only their usual surroundings but time altogether.

Třeboň (Wittingau)

Třeboň (TREH-bohn, pop. 18,000, Wittingau in German), a well-preserved medieval spa town centered around an inviting Renaissance square, is a charming place to experience good living and to explore a unique biosphere of artificial lakes that date back to the 14th century.

Over the centuries, people have transformed what was a flooding marshland into a clever and delightful combination of lakes, oak-lined dikes, wild meadows, Baroque villages, peat bogs, and pine woods. Rather than unprofitable wet fields, the nobles wanted ponds that swarmed with fish—and today Třeboň remains the fish-raising capital of the Czech Republic. Landscape architects in the 16th century managed to strike an amazing balance between civilization and nature, which today is a protected ecosystem (about 15 percent covered by water) with the biggest diversity of bird species in Eastern Europe. Nature enthusiasts come here to bird-watch, bike along dikes held together by the roots of centuries-old oaks, and devour the best fish specialties in the country.

While Třeboň enjoys plenty of tourism, most visitors are Czech vacationers who come for a week every year—meaning establishments work hard to please. These demanding local customers and a booming fish industry make Třeboň's relative affluence feel less touristy than other popular towns. Its peat spas have attracted patients from all over the world for decades, but since the facilities are small, Třeboň is never as overrun as some more famous, pretentious spa towns. Compared to the other Bohemian towns in this book, Třeboň (like Třebíč), feels workaday and real—it's a thriving community that just happens to spread out in a beautiful, tourism-worthy main square. It's the kind of place where an artsy cinema and a theater presenting plays and musical events neighbor the Town Hall.

Třeboň is a good home base for those looking to experience Český Krumlov sans crowds: Stay here, then drive down to Český Krumlov in the evening for a magical, floodlit nighttime tour when the tourists are asleep and the spirits awake (see previous chapter).

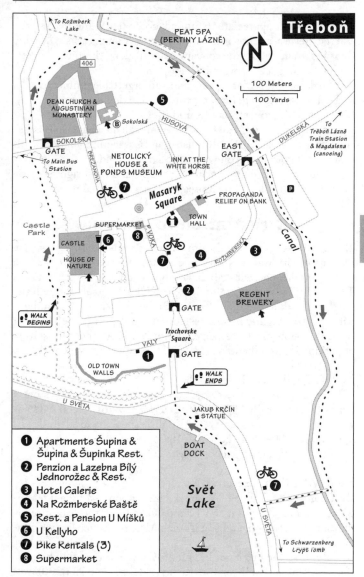

Map labels:

To Rožmberk Lake

PEAT SPA (BERTINY LÁZNĚ)

Třeboň

N

406

100 Meters

100 Yards

DEAN CHURCH & AUGUSTINIAN MONASTERY

B Sokolská

HUSOVA

DUKELSKÁ

To Třeboň Lázně Train Station & Magdalena (canoeing)

SOKOLSKÁ GATE

To Main Bus Station

BŘEZANOVA

NETOLICKÝ HOUSE & PONDS MUSEUM

INN AT THE WHITE HORSE

EAST GATE

P

🚲 7

Masaryk Square

PROPAGANDA RELIEF ON BANK

Canal

Castle Park

SUPERMARKET

DVOKA

TOWN HALL

🚲 7

8

CASTLE

6

4

ROŽMBERSKÁ

3

HOUSE OF NATURE

2

REGENT BREWERY

WALK BEGINS

GATE

Trochovske Square

VALY

1

OLD TOWN WALLS

GATE

WALK ENDS

U SVĚTA

JAKUB KRČÍN STATUE

BOAT DOCK

🚲 7

Svět Lake

U SVĚTA

To Schwarzenberg Crypt Tomb

Legend:
1 Apartments Šupina & Šupina & Šupinka Rest.
2 Penzion a Lazebna Bílý Jednorožec & Rest.
3 Hotel Galerie
4 Na Rožmberské Baště
5 Rest. a Pension U Míšků
6 U Kellyho
7 Bike Rentals (3)
8 Supermarket

PLANNING YOUR TIME

Don't be in a rush here—unlike Telč or Třebíč (which can each essentially be seen in two hours), Třeboň rewards those who take time for a stroll (or, better, a bike ride) outside its walls. Get oriented on the main square, climb the Town Hall Tower, duck through the castle (and consider visiting the House of Nature), and make a point to walk the canals and greenbelt that surround the Old

Town, to better appreciate its unique ecosystem. (The castle itself and the brewery are less interesting.) Try fish soup, catfish, or pike. Rent a bike and follow the educational trail along the ancient dikes. If it's hot, bring a bathing suit.

Soaking yourself at a peat spa is unforgettable; unfortunately, it may be difficult to get a spot (for booking details, see page 353). If you get in, build your day around it.

If you're here in October or November, lend a hand in the fascinating ritual of clearing the fish ponds, warming yourself with shots of potato rum as you wade through the mud.

Note that the town—including the TI and most sights—basically closes down for a lunch break (generally around noon).

Orientation to Třeboň

The Old Town—separated from newer construction by the sparse remains of city walls, Renaissance gates, a water channel, and a castle garden—encircles Masaryk Square (Masarykovo Náměstí). The parallel Husova street—with Dean Church—cuts through the north end, while the huge Regent Brewery anchors the southern part of town. Sights, hotels, restaurants, and ATMs are all on or within a couple blocks of Masaryk Square. From the train station or parking lot, you'll enter the square through the east gate.

TOURIST INFORMATION
The TI, next to the Town Hall on Masaryk Square, gives out a handy brochure called *The Region of Třeboň*. With several days advance notice, they can reserve an English-speaking local guide (TI open daily 9:00-12:00 & 12:45-18:00, shorter hours off-season, tel. 384-721-169, www.trebon-mesto.cz).

ARRIVAL IN TŘEBOŇ
By Train: Get off at the Třeboň-Lázně station—*not* the Třeboň-Město station. From Třeboň-Lázně, walk along the road directly in front of the station, and you'll reach Masaryk Square in five minutes.

By Bus: The bus from Prague leaves you at the main bus station, a 20-minute walk (or 100-Kč taxi ride, tel. 384-722-200) west of the Old Town. Most buses arriving from České Budějovice continue from the main station to the Sokolská stop, which is a short walk through the castle park to Masaryk Square.

By Car: Approaching town, follow blue *P/Centrum* signs. You'll drive through a gate into the Old Town, zip past the Dean Church, cut across the bottom of the main square, then exit through another gate. A handy pay parking lot is along the canal just outside, on your right.

HELPFUL HINTS

Exchange Rate: 25 Kč = about $1

Country Calling Code: 420 (see page 464 for dialing instructions)

Wi-Fi: The **TI** offers free Wi-Fi for up to 15 minutes. If you need a computer try the **town library** (Mon-Fri 8:00-17:00, closed Sat-Sun, near the castle park at Na Sadech 349) or the peat spa, **Bertiny Lázně,** just outside the east gate (long hours daily).

Bike Rental: You'll see lots of bikes around town. If you want to join in the fun, you can rent decent bikes near the main square: at the bowling alley in **Hotel Zlatá Hvězda** (accessible from Žižkovo Náměstí—from the main square it's a few yards past the Pramen supermarket, mobile 720-537-438) and the **newsstand** directly across the square from the Pramen supermarket at #85 (look for *tabák* sign; mobile 602-151-756; prices at both 200 Kč/five hours, 300 Kč/day, bring driver's license as a deposit). If you are more serious about the quality of your bike or would like an electric push (despite the generally flat terrain), walk through the three gates past the bowling alley, turn left, and continue another 200 yards to the **Třeboň Centrum** sports shop (daily 9:00-18:00, mountain bike-350 Kč/day, electric bike-550 Kč/day, helmet-60 Kč, mobile 777-998-560, www.treboncentrum.cz).

Local Guide: Hana will take you on a town walk that may include the castle and the Neo-Gothic Schwarzenberg family tomb (500 Kč/hour, mobile 724-309-987, hana.pechova@gmail.com).

Sights in Třeboň

▲▲Masaryk Square (Masarykovo Náměstí)

Třeboň's fine main square is typical of squares in the region: lined with colorful facades artfully blending both Renaissance and Ba-

roque building styles. It was built by the town's 17th-century burghers, whose wealth came from the booming fish industry. The rectangular market plaza with a humble plague column and fountain in the middle— feels just right. Grab a seat at one of the outdoor cafés, and watch local life circulate with the serenity of ducks on a lake.

While the tranquility comes naturally today, until 1989 it was a government requirement. At the square's lower end, above the bank door (yellow *spořitelna* building), a **propaganda relief** in the

SOUTHERN CZECH TOWNS

Social Realist style of the Soviet Union extols the virtue of working hard and stowing your money here for the common good (and shows how much the avant-garde of the time embraced a radical-left ideology with its accompanying aesthetic). Higher up, a happy fisherman cradles a big fish, the reason for his wealth—and, since the 15th century, the wealth of Třeboň.

The nearby **Town Hall Tower,** whose moderate height of 100 feet just fits with the size of the square, is well worth the climb (exactly 100 steps). Surveying the view from its top, you feel as if you can reach out and touch the circular Old Town. Beyond that, the lakes glimmer against the green backdrop of stately oaks (30 Kč, pay and borrow key at TI—typically available at the top of each hour, same hours as TI).

Across from the Town Hall, the impossible-to-miss, rampart-like white gable marks the 16th-century **Inn at the White Horse** (U Bílého Koníčka—look for the small horse on the facade). A few houses to the left is the state-of-the-art **Štěpánek Netolický House and Pond-Building Heritage Museum,** with an exhibit on the region's innovative, centuries-old system of dikes, lakes, and canals (described later).

At the other end of the square, notice the only modern building here, a **Pramen supermarket.** Some 30 years ago, when the square was veiled in the shabby gray of communism, the regime decided to give it a facelift with a modern building that fit the medieval space like a UFO. After 1989, locals carefully added a facade and a new gabled roof to the concrete box, effectively blending the former eyesore into the Old World townscape.

Get oriented to this tiny town: Stand in the middle of the square and face west (with the station and gate at your back). The street to the left, past the Pramen supermarket, leads to the brewery, the recommended Šupina & Šupinka and Bílý Jednorožec restaurants, and Svět lake. Now walk a few steps forward, to the top end of the square. The street to your right leads to Husova (which parallels this square) and the pointy spire of the Dean Church. The ornamental red gateway to your left opens up into the castle courtyard; cut through there, and emerge at the park on the other side, to find the House of Nature (with the recommended "Man and the Landscape" exhibit). All of these sights are described below.

Štěpánek Netolický House and Pond-Building Heritage Museum

Set in a Renaissance townhouse on the main square—and recently lavishly renovated with generous European Union funding—this museum gives you a chance to appreciate the typical floor plan of the time. The downstairs exhibit (including a running-water model on the patio) illustrates how the nearby pond system is ingeniously tied to a 16th-century canal called the Golden Channel, designed by fishpond builder and architect Josef Štěpánek Netolický (see sidebar on the lakes of Třeboň). The upper level functions as a gracious gallery space that showcases temporary exhibits by top Czech contemporary artists.

Cost and Hours: 50 Kč; July-Aug daily 10:00-20:00; May-June and Sept daily 10:00-12:00 & 13:00-17:00; Oct-April Wed-Mon 10:00-12:00 & 13:00-16:00, closed Tue; tel. 380-130-004.

Dean Church and Augustine Monastery (Děkanský Kostel a Augustiánský Klášter)

This Gothic church, with its unusual double nave (and obtrusive columns down the middle), is worth a look if open. (If it's closed, peer

through the gate at the back of the church; you can also look through the door around the right side.) A highlight is its delicately curved statue of the *Madonna and Child* (c. 1390, painted limestone, at the bottom of the third pillar in from the back). Its Ivory Soap sweetness and slinky S-shaped body are typical of late "beautiful style" Gothic. The artist, though anonymous, is known as the "Master of the Třeboň Madonna." The church once showcased more marvelous Gothic sculptures and altars, but these were deemed too valuable, so they were zipped off to the Museum of Medieval Art in Prague's St. Agnes Convent (see page 58). Frescoes in the adjoining cloister, badly neglected until after 1989, show scenes from the life of St. Augustine. While the monastery library is long gone, Augustinians were some of the most ardent medieval copyists in the time before Gutenberg's movable type revolutionized printing. Through the efforts of monks in this monastery, Třeboň became a center of medieval learning for Czechs and Austrians alike.

Cost and Hours: Donation requested; July-Aug daily 9:00-11:30 & 13:30-17:00, or pop in just before the nearly nightly 18:30 Mass, shorter hours off-season; if closed, ring the parish home next door; Husova 142, rectory tel. 384-722-390.

Castle (Zámek)

In a land of great castles, Třeboň's is unusually dull. Perhaps what makes the castle unique is how it blends with the rest of the town as if the local aristocrat were just another burgher. From the main square, step through the red gateway into the courtyard, which is covered with rectangular sgraffiti—a

characteristic faux-stone-block decoration of the late 1500s (made by etching a design in plaster, revealing a different color underneath). As with other South Bohemian towns, all this sgraffiti is a reminder that the 16th century was Třeboň's heyday.

Třeboň belonged to the Český Krumlov-based Rožmberk family. In 1600, Petr Vok—the last of the Rožmberks—moved here permanently after selling Český Krumlov to the emperor. He brought along his archive, still considered the most valuable collection of medieval documents in this part of Europe. It was here that the historian František Palacký—pictured on the 1,000-Kč bill—did much of the research for his history of the Czech nation (including details on Reformer Jan Hus) that came to define modern Czech identity; his "History of the Czech Nation in Bohemia and Moravia" (1836-1867) remains an authoritative work on the subject.

The castle can only be visited with an escorted tour (likely in Czech, with an English flier). Your best basic castle visit is Route A, which includes Petr Vok's Renaissance rooms. Route B covers the 19th-century apartments, kitchens, and stables of the later, equally distinguished Schwarzenbergs.

Cost and Hours: 100 Kč for either tour in Czech, English-language flier provided, buy at "cash box" ticket desk, English tours cost more and must be reserved a week ahead by emailing zamek. trebon@seznam.cz; tours go at least hourly April-Oct Tue-Sun 9:00-11:45 & 12:45-17:00, possibly shorter hours in spring and fall, closed Nov-March and Mon year-round, tel. 384-721-193, www. zamek-trebon.eu.

Nearby: To reach the House of Nature, listed next, go through the little gate at the far end of the castle's big courtyard. You'll emerge into the big park; to find the museum, look right.

▲House of Nature (Dům Přírody)

Located inside the castle, this is the best sight in town. Its "Man and the Landscape" exhibit is surprisingly modern, thoughtfully described in English, and further illuminated by excellent little video-on-demand terminals. It covers the things that make this town distinct: lake-making, the fish industry, the peat spa treatment, and the natural environment. A highlight is the theater (just after the stuffed animals), where you can watch a 13-minute video that takes you fishing early in the morning, and a 20-minute video that speeds you through a year with nature in Třeboň. An hour here is time well-invested.

Cost and Hours: 50 Kč; May-Sept daily 9:00-12:00 & 13:00-17:00; Oct-April Sat-Sun 13:00-15:00, closed Mon-Fri; enter from garden just outside castle and city wall, tel. 384-724-912.

Nearby: After touring the museum, head out into the park, and consider circling the town (described below).

ACTIVITIES
▲▲Walking the City Park and Canals

Given how closely tied Třeboň is to its landscape, limiting your visit to the main square and castle area misses the big picture.

Take a 20-minute circular walk around the Old Town, seeing fragments of the city wall and the canals and lakes that define the local identity. While you could begin and end your stroll anywhere, I've described the route clockwise, starting at the city park just outside the castle and House of Nature. To trace your route, see the map on page 345.

First, linger in the broad, lush **park,** which the town's inhabitants clearly enjoy. Bear right, working your way around to the gateway into town (it's easy to imagine how the entire town was once encircled by a protective wall—even if today you mostly see only the backs of houses). Cross the street and find the **canal** on the other side; follow it, bearing right when the canal forks. Here you'll enjoy a lush canalside garden scene, with a handy bike path and the wimpy, sgraffito-etched, crenellated remains of the city wall as a backdrop. As you stroll the delightful canal, notice the modern building on your left—Třeboň's famous peat spa (described later).

Soon you'll emerge from the park at the town's **east gate,** facing the parking lot and train station—handy if you're in a hurry to head out. Better yet, keep going straight, following the canal into a more rugged park with tall trees. As you stroll, you'll see the yellow-with-brick-trim **Regent Brewery,** a few more impressive chunks of the city wall overlooking the moat-like canal, and—very likely—a few old-timers throwing a line into the canal or trying to pull fish up with a net from the bottom of a sluice.

Keep going along the canal, passing (across the water) an industrial zone, then a welcoming park. Cross the next footbridge, walk up the lane to cross the busy road, then angle up to the top of the dike and turn right. You're circling **Svět,** the second-largest of Třeboň's

lakes. Just ahead, near the statue of Jakub Krčín, who built this lake

The Lakes of Třeboň

The medieval lake-builders of Třeboň created an ingenious landscape of regulated channels, marshes turned into lakes, and fields changed into marshes. Birds and animals new to the region began to dwell here. Peat provided a rich soil for pine trees and blueberry bushes.

The good lake-builders knew that small is beautiful... but, of course, not all of them were good. The most famous of Třeboň lake-builders was Jakub Krčín, the architect of the largest lakes, Svět and Rožmberk. Krčín was a man driven more by his ego than by practical considerations. Much of the water in his huge, deep lakes is a dead zone, lacking enough oxygen to support large fish colonies. Though less celebrated, his predecessor, Štěpánek Netolický, was more of a fishing expert. He built small lakes, and the fish in them thrived. His Golden Channel, which connects dozens of lakes, is the region's biggest marvel.

The Třeboň lakes were built for flood control as well as fishing. The marshy area around the town used to be regularly flooded by the Lužnice River, and the artificial lakes were designed to absorb the floods. In 2002, the largest floods in Czech history tested the work of those medieval lake-builders. While the 20th-century dams built on the Vltava River to protect Prague failed, Třeboň's 16th-century dams held, vindicating Krčín and keeping Třeboň's feet dry.

(badly—see sidebar), you'll find a dock for **boat trips** (60 Kč/30 minutes, 90 Kč/45 minutes, departs hourly, daily 10:00-19:00).

From here, you have some choices: You can continue along the dike (the nearest sandy **beach** is a 10-minute walk past the boat dock). Or, to head back into **town,** cross the street behind Jakub Krčín, go up the lane (noticing that the castle park is just to your left), and go through the gate. If you're ready for a meal or a drink, the recommended **Bílý Jednorožec** restaurant is immediately on your right, and the **Šupina & Šupinka** restaurants are to your left, under the arch. Otherwise, head straight, through the tall white gate, and in a long block you'll be back on **Masaryk Square.**

Biking

The area is flat, so biking is a fun and convenient way to get around. A bike trip along the dirt trails on the ancient dikes is a great way to experience the land and water. Buy a cycling map from the TI, then follow the marked trails that snake along channels and through traditional villages. For bike-rental options, see "Helpful Hints," earlier.

Hiking, Bird Watching, and Fishing

Head north or south of town to find outdoor activities around the Golden Channel system, the Rožmberk Lake, and original peat bogs and marshes such as Červené Blato. Trails are clearly indicated by markers on trees. Serious bird-watchers or fishers should get in touch ahead of time with Petr Muller at the recommended Šupina restaurant (muller@supina.cz), who can set you up with a guide (likely one of his former high school buddies) to lead you on an outing.

▲▲Canoeing

The Lužnice River, which feeds the system of ponds in Třeboň, is just as popular with Czech boaters as is the Vltava River around Český Krumlov. To gain a full appreciation for this wild landscape of pine woods, meadows, peat marshes, bogs, bugs, and authentic riverside beer stalls, consider canoeing the meandering, 7.5-mile stretch of the Lužnice River from the small town of Suchdol nad Lužnicí to the village of Majdalena.

You can either drive or bike the six miles to Majdalena where **Martin Dunaj**'s canoe-rental company is based, or for 400 Kč extra Dunaj and his team will pick you up and drop you back off at your hotel in Třeboň (canoe rental—300 Kč/two people, includes transport from Majdalena to Suchdol, allow 3-4 hours, buy bug repellent at the Pramen supermarket in Třeboň, mobile 724-919-143, www.pujcovnalodidunaj.cz).

Regent Brewery Tour

The Regent Brewery is proudly locally owned rather than part of a multinational corporation. While the recently spiffed-up, tour-group-oriented beer hall is a safe miss, the brewery tour itself is worthwhile. Run in Czech by area youngsters who will hand you an English leaflet at the start (English tour on request), the tour takes you through some of the oldest brewery operations in the country (150 Kč, 250 Kč for porch-lit night tour, daily 10:00-17:00 on the hour, night tour Fri-Sat in July-Aug at 21:00, mobile 777-357-090, www.pivovar-regent.cz).

Peat Spa (Bertiny Lázně)

Třeboň is home to an important peat spa. Patients from all over the world come here for weeklong stays to get naked and buried in the black, smelly sludge that's thought to cure aching joints and spines. Well...I guess it doesn't hurt to try. The complete peat bath *(slatinná koupel celková)* is combined with a full-body massage (don't ever try to sneak away before the nurse is finished with you). It's worth it to have the opportunity to fully judge the power of peat and experience the surreal *One Flew Over the Cuckoo's Nest* atmosphere of Czech medical institutions.

While it's smart to book a spa treatment several months ahead (you'll receive a prompt confirmation and a reminder one month before your appointment), you can often snare a last-minute spot if there's a cancellation. Call the spa or, better yet, ask your hotelier to inquire, as locals can pull strings for you (tel. 384-754-457, www. berta.cz). To get to the spa, go through the east gate of the city walls; the spa is just off to your left.

Sleeping in Třeboň

($$$$ = Splurge, $$$ = Pricier, $$ = Moderate, $ = Budget)
Although there are many pensions in Třeboň, many work in conjunction with the spa and only take guests for a week or more. The places listed here welcome guests for short stays.

$$ Apartments Šupina, with four gorgeously renovated rooms and suites in the former home of the town's chief pond supervisor, is a stylish treat. The back windows face a private garden, former moat, and the oak-lined dam of the Svět Lake. Petr, who runs the inn and the recommended restaurant next door with his family, can link you up with his bird-watching and fishing buddies, and may be able to help with last-minute spa reservations. The on-sale paintings of nearby landscapes that decorate the rooms were done by Petr's grandfather (Valy 155, mobile 720-993-825, www. supina.cz, office@supina.cz). This place is located next to and operated by the same family as the recommended Šupina & Šupinka restaurants, listed later.

$$ Hotel Galerie with twelve simple rooms and an artistically decorated breakfast area may have space even at last minute. Notice the slightly buried storage room by the reception hall that now serves as a semi-open wine cellar—since Třeboň stands on floating sands, no house in town has a basement. The manager may be able to set up a spa appointment on short notice (Rožmberská 35, 724-093-876, www.hotel-trebon.cz, galerie@hoteltrebon.cz).

$ Penzion a Lazebna Bílý Jednorožec ("White Unicorn") is a modern, tastefully opulent place with 12 rooms and an in-house spa and wellness center. Linda, the manager, keeps up high standards on all fronts and is a wealth of information (Žižkovo Náměstí 46, mobile 724-065-785, www.bilyjednorozec.cz, recepce@bilyjednorozes.cz).

Eating in Třeboň

Since the 1200s, Třeboň has lived on a steady diet of fish. The abundant variety of fish raised here is amazing...as are the chefs who cook that abundance. Austrians and Czechs alike drive for hours just to dine here. While you can find trout and carp through-

out the country, the catfish, pike, and pike perch (also called "tender") from these lakes are unique. Pike perch is nicknamed "royal" fish due to its delicate meat (for some, it's overly tender). Catfish *(sumec)* is hardier and somewhat fattier, with no bones. Pike is the only widely available predator fish. Carp, imported to Bohemia some thousand years ago from Turkey, is prepared in the most imaginative ways. Pike and pike perch may be stored frozen even during the season—check with your server to find out if your fish is fresh. Eel and salmon are not locally produced.

$$$ Šupina & Šupinka ("Scale" and "Little Scale"), set in modern interiors across the street from one other (and with an airy, quiet terrace), are top-notch places run by a committed local staff. In 1990, the Muller family opened a beer- and-hot-dog window, a business that has now evolved into the classiest restaurant in town. It's now run by proud second-generation brothers Petr and Pavel, who blend professional dedication with a personal approach. Everything is just right. Dig into the rare and refined appetizers, which include fried carp sperm. While expensive by local standards, you'll feel like royalty as you dine for half the price of a similar meal in Prague (daily 11:00-24:00; accommodations upstairs—see listing under "Sleeping in Třeboň"; Valy 155, tel. 384-721-149).

$$ Bílý Jednorožec ("White Unicorn"), just before the first gate, is a sleek, modern, one-room place with an imaginative chef who will not touch any ingredient that's not entirely fresh. Rather than stick with a permanent wide-ranging fish menu, the restaurant serves whatever fresh ingredients the chef choses to cook that night. Fish is complemented by game and meat from local small farms. Gourmet yet relatively inexpensive, this is the best value in town (daily 9:00-23:00, mobile 777-696-833).

$$ Na Rožmberské Baště ("Fisherman's Bastion") is a cozy wood-paneled family eatery with nets hanging overhead and stuffed fish of all sorts staring from the walls. Ask Vlasta, the owner, to tell you which is which (in Czech), then use the menu to decipher and assess the English equivalents; the biggest, fiercest looking specimen is *sumec* (catfish). Outside the main season, confirm which fish is fresh (daily 11:00-21:00, Fri-Sat until 22:30; on Rožmberská, the street that runs parallel to the main square behind the Town Hall tower; mobile 728-777-068).

$$ Restaurace a Pension U Míšků, an antique-filled family establishment, prides itself on fish caught every morning in their own pond. They also have a long non-fish menu that includes pasta.

The richly decorated interior is more refined than rustic. They also rent five classy rooms (daily 11:00-23:00, near the Dean Church at Husova 11—look for the prettiest facade on the street, tel. 384-721-698).

To grab a quick beer in a student-packed den, head to **$ U Kellyho** (daily 12:00-sunrise) in the castle basement off the passageway from the main square to the castle park.

Třeboň Connections

While buses between Třeboň and Prague are about as fast as the train (2.5 hours), bus departures are less frequent, and the bus station is far from the center of Třeboň. For bus and train schedules, see www.idos.cz.

From Třeboň by Train to: Prague (7/day, 2.5 hours, transfer at Veselí nad Lužnicí). If going from Prague to Třeboň, get off at Třeboň-Lázně, not Třeboň-Město.

From Třeboň by Bus to: Prague (2/day, 2.5 hours), **Český Krumlov** (10/day to České Budějovice, 30 minutes; then transfer to Český Krumlov—see page 313), **Telč** (3/day Mon-Fri, 2/day Sat-Sun, 2 hours), **Třebíč** (3/day Mon-Fri, 2/day Sat-Sun, 3 hours), **Brno** (3/day Mon-Fri, 2/day Sat-Sun, 4 hours).

Telč

Telč (pronounced "telch," pop. 6,000) is famous for its glorious square, considered by many to be the country's best. The Old Town—just a fat square with a thin layer of buildings—is surrounded by a sophisticated system of protective ponds and defensive walls. The general lay of the land has changed little since the 1300s. After 1800, all new construction took place outside the core. Today, Telč remains an unspoiled, sleepy Czech town where neighbors chat in pastry shops, Vietnamese traders in medieval arcade stalls sell dirt-cheap textiles to country folks, and the smell of goat dung from a pasture across the lake permeates the town after nightfall.

With few attractions aside from the square and the castle, Telč is made to order as a lunch stop on the way to or from Slavonice, Třeboň, and Třebíč, or on the longer haul between Prague, Brno, and Vienna. An overnight stay here can be a relaxing village experience.

Orientation to Telč

Everything you'll need—including ATMs, shops, hotels, and restaurants—is on the main square (Náměstí Zachariáše z Hradce).

TOURIST INFORMATION

The TI has information on area activities, and train and bus schedules (July-Aug Mon-Fri 8:00-18:00, Sat-Sun from 10:00, shorter hours off-season, two public computers, tel. 567-112-407, www.telc.eu). They hand out several different, well-produced materials about the town and region and offer a free town audioguide. They can also help you find a room in one of the pensions on the square (see "Sleeping in Telč," later).

ARRIVAL IN TELČ

The main square is easily reachable on foot from the bus station. If arriving by car, don't park right on the square (spaces there are reserved for residents). Instead, use the P1 lot along the main road just north of town (an easy 5-minute walk through the park to the castle), or the P2/P3 lots at the east end of town, near the top of the square (10 Kč/hour, up to 50 Kč/day).

HELPFUL HINTS

Festivals: Every year during the first two weeks of July, young musicians pour into Telč from all over Europe for the **French-Czech Music Academy,** which hosts workshops on classical music interpretation. The young virtuosos show off their skills in a number of concerts and recitals (www.academie-telc.cz). The **Telč Vacations** (Prázdniny v Telči) festival, held during the first two weeks of August, makes the squares, gardens, and castle chambers come alive with folk music, open-air theater, and exhibitions (www.prazdninyvtelci.cz/eng).

Bike Rental: You can rent bikes at the train station, or at the shop next to the TI (150 Kč/day, open daily 8:30-19:00, tel. 567-243-562). Locals enjoy the half-day bike trip to the castle ruin of Roštejn and back (10 miles round-trip).

Taxi: For a taxi, call 603-255-048 and expect basic English.

Boat Rental: During the summer, you can rent a boat for a lazy lake cruise. To get to the rental boats, walk through the gate between the castle and the square, then turn right on the path along the lake (25 Kč/30 minutes; July-Aug daily 10:00-14:00 & 14:30-18:00; June Fri 13:00-18:00, Sat-Sun from 10:00, closed Mon-Thu; no rentals Sept-May).

Telč Main Square Walk

Telč's spacious **square** (Náměstí Zachariáše z Hradce) is lined by fairy-tale gables resting on the characteristic vaulted arcades that still cover local shops and bakeries. It's the most impressive square in the Czech Republic and worth ▲▲. The uniqueness of the square lies in its enormous size, unexpected proportions in such a small town, and the purity of its style—of the 40 houses lining the square, there isn't a single one younger than 300 years. A fire devastated the town in 1553, and it was

rebuilt of stone. A plague that ravaged the region in 1780 skipped Telč, so the plague column was built on the square to thank God.

Begin this self-guided walk at the narrow/bottom end, near the castle complex (described later), and stroll slowly up the square. The tallest, turreted facade, with the little onion dome (on the right, at #10), is the **Town Hall,** and home to the TI. Farther along on the same side is the dramatic green building at #15—the only one with a turret on the corner. Like many Telč buildings, it's covered in sgraffito designs (etched into wet plaster); the bottom half has the standard "envelope" sgraffito, while the upper half boasts dramatic scenes. The narrow lane alongside this house (with more sgraffito scenes on the upper story) leads to a little **footbridge** that offers fine views of the church and castle. This gives a sense of the fortifications that protected Telč—which is ringed with fish ponds *(rybník)* that both provide food and are a strategic barrier to would-be invaders.

Directly across the square from the green house are several of the finest **facades** around. At #61, the black-and-white designs (including Old Testament figures) and Venetian-inspired flare gable were commissioned in 1555 by a local bigwig determined to impress. Two doors up, the coral-colored #59 brings some bubbly Baroque curves to the square (which, until this point, had been more rigidly Renaissance); #57, two houses up, followed suit and upped the ante, planting chubby cherubs on the crests of the gables.

A bit farther up, #54 and #55 are joined with a crenellated top and resemble some fantasy fortress. Notice the gaps in the gables partway up, where the actual roof ends; this makes it easier to clear snow off the rooftops.

By this point, you've worked your way up to the charming little **park** that surrounds the plague column. Grab the handle on the well just below the park and give it a few pumps—it still works. At the corner of the park, notice the clever little "Retro-culcar" sound box. Spin the crank a few times, press the button, and you've powered a few minutes of English commentary about the square.

Farther up, the stretch of houses on the left is some of the square's prettiest—especially #51, with its rich burgundy color. Near the top corner, look for #47, with a rectangular facade. The two top windows on the sides are obviously fake—added to the facade to create the illusion of symmetry. Poking up over the right end of the square is the pointy spire of a **church** on the next street over, which marks two recommended restaurants.

While there's not much else to see in this little town, it's worth strolling through the castle complex or heading out to the lakes that flank the town for a different view on Telč.

Sights in Telč

Telč Castle

The castle is located at the end of the main square—you can't miss it. In its early years, this castle belonged to the clan of the Five Roses (symbolized by a golden rose on a blue field; see the "Parting of the Roses" sidebar on page 319). In the 1500s, the noble-man Zachariáš z Hradce (for whom the grand main square is named) imported a team of Italian artists, who turned the earlier Gothic palace into a lav-

ish Renaissance residence. (Their work also influenced most of the burgher houses in the square.)

If the castle is open, step inside and explore its fine courtyards. Placards posted throughout the grounds identify movies that were filmed in this very atmospheric space (most of them Czech). Don't miss the fine garden just to the right as you enter (it's the walled area that you see from outside, on the square). Savor this tranquil space, surrounded on two sides by a perfectly harmonious Renais-sance arcade. The little museum along one part of the arcade dis-plays special exhibits.

Cost and Hours: Free to enter courtyards and garden, inte-rior by tour only; open May-Sept Tue-Sun 9:00-12:00 & 13:00-17:00, July-Aug until 18:00, April and Oct Tue-Sun 10:00-11:45

Gustav Mahler and Jihlava

Gustav Mahler (1860-1911) was the most important composer in Vienna at the turn of the 20th century. Mahler composed some of the last of the classical symphonies and was the first to venture into the musical never-never land of atonality (while his contemporary Arnold Schönberg, also Jewish, took up residence there). The age of harmony ended—by 1910 there was nothing to hold the world together, and shifts in art preceded the shots of World War I.

Mahler, born in the Czech village of Kaliště, spent the first 15 years of his life in Jihlava (about 30 minutes north of Telč), at a house at Znojemská 4 that now functions as a vibrant cultural center and the composer's museum (50 Kč, tel. 567-167-132, www.mahler.cz/en/dgm). This is a worthwhile stop for music buffs en route from Prague to Telč.

& 13:00-16:00, closed Nov-March and Mon year-round, last tour one hour before closing, www.zamek-telc.eu.

Interior Tours: The interior can be visited only with an escort. Tour A, the best basic castle tour, takes you through stately Renaissance chambers (110 Kč, 50 minutes). Tour B goes through the 19th-century apartments of the Lichtenstein family, who lived here until 1945 (90 Kč, 45 minutes). You'll most likely have a Czech-speaking guide and be given an English description to read as you go.

Highlands Museum (Muzeum Vysočiny)

While humble, this five-room exhibit upstairs in the castle—a branch of a much bigger collection in the town of Jihlava—gives you an interesting insight into the town (check out the 1895 town model and the WWI and WWII photos). Everything is well-explained in the English pamphlet you can borrow as you enter.

Cost and Hours: 30 Kč, similar hours to castle but can be a bit shorter.

Sleeping in Telč

Many families living on or near the main square have turned parts of their homes into pleasant pensions that meld perfectly with the mellow feel of this town. At a pension, you get nicer rooms and more personal service for about half the price of the hotels, which bank on being the only places in town able to accommodate groups.

$$ Hotel Telč, under the church tower across the square from the castle, has six spacious apartments above a delightful café (Na Mustku 37, mobile 733-141-300, http://cafetelc.cz/hotel, hoteltelc@gmail.com).

$$ Hotel Celerin, has 12 rooms, half of which face the main square (slightly more expensive). Some rooms have traditional burgher furniture (tel. 567-243-477, www.hotelcelerin.cz, office@ hotelcelerin.cz).

$ Penzion Danuše is a well-managed, quiet place with four solid rooms (30 yards off the main square at the corner of Palackého and Hradební 25, mobile 603-449-188, www.penziondanusetelc. cz, danuse.telc@seznam.cz).

¢ Penzion Patricia is run by a talkative former high-school teacher who, after 14 years in the US, returned to Telč with a mission: to turn her family's house into a showcase of Telč's hospitality. She runs the place with her four-legged teammates Sophie, Omar, Bibi, and lab Ron. The five apartments vary in size and style, but all come with a kitchenette and queen-size beds imported from California. While the entrance is at the end of the main square, the secluded garden and the back terrace under the Romanesque church tower facing the former town walls are perfect for bonfires, grilling meats, or munching seasonal fruits (breakfast extra on request or at the next door Hotel Telč café, on the main square at #38, mobile 776-691-300, patricia.telc@gmail.cz).

¢ Penzion Steidler has the most tastefully furnished rooms in town and a narrow, blooming garden that stretches all the way to the lake (breakfast extra, pay parking, look for house #52 on the main square, mobile 721-316-390, www.telc-accommodation.eu, steidler@volny.cz).

Eating in Telč

The first two places are just up the street from the wide end of the main square (with the plague column and park), below the pointy steeple; the third one sits on the square itself.

$$ Restaurant Zach serves variations on Czech classics as well as a more cosmopolitan fair, cooked using local ingredients in a renovated, modern interior. There's also a terrace on the square (at #33, good selection of local and international wines, daily 11:00-23:00, tel. 567-243-672).

$$ Amigo Restaurant serves pizzas, tortillas, salads, steaks, and homemade burgers in a modern, bar-like interior (at #22, local Telč beer on tap, daily 9:00-23:00, mobile 722-406-402). Delivery and takeout are available—consider using this place as a supply base for a lakeside picnic.

$$ Šenk pod Věží ("Under the Tower") serves up Czech classics in a small, nondescript interior with 100-year-old photographs. Or you can eat out back, in a tranquil space on the former town wall (Mon-Sat 11:00-15:00 & 18:00-22:00, Sun 11:00-16:00, tel. 567-243-889).

$$ Osvěžovna u Marušky, also directly beneath the tower, is popular with young locals who congregate here for coffee and cigarettes as much as for the food and beer. The walls are decorated by local artists and vacationing out-of-towners; jazz and classical concerts take place here twice a month (daily 11:00-24:00, mobile 603-398-128).

Telč Connections

From Telč to: Třeboň (3 buses/day Mon-Fri, 2/day Sat-Sun, 2 hours), **Třebíč** (3 buses/day Mon-Fri, 2/day Sat-Sun, 1 hour), **Brno** (3 buses/day Mon-Fri, 2/day Sat-Sun, 2 hours), **Slavonice** (5 trains/day, 1 hour), **Prague** (3 trains/day, 4-5 hours, requires 2 changes—bus is better; 5 buses/day Mon-Fri, 3/day Sat-Sun, 2-3 hours; more with a transfer in Jihlava—3 hours total). Note that some buses to Prague may arrive at Prague's Roztyly station (on the red Metro line) rather than the main bus station, Florenc. For bus and train schedules, see www.idos.cz.

Třebíč

A few miles east of Telč is the big, busy town of Třebíč (TREH-beech, pop. 40,000), with another wonderful main square and, just over its river, the largest intact Jewish ghetto in the country. While Prague's Jewish Quarter is packed with tourists, in Třebíč you'll have an entire Jewish town to yourself. Třebíč's Jewish settlement was relatively small. Though lonely and neglected, its remains are amazingly authentic.

Orientation to Třebíč

Three hours in Třebíč is sufficient—everything's close by. The main square affords a fun slice-of-local-life look at a humble yet vibrant community, while the near-ghost town across the river was once the Jewish ghetto. The two main streets that run parallel to the river (which separates the ghetto from the Christian town) are connected by a maze of narrow passages, courtyards, and tunnels.

TOURIST INFORMATION

The TI has two helpful branches: one on the main square and one in the ghetto's Rear Synagogue (both open daily 10:00-12:00 & 13:00-17:00, rental bikes at main square location, tel. 568-823-005, www.mkstrebic.cz).

ARRIVAL IN TŘEBÍČ

From the train station (with safe 24-hour luggage storage), cross the street behind the large waiting hall, and walk to the main square. To continue on to the ghetto, cross the river, following *Židovské Město* signs, marked with Stars of David. The cemetery is uphill.

Sights in Třebíč

▲Charles Square (Karlovo Náměstí)

Třebíč's main square is the third-biggest in the Czech Republic. A market square since the 13th century, it's still busy with a farmers market every morning. Třebíč was historically a mix of Christians and Jews, all living on the easy-to-defend bit of land between the river and the hill. As you'll see, that area is pretty tiny—and eventually the Christian community packed up and moved across the river for more space, establishing this square as the town's nucleus.

The statue of two Macedonian brothers—the saints Cyril and Methodius, who brought Christianity to Moravia and the Slavs in their own language, rather than Greek or Latin—was erected a thousand years after Methodius' death in 885. But forget all that history. Just circle the square, surveying today's Moravian scene. There are several fine pubs and cafés from which to people-watch. The small gallery in the four delightful vaulted rooms of the Painted House on the upper corner of the square is worth checking out to feel the artistic pulse of Moravia (next to the TI, displays temporary exhibits).

Opposite the bell tower, at #11, a lane leads across the river into the Jewish quarter, taking you directly to the Rear Synagogue (with a TI and small museum). Notice the grand views of the ghetto from the bridge.

▲Jewish Ghetto (Židovské Město)

The population of Třebíč's ghetto peaked in the 19th century at about 1,500. Only 10 Třebíč Jews survived the Holocaust. In the

1970s, the ghetto was slated for destruction, to be replaced by another ugly communist highrise housing complex. But because the land proved unable to support a huge building project, the neighborhood survived. Today, it's protected by the government as the largest preserved Jewish quarter in Europe. It comes back to life for one weekend a year during the Jewish festival (usually in late July).

Coming here, you enter a place where time has stopped: The

houses are essentially as the Jews left them more than 60 years ago. Many of the houses were resettled by Roma (see sidebar, page 331), who have done little to change the look and feel of the place. In Třebíč today, only one woman has a Jewish father. (Because you must have a Jewish mother to be legally Jewish, the Jewish population is officially zero.) The government wants the ghetto to be a living neighborhood, not a museum. Lines of drying clothes and kids kicking around a soccer ball on the cobblestones make today's ghetto come alive. After dark, it's *the* place for edgy nightlife.

The **Rear Synagogue** (Zadní Synagoga) is the visitors center, with a branch of the TI, plus displays of artifacts and a model of the once-thriving local Jewish community (40 Kč, daily 10:00-12:00 & 13:00-17:00). You can also hire a guide here. At the TI, confirm the hours of the nearby cemetery (listed below).

The **Front Synagogue** (Přední Synagoga) has functioned since 1954 as a Hussite Christian church. Though the synagogue is generally locked, you can peek through its gate to see how it was retooled for the plain Hus-style worship.

Jewish Cemetery (Židovský Hřbitov)

A 20-minute walk above the ghetto, this evocative memorial park is covered with spreading ivy, bushes of wild strawberries, and a commotion of 9,000 gravestones (the oldest dating to 1631). Notice how the tombstones follow the assimilation of the Jews, from simple markers to fancy 19th-century headstones that look exactly like those of the rich burghers in Christian cemeteries.

Cost and Hours: Free, daily May-Sept 8:00-20:00, March-April and Oct 8:00-18:00, Nov-Feb 9:00-16:00, confirm hours at the Rear Synagogue TI before ascending the hill.

St. Procopius Basilica (Bazilika sv. Prokopa)

This enormous church looms over the town on a hill a five-minute walk above the main square and the ghetto. In a region of Baroque churches, this rich fusion of late Romanesque and early Gothic styles is a striking contrast. Unfortunately, it's viewable only with a tour.

Cost and Hours: 40 Kč, 45-minute tours start every 30 minutes, May-Sept Tue-Fri 9:00-12:00 & 13:00-17:00, Sat-Mon 13:00-17:00, shorter hours and less-frequent tours Oct-April, tel. 568-610-022.

Sleeping in Třebíč

$ Hotel Solaster, near the bus station, is an attractive little place with 13 comfortable rooms, two suites, and flowers in the windows (no elevator, free parking, V. Nezvala 8, tel. 568-841-506, www. hotel-solaster.cz, recepce@hotel-solaster.cz).

¢ Penzion u Synagogy, with seven rooms next to the Rear Synagogue, is as close as you can get to living in a Jewish ghetto, and includes free entry to the exhibits at the synagogue (breakfast extra, Subakova 43, check in at Rear Synagogue TI, mobile 775-707-506, penzionsynagoga@mkstrebic.cz).

¢ Travellers' Hostel, near the Front Synagogue, has 55 dorm beds fitted into the meticulously restored home of a 16th-century baker. The oven still turns out warm bread, and a beer tap was installed even before the new roof, ensuring no guest leaves this party place without the two key elements of life (private rooms available, Žerotínovo 19, mobile 777-637-417, www.travellers.cz, trebic@travellers.cz).

Eating in Třebíč

$$ Neptune Restaurant, facing the Front Synagogue, serves good soup, fish dishes, and cheap daily lunch specials. This is the best place in the Jewish quarter, with fine indoor or outdoor seating (daily 11:00-22:00, mobile 776-350-850).

$$ Měsíční Čajovna ("Moon Teahouse"), on the upper street in the middle of the ghetto, is made for contemplating times gone by in the company of young English-speaking locals (Sun and Tue-Fri 15:00-21:00, Sat 16:00-23:00, closed Mon, Skalní 2).

$ Občerstvení Jordan, in the midst of the action at #23 on the main square, has outside seating perfect for a fast salad, sandwich, or ready-made daily special. Go inside and order by pointing at what you want (Mon-Fri 6:30-18:00, Sat 8:00-12:00, Sun 14:00-18:00).

Třebíč Connections

From Třebíč to: Telč (3 buses/day Mon-Fri, 2/day Sat-Sun, 1 hour), **Třeboň** (3 buses/day Mon-Fri, 2/day Sat-Sun, 3 hours), **Brno** (3 buses/day Mon-Fri, 2/day Sat-Sun, 1 hour; also 10 trains/day, 1.5 hours), **Prague** (nearly hourly trains, 4-5 hours, transfer in Brno—bus is better; 7 buses/day, 2.5 hours). Note that some buses to Prague may arrive at Prague's Roztyly station (on the red Metro line), not the main bus station, Florenc. For bus and train schedules, see www.idos.cz.

Slavonice (Zlabings)

The rail tracks end. Time has stopped. You may think you have arrived in a ghost town in the middle
of Arizona desert, except that the
buildings huddling in the shadow of
the dark church tower are all stone,
their gables Renaissance. Slavonice
(SLAH-voh-neet-seh), a humble
town of 2,700 a stone's throw from
the Austrian border with a low-key
artistic community, can be under-
whelming on a passing visit. But with more time it makes a perfect
base for exploring the thought-provoking surrounding landscape.

The town centers on two once-elegant Renaissance squares
separated by a Gothic church and the Town Hall. In the surrounding countryside—a region marketed as "Czech Canada" since the
1920s—hulking castle ruins top forested hills, and deep woods
surround run-down Gothic churches, Jewish cemeteries, and abandoned villages. WWII bunkers covered with sprawling blueberry
bushes evoke the harsh realities of being a border town.

Centuries ago, this thinly populated borderland between Bohemia, Moravia, and Austria was filled with thieves and thugs—
and was, therefore, nearly impossible to tax. Founded in the 1200s,
the town was originally named Zlabings by the German settlers
invited to colonize and civilize the region. During the 14th century, when the main trade route between Prague and Vienna passed
through here, Zlabings boomed. Most of the town's finest buildings date from this period. After the Thirty Years' War (1618-1648)
the town declined, and few new buildings broke the medieval architectural harmony. In late 19th century a rail line connected the
town north to Brno and south to Vienna.

Following World War II, German residents of Zlabings and
the surrounding villages—90 percent of the population—were
forced out (see the sidebar on page 324). The Czech "visitors" who
took over the deserted homes were evicted ten years later with the
creation of a buffer zone bordering Austria. Curtains of barbed
wire sealed the town off on three sides.

Starting in 1988, free-spirited artists began coming to Slavonice to retreat from the fast pace of Prague city life. Most came
for short visits, but quite a few stayed, imbuing the sleepy town with
a creative soul. Roaming the town's backstreets, you are bound to
chance upon a hidden workshop. Among the artists who stayed on
was Kryštof Trubáček, a designer of colorful pottery, who founded

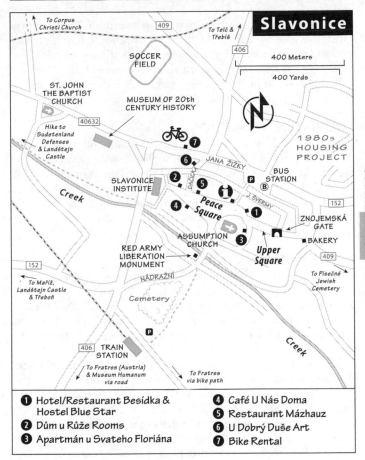

Slavonice

To Corpus Christi Church • 409 • To Telč & Třebíš • 406

400 Meters
400 Yards

SOCCER FIELD

ST. JOHN THE BAPTIST CHURCH

MUSEUM OF 20th CENTURY HISTORY

Hike to Sudetenland Defenses & Landštejn Castle

40632

1980s HOUSING PROJECT

JANA ŽIŽKY

BUS STATION

SLAVONICE INSTITUTE

Creek

DAČICKÁ

Peace Square

J. ŠVERMY

152

ZNOJEMSKÁ GATE

BAKERY

ASSUMPTION CHURCH

Upper Square

RED ARMY LIBERATION MONUMENT

152

To Mařiž, Landštejn Castle & Třeboň

NÁDRAŽNÍ

Cemetery

409

To Písečné Jewish Cemetery

TRAIN STATION

406

To Fratres (Austria) & Museum Humanum via road

To Fratres via bike path

Creek

SOUTHERN CZECH TOWNS

❶ Hotel/Restaurant Besídka & Hostel Blue Star
❷ Dům u Růže Rooms
❸ Apartmán u Svatého Floriána
❹ Café U Nás Doma
❺ Restaurant Mázhauz
❻ U Dobrý Duše Art
❼ Bike Rental

the now-legendary workshop and informal school in the nearby village of Mařiž. You'll see his trademark ceramics all around town.

After a tumultuous history, the only battle waging today across Slavonice's square is between rival shops promoting "uniquely Czech ice-cream" and "genuine Adriatic gelato." An hour's drive from the closest mall, locally owned stores still line the streets. The formerly cultured countryside west of town is now engulfed by wilderness.

Orientation to Slavonice

The fancy burgher houses on Slavonice's two main squares, Peace Square (Náměstí Míru) and Upper Square (Horní Náměstí), are ringed by another layer of centuries-old single-story houses with tiny gardens. A more contemporary residential district stretches west along Jana Žižky street, past the Museum of 20th Century History and John the Baptist Church. A linden-lined path leads up to the Corpus Christi pilgrimage site, which offers the town's best views. On the other side of town above the bus station, a low-key 1980s communist housing project surrounds a school and a health center, adding some grit to all the wistful Renaissance fancifulness.

TOURIST INFORMATION

The TI and its helpful staff, on the main square, offer free tourist maps of the Slavonicko region, an English audioguide, and walking-tour brochures including a useful three-language guide. They also sell the detailed *Česká Kanada* hiking map (May-Sept daily 8:00-17:00; Oct-April Mon-Fri until 16:00, closed Sat-Sun; free Wi-Fi and public computer, Peace Square, tel. 384-493-320, www. slavonice-mesto.cz).

ARRIVAL IN SLAVONICE

Drivers can park for free in the lot just north of the main square (near the bus station), or can pay to park on the square itself. The **train and bus stations** are each within a few minutes' walk of the center. Head straight for the church tower, which overlooks the square, and get a little introduction to Slavonice by following the routes below.

From the Train Station: As you exit, look down the tracks that continue toward Austria, lined with mountain ash trees and gradually disappearing under a carpet of elder and blackberry bushes, and medicinal herbs like mullein and St. John's wort. On the other side of the border, the track has been converted into a bike path. Next to the station, young spruce logs pile around a 1960s sawmill. Follow the narrow dirt path that starts across the street from the repaired (but closed up) Austro-Hungarian station building. On the left, peek through the fence into the cemetery where old, unkempt German tombstones contrast with a few flower-decorated Czech graves. As you enter the open space in front of the cemetery, notice the small, two-part Liberation monument (a stone with hammer and sickle), and a statue of a Red Army soldier carrying a little girl. The archaic-sounding caption reads: "You we thank and You we love." From here the town's main square is just up the street.

From the Bus Station: Walk down a little staircase and then along a path through two tunnel-like passages to reach the town center. In the first passage you can peek into a classic local "refreshment" station consisting of a single room where aged locals down their bottled beers during prime working hours.

HELPFUL HINTS

Bike Rental: U Čápa rents road and mountain bikes (daily 9:00-18:00, 30 Kč/hour, 250 Kč/day, Jana Žižky 51, from the square follow Dačická street and turn left at the intersection at Hotel U Růže, mobile 728-828-837).

Pharmacy: A medical complex is above the bus station (Mon-Fri 7:30-12:30 & 13:30-15:00, longer hours Tue and Wed, Brněnská 214, tel. 384-493-140).

Local Guide: Tomáš Heczko, who lives in nearby Muteňice and works at the American-owned Slavonice Institute, is the perfect person to give a first-hand account of recent history. For an even more fascinating exchange that will include some friendly heated argument, ask Tomáš to bring along his Austrian friend and colleague Alexander Stipsits (600 Kč/hour, 1,200 Kč for a back-and-forth session with Alexander, mobile 775-030-186, tom@centreforthefuture.cz).

Sights in Slavonice

On Peace Square (Náměstí Míru), the **city tower** and the simple **town museum** are nothing special (both open daily June-Aug, weekends only May and Sept, closed Oct-April). Some of the houses have worthy interiors, such as the **Lutheran prayer room** at #517 (100 Kč, tours daily at 11:00, 14:00, and 16:00, mobile 605-068-546) and the **Fresco House** at #480 (daily 10:00-16:00).

Other than these, consider the following attractions.

Underground Passages

The medieval cellars under the town, connected by an intricate network of underground passages, are a hit with children and thin, short people. Starting from the entrance (on the main square, next to the TI), you can slip on boots and an overcoat and follow your guide's flashlight, squeezing through a subterranean tour of the town. While you'll see little more than dirty bricks, it's certainly a unique experience.

Cost and Hours: To join an existing tour, it's 60 Kč/30-minute tour or 80 Kč/1-hour tour. If you're visiting when a tour isn't already scheduled, you'll pay 400 Kč (daily July-Aug 9:00-17:00, call 777-038-978 to arrange a visit).

Museum of 20th Century History

A proud grandson of one of the designers of the border defense system, WWII buff Jiří Duchoň first reconstructed a complex of bunkers outside town (see "Sudetenland Defenses" later) and then eventually moved to Slavonice along with his wife Nataša to open this museum. Set in a repurposed farm building, it faithfully re-creates both the pre- and post-war atmosphere (50 Kč; July-Aug daily 10:00-17:00, May-June and Sept open Sat-Sun only, Oct-April pre-arranged tours possible on weekends; descriptions in Czech, ask for the simple English flier; mobile 606-124-829).

Pilgrimage Route to Corpus Christi Church

For a meditative spot with beautiful views, follow Žižkova street from the center of town, peek inside the Gothic John the Baptist Church, then turn right, cross the rail tracks, and walk the linden-lined Stations of the Cross up the hill. According to legend, thieves who robbed the main church dropped the consecrated altar bread on this spot during their flight. Despite attempts to transport it back to the main church, the Eucharist kept reappearing here until a pilgrimage church dedicated to the cult of the body of Christ (rare in this region) was built on the spot. Note the colorful mosaic of St. Christopher added to the church exterior in 1933. (To see the interior, prearrange a tour by calling mobile 723-871-181.)

1980s Slavonice

To see a slice of more contemporary life, leave the Upper Square (Horní Náměstí) through the Znojemská Gate. Stop in the cute little bakery on the right, then cross the main street to a modern marketplace that caters exclusively to locals. Then walk up the hill to survey a 1980s housing project that includes a central heating plant, school, and medical center. Notice how most of the buildings have added color, while a few others have remained the old shabby gray.

Shopping

This town filled with ceramics and art studios is designed for thoughtful shopping. Consider in particular **U Dobrý Duše** on Dačická street (50 yards from the main square down the street next to the U Růže Hotel), where local artist Jana Dušková sells a wide array of her decorative creations. Jana is also the best person to connect you to other members of the local artistic community (open July-Aug daily 10:00-18:00, off-season ring the bell—the owners live upstairs, tel. 384-493-515, dobraduse.jana@seznam.cz).

Ceramics

Six different establishments around the main square give you a chance to paint your own cups (bake overnight, pick up next day) or buy locally produced wares. The glossier ones are copyrighted, the less shiny ones are more imaginative and eco-friendly. While the places on the square are just fine to get a basic sense for the craft, to fully appreci-

ate the story behind the famous local ceramics, bike or drive to nearby **Maříž,** where there are two workshops. I prefer the smaller one in the starkly modern bronze-roofed shack on the bank of the pond (open July-Aug daily 9:00-18:00, May-June and Sept weekends only). The other, larger studio has a good restaurant.

Sights near Slavonice

Hiking

For a pleasant five-mile, three-hour **hike,** consider the following (get a detailed map at the TI): From the bottom end of the square (by the Slavonice Institute), turn left, walk fifty yards along a footpath to a stream, cross the road, and then walk upstream along a birch-lined path. Once you clear a railway underpass, turn right up the hill, following the red-and-white markers (a red line between two white lines).

As you walk up the forest, note the rare place where a patch of young beech trees has been planted to replace the ubiquitous spruce, a non-native industrial crop that is suffering all across Central Europe as a result of global warming. (Were you to cross the border into Austria, you would find a similar single-minded adherence to spruce monoculture forestry that dates back to 19th century.) Atop the hill, less than a mile out of town, you enter the **Museum of Fortifications** complex (described later).

From here, follow the green-and-white trail markers (diagonal green line in a white square) for a mile-long walk along the bunkers. At the end, up above the third fishing pond, pick up the red-and-white-marked trail again. After a mile walk through the forest you will reach a trail intersection. From here you can either continue along the red-and-white trail to Landštejn Castle (see below), or you can turn right on a green-and-white trail.

If you turn right, in couple hundred yards you'll reach a magic spot: a briar-covered meadow with views of the medieval village of **Pfaffenschlag.** Discovered by archaeologists in the 1960s, the village was excavated in the following decade by a Slavonice teacher with help from his 8th and 9th grade students. The clean, reedfringed pond down below the meadow is easily accessible for swimming from the stone steps.

Continue along the green-and-white trail and cross a paved road. Then turn right on the next paved forest road you reach. Now follow markers composed of a yellow spiral in a white circle. After about a mile, the trail markers will divert you on a path to the left, take you past a few more forest fishing ponds, and deliver you back to the Corpus Christi church on the hill overlooking Slavonice.

The Never-Used Fortifications

As Adolf Hitler came to power in Germany, Czechoslovakia grew nervous about invasion. Starting in 1935 it began to systematically build up its army and to construct borderline defenses such as steel-reinforced concrete bunkers that could resist the German guns. Unfortunately these fortifications were not shored up with successful diplomacy: Czechoslovakia never managed to repair its relations with Poland, with which it

had fought a war in 1919 over a disputed area, and by 1937 it had lost its principal local allies Romania and Yugoslavia, which signed ill-advised neutrality pacts with Hitler. Inside Czechoslovakia, the country's German and Slovak populations were losing interest in the fate of the Czech-dominated democracy. The creator of Czechoslovakia's inter-war foreign policy, Edvard Beneš, bet his nation's future on France, determined to ignore the increasing French and British lean toward popular "appeasement" policy.

By September 1938, when Hitler and Mussolini met with the French and British in Munich to claim the Sudetenland, these still-unfinished fortifications were filled with 1.5 million mobilized Czechs and Slovaks. Morale was high, and few doubted that the

▲Sudetenland Defenses

Hidden in a thick pine forest near Slavonice is a network of armadillo-like concrete pillboxes and gun emplacements built by the

Czechs in the 1930s, in anticipation of the Nazi takeover (see sidebar above). Exploring the area is interesting to anyone, but worth ▲▲ to WWII buffs with good imaginations. It's free to walk through the woods and see the bunkers from the outside, but there's a small fee to go inside the bunkers.

Cost and Hours: Site is free and always open; one bunker interior-40 Kč, both interiors-60 Kč; bunkers open July-Aug daily 9:00-17:00; May-June and Sept Sat-Sun 9:00-17:00, closed Mon-Fri and off-season.

Getting There: By foot, hike from Slavonice (1.25 miles) along the red-marked trail in the direction of Landštejn (see "Suggested Day Hike," later). Or you can drive west of town on the Slavonice-

French and British would honor treaties with Czechoslovakia. But instead, British Prime Minister Chamberlain proclaimed to the British public, "Why should we care about the fate of a quarreling people about whom we know nothing?"—and, along with the French Prime Minister Daladier and without Czech input, signed off on the Munich Agreement, ceding the ethnic German populated areas of Czechoslovakia to Hitler. Alone, the Czechoslovak army—outnumbered by the Germans three to one—stood little chance. The frustrated soldiers were ordered home, and Czechs were forced out of the Sudetenland. Within six months, Hitler occupied the rest of the territory. Beneš and most Czechslovaks saw themselves as victims, a passive stance that would prevail in the national consciousness for much of the 20th century.

Today, the never-used bunkers and anti-tank obstacles in the countryside near Slavonice stand witness not only to the futility of appeasement policies and to the Czechs' bitter sense of betrayal, but also to the fact that a small democracy cannot survive without a collective security arrangement. Ironically, the Munich Agreement probably saved Czechoslovakia from Poland's fate (it was reduced to rubble during the war). For many young Czechs today, these almost mythical fortresses are a symbol of determination to defend freedom at all costs and an inspiration to take up a career in the armed services (the teenage guides in the bunkers under Landštejn Castle dream of serving in the US Marines).

Nová Bystřice road, and keep a careful eye out (on the right) for the turnoff with the green *Pevnostní Areál Slavonice 300 m* sign, and the brown *Bejčkův mlýn* sign. Just a few hundred feet down this road, watch for the low-profile pullout on the left, and hike five minutes into the lonely woods as if you were a 20th-century invader.

Visiting the Bunkers: The small area contains 11 mothballed bunkers—strategically staggered on a slight slope toward a pond, which was also part of the defensive network. While information plaques are scattered around, there's very little in English, making it difficult to get details—but the eerie ambience of the place transcends language. As you walk around the camouflaged mini-forts, barbed wire, and toy-like tank barriers, you'll ponder the fine line between heroism and folly.

Two of the bunkers have been refurbished with original equipment and are now the **Museum of Fortifications.** When open, they offer an intimate look at 1930s periscopes and machine guns. Imagine being a Czech soldier cowering in this bunker, terrified but determined to defend your homeland from a lunatic dictator across the border.

Landštejn Castle (Hrad Landštejn)

This region of thick forests and softly rolling hills is overseen by dramatic, reconstructed ruins of the Gothic castle that once guarded the border, an evocative reminder that the conflicts along here date to well before World War II. You can hike to the top of the complex for a view over the entire region. While it may seem like there's little to see other than forests, you're actually peering into three distinct lands: Bohemia (west), Moravia (east), and Austria (south)—illustrating this fort's strategic importance. On summer weekends, the castle serves as a venue for open-air folk and rock concerts.

Cost and Hours: 70 Kč; May-Sept Tue-Sun 9:00-15:30, June-Aug until 16:30, closed Mon; April and Oct Sat-Sun 9:00-15:30, closed Mon-Fri; closed Nov-March.

Getting There: Landštejn Castle is seven miles west of Slavonice, on the road to Nová Bystřice. Hikers can reach the castle on foot (follow red-marked trail, see above and "Suggested Day Hike," below) or by bike (follow the road or get map at TI to go through the countryside). You can also reach it by bus (Slavonice-Nová Bystřice line, 3/day, weekdays only, 15 minutes, ask to be let off at Landštejn) or car (drive toward Nová Bystřice).

Eating: The best dining option for miles around, the **$$ Landštejnský Dvůr** restaurant is set in a dark-wood mountain lodge that once served as a school. Try their tender venison in lingonberry sauce, tart soft duck leg with cabbage and dumplings, Hungarian style spicy fish soup, or any of the fish choices delivered daily from Třeboň (daily 11:00-23:00, fresh fish only on weekends during off-season, mobile 777-111-767).

Suggested Day Hike: Follow the red-marked trail from Slavonice to Landštejn via the Museum of Fortifications (described earlier), visit the castle (have lunch here), then descend along the yellow-marked trail to Stálkov (with an American buffalo farm and an excellent restaurant). Then continue to Velký Troubný lake, and from there, return to Slavonice along the trail marked with a yellow spiral inside a white circle.

▲Museum Humanum and Cultural Bridge Fratres

Just across the Austrian border, tiny Fratres, with its handful of Baroque-front village houses, feels even more remote than Slavonice. That is perhaps why Austrian writer Peter Coreth chose to follow *feng shui* here and rebuilt an ancient farmstead into a monastery-like exhibition space for his unique art collection. More than 200 art objects from Asia, Americas, Africa—and, yes, Europe—are displayed in a dense formation that is not intended to instruct but encourages the viewer to discover new connections and make fresh comparisons. Ignoring time and place of origin, Peter places his treasures in a provocative anthropological/evolutionary framework: from animal subjects progressing to gods to man, and from survival to myth to meaning to power to self-reflection.

Peter, a soft-spoken philosopher of life, will be happy to debate with you ideas of traditional categories and universal context. Or you can quietly pass from piece to piece, meditating over the magnificent highlights of the collection, such as the frightening Tibetan protective deity Kalacakra. To complement the permanent collection, on summer weekends Peter invites unusual speakers for inspiring lectures and discussions on timely topics. With space also allotted to rotating exhibits, Museum Humanum is sure to surprise no matter what expectations you bring.

Cost and Hours: €5; May-Oct Tue-Sun 10:00-18:00, closed Mon and Nov-April; Fratres 11, A-3844 Waldkirchen/Thaya, Austria; Austrian mobile (+43) 2843-2874, Austrian tel. (+43) 664-150-8282, www.museumhumanum.com.

Getting There: Fratres is in Austria, about 2 miles south of Slavonice. Either drive along the southbound (signposted) road that passes the railway station, or hike/bike down the new bike path that starts at the train station and follows the former railway track. After the border, turn right on a single-track paved road that takes you some 200 yards straight to Fratres.

Eating: On Friday evenings and on weekends, the neighboring **$$ Casa Angelina Restaurant** serves excellent Italian home cooking of the South Tyrolean region (Fri 17:00-23:00, Sat-Sun from 11:00, closed Mon-Thu, Austrian tel. (+43) 664-7301-2532).

Biking

With the surrounding rolling hills filled with unusual attractions connected by paved back roads, the region on both sides of the border is a cyclist's heaven. Many specially marked bike trails follow various themes (such as disappeared villages, the local robber Grassel, border defenses, and pond building). Buy a good map at the TI (the best is the 1:50,000 *Česká Kanada a Slavonicko* by Klub Českých Turistů). In the spring, one of the highlights is Jewish cemetery at Písečné, which blooms with lily of the valley and liverwort.

Sleeping in Slavonice

All three recommended hotels are on the main square.

$ Hotel Besídka, between the two parts of the square separated by the church, hides twelve rooms (eight in the Old Town house, four in an adjacent, fascinating post-modern annex) behind a magnificent Renaissance facade. The hotel won a Czech Architects' Society award for "adding extra value to a historic house where history complements the present, and the present complements the past." Every room is uniquely designed by a different architect, striking a perfect balance of ancient and modern. The combination of cutting-edge art and wistful decadence is quintessential Slavonice, and attracts a well-to-do Bohemian crowd (Horní Náměstí 522, tel. 384-493-293, mobile 606-212-070, www.besidka.cz, besidka@besidka.cz). The hotel also runs the ¢ **Hostel Blue Star** (Modrá Hvězda) next door and a recommended restaurant downstairs.

$ Dům u Růže has 12 modern, tasteful rooms in a restored late-19th-century house on the square, and three apartments in an annex next door. An art exhibition enlivens the breakfast room. Each room has its own kitchenette. Access to the sauna and pool are 100 Kč/person extra (Náměstí Míru 452, tel. 384-493-004, mobile 603-493-879, www.dumuruze.cz, rezervace@hoteluruze.cz). They also rent bikes (30 Kč/hour, 200 Kč/day).

¢ **Apartmán u Svatého Floriána** consists of three rooms in a Gothic house newly renovated by a local piano teacher. The classy Janáček apartment has its own bath and kitchen; the economic Smetana and Dvořák doubles share kitchen and bath amenities. There are plenty of private rooms being rented around town, but these are the most atmospheric (no breakfast, Horní Náměstí 531, mobile 603-838-014 or 777-838-014, www.apartman-u-sv-floriana-slavonice.com, jan.palenicek@gmail.com).

Eating in Slavonice

$$ Restaurant Besídka is the unofficial cultural center of town—the vaulted, artsy interior always pulses with life. Their thin-crust pizzas, croissants, and daily specials are hard to beat. The adjacent ceramics-painting workshop is run in a more individualistic fashion than the other copyrighted establishments around town (daily 11:00-22:00, tel. 384-493-293).

$ Café U Nás Doma ("At Our Home"), with its mellow, art-filled Renaissance interior (the wooden floor likely remembers the Thirty Years War) and a quiet outside terrace overlooking a patio, fits the town perfectly. Run by the youngest generation of an old Slavonice family, the café serves pastries made fresh by the grandmothers and aunts and fragrant coffee made from beans flown in straight from Columbia. An art gallery and gift store are integral parts of the experience (July-Aug daily 9:00-19:00, June and Sept closed Mon-Thu, closed Oct-May, Náměstí Míru 465, mobile 606-933-587).

$$ Restaurant Mázhauz, on the square, serves straightforward steaks and other meats in a medieval-themed interior (Sun-Thu 10:00-21:00, Fri-Sat 10:00-24:00, mobile 606-831-886).

Slavonice Connections

The easiest way in and out of Slavonice is by train via **Telč** (5/day, 1 hour; see "Telč Connections" on page 362). Most buses require a transfer in Dačice. For train and bus schedules, see www.idos.cz.

OLOMOUC

Olomouc (OH-loh-moats), the historical capital of Moravia, is a showcase of Baroque city planning. Today, it's the Czech Republic's fifth-largest city (pop. 100,000) and harbors Moravia's oldest university. Students rule the town. With its wealth of cafés, clubs, and restaurants, Olomouc is the place to taste vibrant local culture—without the hassles and scams of Prague.

Olomouc has pride. It's at a crossroads about 150 miles from each of the other great cities of the region (Prague, Wrocław, Kraków, Bratislava, and Vienna) and wants to play with the big boys. While it ruled Moravia from the 11th century until 1642, today it's clearly playing second fiddle to Brno, the booming industrial city four times its size an hour south. Locals brag that Olomouc has the country's second-most-important archbishopric and the tastiest diet cheese (less than one percent fat) in the world. Like Prague, it has its own fancy astronomical clock. Olomouc actually built its bell tower in the 19th century to be six feet taller than Prague's. Olomouc is unrivaled in one category: Its plague monument is the tallest and most grandiose anywhere.

Although Olomouc's suburbs sprawl with 1960s apartment complexes and factories, its historic core was spared experiments in urban design. It's not lost in a time warp like the old-town areas of Český Krumlov, Telč, and Slavonice. It's simply workaday Moravia. Trams clatter through the streets, fancy boutiques sell stylish Versace fashions, and locals pack the busy pubs. Few tourists come here, so the town thrives on its own economy.

In the mornings, proud farmers dig out their leeks and carrots and descend upon the colorful open-air market. Haná, the region that immediately surrounds Olomouc, is among the most fertile in the Czech Republic. The big landowners here have never had trouble converting their meat, milk, and bread into gold and power. The

Olomouc's History

The fortune and misfortune of Olomouc has always come from

its strategic location at the intersection of Eastern Europe's main east-west and south-north routes: Merchants, pilgrims, kings, and armies had to pass through the city.

Until the 1640s, Olomouc was the second-largest city in the Czech lands. The king's younger brother governed Moravian politics from here, while the archbishop kept the spirits (and the lands) of Moravians in God's hands—that is, his own.

Olomouc was trashed by passing armies during the Thirty Years' War (1618-1648) and occupied by the Swedes for the last eight of those years. More than 70 percent of the town's population died in battles or from plagues, and the Moravian capital was moved to Brno. In 1709, Olomouc burned to the ground... only to emerge from the ashes with a Baroque flair during the Habsburg years. The new Olomouc—filled with churches, colleges, statues, and fountains—became the largest Baroque town in the country. But its prosperity again ended abruptly, as Prussia (occupying what is now western Poland and eastern Germany) threatened to invade Vienna—and Olomouc was right in the way. The Habsburgs had Olomouc's students and monks leave, and replaced them with soldiers who would defend the city. They surrounded Olomouc with tall, thick walls, and what once was a cultural center became an immense fortress. The Prussians laid siege to the city, but never managed to take it. The ring of walls and moats that protected the town also ended up preventing the encroachment of modern-day architecture into the historic center.

Olomouc eventually began to thrive again, but it remains overshadowed by Brno. Today, it still comes in second as the economic powerhouse of Moravia. But ever since Palacký University was founded here in 1946—on the grounds of the centuries-old theological university—Olomouc has been Moravia's intellectual center.

most distinguished landowner of all has always been the Church. Archbishops have ruled from here for a thousand years, filling the town with churches and monasteries. In 1946, these buildings were turned into departments of the new Palacký University.

Being a student town, Olomouc feels young and alive (though quiet during summer weekends and school vacations, when the students clear out). It's also noticeably artistic, with more than its share of oddball characters roaming the streets. Olomouc has managed to blend the old and the new better than any other town in the country. The McDonald's on the Baroque main square is not an intruder, but simply a contented acknowledgment of modern times.

To generalize, the Moravians are seen as friendlier and more community-oriented than the more individualistic Bohemians. This shows in voting patterns. In Moravia, left-leaning parties tend to do better than the pro-business candidates who dominate the electorates in Prague and Plzeň (a city in western Bohemia). Moravians are also more Catholic and eco-minded. Traditions are prized in Moravia: Diverse regional dialects and folk customs have flourished here but have long since disappeared in Bohemia.

Anything labeled "Haná" is from this particular part of Moravia—you'll notice plenty of Haná pride here. Olomouc is a fine place to just kick back for a day or two in a beautiful Baroque town with its Haná-centric gaze fixed on the future. Nearby Kroměříž, an hour away by train, beckons day-trippers with its lavish castle and gardens. And to delve even more deeply into the Moravian countryside, linger in Wallachia—tucked in the forested hills between Olomouc and the Polish border.

PLANNING YOUR TIME

Olomouc is a delightful mix of Baroque space and 21st-century life. Don't approach the city as a sightseer; Olomouc is to be experienced and enjoyed. The only must-see "sights"—the two squares and the plague column—can be covered in an hour, but you can enjoy additional time in the city's restaurants, bars, and clubs.

If you're passing through, hop off the train for a three-hour lunch stop on the main square. Better yet, stay the night to relax and sample the rich nightlife. I enjoy the city enough to visit it as a long day trip from Prague. On a more leisurely visit, consider the worthwhile side trips to Kroměříž (with a sumptuous château) and the Wallachia region (a rural, rustic corner of Moravia).

Orientation to Olomouc

Olomouc's historic core is small, compact, and just five tram stops from the train station. The core has two parts: the original settlement around the former royal palace and cathedral, and the royal town (west of the cathedral). The royal town is concentrated around two connected squares: Upper Square (Horní Náměstí), with the Town Hall and plague column; and Lower Square (Dolní Náměstí), with many restaurants.

Part of Olomouc's charm is that it's a Baroque town on a medieval street plan. Everything of sightseeing interest is contained within its historic core, defined by the circular greenbelt that follows the town's old wall (much like the famous Planty in Kraków).

TOURIST INFORMATION

Olomouc's main TI, in the Town Hall on the Upper Square, has plenty of maps and well-written fliers describing the town's main sights (daily 9:00-19:00, tel. 585-513-385, http://tourism.olomouc. eu). They sell tickets to concerts, organize tours of individual sights, and can set you up with a local guide (500 Kč/hour, reserve ahead).

ARRIVAL IN OLOMOUC

By Train: Olomouc's circa-1950s train station (Hlavní Nádraží) is downright cute. Bright, happy peasants still greet you with their banners, rakes, and trays of *koláče* (pastries). As you exit through the main station hall, on your left you'll see the Czech state railways center, with 24-hour help on train connections (tel. 972-741-620). On your right are ticket windows for RegioJet and LEO Express (private railway companies with service to Prague), and the city transit office with information about trams and tickets (Sun 14:00-19:00, Mon-Fri 5:00-19:00, closed Sat).

Take the **tram** into the center. Trams #2, #4, and #6 stop in front of the train station and go past the cathedral (U Dómu, third stop), then continue to Koruna (fifth stop), right by the main square. Even if you're not arriving by train, consider riding the tram for an easy orientation to the city (described later).

Taxis are inexpensive (figure on 100 Kč to the center). Call Atlant-taxi (toll-free tel. 800-113-030) or Citytaxi (toll-free tel. 800-223-030).

By Car: Several streets in the city center are closed to traffic; others allow street parking (pay at meter Mon-Fri 8:00-18:00). The best plan is to park your car at a pay garage. Garages that are handy to the Upper Square include one at the corner of Mlýnská and Pavelčákova, and another a couple of blocks away, at Palachovo Náměstí.

HELPFUL HINTS

Exchange Rate: 25 Kč = about $1
Country Calling Code: 420 (see page 464 for dialing instructions)
Festivals: Olomouc's **Festival of Song** (early June, www.
festamusicale.com) kicks off the event calendar. During the summer (July-Sept), the town organizes a cultural festival. Top Czech artists perform weekly under the open sky in the Town Hall courtyard or in one of the numerous churches and student clubs around town (www.olomouckekulturniprazdniny. cz). The Jesuit Konvikt (former monastery) simultaneously hosts a Baroque music festival. Outside of festival time, when school is in session (Sept-May), Olomouc is hopping, with good independent movie theaters and live music in bars. The town's main theater, **Moravské Divadlo,** regularly puts on

OLOMOUC

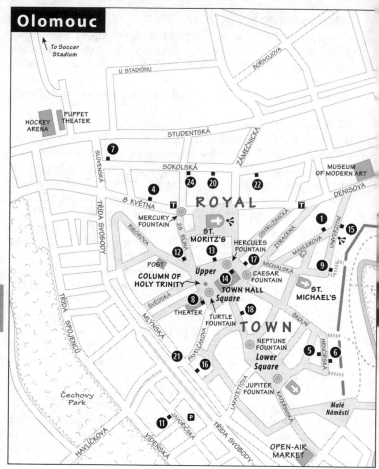

Olomouc

opera performances (ticket office open Mon-Fri 9:00-18:00, closed Sat-Sun, located on the Upper Square next to the recommended Moravská Restaurace, tel. 585-223-533, www.moravskedivadlo.cz, pokladna@moravskedivadlo.cz).

Beer Spa: For an unforgettable memory, it's hard to beat soaking in a sudsy beer bath at the **Svatováclavský Pivovar** brewery (see page 395).

Pharmacy: A 24-hour pharmacy is on Aksamitova street.

Wi-Fi: Slam.cz copy center is across the street from the Dominican monastery (at the corner of Sokolská and Slovenská).

Bike Rental: Cosy Corner Hostel rents wheels by the day (for details, see hostel listing under "Sleeping in Olomouc," later).

Rickshaws: To cycle around on a rickshaw, look for the main stand in front of the TI on the square (50 Kč/ride, 100-Kč circuit goes around all fountains, 200 Kč also includes parks).

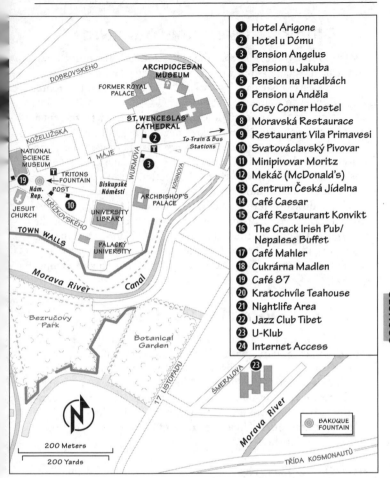

1. Hotel Arigone
2. Hotel u Dómu
3. Pension Angelus
4. Pension u Jakuba
5. Pension na Hradbách
6. Pension u Anděla
7. Cosy Corner Hostel
8. Moravská Restaurace
9. Restaurant Vila Primavesi
10. Svatováclavský Pivovar
11. Minipivovar Moritz
12. Mekáč (McDonald's)
13. Centrum Česká Jídelna
14. Café Caesar
15. Café Restaurant Konvikt
16. The Crack Irish Pub/ Nepalese Buffet
17. Café Mahler
18. Cukrárna Madlen
19. Café 87
20. Kratochvíle Teahouse
21. Nightlife Area
22. Jazz Club Tibet
23. U-Klub
24. Internet Access

OLOMOUC

Local Guide: Štefan Blaho, who speaks English well, is a rare Olomouc guide ready to connect with curious visitors who figure out how much fun Olomouc is to visit—especially with a local (500 Kč/hour, tel. 581-208-242, mobile 602-729-613, www.olomouc-guide.cz, stefan@olomouc-guide.cz).

GETTING AROUND OLOMOUC

Although Olomouc is walkable, I recommend taking a tram ride for a good orientation (described later). Tickets are good for 40 minutes, so you can hop on and off (14 Kč, buy at *tabák* shops or yellow machines, or pay a little extra to buy on board from the driver).

Olomouc Overview Tram Ride

This 10-minute tram ride from the train station (Hlavní Nádraží) to the Upper Square (stop: Koruna) is a handy way to get an overview of the city. It's easy. Trams #2, #4, and #6 make the route, going every few minutes.

In front of the train station stretches a modern town center with planned communist-era apartment blocks. While there are plenty of drawbacks to the city's communist heritage, one good leftover from that era is Olomouc's fine, still-subsidized public transit. As you ride, notice that people often forgo owning a car because of dirt-cheap monthly passes. It's second nature here.

Going downtown from the station, you peel through the city's architectural layers of history. Crossing the three branches of the river, you pass through the university district before reaching the center. A red light at the front of the car indicates your next stop. Hop out at "Koruna," and head toward the big square (Upper Square) a block to your left.

Sights in Olomouc

Olomouc is divided between its royal town (surrounding the magnificent Upper Square, with its famous plague column) and its bishop's town, or cathedral district (the other end of town, with the bishop's palace and Archdiocesan Museum). The huge university sprawls between these two former centers of power. Visitors connect the two zones with an easy 10-minute walk. The sights here are listed in that order: Upper Square and its surroundings, crosstown walk, and cathedral.

THE ROYAL TOWN
▲▲Upper Square (Horní Náměstí)

Standing in front of the Town Hall, surrounded by the vast square and the many beautiful noble and bourgeois residences, you can imagine Olomouc's importance over the centuries.

The square is dominated by the Column of the Holy Trinity (Sousoší Nejsvětější Trojice). The artistic pride of Olomouc is the tallest **plague column** in Europe. Squares throughout Central and Eastern Europe are dotted with similar structures, erected by locals to give thanks for surviving the plague. This one was started in 1716 by a local man named Render, who announced—with a confidence characteristic of the

Haná region—that he would create a work that in "its height and ornamentation would not have a peer in terms of excellence." He donated his entire fortune, employing many great artists for decades to build the monument. Sadly, he died before its consecration, which occurred in the presence of the Habsburg ruler Maria Theresa, the Holy Roman Empress.

The Holy Trinity group on the highest point of the column features God the Father making a blessing, Christ with a cross

sitting on a globe, and the dove in gold (representing the Holy Spirit) crowning everything. Tumbling with the Trinity, the archangel Michael—holding his fiery sword and shield—reminds us that the Church is in a constant struggle with evil. A third of the way down from the top of the column (past the golden cannonball—embedded there as a reminder of the 1758 Prussian siege), we see Mary—the mediator between heavenly and earthly spheres—carried off by angels during the Assumption.

The bottom third features three reliefs with allegories of the Christian virtues (Faith, Hope, and Charity), surrounded by six saints. Four of the saints are closely connected with the life of Jesus (saints Joachim and Anne—the parents of the Virgin Mary—as well as St. Joseph and St. John the Baptist); the other two are the patron saints of Olomouc (saints Jerome and Lawrence). This particular arrangement of saints shows that universal faith is often combined with a distinctly local myth and belief.

It all sits atop a tiny (and rarely open) chapel where Maria Theresa knelt to pray—devout, yet green with envy. Olomouc had a plague column grander than Vienna's.

Olomouc's grand **Town Hall** is a testament to the city's 600 years of prominence in Moravia. The three wings around a rectangular courtyard once served as both council chambers and market halls. In the late 1400s, part of the building was converted into an armory, guards' house, and jail. The Town Hall is busy with local weddings—if you see a festively decorated car parked on the square, it's probably waiting to zip a bride and groom away. You can visit the Town Hall's interior and climb the tower only with an escort (30 Kč for 30-minute tour, 6/day in summer, 2/day off-season, book tickets and depart from the TI located within the Town Hall).

The huge **astronomical clock** on the Town Hall was once far more complex than the one in Prague. Originally, it depicted the medieval universe divided into three spheres, but it was periodi-

OLOMOUC

The Baroque Fountains of Olomouc

Sprinkled around Olomouc's old town is a series of seven alle-gorical fountains with statues. Since pagan times, Olomouc—whose wealth has always been based on agriculture—has had a close relationship with water. Most of the fountains were in-spired by classical mythology.

One features a statue of **Neptune,** the god of water. An-other shows **Hercules** depicted as the guardian of Olomouc, holding the Moravian checkered eagle in his left hand and a mace in his right. **Jupiter,** the overlord of the gods, replaced an earlier sculpture of the only Christian saint who appeared on the fountains: St. Florian, protector from fires and floods.

The **Tritons** fountain—closely based on the one at Rome's Piazza Barberini—has the most developed composition: a pair of water spirits and a dolphin carrying a conch, with a fragile boy leading two dogs.

The culmination of the cycle is the equestrian statue of **Caesar,** who looks proudly to-ward Michael Hill (where legend says he founded Olomouc). The water gods Morava and Danubi-us carry the coats of arms of Moravia and Lower Austria, and the dog represents Olomouc's fi-delity to the Austrian emperor.

The **Mercury** statue (by the tram stop near the Upper Square) is artistically the most successful. Mercury fulfilled the same role in classical mythology as the archangel Michael did in the Old Testament: He was the guide through the land of the dead and the messenger of the gods.

The modern **turtle fountain,** at the end of the Town Hall, is the most entertaining. The turtle, who lives a long life, sym-bolizes ancient Olomouc's ability to hang in there. The city's history in maps and documents is inscribed on the turtle's pil-lar. Contribute to a new tradition—though the statue is only a few years old, the tail (on the dolphin statue) already shows signs of being rubbed by visitors to assure their return to Olo-mouc. This fountain is a meeting place for young mothers and a fun place to watch toddlers enjoy the art.

The placement of the fountains and statues at the inter-sections of roads and squares—reminiscent of stage props in Baroque theater—imitates the spectacular cycle of Bernini's fountains in Rome. Since the second half of the 18th century, every view down any main street in Olomouc has ended with a sculpture. Look for these as you sightsee, and you'll better appreciate the town as theater.

cally rebuilt to correspond with new advances in knowledge. In 1898, purists worked to restore it to its original state.

Like Prague's clock, Olomouc's astronomical clock was intentionally destroyed by the Nazis in World War II. Today's version was rebuilt in 1953 by the communists, who had a flair for kitschy propaganda. In this one-of-a-kind clock made in the Socialist Realist style, you have earnest chemists and heroic mothers rather than saints and Virgin Marys. High noon is marked by a proletarian parade, when, for six minutes, a mechanical conga line of milkmaids, clerks, blacksmiths, medics, and teachers are celebrated as the champions of everyday society. Study the mosaic symbols of the 12 months (*leden* is January; circle down on the left—*červen* is June). The Haná region is agriculturally rich, so each month features a farm activity. As with any proper astronomical clock, there's a wheel with 365 saints, so you'll always know whose special day it is. But this clock comes with a Moscow-inspired bonus—red bands on the wheel splice in the birthdays of communist leaders (Lenin was born on the 112th day of the year in 1870; Stalin's saint was Toman—day 355). Note that the clock's designers were optimists—the year mechanism (on the bottom) is capable of spinning until A.D. 9999.

Locate the **town model,** near the fountain just in front of the clock. While designed for blind people, it gives anyone interested a feel—literally—for the medieval street plan, otherwise easily overlooked among all the Baroque grandeur.

Circle around the left side of the Town Hall to find another fountain, with an equestrian statue of **Julius Caesar.** This is dedicated to the legendary founder of the town (excavations reveal that it actually originated as a third-century A.D. Roman military camp—centuries after Caesar). For more on the fountains that are strategically scattered around Olomouc's core, see the sidebar on page 386.

Just behind Caesar, **Café Mahler** is a reminder of the great composer Gustav Mahler (1860-1911). He lived and worked here until he moved to Vienna, claiming he needed better food.

On this side of the Town Hall, notice the beautiful Mannerist

loggia, used for the entry into the council chambers and for ceremonial purposes (such as the mayor's declarations to the public). The coats of arms of many nations show that Moravia was part of the vast and multiethnic Habsburg Empire.

Circling the rest of the way around the Town Hall, you'll see the wide street leading down to Olomouc's Lower Square.

Lower Square (Dolní Náměstí)

Below the Upper Square stretches the more workaday Lower Square. This space was ripped up and renovated from 2011 to 2013. The dark blocks in the paving stones mark the site of an old chapel's foundation, which was discovered during the renovation. Today the square enjoys a sparkle that rivals its big brother—it even has its very own, twisty plague column.

Open-Air Market

As was the norm in medieval times, poor people traded tax- and duty-free items just outside the town walls. The city's market remains in the same spot, just outside the town wall a long block below the Lower Square. The town's circa-1900 brick market hall is of no interest today, but around it sprawls a colorful open-air market. While Moravian farmers sell their vegetables and herbs, Vietnamese traders hawk knockoff jeans and cheap sunglasses (closed Sun, busiest on Wed and Sat, but fun any morning). The rough little snack bar sells *langoš* (a Hungarian cheese-and-garlic savory doughnut), cheap coffee, and good beer.

Churches

Since its origin, Olomouc has been the seat of bishops. The great number of churches—concentrated in such a small area—shows the strong presence of the Church here. Of the many churches in town, two are worth a peek (each one is a block off the Upper Square; both are free to enter—though donations are appreciated—and open daily 7:00-18:00, shorter hours off-season).

St. Michael's Church (Sv. Michal), located at the highest point in town, dominates Olomouc's skyline. It's a fine, single-nave Baroque church full of illusory paintings, fake armor, and lovely Gothic frescoes hidden under Baroque whitewash. As it was rebuilt after looting by the Protestant Swedes during the Counter-Reformation, the Catholic propaganda is really cranked up. The three-domed ceiling—a reminder of the Trinity—is an unusual feature. From the cloister, stairs lead down to the 11th-century "rock chapel" and its tiny lake. The chair in the dark hole on the left is an invitation to pray or meditate. This humble grotto was the site of the first hermitage here on Olomouc's high rock. As Michael is the Christian antidote to paganism, archaeologists assume that this church sits upon a pagan holy spot.

St. Moritz's Church (Sv. Mořic) is a must-see for its pair of asymmetrical towers, which look more like fortresses. The church has an original Gothic vault, but its Gothic treasures are in a Prague museum. The altar and windows, while lovely, are Neo-Gothic, dating only from the 19th century. Climb the 206 steps to the tower to enjoy a commanding city view (20 Kč).

STROLLING BETWEEN THE ROYAL TOWN AND THE CATHEDRAL

Connect the two sightseeing zones with a short walk along the city's main drag. Leaving the Upper Square on **Ostružnická** street, you'll pass real-estate offices (a home in a village or an apartment here goes for about 1.5 million Kč, or about $75,000) and lots of bookstores (supplying 17,000 local university students).

When you hit the main road, **Denisova,** turn right. In the little square, notice the fine gas streetlamp that lit the street in 1899, when the tram first ran. Follow the tram line toward the lacy spire of the cathedral in the distance. The mix of facades, from Gothic to Art Nouveau, masks narrow medieval buildings.

At Univerzitní street (a block after the lamppost), a quick detour to the right leads past the Vertigo Bar (where students believe

a mind is a wonderful thing to waste) to the grand and renovated **University building** on the left (with its recommended Café Restaurant Konvikt and a courtyard with a nice view over the town wall).

Continuing up the main drag, you pass the Museum of Modern Art (interesting) and the Natural Science Museum (boring). The collection at the **Museum of Modern Art** (Muzeum Umění) spans the 20th century from Expressionism and Cubism to more recent conceptual and Postmodernist works (70 Kč, 100 Kč combo-ticket with worthwhile Archdiocesan Museum—described later, free on Sun and first Wed of the month; open Tue-Sun 10:00-18:00, closed Mon, last entry 30 minutes before closing; Denisova 47, tel. 585-514-111, www.olmuart.cz).

OLOMOUC

"From Armories Make Libraries": John Amos Comenius (1592-1670)

This motto, which inspired the transformation of Olomouc's military fortress into a lively university campus, came from John Amos Comenius (aka Jan Amos Komenský), one of the Czech Republic's most influential teachers and writers (pull out a 200-Kč banknote to have a look at him). You'll find his dictum embedded in the pavement at the entrance to Olomouc's former central armory, which is the main university library today.

Comenius was born into the Moravian Brethren faith, which was founded on the pacifist ideals of the Czech religious reformer Petr Chelčický (c. 1390-1460). Having studied at universities in Germany, Comenius returned to Moravia as a young pastor to run the Protestant schools in Fulnek and Přerov. The beginning of the Thirty Years' War had a direct impact on him: His wife and two children died in a plague epidemic, and following the defeat of the Czech Protestants by the Catholic Habsburgs, Comenius had to choose exile over abandoning his faith. Personal misfortune went hand-in-hand with a professional one: During his escape through Poland, his entire library went up in flames, a fate that later befell many of his personal writings.

Surrounded by the chaos and destruction of war, Comenius believed that guns were no way to restore order—what the world really needed was a revolution in learning. He envisioned a liberal-arts education that would create citizens rather than specialists, and proposed a new teaching system based on the novel principle of "school through play." To promote this idea, he wrote extensively. His works included a textbook aimed at making learning Latin fun for children, one of the first scholarly treatments of preschool education, and *Orbis Pictus* ("World in Pictures"), the first children's encyclopedia. His most famous and acclaimed work,

The big square called **Náměstí Republiky** is marked by a fountain inspired by Bernini's Triton Fountain in Rome (see sidebar on page 386). The Jesuits, whose gorgeous church faces the square, founded the original university in the 16th century. This square marks the division between the royal town and the bishop's town.

Ahead (past the square, veering a bit to the right), **Mariánská** street leads to the archbishop's stately 17th-century palace (closed to the public). On the slopes below the palace are Jesuit colleges (now university classrooms) and a Clarist convent (now a museum). When you reach the archbishop's palace, turn left, head down the street, cross the tram tracks, and continue straight ahead up Dómská to reach the next two sights.

The Labyrinth of the World and the Paradise of the Heart (written in Czech, not Latin), argued that all human knowledge and ambition are futile if unaccompanied by faith and charity. His fame spread across the Atlantic: In 1636, Comenius was asked to become the first president of Harvard University. Still hoping to return home (and afraid of sea journeys after he almost lost his life in a storm in the North Sea), Comenius declined the offer.

For the remainder of his wandering life, Comenius taught and wrote in Poland, Hungary, the Netherlands, England, and Sweden, never able to return home. Alfons Mucha powerfully captured Comenius' tragic fate as a homeless exile—a fate later to be shared by thousands of free-spirited Czechs—in one of the canvases of his *Slav Epic* (see page 158).

During the communist era, Comenius' grave (in Naarden, near Amsterdam) became a shrine for Czech exiles; immediately after the fall of the Iron Curtain, the site was swamped with Czechs who came to pay their respects. Today, Comenius is considered one of the founders of modern education, and his legacy is alive far beyond Olomouc. In the Czech Republic and Slovakia, Comenius' birthday is celebrated as Teachers' Day, and the Comenius Medal is the highest UNESCO award for achievement in education.

OLOMOUC

IN THE BISHOP'S TOWN, NEAR THE CATHEDRAL
St. Wenceslas' Cathedral (Dóm Sv. Václava)

Supposedly, this has been the resident church of Olomouc's bishops ever since the Christian missionaries Cyril and Methodius visited in the ninth century. The present church has been rebuilt many times. While it maintains its Gothic lines, what you see is 19th-century pseudo-Gothic, with Neo-Renaissance paintings. On the walls under the organ loft and on big black panels flanking the main door, you can trace the lineage of local archbishops back 68 men—from today's archbishop to St. Methodius in 869. Step up to the cavernous, gated-off choir area, where a Neo-Gothic altarpiece glitters at the far end. Nearby, look for photos from Pope John Paul II's visit here in 1995. The crypt (entrance to the left as you face the choir) houses a collection of liturgical ornaments—the second-largest in the country, after Loreta Church in Prague.

Cost and Hours: Small fee possible, crypt generally open daily May-Oct 10:00-17:00, closed off-season.

▲Archdiocesan Museum

Opened in 2006, this is Olomouc's pride and joy. After his 1995 visit, Pope John Paul II asked the city to build this museum. The mission of this state-of-the-art museum is "In Glory and Praise—To Share a Thousand Years of Spiritual Culture in Moravia"...and it does just that. Enter it through the gated park just to the left as you face the cathedral.

Cost and Hours: 70 Kč, 100-Kč combo-ticket with Museum of Modern Art, free on Sun and first Wed of the month; open Tue-Sun 10:00-18:00, closed Mon; audioguide-20 Kč, Václavské Náměstí 3, tel. 585-514-111, www.olmuart.cz.

Visiting the Museum: This former royal castle, once the king's principal Moravian residence, later became home to Olomouc's archbishop. The exterior is a mix of Romanesque and Gothic elements. Inside you'll wander among a small collection of some of the finest medieval art in Eastern Europe. While English descriptions are posted, renting the audioguide can deepen your appreciation of the art.

The mazelike floor plan is confusing, but attendants will point the way. Entering the main collection, you'll be wowed by the bishop's gilded coach, which understandably gave the Holy Roman Empress Maria Theresa more reason for envy. The adjacent treasury—one small room—displays several priceless items, including its remarkable centerpiece: a monstrance (Communion wafer holder) with 1,800 diamonds and seven pounds of pure gold (from 1750). From here, you'll circle on several levels through the rest of the collection, from archaeological finds in the cellar, to lots of S-curve Madonna-and-Child altarpiece statues, to the fine little cloister with its well-tended herb garden.

Finally, head back to the ticket desk and go upstairs to find the painting gallery. You'll slide on slippers to protect the not-so-hardwood floor and shuffle through the staterooms lined with well-lit paintings.

Entertainment in Olomouc

Consider filling your evenings at one of the following venues:

Vodní Kasárna, Mi Casa Su Casa Music Bar, and **The Crack Irish Pub** fill the massive red-brick 18th-century town wall with nightlife inspired by various corners of Europe. Fueled by the vibrant local crowd, these spots are open much of the day, but they don't really start to swing until around 21:00, when the disco and live music begin. Head to the corner of Mlýnská and Pavelčákova, just across the Třída Svobody from Maria Theresa Gate.

Jazz Club Tibet has nothing to do with Tibet, but it does offer good food and live jazz twice a week in a modern, pub-like setting (Mon-Sat 11:00 until late, closed Sun, Sokolská 48, tel. 585-230-399). Across the street, the **Metropol** movie theater screens a mixture of artsy and mainstream flicks.

Konvikt is a hip club right next to the restaurant of the same name (described earlier). In summer, it's a popular hangout for foreign students (Mon-Sat 14:00-24:00, closed Sun, tel. 585-631-191).

U-Klub, a 10-minute walk out of the center in the dorms, is the university's concert hall. Bands play folk, jazz, rock, punk...you name it (Šmeralova 12, tel. 585-638-117).

Sleeping in Olomouc

$$ Hotel Arigone, filling three tastefully renovated townhouses, is on the hill by St. Michael's Church. While some of the 53 rooms have 17th-century wooden ceilings and 19th-century-style furniture, most are furnished in a modern style and are accessible by elevator (rental bikes, parking, Univerzitní 20, tel. 585-232-351, www.arigone.cz, hotel@arigone.cz).

$$ Hotel u Dómu, a six-room place on a quiet street next to the cathedral, is run with a personal touch that makes it popular with quirky visiting professors (free parking, Dómská 4, tel. 585-220-502, www.hoteludomu.cz, hoteludomu@email.cz).

$$ Pension Angelus rents four rooms in a Baroque house with wooden beams and solid furniture (free parking, Wurmova 1, mobile 776-206-936, www.pensionangelus.cz, pensionangelus@email.cz).

$ Pension u Jakuba rents six self-contained, Ikea-furnished apartments in a 400-year-old house on a busy street. The business-style pension also has seven quiet, modern rooms in an annex in the courtyard (family rooms available, parking, 8 Května #9, to reach reception walk through passage into courtyard, tel. 585-209-995, mobile 777-747-688, www.pensionujakuba.com, ujakuba@iol.cz).

$ Pension na Hradbách rents four modern rooms, each with

Sleep Code

Hotels are classified based on the average price of a standard double room with breakfast in high season. I've given *very* rough conversions to dollars using 25 Kč = $1.

$$$$ **Splurge:** Most rooms over 3,400 Kč (roughly $135)
$$$ **Pricier:** 2,600-3,400 Kč ($105-135)
$$ **Moderate:** 1,800-2,600 Kč ($70-105)
$ **Budget:** 1,000-1,800 Kč ($40-70)
¢   **Backpacker:** Under 1,000 Kč ($40)
RS%   **Rick Steves discount**

Unless otherwise noted, credit cards are accepted, hotel staff speak basic English, and free Wi-Fi is available. Comparison-shop by checking prices at several hotels (on each hotel's own website, on a booking site, or by email). For the best deal, *book directly with the hotel*. Ask for a discount if paying in cash; if the listing includes **RS%,** request a Rick Steves discount.

---

a personal touch (no breakfast, Hrnčířská 3, tel. 585-233-243, mobile 602-755-848, www.pensionnahradbach.wz.cz, nahradbach@quick.cz).

¢ Pension u Anděla, across the street, is well-suited to be on Hrnčířská ("Potter's street"), a quiet row of two-story village houses with brightly painted facades and window-boxes full of geraniums. Two of the four simply furnished rooms overlook the bastion and park (no breakfast but in-room fridge, downstairs restaurant can make breakfast the night before on request, Hrnčířská 10, tel. 585-228-755, mobile 602-512-763, www.uandela.cz, info@uandela.cz).

¢ *Hostel:* Cosy Corner Hostel fills two 1930s apartments near the town center. Tastefully furnished and immaculate, it's run as a family business by a friendly couple, Ian Martin (who's Australian) and Lucie Kyvalova (who's Czech). They have two young kids and a great enthusiasm for Olomouc. The hostel fits in perfectly with Olomouc's character as a student town and ultimate Back Door destination. The common room has sofas, armchairs, a decent library, Czech CDs (and no TV), and holds a wealth of information on Olomouc and the surrounding area (private rooms available, laundry service, ring doorbell at entryway to the right of the Charley Secondhand shop to get into Sokolská 1, mobile 777-570-730, www.cosycornerhostel.com, reservation@cosycornerhostel.com). The hostel also rents bicycles (100-200 Kč/day) and offers walking tours for guests.

Eating in Olomouc

Try the sour, foul-smelling, yet beloved specialty of the Haná region, Olomouc cheese sticks *(olomoucké tvarůžky)*. The milk goes through a process of natural maturation under chunks of meat. Czechs figure there are two types of people in the world: *tvarůžky* lovers and sane people. The *tvarůžky* are so much a part of the Haná and Czech identity that when the European Union tried to forbid the product, the Czech government negotiated for special permission to continue to rot their milk. Zip a few of these stinkers into a baggie, and you can count on getting a train compartment to yourself.

RESTAURANTS

$$$ Moravská Restaurace ("Moravian Restaurant"), on the Upper Square, is the one touristy place in town. If you're feeling homesick, step into this cozy, woody space, and you'll see happy tourists attracted by ads all over town, "authentic" Moravian folk costumes on the waiters, walls decorated with Moravian painted ceramics... and prices that will make you feel like you're back at home (daily 11:30-23:00, reservations recommended, Horní Náměstí, tel. 585-222-868, www.moravskarestaurace.cz).

$$ Restaurant Vila Primavesi, to the left of St. Michael's Church, is located in a renovated, classy Art Nouveau villa—arguably one of Moravia's finest. The creative menu is rich in fish and Italian fare (the owner is Italian), and they have daily specials and a good wine selection. Seating is either inside, with ironed tablecloths, or on the terrace overlooking the city park (daily 11:00-23:00, Univerzitní 7, tel. 585-204-852, mobile 777-749-288).

$$ Svatováclavský Pivovar ("St. Wenceslas Brewery") is justifiably popular. It features seven kinds of unpasteurized beer brewed on the premises; an extensive menu of unimaginative, stick-to-your ribs Czech dishes; and the first "beer spa" in Olomouc. Reservations are recommended for dinner (restaurant open daily 11:00-24:00 except Sun until 21:00; spa open daily 14:00-20:00; beer bath-1,000 Kč, 2,000 Kč/2 people; free Wi-Fi for customers, Mariánská 4, tel. 585-207-517, www.svatovaclavsky-pivovar.cz).

$$ Minipivovar Moritz, which brews fresh yeasty beer on-site, serves Bohemian cuisine and specialties from Galicia (the region of Poland just east of here). Dine in their atmospheric circa-1900 cellar or on the park-like square, in front of the dilapidated, picturesque Maria Theresa Gate. Taking its name from a German-Jewish industrialist (Moritz Fischer), it opened near a former syn-

Restaurant Price Code

I've assigned each eatery a price category, based on the average cost of a typical main course. Drinks, desserts, and splurge items (steak and seafood) can raise the price considerably. I've given *very* rough conversions to dollars using 25 Kč = $1.

$$$$ **Splurge:** Most main courses over 500 Kč (roughly $20)

$$$ **Pricier:** 250-500 Kč ($10-20)

$$ **Moderate**: 120-250 Kč ($5-10)

$ **Budget:** Under 120 Kč ($5)

In the Czech Republic, a pub, basic sit-down eatery, and less-touristy café or teahouse is **$**; a typical restaurant—or a fancy café with coffee over 50 Kč and tea over 100 Kč—is **$$**; an upscale restaurant is **$$$**; and a swanky splurge is **$$$$**.

agogue in 2006 (precisely 100 years after the death of the man responsible for developing Olomouc into a modern manufacturing center). Today Moritz is one of the trendiest places in town. Head down to the basement to check out the kosher beer-making process, the unique *pivovod* (system of beer pipes that leads under the street to the outdoor bar on the square), and the portrait of Moritz's grandmother, who set the standard for hospitality that the owners hope to match (daily 11:00-23:00, on Palachovo Náměstí at Nešverova 2, tel. 585-205-560, reservations recommended in the evenings, www.hostinec-moritz.cz).

$ Mekáč (McDonald's), on the Upper Square, is filled with teenagers and moms with kids during the week. On a weekend, you can sit here and watch folks from the countryside, dressed in their Sunday best and coming to town for a "Bikmek" taste of the world.

$ Centrum Česká Jídelna ("Czech Eatery") is ideal if you're short on time and want some local-style fast food. They offer a world of traditional Czech dishes, ready and warmed, as well as an array of sandwiches and salads. Choose your meal by pointing at what you want (Mon-Fri 6:30-18:00, Sat 7:30-12:00, closed Sun, directly opposite the astronomical clock on the Upper Square).

$ Café Caesar, filling the Gothic vaults in the Town Hall, is a popular pizza place with fine outside seating within a flea's hop of the plague monument (daily 9:00-24:00, tel. 585-229-287). The little gallery next door, run by the café, promotes local artists.

$$ Café Restaurant Konvikt is a modern-feeling place in the delightfully restored former Jesuit college. They cater primarily to businessmen, though some philosophy students also wander in here from the classrooms upstairs. In summer, they offer seating in a peaceful courtyard above the city walls and greenbelt (daily 11:00-24:00, Univerzitní 3, tel. 585-631-190).

$ The Crack Irish Pub, under red-brick vaulted ceilings inside the city wall barracks, doubles as a Nepalese restaurant with an eat-what-you-can weekday lunch buffet for an incredible 110 Kč (restaurant open daily 11:00-22:00, pub stays open later, Mlýnská 4, tel. 585-208-428).

CAFÉS AND TEAHOUSES
Olomouc is the Moravian university town, and every aspect of student life (except sleeping) happens right in the old center. Being a student town, Olomouc is lively and cheap during the school year but slower in July, August, and September (although foreign students coming here for summer programs in languages, music, and history are doing their best to make up for the annual vacation energy drain).

$ **Café Mahler,** on the Upper Square, is a stylish place for coffee and cake (Mon-Sat 8:00-22:00, Sun 10:00-21:00, mobile 605-279-012), while **Cukrárna Madlen,** between the Upper Square and the Lower Square, is the local ice-cream paradise (daily 9:00-21:00).

$ **Café 87** has the longest list of espresso drinks, iced coffees, frappés, pancakes, and desserts in town. The handful of Olomouc expats converge here daily just before lunch to have the chocolate cake, which is heavenly but highly addictive (daily 10:00-19:00, between the art and natural-history museums on Náměstí Republiky, tel. 585-202-593).

$ **Kratochvíle Teahouse** offers a wide array of freshly harvested tea leaves, as well as coffee, Moravian wines, and the increasingly popular hookahs (water pipes). This contemplative, bamboo-lined space also hosts exhibitions, concerts, and author readings (Mon-Fri 11:00-23:00, Sat-Sun 15:00-23:00, Sokolská 36, mobile 603-564-120).

Olomouc Connections

Olomouc is on several major rail lines (including the one from Prague to Kraków). Three companies serve the Prague-Olomouc route. The Czech railway's Pendolino trains are fastest. But the private companies are also worth considering: LEO Express is the most comfortable and RegioJet serves the best (free) coffee. For bus and train schedules, see www.idos.cz.

From Olomouc by Train to: Kroměříž (hourly, 1-1.5 hours, transfer in Hulín), **Prague** (at least hourly, 2-3 hours), **Brno** (buses and trains at least hourly, 1.5 hours), **Rožnov pod Radhoštěm** (7/day, most connections require transfer in Valašské Meziříčí, allow 2 hours total; also consider bus), **Břeclav** (10/day, 2 hours, may transfer in Brno or Přerov), **Kraków** (5/day, 4.5-6 hours, transfer in Katowice, Poland, and possibly Přerov, Czech Republic; one

5-hour overnight train), **Vienna** (8/day, 3-4 hours, transfer in Brno, Břeclav, or Přerov), **Budapest** (6/day, 5-8 hours, transfer in Brno or Přerov).

From Olomouc by Bus to: Třeboň, Telč, and **Třebíč**—take the bus or train to **Brno** (listed earlier), then take the bus in the direction of **České Budějovice** (3/day Mon-Fri, 2/day Sat-Sun—see page 338 for connections out of České Budějovice), **Rožnov pod Radhoštěm** (hourly, 2 hours, most with change in Valašské Meziříčí).

Near Olomouc: Kroměříž

Whereas Olomouc was the official seat of the Moravian archbishops, Kroměříž (KROH-myehr-eezh) was the site of their lavish summer château. In 1948, this castle and its enormous gardens were nationalized and opened to the public. Kroměříž—showing off the richness of this corner of the Czech Republic—is the most lavish and best-renovated Rococo castle in the country. The 19th-century English-style park, with lakes, woods, and Chinese pavilions, is good for a walk or picnic.

While there are no other worthwhile sights in town, the pleasant square and streets filled with little bakeries offer a perfect complement to the grandeur of the archbishop's estate. The town and château of Kroměříž combine for a perfect half-day excursion from Olomouc, a wonderful opportunity to enjoy the genteel art and gentle life of small-town Moravia.

GETTING THERE

From Olomouc, take one of the frequent trains in the direction of Přerov and Břeclav (hourly, 7:20 or 9:20 train is convenient). Get off at Hulín (the stop after Přerov on fast trains, 45 minutes), walk through the train station to the other side of the building, and hop on the small motor train to Kroměříž (departure scheduled to coincide with the arrival of Břeclav-bound trains, 8 minutes). Turn right out of the train station, then take the first left over the bridge. The main square (Velké Náměstí) and the entrance to the château are an easy 10-minute walk away.

On the way back, most trains from Kroměříž to Hulín connect with an Olomouc-bound train. For bus and train schedules, see www.idos.cz.

Orientation to Kroměříž

TOURIST INFORMATION

The TI is on the main square, next to City Hall, and hands out a useful map with brief descriptions of all major sights, as well as a list of events (Mon-Fri 8:30-17:00, Sat Sun 9:00-13:00, open weekdays until 16:00 May-Sept, closed Sun Oct-April, Velké Náměstí 115, tel. 573-321-408, www.kromeriz.eu).

HELPFUL HINTS

Music: Throughout the summer, the city government joins forces with art schools and conservatories to enliven historical spaces with weekly concerts. The quality of the performers and the unique setting—in château halls and gardens—make a visit worthwhile (ticket booking and purchase at the TI on Velké Náměstí). The **Kroměříž Music Summer Festival** is in September (tel. 573-341-400).

Wi-Fi: The **TI** offers Internet access (first 15 minutes free). **DC Internet Café,** located on the main square, is right below the town museum (40 Kč/hour, Mon-Fri 10:00-19:00, Sat-Sun 13:00-19:00, Velké Náměstí 39).

OLOMOUC

Sights in Kroměříž

Archbishop's Château (Arcibiskupský Zámek)

Dominating the main square and the whole town, this château was rebuilt in Baroque style by archbishop Karel Lichtenstein (dubbed

the "Moravian Richelieu") after an earlier castle was severely damaged in the Swedish siege during the Thirty Years' War. The furniture and decorations are in the Rococo style (from the second half of the 18th century). The breathtaking chandeliers are made of Czech crystal.

The château is famous for one historic event: The Austrian parliament moved here from unstable Vienna during the tumultuous year of 1848, when a wave of revolutions spread across the Habsburg lands. The Parliament drafted the first Austrian constitution in the château's main hall.

Cost and Hours: Château-140 Kč or more (by tour only— see below), art gallery-90 Kč, tower-50 Kč; May-Sept Tue-Sun 9:00-17:00, closed Mon; April and Oct Sat-Sun 9:00-16:00, closed

Mon-Fri; closed Nov-March; tel. 573-502-011, www.zamek-kromeriz.cz.

Tours: You can see the art gallery (described next) and climb the tower on your own, but to visit the château interior, you must go with a guide. It's 140 Kč to join a Czech-speaking group; you can ask for an English-language tour—but be aware that you'll pay double, and you might be the only one on the tour. Tours run about every hour and last 70 minutes, with the time about evenly split between the first floor (eight rooms) and second floor (which has a beautifully painted ceiling depicting the history of the bishopric, and overlooks a stunning library interior with 80,000 books).

Art Gallery: Art lovers should consider visiting the bishop's art gallery. Sure, it's not the Louvre, but it's the best Moravian collection of European paintings from 1400 to 1800, with works by Titian, Lucas Cranach, Albrecht Dürer, and Paolo Veronese.

Castle Garden (Podzámecká Zahrada)

This green space, filled with little ponds, exotic trees, and Chinese pavilions, offers a peaceful refuge. It's in the English style—wilder and more natural than the geometrically designed French gardens.

Cost and Hours: Free, July-Aug daily 5:30-20:30; May-June and Sept Tue-Sun 9:00-17:00, closed Mon; April and Oct Sat-Sun only, closed Mon-Fri; closed Nov-March.

Sleeping and Eating in Kroměříž

Kroměříž works best as a day trip from Olomouc, but if you want to attend a concert and stay the night, try **$ Hotel Bouček.** This well-renovated, traditional townhouse on the main square rents 11 decent rooms (Velké Náměstí 108, tel. 573-342-777, www.hotelboucek.cz, hotel.boucek@seznam.cz).

Several good eateries are on or just off the main square (Velké Náměstí).

$ Bistro u Zámku is a popular place to sip a frappé or iced coffee (daily, on the corner of main square next to the château).

$$ Zámecká Myslivna ("Château Hunting Lodge") specializes in game. Your venison might have been shot by the archbishop, who still comes here during the summer (daily 11:00-22:00 except Fri-Sat until 24:00, just off main square, Sněmovní Náměstí 41).

$$ Radniční Kavárna is perfect if you want to eat on cushioned chairs outside, because it's a bit stuffy inside (daily 9:00-22:00, at top of main square across street from Town Hall).

$ Bistro Avion, a blue-collar self-service cafeteria on the main square, is good for a basic, filling meal (Mon-Fri 6:00-18:00, Sat 8:00-15:00, Sun 7:00-14:00). The place has no menu—just point to what looks good, and wash it down with Slovakia's best beer, Zlatý Bažant ("Golden Pheasant").

Near Olomouc: Wallachia

About an hour east of Olomouc, the mountainous region of Wallachia (vah-LAH-chee-ah)—where Slovakia and Poland meet the eastern edge of the Czech Republic—is ideal for an escape into nature. Here you can enjoy both the ruggedness of the mountains and the easy tourist facilities of an accessible recreational area.

Wallachia (Valašsko) comprises three east-west ridges separating three long valleys. The Beskydy Mountains—the westernmost part of the Carpathian mountain range—make an impressive backdrop.

Wallachia has a sparse but proud population: the Wallachians (Valaši). They were originally Romanian shepherds who, following their sheep, drifted west along the pristine meadows and rugged canyons of the hauntingly beautiful Carpathians. In exchange for guarding the border, these shepherds received many privileges—most importantly, exemption from taxes.

Today, the Wallachians have their own tongue-in-cheek, tax-free "kingdom." In local restaurants and hotels, you can buy Wallachian "passports," which come with a brochure explaining in English why you should emigrate. The 90 Kč is a small price to pay for a passport when you consider that it frees you from the far-reaching clutches of the IRS.

For the easiest and quickest foray into this region, visit the pretty, touristy village of Štramberk, which sits at the edge of Wallachia. For greater immersion into this region, venture to the open-air folk museum at Rožnov pod Radhoštěm, and hang your hiking boots at the hilltop refuge called Pustevny.

GETTING AROUND WALLACHIA

This region is best with a car, though it is doable by public transportation. From Olomouc, the closest major transit hub, it's at least 1.5 hours by train to Štramberk and 2-2.5 hours by train or bus to

OLOMOUC

Rožnov pod Radhoštěm. From Rožnov, you can catch a 45-minute direct bus to Pustevny (for details, see "Getting There" under each destination).

Štramberk

The endearing cover-girl village of Štramberk (SHTRAM-berk) is the delightful gateway to wild Wallachia. Štramberk dates way back—remains in the nearby Šipka Cave suggest there was a Neanderthal settlement here as far back as 40,000 B.C.—but today it's a sleepy tourist town, ideal for a low-impact, stretch-your-legs lunch stop. Sitting just a few minutes' drive off of the expressway (between Olomouc and Ostrava, near the border with Poland), it offers an enticing and accessible glimpse at the region.

The **TI** is in the big House of Culture (Kulturní Dům) near the main parking lot (Zauličí 456, tel. 558-840-617, www.stramberk. info).

Getting There: For **drivers,** Štramberk is well-marked from the D-1 expressway east of Olomouc. Approaching town, follow the one main road as it curls around the base of the hill. Most spaces near the main square are reserved for locals (and are scrupulously monitored by overeager cops), so it's safest to park in the large public lot at the far end of town (near the House of Culture/Kulturní Dům, which houses the TI). From there, walk back along the main road 10 minutes to the square.

To get to Štramberk without a car, take a **train** from Olomouc to Studénka (1 hour, may require a transfer), then hop on the hourly spur line to Štramberk (30 minutes). While the town is pretty, I wouldn't bother making the trip by public transportation.

Visiting Štramberk: The hamlet is huddled tightly against the base of a forested hill. The sloped main square boasts a quaint gurgling fountain, watched over by a postcard-perfect Baroque church with a pink onion dome. A short but steep hike brings you to the crest of the hill and Štramberk's "castle"—really more of a rustic defensive tower, called the Trúba. You can pay a modest fee to spiral up to the tower's summit for cozy views of a square hemmed in by rolling countryside.

Other than the tower climb and a few tacky amusements, there's not much to see or do in Štramberk; just let your pulse slow and enjoy its tranquil (if touristy) square. Several decent restaurants ring the square, including the Městský Pivovar ("Town

Brewery"), serving its own unfiltered Trubač beer. Save room for the local temptation—"Štramberk ears" *(Štramberské uši)*, a soft, flat gingerbread cookie rolled into a cone shape (sometimes filled with whipped cream and fruit). While munching, try not to be turned off by their gruesome origin story: During the Tatar incursions in 1241, invaders would lop off the ears of their victims as trophies to be brought back to the Khan. But after clever locals broke a dam and flooded the enemy camp, the Tatars were driven away, leaving bags of ears behind.

Rožnov pod Radhoštěm

Rožnov pod Radhoštěm (ROHZH-novh pohd rahd-hosh-tyem), the largest town in the region and once a popular spa resort, may not be worth an overnight stay, but it certainly merits a visit for its Wallachian Open-Air Folk Museum.

Getting There: To reach Rožnov pod Radhoštěm by train or bus from Olomouc, you'll need to transfer in Valašské Meziříčí (7 trains/day, allow 2 hours total; hourly bus, 2-2.5 hours). From Rožnov's main square, it's a 10-minute walk to the museum (look for direction markers).

▲Wallachian Open-Air Folk Museum (Valašské Muzeum v Přírodě)

The museum, which re-creates a traditional Wallachian village, is divided into three parts. Touring the "Little Wooden Town" is

sufficient to give you a good sense of Eastern European mountain architecture, which blends here with elements of Moravian house-building. The museum is also the resting place for the most distinguished Wallachians, among them the incredible runner Emil Zátopek, who won three gold medals at the Helsinki Olympics in 1952.

Cost and Hours: 180 Kč for all three parts; May-Sept daily 9:00-17:00; April Tue-Sun 9:00-17:00, closed Mon; Jan-March and Oct Tue-Sun 9:00-16:00, closed Mon; closed most of Nov and part of Dec (www.vmp.cz).

Tours: Although you can visit the complex on your own, you can more fully appreciate the sight with an English-speaking guide—call a few days ahead to reserve (400 Kč for an hour-long tour, reserve at tel. 571-757-111 between 6:00 and 14:00, or email prohlidka@vmp.cz).

Pustevny

Pustevny (POO-stehv-nee, "Hermitage") is a small, pleasant resort atop the Beskydy (BEH-skih-dee) Mountains' most sacred ridge, in a spot where a legendary hermit once lived. The style of the mountain huts here is an imaginative combination of Art Nouveau and wooden village architecture. Peak season is June through August for hiking, and Christmas through Easter for skiing. During other months restaurants are open only on weekends.

Getting There: To get to Pustevny by **public transportation,** take a direct bus from Rožnov pod Radhoštěm (4/day, 45 minutes, stop is marked *Prostřední Bečva/ Pustevny*).

If you're **driving,** you can reach the summit either from the south via Rožnov pod Radhoštěm and Prostřední Bečva, or from the north via Frenštát pod Radhoštěm and Trojanovice (which is linked to Pustevny by a scenic chairlift). From Frenštát, follow signs for Trojanovice, drive to the end of the road at the Ráztoka Hotel, then walk 500 yards to find the chairlift (50 Kč one-way, 80 Kč round-trip, in summer runs daily once an hour 9:00-18:00, off-season until 16:00, 15-minute ride). On arrival in Pustevny, be sure to check the schedule for the last chairlift back down to Trojanovice.

Hiking in Pustevny: The 30-minute hike from Pustevny along the red-marked trail on the ridge toward the west will take you to a statue of Radegast, the old Slavic god of sun, friendship, and harvest. If you hike farther along the ridge for two miles, you'll reach the top of the sacred Radhošť mountain and statues of the Slavic ninth-century missionaries St. Cyril and St. Methodius. They hold a page of the beginning of the Gospel according to John, which they translated for the Slavic

people more than 1,100 years ago. A wooden church dedicated to these two patrons of all Slavs stands behind the statue.

Hiking along the ridge from Pustevny in the opposite direction takes you through less-visited woods and into a virgin forest preserve at Kněhyně.

Sleeping and Eating in Pustevny: A century-old historical landmark, **$ Hotel Maměnka** fits sumptuously furnished rooms into a wooden structure that uniquely blends Art Nouveau with regional architecture (tel. 556-836-207, mobile 736-682-289, www.libusin-mamenka.cz, libusin@libusin-mamenka.cz). Its **Koliba Valaška** annex, with similar rooms, is an opulent imitation of a shepherd's lodge. The complex has two restaurants: The famous Art Nouveau **Restaurant Libušín,** which burnt down in 2014, is slated to open in 2019 after a thorough, beam-by-beam reconstruction. **$$ Restaurant Koliba** serves mountain fare in a traditional setting.

$ Hotel Tanečnica, large and modern, is a solid, standard, circa-1980 Czech mountain lodge (Db-1,250 Kč, swimming pool, pay parking, tel. 556-835-341, www.hoteltanecnica.cz, hoteltanecnica@seznam.cz). The nearby **$ Koliba u Záryša** restaurant, with a more down-to-earth, scruffy shepherd's-hut setting than Restaurant Koliba, serves Wallachian food (such as cabbage soup and the pan-Carpathian specialty *halušky*—potato and flour gnocchi with sheep cheese and bacon) as well as the owner/cook's imaginative creations (such as oven-baked *živáňská pečeně*—a mixture of beef tenderloin, pork, or lamb in spices, wine, and vegetables).

OLOMOUC

MIKULOV WINE REGION

Mikulov • Pavlov and the Pálava Hills • Lednice and Valtice

Blessed by a warm climate and limestone geology, the Mikulov region produces the Czech Republic's most famous wines. Like the spine of a colossal humpback whale, the limestone ridge of the Pálava Hills rises out of the fertile alluvial plains of the Morava and Thaya rivers. Some 40,000 years ago, this region's inhabitants made the world's first-ever ceramic sculpture: the voluptuous Venus of Věstonice. The area has been continuously inhabited since. Slavs founded their first state from here, and for good reason: This is a land where it's said the wine flows from the tap and plums fall from the sky. To back up their word the Moravians generously share their riches: Whether in a chance encounter or as a paying guest, you will soon find out that the people here are dedicated to matter-of-fact, non-intrusive hospitality.

At the southern end of the ridge, the historic town of **Mikulov,** long the cultural center of South Moravia, has the look and

feel of an Italian hill town—and some particularly vivid artifacts of a rich Jewish heritage. Seven miles north, on the slopes of the 300-yard-high "hump" of Děvín Hill, the village of **Pavlov** boasts unique rustic architecture and hillside wine cellars. To the east, straddling the banks of the Thaya, the **Lednice-Valtice** complex of two châteaux and 19th-century English-style parks is one of the largest man-made landscapes in Europe. The glistening white Lednice Château is the ideal starting point for exploring the area's meandering waterways, oak- and cypress-dotted meadows, and romantic structures. Bordered by parks on one side, the town of Valtice is encircled by vine-yards on the other. The deep cellars of its château hide the country's official wine salon—with all regions represented—while a local winery has become one of the country's largest brands. The Iron Curtain that once loomed on the hill just above town, separating Czechoslovakia from Austria, is thoughtfully documented.

As this area is right off the main highway and rail line between Prague/Brno and Vienna/Bratislava, it's a natural stop for those traveling from the core of the Czech Republic to Austria or Hungary. While popular with Czech, Slovak, and Austrian holiday makers, this region remains relatively undiscovered by American tourists—adding to its many charms.

CHOOSING A HOME BASE

Mikulov or Pavlov are both fine home base from which to explore the region. Mikulov's advantages are its hillside setting, cultured small-town feel, and restaurants and wine bars. Pavlov's romantic upper street is best at dusk when vintners serve wines directly by their cellars; you'll be glad to be in stumbling distance of your bed.

GETTING AROUND THE MIKULOV WINE REGION

The main railway junction of Břeclav is the gateway to the Mikulov wine region, whether you come through as a public transit transfer point or stop here to rent a car or bike. For bus and train schedules, see www.idos.cz.

By Train from Břeclav to: Mikulov (10/day, 30 minutes, goes through Valtice), **Valtice** (10/day, 15 minutes), **Lednice** (on summer weekends, a cute historical train runs 4/day, 20 minutes), **Prague** (9/day direct, 3 hours), **Olomouc** (10/day, 2 hours, may transfer in Brno or Přerov), **Vienna** (5/day, 1 hour).

By Bus from Břeclav to: Mikulov (10/day Mon-Fri, 5/day Sat-Sun, 1 hour), **Lednice** (10/day Mon-Fri, 5/day Sat-Sun, 15 minutes), **Pavlov** (10/day Mon-Fri, 5/day Sat-Sun, 45 minutes), **Prague** (1-2/hour, fewer on weekends, 5-6 hours, train is better—see above).

By Car: Although it's perfectly feasible to connect these destinations by public transportation, a car speeds things up substantially. Mikulov, Pavlov, Lednice, and Valtice form a handy little rectangle, each about 10-15 minutes' drive from the next. This makes it easy to home-base in one and side-trip to the others. Get a good map. You can pick up a rental car in Břeclav (see "Helpful Hints," next page). This is especially handy if you're arriving in the Czech Republic by train from Vienna or Budapest and want to rent a car.

By Bike: Many Czechs—and even more Austrians—connect their Mikulov area wine-cellar visits by bicycle. To bike on

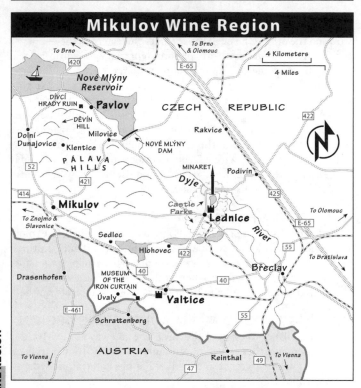

Mikulov Wine Region

flat terrain, stay within the Břeclav-Lednice-Valtice parks complex. From Valtice to Mikulov expect small hills, and out of Mikulov to Pavlov there is one gradual climb. From Pavlov to Lednice is level terrain. Figure about 35 miles for a full-day circuit connecting Valtice, Mikulov, Pavlov, and Lednice; starting in Břeclav adds another ten miles. Also consider side-tripping to the nearby hillside winemaking villages of Bavory, Perná, and Věstonice. Bike paths, both paved and gravel, are well-marked and filled with bikers who can provide needed directions or assistance. Bikes are allowed on trains.

For bike rentals, see "Helpful Hints," next.

HELPFUL HINTS

Exchange Rate: 25 Kč = about $1

Country Calling Code: 420 (see page 464 for dialing instructions)

Bike Rental: Reserve ahead in summer (particularly on weekends). Figure about 300-400 Kč/day depending on bike quality. Bikes come in all varieties—specify your preferences when you reserve.

MIKULOV WINE REGION

Taxis: Catch one in front of the Břeclav train station. In or around Mikulov, call Patrik Špiřík (775-959-295).

In Břeclav: Get to Břeclav early, drop your luggage at the train station baggage check, and walk (or taxi) up the main street to one of two places that rent bikes: the **TI** (U Tržiště 8, tel. 519-326-290, tic@ticbreclav.cz) or **Cyklosfera Café** (Pod Zámkem 3, mobile 774-027-549, http://cyklosfera.cz) in the park by the Břeclav castle. For the TI, follow the green *TI* sign to the left after about a mile. For Cyklosfera, go farther along the main street past an intersection, then continue on a bike path for another 300 yards.

In Mikulov: **Cyklopomoc** is a very friendly bike repair and rental shop (daily 8:30-18:00, Pavlovská 24, mobile 773-523-120, www.funmorava.cz). Recommended **Hotel Templ** also rents bikes.

In Pavlov: The most professional service in the region with the widest selection is provided by the Brno-based **Rent-bike.** Currently they distribute bikes and electrobikes only out of Penzion Nad Jezerem in Pavlov, but they may soon open a branch in Mikulov (23 Dubna 165e, www.rentbike.cz).

In Valtice: **Cykloráj** rents bikes and sells sport equipment in a purpose-built facility just across the big intersection off the main square (tel. 539-050-773, mobile 605-983-978, http://cykloraj.com).

Car Rental: The **Bors** rental office in Břeclav is convenient and rents Renaults (from 900-1,300 Kč/day, includes insurance, Mon-Fri 8:00-17:00, Sat 8:00-11:00, closed Sun, tel. 519-444-241, mobile 731-606-243, www.bors.cz). To get to Bors from Břeclav's train station, it's a quick taxi ride (under 50 Kč) or a 10-minute walk (exit train station into park, turn left, walk along main street past the post office, go under a railway bridge, and find the Bors Renault dealership next door to the gas station).

Local Guides: Barbora Hammond, based in Valtice, guides individuals on bikes or by foot. With her insights on local customs, nature, and architecture, she makes the wine region's dreamy landscapes come alive (500 Kč/hour, tel. 519-353-221, mobile 728-983-858, barboraham@gmail.com).

Mikulov

An important border town on the ancient "Amber Road" from the Baltic Sea to the Adriatic, Mikulov (MEE-kuh-lohv; think "Mikulov, not war") was briefly the unofficial capital of Moravia. When the Austrian kings expelled the Jews from Austria in the early 1400s, they settled here on the border. As Jews in Moravia were soon forced to find

protection in towns under aristocratic (rather than royal) jurisdiction, aristocrat-ruled Mikulov further grew. Jewish philosopher and scholar Judah Loew ben Bezalel—the famous Rabbi Loew—was the head Moravian rabbi here in the 16th century before moving to Prague. In 1835, Mikulov's 3,500 Jewish residents made up half the town's population and formed the largest Jewish community in what is now the Czech Republic outside of Prague. When the railway line to Vienna bypassed Mikulov a few years later, the town was fated to a stagnation that mercifully protected it from Industrial Age construction.

Set between two hills that act as twin viewpoints—and with a beautifully restored main square dotted with cafés and wine bars—Mikulov today is the cultural hub of South Moravia. It's an almost startlingly beautiful and sophisticated-feeling town, with a tight and tidy cobbled core of pretty pastel buildings, huddled under a grand château. The main square exudes a certain gentility, with ivy-blanketed buildings, thoughtfully tended flower boxes, pristine gurgling fountains, and bubbly Baroque sculptures. A piano sits under the arches at the bottom part of the square for anyone to play. And tucked behind the hill are the town's Jewish sights, including a newly renovated synagogue and a soulful cemetery.

TOURIST INFORMATION

The TI on the main square is a wealth of information about the entire region. They have good biking information and can help you arrange accommodations (Mon-Fri 8:00-18:00, Sat-Sun 9:00-18:00; shorter hours and closed Sat-Sun off-season; public computer—small fee, Náměstí 1, tel. 519-510-855, www.mikulov.cz).

ARRIVAL IN MIKULOV

The train and bus stations are right next to each other, a little over a half-mile south of town. To reach Mikulov's main square, you can either walk along Nádražní street toward the hilltop château, take a taxi, or ride bus #550 or #585 bus for two stops.

Sights in Mikulov

The major sights in Mikulov are scattered between its hills and the town square. I've connected them with easy up-and-down walking directions.

Main Square

Start in the upper part of the main square. Stand near the TI, between the plague column and the fountain. The **Holy Trinity Column** in the middle of the square is a fine piece of late Baroque sculpture.

Look up at Holy Hill with the Church of St. Sebastian at the top (to reach this panoramic spot from the main square, follow the blue-marked trail down the alley and then past the Stations of the Cross). On the first Sunday in September, this is the destination of the annual pilgrimage to the **Black Madonna of Mikulov** (a statue of the Virgin Mary based on the famous Black Madonna of Loreto, Italy). The Madonna is housed in the large **Church of St. Wenceslas**—you can see its onion dome (with a big clock face) jutting up above the square. Inside, you can also visit the ossuary in the church's crypt (free; church open July-Aug daily 10:00-12:00 & 13:00-18:00; Sept-June only during Mass Sun at 8:00, Tue at 17:30, and Thu at 7:00; mobile 605-900-544).

At the foot of the square—between you and the Holy Hill—stands a prominent, Italian-feeling, churchlike building, the **Tomb of the Dietrichstein Family.** These aristocrats ruled Mikulov from the 16th century to 1945 (60 Kč, daily June-Sept 9:00-18:00, April-May and Oct 10:00-17:00, closed Nov-March).

Above the square is the town's **château.** The original castle burned down at the end of World War II and was rebuilt in 1950, so it lacks the period interiors of neighboring châteaux in Valtice and Lednice and isn't worth the price of admission.

• *From the top of the square, step into the first castle courtyard (free to enter). Note the wrought-iron gate and coat-of-arms of the Dietrichstein family, with two vintners' knives in the center. Walk through the castle's small park, past a fountain, and take the switchback trail toward the castle. As you gain altitude, the surrounding countryside comes into view.*

You'll circle gradually around behind the castle. After passing the stout round tower, continue ahead 30 yards and take the staircase that

MIKULOV WINE REGION

Mikulov Wines

Czech wine is more than just a drink—it's a way of life. Although the Moravians might not have captured the sweetness of the Portuguese varieties, they did manage to ferment the taste of grapes into their own authentic culture. Without experiencing the wine tradition of southern Moravia, you will have missed a good part of the country's spirit.

Wine has been made in the Mikulov region since Roman times. Because no Roman soldier would fight without his daily two-liter ration of wine, and because it was difficult to transport unpasteurized wine over long distances, the 10th legion of Marcus Aurelius planted its own vines on this region's limestone hills (which reminded them of their homes in Tuscany). The Slavs and the Germans found the vines long after the Romans were gone and continued the tradition. In the 16th century, Anabaptist refugees from Switzerland brought new energy to the winemaking process. Today, the warm climate and the soil rich in calcium (from the limestone) make the Mikulov region one of the best wine-producing areas in Eastern Europe.

The most commonly used grapes are ryzlink (riesling), veltlínské zelené (grüner veltliner), rulandské bílé (pinot blanc), chardonnay, and sauvignon for whites. Svatovavřinecké (St. Laurent), frankovka (blaufränkish, aka lemberger), and cabernet sauvignon are used for reds. The locally bred grapes are pálava and aurelius.

The variety of grape is only one factor that contributes to each wine's distinct taste. Vintners discern wines by the type of soil in which they grow; the orientation of the slope (which de-

descends down to Husova street—noticing the Star of David topping the tent-like red roof ahead of you. At the bottom of the stairs, enter the...

▲▲Synagogue

Gorgeously renovated from top to bottom (as part of the EU-funded "Ten Stars" project which improved synagogues around the country), Mikulov's upper synagogue is now a museum and a regional Jewish cultural center. Step inside the blueish, spiritually charged space to appreciate the unique design: a bema with oversized marble pillars that carry four finely carved ceiling cupolas, a lavish Baroque ark (rebuilt from scratch from old plans and photographs), and an upstairs gallery that lets you look down and take it all in. While the exhibits—pertaining to the history of the local community, including two panels on Rabbi Loew—are only

termines the amount of sun); and—most importantly—the sugar content. The best wines are from hand-picked late vintages, with sugar content reaching 27 percent.

The quirky local specialties are straw and ice wines. The grapes for straw wines mature in barns for months spread on dry straw. Ice wines—a Moravian and German specialty—are made from late-season grapes left to freeze while they are still on the vine. Since sugars and other solids do not freeze, pressing these grapes results in a small amount of concentrated, sweet wine. As these two wines are very difficult to make—the process is practically alchemy, and even the best vintners cannot predict which grapes will turn into a good straw or ice wine—they are also the most expensive. A tiny .3-liter bottle (about 10 oz.) costs more than 700 Kč.

The communists mismanaged wine production by planting bad shoots prone to diseases. Over the last 20 years, vintners have replaced most of these old vines with younger, better-quality ones. Moravian wines improve from year to year. Look for vintages from odd years—in the past decade these have been better than even years. Among older vintages, 2007 was outstanding.

The wine salon in the basement of Valtice Château offers tastings and promotes 100 wines that have been chosen by experts as the best in the Czech Republic (see page 423). And the town of Pavlov is home to many small vintners as well as a few prominent—although still relatively small—wine companies like Reisten, the exclusive supplier to Prague's luxury restaurants and the president of the Czech Republic (see page 418).

in Czech, you can pick up a blue plastic folder with English translations as you enter.

Cost and Hours: 50 Kč, Tue-Sun 9:00-18:00, closed Mon, shorter hours off-season.

• *Exiting the synagogue, turn right on Husova street. Where you emerge at the little square, turn left, then veer right and uphill, following the brown* Židovský hřbitov *sign.*

Jewish Cemetery

Buy your ticket at the white, Baroque-frilled Ceremonial Hall (which houses several small exhibits on the history and customs of the local Jewish community). Then continue up into the extremely evocative cemetery, peacefully filling the hillside. It's larger and less crowded—

both with graves and with tourists—than the one in Prague. The oldest tombstone dates from 1603.

Cost and Hours: 30 Kč; June-Sept daily 10:00-18:00; April-May and Oct Tue-Sun until, closed Mon; closed Nov-March; Hřbitovní Náměstí, tel. 519-510-388.

• *Upon leaving the cemetery, veer to the hillside on a small street, then turn left up a narrow staircase to walk up to the brick tower on the adjacent **Kozí Hrádek** hilltop—offering fine views over Mikulov and into Austria. From here, walk down the narrow staircase back to the main square. Or continue in the opposite direction toward **Turold Hill** for a magnificent eight-mile hike along the Pálava Ridge to Pavlov (see below).*

NEAR MIKULOV
▲Hiking in the Mikulov-Pavlov Hills

The Pálave Nature Preserve packs an incredible amount of biological and geological diversity into a small area. For a highly enjoyable, vista-filled seven-mile hike through a protected natural area filled with limestone formations, hillside meadows, vineyards, forests, and castle ruins, consider the red-and-white-marked trail from Mikulov to Pavlov.

Before heading out, pick up picnic supplies in the recommended Sojka & Spol store on the main square. On the opposite end of the square, walk up the steps to the **Kozí Hrádek** ("Goat Castle") ruins. On the other side of the ruins, the trail gently descends into a newer part of town. Continue straight along a residential street, and after an intersection, turn left on a path leading up to **Turold Hill,** topped with a radio tower. After a short descent, the trail briefly skirts a vineyard along the Mikulov-Pavlov country road. On the right, appreciate the rare limestone geology of the craggy outcrop known as Cats' Rocks.

Just as you turn left off the road on a footpath to scale the Stolová Hora ("Table Hill"), consider stopping for a snack at the Wild West-themed **Pony Ranch** (look for the Confederate flag some 20 yards after the turnoff—the owners' idea of a symbol for "American country life," open daily May-Oct). First you only see a scrub of bushes, but as you walk through this natural palisade, you enter a hidden, white-cliff-enclosed gulch seemingly fitted for a Western movie set: a horse-filled corral in the middle, a two-story saloon at the far end, and a beer-and-sausage kitchen shack on the side. No movie was ever shot here. Rather, the Pony Ranch is part of an Old West-inspired Czech phenomenon that began in the 1930s but really took off in the 1970s (when the political situation turned from bad to worse). With the barbed wire of the Iron Curtain scratching the southern edge of town, locals were reminded daily that they lived in a prison, rather than a free land. As if to say, "You can trap our bodies but not our spirits," hundreds of similar Western-themed stage sets popped up around the country. On Fridays locals rushed here to live, and on Sundays they returned to town to survive. The authorities didn't mind these tiny Americas...as long as they kept the people quiet. The strategy seemingly worked—until 1989. Today the scruffy Pony Ranch is run by a friendly Mikulov couple in their sixties who seem to never have left their 1980s paradise. You may be the first flesh-and-blood American to stumble upon their campfire.

As you reach the meadow-covered **Stolová Hora,** survey the land. Here you are at Europe's crucial geopolitical juncture: The mountain range rising in the east is the beginning of the Carpathians, while to the south—on a clear day—you can see the Alps. In between these two principal mountain ranges of Europe, the grey-green **Danube River** dashes southeast. For millennia, cultures and armies followed it in either direction. Four centuries ago, the Turks ruled in Budapest, while the Habsburgs desperately clung to Vienna. Today, three country capitals straddle its banks within 100 miles of here.

Consider the contrasting energy policies: South of the border you see a sea of wind farms, while due west notice the four cooling towers of the Dukovany nuclear plant rising like mushrooms on the horizon. Austrians have always been opposed to nuclear energy, while Czech politicians are still expanding this Soviet legacy, although no permanent storage place for waste has been found in the country.

Descend toward the Sirotčí Hrádek **castle ruin** (one of many ancient fortifications along the ridge where, ever since Neolithic times, people from surrounding countryside took refuge during invasions). Just before the ruin itself, you have an option of turning down to the right to reach the village of **Klentnice,** with two good, sit-down restaurants (if you pass through the village, notice the rare monument to fallen Red Army soldiers in front of the church—with a cross in place of the typical star or hammer and sickle). Otherwise, continue along the trail to the ruins, then descend on the other side and touch the road at the far end of the village. After a small intersection, the trail turns into an oak, maple, and linden forest and eventually climbs to the radio tower-topped **Děvín Hill.** From here it's a sharp descent to **Dívčí Hrady** ("Maidens Castle"), a spectacularly set ruin over the village of Pavlov, and then—following the green-and-white marked path (a green line between white lines)—to **Pavlov** itself.

You can also do this hike in the opposite direction, but the initial ascent to Děvín Hill is steeper than the gradual climb from Mikulov. Buses run every hour in both directions.

Sleeping in Mikulov

($$$$ = Splurge, $$$ = Pricier, $$ = Moderate, $ = Budget)
Two of my recommended hotels lie along Husova street, in the heart of the former Jewish district under the castle, while the other one is near the Jewish Cemetery.

$$ Hotel Templ is situated in two delightfully restored houses, one Renaissance (with a former synagogue in the back), the other Art Nouveau (with a private garden). Each room is uniquely decorated, and all attic rooms have air-conditioning. Summer weekends book well ahead; on weekdays you may be able to land a room on short notice. An excellent restaurant is part of the business (apartment with fireplace—firewood provided, bike rental, pool, Husova 50, tel. 519-323-095, www.templ.cz, info@templ.cz).

$ Penzion Baltazar is a 19th-century house that uniquely preserves its historic spirit amid modern amenities (Husova 44, tel. 519-324-327, mobile 720-611-712, www.pensionbaltazar.cz, info@pensionbaltazar.cz).

¢ Penzion and Café Bárta is a family-run place with simple, clean rooms and an excellent café cuddling on the side of Kozí Hrádek hill. While the website is only in Czech, the owner speaks English as well as Hebrew (breakfast extra—available at the café; drivers park in the small square in front of the cemetary, then walk right; otherwise, from the upper end of the main square walk up the narrow staircase; mobile 608-833-821, www.penzion-mikulov.cz, info@penzion-mikulov.cz).

Eating in Mikulov

$$ Restaurant Templ, in the recommended Hotel Templ, serves the most exquisite food in town in an interior that combines ancient and modern—check out the synagogue-turned-conference room in the back. It is somewhat quiet and away from the action on the square.

$ Sojka & Spol is a trendy, spirited, family-run food store with an airy restaurant upstairs serving imaginative dishes, from creamy mushroom risotto to Thai curry (perfect for picnic supplies, Náměstí 10, tel. 518-327-862).

$ U Obřího Soudku ("By the Giant Keg"), just across the square, with two small rooms inside or on the square-side terrace, is the best choice for a more traditional Czech menu (daily 10:00-20:00, Náměstí 24, tel. 519-510-004).

$ Kafe Pala serves both sweet and savory buckwheat crêpes in a pleasant, secluded little Renaissance courtyard just off the main square (daily 9:00-20:00, mobile 775-699-990).

Dobrý Ročník ("Good Vintage Year") is an excellent wine bar on the main square.

Mikulov Connections

BY PUBLIC TRANSPORTATION

From Mikulov by Train to: Valtice (10/day, 15 minutes), Břeclav (10/day, 30 minutes; connect from here to Prague), Vienna (8/day, 2 hours, transfer in Břeclav).

From Mikulov by Bus to: Pavlov (10/day Mon-Fri, 5/day Sat-Sun, 20 minutes), Lednice (10/day Mon-Fri, 5/day Sat-Sun, 45 minutes), Břeclav (10/day Mon-Fri, 5/day Sat-Sun, 1 hour). For bus and train schedules, see www.idos.cz.

ROUTE TIPS FOR DRIVERS

From Mikulov to Pavlov: Mikulov sits just below the plateau of the Pálava Hills. The most scenic route to Pavlov is through the hills and vineyards; get careful directions in town for how to find the road (to avoid circling around via Milovice, which is easier driving but less scenic). Leaving town, you'll climb up into hills blanketed with cornfields and vines, and vineyards tucked beneath white limestone hills (while not exactly breathtaking, it's pleasant). Passing through the winemaking town of Klentnice, carefully track *Pavlov* signs. You'll cruise downhill, with vineyards all around and a big reservoir on the horizon, then come down through the top of Pavlov—a confusing spaghetti of narrow streets that suddenly become gravel wine roads; set your sights on the lower church tower, where you can park and hike up Česká street to explore the cellars. You can return to Mikulov the way you came.

From Pavlov to Lednice and Onward: Drop down on Pavlov's main street to the road that parallels the reservoir, turn right, and follow *Břeclav,* then *Lednice* signs through villages to the castle.

From Lednice, you're just 10 minutes from the expressway, which takes you in about 1.5 hours north to Olomouc (via Brno) or 1 hour south to Bratislava. To reach Vienna (1.5 hours), head south from Lednice through Valtice to the Austrian border, then pick up the A-5 expressway south into the capital.

Pavlov and the Pálava Hills

The traditional, sleepy, endearingly ragtag winemaking village of Pavlov—no relation to the Russian physiologist or his drooling dogs—stretches from the banks of a water reservoir toward the dramatic hilltop ruin of Dívčí Hrady ("Maidens' Castle"). In

MIKULOV WINE REGION

deep brick cellars, you can taste local wines and spicy Hungarian salami while listening to a local dulcimer band. Or take nature walks along the wooded slopes of the white, limestone Pálava Hills to Bavory, Perná, and Věstonice, other cute winemaking villages on the opposite side of the ridge. Either way, you'll see Moravian village architecture at its best. The town of Pavlov, which slopes severely downhill toward the reservoir, has two distinct sections: the upper part—an attractive traditional village with a wine-cellar atmosphere—and a more disorganized area catering to sports fishermen that's recently sprung up closer to the reservoir. If you stay in the upper part, you won't even know the reservoir exists.

Sights in Pavlov

Wandering the Town

Sloping Na Návsi ("on the village green") street, stretching from under the hill to a parking lot above the church, is lined with magnificent examples of rustic Baroque architecture. Two parallel hillside streets up above, Česká and Vinařská, are host to many traditional wine cellars. The owners typically live or rent out the

first floor, wine is pressed on the ground floor, and extensive cellars run deep into the mountain. The atmosphere at dusk is unbeatable.

Wine Cellars

Thirteen family wineries here open their cellars to passers-by on a regular basis. Sipping your way from one to the next is a highlight of any visit. Ask your host whether a dulcimer band is playing in any of the wine cellars. September can be a wild month here as many arrive for harvest festivals and to drink the popular, slightly fermented wine juice called *burčák*.

To buy a famous bottle, consider one of the top wineries in the Czech Republic—**Reisten**—which produces its wines in Pavlov on Vinařská street (April-Oct Mon-Sat 9:00-18:00, Sun 10:00-14:00, Nov-March shorter hours and closed Sun, mobile 724-793-429, www.reisten.net). **Paulus Winery,** in a recently renovated wine cellar, combines tradition with modern trends and is the most accessible of Pavlov's many wine cellars (Mon-Thu 10:00-20:00, Fri-Sat until 24:00, Sun until 19:00; weekends only in off-season; follow the green-and-white marked trail uphill in the direction of the castle to Na Cimbuří 159, mobile 773-334-433, www.vinarstvipaulus.cz). Just below, on the corner of Česká and Na Cimbuří, the modern **U Venuše Wine Bar** offers a wide sampling of local wines (mobile 773-644-183).

Nové Mlýny Reservoir

Three successive dams, planned for decades as part of an immense water regulation project, were built here shortly before the Velvet Revolution. They caused an ecological disaster: In the name of flood prevention, one of the last wetland forests in the Czech Republic was inundated—destroying precious flora and fauna. One of the intended benefits of the plan—to irrigate southern Moravia—also did not pan out. By the early 1990s, the collectivized fields and vineyards had been returned to individual owners. For these small producers, building channels or pumping water from the dams turned out to be too expensive. Still, the townspeople try to make the best of it. During the day, the yacht club at the bottom of the village rents paddleboats, canoes, and windsurfing boards. The relatively shallow water is warm for most of the summer and, as long as you bring flip-flops or are careful about mussels, excellent to swim in. Fishermen delight in the waters here: Recently one Pálava native caught a seven-foot sheatfish (a large, freshwater catfish) here.

Hiking in the Pálava Hills

For a good half-day hike to Mikulov, follow the route recommended earlier, under "Sights in Mikulov," in reverse (see page 414). Or use that same green-and-white marked trail to hike up to the Maidens' Castle (1 mile, 30 minutes) and then descend on the other side to the winemaking villages of Věstonice, Perná, and Bavory. An educational winemaking route (marked by white signs with diagonal green stripes) passes through these vineyards west of the hills.

Sleeping and Eating in Pavlov

During the hot summer months and in September, getting a room on short notice can be difficult—book ahead.

$ Hotel Pavlov is a suitable fallback if the pensions (listed next) are full (Klentnická 174, tel. 519-324-246, www.hotelpavlov. cz, info@hotelpavlov.cz).

Part of **$$ Café Fara** ("The Parish House"), in the nearby village of Klentnice, is a relatively new, all-wood building, inspired by traditional Moravian architecture. Winner of a historical renovation award, it has become almost too popular with trendy Czechs from across the country, and rents nine contemporary-cozy rooms (family rooms available). The historic parish house next door serves homemade meals and cakes on a large outdoor terrace (restaurant open daily until 20:00, mobile 720-611-161, www.cafefara.cz, info@cafefara.cz).

¢ Pension Pod Hradem ("Under the Castle") and **Nad Starým Sklepem** ("Above the Old Wine Cellar"), across the street from each other with seven rooms between them, are built above 400-year-old wine cellars and are run by the Garčica vintner family. They pride themselves on having a garden with the best views of the Pálava Hills and Dívčí Hrady (Maidens' Castle). The young owners studied winemaking in France and speak both French and English. Tours of the wine cellars, with samples of home-made wines, are available on request (cheaper rooms with shared bath, Vinařská 237, tel. 519-515-375, mobile 728-746-500, www. garcicovi.cz, penzion@garcicovi.cz).

Lednice and Valtice

The twin towns of Lednice and Valtice, each boasting a palatial castle-château, are just four miles apart and connected by a lush, bikeable greenbelt.

Since the 1200s, Lednice (LEHD-neet-seh, pop. 2,400) and Valtice (VAHLT-eet-seh, pop. 3,600) have been under the control of the Mikulov-based Lichtenstein family. The Lichtensteins were to South Moravia what the Rožmberks were to South Bohemia: either caring benefactors who turned marshes and beech woods into the promised land, or despotic aristocrats who mercilessly impoverished their serfs...depending on whom you ask. While the Rožmberks died out in the early 1600s, the Lichtensteins thrived during the Thirty Years' War (they wisely stayed loyal to the victorious Habsburgs) and continued to enrich the region until the 1940s. Valtice was their winter residence, but they summered at cooler Lednice (Lednice means "fridge," so named because this stretch of the Dyje River is known for frequent frosts). Of the two châteaus, Lednice is more interesting to tour.

An even more compelling reason to make the short side-trip from Mikulov, Pavlov, or Břeclav is the spectacular 19th-century English-style park, which extends for miles between the two châteaus. While less manicured than similar elegant gardens in France or Austria, its ruggedness is part of its charm. Native oaks and exotic cedars span their gnarled branches over wild meadows and green lakes, Romantic castles and Taj Mahal-style minarets rise in the middle of woods like apparitions, and rare birds silently glide through the sky.

TOURIST INFORMATION

Lednice's TI, by the main parking lot across from the entrance to Lednice Château, sells an inexpensive info brochure and maps of the garden complex (June-Sept Mon-Fri 8:00-17:00, Sat-Sun from

9:00; shorter hours off-season and closed Sat-Sun Nov-March; free Wi-Fi, Zámecké Náměstí 68, tel. 519-340-986, www.lednice.cz).

Valtice's TI is on the town's main square (April-Sept daily 9:00-17:00; Oct-March Mon-Fri 7:00-15:30, closed Sat-Sun; Svobody Náměstí 4, tel. 519-352-978, www.valtice.eu).

ARRIVAL IN LEDNICE AND VALTICE

From **Lednice** train station, follow the bike path along the greenbelt for half a mile to the castle complex. Buses from Břeclav and Valtice stop right in front of the castle entrance.

In **Valtice,** the train station is a bit over a half-mile walk along a sidewalk from the center—take the main road to the main square, where you'll find the castle entrance.

Sights in and near Lednice and Valtice

LEDNICE
▲Lednice Château (Zámek Lednice)

Lednice, the Moravian answer to England's Windsor Castle, is an immense structure built in the English Neo-Gothic style (1846-58).

Today, the castle houses a university for winemakers; anyone is welcome to sign up for a short summer course. To tour the palace, choose between three routes: Route I (ground-floor halls), Route II (prince's apartments), or Route III (picture gallery).

Cost and Hours: Route I or II-150 Kč each, Route III-50 Kč, English tour-50 Kč extra; May-Aug Tue-Sun 9:00-18:00; Sept Tue-Sun until 9:00-17:00, closed Mon; April and Oct Sat-Sun 9:00-17:00, closed Mon-Fri except by reservation; closed Nov-March and Mon year-round; tel. 519-340-128, www.zamek-lednice.info.

Castle Parks

From Lednice Château, parks extend both north and south. The 19th-century nobles loved everything Romantic, peppering these woods with a quirky architectural hodgepodge: a Neo-Roman aqueduct, a Neo-Gothic castle ruin, a Neo-Greek temple, a victory column, a rendezvous pavilion, a minaret, and so on. Navigate between these spots with the help of the map from the TI.

Cost and Hours: Depending on how many of the recommended park attractions you visit, plan on spending about 190-230 Kč per person. Hours vary per sight.

Getting There: To reach the minaret from Lednice Château, you can walk (one mile), hire a horse carriage (100 Kč/person, 30

MIKULOV WINE REGION

minutes), or take a boat. Boats and carriages depart from the little dam just behind the castle; prices depend on the number of riders. Although most horse-carriage rides throughout Europe are tourist traps, here it feels appropriate to ride through the alleys like the nobles once did—even the school groups do it. A good plan is to ride to the minaret and walk back.

Visiting the Parks: Here are some highlights of the parks.

The **Palm Greenhouse,** located near the château entrance, takes you from Moravia to the tropics (60 Kč, similar hours as castle but open even during winter). Notice the construction above you: one of the oldest examples of a cast-iron roof in Europe. Created in England in the 1830s, this innovation was one of the great

technical marvels of the 19th century, enabling the construction of ever-more spacious train stations and market halls as its use gradually spread through Europe.

From the greenhouse, it's a five-minute walk to the predator bird show; en route, you'll see a small **archery stand,** where you can try your skill on the medieval and modern crossbows (60 Kč for five shots, daily in summer, weekends only in spring and fall).

The 45-minute show of live **predator birds** features more than 20 kinds of birds from all over the world. The falcons, merlins, marsh harriers, buzzards, and goshawks demonstrate their hunting skills on simulated rabbits and quails. Some are breathtakingly fast, others comically slow. You can leave whenever you want (short visit-35 Kč, whole show-70 Kč, pick up English brochure in ticket tent that describes every bird; July-Aug Tue-Sun at 12:00, 14:00, and 16:00; April-June and Sept-Oct Sat-Sun at 12:00 and 14:00; tel. 608-100-440).

My favorite part of the park stretches north, from the château to the minaret. The **minaret** is an impressive bit of Romantic-era garden planning that copies the kind of Muslim-style minarets that flank the Taj Mahal in India. Those who climb its 302 winding steps (40 Kč) are rewarded with a grand view. Locals say that Count Alois Josef I intended to build a new church for the village of Lednice, but no plan seemed quite right to the villagers. Their pickiness finally irritated the count so much that he decided to build a mosque with a minaret instead of a church. The mosque never materialized, but the minaret did (completed in 1804). Since the ground around the Dyje River is made up of moving sands, the 200-foot-tall tower had to be anchored almost as deep underground, on beech and oak pilings. The minaret's architect, Josef Hardtmuth, was a versatile genius. The most successful of his patents was the idea of mixing graphite and mud and coating it with wood. The pencil factory he founded (which bears his name) is still one of the largest in Europe.

The four Arabic inscriptions on the sides of the minaret roughly translate as: "There is no God except God, and Muhammad is his prophet. The world betrayed its people. Do not forsake your worldly possessions. There is no difference between wealth and renunciation. True happiness can be reached only in the world beyond. Only through industry and hard work can you reach well-being in this world. When fate stands against you, all plans lose meaning; indeed, without the help of fate, man does not reach redemption." Whoever utters the contents of the first inscription aloud is technically considered a Muslim.

VALTICE
Valtice Château
While not as appealing as Lednice, this winter residence of the Lichtenstein family is home to the Wine Salon of the Czech Republic, enormous castle cellars, and an extensive herb garden.

The **Wine Salon of the Czech Republic** exhibits the best 100 Czech wines—selected annually in a vote by wine experts. The 1.5-hour wine tasting lets you make your own selections from featured wines (335 Kč; June-Sept Mon and Wed-Thu 9:30-17:00, Fri-Sun from 10:30, closed Tue; Oct-Jan and March-May similar hours and closed Sun; closed Feb; enter through the basement of the main château entrance, tel. 519-352-072, www.salonvin.cz).

The 15th- and 17th-century **cellars** are rented by the leading local wine producer—Víno Château Valtice. Tours here include a look at the vats and tastes of three wines (60 Kč, July-Aug daily 10:00-18:00, May-June and Sept Sat-Sun only, closed Oct-April, enter to left of castle entrance, call ahead for tours in English, tel. 519-361-314, www.vsvaltice.cz).

The castle's **Tiree Chmelar Herb Garden** was founded by an American couple with Czech roots; it was designed by students at the Mendel University in Lednice (60 Kč; July-Aug daily 10:00-18:00; May-June and Sept Tue-Fri from 16:00, Sat-Sun from 10:00, closed Mon; closed Oct-April; enter to left of château entrance, mobile 776-251-058, www.bylinkovazahradavaltice.cz).

Valtice Underground (Valtické podzemí)

This complex is a unique labyrinth of interconnected cellars that has been restored and is now run by the winery. It's a great spot for dinner or wine tasting. To get there, follow the red-marked trail from the main square along Růžová and then turn right onto Vinařská.

Cost and Hours: Cost varies with tour, May-Sept Tue-Fri 17:00-22:00, Sat 10:00-22:00, Sun 10:00-17:00, closed Mon; longer hours July-Aug; closed Mon-Thu and shorter weekend hours in April and Oct; closed Nov-March, mobile 724-331-563, www.valtickepodzemi.cz.

BEYOND VALTICE

The sights outside of town are best connected by bike (too far to walk, too close to drive).

▲Museum of the Iron Curtain (Muzeum Železné Opony)

Near the border with Austria is a stark reminder of the Cold War. This museum exhibits uniforms, guns, and old photographs in the rooms of a former border-crossing station. You'll see the guards' quarters, a detention cell, and a piece of the barbed-wire fence that once divided Czechoslovakia and Austria. One room documents various imaginative attempts at illegal crossings, and a sober memorial lists the names and dates of those who were killed during their unsuccessful attempts. Your visit ends with a chilling 1980s propaganda film about the work of hunting down a "trespasser" *(narušitel)*. The museum's motto is "Freedom is the right to hit the road."

Cost and Hours: 70 Kč; July-Aug daily 10:00-17:00, April-June and Sept-Oct Fri-Sun only, closed Nov-March; to arrange a visit outside normal hours or a guided tour call 519-340-130 or 608-968-388, Hraniční Přechod 483, www.muzeumopony.cz.

Getting There: From Valtice, you can either walk or bike the 1.5 miles to the museum—follow the paved bike path that starts by the large Vinné Sklepy Valtice winery. By car (drive or take a taxi), follow the road to Schrattenberg in Austria.

Úvaly Village

Continuing another mile and a half west past the Museum of the Iron Curtain (see "Getting There," above), you'll reach the remote, cut-off village of Úvaly with its appealing, professionally run, recommended pension and restaurant **Villa Daniela.** Lunch is served on a pleasant, rustic summer patio with manicured lawns, a fountain, and Moravian dulcimer music on the loudspeakers. Another six miles along the 1950s-era paved military signal road (now an endearingly rough bike path) takes you to Mikulov, past panels illustrating stories of attempted escapes across the Iron Curtain.

MIKULOV WINE REGION

Sleeping in Valtice and Úvaly

$$ Château La Veneria has six meticulous rooms, lavishly reno-
vated and richly decorated with a woman's touch, in the former
residence of the castle's chief groundskeeper. Breakfast is served in
a gorgeous, secluded garden with a small waterfall and a summer
kitchen; from here you have direct access to the castle parks. One
could not find a better fit for visiting the opulent Lednice-Valtice
complex (in summer and on weekends reserve two months ahead,
walk to the far end of the main square and then continue 200 yards
along Růžová before turning left, K. Venerii 82, mobile 737-684-
308, www.valtice-ubytovani-zamecek.cz, ivanabenadova@tiscali.
cz).

$ Villa Daniela has 14 standard rooms in a newly built man-
sion that very successfully imitates a red-brick traditional farm-
stead. Set in the middle of the "end-of-the-road" village of Úvaly,
this is a perfect base not just for wine tasting but also to get a sense
for the borderlands in this part of Europe. Before 1989, visitors
to the village had to be accompanied to their stated destination
by guards and couldn't stay past the 18:00 curfew. Yet a group of
four youngsters, one of whose grandmother lived here, managed
to dig a tunnel under the border 300 yards away. Today, the patio
atmosphere is so quietly perfect that all that history seems surreal
(at the end of the road in Úvaly, about 3 miles from Valtice, mobile
776-245-851, www.sklepuvaly.cz, recepce@villadaniela.cz).

Lednice and Valtice Connections

This area is made for biking. Or consider taking the bus to Lednice,
walking through the gardens to Valtice (a level four-mile stroll),
and then taking the train from there. For bus and train schedules,
see www.idos.cz.

From Lednice to: Mikulov (10 buses/day Mon-Fri, 5 buses/
day Sat-Sun, 45 minutes), **Vienna** (8 trains/day, 2 hours, transfer
in Břeclav).

From Valtice to: Mikulov (10 trains/day, 15 minutes), **Prague**
(hourly trains, 4 hours, 1 transfer), **Olomouc** (3 trains/day, 2.5-4
hours, several transfers).

MIKULOV WINE REGION

CZECH HISTORY

The Czechs have always been at a crossroads of Europe—between the Slavic and Germanic worlds, between Catholicism and Protestantism, and between Cold War East and West. As if having foreseen all of this, the mythical founder of Prague—the beautiful princess Libuše—named her city "Praha" (meaning "threshold" in Czech). Despite these strong external influences, the Czechs have retained their distinct culture...and a dark, ironic sense of humor to keep them laughing through it all.

CHARLES IV AND THE MIDDLE AGES (500s-1300s)

The pagan, Slavic tribes that arrived in this part of Europe in the sixth century A.D. were first united by the Prague-based Přemysl dynasty. The main figure of this era was Duke Václav I (A.D. 907-935)—later immortalized in a Christmas carol as "Good King Wenceslas"—who converted the Czechs to Christianity and founded a cathedral at Prague Castle, on a bluff overlooking the Vltava River.

In 1004, Bohemia was incorporated into the Holy Roman Empire (an alliance of mostly German-speaking kingdoms and

dukedoms). Within 200 years—thanks to its strategic location and privileged status within the empire—Prague had become one of Europe's largest and most highly cultured cities.

The 14th century was Prague's Golden Age, when Holy Roman Emperor Charles IV (1316-1378) ruled. Born to a Luxembourger nobleman and a Czech princess, Charles IV was an ambitious man on the cusp of the

Renaissance. He lived and studied in several European lands, spoke five languages, and counted Petrarch as a friend—but always felt a deep connection to his mother's Czech roots. Selecting Prague as his seat of power, Charles imported French architects to make the city a grand capital, founded the first university north of the Alps, and invigorated the Czech national spirit. (He popularized the legend of Wenceslas to give his people a near-mythical, King Arthur-type cultural standard-bearer.) Much of Prague's history and architecture—including the famous Charles Bridge, Charles University, St. Vitus Cathedral, and Karlštejn Castle—can be traced to this dynamic man's rule. Under Charles IV, the Czech people gained esteem among Europeans. Charles was born under a lucky star: During his time the dominance of divinely sanctioned monarchs peaked. A generation later, after a religious and social upheaval, his son faced much stronger opposition when trying to implement Charles-like absolute power.

JAN HUS AND RELIGIOUS WARS (1300s-1600s)

Jan Hus (c. 1369-1415) was a local preacher and professor who got in trouble with the Vatican a hundred years before Martin Luther.

Like Luther, Hus preached in the people's language rather than in Latin. To add insult to injury, he complained about Church corruption. Tried for heresy and burned in 1415, Hus became both a religious and a national hero. While each age has defined Hus to its liking, the way he challenged authority while staying true to his beliefs has long inspired and rallied the Czech people. (For more on Hus, see page 103.)

Inspired by Hus' reformist ideas, the Czechs rebelled against both the Roman Catholic Church and German political control. This burst of independent thought led to a period of religious wars. Protestant Czech patriots—like the rough-and-rugged war hero Jan Žižka (often depicted in patriotic art with his trademark eye patch)—fought to maintain Czech autonomy. But ultimately, these rebels were overwhelmed by their Catholic opponents. The result of these wars was the loss of autonomy to Vienna.

Ruled by the Habsburgs of Austria, Prague stagnated—except during the rule of King Rudolf II (1552-1612), a Holy Roman Emperor. With Rudolf living in Prague, the city again emerged as a cultural and intellectual center. Astronomers Johannes Kepler and Tycho Brahe flourished, as did other scientists, and much of

Typical Church Architecture

History comes to life when you visit a centuries-old church. Even if you wouldn't know your apse from a hole in the ground, learning a few simple terms will enrich your experience. Note that not every church has every feature, and a "cathedral" isn't a type of church architecture, but rather a designation for a church that's a governing center for a local bishop.

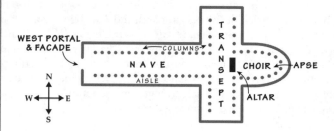

Aisles: The long, generally low-ceilinged arcades that flank the nave.

Altar: The raised area with a ceremonial table (often adorned with candles or a crucifix), where the priest prepares and serves the bread and wine for Communion.

Apse: The space beyond the altar, generally bordered with small chapels.

Barrel Vault: A continuous round-arched ceiling that resembles an extended upside-down U.

Choir: A cozy area, often screened off, located within the church nave and near the high altar, where services are sung in a more intimate setting.

Cloister: Covered hallways bordering a square or rectangular open-air courtyard, traditionally where monks and nuns got fresh air.

Facade: The front exterior of the church's main (west) entrance, viewable from outside, usually highly decorated.

Groin Vault: An arched ceiling formed where two equal barrel vaults meet at right angles. Less common usage: term for a medieval jock strap.

Narthex: The area (portico or foyer) between the main entry and the nave.

Nave: The long, central section of the church (running west to east, from the entrance to the altar) where the congregation sits or stands through the service.

Transept: In a traditional cross-shaped floor plan, the transept is one of the two parts forming the "arms" of the cross. The transepts run north-south, perpendicularly crossing the east-west nave.

West Portal: The main entry to the church (on the west end, opposite the main altar).

Typical Castle Architecture

Castles were fortified residences for medieval nobles. Castles come in all shapes and sizes, but knowing a few general terms will help you understand them.

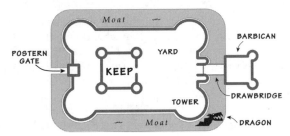

Barbican: A fortified gatehouse, sometimes a stand-alone building located outside the main walls.

Crenellation: A gap-toothed pattern of stones atop the parapet.

Drawbridge: A bridge that could be raised or lowered, using counterweights or a chain-and-winch.

Great Hall: The largest room in the castle, serving as throne room, conference center, and dining hall.

Hoardings (or Gallery or Brattice): Wooden huts built onto the upper parts of the stone walls. They served as watchtowers, living quarters, and fighting platforms.

Keep (or Donjon): A high, strong stone tower in the center of the complex; the lord's home and refuge of last resort.

Loopholes (or Embrasures): Narrow wall slits through which soldiers could shoot arrows.

Machicolation: A stone ledge jutting out from the wall, with holes through which soldiers could drop rocks or boiling oil onto wall-scaling enemies below.

Moat: A ditch encircling the wall, sometimes filled with water.

Parapet: Outer railing of the wall walk.

Portcullis: An iron grille that could be lowered across the entrance.

Postern Gate: A small, unfortified side or rear entrance. In wartime, it became a "sally-port" used to launch surprise attacks, or as an escape route.

Towers: Square or round structures with crenellated tops or conical roofs serving as lookouts, chapels, living quarters, or the dungeon.

Turret: A small lookout tower rising from the top of the wall.

Wall Walk (or Allure): A pathway atop the wall where guards could patrol and where soldiers stood to fire at the enemy.

Yard (or Bailey): An open courtyard inside the castle walls.

the inspiration for Prague's great art can be attributed to the king's patronage.

Not long after this period, Prague entered one of its darker spells. The Thirty Years' War (1618-1648) began in Prague when Czech Protestant nobles, wanting religious and political autonomy, tossed two Catholic Habsburg officials out the window of the castle. (This was one of Prague's many defenestrations—a uniquely Czech solution to political discord, in which offending politicians were literally thrown out the window.) The Czech Estates Uprising lasted two years, ending in a crushing defeat in the Battle of White Mountain (1620), which marked the end of Czech freedom. Twenty-seven leaders of the uprising were executed (today commemorated by crosses on Prague's Old Town Square), most of the old Czech nobility was dispossessed, and Protestants had to convert to Catholicism or leave the country.

Often called "the first world war" because it engulfed so many nations, the Thirty Years' War was particularly tough on Prague. During this period, its population dropped from 60,000 to 25,000. The result of this war was 300 years of Habsburg rule from afar, as Prague became a German-speaking backwater of Vienna. While the Austrian rule contributed to economic prosperity—and was fairly liberal compared to its Russian and Prussian neighbors—Czechs still tend to despise the Habsburgs. They see them as a pompous royal family that invented the concept of the modern zoo (at Vienna's Schönbrunn Palace) and then tried to impose it on the people of their empire (before deciding it was better to turn them into cannon fodder).

CZECH NATIONAL REVIVAL (1800s-1918)

The end of Prague as a German city came gradually. During the centuries that the Czech language and culture were suppressed, "Prag" and other cities were populated mainly by German-speaking urbanites, while "backwards" peasants kept the old Czech ways alive in the countryside. But as the Industrial Revolution attracted Czech farmers and peasants to the cities, the demographics of the Czech population centers began to shift. Between 1800 and 1900—though it remained part of the Habsburg Empire—Prague went from being an essentially German town to a predominantly Czech one.

As in the rest of Europe, the 19th century was a time of great nationalism, when the age of divine kings and ruling families came to a fitful end. The Czech spirit was first stirred by the work of historian František Palacký, who dug deep into the Czech archives to forge a national narrative. During this time, Czechs were inspired by the completion of Prague's St. Vitus Cathedral, the symphonies of Antonín Dvořák, and the operas of Bedřich Smetana, which were performed in the new National Theater.

Alfons Mucha, a prodigiously talented Czech artist who made a name for himself in the high society of turn-of-the-century Paris,

 embodied this wave of nationalism. When he could have lived out his days in the lap of luxury in Paris or New York City, Mucha chose instead to return to his homeland and spend decades painting a magnum opus celebrating the historic journey of the Czechs and all Slavs—the *Slav Epic.*

After the Habsburgs' Austro-Hungarian Empire suffered defeat in World War I, their vast holdings broke apart and became independent countries. Among these was a union of Bohemia, Moravia, and Slovakia, the brainchild of a clever politician named Tomáš Garrigue Masaryk (see sidebar on page 174). The new nation, Czechoslovakia, was proclaimed in 1918, with Prague as its capital.

TROUBLES OF THE 20TH CENTURY (1918-1989)

Independence lasted only 20 years. In the notorious Munich Agreement of September 1938—much to the dismay of the Czechs and Slovaks—Great Britain and France peacefully ceded to Hitler the so-called Sudetenland (a fringe around the edge of Bohemia, populated mainly by people of German descent; see sidebar on page 372). It wasn't long before Hitler seized the rest of Czechoslovakia...and the Holocaust began. Under the ruthless Nazi governor Reinhard Heydrich, tens of thousands of Jews were sent first to the concentration camp at Terezín, and later to Auschwitz and other death camps. After Heydrich was assassinated by a pair of Czech paratroopers, the campaign of genocide grew even worse. Out of the 55,000 Jews living in Prague before the war, more than 80 percent perished during the Holocaust; throughout Czechoslovakia, an estimated 260,000 Jews were murdered.

For centuries, Prague's cultural makeup had consisted of a rich mix of Czech, German, and Jewish people—historically, they were almost evenly divided. With the Jewish population decimated, part of that delicate tapestry was gone forever. And after World War II ended, more than 2 million people of Germanic descent who lived in Czechoslovakia were pushed into Germany. Their forced resettlement—which led to the deaths of untold numbers of Germans (what some today might call "ethnic cleansing")—was demanded by the public and carried out by Czechoslovak President Edvard Beneš, who had ruled from exile in London throughout the war.

Czech Borders 1914–Today

Legend:
- ▨ Habsburg Empire in 1914
- ▨ Czechoslovakia (1918-1993)
- ▬ Current Czech Republic Border
- ─ Current National Borders

Today's Czech Republic is largely homogenous—about 95 percent Czechs.

Although Prague escaped the bombs of World War II, it went directly from the Nazi frying pan into the communist fire. A local uprising freed the city from the Nazis on May 8, 1945, but the Soviets "liberated" them on May 9.

The period of 1945 to 1948 is a perfect case study of how, in trying times, a country can lose its freedom through its own folly. The popular perception that Czechoslovakia simply fell into the Soviet sphere of influence is only partly true. While the Soviets had special interest in controlling Czechoslovakia (particularly because of its uranium deposits), Czechoslovakia was represented by an internationally recognized exile government during the war.

This government was allowed to come back and rule until the 1946 election. And up until 1948, Czechoslovakia was still a sovereign state (though it was under pressure) whose elected leaders were responsible for shaping its eventual orientation.

The first mistake was that the government in exile (despite Churchill's warnings) signed a binding cooperation pact with the Soviet Union in 1943. Then the communists won the most seats in the 1946 election—garnering over 40 percent of the vote in the Czech lands (they came in only second in Slovakia). In 1947 the Parliament voted against the Marshall Plan. When the country's leaders and electorate realized the communists weren't playing according to any rule book, it was too late. By 1948 the communists controlled all the powerful ministries and suppressed student-led protests calling for democracy. For over 40 years they would not hold a free election.

The early communist era (1948-1968) was a mixture of misguided zeal, Stalinist repressions, and attempts to wed socialism with democracy. The "Prague Spring" period of reform—initiated by a young generation of progressive communists in 1968, led by the charismatic Slovak politician Alexander Dubček—came to an abrupt halt under the treads of Warsaw Pact tanks (for details,

see page 146). Dubček was exiled (and made a backwoods forest ranger), and the years of "normalization" following the unsuccessful revolt were particularly disheartening. A wave of protests spread through the country in 1969, as furious young Czechs and Slovaks lit themselves on fire to decry communist oppression. But the status quo would hold strong for another 20 years.

In the late 1980s, the communists began constructing Prague's huge Žižkov TV tower (now the city's tallest structure)—not only to broadcast Czech TV transmissions, but also to jam Western signals. The Metro, built at about the same time, was intended for mass transit, but was also designed to be a giant fallout shelter for protection against capitalist bombs.

Every small town had its own set of loudspeakers for broadcasting propaganda. (You'll still see these if you look closely as you pass through the countryside.) Locals remember growing up with these mouthpieces of government boasting of successes ("This year, despite many efforts of sabotage on the part of certain individuals in service of imperialist goals, we have surpassed the planned output of steel by 195 percent"); calling people to action ("There will be no school tomorrow as all will join the farmers in the fields

Notable Czechs

These prominent historical figures are listed in chronological order.

St. Wenceslas (907-935): Bohemian duke who allied the Czechs with the Holy Roman Empire. He went on to become the Czech Republic's patron saint, and it is he who is memorialized as a "good king" in the Christmas carol. For more on Wenceslas, see page 60.

Jan Hus (c. 1369-1415): Proto-Protestant Reformer who was burned at the stake (see page 427).

John Amos Comenius (Jan Amos Komenský in Czech, 1592-1670): "Teacher of Nations" and Protestant exile, whose ideas paved the way for modern education (see page 390).

Antonín Dvořák (1841-1904): Inspired by a trip to America, he composed his New World Symphony. For more on Czech composers, see page 246.

Tomáš Garrigue Masaryk (1850-1937): Sociology professor, writer, politician, and spiritual reformer. He was idolized during his lifetime as the "dearest father" of the Czechoslovak democracy (see sidebar in this chapter).

Jára Cimrman (c. 1853-1914): Illustrious but fictional inventor, explorer, philosopher, and all-around genius. Despite being overwhelmingly voted the "Greatest Czech of All Time" in a nationwide poll, he was not awarded the title (see page 74).

Alfons Mucha (1860-1939): You might recognize his turn-of-the-century Art Nouveau posters of pretty girls entwined in vines. Visit his museum in Prague, marvel at his stained-glass window

for an abundant harvest"); or quelling disturbances ("Some citizens may have heard about alien forces in our society taking advantage of this week's anniversary to spread unrest. This is to reassure you that the situation is firmly under control and nothing is happening in Olomouc or in Prague. Nevertheless, for their own safety, we suggest all citizens stay home.").

Eventually the Soviet empire crumbled, beginning with reforms in Hungary in the summer of 1989 and culminating in the fall of the Berlin Wall that October. A few weeks later, Czechoslovakia regained its freedom in the student- and artist-powered 1989 "Velvet Revolution," so-called because there were no casualties... or even broken windows (see page 151).

Václav Havel, a poet, playwright, and philosopher who had been

in St. Vitus Cathedral, and view his magnum opus, the *Slav Epic*, once it returns from a world tour in 2019 (see page 158).

Franz Kafka (1883-1924): While working for a Prague insurance firm, he wrote (in German) *The Metamorphosis* (man awakens as a cockroach), *The Trial*, *The Castle*, and other psychologically haunting stories and novels.

Milan Kundera (1929—): Wrote the novel *The Unbearable Lightness of Being* (which became a film), among others. For more on Czech authors, see page 484.

Miloš Forman (1932—): The director of *One Flew Over the Cuckoo's Nest*, *Amadeus*, and other award-winning films, Forman is one of many Czech filmmakers who has made his mark on Hollywood. For more on Czech filmmakers, see page 485.

Václav Havel (1936-2011): The country's first post-Communist president, also well-known as a playwright and philosopher (see page 152).

Madeleine Albright (1937—): Born in Prague as Marie Jana Korbelová, Albright was the first woman to serve as US Secretary of State, from 1997-2001, under President Bill Clinton.

Martina Navrátilová (1956—) and **Ivan Lendl** (1960-): Tennis stars of the 1980s.

Dominik Hašek (1965—) and **Jaromír Jágr** (1972-): Hockey players and NHL stars. For more on Czech sports, see page 250.

David Černý (1967—): Wildly controversial, iconoclastic artist who (in good Czech form) misses no opportunity to thumb his nose at authority (see page 153).

imprisoned by the communist regime, became Czechoslovakia's first post-communist president (see page 152).

"IT'S NOT YOU, IT'S ME": THE PEACEFUL BREAKUP (1989-1993)

In the post-communist age of new possibility, the two peoples of Czechoslovakia began to wonder if, in fact, they belonged together.

Ever since they joined with the Czechs in 1918, the Slovaks felt overshadowed by Prague (unmistakably the political, economic, and cultural center of the country). Slovakia, which in the preceding 50 years had been stripped even of the right to run schools in its own language, stood no chance of independence on its own after World War I. And over the years, the Czechs resented the financial burden of carrying their poorer neighbors to the east. In this new world of flux and freedom, longstanding trends and tensions came to a head. You could argue that Austro-Hungary's multiethnic successor states—such as Czechoslovakia and Yugoslavia—were miniature copies of the mother country. Once the idea of a multiethnic state represented by that mother fell apart, it was only a matter of time until the children would dissolve into national states as well.

The dissolution of Czechoslovakia began over a hyphen, as the Slovaks wanted to rename the country Czecho-Slovakia. Ideally, this symbolic move would come with a redistribution of powers: two capitals and two UN reps, but one national bank and a single currency. This idea was rejected, and in June 1992, the Slovak nationalist candidate Vladimír Mečiar fared surprisingly well in the elections—suggesting that the Slovaks were serious about secession. The politicians plowed ahead, getting serious about the split in September 1992. The transition took only three months from start to finish.

The split became official on January 1, 1993, and each country ended up with its own capital, currency, and head of state. For most, the breakup dissolved tensions, and a decade and a half later, Czechs and Slovaks still feel closer to each other than to any other nationality.

THE CZECH REPUBLIC TODAY (1990s TO PRESENT)

In recent times, the Czech Republic has had three significant turning points. In March 1999, it joined NATO. Then on May 1, 2004, the country joined the European Union (see sidebar on page 93). Three and a half years later, it entered the Schengen Agreement, effectively erasing its borders for the purposes of work and travel.

After 14 years in office, a term-limited Václav Havel stepped down in 2003. He died in 2011. While he's fondly remembered by Czechs as a great thinker, writer, and fearless leader of the opposition movement during the communist days, many consider him to have been less successful as a president.

The next president, Václav Klaus, had been the pragmatic author of the economic reforms in the 1990s. Klaus' surprising win in the 2003 election symbolized a change from revolutionary times, when philosophers became kings, to modern humdrum politics, when offices are gained by bargaining with the opposition (Communist Party votes in the Parliament were the decisive factor in Klaus' election).

Behind-the-scenes deals in Parliament allowed Klaus to be re-elected, drawing public outrage and eventually a change in the country's constitution, which allowed for the first election of a president directly by the people (rather than by Parliament) in January 2013.

The winner of this historic presidential election was Miloš Zeman, the other political heavyweight of the 1990s. President Zeman, a tobacco, pork, and Becherovka-powered man of the

Freedom Versus Babies

In communist times, it was routine to be married and start a family by age 22. Once a Czech finished training school and (for men) the compulsory two-year military service, there was little else to aspire to. Everyone was assigned essentially the same mediocre job ("They pretended to pay us, we pretended to work"), with little hope of career progress—unless you were willing to cut ties with your friends by entering the Communist Party or by working for the secret police. Children (and summer homes) were the only way for people to project their dreams. Parenting was subsidized. In the countryside, young families were guaranteed housing, and in cities, flats were allocated according to long waiting lists that gave priority to married couples with children.

But after the fall of communism in 1989, many more options became available to young people who had not previously dreamed of such possibilities. Young Czechs embraced the new freedoms: Everyone wanted to travel—to the West to study law, or to the East to meditate. And everyone wanted to work—for big bucks at a multinational investment bank, or for pennies at a nonprofit organization in Afghanistan. Marriage was no longer the expected "next step." And shacking up was no longer a problem; you needed money, rather than a marriage certificate, to get a place to live. More and more young adults waited until after 30 to get married, and those already married reconsidered their choices. Fewer Czechs had children, and many divorced.

By 2004, the falling birthrate was a regular topic in newspaper columns. To stimulate production, the socialist government began paying new parents a baby bonus—one month's wages—in addition to the standard three years of paid maternity leave already promised to one parent.

Ironically—as if to prove that Czechs will never listen to what the government tells them to do—as soon as the newly elected conservatives revoked the monthly baby bonus in 2006, everyone decided to have children. The biggest baby boom in a generation is still on: Maternity wards are overflowing, signs regulating stroller traffic are popping up in public parks, and politicians are blaming each other for imprudently closing down many state-run nurseries.

Yet, even though they're faced with a bright and baby-filled future, some Czechs maintain a healthy dose of pessimism and seem reluctant to dive headlong into the Western rat race. Life still goes a little slower here, and people find pleasure in simple things.

CZECH HISTORY

The Wisdom of Babička Míla ("Granny Míla")

Co-author Honza Vihan's grandmother, Bohumila Vihanová (February 17, 1907-August 18, 2008), was born in the Austro-Hungarian town of Prag (today's Praha), which was then ruled from Vienna. In the 101 years of her life, she lived under seven different governments: Habsburgs, Masaryk's interwar Czechoslovakia, Nazis, communists, post-communist Czechoslovakia, the Czech Republic, and the European Union. Wise beyond even her many years, she counseled family and visitors alike as follows:

- "I liked each change, because it always brought something new."
- "You must be able to take the best from whatever comes."
- "Nothing good that you do is ever lost; it always stays somewhere and surfaces when needed."
- "When the communists took over, that was bad—really bad. But then, my mother used to say, 'There's no point in crying over spilled milk. There's enough water in it already.' So I tried to get by, and somehow we managed to live through it all."
- "The main thing is to keep your inner balance."
- "You should never take yourself too seriously."
- "Let everyone believe whatever they want, as long as they behave accordingly."
- "Money will always be here. We won't."
- "Parents should never mix in their children's lives."
- "Good health and happy mind!"

people, has since suffered ill health, and critics say he's become so confused that he can no longer tell East from West. He's been criticized for courting Russian President Vladimir Putin, and during the 2016 visit of Chinese President Xi Jinping, Zeman took a page from Prague circa-1980, ordering a police assault on peaceful protesters.

But the president is largely a symbolic head. The main power broker, the prime minister, is chosen in the parliamentary elections. In 2017, the country faces a choice: settle for its imperfect traditional parties, or empower a recently emerged antiestablishment candidate—food industry mogul and former secret police collaborator Andrej Babiš, head of the Action of Dissatisfied Citizens party. Wary Czechs debate whether the out-of-control Zeman or the cunning finance minister Babiš, who seems to be a cross between Vladimir Putin and former Italian Prime Minister Silvio Berlusconi, is more dangerous for the country overall.

But every country has its political wrangling and corruption scandals. Overall, the recent trajectory of Czech history is trending positive. Both in the capital and in rural villages, the country feels more affluent than ever before, all while celebrating its inherent Czech-ness. And Prague is, quite justifiably, one of the most popular tourist destinations in Europe.

PRACTICALITIES

Contents

This chapter covers the practical skills of European travel: how to get tourist information, pay for things, sightsee efficiently, find good-value accommodations, eat affordably but well, use technology wisely, and get between destinations smoothly. To study ahead and round out your knowledge and skills, check out "Resources from Rick Steves."

Tourist Information

The Czech national tourist office **in the US** is a wealth of information (www.czechtourism.com). Their website includes a number of planning tools, descriptions of tourist regions and popular sights, and downloadable apps and brochures.

In the Czech Republic, a good first stop is generally the tourist information office—abbreviated **TI** in this book. You can get plenty of information online, but I still make a point to swing by the local TI to confirm sightseeing plans, pick up a city map, and get information on public transit (including bus and train schedules), walking tours, special events, and nightlife. Prepare a list of questions and a proposed plan to double-check. Some TIs have information on the entire country or at least the region, so try to pick up maps and printed information for destinations you'll be visiting later in your trip. If you're arriving in town after the TI closes, call ahead with your questions or pick up a map in a neighboring town. Almost all the TIs in the Czech Republic are run by local governments, which means their information isn't colored by a drive for profit.

Some TIs offer a room-booking service for a fee, though they're unable to give hard opinions on the relative value of one place over another. It's best to go direct with the listings in this book. But in a pinch, you could use the TI's help (or consult an online booking site, which can provide a broader range of options).

Travel Tips

Emergency and Medical Help: In Prague, dial 112 for medical or other emergencies and 158 for police. To summon an ambulance, call 155. If you get sick, do as the Czechs do and go to a pharmacist for advice. Or ask at your hotel for help—they'll know the nearest medical and emergency services. (See "Medical Help" on page 27 for pharmacy and hospital locations in Prague.)

Theft or Loss: To replace a passport, you'll need to go in person to an embassy (see page 481). If your credit and debit cards disappear, cancel and replace them (see "Damage Control for Lost Cards" on page 445). File a police report, either on the spot or within a day or two; you'll need it to submit an insurance claim for lost or stolen rail passes or travel gear, and it can help with replacing your passport or credit and debit cards. For more information, see www.ricksteves.com/help.

Time Zones: The Czech Republic, like most of continental Europe, is generally six/nine hours ahead of the East/West Coasts of the US. The exceptions are the beginning and end of Daylight Saving Time: Europe "springs forward" the last Sunday in March (two weeks after most of North America) and "falls back" the last Sunday in October (one week before North America). For a handy online time converter, try www.timeanddate.com/worldclock.

Business Hours: Most stores are open Monday through Friday from roughly 9:00 or 10:00 until 17:00 or 18:00, Saturday morning until lunchtime, and closed Sunday. Souvenir shops in Prague's Old Town, and other businesses serving both urbanites and tourists (like small grocery stores), are open daily until at least 20:00.

Sundays have the same pros and cons as they do for travelers in the US—sights are generally open but may have limited hours, many shops and all banks are closed, city traffic is light, and public-transportation options are fewer.

Watt's Up? Europe's electrical system is 220 volts, instead of North America's 110 volts. Most newer electronics (such as laptops, battery chargers, and hair dryers) convert automatically, so you won't need a converter plug, but you will need an adapter plug with two round prongs, sold inexpensively at travel stores in the US. Avoid bringing older appliances that don't automatically convert voltage; instead, buy a cheap replacement in Europe.

Discounts: Discounts for sights are generally not listed in this book. However, many sights offer discounts for youths (up to age 18), students (with proper identification cards, www.isic.org), families, seniors (loosely defined as retirees or those willing to call themselves a senior), and groups of 10 or more. While some discounts are technically available only for Czechs or citizens of the European Union (EU), they are sometimes are granted to travelers too—always ask.

Online Translation Tip: Google's Chrome browser instantly translates websites. You can also paste text or the URL of a foreign website into the translation window at http://translate.google.com. The Google Translate app converts spoken English into most European languages (and vice versa) and can also translate text it "reads" with your mobile device's camera.

Money

This section offers advice on how to pay for purchases on your trip (including getting cash from ATMs and paying with plastic), dealing with lost or stolen cards, VAT (sales tax) refunds, and tipping.

WHAT TO BRING

Bring both a debit card and a credit card. You'll use the debit card at cash machines (ATMs) to withdraw local cash for most purchases, and the credit card to pay for larger items. (Due to problems with fraud, try to avoid using your credit card to pay for goods or services in Prague.) Some travelers also carry a third card, in case one gets demagnetized or eaten by a temperamental machine.

For an emergency stash, bring $100-200 in US cash. Although banks in some countries don't exchange dollars, in a pinch you can always find exchange desks at major train stations or airports—convenient but with crummy rates.

CASH

Although credit cards are widely accepted in Europe, day-to-day spending is generally more cash-based. I find local cash is the easi-

PRACTICALITIES

est—and sometimes only—way to pay for cheap food, bus fare, taxis, and local guides. Some vendors will charge you extra for using a credit card, some won't take credit cards at all. Having cash on hand can help you avoid a stressful predicament if you find yourself in a place that won't accept your card.

Throughout Europe, ATMs are the easiest and smartest way for travelers to get cash. They work just like they do at home. To

 withdraw money from an ATM (called a *Bankomat* in the Czech Republic), you'll need a debit card (ideally with a Visa or MasterCard logo), plus a PIN code (numeric and four digits). For increased security, shield the keypad when entering your PIN code, and don't use an ATM if anything on the front of the machine looks loose or damaged (a sign that someone may have attached a "skimming" device to capture account information). Try to withdraw large sums of money to reduce the number of per-transaction bank fees you'll pay.

When possible, use ATMs located outside banks—a thief is less likely to target a cash machine near surveillance cameras, and if your card is munched by a machine during banking hours, you can go inside for help. Stay away from "independent" ATMs such as Travelex, Euronet, Moneybox, Cardpoint, and Cashzone, which charge huge commissions, have terrible exchange rates, and may try to trick users with "dynamic currency conversion" (described later). Although you can use a credit card to withdraw cash at an ATM, this comes with high bank fees and only makes sense in an emergency.

While traveling, if you want to access your accounts online, be sure to use a secure connection (see page 463).

Pickpockets target tourists. To safeguard your cash, wear a money belt—a pouch with a strap that you buckle around your waist like a belt and tuck under your clothes. Keep your cash, credit cards, and passport secure in your money belt, and carry only a day's spending money in your front pocket or wallet.

CREDIT AND DEBIT CARDS

For purchases, Visa and MasterCard are more commonly accepted than American Express. Just like at home, credit or debit cards work easily at larger hotels and shops. Although larger restaurants take credit cards, I still try to pay in cash.

I typically use my debit card to withdraw cash to pay for daily purchases. I use my credit card sparingly: to book and pay for hotel rooms, to buy advance tickets for events or sights, to cover

PRACTICALITIES

Exchange Rate

Though the Czech Republic joined the EU in 2004, it continues to use its traditional currency, the Czech crown (*koruna*, abbreviated Kč).

25 Czech crowns (Kč) = about $1

To roughly convert prices in crowns to dollars, drop the last digit, multiply by 4, then drop the last digit again. So that tasty lunch for 160 Kč is about $6, the souvenir Czech puppet for 450 Kč costs roughly $18, and the taxi ride for 2,300 Kč from the airport is...uh-oh.

Many hotels, restaurants, and shops accept euro bills (but not coins or large bills). You may even see hotel rooms or souvenirs priced in euros (€). In this case, remember that €1 = 27 Kč = about $1.10. If you're using euros, expect bad rates and your change in *korunas*. If you're just passing through, your euros will probably get you by—and they can actually be helpful in an emergency. But if you're staying awhile, get the local currency.

Check www.oanda.com for the latest exchange rates.

---

major expenses (such as car rentals or plane tickets), and to pay for things online or near the end of my trip (to avoid another visit to the ATM). While you could instead use a debit card for these purchases, a credit card offers a greater degree of fraud protection.

Ask Your Credit- or Debit-Card Company: Before your trip, contact the company that issued your debit or credit cards.

Confirm that your **card will work overseas,** and alert them that you'll be using it in Europe; otherwise, they may deny transactions if they perceive unusual spending patterns.

Ask for the specifics on transaction **fees.** When you use your credit or debit card—either for purchases or ATM withdrawals—you'll typically be charged additional "international transaction" fees of up to 3 percent (1 percent is normal). If your card's fees seem high, consider getting a different card just for your trip: Capital One (www.capitalone.com) and most credit unions have low-to-no international fees.

Verify your daily ATM **withdrawal limit,** and if necessary, ask your bank to adjust it. I prefer a high limit that allows me to take out more cash at each ATM stop and save on bank fees; some travelers prefer to set a lower limit in case their card is stolen. Note that foreign banks also set maximum withdrawal amounts for their ATMs.

• Get your bank's emergency **phone number** in the US (but

not its 800 number, which isn't accessible from overseas) to call collect if you have a problem.

• Ask for your credit card's **PIN** in case you need to make an emergency cash withdrawal or encounter payment machines using the chip-and-PIN system; the bank won't tell you your PIN over the phone, so allow time for it to be mailed to you.

Chip-and-PIN Credit Cards: Europeans use chip-and-PIN credit cards (embedded with an electronic security chip and re-

quiring a four-digit PIN). Most of the chip cards now being offered by major US banks are not true chip-and-PIN cards, but instead are chip-and-signature cards, so you'll be asked to sign a receipt rather than type in the PIN code. These cards work in Europe for live transactions and at most payment machines, but won't work for offline transactions such as at unattended gas pumps.

Older American cards with just a magnetic stripe also may not work at unattended payment machines, such as those at train and subway stations, toll plazas, parking garages, bike-rental kiosks, and gas pumps. If you have problems with either type of American card, try entering your card's PIN, look for a machine that takes cash, or find a clerk who can process the transaction manually.

If you're concerned, ask if your bank offers a true chip-and-PIN card. Andrews Federal Credit Union (www.andrewsfcu.org) and the State Department Federal Credit Union (www.sdfcu.org) offer these cards and are open to all US residents.

Dynamic Currency Conversion: If merchants or hoteliers offer to convert your purchase price into dollars (called dynamic currency conversion, or "DCC"), refuse this "service." You'll pay extra for the expensive convenience of seeing your charge in dollars. Some ATMs and retailers try to confuse customers by presenting DCC in misleading terms. If an ATM offers to "lock in" or "guarantee" your conversion rate, choose "proceed without conversion." Other prompts might state, "You can be charged in dollars: Press YES for dollars, NO for Czech crowns." Always choose the local currency.

Damage Control for Lost Cards

If you lose your credit or debit card, you can stop people from using your card by reporting the loss immediately to the respective global customer-assistance centers. Call these 24-hour US numbers collect: Visa (tel. 303/967-1096), MasterCard (tel. 636/722-7111), or American Express (tel. 336/393-1111). In the Czech Republic, to make a collect call to the US, dial 00-800-222-55288. Press zero or stay on the line for an English-speaking operator. European toll-free numbers (listed by country) can be found at the websites for Visa and MasterCard.

If you are the secondary cardholder, you'll need to provide the primary cardholder's identification–verification details (such as birth date, mother's maiden name, or your Social Security number). You can generally receive a temporary card within two or three business days in Europe (see www.ricksteves.com/help for more).

If you report your loss within two days, you typically won't be responsible for any unauthorized transactions on your account, although many banks charge a liability fee of $50.

TIPPING

Tipping in the Czech Republic isn't as automatic and generous as it is in the US. For special service, tips are appreciated, but not expected. As in the US, the proper amount depends on your resources, tipping philosophy, and the circumstances, but some general guidelines apply.

Taxis: For a typical ride, round up your fare about 5 percent. If the cabbie hauls your bags and zips you to the airport to help you catch your flight, you might want to toss in a little more. But if you feel like you're being driven in circles or otherwise ripped off, skip the tip.

Services: In general, if someone in the tourism or service industry does a super job for you, a small tip (about 50 Kč) is appropriate...but not required. If you're not sure whether (or how much) to tip, ask a local for advice.

GETTING A VAT REFUND

Wrapped into the purchase price of your Czech souvenirs is a Value-Added Tax (VAT) of 21 percent. You're entitled to get most of that tax back if you purchase more than 2,001 Kč (about $80) of goods at a store that participates in the VAT-refund scheme. Typically, you must ring up the minimum at a single retailer—you can't add up your purchases from various shops to reach the required amount.

Getting your refund is usually straightforward and, if you buy a substantial amount of souvenirs, well worth the hassle. (Note that if the store ships the goods to your US home, VAT is not assessed on your purchase.) You'll need to:

Get the paperwork. Have the merchant completely fill out the necessary refund document. You'll have to present your passport.

Get the paperwork done before you leave the store to ensure you'll have everything you need (including your original sales receipt).

Get your stamp at the border or airport. Process your VAT document at your last stop in the Czech Republic (such as at the airport) with the customs agent who deals with VAT refunds. (For the location of customs desks at Prague's Václav Havel Airport, see page 258). Arrive an additional hour before you need to check in for your flight to allow time to find the customs office—and to stand in line. It's best to keep your purchases in your carry-on. If they're too large or dangerous to carry on (such as knives), pack them in your checked bags and alert the check-in agent. You'll be sent (with your tagged bag) to a customs desk outside security; someone will examine your bag, stamp your paperwork, and put your bag on the belt. You're not supposed to use your purchased goods before you leave. If you show up at customs wearing your new chic Czech outfit, officials might look the other way—or deny you a refund.

Collect your refund. You'll need to return your stamped document to the retailer or its representative. Many merchants work with services, such as Global Blue or Premier Tax Free, that have offices at major airports, ports, or border crossings (either before or after security, probably strategically located near a duty-free shop). These services, which extract a 4 percent fee, can refund your money immediately in cash or credit your card (within two billing cycles). Other refund services may require you to mail the documents from home, or more quickly, from your point of departure (using an envelope you've prepared in advance or one that's been provided by the merchant). You'll then have to wait—it can take months.

CUSTOMS FOR AMERICAN SHOPPERS

You are allowed to take home $800 worth of items per person duty-free, once every 31 days. You can take home many processed and packaged foods: vacuum-packed cheeses, dried herbs, jams, baked goods, candy, chocolate, oil, vinegar, mustard, and honey. Fresh fruits and vegetables and most meats are not allowed, with exceptions for some canned items. As for alcohol, you can bring in one liter duty-free (it can be packed securely in your checked luggage, along with any other liquid-containing items).

To bring alcohol (or liquid-packed foods) in your carry-on bag on your flight home, buy it at a duty-free shop at the airport. You'll increase your odds of getting it onto a connecting flight if it's packaged in a "STEB"—a secure, tamper-evident bag. But stay away from liquids in opaque, ceramic, or metallic containers, which usually cannot be successfully screened (STEB or no STEB).

PRACTICALITIES

For details on allowable goods, customs rules, and duty rates, visit http://help.cbp.gov.

Sightseeing

Sightseeing can be hard work. Use these tips to make your visits to the Czech Republic's finest sights meaningful, fun, efficient, and painless.

MAPS AND NAVIGATION TOOLS

A good map is essential for efficient navigation while sightseeing. The maps in this book are concise and simple, designed to help you locate recommended destinations, sights, and local TIs, where you can pick up more in-depth maps. Maps with even more detail are sold at newsstands and bookstores.

You can also use a mapping app on your mobile device. Be aware that pulling up maps or looking up turn-by-turn walking directions on the fly requires an Internet connection: To use this feature, it's smart to get an international data plan (see page 462) or only connect using Wi-Fi. With Google Maps or Apple Maps, it's possible to download a map while online, then go offline and navigate without incurring data-roaming charges, though you can't search for an address or get real-time walking directions. A handful of other apps—including City Maps 2Go, OffMaps, and Nav-free—also allow you to use maps offline.

PLAN AHEAD

Set up an itinerary that allows you to fit in all your must-see sights. For a one-stop look at the best sightseeing options, see "Prague at a Glance" (page 46), and "Day Trips from Prague at a Glance" (page 264); also see "Daily Reminder" on page 38). Most sights keep stable hours, but you can easily confirm the latest by checking with the TI or visiting museum websites.

Don't put off visiting a must-see sight—you never know when a place will close unexpectedly for a holiday, strike, or restoration. Many museums are closed or have reduced hours at least a few days a year, especially on holidays such as Christmas, New Year's, and Labor Day (May 1). Prague's Jewish Quarter—and other Jewish sites around the country—are closed on Jewish holidays, which are particularly frequent in the fall. A list of major holidays is on page 482; check online for possible museum closures during your trip. In summer, some sights may stay open late; off-season, hours may be shorter.

Going at the right time helps avoid crowds—especially in jam-packed Prague. This book offers tips on the best times to see specif-

PRACTICALITIES

ic sights. Try visiting popular sights very early or very late. Evening visits (when available) are usually peaceful, with fewer crowds.

Study up. To get the most out of the self-guided walks and sight descriptions in this book, read them before you visit.

AT SIGHTS

Here's what you can typically expect:

Entering: Be warned that you may not be allowed to enter if you arrive less than 30 to 60 minutes before closing time. And guards start ushering people out well before the actual closing time, so don't save the best for last.

Many sights have a security check, where you must open your bag or send it through a metal detector. Allow extra time for these lines in your planning. Some sights require you to check daypacks and coats. (If you'd rather not check your daypack, try carrying it tucked under your arm like a purse as you enter.)

Castle Tours: Getting inside a castle often means taking a mandatory guided tour—which may be offered infrequently in English. Typically a castle will have two or three different, numbered "routes" highlighting different aspects of the architecture or history; for the castles described in this book, I've noted the best choice. It's smart to check the castle's website or call ahead to ask about English tours; if they expect crowds, reserve a spot (generally for a small extra fee). To be more spontaneous, show up and join whichever tour departs next (usually in Czech)—they'll give you an English handout to follow along.

Photography: If the museum's photo policy isn't clearly posted, ask a guard. Generally, taking photos without a flash or tripod is allowed (although some Czech sights charge a photography fee). Some sights ban photos altogether; others ban selfie sticks.

Temporary Exhibits: Museums may show special exhibits in addition to their permanent collection. Some exhibits are included in the entry price, while others come at an extra cost (which you may have to pay even if you don't want to see the exhibit).

Expect Changes: Artwork can be on tour, on loan, out sick, or shifted at the whim of the curator. Pick up a floor plan as you enter, and ask museum staff if you can't find a particular item.

Audioguides and Apps: Many sights rent audioguides, which generally offer good recorded descriptions in English. If you bring your own earbuds, you can enjoy better sound and avoid holding the device to your ear. To save money, bring a Y-jack and share one audioguide with your travel partner. Museums and sights often offer free apps that you can download to your mobile device (check their websites).

🎧 I've produced a free downloadable Prague City Walk audio tour; see page 10.

Services: Important sights may have a reasonably priced on-site café or cafeteria (handy places to rejuvenate during a long visit). The WCs at sights are usually free and generally clean.

Before Leaving: At the gift shop, scan the postcard rack or thumb through a guidebook to be sure that you haven't overlooked something that you'd like to see.

Every sight or museum offers more than what is covered in this book. Use the information in this book as an introduction—not the final word.

Sleeping

I favor hotels and restaurants that are handy to your sightseeing activities. Rather than list lodgings scattered throughout a city, I choose hotels in my favorite neigh-borhoods. My recommendations run the gamut, from dorm beds to fancy doubles with all the comforts.

Extensive and opinionated list-ings of good-value rooms are a major feature of this book. I like places that are clean, central, relatively quiet at night, reasonably priced, friendly, small enough to have a hands-on owner or manager and stable staff, and run with a respect for Czech traditions. I'm more impressed by a convenient location and a fun-loving philosophy than flat-screen TVs and a fancy gym. Most places I recommend fall short of perfection. But if I can find a place with most of these features, it's a keeper.

Book your accommodations well in advance, especially if you want to stay at one of my top listings or if you'll be traveling during busy times. See page 482 for a list of major holidays and festivals in the Czech Republic; for tips on making reservations, see page 452.

Some people make reservations as they travel, calling hotels a few days to a week before their arrival. If you anticipate crowds (weekends are worst) on the day you want to check in, call ho-tels at about 9:00 or 10:00, when the receptionist knows who'll be checking out and which rooms will be available. Some apps—such as HotelTonight.com—specialize in last-minute rooms, often at business-class hotels in big cities. If you encounter a language bar-rier, ask the fluent receptionist at your current hotel to call for you.

RATES AND DEALS

I've categorized my recommended accommodations based on price, indicated with a dollar-sign rating (see sidebar). The price ranges suggest an estimated cost for a one-night stay in a standard dou-

Sleep Code

Hotels are classified based on the average price of a standard double room with breakfast in high season. I've given *very* rough conversions to dollars using 25 Kč = $1.

$$$$	**Splurge:**	Most rooms over 3,400 Kč (roughly $135)
$$$	**Pricier:**	2,600-3,400 Kč ($105-135)
$$	**Moderate:**	1,800-2,600 Kč ($70-105)
$	**Budget:**	1,000-1,800 Kč ($40-70)
¢	**Backpacker:**	Under 1,000 Kč ($40)
RS%	**Rick Steves discount**	

Unless otherwise noted, credit cards are accepted, hotel staff speak basic English, and free Wi-Fi is available. Comparison-shop by checking prices at several hotels (on each hotel's own website, on a booking site, or by email). For the best deal, *book directly with the hotel.* Ask for a discount if paying in cash; if the listing includes **RS%,** request a Rick Steves discount.

ble room with a private toilet and shower in high season, include breakfast, and assume you're booking directly with the hotel (not through a booking site, which extracts a commission and logically closes the door on special deals). Room prices can fluctuate significantly with demand and amenities (size, views, room class, and so on), but these relative price categories remain constant.

Room rates are especially volatile at larger hotels that use "dynamic pricing" to predict demand. Rates can skyrocket during festivals and conventions, while business hotels can have deep discounts on weekends when demand plummets. For this reason, of the many hotels I recommend, it's difficult to say which will be the best value on a given day—until you do your homework.

Once your dates are set, check the specific price for your preferred stay at several hotels. You can do this either by comparing prices online on the hotels' own websites, or by emailing several hotels directly and asking for their best rate. Even if you start your search on a booking site such as TripAdvisor or Booking.com, you'll usually find the lowest rates through a hotel's own website.

Many hotels offer a discount to those who pay cash or stay longer than three nights. To cut costs further, try asking for a cheaper room (for example, with a shared bathroom or no window) or offer to skip breakfast.

Additionally, some accommodations offer a special discount for Rick Steves readers, indicated in this guidebook by the abbreviation "**RS%**." Discounts vary: Ask for details when you book. Generally, to qualify you must book direct (that is, not through a booking site), mention this book when you reserve, show the book upon arrival, and sometimes pay cash or stay a certain number of

PRACTICALITIES

Making Hotel Reservations

Reserve your rooms several weeks or even months in advance—or as soon as you've pinned down your travel dates. Note that some national holidays merit your making reservations far in advance (see page 482).

Requesting a Reservation: It's easiest to book your room through the hotel's website. (For the best rates, use the hotel's official site and not a booking agency's site.) If there's no reservation form, or for complicated requests, send an email (see next page for a sample). Most recommended hotels take reservations in English.

The hotelier wants to know:

- the size of your party and type of rooms you need
- your arrival and departure dates, written European-style—day followed by month and year (for example, 18/06/17 or 18 June 2017); include the total number of nights
- special requests (such as en suite bathroom vs. down the hall, cheapest room, twin beds vs. double bed, quiet room)
- applicable discounts (such as a Rick Steves reader discount, cash discount, or promotional rate)

Confirming a Reservation: Most places will request a credit-card number to hold your room. If they don't have a secure online reservation form—look for the *https*—you can email it (I do), but it's safer to share that confidential info via a phone call or fax.

Canceling a Reservation: If you must cancel, it's courteous—and smart—to do so with as much notice as possible, especially

nights. In some cases, you may need to enter a discount code (which I've provided in the listing) in the booking form on the hotel's website. Rick Steves discounts apply to readers with ebooks as well as printed books. Understandably, discounts do not apply to promotional rates.

TYPES OF ACCOMMODATIONS
Hotels

Hotel prices in Prague are at Western European levels, but once you get out of the city, you'll pay half as much for a similar room. Plan on spending $80-200 per hotel double in Prague and $40-100 in smaller towns.

In addition to doubles, most hotels also offer single rooms, and some offer larger rooms for four or more people (I call these "family rooms" in the listings). Some hotels can add an extra bed (for a small

From:	rick@ricksteves.com
Sent:	Today
To:	info@hotelcentral.com
Subject:	Reservation request for 19-22 July

Dear Hotel Central,

I would like to stay at your hotel. Please let me know if you have a room available and the price for:
• 2 people
• Double bed and en suite bathroom in a quiet room
• Arriving 19 July, departing 22 July (3 nights)

Thank you!
Rick Steves

for smaller family-run places. Cancellation policies can be strict; read the fine print or ask about these before you book. Many discounts require prepayment, with no refunds for cancellations.

Reconfirming a Reservation: Always call to reconfirm your room a few days in advance. For smaller hotels and pensions, I call again on my day of arrival to tell my host what time I expect to get there (especially important if arriving after 17:00).

Phoning: For tips on calling hotels overseas, see page 464

charge) to a double into a triple. In general, a triple room is cheaper than the cost of a double and a single. Traveling alone can be expensive: A single room can be close to the cost of a double.

Breakfast is generally included (sometimes continental, but often buffet). Hotel elevators, while becoming more common, are often very small—pack light. You may need to send your bags up one at a time.

If you're arriving early in the morning, your room probably won't be ready. Check your bag safely at the hotel and dive right into sightseeing.

Hoteliers can be a good source of advice. Most know their city well, and can assist you with everything from public transit and airport connections to finding a good restaurant, the nearest launderette, or a late-night pharmacy.

Even at the best places, mechanical breakdowns occur: Sinks leak, hot water turns cold, toilets may gurgle or smell, the Wi-Fi goes out, or the air-conditioning dies when you need it most. Report your concerns clearly and calmly at the front desk. For more complicated problems, don't expect instant results.

PRACTICALITIES

If you find that night noise is a problem (if, for instance, your room is over a pub), ask for a quiet room in the back or on an upper floor. To guard against theft in your room, keep valuables out of sight. Some rooms come with a safe, and other hotels have safes at the front desk. I've never bothered using one.

While it's customary to pay for your room upon departure, it can be a good idea to settle your bill the day before, when you're not in a hurry and while the manager's in. That way you'll have time to discuss and address any points of contention.

Above all, keep a positive attitude. Remember, you're on vacation. If your hotel is a disappointment, spend more time out enjoying the place you came to see.

Short-Term Rentals

A short-term rental—whether an apartment, house, or room in a local's home—is an increasingly popular alternative to a hotel, especially if you plan to settle in one location for several nights. For stays longer than a few days, you can usually find a rental that's comparable to—or even cheaper than—a hotel room with similar amenities. Plus, you'll get a behind-the-scenes peek into how locals live.

The rental route isn't for everyone. Many places require a minimum night stay, and compared to hotels, rentals usually have less-flexible cancellation policies. Also you're generally on your own: There's no hotel reception desk, breakfast, or daily cleaning service.

Finding Accommodations: Websites such as www.airbnb.com, www.roomorama.com, and www.vrbo.com let you browse properties and correspond directly with European property owners or managers. Or, for more guidance, consider using a rental agency such as www.interhomeusa.com or www.rentavilla.com. Agency-represented apartments may cost more, but this route often offers more help and safeguards than booking direct.

Before you commit to a rental, be clear on the details, location, and amenities. I like to virtually "explore" the neighborhood using the Street View feature on Google Maps. Also consider the proximity to public transportation, and how well-connected it is with the rest of the city. Ask about amenities that are important to you (elevator, laundry, coffee maker, Wi-Fi, parking, etc.). Reading reviews from previous guests can help identify trouble spots that are glossed over in the official description.

Private and Shared Rooms: A cheap option in the Czech Republic is a room in a private home (called a **"pension,"** some-

PRACTICALITIES

The Good and Bad of Online Reviews

User-generated review sites and apps such as Yelp, Booking. com, and TripAdvisor are changing the travel industry. These sites can give you a consensus of opinions about everything from hotels and restaurants to sights and nightlife. If you scan reviews of a hotel and see several complaints about noise or a rotten location, it tells you something important that you'd never learn from the hotel's own website.

But review sites are only as good as the judgment of their reviewers. And while these sites work hard to weed out bogus users, my hunch is that a significant percentage of user reviews are posted by friends or enemies of the business being reviewed.

As a guidebook writer, my sense is that there is a big difference between this uncurated information and a guidebook. A user-generated review is based on the experience of one person, who stayed at one hotel and ate at a few restaurants, and doesn't have much of a basis for comparison. A guidebook is the work of a trained researcher who visited many alternatives to assess their relative value. I recently checked out some top-rated user-reviewed hotel and restaurant listings in various towns; when stacked up against their competitors, some were gems, while just as many were duds.

Both types of information have their place, and in many ways, they're complementary. If something is well-reviewed in a guidebook, and also gets good ratings on one of these sites, it's likely a winner.

times advertised with the German phrase *Zimmer frei*, "room free," meaning vacancy). Pensions are inexpensive and at least as comfortable as a cheap hotel. While you can't expect your host to also be your tour guide—or even to provide you with much info— some may be interested in getting to know the travelers who come through their home. Beds range from air-mattress-in-living-room basic to plush-B&B-suite posh. The boss changes the sheets, so people staying several nights are most desirable—and stays of less than three nights are often charged up to 30 percent more. A pension is also a good option for those traveling alone, as you're more likely to find true single rooms. If staying for several nights, you can buy groceries just as you would in an apartment or rental house.

Apartments: If you're staying somewhere for four nights or longer, it's worth considering an apartment (anything less than that isn't worth the extra effort involved, such as arranging key pickup, buying groceries, etc.). Apartment rentals can be especially cost-effective for groups and families. European apartments, like hotel rooms, tend to be small by US standards. But they often come with laundry machines and small, equipped kitchens, making it easier and cheaper to dine in. If you make good use of the kitchen (and Europe's great produce markets), you'll save on your meal budget.

Other Options: Swapping homes with a local works for people with an appealing place to offer, and who can live with the idea of having strangers in their home (don't assume where you live is not interesting to Europeans). A good place to start is HomeExchange (www.homeexchange.com).

To sleep for free, Couchsurfing.com is a vagabond's alternative to Airbnb. It lists millions of outgoing members, who host fellow "surfers" in their homes.

Hostels

A hostel provides cheap beds in dorms where you sleep alongside strangers for about $20-25 per night. Travelers of any age are welcome if they don't mind dorm-style accommodations and meeting other travelers. Most hostels offer kitchen facilities, guest computers, Wi-Fi, and a self-service laundry. Hostels almost always provide bedding, but the towel's up to you (though you can usually rent one for a small fee). Family and private rooms are often available. Unlike in Western Europe, many hostels in the Czech Republic are in university dorms where two- or three-person rooms are the norm.

Independent hostels tend to be easygoing, colorful, and informal (no membership required; www.hostelworld.com). You may pay slightly less by booking direct with the hostel. **Official hostels** are part of Hostelling International (HI) and share an online booking site (www.hihostels.com). HI hostels typically require that you be a member or pay extra per night.

Eating

You'll find that the local cafés, cuisine, beer, and wine are highlights of your Czech adventure. This is affordable sightseeing for your palate.

When restaurant-hunting, choose a spot filled with locals, not the place with the big neon signs boasting "We Speak English and Accept Credit Cards." Incredible deals abound in the Czech Republic, where locals routinely eat well for $5. Venturing even a block or two off the main drag leads to authentic, higher-quality food for less than half the price of the tourist-oriented places. Locals eat better at lower-rent locales. Most restaurants tack a menu onto their door for browsers and have an English menu inside.

In general, Czech restaurants are open Sunday through

Restaurant Price Code

I've assigned each eatery a price category, based on the average cost of a typical main course. Drinks, desserts, and splurge items (steak and seafood) can raise the price considerably. I've given *very* rough conversions to dollars using 25 Kč = $1.

$$$$ **Splurge:** Most main courses over 500 Kč (roughly $20)

   $$$ **Pricier:** 250-500 Kč ($10-20)

     $$ **Moderate:** 120-250 Kč ($5-10)

      $ **Budget:** Under 120 Kč ($5)

In the Czech Republic, a pub, basic sit-down eatery, and less-touristy café or teahouse is **$**; a typical restaurant—or a fancy café with coffee over 50 Kč and tea over 100 Kč—is **$$**; an upscale restaurant is **$$$**; and a swanky splurge is **$$$$**.

Thursday 11:00-22:00, and Friday and Saturday 11:00-24:00. Only a rude waiter will rush you. Good service is relaxed (slow to an American). You can stay in a pub as long as you want—no one will bring you the *účet* (bill) until you ask for it: *"Pane vrchní, za-platím!"* (PAH-neh VURCH-nee zah-plah-TEEM; "Mr. Waiter, now I pay!").

In Prague, it's generally better to pay cash for your meals rather than use your credit card. Tipping is an issue only at restaurants that have table service. If you order your food at a counter, don't tip. At Czech restaurants that have a waitstaff, service is included, although it's common to round up the bill after a good meal (usually 5-10 percent; e.g., for a 370-Kč meal, pay 400 Kč). If you warm up the waiter with a few Czech words, such as "please" (*prosím;* PROH-zeem) and "thank you" (*děkuji;* DYACK-khuyi), you'll get better service and won't be expected to tip more than a local. But if you greet your waiter in English, he'll want a 15 percent tip. Believe me: The slightest attempt at speaking Czech (see phrases on page 491) turns you from a targeted tourist into a special guest, even in the most touristy restaurants.

When you're in the mood for something halfway between a restaurant and a picnic, look for takeout food stands, bakeries (with sandwiches and small pizzas to go), delis with stools or a table, department-store cafeterias, salad bars, or simple little eateries for fast and easy sit-down restaurant food.

Venues are required to post stickers on the exterior of their premises indicating whether they allow smoking, prohibit it, or provide a nonsmoking section.

RESTAURANT PRICING

I've categorized my recommended eateries based on price, indicated with a dollar-sign rating (see sidebar). The price ranges suggest the average price of a typical main course—but not necessarily a complete meal. Obviously, expensive items (like steak and seafood), fine wine, appetizers, and dessert can significantly increase your final bill.

The dollar-sign categories also indicate the overall personality and "feel" of a place (outside of Prague, your money goes farther—you can eat well in a fancy place for moderate prices):

$ Budget eateries include street food, takeaway, order-at-the-counter shops, basic cafeterias, bakeries selling sandwiches, and so on.

$$ Moderate eateries are typically nice (but not fancy) sit-down restaurants, ideal for a straightforward, fill-the-tank meal. Most of my listings fall in this category—great for getting a good taste of the local cuisine on a budget.

$$$ Pricier eateries are a notch up, with more attention paid to the setting, presentation, and cuisine. These are ideal for a memorable meal that's relatively casual and doesn't break the bank. This category often includes affordable "destination" or "foodie" restaurants.

$$$$ Splurge eateries are dress-up-for-a-special-occasion-swanky—Michelin star-type restaurants, typically with an elegant setting, polished service, pricey and intricate cuisine, and an expansive (and expensive) wine list.

I haven't categorized places where you might assemble a picnic, snack, or graze: supermarkets, delis, ice-cream stands, cafés or bars specializing in drinks, chocolate shops, and so on.

CZECH FOOD

The Czechs have one of Europe's most stick-to-your-ribs cuisines. Heavy on meat, potatoes, and cabbage, it's hearty and tasty—designed to keep peasants fueled through a day of hard work. Some people could eat this stuff forever, while others seek a frequent break in the form of ethnic restaurants (bigger towns such as Prague, Český Krumlov, and Kutná Hora have several options).

A Czech restaurant is a social place where people come to relax. Tables are not private. You can ask to join someone, and you will most likely make some new friends. After a sip of beer, ask for the *jídelní lístek* (menu).

Soups: *Polévka* (soup) is the most essential part of a meal. The saying goes: "The soup fills you up, the dish plugs it up." Some of the thick soups for a cold day are *zelná* or *zelňačka* (cabbage),

Czech Dumplings

Czech dumplings (knedlíky) resemble steamed white bread. They come in plain or potato (bramborové) varieties; are meant to be drowned in gravy (dumplings never accompany sauceless dishes); and are eaten with a knife and fork.

Sweet dumplings, listed in the dessert section on a menu, are a tempting option in summer, when they are loaded with fresh strawberries, blueberries, apricots, or plums, and garnished with custard and melted butter. Beware, though, that many restaurants cheat by filling the sticky dough with a smattering of jam or fruit preserve; before ordering, ask the waiter for details, or discreetly inspect that plate at your neighbor's table. Dumplings with frozen fruit lose some of the flavor, but are still worth trying.

čočková (lentil), fazolová (bean), and dršťková (tripe—delicious if fresh, chewy as gum if not). The lighter soups are hovězí or slepičí vývar s nudlemi (beef or chicken broth with noodles), pórková (leek), and květáková (cauliflower).

Bread: Pečivo (bread) is either delivered with the soup, or you need to ask for it; it's always charged separately depending on how many rohlíky (rolls) or slices of chleba (yeast bread) you eat.

Main Dishes: These can either be hotová jídla (quick, ready-to-serve standard dishes, in some places available only during lunch hours, generally 11:00-14:30) or the more specialized jídla na objednávku or minutky (plates prepared when you order).

The word pečené (roasted) shows up frequently on menus, whether it's vepřová pečeně (pork roast), pečené kuře (roasted chicken), or pečená kachna (roasted duck). Other popular meat dishes are smažený řízek (fried pork fillet, like Wiener schnitzel), guláš (a thick, meaty stew), and svíčková na smetaně (beef tenderloin in cream sauce). If you're spending the night out with friends, have a beer and feast on the huge vepřové koleno (pork knuckle), usually served with mustard (hořčicí), horseradish sauce (křenem), and yeast bread (chleba).

In this landlocked country, fish options are typically limited to kapr (carp) and pstruh (trout), prepared in a variety of ways and served with potatoes or fries—although recently, Czech perch and Norwegian salmon have cropped up on many local menus.

Vegetarians can go for the delicious smažený sýr s bramborem (fried cheese with potatoes) or default to *čočka s vejci* (lentils with fried egg).

Starches and Garnishes: *Hotová jídla* come with set garnishes, but if ordering à la carte *(jídla na objednávku)*, you'll typically need to order your garnishes separately (otherwise you'll get only the main dish). In either case, the most common sides are *knedlíky* (bread dumplings, described in the sidebar), *zelím* (cabbage), and *bramborem* (potatoes).

Salad: *Šopský salát*, like a Greek salad, is usually the best salad option (a mix of tomatoes, cucumbers, peppers, onion, and feta cheese with vinegar and olive oil). The waiter will bring it with the main dish, unless you specify that you want it before.

Dessert: For *moučník* (dessert), there are *palačinka* (crêpes served with fruit or jam), *lívance* (small pancakes with jam and curd), *zmrzlinový pohár* (ice-cream sundae), or fruit-filled dumplings. Many restaurants will offer different sorts of *koláče* (pastries) and *štrůdl* (apple strudel), but it's much better to get these directly from a bakery. A

větrník is a super-decadent, glazed cream puff.

All over Prague's Old Town, you'll find kiosks selling a treat called *trdlo* or *trdelník*. This is a long ribbon of dough wrapped around a stick, slowly cooked on a rotisserie, then rolled in cinnamon, sugar, or other toppings. While these aren't "traditional Czech" (they were imported quite recently from Hungary), they do offer a fresh, sweet treat. Try to get one that's still warm, rather than one wrapped in plastic—it makes a big difference.

Beverages: No Czech meal is complete without a cup of strong *turecká káva* (Turkish coffee—finely ground coffee that only partly dissolves, leaving "mud" on the bottom, highly caffeinated and drunk without milk). Although espressos and instant coffees have made headway in the past few years, some Czechs regard them as a threat to tradition.

Czech mineral waters *(minerálka)* have a high mineral content. They're naturally carbonated because they come from the springs in the many Czech spas (Mattoni, the most common brand, is from Carlsbad). If you want still water, ask for *voda bez bublinek* (water without bubbles). Tap water is generally not served. Water comes bottled and generally costs more than beer.

Bohemia is beer country, with Europe's best and cheapest brew (see the sidebar on page 216). Moravians prefer wine and *slivovice* (SLEE-voh-veet-seh)—a plum brandy so highly valued that it's the de facto currency of the Carpathian Mountains (often used to barter with farmers and other mountain folk). *Medovina* ("honey wine") is mead.

In bars and restaurants, you can go wild with memorable liqueurs, most of which cost about a dollar a shot. Experiment. *Fernet,* a bitter drink made from many herbs, is the leading Czech aperitif. Absinthe, made from wormwood and herbs, is a watered-down version of the hallucinogenic drink that's illegal in much of Europe. It's famous as the muse of many artists (including Henri de Toulouse-Lautrec in Paris more than a century ago). *Becherovka,* made of 13 herbs and 38 percent alcohol, was used to settle upset aristocratic tummies and as an aphrodisiac. This velvety drink remains popular today. *Becherovka* and tonic mixed together is nicknamed *beton* ("concrete"). If you drink three, you'll find out why.

Staying Connected

One of the most common questions I hear from travelers is, "How can I stay connected in Europe?" The short answer is: more easily and cheaply than you might think.

The simplest solution is to bring your own device—mobile phone, tablet, or laptop—and use it just as you would at home (following the tips below, such as connecting to free Wi-Fi whenever possible). Another option is to buy a European SIM card for your mobile phone—either your US phone or one you buy in Europe. Or you can travel without a mobile device and use European landlines and computers to connect. Each of these options is described below; more details are at www.ricksteves.com/phoning. For a very practical one-hour lecture covering tech issues for travelers, see www.ricksteves.com/travel-talks.

USING YOUR OWN MOBILE DEVICE IN EUROPE

Without an international plan, typical rates from major service providers (AT&T, Verizon, etc.) for using your device abroad are about $1.70/minute for voice calls, 50 cents to send text messages,

5 cents to receive them, and $10 to download one megabyte of data. At these rates, costs can add up quickly. Here are some budget tips and options.

Use free Wi-Fi whenever possible. Unless you have an unlimited-data plan, you're best off saving most of your online tasks for Wi-Fi. You can access the Internet, send texts, and make voice calls over Wi-Fi.

Many cafés (including Starbucks and McDonald's) have free hotspots for customers; look for signs offering it and ask for the Wi-Fi password when you buy something. You'll also often find Wi-Fi at TIs, city squares, major museums, public-transit hubs, airports, and aboard trains and buses.

Sign up for an international plan. Most providers offer a global calling plan that cuts the per-minute cost of phone calls and texts, and a flat-fee data plan. Your normal plan may already include international coverage (T-Mobile's does).

Before your trip, call your provider or check online to confirm that your phone will work in Europe, and research your provider's international rates. Activate the plan a day or two before you leave, then remember to cancel it when your trip's over.

Minimize the use of your cellular network. When you can't find Wi-Fi, you can use your cellular network to connect to the Internet, text, or make voice calls. When you're done, avoid further charges by manually switching off "data roaming" or "cellular data" (in your device's Settings menu; for help, ask your service provider or Google it). Another way to make sure you're not accidentally using data roaming is to put your device in "airplane" or "flight" mode (which also disables phone calls and texts), and then turn on Wi-Fi as needed.

Don't use your cellular network for bandwidth-gobbling tasks, such as Skyping, downloading apps, and streaming video: Save these for when you're on Wi-Fi. Using a navigation app such as Google Maps over a cellular network can take lots of data, so do this sparingly or use it offline.

Limit automatic updates. By default, your device constantly checks for a data connection and updates apps. It's smart to disable these features so your apps will only update when you're on Wi-Fi, and to change your device's email settings from "auto-retrieve" to "manual" (or from "push" to "fetch").

It's also a good idea to keep track of your data usage. On your device's menu, look for "cellular data usage" or "mobile data" and reset the counter at the start of your trip.

Use Skype or other calling/messaging apps for cheaper calls and texts. Certain apps let you make voice or video calls or send texts over the Internet for free or cheap. If you're bringing a tablet or laptop, you can also use them for voice calls and texts. All you

Tips on Internet Security

Using the Internet while traveling brings added security risks, whether you're getting online with your own device or at a public terminal using a shared network. Here are some tips for securing your data:

First, make sure that your device is running the latest version of its operating system and security software, and that your apps are up-to-date. Next, ensure that your device is password- or passcode-protected so thieves can't access it if your device is stolen. For extra security, set passwords on apps that access key info (such as email or Facebook).

On the road, use only legitimate Wi-Fi hotspots. Ask the hotel or café staff for the specific name of their Wi-Fi network, and make sure you log on to that exact one. Hackers sometimes create a bogus hotspot with a similar or vague name (such as "Hotel Europa Free Wi-Fi"). The best Wi-Fi networks require a password. If you're not actively using a hotspot, turn off your device's Wi-Fi connection so it's not visible to others.

Be especially cautious when accessing financial information online. Experts say it's best to use a banking app rather than sign in to your bank's website via a browser (the app is less likely to get hacked). Refrain from logging in to any personal finance sites on a public computer. Even if you're using your own mobile device at a password-protected hotspot, there's a remote chance that a hacker who's logged on to the same network could see what you're doing.

Never share your credit-card number (or any other sensitive information) online unless you know that the site is secure. A secure site displays a little padlock icon, and the URL begins with *https* (instead of the usual *http*).

have to do is log on to a Wi-Fi network, then contact any of your friends or family members who are also online and signed into the same service.

You can make voice and video calls using Skype, Viber, Face-Time, and Google+ Hangouts. If the connection is bad, try making an audio-only call. WhatsApp only offers voice calls. You can also make voice calls from your device to telephones worldwide for just a few cents per minute using Skype, Viber, or Hangouts if you buy credit first.

To text for free over Wi-Fi, try apps like Google+ Hangouts, WhatsApp, Viber, Facebook Messenger, and iMessage. Make sure you're on Wi-Fi to avoid data charges.

USING A EUROPEAN SIM CARD IN A MOBILE PHONE

This option works well for those who want to make a lot of voice calls at cheap local rates, and those who need faster connection

PRACTICALITIES

How to Dial

International Calls

Whether phoning from a US landline or mobile phone, or from a number in another European country, here's how to make an international call. I've used one of my recommended Prague hotels as an example (tel. 257-311-150).

Initial Zero: Drop the initial zero from international phone numbers—except when calling Italy.

Mobile Tip: If using a mobile phone, the "+" sign can replace the international access code (for a "+" sign, press and hold "0").

US/Canada to Europe

Dial 011 (US/Canada international access code), country code (420 for the Czech Republic), and phone number.

▶ To call the Prague hotel from home, dial 011-420-257-311-150.

Country to Country Within Europe

Dial 00 (Europe international access code), country code, and phone number.

▶ To call the Prague hotel from Germany, dial 00-420-257-311-150.

Europe to the US/Canada

Dial 00, country code (1 for US/Canada), and phone number.

▶ To call from Europe to my office in Edmonds, Washington, dial 00-1-425-771-8303.

Domestic Calls

To call within the Czech Republic (from one Czech landline or mobile phone to another), simply dial the phone number, including the initial 0 if there is one.

▶ To call the Prague hotel from Český Krumlov, dial 257-311-150.

More Dialing Tips

Czech Phone Numbers: All Prague landlines numbers begin

speeds than their US carrier provides. With a European SIM card, you get a European phone number—and European rates.

You can buy a basic cell phone in Europe (as little as $20 from mobile-phone shops anywhere, including a SIM card). Or you can bring an "unlocked" US phone (check with your carrier about unlocking it) and swap out the original SIM card for one you buy in Europe. SIM cards are sold at mobile-phone shops, department-store electronics counters, newsstands, and vending machines. Costing about $5-10, they usually include about that much pre-paid calling credit, with no contract and no commitment. A SIM card that also includes data (including roaming) will cost $20-40 more for one month of data within the country in which it was pur-

with a 2. Mobile numbers begin with the three digits running from 601 to 777 and are substantially more expensive to call than a landline.

Toll and Toll-Free Calls: International rates apply to US toll-free numbers dialed from the Czech Republic—they're not free.

More Phoning Help: See www.howtocallabroad.com.

European Country Codes			
Austria	43	Italy	39
Belgium	32	Latvia	371
Bosnia-Herzegovina	387	Montenegro	382
Croatia	385	Morocco	212
Czech Republic	420	Netherlands	31
Denmark	45	Norway	47
Estonia	372	Poland	48
Finland	358	Portugal	351
France	33	Russia	7
Germany	49	Slovakia	421
Gibraltar	350	Slovenia	386
Great Britain	44	Spain	34
Greece	30	Sweden	46
Hungary	36	Switzerland	41
Ireland & N. Ireland	353 / 44	Turkey	90

chased. This can be faster than data roaming through your home provider. To get the best rates, buy a new SIM card whenever you arrive in a new country.

I like to buy SIM cards at a mobile-phone shop where there's a clerk to help explain the options and brands. Certain brands—including Lebara, Lycamobile, and Vodafone, which are available in multiple European countries—are reliable and especially economical. Ask the clerk to help you insert your SIM card, set it up, and show you how to use it. In some countries you'll be required to register the SIM card with your passport as an antiterrorism measure (which may mean you can't use the phone for the first hour or two).

Find out how to check your credit balance. When you run out

Hurdling the Language Barrier

The language barrier in the Czech Republic is no bigger than in Western Europe. In fact, I find that it's even easier to communicate in Český Krumlov than it is in Madrid. You'll find that most people in the tourist industry—and just about all young people—speak English well.

Of course, not everyone speaks English. You'll run into the most substantial language barriers when you need to deal with a clerk or service person over age 50 (train station and post-office staff, maids, museum guards, bakers, and so on). Be reasonable in your expectations. Czech post-office clerks and museum ticket-sellers are every bit as friendly, cheery, and multilingual as ours are in the US. Luckily, it's relatively easy to get your point across. I've often bought a train ticket simply by writing out the name of my destination; the time I want to travel (using the 24-hour clock); and, if necessary, the date I want to leave (day first, then month, then year). Here's an example of what I'd show a ticket seller at a train station: "Olomouc - 17:30 - 15.7.2018."

Czech is a Slavic language closely related to its Polish and Slovak neighbors. Slavic pronunciation can be tricky. In fact, when the first Christian missionaries, Cyril and Methodius, came

of credit, you can top it up at newsstands, tobacco shops, mobile-phone stores, or many other businesses (look for your SIM card's logo in the window), or online.

UNTETHERED TRAVEL: PUBLIC PHONES AND COMPUTERS

It's possible to travel in Europe without a mobile device. You can check email or browse websites using public computers and Internet cafés, and make calls from your hotel room and/or public phones.

Phones in your **hotel room** generally have a fee for placing local and "toll-free" calls, as well as long-distance or international calls—ask for the rates before you dial. Since you're never charged for receiving calls, it's better to have someone from the US call you in your room.

If these fees are low, hotel phones can be used inexpensively for calls made with cheap international phone cards (sold at many

to Eastern Europe a millennium ago, they invented a whole new alphabet to represent these strange Slavic sounds. A variation of their alphabet, called Cyrillic after its inventor, is still used today in the eastern Slavic countries (such as Serbia and Russia).

Fortunately, the Czechs long ago converted to the same Roman alphabet we use, but they've added lots of different diacritics—little markings below and above letters—to represent a wide range of sounds. An acute accent (*á, é, í, ó, ú, ý*) means you linger on that vowel; it does not indicate stress, which invariably falls on the first syllable. The letter *c* always sounds like "ts" (as in "cats"). The little accent (*háček*) above the *č, š,* or *ž* makes it sound like "ch," "sh," or "zh" (as in "leisure"). A *háček* over *ě* makes it sound like "yeh."

Czech has one sound that occurs in no other language: *ř* (as in "Dvořák"), which sounds like a cross between a rolled "r" and "zh." Another unusual sound is *ň*, which is pronounced "ny" (as in "canyon"). These sounds are notoriously difficult for foreigners to duplicate; it's easiest just to replace them with simple "r" and "n" sounds.

Study the Czech survival phrases on page 491 and give it your best shot. The locals will appreciate your efforts. When navigating a town, these words can be helpful: *město* (MYEHS-toh, town), *náměstí* (NAH-myehs-tee, square), *ulice* (OO-leet-sah, street), *nábřeží* (NAH-bzheh-zhee, embankment road), and *most* (mohst, bridge).

If you speak German, it can come in handy—especially in the south of the country, where the economy depends in part on Austrian tourists from across the border.

newsstands, street kiosks, tobacco shops, and train stations). You'll either get a prepaid card with a toll-free number and a scratch-to-reveal PIN code, or a code printed on a receipt.

You'll see **public pay phones** in a few post offices and train stations. The phones generally come with multilingual instructions, and some work with insertable phone cards sold at post offices, newsstands, etc.). With the exception of Great Britain, each European country has its own insertable phone card—so your Czech card won't work in an Austrian phone.

Public computers are easy to find. Many hotels have one in their lobby for guests to use; otherwise you can find them at Internet cafés and public libraries (ask your hotelier or the TI for the nearest location). If typing on a European keyboard, use the "Alt Gr" key to the right of the space bar to insert the extra symbol that appears on some keys. If you can't locate a special character (such as @), simply copy it from a Web page and paste it into your email message.

MAIL

You can mail one package per day to yourself worth up to $200 duty-free from Europe to the US (mark it "personal purchases"). If you're sending a gift to someone, mark it "unsolicited gift." For details, visit www.cbp.gov, select "Travel," and search for "Know Before You Go." The Czech postal service works fine, but for quick transatlantic delivery (in either direction), consider services such as DHL (www.dhl.com).

Transportation

Within Prague, a car is a worthless headache. If you're staying mostly in Prague and tackling a few convenient side-trips (such as Kutná Hora and Český Krumlov), public transportation works well. If you'll be venturing farther into the countryside, trains and buses will get you where you need to go—but renting a car gives you greater flexibility. I find the Czech Republic a delightful place to drive; outside of the congested Prague area, the roads are uncrowded and in generally good repair, and the rolling countryside is gently scenic. For connecting Prague to international destinations (like Budapest or Kraków), stick with the train.

Trains

Trains are fairly punctual (although you can expect the occasional late arrival) and cover cities well, but frustrating schedules make a few out-of-the-way destinations I recommend not worth the time and trouble for the less determined (try buses instead—described later).

Schedules: For Czech train and bus timetables, visit www.idos. cz (train info tel. 221-111-122, little English spoken). For trains, you can also check out Germany's excellent Europe-wide timetable at www.bahn.com. Consider buying the *Traťové Jízdní Řády,* a comprehensive, easy-to-use schedule of all trains in the country (includes English instructions, sold at major station ticket windows for 30 Kč). Although it's easy to look up a connection online, having the printed schedule and a map of railway lines gives you the freedom to easily change or make new plans as you travel.

Tickets and Tips: Tickets within the Czech Republic are valid for two days, and international tickets are good from three days to two weeks (the shorter-term ones are often cheaper). Your ticket is valid for travel along the entire stretch from Prague to your destination, not just for one trip on a specific train—so enjoy the flexibility it gives you, and hop on and hop off along the way. You'll rarely need a reservation, except for international night trains.

If you are traveling by train with one or more companions, ask for a group ticket. This gets you a 50 percent discount for every extra ticket (only the first person pays full price).

The Czech railway network has a rather complex system for discounts on international tickets. If you're heading to a city near the Czech border (such as Vienna, Bratislava, Dresden, or Nürnberg), it sometimes pays to buy two separate tickets: one to the Czech border, and another from the border to your destination. This also allows you to take advantage of particular discounts (such as the group discount) that apply only to domestic travel.

Rail Passes: The Czech Republic is covered by a Czech Republic pass, a Central Europe Triangle Pass (Vienna-Budapest-Prague or Vienna-Salzburg-Prague), a four-country European East pass, the Global Pass, and the Select Pass. If your train travel will be limited to a handful of rides and/or short distances (for example, within the Czech Republic), you're probably better off without a pass—Czech tickets are cheap to buy as you go. But if you're combining Prague with international destinations, a rail pass could save you money.

For more detailed advice on figuring out the smartest rail pass options for your train trip, visit the Trains & Rail Passes section of my website at www.ricksteves.com/rail.

Buses

To reach many of the destinations in this book, buses are faster and cheaper than trains, and may be more punctual. No reserva-

tions are necessary, but they're highly recommended if you're traveling on a popular route (such as from Prague to Český Krumlov). Bus timetables are online at www.idos.cz. To make online reservations, use www.studentagency.cz; if you're in Prague, visit the ticket office at the Florenc bus station (Metro: Florenc) or the main train station (Metro: Hlavní Nádraží). For other routes, buy tickets online or directly from the driver as you board (exact change is appreciated; the driver might have difficulty breaking large bills). You'll be required to put big bags in the luggage compartment under the bus (12-24 Kč extra, depending on the distance), so have a small day bag ready to take on the bus with you. Most buses don't have bathrooms, nor do they stop for bathroom breaks.

Always let the bus driver know where you want to get off.

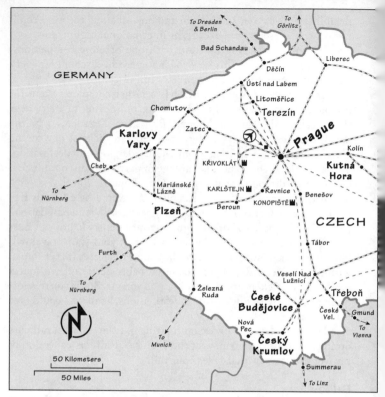

Some stops may require a request (for example, the Small Fortress at Terezín Memorial), and most bus drivers are happy to let you know when your stop is coming up.

RENTING A CAR

If you're renting a car in the Czech Republic, bring your driver's license. You're also required to have an International Driving Permit—an official translation of your driver's license (sold at your local AAA office for $15 plus the cost of two passport-type photos; see www.aaa.com). While that's the letter of the law, I've often rented cars without having this permit. How this is enforced varies from country to country: Get advice from your car rental company.

Rental companies require you to be at least 21 years old and to have held your license for one year. Drivers under the age of 25 may incur a young-driver surcharge, and some rental companies do not rent to anyone 75 or older. If you're considered too young or old, look into leasing (covered later), which has less-stringent age restrictions.

Research car rentals before you go. Especially during peak season, the best deals at Czech car-rental companies need to be

Czech Public Transportation

arranged two to three weeks ahead. Most of the major US rental agencies (including Avis, Budget, Enterprise, Hertz, and Thrifty) have offices throughout Europe, including the Czech Republic. Also consider the two major Europe-based agencies, Europcar and Sixt. It can be cheaper to use a consolidator, such as Auto Europe/Kemwel (www.autoeurope.com—or the often cheaper www.autoeurope.eu) or Europe by Car (www.europebycar.com), which compares rates at several companies to get you the best deal—but because you're working with a middleman, it's especially important to ask in advance about add-on fees and restrictions.

Always read the fine print carefully for add-on charges—such as one-way drop-off fees, airport surcharges, or mandatory insurance policies—that aren't included in the "total price." You may need to query rental agents pointedly to find out your actual cost.

For the best deal, rent by the week with unlimited mileage. To save money on fuel, ask for a diesel car. I normally rent the smallest, least-expensive model with a stick shift (generally much cheaper than an automatic). Almost all rentals are manual by default, so if you need an automatic, request one in advance; be aware that

PRACTICALITIES

Czech Place Names

Here's a rough pronunciation key for places mentioned in this book. For pronunciation help for specific sights and neighborhoods in Prague, see the "Prague Pronunciations" sidebar in the Orientation chapter.

Beskydy (mountains)	BEH-skih-dee
Brno	BURR-noh
České Budějovice	CHESS-keh BOO-dyeh-yoh-vee-tseh
Český Krumlov	CHESS-key KROOM-loff
Karlovy Vary	KAR-loh-vee VAH-ree
Karlštejn (castle)	KARL-shtayn
Konopiště (castle)	KOH-noh-peesh-tyeh
Křivoklát (castle)	KREE-vohk-laht
Kroměříž	KROH-myehr-eezh
Kutná Hora	KOOT-nah HO-rah
Lednice	LEHD-nee-tseh
Litoměřice	LEE-toh-myer-zhee-tseh
Mikulov	MEE-kuh-lohv
Olomouc	OH-loh-moats
Pálava (hills)	PAH-lah-vah
Pavlov	PAHV-lohv
Pustevny	POO-stehv-nee
Rožnov	ROHZ-nohv
Slavonice	SLAH-voh-neet-seh
Šumava (mountains)	SHOO-mah-vah
Telč	telch
Terezín	TEH-reh-zeen
Třebíč	TREH-beech

these cars are usually larger models (not as maneuverable on narrow, winding roads).

Czechs are once again proud of their locally built Škoda cars (since the 1920s, the Ford of Eastern Europe). Now owned by Volkswagen, Škoda is the biggest post-communist success story in the country. By renting one, you'll learn why most Eastern Europeans stay loyal to the brand, even as cheap Japanese cars are now available. (In an ironic twist, the word "Škoda"—the family name of an early owner of the company—also means "damage" in Czech.)

When renting, I usually get a Škoda Fabia; for more luggage space and more oomph, step up to the Škoda Octavia. On average, you should be able to get a Škoda with full insurance and unlimited mileage for $40-65 per day. Škodas usually have manual transmission and come with alarms; you might want to supplement the alarm with a lock for the steering wheel or stick shift.

For trips of three weeks or more, leasing can save you money on insurance and taxes. Be warned that international trips—say, picking up in Prague and dropping off in Vienna—can be expensive if the rental company assesses a drop-off fee for crossing a border.

As a rule, always tell your car-rental company up-front exactly which countries you'll be entering. Some companies levy extra insurance fees for trips taken in certain countries with certain types of cars (such as BMWs, Mercedes, and convertibles). Double-check with your rental agent that you have all the documentation you need before you drive off (especially if you're crossing borders into non-Schengen countries, such as Croatia, where you might need to present proof of insurance).

Picking Up Your Car: Big companies have offices in most cities, but small local rental companies can be cheaper.

Compare pickup costs (downtown can be less expensive than the airport) and explore drop-off options. Always check the hours of the location you choose: Many rental offices close from midday Saturday until Monday morning and, in smaller towns, at lunchtime.

When selecting a location, don't trust the agency's description of "downtown" or "city center." In some cases, a "downtown" branch can be on the outskirts of the city—a long, costly taxi ride from the center. Before choosing, plug the addresses into a mapping website. You may find that the "train station" location is handier. But returning a car at a big-city train station or downtown agency can be tricky; get precise details on the car drop-off location and hours, and allow ample time to find it.

When you pick up the rental car, check it thoroughly and make sure any damage is noted on your rental agreement. Rental agencies in Europe are very strict when it comes to charging for even minor damage, so be sure to mark everything. Before driving off, find out how your car's gearshift, lights, turn signals, wipers, radio, and fuel cap function, and know what kind of gas the car takes (diesel vs. unleaded). When you return the car, make sure the agent verifies its condition with you. Some drivers take pictures of the returned vehicle as proof of its condition.

Car Insurance Options

When you rent a car, you are liable for a very high deductible, sometimes equal to the entire value of the car. Limit your financial risk with one of these three options: Buy Collision Damage Waiver (CDW) coverage from the car-rental company, get coverage through your credit card (if your card automatically includes zero-deductible coverage), or get collision insurance as part of a larger travel-insurance policy.

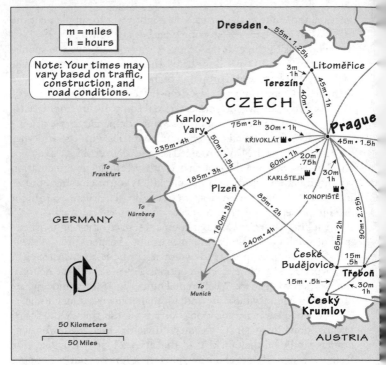

Basic **CDW** includes a very high deductible (typically $1,000-1,500), costs $10–30 a day (figure roughly 30 percent extra) and reduces your liability, but does not eliminate it. When you reserve or pick up the car, you'll be offered the chance to "buy down" the basic deductible to zero (for an additional $10-30/day; this is sometimes called "super CDW" or "zero-deductible coverage").

If you opt for **credit-card coverage,** you'll technically have to decline all coverage offered by the car-rental company, which means they can place a hold on your card (which can be up to the full value of the car). In case of damage, it can be time-consuming to resolve the charges with your credit-card company. Before you decide on this option, quiz your credit-card company about how it works.

If you're already purchasing a **travel-insurance policy** for your trip, adding collision coverage can be an economical option. For example, Travel Guard (www.travelguard.com) sells affordable renter's collision insurance as an add-on to its other policies; it's valid everywhere in Europe except the Republic of Ireland, and some Italian car-rental companies refuse to honor it, as it doesn't cover you in case of theft.

For more on car-rental insurance, see www.ricksteves.com/cdw.

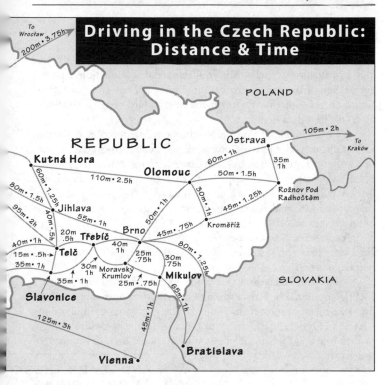

Driving in the Czech Republic: Distance & Time

Leasing

For trips of three weeks or more, consider leasing (which automatically includes zero-deductible collision and theft insurance). By technically buying and then selling back the car, you save lots of money on tax and insurance. Leasing provides you a brand-new car with unlimited mileage and a 24-hour emergency assistance program. You can lease for as little as 21 days to as long as five and a half months. Car leases must be arranged from the US, and cars must be picked up and dropped off outside the Czech Republic (Munich is the closest city to Prague that has leasing services). One of many companies offering affordable lease packages is Europe by Car (www.europebycar.com/lease).

Navigation Options

If you'll be navigating using your phone or a GPS unit from home, remember to bring a car charger and device mount.

Your Mobile Device: The mapping app on your mobile phone works fine for navigation in Europe, but for real-time turn-by-turn directions and traffic updates, you'll generally need access to a cellular network. A helpful exception is Google Maps, which provides turn-by-turn driving directions and recalibrates even when it's offline.

To use Google Maps offline, you must have a Google account and download your map while you have a data connection. Later—even when offline—you can call up that map, enter your destination, and get directions. View maps in standard view (not satellite view) to limit data demands.

GPS Devices: If you prefer the convenience of a dedicated GPS unit, consider renting one with your car ($10-30/day). These units offer real-time turn-by-turn directions and traffic without the data requirements of an app. Note that the unit may only come loaded with maps for its home country; if you need additional maps, ask. Also make sure your device's language is set to English before you drive off.

A less-expensive option is to bring a GPS device from home. Be aware that you'll need to buy and download European maps before your trip.

Maps and Atlases: Even when navigating primarily with a mobile app or GPS, I always make it a point to have a paper map. The free maps you get from your car-rental company usually don't have enough detail. It's smart to buy a better map before you go, or pick one up at a European gas station, bookshop, newsstand, or tourist shop.

Driving

Road Rules: Learn the universal road signs. Seat belts are required, and two beers under those belts are enough to land you in jail. Children under age 12 must ride in the back, and children under 80 pounds must have a child safety seat. Be aware of typical European road rules; for example, many countries require headlights to be turned on at all times, and nearly all forbid talking on a mobile phone without a hands-free headset. In Europe, you're not allowed to turn right on a red light, unless there is a sign or signal specifically authorizing it, and on expressways it's illegal to pass driv-

AND LEARN THESE ROAD SIGNS

Speed Limit (km/hr) — Yield — No Passing — End of No Passing Zone

One Way — Intersection — Main Road — Expressway

Danger — No Entry — Cars Prohibited — All Vehicles Prohibited

No Through Road — Restrictions No Longer Apply — Yield to Oncoming Traffic — No Stopping

Parking — No Parking — Customs or Toll Road — Peace

ers on the right. Ask your car-rental company about these rules, or check the US State Department website (www.travel.state.gov, search for your country in the "Learn about your destination" box, then click on "Travel and Transportation").

Freeways: During the communist era, Eastern Europe's infrastructure lagged far behind the West's. With the Iron Curtain gone, big cities gradually were connected by superhighways. A new expressway connects Prague to Nürnberg, and the old nightmare of a freeway between Prague, Brno, and Olomouc has been almost entirely upgraded. Currently the biggest project is the freeway connecting Prague to České Budějovice (toward Český Krumlov). Other than these, you will likely be traveling on backcountry roads (particularly in the southern Czech Republic). These can vary from smooth and new to bumpy and slow, but they're always paved (or, at least, they once were).

Fuel: Be sure you know which type of fuel your rental car takes. At about $1.25 per liter ($5 per gallon) for unleaded ("Natural 95"), gas in the Czech Republic is still somewhat cheaper than in Western Europe. If driving a diesel car, you're in luck—it's called "diesel" at the pump.

Tolls: If you're driving on highways in the Czech Republic, you're required to buy a toll sticker *(dálniční známka)* at the border, a post office, or a gas station (310 Kč/10 days, 440 Kč/1 month). Your rental car may already come with the necessary sticker—ask.

Parking: You'll pay about $10-15 a day to park safely in Prague. Formerly notorious for its Russian car-theft gangs, Prague is safer now—but it's still wise to be careful. Ask at your hotel for advice. In small towns, such as Třeboň or Slavonice, it's better to stay on the safe side when parking overnight. Again, ask your hotelier for advice. I keep a pile of coins in my car console for parking meters, launderettes, and wishing wells.

FLIGHTS

The best comparison search engine for both international and intra-European flights is www.kayak.com. For inexpensive flights within Europe, try www.skyscanner.com.

Flying to Europe: Start looking for international flights at least four to six months before your trip, especially for peak-season travel. Off-season tickets can usually be purchased a month or so in advance. Depending on your itinerary, it can be efficient to fly into one city and out of another. If your flight requires a connection in Europe, see my hints on navigating Europe's top hub airports at www.ricksteves.com/hub-airports.

Flying Within Europe: If you're considering a train ride that's more than five hours long, a flight may save you both time and

PRACTICALITIES

money. When comparing your options, factor in the time it takes to get to the airport and how early you'll need to arrive to check in.

Well-known cheapo airlines include easyJet (www.easyjet. com) and Ryanair (www.ryanair.com). Smart Wings (www. smartwings.com) is based in the Czech Republic. But be aware of the potential drawbacks of flying on the cheap: nonrefundable and nonchangeable tickets, minimal or nonexistent customer service, pricey and time-consuming treks to secondary airports, and stingy baggage allowances with steep overage fees.

If you're traveling with lots of luggage, a cheap flight can quickly become a bad deal. To avoid unpleasant surprises, read the small print before you book. These days you can also fly within Europe on major airlines affordably—and without all the aggressive restrictions—for around $100 a flight.

Flying to the US and Canada: Because security is extra tight for flights to the US, be sure to give yourself plenty of time at the airport. It's also important to charge your electronic devices before you board as security checks may require you to turn them on (see www.tsa.gov for the latest rules).

Resources from Rick Steves

Begin your trip at www.ricksteves.com: My **website** is *the* place to explore Europe. You'll find thousands of fun articles, videos, photos, and radio interviews organized by country; a wealth of money-saving tips for planning your dream trip; monthly travel news dispatches; a collection of over 30 hours of practical travel talks; my travel blog; my latest guidebook updates (www. ricksteves.com/update); and my free Rick Steves Audio Europe app. You can also follow me on Facebook and Twitter.

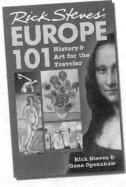

Our **Travel Forum** is an immense, yet well-groomed collection of message boards, where our travel-savvy community answers questions and shares their personal travel experiences—and our well-traveled staff chimes in when they can be helpful (www.ricksteves.com/forums).

Our **online Travel Store** offers travel bags and accessories that I've designed specifically to help you travel smarter and lighter. These include my popular carry-on bags (which I live out of four months a year), money belts, totes, toiletries kits, adapters, other accessories, and a wide selection of guidebooks and planning maps (www.ricksteves.com/shop).

Choosing the right **rail pass** for your trip—amid hundreds of options—can drive you nutty. Our website will help you find the perfect fit for your itinerary and your budget: We offer easy, one-stop shopping for rail passes, seat reservations, and point-to-point tickets.

Tours: Want to travel with greater efficiency and less stress? We organize **tours** with more than three dozen itineraries and more than 900 departures reaching the best destinations in this book...and beyond. We offer several tours that visit Prague and destinations in the Czech Republic, including our 8-day Prague and Budapest tour; our 12-day Berlin, Prague, and Vienna tour (which includes the charming village of Český Krumlov); and our 14-day Eastern Europe tour. You'll enjoy great guides, a fun bunch of travel partners (with small groups of 24 to 28 travelers), and plenty of room to spread out in a big, comfy bus when touring between towns. You'll find European adventures to fit every vacation length. For all the details and to get our Tour Catalog, visit www.ricksteves.com/tours or call us at 425/608-4217.

Books: *Rick Steves Prague & the Czech Republic* is one of many books in my series on European travel, which includes country guidebooks, city guidebooks (Rome, Florence, Paris, London, etc.), Snapshot guidebooks (excerpted chapters from my country guides), Pocket guidebooks (full-color little books on big cities, including Prague), "Best Of" guidebooks (condensed country guides in a full-color, easy-to-scan format), and my budget-travel skills handbook, *Rick Steves Europe Through the Back Door*. Most of my titles are available as ebooks.

My phrase books—for French, Italian, German, Spanish, and Portuguese—are practical and budget-oriented. My other books include *Europe 101* (a crash course on art and history designed for travelers); *Mediterranean Cruise Ports* and *Northern European Cruise Ports* (how to make the most of your time in port); and *Travel as a Political Act* (a travelogue sprinkled with tips for bringing home a global perspective). A more complete list of my titles appears near the end of this book.

TV Shows: My public television series, *Rick Steves' Europe*, covers Europe from top to bottom with over 100 half-hour episodes. To watch full episodes online for free, see www.ricksteves.com/tv.

Travel Talks on Video: You can raise your travel I.Q. with video versions of our popular classes (including talks on travel skills, packing smart, cruising, tech for travelers, European art for travelers, travel as a political act, and individual talks covering most European counties). See www.ricksteves.com/travel-talks.

Audio: My weekly public radio show, *Travel with Rick Steves,* features interviews with travel experts from around the world. A complete archive of 10 years of programs (over 400 in all) is available at www.ricksteves.com/radio. I've also produced a free, self-guided **audio tour** for my Prague City Walk. Most of this free audio content is available for free through my **Rick Steves Audio Europe app,** an extensive online library organized by destination. For more on my app, see page 10.

APPENDIX

Contents

Useful Contacts

Emergency Needs
Police, Fire, and Ambulance (Europe-wide): 112
Police: Tel. 158
Ambulance: Tel. 155
Road Service: 1240

Embassies
US Embassy: Tel. 257-022-000 (24-hour line), emergency passport services Mon-Fri 8:15-11.30, in Prague's Little Quarter below the castle at Tržiště 15, http://prague.usembassy.gov, ACSPrg@state.gov
Canadian Embassy: Tel. 272-101-800, consular services Mon-Thu 9:00-12:00, Fri and afternoons by appointment, north of the Castle Quarter at Ve Struhách 95/2, www.canadainternational.gc.ca/czech-tcheque, prgue-cs@international.gc.ca

Directory Assistance

Directory Assistance within the Czech Republic: Tel. 1188 (12-27 Kč/minute)

Online "Yellow Pages" and "White Pages": www.zlatestranky.cz

Holidays and Festivals

This list includes selected festivals in Prague and the Czech Republic, plus national holidays observed throughout the country. Many sights and banks close down on national holidays—keep this in mind when planning your itinerary. The sights in Prague's Jewish Quarter close on Jewish holidays (the major ones are listed below). Before planning a trip around a festival, verify its dates by checking the festival's website or TI sites. The Czech national TI (www.czechtourism.com) can provide specifics and a more comprehensive list of festivals.

Jan 1	New Year's Day; Restoration of Czech Independence Day
Jan 19	Anniversary of Jan Palach's death (flowers in Prague's Wenceslas Square)
March	One World International Human Rights Film Festival, Prague (www.oneworld.cz)
March-April	Pesach (Passover) begins: April 10, 2017; March 30, 2018
April	Easter Sunday and Monday: April 16-17, 2017; April 1-2, 2018
April 30	Witches' Night (similar to Halloween, with bonfires)
May 1	Labor Day and Day of Love (akin to Valentine's Day)
Early May	Prague International Marathon (www.runczech.com)
May 8	Liberation Day
Mid-May	Czech Beer Festival, Prague
May-June	Shavu'ot (Jewish "Feast of Weeks"): May 30-June 1, 2017; May 19-21, 2018
May-June	Corpus Christi: June 15, 2017; May 31, 2018
Mid-May-early June	"Prague Spring" Music Festival (www.festival.cz)
Late May	Prague Food Festival (food booths in Royal Gardens of Prague Castle, www.praguefoodfestival.cz)

APPENDIX

Late May	Khamoro World Roma Festival, Prague (celebration of Roma culture)
Early June	Festival of Song, Olomouc (www.festamusicale.com)
Mid-June	United Islands of Prague (cultural events and world music on the city's islands)
Mid-June-late July	Prague Proms (music festival, www.pragueproms.cz)
Late June	Celebration of the Rose, Český Krumlov (medieval festival and knights' tournament, www.ckrumlov.info)
July 5	Sts. Cyril and Methodius Day
July 6	Jan Hus Day
July-Aug	Summer of Culture, Olomouc (www.olomouckekulturniprazdniny.cz)
Mid-July-mid-Aug	International Music Festival, Český Krumlov (classical music and opera, www.festivalkrumlov.cz)
Late July-Early Aug	Telč Vacations Festival (folk music, open-air theater, exhibitions, www.prazdninyvtelci.cz)
Sept	Dvořák's Prague Music Festival (www.dvorakovapraha.cz)
Sept	Rosh Hashanah: Sept 21-22, 2017; Sept 10-11, 2018
Sept	Yom Kippur: Sept 30, 2017; Sept 19, 2018
Sept 28	St. Wenceslas Day (celebrates national patron saint and Czech statehood)
Sept-Oct	Sukkot (Jewish "Feast of Tabernacles"): Oct 5-6, 2017; Sept 24-25, 2018
Oct	Shemini Atzeret and Simchat Torah (Jewish holidays): Oct 12-13, 2017; Oct 1-2, 2018
Mid-Oct-early Nov	Prague International Jazz Festival
Oct 28	Independence Day
Nov 1	All Saints' Day/Remembrance Day (religious festival)
Nov 17	Velvet Revolution Anniversary
Dec	Christmas markets, Prague
Dec 5	St. Nicholas Eve, Prague (St. Nicholas, devils, and angels walk the streets in search of nice—and naughty—children)
Dec 24-25	Christmas Eve and Christmas Day

APPENDIX

Dec 26	St. Stephen's Day
Dec 31	St. Sylvester's Day (fireworks)

Recommended Books and Films

To learn more about the Czech Republic past and present, check out a few of these books or films.

NONFICTION

Alice's Piano: The Life of Alice Herz-Sommer (Melissa Müller, 2012). A classical pianist uses music to bring hope to fellow prisoners at the Terezín concentration camp.

My Crazy Century (Ivan Klíma, 2009). Celebrated Czech author Ivan Klíma chronicles events spanning from his childhood in a concentration camp to the aftermath of the Velvet Revolution, painting a dynamic portrait of 20th-century Czechoslovakia.

Prague Winter: A Personal Story of Remembrance and War, 1937-1948 (Madeleine Albright, 2012). Former Secretary of State Albright describes her early years in Czechoslovakia during the Nazi occupation and World War II.

The Twelve Little Cakes (Dominika Dery, 2004). Dery details a childhood spent near Prague at the end of the communist era.

Under a Cruel Star: A Life in Prague, 1941-1968 (Heda Kovály, 1997). Kovály's clear-eyed memoir recounts a Czechoslovakian's fate under the Nazis and then during the Stalin regime.

The Wall: Growing Up Behind the Iron Curtain (Peter Sís, 2007). An illustrated children's book depicts the author's childhood in communist Czechoslovakia.

FICTION

City Sister Silver (Jáchym Topol, 1994). In this definitive novel of the 1989 generation, Topol explores the zeitgeist of post-liberation Czech Republic in a rich mixture of colloquial Czech and neologisms.

The Cowards (Josef Škvorecký, 1958). A Czech teen comes of age in post-WWII Bohemia.

Dita Saxová (Arnošt Lustig, 1962). A young concentration camp survivor struggles to resume a normal life in Prague.

The Garden Party and Other Plays (Václav Havel, 1994). The renowned playwright, the country's first post-communist president, fuses political commentary and dry humor in these absurdist plays.

Good Soldier Švejk (Jaroslav Hašek, 1923). This darkly comic Czech classic follows the fortunes of a soldier in World War I's Austro-Hungarian army.

How I Came to Know Fish (Ota Pavel, 1974). Pavel's imaginative memoir juxtaposes the simple act of fishing with the complexities and terror of World War II.

I Served the King of England (Bohumil Hrabal, 1971). An eccentric busboy at a luxurious Prague hotel rises and falls in the years before WWII. Hrabal's writing captures the Czech spirit and sense of humor.

The Metamorphosis (Franz Kafka, 1915). The famous Czech writer and existentialist wrote this novella in German, about a man turning into a giant cockroach.

R.U.R. (Karel Čapek, 1920). Čapek created the robot in this 1920s play.

Too Loud a Solitude (Bohumil Hrabal, 1976). Hrabal's stream-of-consciousness style explores the endurance of knowledge and written-word.

The Trial (Franz Kafka, 1925). An urbanite is pursued and persecuted for crimes he knows nothing about.

The Unbearable Lightness of Being (Milan Kundera, 1981). Set during the 1968 Prague Spring uprising, this novel follows the lives and choices of two men and two women.

FILMS

Alice (1988). Inspiring Czech artist Jan Švankmajer adapts Lewis Carroll's *Alice's Adventures in Wonderland* in stop-motion animation combined with live action.

All My Loved Ones (1999). A Jewish family's son is sent to England in the "Kindertransports" organized by Nicholas Winton, the British humanitarian who saved almost 700 Czech Jewish children.

Burning Bush (2013). This miniseries details the communist occupation of Czechoslovakia and the Prague Spring, focusing on Jan Palach, the Czech student who set himself on fire and died in protest against the Soviet occupation.

Closely Watched Trains (1966). This Oscar-winner follows a young Czech man working at a German-occupied train station during WWII.

Czech Dream (2004). Two film students advertise and document the opening of a fake hypermarket in this hilarious, disturbing commentary on consumerism.

Divided We Fall (2000). A Czech couple hides a Jewish friend during Nazi occupation in this Academy Award-nominated film.

The Elementary School (1991). Set in the late 1940s, a rowdy classroom in suburban Prague faces reform under the strict guidance of a war hero teacher.

I Served the King of England (2006). In this adaptation of Bohumil Hrabal's novel, a man reminisces about his past as an ambitious waiter who suffers the consequences of World War II.

In the Shadow (2012). A burglary in 1950s Czechoslovakia sets off a political investigation of Jewish immigrants and a detective's struggle for justice amid German prosecutors.

Intimate Lighting (1965). Two musicians reunite in a small town in this showcase of 1960s Czech New Wave.

Kolya (1996). A concert-cellist in Soviet-controlled Czechoslovakia must care for an abandoned Russian boy.

Larks on a String (1990). Under the communist regime, bourgeois Czechs are forced into labor camps and struggle to maintain their humanity.

Loves of a Blonde (1965). Before he directed *One Flew Over the Cuckoo's Nest* and *Amadeus,* Czech Miloš Forman directed this film about the relationship between a rural Czech woman and a jazz pianist from Prague.

Protektor (2009). In this WWII Czech drama, a man must reconcile his job at a Nazi-propaganda radio station and his relationship with his Jewish wife.

ANIMATION

The Czechs have a wonderful animation tradition that successfully competes with Walt Disney in Eastern Europe and China. During communism when Western cartoons weren't widely available, Czechoslovakia produced several that were beloved throughout the Soviet Bloc. Since the 1950s, every night at 18:45 a block of cartoons is shown on Czech television's channel 1, with the lineup introduced by a character called Večerníček ("Bedtime"—a little boy with starry eyes and a sleeping cap). The most popular character is Krtek (or Krteček, "Little Mole"), who gets in and out of trouble. You'll see plush black-and-white Krtek figures everywhere. Křemílek and Vochomůrka are brothers who live in the woods, Maxipes Fík is a clever dog, and the duo Pat and Mat are builders who can't seem to get anything right.

Conversions and Climate

NUMBERS AND STUMBLERS

- Europeans write a few of their numbers differently than we do. 1 = 1, 4 = 4, 7 = 7.
- In Europe, dates appear as day/month/year, so Christmas in 2018 is 25/12/18.
- Commas are decimal points and decimals are commas. A dollar and a half is 1,50; one thousand is 1.000; and there are 5.280 feet in a mile.

- When counting with fingers, start with your thumb. If you hold up your first finger to request one item, you'll probably get two.
- What Americans call the second floor of a building is the first floor in Europe.
- On escalators and moving sidewalks, Europeans keep the left "lane" open for passing. Keep to the right.

METRIC CONVERSIONS

A kilogram is 2.2 pounds and 1 liter is about a quart, or almost four to a gallon. A kilometer is six-tenths of a mile. I figure kilometers to miles by cutting them in half and adding back 10 percent of the original (120 km: 60 + 12 = 72 miles, 300 km: 150 + 30 = 180 miles).

1 foot = 0.3 meter	1 square yard = 0.8 square meter
1 yard = 0.9 meter	1 square mile = 2.6 square kilometers
1 mile = 1.6 kilometers	1 ounce = 28 grams
1 centimeter = 0.4 inch	1 quart = 0.95 liter
1 meter = 39.4 inches	1 kilogram = 2.2 pounds
1 kilometer = 0.62 mile	32°F = 0°C

CLOTHING SIZES

When shopping for clothing, use these US-to-European comparisons as general guidelines (but note that no conversion is perfect).

Women: For clothing or shoe sizes, add 30 (US shirt size 10 = European size 40; US shoe size 8 = European size 38-39).

Men: For shirts, multiply by 2 and add about 8 (US size 15 = European size 38). For jackets and suits, add 10. For shoes, add 32-34.

Children: For clothing, subtract 1-2 sizes for small children and subtract 4 for juniors. For shoes up to size 13, add 16-18, and for sizes 1 and up, add 30-32.

APPENDIX

THE CZECH REPUBLIC'S CLIMATE

First line, average daily high; second line, average daily low; third line, average number of days with some rain. For more detailed weather statistics for destinations throughout the Czech Republic (as well as the rest of the world), check www.wunderground.com.

J	F	M	A	M	J	J	A	S	O	N	D
31°	34°	44°	54°	64°	70°	73°	72°	65°	53°	42°	34°
22°	24°	30°	38°	46°	52°	55°	55°	49°	41°	33°	27°
13°	11°	10°	11°	13°	12°	13°	12°	10°	13°	12°	13°

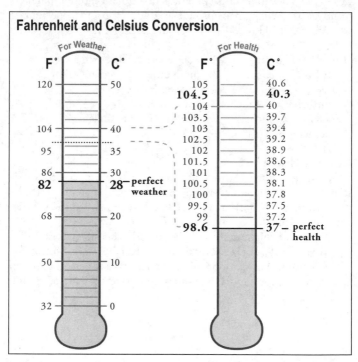

Fahrenheit and Celsius Conversion

Europe takes its temperature using the Celsius scale, while we opt for Fahrenheit. For a rough conversion from Celsius to Fahrenheit, double the number and add 30. For weather, remember that 28°C is 82°F—perfect. For health, 37°C is just right. At a launderette, 30°C is cold, 40°C is warm (usually the default setting), 60°C is hot, and 95°C is boiling. Your air-conditioner should be set at about 20°C.

Packing Checklist

Whether you're traveling for five days or five weeks, you won't need more than this. Pack light to enjoy the sweet freedom of true mobility.

Clothing

- ☐ 5 shirts: long- & short-sleeve
- ☐ 2 pairs pants (or skirts/capris)
- ☐ 1 pair shorts
- ☐ 5 pairs underwear & socks
- ☐ 1 pair walking shoes
- ☐ Sweater or warm layer
- ☐ Rainproof jacket with hood
- ☐ Tie, scarf, belt, and/or hat
- ☐ Swimsuit
- ☐ Sleepwear/loungewear

Money

- ☐ Debit card(s)
- ☐ Credit card(s)
- ☐ Hard cash ($100-200 in US dollars)
- ☐ Money belt

Documents

- ☐ Passport
- ☐ Tickets & confirmations: flights, hotels, trains, rail pass, car rental, sight entries
- ☐ Driver's license
- ☐ Student ID, hostel card, etc.
- ☐ Photocopies of important documents
- ☐ Insurance details
- ☐ Guidebooks & maps
- ☐ Notepad & pen
- ☐ Journal

Toiletries Kit

- ☐ Basics: soap, shampoo, toothbrush, toothpaste, floss, deodorant, sunscreen, brush/comb, etc.
- ☐ Medicines & vitamins
- ☐ First-aid kit
- ☐ Glasses/contacts/sunglasses

- ☐ Sewing kit
- ☐ Packet of tissues (for WC)
- ☐ Earplugs

Electronics

- ☐ Mobile phone
- ☐ Camera & related gear
- ☐ Tablet/ebook reader/media player
- ☐ Laptop & flash drive
- ☐ Headphones
- ☐ Chargers & batteries
- ☐ Smartphone car charger & mount (or GPS device)
- ☐ Plug adapters

Miscellaneous

- ☐ Daypack
- ☐ Sealable plastic baggies
- ☐ Laundry supplies: soap, laundry bag, clothesline, spot remover
- ☐ Small umbrella
- ☐ Travel alarm/watch

Optional Extras

- ☐ Second pair of shoes (flip-flops, sandals, tennis shoes, boots)
- ☐ Travel hairdryer
- ☐ Picnic supplies
- ☐ Water bottle
- ☐ Fold-up tote bag
- ☐ Small flashlight
- ☐ Mini binoculars
- ☐ Small towel or washcloth
- ☐ Inflatable pillow/neck rest
- ☐ Tiny lock
- ☐ Address list (to mail postcards)
- ☐ Extra passport photos

Czech Survival Phrases

The emphasis in Czech words usually falls on the first syllable—though don't overdo it, as this stress is subtle. A vowel with an accent (á, é, í, ú, ý) is held longer. The combination ch sounds like the guttural "kh" sound in the Scottish word "loch." The uniquely Czech ř (as in Dvořák) sounds like a cross between a rolled "r" and "zh"; in the phonetics, it's "zh." Here are a few English words that all Czechs know: super, OK, pardon, stop, menu, problem, and no problem.

English	Czech	Pronunciation
Hello. (formal)	*Dobrý den.*	**doh**-bree dehn
Hi. / Bye. (informal)	*Ahoj.*	**ah**-hoy
Do you speak English?	*Mluvíte anglicky?*	**mloo**-vee-teh **ahn**-glits-kee
Yes. / No.	*Ano. / Ne.*	**ah**-noh / neh
I don't understand.	*Nerozumím.*	**neh**-roh-zoo-meem
Please. / You're welcome. / Can I help you?	*Prosím.*	**proh**-seem
Thank you.	*Děkuji.*	**dyeh**-kwee
Excuse me. / I'm sorry.	*Promiňte.*	**proh**-meen-teh
Good.	*Dobře.*	**dohb**-zheh
Goodbye.	*Nashledanou.*	**nah**-skleh-dah-noh
one / two / three	*jeden / dva / tři*	**yay**-dehn / dvah / tzhee
four / five / six	*čtyři / pět / šest*	**chtee**-zhee / pyeht / shehst
seven / eight	*sedm / osm*	**seh**-dum / **oh**-sum
nine / ten	*devět / deset*	**dehv**-yeht / **deh**-seht
hundred / thousand	*sto / tisíc*	stoh / **tee**-seets
How much?	*Kolik?*	**koh**-leek
local currency	*koruna (Kč)*	koh-**roo**-nah
Write it?	*Napište to?*	**nah**-pish-teh toh
Is it free?	*Je to zadarmo?*	yeh toh **zah**-dar-moh
Is it included?	*Je to v ceně?*	yeh tohf **tsay**-nyeh
Where can I find / buy...?	*Kde mohu najít / koupit...?*	guh-**deh** moh-hoo **nah**-yeet / **koh**-pit
I'd like... (said by a man)	*Rád bych...*	rahd bikh
I'd like... (said by a woman)	*Ráda bych...*	**rah**-dah bikh
We'd like...	*Rádi bychom...*	**rah**-dyee bee-khohm
...a room.	*...pokoj.*	**poh**-koy
...a ticket to ___. (destination)	*...jízdenka do ___.*	**yeez**-dehn-kah doh ___
Is it possible?	*Je to možné?*	yeh toh **mohzh**-neh
Where is...?	*Kde je...?*	guh-**deh** yeh
...the train station	*...nádraží*	**nah**-drah-zhee
...the bus station	*...autobusové nádraží*	**ow**-toh-boo-soh-veh **nah**-drah-zhee
...the tourist information office	*...turistická informační kancelář*	**too**-rih-stit-skah **een**-for-mahch-nee **kahn**-tseh-lahzh
...the toilet	*...vécé*	**veht**-seh
men / women	*muži / ženy*	**moo**-zhee / **zheh**-nee
left / right / straight	*vlevo / vpravo / rovně*	**vleh**-voh / **fprah**-voh / **rohv**-nyeh
At what time...?	*V kolik...?*	**fkoh**-leek
...does this open / close	*...otevírají / zavírají*	**oh**-teh-vee-rah-yee / **zah**-vee-rah-yee
Just a moment, please.	*Moment, prosím.*	moh-mehnt **proh**-seem
now / soon / later	*teď / brzy / později*	tedge / **bir**-zih / **pohz**-dyeh-yee
today / tomorrow	*dnes / zítra*	duh-**nehs** / **zee**-trah

In a Czech Restaurant

English	Czech	Pronunciation
I'd like to reserve... (said by a man)	Rád bych zarezervoval...	rahd bikh **zah**-reh-zehr-voh-vahl
I'd like to reserve... (said by a woman)	Ráda bych zarezervovala...	**rah**-dah bikh **zah**-reh-zehr-voh-vah-lah
...a table for one / two.	...stůl pro jednoho / dva.	stool proh **yehd**-noh-hoh / dvah
Nonsmoking.	Nekuřácký.	neh-kuhzh-aht-skee
Is this table free?	Je tento stůl volný?	yeh **tehn**-toh stool **vohl**-nee
Can I help you?	Mohu vám pomoci?	**moh**-hoo vahm poh-**moht**-see
The menu (in English), please.	Jídelní lístek (v angličtině), prosím.	**yee**-dehl-nee **lee**-stehk (**fahn**-gleech-tee-nyeh) **proh**-seem
Service is / isn't included.	Spropitné je / není zahrnuto.	**sproh**-pit-neh yeh / **neh**-nee **zah**-har-noo-toh
"to go"	s sebou	**seh**-boh
with / and / or	s / a / nebo	suh / ah / **neh**-boh
ready-to-eat meal	hotová jídla	**hoh**-toh-vah **yeed**-lah
meal on request	minutky	**mih**-noot-kee
appetizers	předkrm	**pzhehd**-krim
bread	chléb	khlehb
cheese	sýr	seer
sandwich	sendvič	**sehnd**-vich
soup / salad	polévka / salát	poh-**lehv**-kah / **sah**-laht
meat	maso	**mah**-soh
poultry	drůbež	**droo**-behzh
fish	ryby	**rih**-bih
fruit / vegetables	ovoce / zelenina	**oh**-voht-seh / **zeh**-leh-nyee-nah
dessert	dezert	**deh**-zehrt
(tap) water	voda (z kohoutku)	**voh**-dah (**skoh**-hoht-koo)
mineral water	minerální voda	**mih**-neh-rahl-nyee **voh**-dah
carbonated / not carbonated (spoken)	s bublinkami / bez bublinek	**sboob**-leen-kah-mee / behz **boo**-blee-nehk
carbonated / not carbonated (printed)	perlivá / neperlivá	**pehr**-lee-vah / **neh**-pehr-lee-vah
milk	mléko	**mleh**-koh
(orange) juice	(pomerančový) džus	(**poh**-mehr-ahn-choh-vee) "juice"
coffee / tea	káva / čaj	**kah**-vah / chai
wine	víno	**vee**-noh
red / white	červené / bílé	**chehr**-veh-neh / **bee**-leh
sweet / dry	sladké / suché	**slahd**-keh / **soo**-kheh
glass / bottle	sklenka / lahev	**sklehn**-kah / **lah**-hehv
beer	pivo	**pee**-voh
light / dark	světlé / tmavé	**svyeht**-leh / **tmah**-veh
Cheers!	Na zdraví!	nah zdrah-**vee**
Enjoy your meal.	Dobrou chuť.	**doh**-broh khoot
More. / Another.	Více. / Další.	**veet**-seh / **dahl**-shee
The same.	To samé.	toh **sah**-meh
The bill.	Účet.	**oo**-cheht
I'll pay.	Zaplatím.	**zah**-plah-teem
tip	spropitné	**sproh**-pit-neh
Delicious!	Výborné!	**vee**-bohr-neh

INDEX

INDEX

INDEX

INDEX

MAP INDEX

Our website enhances this book and turns

Explore Europe

At ricksteves.com you can browse through thousands of articles, videos, photos and radio interviews, plus find a wealth of money-saving travel tips for planning your dream trip. And with our mobile-friendly website, you can easily access all this great travel information anywhere you go.

TV Shows

Preview the places you'll visit by watching entire half-hour episodes of Rick Steves' Europe (choose from all 100 shows) on-demand, for free.

ricksteves.com

your travel dreams into affordable reality

Radio Interviews

Enjoy ready access to Rick's vast library of radio interviews covering travel

tips and cultural insights that relate specifically to your Europe travel plans.

Travel Forums

Learn, ask, share! Our online community of savvy travelers is a great resource for first-time travelers to Europe, as well as seasoned pros. You'll find forums on each country, plus travel tips and restaurant/hotel reviews. You can even ask one of our well-traveled staff to chime in with an opinion.

Travel News

Subscribe to our free Travel News e-newsletter, and get monthly updates from Rick on what's happening in Europe.

Audio Europe™

Rick's Free Travel App

Get your FREE **Rick Steves Audio Europe**™ app to enjoy...

- Dozens of self-guided tours of Europe's top museums, sights and historic walks

- Hundreds of tracks filled with cultural insights and sightseeing tips from Rick's radio interviews

- All organized into handy geographic playlists

- For Apple and Android

With Rick whispering in your ear, Europe gets even better.

Find out more at ricksteves.com

Pack Light and Right

Gear up for your next adventure at ricksteves.com

Light Luggage

Pack light and right with Rick Steves' affordable, custom-designed rolling carry-on bags, backpacks, day packs and shoulder bags.

Accessories

From packing cubes to moneybelts and beyond, Rick has personally selected the travel goodies that will help your trip go smoother.

Rick Steves has

great tours, too!

with minimum stress

guides and small groups of 28 or less. We follow Rick's favorite itineraries, ride in comfy buses, stay in family-run hotels, and bring you intimately close to the Europe you've traveled so far to see. Most importantly, we take away the logistical headaches so you can focus on the fun.

travelers—nearly half of them repeat customers—along with us on four dozen different itineraries, from Ireland to Italy to Istanbul. Is a Rick Steves tour the right fit for your travel dreams? Find out at ricksteves.com, where you can also request Rick's latest tour catalog. Europe is best experienced with happy travel partners. We hope you can join us.

Join the fun

This year we'll take thousands of free-spirited

Rick Steves

BEST OF GUIDES

Best of England
Best of France
Best of Germany
Best of Ireland
Best of Italy
Best of Spain

EUROPE GUIDES

Best of Europe
Eastern Europe
Europe Through the Back Door
Mediterranean Cruise Ports
Northern European Cruise Ports

COUNTRY GUIDES

Croatia & Slovenia
England
France
Germany
Great Britain
Ireland
Italy
Portugal
Scandinavia
Scotland
Spain
Switzerland

CITY & REGIONAL GUIDES

Amsterdam & the Netherlands
Belgium: Bruges, Brussels, Antwerp & Ghe
Barcelona
Budapest
Florence & Tuscany
Greece: Athens & the Peloponnese
Istanbul
London
Paris
Prague & the Czech Republic
Provence & the French Riviera
Rome
Venice
Vienna, Salzburg & Tirol

SNAPSHOT GUIDES

Basque Country: Spain & France
Berlin
Copenhagen & the Best of Denmark
Dublin
Dubrovnik
Edinburgh
Hill Towns of Central Italy
Krakow, Warsaw & Gdansk
Lisbon

Maximize your travel skills with a good guidebook.

Credits

CONTRIBUTOR
Gene Openshaw

Gene has co-authored a dozen *Rick Steves* books, specializing in writing walks and tours of Europe's cities, museums, and cultural sights. He also contributes to Rick's public television series, produces tours for Rick Steves Audio Europe, and is a regular guest on Rick's public radio show. Outside of the travel world, Gene has co-authored *The Seattle Joke Book*. As a composer, Gene has written a full-length opera called *Matter* (soundtrack available on Amazon), a violin sonata, and dozens of songs. He lives near Seattle with his daughter, enjoys giving presentations on art and history, and roots for the Mariners in good times and bad.

ACKNOWLEDGMENTS
Co-author Honza Vihan would like to offer special thanks to Victor Chen, Cimrmanologist par excellence, who wrote the "Jára Cimrman: The Greatest Czech?" sidebar on page 74. He would also like to thank Cameron Hewitt for his work on the Karlovy Vary and Shopping in Prague chapters.

Avalon Travel
An imprint of Perseus Books
A Hachette Book Group company
1700 Fourth Street
Berkeley, CA 94710

Printed in Canada by Friesens. First printing April 2017.

ISBN: 978-1-63121-619-0
ISSN: 1554-3870
9th Edition

For the latest on Rick Steves' talks, guidebooks, Europe tours, public radio show, free audio tours, and public television series, contact Rick Steves' Europe, 130 Fourth Avenue North, Edmonds, WA 98020, tel. 425/771-8303, www.ricksteves.com, rick@ricksteves.com.

Rick Steves' Europe
Managing Editor: Jennifer Madison Davis
Special Publications Manager: Risa Laib
Editors: Glenn Eriksen, Tom Griffin, Cameron Hewitt, Suzanne Kotz, Cathy Lu, Carrie Shepherd
Editorial & Production Assistant: Jessica Shaw
Editorial Intern: Megan Simms
Graphic Content Director: Sandra Hundacker
Maps & Graphics: David C. Hoerlein, Lauren Mills, Mary Rostad

Avalon Travel
Senior Editor & Series Manager: Madhu Prasher
Editor: Jamie Andrade
Associate Editor: Sierra Machado
Copy Editor: Patrick Collins
Proofreader: Kelly Lydick
Indexer: Claire Splan
Production & Typesetting: Sarah Wildfang, Jane Musser
Cover Design: Kimberly Glyder Design
Maps & Graphics: Kat Bennett, Mike Morgenfeld

Photo Credits
Front Cover: Prague's Old Town Square © Francesco Iacobelli/Getty Images
Title Page: Český Krumlov © Dominic Arizona Bonuccelli
Additional Photography: Dominic Arizona Bonuccelli, Ben Cameron, Barb Geisler, Cameron Hewitt, David C. Hoerlein, Sandra Hundacker, Suzanne Kotz, Lauren Mills, Michael Potter, Rick Steves, Honza Vihan, Robyn Stencil, Gretchen Strauch, Mucha Trust 2014, Wikimedia Commons—PD-Art/PD-US (photos are used by permission and are the property of the original copyright owners).

More for your trip!
Maximize the experience with Rick Steves as your guide

Guidebooks
Rick's Eastern Europe guide makes side-trips smooth and affordable

Rick's TV Shows
Preview where you're going with 2 shows on Prague and surroundings

Free! Rick's Audio Europe™ App
Get a free audio tour for Prague

Small Group Tours
Rick offers 3 great itineraries that include Prague

For all the details, visit ricksteves.com